MANAGEMENT ACCOUNTING

text and cases

MANAGEMENT ACCOUNTING

text and cases

John Dearden

HARVARD UNIVERSITY

PRENTICE-HALL INTERNATIONAL, INC.

Editorial/production supervision and
    interior design: Esther S. Koehn
Manufacturing buyer: Ed O'Dougherty

©1988 by Prentice-Hall, Inc.
A Division of Simon & Schuster
Englewood Cliffs, New Jersey 07632

Printed in the United States of America

10   9   8   7   6   5   4   3

ISBN 0-13-551359-6

Prentice-Hall of Australia Pty. Limited, *Sydney*
Prentice-Hall Canada Inc., *Toronto*
Prentice-Hall Hispanoamericana, S.A., *Mexico City*
Prentice-Hall of India Private Limited, *New Delhi*
Prentice-Hall of Japan, Inc., *Tokyo*
Prentice-Hall of Southeast Asia Pte. Ltd., *Singapore*
Editora Prentice-Hall do Brasil, Ltda., *Rio de Janeiro*
Prentice-Hall Inc., *Englewood Cliffs, New Jersey*

To Rachel and David

CONTENTS

chapter 3

HISTORICAL AND COMBINATION COST ACCOUNTING SYSTEMS 50

chapter 4

ASSIGNING OVERHEAD COSTS TO PRODUCTS 96

chapter 5

MISCELLANEOUS TOPICS IN COST ACCOUNTING 135

PART II Decision Support Systems

chapter 6

DECISION SUPPORT SYSTEMS: TACTICAL MARKETING DECISIONS 163

chapter 7

DECISION SUPPORT SYSTEMS: DISINVESTMENT DECISIONS   184

*Identification of Problem Areas 185   Screening and Action 187
Differences Between Variable Costs and Unique Costs 189   Joint Costs 190
Inflation 190   Summary 191*

chapter 8

DECISION SUPPORT SYSTEMS: CAPITAL INVESTMENT DECISIONS   206

*Part 1: Measuring Profitability 207   Part 2: Estimating Cash Flows 213
Part 3: Follow-Up Procedures 219   Part 4: Some Theoretical
Considerations 220*

PART III Financial Control Systems

chapter 9

MANUFACTURING COST VARIANCE ANALYSIS   252

*Requirements of Good Variance Analysis 253   Disaggregation of
Manufacturing Variances 254   Accounting for Variances 261*

chapter 10

FINANCIAL CONTROL OF MANUFACTURING OVERHEAD EXPENSES   277

*Flexible Overhead Budgeting 277   Management Considerations of
Manufacturing Cost Control Systems 290   Chapter 10 Appendix: Line
Fitting 291*

chapter 11

FINANCIAL CONTROL OF DISCRETIONARY EXPENSES   319

*Characteristics of Discretionary Expense Budgets   320   Types of
Discretionary Expense Budgets   322*

chapter 12

PROFIT ANALYSIS   355

*The Profit Budget   355   Profit Budget Variance Analysis   356
The Revenue Variance   358   Cost Variances   360   Break-Even and
Profit-Volume Analysis   367   Chapter 12 Appendix: Model Profit Budget
Analysis   377*

PART IV Management Control Systems

chapter 13

PROFIT CENTERS   403

*Characteristics of Management Control   403   Financial Control versus
Management Control   404   Profit Center versus Functional Organization   405*

chapter 14

TRANSFER PRICING   440

chapter 15

MEASUREMENT OF PERFORMANCE   483

chapter 16

COST ACCOUNTING AND CONTROL IN SERVICE INDUSTRIES 550

chapter 17

COMPREHENSIVE CASES   606

PREFACE

The accounting function can be divided into two parts: external accounting and internal accounting. External accounting systems (called financial accounting) provide the accounting data needed for published financial statements. Internal accounting systems (called management accounting) provide management with the accounting information that it needs in addition to that required for external statements. This book is designed for a course in management accounting. It assumes that the student has completed a course in financial accounting and, therefore, only those accounting systems and procedures that are needed to supplement the information provided by the external accounting system are covered.

The emphasis of the book is on the managerial use of accounting information rather than on the mechanical and procedural aspects of cost accounting. Thirty years ago, some business students could have expected to work in a clerical or semi-clerical job involving the collection and processing of plant accounting data. Now these tasks are performed by the computer and the procedures for capturing and processing cost information is largely in the hands of computer and systems specialists. Consequently, the procedural and mechanical aspects of cost accounting have been discussed only to the extent that it is necessary for the student to visualize the flow of the accounting information through the system.

This is a text and case book, and the material has been integrated as much as possible. Because of the integrated nature of a case text, the text material must be supplemented by cases in many instances. Where cases illustrated some aspect of managerial accounting, similar material was not covered in the text; for example, Chapter 2, "Standard Cost Accounting Systems," includes the Black Meter Company (Case 2.1) that describes an entire cost accounting system. One advantage of a case text is that the combination of text and cases can provide considerable flexibility in course design. The selection of case material to be assigned allows an instructor to emphasize the topics believed to be important.

Markets

This book has been designed to serve two principal markets. First, it has been designed to be used as a second-semester course in Management Accounting, to supplement the traditional financial accounting course. Second, it is designed to be used in an advanced course in management accounting, even if a student has had a traditional course in management accounting and/or cost accounting. If it were to be used for an initial course, the instructor should emphasize the first three parts and rely more on the problems and the shorter, easier cases. If it were to be used in an advanced course, the emphasis should be placed on the last three parts and on the more difficult and comprehensive cases.

All of the text and most of the cases in this book have been used at the Harvard Business School in the first-year Control course. Much of the material has been used also in management programs and many of the cases in the last three parts of the book do not require a detailed knowledge of accounting or finance.

Acknowledgments

I am very much indebted to the scholars who have written cases included in this book. Each has been recognized in the citation to the cases. I also wish to thank the following scholars who reviewed the manuscript and made many helpful suggestions: William N. Lanen, University of Pennsylvania; Srinivason Umapathy, Babson College; and S. Mark Young, University of Arizona.

I wish to thank Dean John McArthur of the Graduate School of Business Administration, Harvard University, for providing me with this opportunity and, also, for allowing me to use fifty-four cases that hold Harvard copyrights.

I also wish to thank Dean Derrick Abell of IMEDE, Management Development Institute, Lausanne, Switzerland, for permission to use six cases that hold IMEDE copyrights.

Finally, I wish to thank my secretary, Pauline B. Henault, for typing and otherwise preparing the manuscript.

John Dearden

INTRODUCTION

If there is a single verb that describes the accounting function, that verb is *measure*. In business, the accounting function measures past economic events. *Financial accounting* is the measurement of economic changes that have occurred in an entire business. *Management accounting* measures the economic changes that have occurred in segments of a business.

In addition to measuring, the management accountant is responsible for communicating the results to management. Managers use accounting information to make decisions. If accounting information is not understood, it is not useful. It could even be counterproductive if misunderstandings resulted in suboptimum decisions.

Financial accounting measures past economic changes by assigning revenues and expenses to the time period being measured. This is necessary because businesses have indefinite lives. It is not until a business has entirely wound up its affairs that it is possible to measure with precision its economic accomplishments or lack thereof. At that point, it is possible to calculate precisely the timing and amount of the cash flows that have occurred, which is the only way to measure economic performance. In the meantime, however, it is necessary to measure interim performance. Generally accepted accounting principles (GAAP) guide the accountant in doing this.

Management accounting measures past economic changes that have occurred in segments of a business by assigning revenues and expenses to these segments. Some revenues and costs can be directly assigned to a segment of a business; others cannot. *Cost accounting* is the subfield of management accounting that assigns costs to the smallest segment of a business for which meaningful costs can be calculated. These segments are called *products*. The principal problem in cost accounting is to assign indirect costs to product.

Type of Information

Purpose	Measure the past	Plan the future	Purpose
Measure economic changes	I. Financial accounting Management accounting	II. Differential cash flow	Decision support
Control	III. Variance analysis	IV. Budgets	Set objectives

The accompanying diagram is called the accounting and control matrix. This matrix separates accounting information into four mutually exclusive types, each with a different and distinct purpose. Once the purpose is determined, the type of accounting information that is needed can be identified. Much of the confusion that exists in using accounting information results from confusing purposes and types of information. That is, the accounting information used may not be consistent with the type of problem being solved. The purpose of each square and the type of information required for that purpose is described next.

Square I

The left-hand squares (I and III) measure the past. Square I measures the past economic performance of the entire business and sections of the business. This includes all the traditional accounting information, the financial statements of the entire company and of divisions or subsidiaries, and all of the information on profits and costs of smaller business segments. In other words, Square I includes all the basic accounting information for either external or internal use. This information has two principal uses. First, it provides managers, owners, and interested outsiders (such as banks and potential stockholders) with past financial results. Second, it is a data bank from which information required by the other three squares can be derived.

Square II

The two right-hand squares represent the financial planning function and, therefore, use forecast information. Square II assists management in the *resource allocation* process. Management must make decisions on resources: when and where to deploy them and how much to deploy. The accountant assists in these decisions by providing the appropriate financial information to support these decisions. Decision support requires a *forecast* of the future because resource allocation decisions involve attempting to select that course of action that results in the greatest financial benefit to the company in the future.

In addition to overall financial plans, managers make hundreds of *specific* decisions involving the allocation of financial resources. Many of these are short-term marketing decisions involving prices, mix, sales promotion, and so forth. These are called short-term because the consequences of the decisions are resolved within a "short" period of time.

A second set of resource-allocation decisions involves discontinuing products, markets, or facilities. These are the disinvestment decisions.

A third set of decisions involves long-term investment decisions.

The financial information required to support management in all these decisions is the forecast of the *cash flow* that is expected to occur as a result of each decision. This is called *differential cash flow.* Differential cash flow includes all the changes in cash or equivalent, and only those changes, that are expected to occur as the result of a particular decision.

There are two things to note about this decision process. First, the differential cash flow is not the same as the traditional accounting information presented in the income statement, although it is developed from the basic accounting records. Second, the cash flow estimates are only one of several inputs into the decision process. Judgments on several other dimensions are required in making any resource allocation decision. In particular, assessments of the degree of uncertainty in the timing and amounts of future cash flow require managerial judgment.

Square IV

The purpose of the activities in Square IV is to set management objectives. The information provided in Square IV is forecast, and, as with Square II, this information is used to support resource allocation decisions as well as to set specific objectives for the manager. Each year, each business segment prepares budgets that are projections of future financial performance. Budgets allow top management to review and approve courses of action before they are undertaken. The approval of a budget is an allocation of resources to accomplish the budgetary goals. The budget also represents a commitment on the part of the budgetee to accomplish the goals within the resources provided.

Note that budgets *are* in the form of traditional accounting statements. For example, a profit budget is usually in the form of projected financial statements. This is necessary because actual financial results, which are in the traditional accounting format, are compared periodically to the budget.

In Square IV, the accountant has the responsibility for translating projected managerial actions into projected financial results. The accountant, however, does not have the responsibility for determining these actions.

Square III

The purpose of Square III is control. The information provided in Square III is variance analysis. Square III compares the actual financial results with the budget upon which the resource allocation decision was based. Square III uses the information generated in Squares I and IV to measure how well *managers* have met their objectives. Thus Square III provides a *follow-up* so that managers can be sure approved plans are being implemented.

The accountant has the responsibility of comparing actual results to the budget and analyzing variances. The explanation of the reasons for the variances and the forecast of future results are the responsibility of the manager, although all information relative to budget performance should be reviewed by the accountant for consistency and accuracy.

ORGANIZATION OF THE BOOK

This book is organized around the accounting and control matrix. Part I is concerned with traditional cost accounting systems (Square I). Part II is concerned with decision-support systems (Square II). Part III is concerned with financial planning and control systems (Squares III and IV). Finally, Part IV is concerned with certain broader problems in management control that are of primary concern to management accounting.

chapter 1

AN INTRODUCTION TO MANUFACTURING COST ACCOUNTING SYSTEMS

Cost accounting is the branch of accounting designed to measure the economic resources exchanged or consumed (or that will be exchanged or consumed) in producing goods or providing services. Typically a cost accounting system is used to provide management with information about the costs of products or services being produced and sold, with the estimated costs of good or services to be produced and sold in the future, and with the costs of goods or services produced and consumed within the company. In this part of the book we concentrate on systems that provide the costs of *products* currently being manufactured and sold (i.e., product costs). This is by far the most common use of cost accounting data. Other types of costs are developed by adapting product cost techniques. For example, the technique for determining service costs is similar to that for finding product costs except that service costs do not involve accounting for material. Or, estimated future costs are developed by adjusting current costs for expected changes in future conditions.

All manufacturing organizations must maintain some type of cost accounting system in order to obtain inventory values for the products they produce. This is required by both the public accountant and the Internal Revenue Service. A good cost accounting system, however, also meets the requirements of management for information concerning product costs. That is, it should serve as a data base for decision support and for financial planning and control systems.

INVENTORY VALUATION

The cost of manufactured products must be calculated in order to establish the value of inventories. In merchandising companies, inventory values are the invoice prices of the goods purchased. By contrast, in manufacturing industries, inputs of labor and other manufacturing costs are added to the cost of the purchased material. For example, in operating a textile mill, raw cotton is purchased. The cotton is mixed, carded, spun, woven, and dyed, thus producing cloth. The process of changing raw cotton into cloth adds to its value, and the added value is reflected in the cost of the finished cloth that is kept in inventory. Following the accounting principle of valuing assets at cost, inventories are valued at their costs of production.

Types of Inventories

In a merchandising enterprise, we have only one type of inventory, the inventory of the goods that are to be sold. In a manufacturing enterprise, however, there are three types of inventory: raw material, work-in-process, and finished goods. (There will also be an inventory of supplies in both merchandising or manufacturing. That is, purchased material, such as paper bags in a retail store, that will not be sold but will be used in the process of manufacturing or sales.)

Raw Material.   The raw material inventory consists of goods that have been purchased from outside vendors and that will subsequently be manufactured into finished products. These may be basic commodities such as cotton, steel, or pig iron, or they may be manufactured parts that will become components of finished products, such as spark plugs and tires in automobile manufacture.

Work-in-Process.   Work-in-process inventory consists of products that are in a semifinished state. Work-in-process inventory is valued at cost of the purchased material plus the cost of manufacturing up to the stage of completion at the time that the inventory is valued.

Finished Goods.   As might be expected, the finished goods inventory consists of the goods that have been completed and are awaiting sale. Finished goods are valued at the cost of the material plus the cost of manufacturing. Note that, for any company, finished goods are those goods for which the manufacturing process has been completed for *that* company. From the point of view of the entire production process, the goods may still be semifinished. For example, sheet steel may be finished goods for a steel mill but raw material for an automobile manufacturer. If the goods are available for sale, they are finished goods to the company holding them for sale.

ELEMENTS OF PRODUCT COSTS

Product costs are divided into three elements, which are discussed under the following headings: (1) direct material, (2) direct labor, and (3) manufacturing overhead (also called burden).

Direct Material

Direct material is material that can be directly identified with each unit of finished product, such as raw cotton in textile manufacture, pig iron in a foundry, or sheet steel in a stamping plant. Material that cannot be directly identified with a unit of finished product is called *indirect material*. For example, the coal that is used to heat the furnace is indirect material. Indirect material is included as part of manufacturing overhead.

Direct Labor

Direct labor is labor that can be identified directly with a unit of finished product. For example, the worker who runs a press that produces automobile body sides is considered to be direct labor because the time spent (and, con-sequently, the cost) can be identified directly with the products that are pro-duced.

Labor that cannot be identified with specific products is called *indirect labor* and is included under manufacturing overhead. For example, sweepers and maintenance men are classified as indirect labor.

Manufacturing Overhead

Manufacturing overhead normally includes all manufacturing costs other than direct material and direct labor. In addition to indirect material and indirect labor, manufacturing overhead includes such costs as utilities, maintenance, de-preciation, and taxes.

PRODUCT VERSUS PERIOD COSTS

The cost accounting system assigns material, labor, and overhead costs to prod-ucts. Costs so assigned become assets because they are included in inventory; thus they are called *product costs*. Costs that are written off in the period in which they are incurred are called *period costs*.

The reason for assigning manufacturing costs to inventory is that these ex-penditures increase the value of a product. For example, an automobile fender is more valuable than the sheet steel used to produce it. The theory is that costs that increase the value of a product are product costs and should be capitalized in inventory. This theory is generally interpreted to mean that costs incurred to change the form of a product are product costs. This has further been interpreted to mean manufacturing costs (i.e., costs incurred within a manufacturing plant). When all or most of the manufacturing costs are treated as product costs, we say that we are using a *full costing or full absorption system.* When only the variable costs are treated as product costs, we say that we are using a *direct costing system.* Both the public accounting profession and the Internal Revenue Service require that finished goods inventories be valued at full costs. Therefore, those companies using a direct costing system internally must adjust their inventories to provide full costs for financial statement and tax purposes.

The usual procedure is to include as product costs all costs, and only those costs, for which the plant manager is responsible. There is, however, some latitude in deciding which overhead costs should be included in product costs. (All direct material and direct labor are, of course, considered product costs.) Plant depreciation and/or plant administration are sometimes treated as period costs, and transportation from the factory to a warehouse is sometimes treated as a product cost. These variations are allowable for both financial statement and tax purposes.

TYPES OF PRODUCT COST SYSTEMS

Cost accounting systems are classified by the way in which direct material and direct labor are assigned to product. All cost accounting systems can be divided into historical cost accounting systems, standard cost accounting systems, and combination systems. Each is discussed shortly and considered in more detail in the following four chapters.

Historical Cost Accounting Systems

A historical cost accounting system is one that assigns the actual costs incurred during a period of time in manufacturing a group of products to the products produced in that period. (The usual period is a month, but some systems calculate product costs on a quarterly or annual basis.) Thus actual manufacturing costs are assigned to the products produced on an after-the-fact basis.

In a typical historical cost accounting system, direct material is requisitioned as needed. These requisitions identify the jobs that will use the material. Direct labor time cards identify the jobs upon which the labor was performed. At the end of the period, the overhead incurred during the period is allocated to the jobs worked on during the period. (The method of overhead allocation is discussed in the following chapters.)

Standard Cost Accounting Systems

A standard cost system develops product costs before the fact. That is, an estimate is made before the product is produced of what the costs should be. In general, this is done as follows:

Material. The material specifications are developed for each product. These are called the *standard quantities.* A price, called a *standard price,* is estimated for each type of material. The standard cost of each type of material is obtained by multiplying the standard quantity by the standard price. The sum of the standard costs of all types of material used in the production of a product is the standard material cost of that particular product.

Direct Labor. The amount of direct labor time required to produce each product is estimated. In the best standard cost systems, direct labor times represent industrial engineering time and motion studies of the operations required to produce the various products. Standard labor rates are established for each operation. In general, these rates are determined by union contract or industrial relations policies. Standard direct labor costs for each operation are calculated by multiplying the standard times by the standard rates. The standard direct labor cost for each product is the sum of the cost of all of the operations.

Overhead. Standard overhead is based on the annual overhead budget that is prepared and approved prior to the beginning of the year. The budget overhead is assigned to product using techniques described in later chapters.

Variances. The unique characteristic of a standard cost system is that instead of generating product costs, it generates variances from standard. At the end of each month, it is possible for management to know how much actual costs varied from standard and where the variances have occurred.

Combination Systems

Many actual cost accounting systems are combinations of historical and standard costs. One of the most common variations is to use historical material and labor and standard overhead.

Direct Cost Systems

In a direct cost accounting system, only the variable costs are assigned to the product (i.e., only variable costs are treated as product costs). The term *direct costs* can be confusing because it does not mean costs directly assigned to a product. It means variable cost. Direct cost systems may be either standard or historical.

COST DEFINITIONS

Variable and Fixed Costs

Variable costs are those costs that vary directly and approximately proportionately with the volume of production or sales. *Fixed costs* are those that do not vary with changes in the volume of production or sales. Whether a cost varies or remains constant when volume changes depends upon the circumstances surrounding the change—in particular, the degree and permanency of the change.

Differential Costs

Differential costs are *all* the costs, and *only* the costs, that change as the result of a specific decision. Differential costs have two characteristics that distinguish them from the product costs described earlier.

First, differential costs are estimated future costs. The future for any decision will be the time period over which the impact of the decision is to take place. For example, if it were necessary to decide whether to accept an order for a particular product, the expected cost at the time the product would be produced would be used. This could be quite different from the latest actual cost. In forward decisions, historical cost data are useful only as a basis for estimating future costs.

Second, differential costs include only costs that change as a result of the decision being analyzed. Costs that do not change, such as rent of a building, are ignored. Also, costs previously incurred are ignored. For example, a decision about whether or not to continue a research project should not be affected by costs already incurred on the project. The decision should be based on the additional cost that is expected in the future.

For practical purposes, differential costs can be thought of as the out-of-pocket cash outflow that will result from a decision. Occasionally, other assets are affected, such as additional building space occupied. In such cases, the estimated cash value of these noncash resources is used.

Opportunity Costs

Opportunity costs are the economic resources that have been foregone as the result of accepting one alternative instead of another. For example, assume that a manufacturer can sell a semifinished product to an outside buyer for $1000. It is decided, however, to keep it and finish it. The opportunity cost of the semifinished product is $1000 because this is the amount of economic resources that the manufacturer gave up in order to complete the product. No cash has changed hands, which is the unique feature of an opportunity cost. There is no exchange of economic resources because opportunity costs result from foregoing some action, which means that opportunity costs are never reflected in the regular cost accounting records. This factor represents a decided limitation in using accounting data for making certain kinds of decisions—for example, accounting information for evaluating managerial performance. Accounting data do not show the losses from suboptimum decisions. In other words, a manager could make a series of decisions that resulted in lost profit opportunities, yet, if the total profit were not too low (and there could be many reasons why it was not), the opportunity losses might go completely unrecorded and undetected.

Direct Costs

Direct costs (as contrasted to direct cost systems) are the costs that can be assigned directly to an organization unit or a product. Depreciation of equipment in a department and indirect labor working in a department are examples of direct department costs. Direct material and direct labor are examples of direct product costs. When a cost cannot be assigned directly, it is allocated.

Sunk Costs

Sunk costs represent economic resources that have already been committed and cannot be recovered—for example, the amount of money spent to date on a researach project that has not yet yielded results. Another example of a sunk cost is the difference between the purchase price of a fixed asset and the net amount that could be realized from its sale. The important point about sunk costs is that they are not relevant in calculating the future financial impact of a forward decision.

QUESTIONS

1.1   A company produces about 500 different products annually. Currently it has been just about breaking even. It has never had an adequate cost accounting system. Suppose that a system was installed that provided accurate product costs for most of the products for the past year. As a manager, what would you do with this information?

1.2   Explain how product costs are used to control manufacturing costs.

1.3   Develop a statement that might be included in a contoller's manual that establishes a rule for deciding whether a particular expense is a product cost or a period cost. Include a rationale or justification for this rule.

1.4   Explain the difference between full costs, variable costs, and differential costs. How would management use each of these costs?

1.5   Give several examples of opportunity costs, other than those given in the text.

1.6   Explain the difference between a direct cost and a direct costing system.

1.7   Give several examples of sunk cost, other than those given in the text.

1.8   In what circumstances do you believe that historical costs are most useful?

1.9 In what circumstances do you believe that standard cost systems are most useful?

1.10 In what circumstances do you believe that combination accounting systems are most useful?

PROBLEMS

1.1 Caluclate the missing amounts. (Numbers given are in thousands.) (See Case 1.1, Marrett Manufacturing Company, for an example of the format to be used.)

	A	B	C	D
Raw material inventory, 1/1/71	$ 500	$1600	$2900	$4200
Raw material inventory, 12/31/71	300	1700	3000	?
Purchases of raw material	400	500	900	2000
Direct labor	100	400	300	100
Indirect labor	75	150	200	100
Supplies	35	60	100	25
Utilities	25	75	50	40
Maintenance	130	100	150	50
Depreciation	50	75	150	60
Work-in-process inventory, 1/1/71	600	800	?	1200
Work-in-process inventory, 12/31/71	700	900	1200	1100
Finished goods inventory, 1/1/71	1000	2500	1000	8000
Finished goods inventory, 12/31/71	800	?	600	5000
Cost of goods sold	?	3060	1950	4675

1.2 Calculate the full and variable product cost per unit for each of the products A, B, C, and D.

	PRODUCTS			
	A	B	C	D
Direct material[a]	$ 500	$ 800	$ 1,000	$5,000
Direct labor[a]	100	400	1,000	2,000
Indirect labor[b]	100	300	1,000	1,000
Supplies[a]	50	20	200	500
Utilities[a]	40	20	300	1,500
Maintenance[b]	30	50	500	500
Depreciation[c]	60	100	600	500
Selling expenses[c]	100	400	2,000	1,000
Administrative expenses[c]	75	100	1,500	500
Units produced	1,000	2,000	10,000	5,000

[a]Variable cost.

[b]One-half is variable cost.

[c]Fixed cost.

1.3 Fred Smith estimates that the costs to run his automobile are as follows:

Gas, oil, grease, etc.	$0.03 per mile
Tires and repairs	0.01 per mile
Depreciation	500 per year
Insurance	100 per year

Approximate mileage driven per year: 10,000

(a) What is Smith's total cost per year for running his car?

(b) What is Smith's cost per mile?

(c) If Smith were to rent his car for $.15 a mile, for how many miles would he have to rent it before he would break even (make exactly zero profit)?

(d) Assume Smith has an investment of $3000 in his car. For how many miles would he have to rent it in order to earn 10% on his investment?

(e) Smith estimates he can rent his car for 12,000 miles next year. What price per mile must he charge (1) to break even, (2) to earn 10% on his investment?

CASES

CASE 1.1   MARRETT MANUFACTURING COMPANY

The management of the Marrett Manufacturing Company annually prepared a budget of expected financial operations for the ensuing calendar year. The completed budget provided information on all aspects of the coming year's operations. It included an estimated balance sheet as of the end of the year and an estimated income statement.

The final preparation of statements was accomplished only after careful integration of detailed computations submitted by each department. This was done to ensure that the operations of all departments were in balance with one another. For example, the finance department needed to base its schedules of loan operations and of collections and disbursements on figures that were dependent upon manufacturing, purchasing, and selling expectations. The level of production would be geared to the forecasts of the sales department, and purchasing would be geared to the proposed manufacturing schedule. In short, it was necessary to integrate the estimates of each department and to revise them in terms of the overall effect on operations to arrive at a well-formulated and profitable plan of operations for the coming year. The budget statements ultimately derived from the adjusted estimated transactions would then serve the company as a reliable guide and measure of the coming year's operations.

At this time the 1986 budget was being prepared, in November of 1985, estimated 1985 financial statements were compiled for use as a comparison with the budgeted figures. These 1985 statements were based on nine months' actual and three months' estimated transactions. They appear as Exhibits 1, 2, and 3.

Following is the summary of expected operations for the budget year 1986 as finally accepted:

1. *Sales:* All on credit, $815,000; sales returns and allowances, $7000; sales discounts taken by customers, $15,000. (The sales figure is net of expected bad debts.)
2. *Purchase of goods and services:*
    (a) New assets:
    Purchased for cash: manufacturing plant and equipment, $31,000; prepaid manufacturing taxes and insurance, $12,000.
    Purchased on accounts payable: raw materials, $227,000; supplies, $25,000.

EXHIBIT 1   Marrett Manufacturing Co.

Estimated Balance Sheet, December 31, 1985

ASSETS		
CURRENT ASSETS:		
Cash		$ 70,000
Accounts receivable (net of allowance for doubtful accounts)		123,000
Inventories:		
Raw materials	$119,000	
Goods in process	47,000	
Finished goods	15,000	
Supplies	33,000	214,000
Prepaid taxes and insurance		9,000
Total Current Assets		$416,000
FIXED ASSETS:		
Manufacturing plant	$620,000	
Less: Accumulated deprecation	210,000	410,000
Total Assets		$826,000
LIABILITIES AND CAPITAL		
CURRENT LIABILITIES:		
Notes payable	$ 64,000	
Accounts payable	27,000	
Unpaid estimated federal income taxes	5,000	
Total Current Liabilities		$ 96,000
CAPITAL:		
Capital stock	$670,000	
Retained earnings	60,000	730,000
Total Liabilities and Capital		$826,000

EXHIBIT 2   Marrett Manufacturing Co.

ESTIMATED STATEMENT OF COST OF GOODS SOLD, 1985

Finished goods inventory, 1/1/85			$166,500
Goods in process inventory, 1/1/85		$ 52,000	
Raw materials used		181,000	
Plus: Factory expenses:			
Direct manufacturing labor		97,000	
Factory overhead:			
Indirect manufacturing labor	$38,000		
Power, heat, and light	27,000		
Depreciation of plant	29,000		
Social security taxes	5,500		
Taxes and insurance, factory	5,000		
Supplies	15,800	120,300	
		$450,300	
Less: Goods in process inventory, 12/31/85		47,000	
Cost of goods manufactured (i.e., completed)			403,300
			$569,800
Less: Finished goods inventory, 12/31/85			15,000
Cost of goods sold			$554,800

(b)   Services used to convert raw materials into goods in process,[1] all pur-chased for cash: direct manufacturing labor, $152,000; indirect manufac-turing labor, $56,000; social security taxes on labor, $9,400; power, heat, and light, $41,600. (Accrued payroll was ignored in these estimates.)

(c)   Sales and administrative service, purchased for cash: $234,000.

3.   *Conversion of assets into goods in process:* This appears as an increase in the "value" of goods in process and a decrease in the appropriate asset accounts. Deprecia-tion of building and equipment, $26,000; expiration of prepaid taxes and in-

EXHIBIT 3   Marrett Manufacturing Co.

ESTIMATED INCOME STATEMENT, 1985

Sales		$728,600
Less: Sales returns and allowances	$ 5,600	
Sales discounts allowed	14,000	19,600
Net sales		$709,000
Less: Cost of goods sold (per schedule)		554,800
Gross profit margin		$154,200
Less: Sales and administrative expense		120,200
Net operating profit		$ 34,000
Less: Interest expense		2,000
Net profit before federal income tax		$ 32,000
Less: Estimated income tax		9,000
Net profit after federal income tax		$ 23,000

---

[1]In a manufacturing company, inventory is assumed to increase in value by the amounts spent to convert raw material into salable products. These amounts include the items listed in 2(b) plus the items listed in 3.

surance, $8000; supplies used in manufacturing, $29,000; raw materials put into process, $259,000.

4. *Transfer of goods in process into finished goods:* This appears as an increase in finished goods and a decrease in goods in process. Total cost accumulated on goods that have been completed and transferred to finished goods inventory, $549,000.

5. *Cost of finished goods sold to customers:* $499,000.

6. *Financial transactions:*
   (a) $180,000, borrowed on notes payable to bank.
   (b) Bank loans paid off (i.e., retired), $210,000.
   (c) Cash payment to bank of $3,000 for interest on loans.

7. *Cash receipts from customers on accounts receivable:* $807,000.

8. *Cash payments of liabilities:*
   (a) Payment of accounts payable, $249,000.
   (b) Payment of 1985 income tax, $5,000.

9. *Estimated federal income tax on 1986 income:* $28,000, of which $10,000 is estimated to be unpaid as of December 31, 1986.

10. *Dividends declared for year and paid in cash:* $11,000.

This summary presents the complete cycle of the Marrett Manufacturing Company's budgeted yearly operations from the purchase of goods and services through their various stages of conversion to completion of the finished product to the sale of this product. All costs and cash receipts and disbursements involved in this cycle are presented, including the provision for federal income tax and the payment of dividends.

Questions

1. Journalize each of the estimated transactions. Set up T accounts with balances as shown on the balance sheet for December 31, 1985 and post the journal entries to these accounts.

2. Prepare an estimated statement of cost of goods sold for 1986, an estimated income statement for 1986, and an estimated balance sheet as of December 31, 1986.

3. Describe the principal differences between the 1986 estimates and the 1985 figures as shown in Exhibits 1, 2, and 3. In what respects is 1986 performance expected to be better than 1985 performance, and in what respects is it expected to be poorer?

CASE 1.2   YARWOOD BLANKET COMPANY

The Yarwood Blanket Company was a large producer of cotton blankets. Since the company performed all the operations from the baled cotton to the finished

This case was prepared by C. A. Bliss and R. C. Walker. Copyright © by the President and Fellows of Harvard College. Harvard Business School case 9-150-005.

blankets, and since a market existed for cotton in various stages of manufacture, an ever-present problem before its management was at what point in the manufacture of a blanket the alternative of selling the uncompleted product was more profitable than continuing with the manufacturing process toward a later market. In the spring of 1985, during a period of under-capacity operations, an incident occurred that raised the question of the validity of using the familiar total average cost accumulations and prorations of the accounting department as a basis for deciding at what point to terminate manufacturing and to sell the product in process.

At a meeting of the principal executives in the spring of 1985, the sales manager proposed that the carding and spinning capacity of the mill be used to produce warp yarn which, he said, could be currently sold at a profit. The production manager on the other hand contended that the loom capacity of the plant rendered it desirable to continue any yarn operations through to the stage of blankets. The sales manager defended his position with the following figures from the cost office, which had based the figures on the cost office's current standard cost sheets.

	COST PER POUND, WARP YARN	COST PER BLANKET*
Labor	$0.1864	$0.4160
Overhead	.1440	.3180
Processing materials	.0172	.1080
Raw materials	.8800	2.6400
	$1.2276	$3.4820
Current selling price	1.2800	3.4600
Profit (loss)	$0.0524	$(0.0220)

*Each blanket contained 1 pound of warp yarn plus filling yarn.

The costs are cumulative in each category. Thus the $0.4160 labor item for blankets covers a $0.1864 per pound charge for the labor needed to make the warp yarn, plus the appropriate labor element in the filling yarn cost and the labor cost of weaving the blanket.

The production manager challenged the validity of any figures that indicated that the optimum move for the management was to shut down the greater part of the mill in the face of a reasonably favorable market that would provide considerable demand for blankets. He argued that the plant was set up to manufacture blankets, not yarn, and to sell yarn was, in effect, to get out of the blanket business in which the company had made its name. Moreover, he wasn't sure but that the company, despite the generally weak market, might do better financially by keeping the blanket room open.

The head of the cost office stated that the figures presented by the sales manager had been the result of painstaking studies of labor and material costs and of methods of distributing burden to products. He admitted that certain allocations were rough and that different kinds of costs were reported together. For example, on being questioned, he said that for both yarn and blankets about 15% of the labor cost was "fixed" and that 60% of overhead was of the same character.

The executives had to reach a decision on the issue. The sales manager was opposed to selling blankets at a loss when he could be selling yarn at a profit. The production manager certainly didn't want to close down his blanket mill.

Required

1. What different courses of action might be taken, and what arguments might be made to support them?

2. What information or forecasts might be necessary to round out the story?

3. On balance and in the light of the probable state of affairs, what would you decide?

4. If the current selling price of warp yarn was $1.367 per pound, instead of $1.28 as given in the case, would your decision be changed?

chapter 2

STANDARD COST
ACCOUNTING SYSTEMS

Chapter 1 briefly described standard costs. The purpose of this chapter is to consider standard cost systems in more detail.

SOME BASIC CONCEPTS

No Actual Costs

Most standard cost accounting systems do not produce actual costs at all; they produce only variances. That is, the difference in costs between one month and the next is expressed in the amount of the variances, not in differences in product costs. In many mass-production factories, there are no practical means for measuring actual product costs. With hundreds of parts, subassemblies and final assemblies being produced simultaneously, it is almost impossible to keep a record of the direct labor time and direct material that is used on each product or assembly. This is one reason for using a standard cost system.

As explained later in this section of the chapter, standard costs provide a better basis for decision-making than actual costs, assuming that standard costs are reasonably accurate. Protection against inaccurate standard costs is provided by variance analysis. If variances are large, an investigation can be made to see if standards should be changed. Consequently, there is normally no need for the actual costs of each product.

When Should Standard Costs Be Used?

A standard cost accounting system is one where product costs are developed before the fact, based on estimates of what the costs should be. Standard costs were originally developed to help control manufacturing costs, and this is still the primary emphasis in standard cost accounting systems. Where standard costs provide effective cost control, they will also provide reliable information for the other uses of product cost information. Consequently, we evaluate standard cost systems in terms of their cost control function.

Effective cost control is obtained by comparing the actual manufacturing costs with the standard and analyzing variances, both in terms of causal factors and organization units responsible. Management's attention is directed to those areas where expenses are higher than standard. It is, then, a system of management by exception. Operating managers are evaluated on their cost performance against standard, and changes are made where cost performance is consistently out of line with standard. Operating managers are *motivated*, therefore, to meet standards because they are being *evaluated* against them.

For a standard cost system to be an effective control tool, two conditions are necessary:

1. It must be possible to set standards that represent a fair and reasonable cost goal for the operating managers: and
2. It must be possible for the line manager to control the performance variables and to isolate the impact on costs of changes in noncontrollable performance variables.

These two conditions are fairly obvious. If an equitable objective cannot be set, how can it be used as a standard to measure how well an operating manager has performed? If a manager cannot control the performance variables or isolate the impact of noncontrollable variables, how can the system accurately measure the efficiency of the operating manager?

The preceding two conditions exist in large, mass-production plants. Precise material specifications have been drawn, production lines laid out, direct labor allowances measured by time and motion study methods, overhead budgets developed, and operating conditions carefully controlled. Consequently we can say that standard costs should be used where mass-production techniques are used, unless there is some compelling reason, unique to the business, that makes some other system necessary.

The use of a standard cost accounting system, therefore, depends on the production technology. The closer a plant is to employing mass-production technology, the more adaptable it is to using standard costs. (Another way of looking at it is, the more repetitive the production cycle, the more useful will be standard cost techniques.)

There is little question that, in most instances, a good standard cost system will provide better management information than a historical cost system. The problem is to decide whether it is practicable to set good standards and whether management needs a sophisticated system of variance analysis. With small businesses, in particular, costs are controlled by personal observation; consequently, the analysis of standard cost variances only tells managers what they already knew.

Advantages of Standard Costs Over Historical Costs

There are three principal limitations to historical cost systems: First, the clerical effort of identifying direct material and direct labor with specific products can be expensive and, in some types of manufacturing processes, almost impossible. Second, cost inefficiencies may be buried in the value of finished goods inventory and not reflected in the income statement until a considerable period after these inefficiencies were incurred. Third, historical cost systems do not provide an adequate means for measuring the efficiency of the manufacturing operation. This part of the chapter describes how standard costs overcome these problems.

Clerical Efficiency. In many production processes, especially in mass-production industries, it is very difficult—if not nearly impossible—to identify specific costs with the products being produced. Literally hundreds of different products flow through a given department during any time period. Even where it is possible to identify costs with products, it can be expensive to maintain the paper work necessary to do this.

In standard cost systems, actual costs are *not* usually identified by product. They are charged only to departments. Products move from work-in-process inventory to finished goods inventory at *standard cost.* Thus it is necessary to know only the number and type of product completed by each department.

Cost Inefficiency. Using a historical cost system, the finished goods inventory is charged with all costs incurred.[1] Suppose, for example, in a given month a major breakdown occurred that doubled the labor cost of certain products. The excess costs would be charged to finished goods inventory and, if the company was on a first-in, first-out basis of inventory valuation, profits might not be affected for several months. If the company was on an average inventory valuation basis, the effect of one month's inefficiencies would gradually affect profits over a much longer period of time.

---

[1]Some historical cost systems provide for unusual expenses to be written off directly against income.

With standard costs, finished goods inventories are valued at standard, and costs in excess of standard are identified as variances and can be written off against income in the period in which they were incurred.

Evaluation.   Standard cost systems provide a means for evaluating manufacturing managers. Ideally, a standard cost should represent the potential efficiency of an operating facility. The difference between the actual and the standard represents how well this potential was realized. This, then, can be a basis for measuring the efficiency of the people responsible. It should be noted, however, that variances alone do not measure efficiency because some variances may be beyond the control of the operating manager. All management evaluation requires some degree of subjective judgment. Variances help in the exercise of this judgment.

Up-To-Date Standards

In order for a standard cost accounting system to provide the advantages described in this part of the chapter, it is vital that the standards be kept up to date. With historical cost systems, product costs always reflect the latest condition and, thus, are automatically updated. In standard cost systems, on the other hand, there must be specific procedures for changing standards as conditions change.

Out-of-date standards are usually worse than no standards at all. In cost control, the variances become a function of volume rather than of efficiency. For example, assume that a set of standards is 15% understated because of changes in economic levels. The variance will be equal to 15% of total costs plus or minus the effect of differences in efficiency. It is obvious that such variances will be useless for cost control.

Costs that are incorrect cannot, of course, be used for making marketing decisions or diagnosing unprofitable operations. Even inventory valuation is distorted. Profit will rise when goods are sold from inventory (assuming that the standards are understated) and fall when production exceeds sales. This can make the monthly income statement a poor measure of financial accomplishment.

Note that the problem is considerably exacerbated by inflation, and the greater the degree of inflation, the more frequently the standards have to be brought up to date.

Level of Standards

When standard cost systems are being developed, the question usually occurs as to how difficult the standards should be. One school of thought is that the standards should represent nearly perfect performance. That is, the standard would be met only if all conditions were optimum. Consequently, the standard could never be bettered, only equaled. The arguments for such difficult standards are

1. Management is provided with a precise measure of efficiency. This is more meaningful than that resulting from a looser standard because there can be many degrees of looseness.
2. It is psychologically better to make operating managers reach for the ultimate in efficiency.

A second school of thought is that standards should be attainable with good average performance. The arguments for attainable standards (and consequently the arguments against perfect standards) are:

1. Attainable standards can be used as a basis for decision-support systems. If perfect standards are used, they must be adjusted upward for uses other than cost control.
2. Attainable standards make a better "management by exception" technique because unfavorable variances mean less than satisfactory performance. With perfect standards, there will be unfavorable variances even with satisfactory performance.
3. Attainable standards are psychologically better than perfect standards because perfect standards discourage operating managers.

Many people prefer attainable standards, although it is probably not a vital issue. (If perfect performance standards are used, however, they must be adjusted upward when used for any other purpose than cost control.)

Regardless of the level of the standards, I believe that standard cost elements should always be separated into two types: (a) those that can be controlled by the operating manager; and (b) those out of the control of the operating manager. The former should be developed on the basis of good performance (or perfect performance, if this is the management decision); the latter should be established on the basis of the best forecast of actual conditions. Often-recommended elements of standard cost and level of performance are as follows:

- *Direct material specification:* efficient but attainable material usage with allowance for necessary scrap.
- *Direct material prices:* best estimate of expected levels. In absence of any reliable evidence of change, current prices would be used.
- *Direct labor hours:* efficient but attainable levels of performance.
- *Direct labor rates:* best estimate of expected levels.
- *Overhead:* efficient but attainable levels of cost. Indirect labor salaries, indirect material prices, and purchased utilities prices should be the best estimates of expected levels.

As you can see, a standard cost is a combination of a management commitment to meet a given level of performance and a forecast of price levels. It is important that managers be evaluated on their abilities to meet their commitments, not on their abilities to forecast price levels. Consequently, the analyses of variances should keep the forecast variances separated from the performance variances to the extent possible.

MECHANICS OF STANDARD COST ACCOUNTING

This part of the chapter described the flow of standard cost accounting information through the accounting records.

Direct Material

As indicated previously, standard direct material consists of two elements: standard quantity and standard price. The standard quantities are developed from engineering specifications and represent a performance standard for material usage. Standard prices, however, are almost always a forecast of expected prices and do not represent a standard of performance for the purchasing department. The reason for this is simply that the prices of most materials are not controllable by any one company and that price level fluctuations are not caused by the efficiency or inefficiency of the purchasing function.

When material is purchased, the accounting entry is as follows:

Raw material inventory	Standard cost
Material price variance	Standard minus actual cost
Accounts payable	Actual cost

When material is used the entry is:

Work-in-process inventory: material	Standard cost × actual
Raw material inventory	quantity

In other words, it is customary to separate the material price variance (the difference between the standard price and the actual price) at the time the material is purchased. The reason for this is that notification is given to management of a price variance at the time it occurs. Some systems record material at actual prices and show the variance when it is put into process. The disadvantage of this procedure is that there could be a significant delay between a price change and management's cognizance of this situation, if the purchased material has remained in inventory for any period of time. This book assumes that material price variances are taken at the time of purchase.

During the month, then, as material is requisitioned it is debited to an account called work-in-process-material or something similar. By the end of the month, this account has been credited for the standard material cost of all products completed during the month. The amount left in the material-in-process account represents the differencce between the standard usage and the actual usage.[2] This amount is transferred to the material usage variance account.

---

[2]In this chapter we have assumed that there is no work left in process at either at the beginning or the end of the month. Also, we have assumed a company with a single productive department. For more complicated situations, the same principles apply; the calculations, however, are more complex.

Example of Standard Material Accounting. Assume that the ABC Company produced three products A, B, and C. Each of these products consists of two raw
materials, X and Y. The standard material costs are as follows:

		A	*B*	*C*
Standard pounds per unit	X	1	1	—
	Y	1	—	1
Standard price per pound	X	$1.00	$1.00	—
	Y	2.00	—	$2.00
Standard material cost	X	$1.00	$1.00	—
	Y	2.00	—	$2.00
Total		$3.00	$1.00	$2.00

Purchases during the month are as follows:

- Material X, 1000 pounds at $1.25 per pound
- Material Y, 500 pounds at $1.90 per pound

The accounting entries, then, can be summarized as follows:

(1)

Material X		
Raw material Inventory	$1000	
Purchase price variance	250	
Accounts payable		$1250

(2)

Material Y		
Raw material inventory	$1000	
Accounts payable		$950
Purchase price variance		50

During the month the following quantities were issued from raw material
inventory:

- 210 units of material X
- 205 units of material Y

(3)

Work-in-process inventory: material	$210	
Raw material inventory		$210

(4)

Work-in-process inventory: material	$410	
Raw material inventory		$410

During the month, the following products were completed and transferred to the finished goods inventory: Product A, 50 units; Product B, 150 units; Product C, 150 units. Standard material cost of these three products is calculated as follows:

		STANDARD COST		
PRODUCT	**NUMBER OF UNITS**	*Material X*	*Material Y*	*Total*
A	50	$ 50	$100	$150
B	150	150	—	150
C	150	—	300	300
		$200	$400	$600

This entry would be:

(5)

Finished goods inventory	$600	
Work-in-process inventory: material		$600

Since the work-in-process material account has been debited with a total of $620 and credited with only $600, this leaves $20 still in the account because actual material usage was $20 higher than standard. The entry to remove this amount from work-in-process is:

(6)

Material usage variance	$20	
Work-in-process inventory: material		$20

Direct Labor

Direct labor standards are established by making time studies for each labor operation for each part produced. The result is standard times (or minutes) per part. Next a standard labor rate is established. In some instances, an average rate is developed and this, when multiplied by the total standard minutes per part, becomes the standard direct labor. In other instances, a separate rate is developed for each operation. The rate for each operation is multiplied by the time for that operation. The sum of the direct labor costs for all of the operations is the standard direct labor cost for the part. Obviously, the latter method will be more accurate but more expensive to calculate. The method to be used is determined by whether the extra accuracy is worth the extra cost.

From an accounting point of view, direct labor is handled in a manner very similar to direct material except, of course, there is no inventory. As direct labor costs are incurred the entry is:

$$\left.\begin{array}{l}\text{Work-in-process inventory: direct labor}\\\quad\text{Accrued payroll}\end{array}\right\}\quad\text{actual labor cost}$$

At the end of each month, the finished goods account is debited for the standard cost of the direct labor in the goods transferred and the work-in-process inventory account is credited. The difference between the standard and actual direct labor is transferred to the direct labor variance account.

$$\left.\begin{array}{l}\text{Finished goods inventory}\\\quad\text{Work-in-process inventory: direct labor}\\\text{Direct labor variances}\\\quad\text{Work-in-process inventory: direct labor}\end{array}\right\}\quad\begin{array}{l}\text{standard cost of goods}\\\quad\text{transferred}\\\text{(if actual is greater than}\\\quad\text{standard)}\end{array}$$

or

$$\left.\begin{array}{l}\text{Work-in-process inventory: direct labor}\\\quad\text{Direct labor variance}\end{array}\right\}\quad\begin{array}{l}\text{(if standard is greater than}\\\quad\text{actual)}\end{array}$$

Example of Direct Labor. In the ABC Company just described, the standard direct labor costs are as follows: A, $2.50; B, $3.00; and C, $3.50. During the month, actual direct labor charges of $1200 were incurred. During the period 50 units of A, 150 units of B, and 150 units of C were completed and transferred to finished goods inventory. The entries for these transactions are as follows:

(7)

Work-in-process inventory: direct labor	$1200	
Accrued payroll		$1200

To record the accrued of wage liability:

(8)

Finished goods inventory	$1100	
Work-in-process inventory: direct labor		$1100

To record the transfer to finished goods:

PRODUCT	NUMBER OF UNITS TRANSFERRED	STANDARD COST PER UNIT	STANDARD COST TRANSFERRED
A	50	$2.50	$125
B	150	3.00	450
C	150	3.50	525
			$1100

(9)

Direct labor variance	$100	
Work-in-process inventory: direct labor		$100

This entry removes the difference between actual and standard direct labor from work-in-process inventory and charges it to the direct labor variance account.

Overhead

Techniques for developing standard overhead costs are described in Chapter 4. Once the overhead costs are established, the accounting for overhead follows the same pattern as accounting for direct material and labor. As actual overhead costs are incurred, they are recorded in the appropriate account. For example, the overhead costs incurred during a month could be summarized by the following accounting entry:

Indirect labor ⎫
Indirect material ⎪
Utilities ⎬ actual amount of costs
Expense tools ⎪
Maintenance ⎪
Depreciation ⎭
Accured payroll ⎫
Accounts payable ⎬ actual amounts
Allowance for depreciation ⎭

At the end of the period, the individual overhead costs are closed to work-in-process as follows:

Work-in process inventory: overhead
Indirect labor
Indirect material
Utilities
Expense tools
Maintenance
Depreciation

Next the finished goods account is increased by the standard overhead cost of the goods completed and the work-in-process inventory account is relieved of this amount.

Finished goods inventory	——	
Work-in-process inventory: overhead		——

Finally, the difference between actual cost and standard cost is closed to the overhead variance account.

Overhead variance $\left.\begin{array}{l}\\ \\ \end{array}\right\}$ difference between actual
    Work-in-process inventory: overhead   and standard

Example of Overhead. Assume that in the ABC Company described previously, the standard overhead rate was 200% of the direct labor cost. Overhead costs incurred during the month are recorded as follows:

(10)

Indirect labor	$800	
Indirect material	300	
Utilities	200	
Expense tools	100	
Depreciation	600	
Accrued payroll		$800
Accounts payable		600
Allowance for depreciation		600

At the end of the month, the overhead expenses are entered into the work-in-process inventory account.

(11)

Work-in-process inventory: overhead	$2000	
Indirect labor		$800
Indirect material		300
Utilities		200
Expense tools		100
Depreciation		600

The finished goods account is increased by the standard overhead of the goods completed and the work-in-process inventory account is relieved by this amount.

(12)

Finished goods inventory	$2200	
Work-in-process inventory: overhead		$2200

(This was obtained by multiplying the standard direct labor by the 200% overhead rate. Note that the standard overhead amount is obtained by multiplying the standard overhead rate by the *standard* direct labor, *not* the actual direct labor.)

    Finally, the difference between actual and standard overhead is transferred to the overhead variance account as follows:

(13)

Work-in-process inventory: overhead	$200	
Overhead variance		$200

Exhibit 1 demonstrates in diagrammatic form the flow of information through the ABC cost accounting system.

Actual Systems

The purpose of this part of the chapter has been to give you an idea of the flow of information through a standard cost accounting system. The example has been simplified in several ways. First, a plant with a single department was assumed. Second, there is no work-in-process inventory at either the beginning or the end of the period. Third, a very limited number of accounts was used. If, however, the complexity of the example had been increased for these factors, it would not in any way have changed the principles involved. All that would have been done would be to increase the complexity of the calculations. The mechanics of a standard cost accounting system can be very complex, even though the principles are exactly the same as demonstrated in this part of the chapter.

Management Considerations

A standard cost accounting system is usually so superior to the typical historical cost system for most uses that the manager should always find out why standard costs are not being used. In other words, there should be a positive explanation as to why some other type of cost accounting system is providing more meaningful information. One possible reason is that a plant produces exclusively to customer specifications, which are always different. Even here, it might be possible to divide the production processes into standard elements and to establish standard costs for each element. The standard cost for any product would be the total standard cost for all of the elements required to produce the product. Thus, it would be possible to use a standard cost system even when each product is different.

Any company that uses mass-production techniques and yet does not use a standard cost accounting system should seriously investigate what unique features of their company preclude them from using standard costs effectively. The large majority of mass-production industries has changed successfully over the past twenty or thirty years to standard costs. The question that management must have answered is "What is there about this company that makes a standard cost system impractical?"

QUESTIONS

2.1   Describe some manufacturing conditions where it is not practicable to set fair product cost standards against which a plant manager can be measured.

2.2   Describe some manufacturing conditions where it is not practicable to measure performance fairly.

2.3   How would you control costs in the situations described in 2.1 and 2.2?

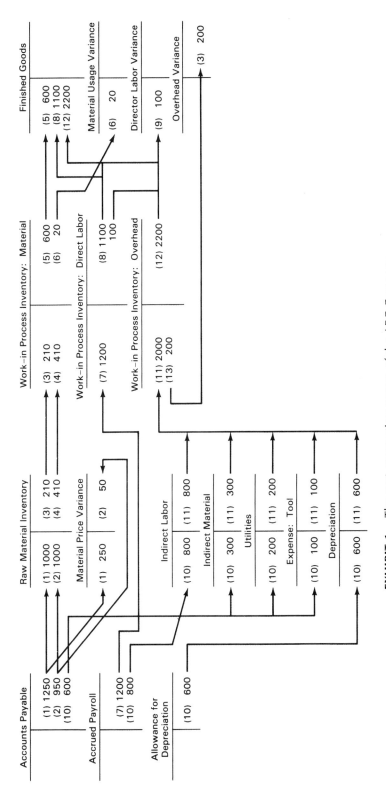

EXHIBIT 1 The cost accounting system of the ABC Company

2.4 Use an example to explain the difference between cost control using historical product costs and cost control using a standard cost accounting system.

2.5 Assume that a company used a standard cost system and that management asked for the "actual" cost of a particular product. How would you go about getting this cost?

2.6 A company uses a historical cost system. One month a production problem shut down most of the plant for nearly two weeks. As a result, the product costs were very high that month. How and when would this condition be reflected in the income statement? If you think that the situation described in the preceding question is unsatisfactory, how would you go about correcting it within the historical cost system?

2.7 The text describes two levels of standards: nearly perfect performance and good but attainable standards. What do you think about setting a standard half-way between these two levels?

2.8 What might be some possible reasons for a mass-production factory not using standard costs?

PROBLEMS

2.1 Listed below is some standard cost information for the Soennecken Company:

	PRODUCTS		
	A	B	C
RAW MATERIAL			
Material 1			
Standard amount required (in lb)	1	2	3
Standard price per lb = $.10			
Material 2			
Standard amount required (in lb)	5	4	3
Standard price per lb = $.50			
Material 3			
Standard amount required (in lb)	1	2	1
Standard price per lb = $5.00			
DIRECT LABOR			
Forging department			
Standard hours	0.5	2	1
Standard labor rate per hour = $3.60			
Machining department			
Standard hours	0.5	1	1.5
Standard labor rate per hour = $4.00			

	PRODUCTS		
	A	B	C
Assembly department			
Standard hours	0.5	0.5	0.5
Standard labor rate per hour = $2.00			

OVERHEAD	DEPARTMENTS		
	Forging	*Machining*	*Assembly*
Total budgeted overhead	$300,000	$450,000	$150,000
Total budgeted standard direct labor	75,000	100,000	100,000

Required

Develop unit standard costs for each of the products described.

2.2 The results of actual operations in the Soennecken Company for January 1986 are as follows:

PRODUCTION COSTS	
Raw materials	$33,420
DIRECT LABOR	
Forging	16,830
Machining	12,900
Assembly	2,800
OVERHEAD	
Forging	60,450
Machining	48,920
Assembly	6,100
PRODUCTION (in units)	
A	900
B	1,200
C	1,500

Required

Calculate the standard cost for each of the actual costs and determine the amount of the variances.

2.3 The president of the Soennecken Company asked the chief accountant to provide him with the "actual" production costs for January. The chief accountant decided that the only way she could calculate the actual costs was to adjust the standard costs by the percentage of the variances. Calculate actual costs by this method. How useful do you think these costs will be to the president?

2.4 Make the journal entries for the material transactions for January for the Soen-necken Company. Material purchases during the month were: 1000 lb of material 1 for $0.09 per lb; 5000 lb of material 2 for $0.52 per lb; 2000 lb of material 3 for $5.25 per lb. There was no work in process at either the beginning or the end of the period.

2.5 Make the journal entries for the direct labor transactions for January for the Soen-necken Company.

2.6 Make the journal entries for the overhead transactions for January for the Soen-necken Company. Supplementary overhead information is provided in the accompanying table.

DIRECT CHARGES	FORGING	MACHINING	ASSEMBLY	SERVICE DEPARTMENT
Indirect labor	$30,730	$18,010	$1,520	$8,040
Indirect material	3,730	3,720	1,000	3,050
Utilities	5,030	5,150	900	2,000
Depreciation	13,310	16,040	1,330	1,910
Total	$52,800	$42,920	$4,750	$15,000

The service departments are allocated to the productive departments on the basis of the relative amounts of direct labor: 51% to Forging; 40% to Machining; 9% to Assembly.

2.7 A company maintains a historical cost accounting system. It produces a single product, X. Given are data for two months. As you can see, the unit costs are identical. Does this mean that the plant was equally efficient in both months? If not, why not? (There was no work-in-process inventory at either the beginning or the end of the month.)

JANUARY 1986

Units produced	1,000
Raw material: A (1000 lb at $0.50 per lb)	$ 500
Raw material: B (2000 lb at $1.00 per lb)	2,000
Direct labor (4000 h at $2.00 per h)	8,000
Variable overhead	8,000
Fixed overhead	4,000
Cost per unit	$22.00

FEBRUARY 1986

Units produced	2,000
Raw material: A (2500 lb at $.40 per lb)	$ 1,000
Raw material: B (4500 lb at $.90 per lb)	4,050
Direct labor (8400 h at $1.90 per h)	15,960
Variable overhead	19,990
Fixed overhead	4,000
Cost per unit	$ 22.50

2.8 Fill in the blocks in the matrix.

	UNITS			
	Dept. 1	*Dept. 2*	*Dept. 3*	*Dept. 4*
BEGINNING WORK-IN-PROCESS INVENTORY				
Units	1000	1000	2000	?
Percent complete	50%	30%	20%	20%
Units completed and transferred	5000	6000	?	3000
Equivalent units produced	?	6500	3200	4400
ENDING WORK-IN-PROCESS INVENTORY				
Units	1000	2000	3000	4000
Percent complete	40%	?	20%	50%

Hint: Translate all partially finished units into equivalent units; for example, 500 half-completed units would be equal to 250 completed units.

CASES

CASE 2.1   BLACK METER COMPANY

The Black Meter Company manufactures water meters in one standard design but in a wide range of sizes. The water meters installed in the basements of most homes are examples of its product. The meters consist basically of a hard rubber piston that is put in motion by the flow of water past it, a gear train that reduces this motion and registers it on a dial, and two heavy bronze castings which are bolted together around the measuring device.

The company has several production departments. The castings and many interior parts of meters are cast in the foundry and then are sent to one of the three machining departments, depending upon their size. Some of the mechanical parts are sent to a subassembly department where they are assembled into gear trains. Other parts go directly to the meter assembly department. There are also several departments that provide service to the production departments.

Overview of System

Since the company ships meters to customers as soon as they are completed, it does not have a Finished Goods Inventory account. It does have Raw Materials

This case was prepared by Professor Robert N. Anthony. Copyright © by the President and Fellows of Harvard College. Harvard Business School case 9-154-007.

Inventory and Goods in Process Inventory accounts. It uses a standard cost system. Standard costs are established for each element of direct labor, direct material, and manufacturing overhead.

During the month, actual costs are accumulated: material is purchased, the earnings of workers are recorded, and manufacturing overhead items, such as water or electricity, are purchased and paid for. These entries are made at actual cost. Elements of cost are debited into inventory at predetermined *standard* costs, however. Since actual costs are different from standard costs, variance accounts are necessary.

Setting up Standard Costs

A standard unit cost is established for every type of maaterial that is purchased. This is done annually by adjusting the current market price for any changes that are expected for the following year. For example, if the current price of copper is 30 cents a pound and no change is predicted, the standard cost for copper for the next year will be 30 cents a pound.

Standard rates for direct labor and manufacturing overhead are also determined annually. These rates are used to assign costs to products according to the number of standard direct labor hours incurred in the manufacture of each product. This is done on a departmental basis. For each production department, the accountants start with data on the actual direct labor payroll and the number of direct labor hours worked in each of the past few years. The departmental foreman gives his opinion as to adjustments that should be made to take account of future conditions. An amount for total labor cost and an amount for hours worked under normal conditions of activity is thus arrived at. By dividing the payroll amount by the normal number of hours, a standard direct labor rate per standard direct labor hour for each department is found.

Overhead costs for a production department include both the overhead costs incurred in that department plus an allocated portion of the costs of service departments. Estimates are made of these amounts for each production department under normal conditions. These estimated total overhead costs are divided by the standard number of direct labor hours for each producing department, the same amount that had been used in calculating the labor rate, to arrive at a manufacturing overhead rate per standard direct labor hour. These rates are given in Exhibit 1.

Developing Standard Product Costs

The standard hourly rates (which include both direct labor and overhead) are used to develop a standard cost for each type of meter. Examples of these calculations are given in Exhibits 2, 3, 4, and 5. The examples show the development of the standard cost of a $\frac{5}{8}$-inch HF Meter.

Exhibit 2 shows the calculation for a $\frac{5}{8}$-inch Chamber Ring, which is manu-

EXHIBIT 1 Black Meter Company

Standard Labor and Overhead Rates Effective January 1

DEPARTMENT NUMBER	DEPARTMENT NAME	LABOR	OVERHEAD	TOTAL RATE
103	Carpenter and pattern shop	$4.06	$3.07	$7.13/hour
104	Toolroom	4.35	3.26	7.61/hour
108	Pattern storage	—	—	8.04/pound
120A	Foundry—molding	4.50	5.78	10.28/hour
120B	Foundry—grinding and snagging	3.50	2.90	6.40/hour
122	Small parts manufacture	3.72	3.38	7.10/hour
123	Interior parts manufacture	3.68	3.73	7.41/hour
124	Case manufacture	3.98	6.02	10.00/hour
125	Plating—rack	—	—	6.50/100 pcs.
130	Train, register, and interior assembly	3.70	3.97	7.67/hour
131	Small meter assembly	3.50	4.01	7.51/hour
132	Large meter assembly	3.90	5.98	9.88/hour
133	Meter testing	4.11	3.56	7.67/hour
134	Meter repair	3.50	3.66	6.16/hour

EXHIBIT 2 Black Meter Company

Foundry Standard Cost

DRAWING NO. D-2408	*PART* 5/8″ HF CHAMBER RINGS	*MATERIAL COST*	$29.712
		PATTERN COST	3.64

MATERIAL GOV'T. BRONZE 100 PCS. 91.0# AT 0.3265/#

Std. Man-hours per 100 Pcs.	Prod. Center	Oper. No.	Operations and Tools	Machine	Std. Rate /hour	Total Cost	Total
1.76	120 A	1	Mold	Match Plate	10.28	18.093	
0.45	120 B	2	Grind	Wheel	6.40	2.88	
0.68	120 B	3	Snag	Bench	6.40	4.35	
							58.675

EXHIBIT 3   Black Meter Company

Parts Department Standard Cost

DRAWING NO. X-2408			PART 5/8″ HF CHAMBER RINGS		MATERIAL COST	
PLATING H.T. & E.T.			**MATERIAL** GOV'T. BRONZE 100 PIECES 89#		$58.675	

Hours per 100 Pcs. *Std.*	*Prod.* *Center*	*Oper.* *No.*	*Operations and Tools*	*Machine*	*Std.* *Rate* */hour*	*Total*
0.75	122	1	Broach outlet #734	P.P.	7.10	5.325
0.55	123	2	Finish tap plate bore and face	Heald	7.41	4.076
0.93	123		Drill 6 holes	Drill	7.41	6.891
0.47	123	3	C-sink 3 holes tap plate side	Drill	7.41	3.483
0.17	123		Tap 3 holes tap plate side	Heskins	7.41	1.260
5.00	123	4	Rough & finish inside & outside	Heald	7.41	37.050
0.20	123		C-sink 3 holes on bottom	Drill	7.41	1.482
0.30	123	5	Tap 3 holes on bottom	Drill	7.41	2.223
0.47	123		Spline inside	Spliner	7.41	3.483
0.50	123	6	Spline outside	Miller	7.41	3.705
5.80	123		Dress	Bench	7.41	42.978
			Total			170.631

factured in the foundry and which is one component of the $\frac{5}{8}$-inch HF Meter. As in the case with most parts, costs are calculated for a lot size of 100 units. The standard material cost is entered in the upper right-hand box. These parts are cast from bronze that has a standard cost of $0.3265 a pound. Since the standard weight of 100 pieces is 91 pounds, the standard material cost is $0.3265 × 91 = $29.712, as shown in the "Material Cost" box. The standard cost of the pattern used in the casting, $3.64, is also entered.

In order to apply the standard direct labor and manufacturing overhead rates to any part, it is necessary to have the standard direct labor hours for the operations involved in making that part. These are obtained from time studies and are entered in the first column of the foundry form. The standard time to mold 100 chamber rings is 1.76 direct labor hours; to grind them, 0.45 hours, and to snag them, 0.68 hours. In the first column of numbers of the right-hand side of the foundry form, the combined standard direct labor and manufacturing

EXHIBIT 4 Black Meter Company

Assembly Department Standard Cost

DRAWING NO. 2400				*ASSEMBLY* 5/8″ DISC INTERIOR					

USED ON ASSEMBLIES OF 5/8″ HF & HD METERS

Parts of Assembly	Cost	Parts of Assembly	Cost
K-2408 Chamber Ring	170.631		
K-2414 Chamber Top Plate	73.550		
K-2418 Chamber Bot. Plate	70.120		
K-2465 Disc Piston Assem.	142.010		
K-2422 Disc. Chbr. Diaphragm	7.660		
		K-4521 Chamber Screw (6)	7.000

Std. Man-hours per 100 Pcs.	Prod. Center	Oper. No.	Operation and Tools	Machine	Std. Rate /hour	Total Cost	Total
2.6	130	1	Assemble Top Plate to Ring	Bench	7.67	19.942	
0.9	130	2	Fit Abutment for Interior	Bench	7.67	6.903	
1.1	130	3	Mill & Scrape Diaphragm for Interior	Bench	7.67	8.437	
2.9	130	4	File Diaphragm Slots in Piston	Bench	7.67	22.243	
							528.496

overhead rate per standard direct labor hour for the operation is recorded. For example, Exhibit 1 shows the labor and overhead rate for molding in Department 120A as $10.28 per standard direct labor hour, and this amount appears on Exhibit 2 as the standard rate per hour for the molding operation. It is multiplied by the standard direct labor time of 1.76 hours to give a standard cost of labor and overhead of $18.093. The same procedure is followed for the other two foundry operations. The total standard foundry cost of 100 chamber rings is $58.675.

Exhibit 3 accumulates additional standard costs for these 100 chamber rings as they pass through the parts manufacture department. They enter the parts department at the standard cost of $58.675, the same cost at which they left the foundry. After the operations listed on Exhibit 3 have been performed on them, they become finished chamber rings. These operations have increased the standard cost to $170.631. As shown in Exhibits 4 and 5, these parts are assembled into $\frac{5}{8}$-inch HF disc interiors, and finally into $\frac{5}{8}$-inch meters. In each of these assembly operations standard costs are added; the total standard cost of 100 meters is $1,760.596.

In the same manner, standard costs are calculated for all the meter sizes that the Black Meter Company manufactures.

EXHIBIT 5 Black Meter Company

Assembly Department Standard Cost

DRAWING NO. 2735		*ASSEMBLY* 5/8″ HF ET FB	
Parts of Assembly	*Cost*	*Parts of Assembly*	*Cost*
2761 Top Case	270.60	K-5030 ⅝″ HF Dur. Bolt (6)	62.880
K-2776 Casting Gasket	13.25	K-4630 ⅝″ HF ac Nut (6)	35.440
X-2770 Bottom Case	100.14	K-5068 ⅝″ HF Washer (6)	20.140
2779 Casting Strainer	16.95	2782 Chamber Pin	3.966
3209 ⅝″ Closed Train	600.01	6172 Misc. Train Conn.	17.120
2400 ⅝″ HF Int. Assem.	528.496		
2412 ⅝″ Sand Plate	15.00		

Rate No.	Std. Man-hours per 100 Pcs.	Prod. Prod. Center	Oper. No.	Operation and Tools	Machine	Std. Rate /hour	Total Cost	Total
	4.6	131	1	Assem. Train and Strainer to Case	Bench	7.51	34.546	
	5.6	131	2	Assem. Int. & Bottom to Meter	Bench	7.51	42.058	
								1760.596

Accounting Entries

All direct material, direct labor, and manufacturing overhead costs are debited to Goods in Process Inventory at standard costs. Actual costs are collected in total for the period, but no actual costs are collected for individual meters.

Material.   As soon as any material is purchased, the standard cost of that material is penciled on the vendor's invoice. Each purchase is journalized in an invoice and check register. This register contains columns in which to credit the actual cost of the material to Accounts Payable, to debit an inventory account for the standard cost, and to debit or credit the difference to a purchase price variance account. When material is issued for use in production, the quantity is the standard amount (e.g., 91 pounds in the example shown in Exhibit 2), and the entry crediting Raw Materials Inventory and debiting Goods in Process Inventory is made at the standard cost (e.g., $29.712 in the example shown in Exhibit 2).

Labor.   The basic document for recording direct labor costs is the job timecard. Each production employee fills out such a card for each order on which he or she works during a week. The timecard illustrated in Exhibit 6 shows that B. Harris worked all week on one order. On the timecard, Harris records the quantity finished, the actual hours worked, and the allowed hours. A payroll clerk

EXHIBIT 6 Black Meter Company

Job Timecard

Mach. No.	Prod. Center	Quantity Ordered	Order Number	
	130	*3,000*	2I - 86572	Clock No. 337
	Part Name			
	5/8" Cl. Trains			
Prev. Quan. Fin.	Oper. No.	Operation Name		
O	*9*	*Finish Assem.*		
Quan. Finished	Std. Hours Per 100	Std. Hours	Std. Rate	Standard Labor	
2,300	*1.75*	*40. | 25*	*3. | 70*	*148.92*	
Quan. Finished			TIME CARD		Name B. Harris
2,300					
	Stop	Actual Hours	D.W. Rate	Earnings	
Sept. 20	*40.0*	*40. | 0*	*3. | 65*	*146. | 00*	
	Start	Foreman		Gain or Loss	
Sept. 16	*00.0*			*2. | 92*	

enters each employee's daywork rate and the standard direct labor rate for that department and extends the actual and standard direct labor cost of the work completed.

By totaling all the job timecards, the payroll clerk obtains the actual wages earned by each employee in each department and also the total standard labor cost of the work done in each department. These amounts are the basis for an entry which credits Wages Payable for the actual amount and debits Goods in Process Inventory account for the standard amount of direct labor. The variance is recorded in a direct labor variance account.

Manufacturing Overhead. For each department, a cost clerk multiplies the standard direct labor hours worked by the manufacturing overhead rate for that department (as obtained from Exhibit 1); this gives the amount of standard manufacturing overhead cost for the department for that month. This amount is debited to Goods in Process Inventory. During the month actual manufacturing overhead expenses have been accumulated in the invoice and check register and in various adjusting entries. The difference between the sum of the actual overhead costs and the standard manufacturing overhead cost is the manufacturing overhead variance, which is debited or credited to an overhead variance account.

When these transactions have been recorded, all material, direct labor, and manufacturing overhead have been charged into the Goods in Process Inventory account at standard cost, and variance accounts have been debited or credited for the difference between actual and standard.

Sales and Cost of Goods Sold

A duplicate copy of each sales invoice is sent to the office where a clerk enters in pencil the standard cost of the items sold (see Exhibit 7). At the end of the month the cost clerk totals the figures on these duplicate invoices to get amounts for sales revenue and for the standard cost of those sales. The standard cost is a credit to the Inventory account and a debit to the Cost of Goods Sold account. The total sales amount is a credit to Sales and a debit to Accounts Receivable. When this work is completed, the accounting department is in a position to obtain the monthly income statement (see Exhibit 8). Note, incidentally, that although the net amount of the variance on this income statement is relatively small, there are sizable detailed variances that tend to offset one another. Management investigates these variances and takes action when warranted.

Refer to the description of Black Meter's cost accounting system, and consider the following:

Questions

1. Trace through the cost accounting procedures described so that you are able to show how the numbers in each exhibit are derived from, and/or help derive, the other exhibits.

2. Try to imagine what an actual cost system for Black Meter would look like. How would it compare with the standard cost system in terms of

  (a) Recordkeeping effort required?
  (b) Usefulness of cost information to Black Meter's management?

EXHIBIT 7 Black Meter Company

Carbon Copy of Sales Invoice

Village of Vernon,
Attn: Village Clerk,
Vernon, N.Y.

Village of Vernon, Water Dept.,
Attn: E. J. Blackburn, Mayor
Vernon, N.Y.

STIBBS   Prepaid

10	5/8″ × 3/4″ Model HF Meters SG SH ET FB & 3/4″		248.00
1	Charge Gear #46X—shipped 8-10-	.88	248.88
		Meters	176.06
		Parts	.48

Ship gear by P. Post

EXHIBIT 8   Black Meter Company

Income Statement: June

Net sales		$1,198,234
Less: Cost of goods sold at standard cost	$831,868	
Variances (detailed below)	5,357	826,511
Gross margin		$ 371,723
Selling expense	$ 92,107	
General and administrative expense	177,362	269,469
Income before income taxes		$ 102,254
Income taxes		49,320
Net income		$ 52,934

VARIANCES

Favorable variances:		
Material price		$ 62,608
Unfavorable variances:		
Material usage	$ 22,457	
Direct labor	16,234	
Overhead	18,560	57,251
Net Variance		$ 5,357

3. Develop a flow chart for Black Meter's system.

4.   Suppose that the direct labor rate for Department 120A was increased to $5.50 per hour, and that for Department 131 was increased to $4.50 per hour. What effect would these changes have on the succeeding exhibits and on the total standard cost of 100 $\frac{5}{8}$-inch HF meters?

5.   As a consultant to Black Meter Company's controller, what would be your evaluation of the present system?

CASE 2.2   **THE GRINBERG COMPANY**

Factory Cost Reporting for Control

In January 1986, the central accounting office of the Grinberg Company, a large steel manufacturer in France, submitted to the board of directors a proposal concerning the use of estimated costs for planning and controlling the company's activities. The controller, Mr. Jannell, had suggested preparing this

This case was prepared by Professor W. Mitchell. Copyright IMEDE (Institut pour l'Etude des Methodes de l'Enterprise), Lausanne, Switzerland.

proposal after criticizing the effectiveness of historical data which were at the time the basis for all reports provided to management.

The Company. Grinberg manufactured steel in a variety of shapes and qualities finished to meet specifications of customers in almost every economic line from mechanics to construction, from shipbuilding to agriculture. It operated a number of plants, scattered throughout the country. Company activities were directed and coordinated from the Amiens headquarters, where the central accounting office was located.

The Existing Accounting System. The company maintained a system of accounts designed to yield year-end financial statement to meet legal and fiscal requirements. In addition, cost records for internal purposes only were maintained in each operating unit. These were designed to determine each month the total costs and unit costs of each product manufactured.

Each factory was divided for accounting purposes into cost centers. These were of two types: producing centers and service centers. Producing centers worked directly on company products; service center, such as utilities, transportation and maintenance, provided services to producing centers.

Each cost center was charged each month for the following costs:

1. *Materials and fuels.* Actual consumption multiplied by the average price paid for the materials. The average price was called a "running average," and was recomputed after each purchase of materials.
2. *Labor.* Actual hours multiplied by current wage rates.
3. *"General services"* costs. Actual costs of facory administration for the month, divided by total factory labor hours (including both producing center labor and service center labor), and assigned to producing centers and service centers by multiplying actual labor hours by average factory administration costs.

At the end of each month, the various producing centers were charged for service center services by multiplying predetermined service rates by the number of service units consumed in each producing center. The predetermined rates were adjusted periodically to reflect more closely the actual costs of the various services.

A record of physical production was maintained for each producing center. At the end of each month, unit cost was determined by dividing the number of product units produced in the center into the center's total cost for the month.

An estimate of the company's administrative, selling and fiscal expenses was prepared each year based on the sales forecast. After the manufacturing cost of each product was established, estimated administrative expenses were apportioned among products on the basis of such manufacturing costs. Estimated selling and fiscal expenses were allocated on the basis of selling price.

At the factory level, historical cost data were examined and discussed by the administrative manager and the head of each of the producing and service departments. The various average costs were compared with average figures for previous periods to identify irregularities in costs and yields. Investigation of the causes of such irregularities was undertaken in order to eliminate or restrict the unfavorable ones and to foster, as far as possible, those which were favorable.

Defects in the System. Cost data were used at company headquarters for studies on cost trends, as an aid for management planning. Mr. Jannell, however, questioned the effectiveness of historical figures for this purpose. He argued that such figures represented combinations of productive factors which had taken place in the past under specific operating and market conditions. Recent years had seen wide market fluctuations which required management to make more frequent revisions of sales forecasts, production plans and inventory and sales policies. Technological progress and the introduction of more efficient methods of production resulted in continuous changes in operating conditions. Furthermore, cost data were not available at the headquarters earlier than twenty days after the close of the period to which they referred. The time lag was not considered excessive in view of the complexities of the operations and the amount of detail provided, but it further reduced the effectiveness of the data for management purposes.

The Proposal. The proposal submitted to the board by the accounting department included the development of estimated costs for each cost center and the preparation of monthly reports showing comparisons of such estimates with actual results. It also recommended that historical cost analyses should be prepared in the future quarterly rather than monthly.

The development of estimated costs was to be based on the company's operating plan for the year. The plan included details as to production quantities by products, quantities and types of materials. In the plan, the activities of the various operating units were balanced and integrated in the attempt to achieve the most effective utilization of the company's production facilities. Underlying the overall plan were individual plans for each operating unit.

Estimated factory unit costs were to be developed as follows:

1. *Materials prices.* Estimated prices to be paid during the year, provided by purchasing department.
2. *Materials yields and recoveries.* Average yields of good products and "recoveries" (by-products, reusable materials, and salvage) in the quarter of the preceding year in which the best percentage yield of good products had been realized from raw materials.
3. *Prices of recoveries.* Estimated prices, from purchasing department.
4. *Utility costs.* Estimated prices times utility quantities used during the quarter of the previous year in which the best percentage yield of good products had been realized from raw materials.
5. *Depreciation.* Replacement cost (rather than historical costs as at present) divided by the economic life of the fixed assets, divided by the *maximum quarterly output* of the preceding year.

6. *Other costs.* Estimated unit costs equal to those achieved during the quarter of the previous year in which the greatest quarterly output had been achieved.

Estimated administrative, selling, and fiscal expenses would be allocated on the same basis used in the existing system.

Once unit cost estimates had been prepared by the central accounting office, they would be submitted for revision and approval to the superintendents of the various operating units. The procedure called for a maximum of responsibility to be placed on the people who, later, would have to explain and justify discrepancies between the cost estimates and actual results.

Proposed Monthly Report. Exhibit 1 shows a sample of the monthly report that Mr. Jannel would prepare for management's use. It shows the results achieved in

EXHIBIT 1   The Grinberg Company

Methods of Determination and Valuation of Actual Costs

	Availability of data (month's day)	Source	Elements Determined			Method of Valuation
			Quantity	Value		
Charges: Primary Raw Materials	2	Manufacturing reports	X		Central Office	"Actual prices"
Auxiliary raw materials (ferric oxide, fluxes, alloys)	2	Manufacturing reports	X		Central Office	
Recoveries	2	Manufacturing reports	X		Factory	Unit prices "by–products and recoveries list"
Manufacturing Expenses						
Fluxes and oxygen enrichment	2	Manufacturing reports	X		Factory	Unit prices previous month
Utilities: gas, tar, coke dust	4	Utilities control report	X		Factory	Unit prices "by–products and recoveries list"
Fuel oil, electricity, blast air, water, steam, anthracite	4	Utilities control report	X		Factory	Unit prices previous month
Indirect materials	1	Cost analyses		X	Factory	Running average^x
Labor	5	Form Per/20	X		Factory	Costs per hour previous month
Refractory materials	11	Cost analyses		X	Factory	Running average^x
Salaries	2	Salaries distribution sheet		X	Factory	Actual cost distributed over production of month
General services	5	Cost analyses		X	Factory	Average percentage of general services to labor in prior months applied to current labor costs
Transportation	1	Cost analyses		X	Factory	Running average^x
Other auxiliary services	1	Cost analyses		X	Factory	Running average^x
Departmental services	2	Cost analyses		X	Factory	Previous months' average distributed over production of month
Maintenance – tool usage	1	Budget		X	Factory	Quota for the month
Usage of cylinders	1	Budget		X	Factory	Quota for the month (normalized when necessary)
Ingot molds	2	Open hearth reports	X		Factory	Average price previous months
Spare parts and equipment	1	Cost analyses		X	Factory	Running average^x
Testing	1	Cost analyses		X	Factory	Most recent unit costs
Molds preparation	2	Manufacturing analyses		X	Factory	

^{x}Average of actual unit costs incurred in previous months of current year.

the production of steel ingots. Mr. Jannel provided the following comments on this report:

1.   The quantities shown in columns 2 and 5 are the physical input quantities necessary to produce 1000 tons of steel ingots. These quantities are expressed in kilograms except for gas and total fuels (expressed in thousands of calories) and labor (expressed in hours and minutes). No physical quantities are shown for most "manufacturing expenses." (A ton is equal to 1000 kg.)
2.   The quantity variances in column 7 are obtained by multiplying the difference between estimated and average quantities per ton (column 5 minus colum 2) by the estimated price (column 1). For account 12—"indirect materials," and account 23—"gas recovery," the entire variation in unit cost is treated as a quantity variance. All prices are quoted in "new francs" (NF).
3.   No quantity variance is shown for accounts 14–17 and 19–22. These are the costs of factory administration and factory service centers and are largely noncontrollable by the foremen of the producing centers.
4.   Average variances per ton are computed for depreciation and company general and administrative expenses. These are also shown as quantity variances.
5.   Actual cost per ton (column 6) is the current price (column 4) multiplied by the actual quantity per ton (column 5). Current price data are derived by the methods described in Exhibit 2.

Mr. Jannel also pointed out that operating supervisors were expected to provide the central accounting office with a brief explanation of the causes of the most significant variances. These would be shown in the right-hand column of the factory cost report, as in Exhibit 1. The forms used for comparisons were to be completed no later than seven days after the end of the month to which they referred.

Advantages of the Proposal.   According to Mr. Jannell, the system's principal advantage lay in that it avoided inventory problems and presented an integrated picture of the operating results attained in the various production stages during one time period. In addition, it would provide operating supervisors with working guides and focus their attention on variances. By promoting the search for causes of variances it would lay the ground for undertaking corrective action. It would also allow comparisons between operating units and foster the exchange of ideas and experiences concerning costs reduction among factory managers.

At the top management level, the system would provide the starting point for taking steps to improve operating performance. It would make possible the determination of profits realized from the sale of the various products under current operating and marketing conditions, thus facilitating better planning of production and sales activities. The information provided would also prove useful in making decisions as to plant modernization and expansion and in long-range forecasting and planning.

FACTORY: STEEL PLANT M. S.

Month: October 1970

	Normal Volume: 47,400 (4 Furnaces)		Actual		
Operations Index = operating time / calendar time =	2,816	HOURS 3,680	= 77%	3,000	HOURS 3,720 = 81%
Utilization Index = productive time / operating time =	2,816	2,816	= 91%	2,737	3,000 = 91%
Production: t/productive hour		18.5			19.4
Manufacturing expenses/productive hour		1605.80			1654.29

Planned production—tons	48,000
Actual Production—tons	53,000

		ESTIMATED COST			ACTUAL COST			Quantity Variance NF/*	No.	MAJOR REMARKS ON VARIANCES
		Price per 100 Kilo	Quantity (in Kg.)	Amount NF/t	Current Price per 100 Kilo	Quantity (in Kg.)	Amount NF/t	Furnace 1 15 / Furnace 2 31 / Furnace 3 22 / Furnace 4 30 / Furnace 5 27 / Furnace 6 — Number of Operating Days		
CHARGES	1 — Pig iron	28.30	600	169.80	28.12	632.9	177.97	+9.31	18.	Higher consumption due to use of flat ingot molds in special steel production
	2 — Scrap steel	33.00	461	152.13	31.89	438.9	139.98	−7.29		
	3 — Minerals and oxides	15.30	50	*7.65	18.33	46.−	8.43	−0.61		
	4 — Alloys	116.43	14	17.70	129.02	12.2	15.74	−2.27		
	5 — TOTAL CHARGES	30.87	1,125	347.28	30.28	1,130	342.12	−0.86		
RECOVERIES	6 — Slag	24.00	27	6.48	24.50	32.−	7.84	+1.20	19. } 20.	Adjustment quotas 4th quarter
	7 — Scrap metal			2.00			1.38	−0.62		
	8 — Waste		98			98.−				
	9 — NET CHARGE	338.80	1,000		332.90	1,000		−0.28		
MANUFACTURING EXPENSES	— Fuel oil Kg.	14.55	65	9.46	14.76	69	10.18			*Includes expenses incurred in coke gas refining
	— Gas Kcal.	1.42*	449	6.37	1.43*	416.7	5.96			
	10 — TOTAL FUELS Kcal.	1.47	1,080	15.83	148	1,087.−	16.14	+0.10		
	11 — Fluxes and oxygen enrichment Kg.	2.25	40	.90	2.63	39.2	1.03	−0.02		
	13 — Indirect materials			14.00			14.52	+0.52		
	12 — Labor h.	570.00	1h 25'**	8.12	591.00	1h 13'**	7.19	−1.14		**Quantity in time
	14 — Salaries			.85			0.87			
	15 — General services			3.40			3.20			
	16 — Transportation			2.55			2.48			
	17 — Other auxiliary services			7.95			8.00			
	18 — Ingot molds Kg.	45.00	15.5	6.98	45.00	16.6	7.47	+0.49		
	19 — Spare parts and equipment			3.65			2.22			
	20 — Ordinary maintenance			3.90			3.00			
	21 — Furnace refining quota			18.50			19.06			
	22 — Extraordinary maintenance			1.72			1.54			
	23 — Gas recovery			−1.55			−1.29	−0.26		
	24 — TOTAL MANUFACTURING EXPENSES			86.80			85.43	−0.31		
	COST OF STEEL INGOTS		1,000	425.60		1,000	418.33	−0.59		
	Depreciation			18.30			18.65	+0.35		
	General and administrative expenses			12.50			12.84	+0.34		
	MANUFACTURING COST		1,000	456.40		1,000	449.82	+0.10		
	Finishing									
	Fiscal expenses									
	Loading and storage									
	Selling expenses									
	TOTAL F.O.B. COST							+0.10		TOTAL VARIANCE NF/t − 6.58

*(Actual quantity − estimated quantity) × estimated prices

EXHIBIT 2 The Grinberg Company

48

Required

1. Verify several of the figures in Column 7 of Exhibit 2 (Quality Variance) to see that they have been computed by the method specified by Mr. Jannel.

2. Compute a price variance for each cost element for which a quantity variance is shown in Exhibit 1, except indirect materials, gas recovery, depreciation, and general and administrative expenses. You may assume that all of these costs are wholly and proportionately variable with volume.

3. To what would you attribute the variance (difference between column 6 and column 3) for each of the other cost elements?

4. To what extent was Mr. Jannel's proposal an improvement over the existing system? What further improvements would you suggest?

chapter 3

HISTORICAL AND COMBINATION COST ACCOUNTING SYSTEMS

There are two basic characteristics that determine the kind of cost accounting system that a company can best use. The first is the production processes and the production control system. The second is the information needs of management. In Chapter 2, we learned that a standard cost system usually required a mass-production type of processing to be practicable. Also, management should require a formal variance analysis system; otherwise, the development of the variances would not be worth the expense of calculating them. In this chapter, we consider alternative cost accounting systems that can be used where a pure standard cost accounting system is not practicable or economic.

Since production processes can take a variety of forms and since management information requirements will differ from company to company, it is rare for any two companies to have exactly the same cost accounting system. These systems, however, can be divided into a few general categories as follows: standard cost systems, historical cost systems, and systems that combine historical and standard costs. The previous chapter discussed standard cost systems. This chapter describes some representative historical and combination cost accounting systems.

HISTORICAL COST ACCOUNTING SYSTEMS

As stated in Chapter 1, a historical cost accounting system assigns all the actual costs incurred during a period (typically a month) to the products produced during that period. This part of the chapter describes two types of historical cost systems: job order cost and process cost. These represent the two extremes in manufacturing processes. A job order cost system applies where each job is unique; a process cost system applies where a homogeneous product is produced. Each of these systems has a number of adaptations for differences in production processes.

Job Order Cost

A job order cost system has the following characteristics:

1. Each job is assigned a number or some other distinguishing symbol and a separate accounting document (usually a job order card) is set up for each job.
2. All direct material and direct labor put into process are assigned to a specific job and recorded on the job order card.
3. Overhead costs are allocated to each job, usually on the basis of the relative amount of direct labor.
4. The work-in-process inventory value is the sum of the costs on the job order cards for the incomplete jobs.

Job Order Card. The job order card takes a variety of forms in actual practice. One of the simplest is an 8½-inch × 11-inch card that specifies the job number and job description on the top and has columns for accumulating material, labor, and overhead costs. The following is an example of such a card.

YZ Company   Job Number 86432
Description 6,000, 6″ Widgets, Chrome-Steel Alloy

DATE	*MATERIAL*	*DEPT. A LABOR*	*DEPT. B LABOR*	*DEPT. A OVERHEAD*	*DEPT. B OVERHEAD*	*TOTAL*
Jan.	$62.00	$10.00	$20.00	$20.00	$20.00	$132.00
Feb.			30.00		30.00	60.00

Direct Material. As material is purchased, the entry is to debit Raw materials inventory and to credit Accounts payable for the cost of the material. Raw materials are issued on requisitions that identify the specific job that will use the material. Periodically, these requisitions are summarized and the amounts applicable to each job are entered on the individual job order cards. The total of the amounts recorded on the job order cards is entered into the general ledger as a debit to Work-in-process inventory and a credit to Raw materials inventory.

For example, assume that during the month of January, material costing $1500 had been requisitioned as follows: Job 101, $900; Job 102, $200; Job 3, $400. The entry is:

Work-in-process inventory	$1500	
Raw materials inventory		$1500

At the same time, the amount of the material requisitioned for each job is recorded on the appropriate job order cards. (The sum of the material costs on the job order cards should be equal to the value of the raw material in process.)

Direct Labor. Direct labor is handled in exactly the same manner as direct material, except, of course, there is no account to correspond to the Raw material inventory. The direct labor payroll is broken down by job; usually, this is done by having each person fill in a time card showing the distribution of time by job number. The accounting entry is to debit Work-in-process inventory and credit Accrued wages payable. At the same time, an entry is made on each job order card to record the direct labor cost applicable to that job.

For example, assume that the following direct labor costs were incurred during the month of January:

JOB	DEPT. A	DEPT. B	TOTAL
101	$ 30	$ 40	$ 70
102	60	50	110
103	90	10	10
Total	$180	$100	$280

The entries are:

Wage expense	$280	
Accrued wages payable (or cash)		$280
Work-in-process inventory	280	
Wage expense		280

The labor cost applicable to each job is recorded on the appropriate job order card at the same time. (The total of the labor on the job order cards is equal to the amount of direct labor in process.)

Overhead. The first problem is to decide on a method for allocating overhead to specific jobs. The usual method is to allocate overhead in proportion to the relative amount of direct labor (either dollars or hours) applicable to each of the jobs. Two other methods are: (a) the relative amount of direct material or (b) the relative number of machine hours. The principle, of course, is to use the base that most closely assigns overhead costs to the jobs that are responsible for generating these costs. This is discussed in more detail in Chapter 4. Throughout this chapter, direct labor dollars will be used as the basis for allocating overhead costs.

Once the basis of allocation has been decided upon, the method of allocating overhead to individual jobs is as follows:

1. Calculate the total direct labor and the total overhead costs incurred during the period. (This is usually done by department.)
2. Divide the direct labor amount into the overhead amount to obtain the overhead rate. (When done by department, there will be several departmental rates.)
3. Apply the overhead rate to the direct labor incurred on each job.
4. Debit work-in-process inventory and credit the overhead account for the total amount.

For example, assume:

DIRECT LABOR:	
Job 101	$ 70
Job 102	110
Job 103	100
Total	$280

OVERHEAD:	
Indirect labor	$200
Supplies	150
Utilities	250
Depreciation	100
Total	$700

The journal entries for overhead are:

(1)

Indirect labor	$200	
Accrued wages payable		$200

(2)

Supplies	$150	
Utilities	250	
Accounts payable		$400

(3)

Depreciation expense	$100	
Accumulated depreciation		$100

(4)

Work-in-process inventory	$700	
Indirect labor		$200
Supplies		150
Utilities		250
Depreciation		100

Note: The overhead rate = 700/280 = 250%. Therefore, Job 101 is charged with $175; Job 102 with $275; Job 103 with $250.

Under this system of overhead allocation, there is never any overhead variance because the rate is calculated *after* the actual direct labor and overhead costs are known and is based, therefore, on the actual costs incurred. The difficulty with this method is that the overhead rate can fluctuate widely from month to month depending upon the volume of operations. Such variation can result in significantly different costs for the same item produced in different periods although cost levels and efficiency may have remained constant. This situation leads to several complications: pricing action, cost control, and even inventory valuation are difficult under such circumstances.

Completed Jobs. When a job is completed, the finished goods inventory is debited and the work-in-process inventory is credited for the cost of the completed job. For example, if the job illustrated on page 51 were completed without further costs, the entry would be:

Finished goods inventory	$192	
Work-in-process inventory		$192

Uses of Job Order Cost Systems. Job order cost systems are typically used where each job is different and where it is useful to know how much each job has actually cost, for example, construction projects, research projects, government contracts to provide nonstandard types of products, printing contracts, or any other products manufactured to special order.

The job order type of cost accounting can be used in general manufacturing companies where production is done in batches. For example, many small and medium-sized companies produce parts for direct sale or inventory in batches. The batch size is determined by the economic production quantity. The production process of such companies consists of scheduling and manufacturing different batches of parts, with many batches frequently being produced simultaneously. A record of the direct material and direct labor is maintained by batch number. When the batch is completed the total cost is calculated by adding an overhead amount to the material and labor. The unit cost is the total cost divided by the number of units produced.

Even in large companies, with sophisticated standard cost accounting systems, job cost accounting is used for special operations. For example, the tool room in a plant will produce tools to be used by the productive departments. These tools are usually included on the books of account at cost, with costs being calculated using a job order system.

Process Cost Accounting

A process cost accounting system is best adapted to a company in which products produced in a particular department at a specific time are identical or nearly identical. (A condition diametric to that found in the usual job order system, which is best adapted to an operation in which all jobs are different.)

The characteristics of a process cost accounting system are

1. Costs are accumulated by department or cost center.
2. The costs of the service departments are allocated to the productive departments so that all costs are eventually charged to some productive department.
3. The number of units produced in each department is divided into the amount of cost incurred by the department.
4. The receiving department is debited and the transferring department is credited for the units transferred to other departments. The amount transferred is the cost per unit multiplied by the number of units transferred.
5. Finished goods inventory is debited and the final transferring department is credited for the units completed and transferred. The amount transferred is the cost per unit multiplied by the number of units transferred.

Direct Departmental Costs. Under a process cost system, costs are charged directly to the department that incurs them to the extent that this is possible. For example, material is requisitioned and charged to the department that uses it; direct labor records are kept by department so that the direct labor cost applicable to each department can be ascertained; the wages of indirect employees (such as foremen, inspectors, or material handlers) are charged to the department for which they work; as supplies are requisitioned, a record is kept of the department to which they are sent.

Usually departmental expense accounts are divided into several subaccounts. For example, there could be the following accounts in Department A:

Dept. A—Direct Material	Dept. A—Supplies
Dept. A—Direct Labor	Dept. A—Utilities
Dept. A—Indirect Labor	Dept. A—Depreciation

The number and type of subaccounts depends upon how much departmental cost information is desired. Some companies use over a hundred subaccounts for each department.

The entries to record departmental costs are quite simple. For material, it is a debit to Department A (Material) and a credit to Raw Materials Inventory; for direct labor, it is a debit to Department A (Direct Labor) and a credit to Accrued Wages Payable. Overhead expenses are handled in the same manner: the debit is to Department A (the particular overhead account to be recorded) and the credit is to Cash, Accounts Payable, and so on.

Allocation of Service Department Expense

In all cost accounting systems, all product costs must eventually be charged to some productive department. Service activities (such as quality control or maintenance) and overall plant cost centers (such as building depreciation or plant manager's office) must be allocated to the productive departments. The allocation process is described in detail in Chapter 4.

The accounting entries for recording charges to service departments are exactly the same as the entries for charging costs to productive departments. At the end of each month, however, the service department is credited and the productive departments are debited for the amount accumulated in the service department accounts.

A Process Cost Problem. The D. French Company has three producing departments, A, B, and C, and two service departments Y and Z. It makes two products, Product 1 and Product 2. Both products enter Department A but Product 1 is completed by Department B and Product 2 is completed by Department C. The costs incurred during the month were:

DEPARTMENT	COSTS FOR THE MONTH
A	$40,000
B	20,000
C	20,000
Y	6,000
Z	4,000

The production statistics were as follows:

DEPARTMENT	UNITS PRODUCED
A	2,500
B	750
C	1,750

Note: There was no beginning or ending work-in-process inventory.

The costs of Service Departments Y and Z are allocated to the production departments on the basis of their relative direct costs.

The entries to record the basic expenses are debits to the department and subclassification (for example, Department A—Material, Department B—Utilities) and credits to Accounts payable, Cash, and so on.

After recording all expenses in some department or cost center, the next step is to allocate all costs to productive departments. In this case the distribution of expenses of Departments Y and Z is as follows:

	DIRECT COSTS		Allocation of costs for service depts.
Department	Amount	Percent of total	
A	$40,000	50	$ 5,000
B	20,000	25	2,500
C	20,000	25	2,500
Total	$80,000	100	$10,000

The entry is:

Department A	$5,000	
Department B	2,500	
Department C	2,500	
Department Y		$6,000
Department Z		4,000

The next step is to show the value of the goods transferred. This is done as follows:

Department B	$13,500	
Department C	31,500	
Department A		$45,000

Department A completed and transferred 2500 units at $18.00 per unit; Department B received 750 units, costing $13,500; Department C received 1750 units costing $31,500.

Finally, the entry to reflect the goods transferred to the Finished goods inventory is made.

Finished goods inventory	$90,000	
Department B		$36,000
Department C		54,000

Department B transferred to Finished goods inventory 750 units of Product 1 at $48.00 per unit or $36,000. Department C transferred to Finished goods inventory 1750 units of Product 2 at $30.86 per unit, or $54,000.

Equivalent Units.   The examples in this chapter have assumed that there was no beginning or ending work-in-process inventory. Thus, all units that were started were completed, and the total production equaled the number of units started. In actual business, it is unusual to find a situation where there is no work-in-process inventory. In many situations, however, the beginning and ending work-in-process inventories are approximately equal. Consequently, work-in-process inventories can be ignored in calculating unit costs. The units started will equal the units completed where there is no change in the work-in-process inventory.

In some instances, the work-in-process inventory at the beginning of the period will change from the work-in-process inventory at the end of the period, and this situation produces an additional complication in process cost accounting. The treatment of work-in-process inventories will differ depending upon whether inventories are valued at average cost or on a first-in, first-out basis.

AVERAGE.   As the term implies, the work-in-process inventory is valued at the average of the beginning of the month values and the costs of production for the current period. The first step is to calculate the *equivalent* units. Equivalent units are the number of units that would have been manufactured if the productive effort had been expended in making completed units only.

The total equivalent production includes the units that have been completed and transferred plus the equivalent units in the ending work-in-process inventory. The latter is calculated by multiplying the units in the ending work-in-process inventory by their degree of completion as a percentage.

For example, suppose that the beginning inventory was valued at $51,250 and that material, labor, and overhead put into process during the month amounted to $150,000. The number of units completed and transferred was 100,000 and the ending work-in-process inventory contained 50,000 units that were 30% completed. The total costs in process are $201,250 (51,250 + 150,000), and the equivalent units produced are 115,000 [100,000 + 0.3 (50,000)]. The average cost per unit for the month, then, is

$$\$201,250 \div 115,000 \quad \text{or} \quad \$1.75 \text{ per unit.}$$

The value of the goods transferred is

$$\$175,000 \ (100,000 \times 1.75),$$

and the value of the work-in-process inventory is

$$\$26,250 \ (15,000 \times 1.75).$$

FIRST-IN, FIRST-OUT.   The process becomes a little more complex when the first-in, first-out method of valuing inventories is used. In this instance, it is necessary to keep track of the costs in the beginning inventory and to transfer them at different value than the units that were started and completed during the month. For example, assume that the beginning work-in-process inventory consisted of 50,000 units that were one-half completed and that the value of this inventory was $25,000. During the month, 100,000 units were started and 120,000 units were completed and transferred. There were 30,000 units in the ending work-in-process inventory and these were one-third completed. The material, labor, and overhead put into process during the month was $115,500. The first step is to find the equivalent production. This is equal to the units completed and transferred plus the equivalent units in the ending work-in-process inventory minus the equivalent units in the beginning work-in-process inventory. This is

$$105,000 \ [120,000 \ + \ \frac{1}{3}(30,000) \ - \ \frac{1}{2}(50,000)].$$

The cost per unit produced, therefore, is

$$\frac{115,500}{105,000}, \quad \text{or} \quad \$1.10.$$

This the value used to calculate the cost of the ending work-in-process inventory. Ending work-in-process inventory is equal to

$$\$11,000 \ [\frac{1}{3}(30,000) \ \times \ 1.10].$$

The cost of the goods transferred is $129,500:

$$(\$25,000 \ + \ 115,500 \ - \ 11,000).$$

This amount can also be reconciled as follows:

25,000 equivalent units at $1.00 per unit in beginning inventory	$25,000
25,000 equivalent units are completed at $1.10	27,500
Value of goods started in previous period and completed in current period	$52,500
70,000 units (120,000 − 50,000) started and completed at $1.10 per unit	77,000
Total value of goods transferred	$129,500

An additional complexity is introduced when the material content has a different degree of completion than the labor and overhead. This occurs when, for example, the entire amount of material is introduced at the beginning of the process. In these instances, it is necessary to make the calculation of material separately from the calculations of labor and overhead.

Uses of Process Cost Accounting Systems.   Process cost accounting systems can be used where all the products in a department are homogeneous or can be expressed in equivalents. For example, suppose a department makes five products, A, B, C, D, and E, all of which can be expressed in terms of a standard product, say A. Assume units of B, C, D, and E were respectively equal to 1.1, 1.5, 0.8, and 0.5 units of A. If the actual production were as follows, the equivalent production would be calculated as follows:

PRODUCT	ACTUAL NUMBER OF UNITS PRODUCED	EQUIVALENT VALUES	EQUIVALENT UNITS
A	1000	1.0	1000
B	2000	1.1	2200
C	3000	1.5	4500
D	1000	0.8	800
E	2000	0.5	1000
			9500

If the actual costs of the department were $19,000 for the month, the cost of an equivalent unit would be $19,000/9500, or $2.00. The cost of the various products would be calculated as follows:

Product	A	B	C	D	E
Cost	$2.00	$2.20	$3.00	$1.60	$1.00

The key, of course, to establishing equivalents is to obtain the relationship between the cost to produce the different units. Sometimes two equivalents are used for each product: one to obtain material cost and a second to calculate labor and overhead costs.

In most instances, there is not much justification in using an historical process cost accounting system. The type of production processes that make process cost systems practicable are also adaptable to a standard cost system. Since a standard cost system usually offers many advantages over an historical cost system, there should be compelling reasons for keeping the process cost system.

Management Considerations of Historical Systems

So far this chapter has been concerned principally with the mechanics of historical cost accounting systems. There are some questions about the value of historical cost data to management. Many companies today use historical cost systems that generate data of questionable value.

There should be a positive need for historical cost information. In producing goods under government contracts, in construction projects, or in special contract work, there are reasons why management should know the actual cost. For one thing, bidding is a very important function in this type of operation, and management must know how actual costs compare to the expected costs on which the bids are based. In manufacturing operations, where the same products are produced each month, the monthly unit cost calculated by an historical cost system often is of no real value to management and, in fact, can be misleading. Therefore, in evaluating any historical cost system, it is vital that the information being generated be analyzed critically to be sure that it is the kind of information that management requires for the decisions that it has to make. It is my opinion that very few historical cost systems satisfy this condition in a repetitive manufacturing operation.

COMBINATION SYSTEMS

As might be expected, many businesses have cost accounting systems that combine elements of standard and historical cost systems. The purpose of this part of the chapter is to describe three typical combination systems.

Actual Material and Labor; Standard Overhead

Probably the most common combination system is one where product costs are calculated using historical material and direct labor and a standard overhead rate. Overhead rates are calculated (usually once a year) by estimating the amount of overhead and direct labor, by department, for the coming year at the expected volume of operation and dividing the estimated direct labor by the estimated overhead. The procedure for calculating these rates is exactly the same as that used in a standard cost system. The difference is that these rates usually reflect a forecast of future conditions rather than a standard of performance. Thus, although it would be possible to analyze the overhead variance, this is generally not done.

There are two principal advantages to using a standard overhead rate:

1. There will not be monthly fluctuations in unit costs resulting from volume fluctuations.
2. It is not necessary to wait until the books are closed at the end of the month before calculating the cost of a job.

Most historical job order cost accounting systems use standard overhead rates because of the disadvantages of having product costs fluctuate each month from changes in volume. In those companies where customer billing is based on actual costs, standard overhead costs are usually required so that the customer may be billed at the time the job is completed. Using actual overhead costs can result in some very particular cost patterns. For example, unit costs soar in the month that the company shuts down for a two-week vacation because all the fixed overhead will be allocated to only two weeks' volume of production. In fact, the problems created by using actual overhead costs are so great that it is almost never a satisfactory method where costs are calculated monthly. About the only valid use of actual overhead is to cost long-term projects or where actual costs are required (as in certain types of government contracts).

Standards Used as a Basis for Allocating Historical Costs

Some companies use standard costs as a basis for allocating historical costs to product. In effect, they use standards as equivalents in somewhat the same way that equivalents are used in process cost accounting. For example, suppose that a company manufactured 80 different products and each of these products had a standard labor amount. The company wishes to calculate "actual" labor cost by product for a month. This can be done by taking the total actual labor cost and dividing it by the total standard labor to get a percent of actual to standard. This percent is then applied to the standard labor amount for each part. Suppose that the standard labor cost for parts A and B were $1 and $2, respectively. For the month of January, total actual labor cost for all 80 parts was $120,000 and total standard cost for all 80 parts was $100,000. This means that actual costs were 120% of standard costs for the month of January. To calculate "actual" labor costs for January, multiply the standard labor cost of each part by 1.2 (120%). Thus Part A would have an "actual" cost of $1.20 and Part B $2.40. All 80 of the parts could be costed in this way. The same procedure can be used to calculate "actual" material and overhead.

In the last paragraph, you will note that the word actual is in quotation marks. This is to indicate that costs calculated in this way are no more actual than are standard costs. In the example above, the off-standard labor could have been caused by a few parts. Allocating this off-standard to all parts will change all products that are produced at standard cost to an incorrect "actual" cost. Even in the best of circumstances, it is most unlikely that off-standard costs will be spread equally on all products. Consequently, *all* that this procedure does is to allocate the total actual costs to some product, thus eliminating the standard cost variances.

It might be logical to ask why anyone would use such a system. There are two basic reasons:

1. Some companies with a standard cost system need to allocate all costs to the products produced. This occurs, for example, in some government contracts where the contracting officer will not accept standard cost as a basis for billing.

2. In many companies that manufacture a complex line of products, it becomes quite difficult to obtain "actual" material and labor costs. The clerical work of assigning all material used to some particular product or of keeping track of the direct labor time spent on each product can be highly impracticable under certain types of production control systems. Consequently, they use a standard amount to allocate total actual costs to product.

Companies sometimes have combinations of all of these methods. For example, certain plants in the automobile industry calculate material cost by assigning material to part on a job order basis: labor, by spreading actual direct labor costs on the basis of standard costs, and overhead, by using standard overhead rates.

Cost Estimating Systems

Many medium- or small-sized businesses cannot effectively employ a standard cost system. There are two main reasons for this: (1) They cannot set consistently good standards; and (2) they cannot control the production variables closely enough to make the variances meaningful. If a company produces to special order, a historical system with a standard overhead rate may be useful. If, however, a company manufactures a group of standard products, historical costs are not particularly useful, even with standard overhead rates, because month-to-month fluctuations in product costs do not provide a basis for management action. These fluctuations can result from changes in price levels, changes in efficiency, or changes in conditions (for example, overtime production). Furthermore, historical cost accounting systems can be expensive to operate, particularly since a fairly large number of cost centers may be necessary if the product costs are going to be even close to accurate.

What kind of a cost system should a company use if it cannot effectively employ a standard cost system and a historical cost system is expensive and yet not very useful? One type of system that has proved effective goes under several names; one of which is *cost estimating systems.*[1]

The principle of a cost estimating system is to estimate product costs periodically (say once a year) and to use these estimates for inventory valuation and decision support. These cost estimates are not reflected in the books of account, so there is no variance analysis. The product cost estimates are made in a manner somewhat similar to the way standard costs are set, except that the cost levels are designed to help management make marketing decisions (such as bidding or pricing) rather than to help management evaluate production efficiency. In other words, a cost estimating system is like a standard cost system except: (1) the cost levels are designed for making marketing decisions; and (2) no variance analyses are calculated.

Cost estimating systems have two advantages over historical cost systems:

1. They are less expensive to maintain.
2. They provide better information for management to make marketing decisions because month-to-month fluctuations are eliminated and the cost levels included are those specifically useful for marketing decisions.

---

[1]For a more complete description of this type of system see "Profit-Planning Accounting for Small Firms" by J. Dearden, *Harvard Business Review,* March–April 1963.

It should be noted, however, that cost estimating systems are useful only where management does not need to control costs through its cost accounting system. In many small- and medium-sized companies, manufacturing costs can be effectively controlled through personal observation and a few special reports. Where this condition exists, cost estimating systems can work very effectively.

SUMMARY OF COST ACCOUNTING SYSTEMS

The purpose of this part of the chapter is to summarize the important management considerations of the cost accounting systems described in Chapters 2 and 3.

1. A standard cost system will be most effective in fulfilling the functions of a cost accounting system. Consequently, standard costs should be used where they are practicable. In order for a standard cost system to be practicable, it should be possible to establish realistic standards and to control the production variables. Obviously, these two requirements are matters of degree. The problem, then, is to decide whether these two conditions can be met well enough to have a useful standard cost system with meaningful variances.

2. If a company manufactures standard type products but cannot meet the conditions of a standard cost system, a cost estimating system is often the next best alternative. Under this alternative, however, some other system of cost control must be available.

3. If a standard cost system is used but actual costs are also required, the variances may be distributed to products in proportion to their standard cost. This does not provide "actual" costs but it is a way of distributing to product all actual costs that have been incurred.

4. Where a company produces on a job order basis, a historical job order cost system can be useful. If the production cycle is short (less than one year), a standard overhead rate should almost always be used.

5. Many companies employ historical cost systems, either because of inertia or because of a belief that they are obtaining "actual" costs. Unless there is a real need for so-called actual costs, these systems can be expensive, while providing little really useful information. Historical cost systems should be evaluated to see if the information that is generated is really necessary and useful and to see if there are no better cost systems that could be employed.

QUESTIONS

3.1 Explain how a cost accounting system is influenced by the production processes and the production control system.

3.2 How would you explain to someone who knew no accounting how a historical cost system differs from a standard cost system?

3.3 Give some examples, other than those listed in the text, where job order costs might be used to advantage.

3.4 Can you think of any instances where a process cost system would be superior to a standard cost system?

3.5 Give some examples of instances where an actual overhead cost, calculated monthly, would be more useful than a standard overhead cost, projected annually.

3.6 Describe some methods for calculating "actual" direct labor costs in a department producing several hundred products by mass-production processes.

3.7 In a cost estimating system, how can you be sure that the costs are accurate enough for revenue decisions? How can you be sure that actual costs have not changed significantly subsequent to their original estimation?

3.8 Which kind of cost control reports would you employ in a cost estimating system?

3.9 In evaluating an existing cost accounting system, what are the critical points that should be considered?

3.10 How would your approach differ to Question 3.9 if you were asked to list the critical points that should be considered in establishing a new cost accounting system?

PROBLEMS

3.1 The ZUR Manufacturing Company employs a job order system. Listed are the financial transactions of the company for January 1986.

INVENTORIES, JANUARY 1, 1986

Raw material	$22,610
Work-in-process inventory	3,940
Finished goods	48,430

DETAILS OF WORK-IN-PROCESS INVENTORY

JOB NO.	MATERIAL	DIRECT LABOR	OVERHEAD	TOTAL
401	$ 410	$150	$ 600	$1160
402	350	200	410	960
403	290	210	430	930
404	280	290	320	890
Total	$1330	$850	$1760	$3940

FINANCIAL TRANSACTIONS

Purchases of raw materials	$2450
Job costs incurred:	

JOB	MATERIAL	LABOR
401	$100	$200
402	150	500
403	50	80
404	300	50
405	250	420
406	360	300
407	180	90

OTHER COSTS INCURRED

Indirect labor	$1580
Indirect materials	730
Utilities	680
Maintenance	980
Depreciation	950

- Jobs 101, 102, and 103 were completed during the month.
- Sales for the month were $10,460: the cost of these goods was $6910.
- Selling and administration costs amounted to $2145.

Required

1. Prepare summary journal entries to reflect the above financial transactions.
2. Prepare an income statement for January 1986.
3. Show the inventory balances as of January 31, 1986.

3.2 Assume that the ZUR Company financial transactions were exactly the same as given in Problem 3.1 except that, beginning in 1986, the company decided to use a standard overhead rate. The standard rate for 1986 was 250%. Make the journal entries that would be different from those in Problem 3.1. Prepare a revised income statement, assuming that the ZUR Company writes off all variances monthly. Show the new balance for the work-in-process and finished goods inventories. (Assume that all of the goods sold during January were made prior to January 1. Also assume that work-in-process prior to January 1 remains valued at the historical cost.)

3.3 The Rich Manufacturing Company employs a job order cost accounting system. Listed below are the financial transactions that affect this system.

	WORK-IN-PROCESS INVENTORY, JANUARY 1, 1986				
	Job 1001	Job 1002	Job 1003	Job 1004	Job total
MATERIAL	$ 1,432	$ 926	$ 2,490	$ 3,360	$ 8,208
DIRECT LABOR					
Dept. A	612	1,014	921	672	3,219
Dept. B	946	1,270	1,349	4,218	7,783
Dept. C	1,621	813	425	962	3,821
OVERHEAD					
Dept. A	1,224	2,028	1,842	1,344	6,438
Dept. B	2,838	3,810	4,047	12,654	23,349
Dept. C	1,621	813	425	962	3,821
	$10,294	$10,674	$11,499	$24,172	$56,639

		JOB COSTS INCURRED		
			Labor	
Job	Material	Dept. A	Dept. B	Dept. C
1001	$ 520	$ 1,490	$ 560	$ 424
1002	690	2,360	440	962
1003	330	720	390	1,322
1004	1,420	4,340	1,420	946
1005	4,160	190	635	2,420
1006	1,320	2,420	3,210	802
	$8,440	$11,520	$6,655	$6,876

	OTHER COSTS INCURRED		
	Dept. A	Dept. B	Dept. C
Indirect labor	$ 5,690	$ 4,640	$ 3,580
Indirect material	2,420	3,480	1,970
Utilities	2,610	4,320	1,130
Maintenance	2,980	4,860	1,870
Depreciation	3,580	2,665	1,764
Total	$17,280	$19,965	$10,314

- Jobs 1001, 1002, and 1003 were completed during January.

Required

1. Prepare the journal entries to record the financial transactions listed above.
2. Prepare a reconciliation of the work-in-process inventory account. (Note that the Rich Manufacturing Company uses departmental cost centers.)

3.4 The Geneva Company produces two products: A and B. It has three productive departrments, 1, 2, and 3, and two service department, Department 4 (maintenance) and Department 5 (general administrative). Both Product A and Product B start in Department 1. Product A is transferred from Department 1 to Department 2, where it is completed. Product B is transferred to Department 3, where it is completed. The Geneva Company uses a historical process cost accounting system. Listed are the financial transactions for January that affect the product costs. From these data, prepare the journal entries that would be required. What is the unit cost of A and B in January?

- Raw material put into process in Department 1: 1000 lb at $2.00 per lb.
- Departmental expense incurred:

	DEPT. 1	DEPT. 2	DEPT. 3	DEPT. 4 (MAINTE-NANCE)	DEPT. 5 (GENERAL ADMIN.)
Direct labor	$1500	$1000	$ 500	—	—
Indirect labor	1500	700	800	$1000	$1500
Indirect material	750	200	300	800	1500
Utilities	800	400	500	300	300
Depreciation	1000	500	400	100	100
	$5550	$2800	$2500	$2200	$3400

- Products finished during January: 750 lb of A and 250 lb of B.
- There was no beginning or ending work-in-process inventory.
- Department 4 is allocated to productive departments and to Department 5 on the basis of relative depreciation. Department 5 is allocated to productive departments on the basis of relative amounts of direct labor.

3.5 Fill in the blanks in the following:

	A	B	C	D
BEGINNING WORK-IN-PROCESS INVENTORY:				
Units	100	200	?	1000
Percent completed	50	40	30	20
Units completed and transferred	500	?	700	800
ENDING WORK-IN-PROCESS INVENTORY:				
Units	300	400	500	600
Percent completed	20	30	40	?
Equivalent units produced	?	640	750	900

3.6 Listed are some cost data for the month of January 1986. Department A transfers all of its completed production to Department B. Department B transfers all of its completed production to Department C. Department C transfers all of its completed production to finished goods inventory. Calculate the amount of each of the transfers made during the month and the value of the work-in-process inventory in each department at the end of the month.

	DEPT. A	DEPT. B	DEPT. C
EXPENSES INCURRED			
Material	$1000	$2000	$ 500
Labor	500	675	500
Overhead	580	1375	1000
Total	$2080	$4050	$2000
BEGINNING WORK-IN-PROCESS INVENTORY:			
Units	500	300	600
Percent completed	40	50	60
Units completed and transferred	1000	900	800
ENDING WORK-IN-PROCESS INVENTORY:			
Units	600	500	300
Percent completed	40	40	50
Value of beginning work-in-process inventory	$ 400	$ 550	$1150

3.7 Assume the same facts as provided in Problem 3.4 except that work-in-process inventories are as follows:

	DEPT. 1		DEPT. 2		DEPT. 3	
	No. of pounds	Percent completed	No. of pounds	Percent completed	No. of pounds	Percent completed
BEGINNING INVENTORY						
Material	500	100	300	100	400	100
Other costs	500	50	300	33⅓	400	25
Value	$3795		$2230		$3325	
ENDING INVENTORY						
Material	500	100	300	100	400	100
Other costs	500	40	300	50	400	50

(The cost of material in both the beginning and ending inventory is $2.00 per pound)

Required

1. How would your entries for Problem 3.4 be different?
2. What are the costs of Products A and B?

3.8 Assume the same facts as provided in Problem 3.4 except that the Geneva Company is on a standard cost system. The standard costs for Products A and B are as follows:

	STANDARD COST PER POUND		
	Dept. 1	*Dept. 2*	*Dept. 3*
Material	$ 1.90	$10.30[a]	$10.30[a]
Direct labor	1.40	1.20	2.70
Overhead	7.00	5.00	12.00
	$10.30	$16.50	$25.00

[a]The standard cost per unit of transfers from Department 1.

Required

Make the journal entries to record the financial transactions in Problem 3.4 that would be different using a standard cost accounting system.

3.9 Calculate the unit costs of each product for January, February, and March. The basic unit of production is Product A. Other products are expressed as equivalents of A. Product B is 1.5 because it is estimated that it costs 50% more to produce it than A. Other equivalents are C = 0.75; D = 1.25; E = 1.10; and F = 0.90.

	PRODUCTION IN UNITS		
Product	*January*	*February*	*March*
A	1000	500	750
B	500	500	500
C	700	500	1000
D	600	700	800
E	800	700	600
F	400	300	700
Total production costs	$4265	$3894	$5148

3.10 The standard unit costs of Products W, X, Y, and Z are as follows:

PRODUCT	DIRECT MATERIAL	DIRECT LABOR	OVERHEAD	TOTAL
W	$1.00	$2.00	$3.00	$6.00
X	.50	3.00	4.00	7.50
Y	2.00	1.00	3.00	6.00
Z	.80	.40	1.20	2.40

The overall plant cost performance for January was as follows:

- Direct material: 10% better than standard
- Direct labor: 5% worse than standard
- Overhead: 7% worse than standard

Required

Calculate the "actual" costs for Products W, X, Y, and Z for January.

CASES

CASE 3.1 HARTFORD CONFECTIONERS, INC.

Introduction

The Hartford Confectioners Company, founded in Hartford, Connecticut, in 1953, manufacturered low-priced general candies. In 1985 the company employed between 250 and 300 people, and reached a new sales peak of almost $6 million. Management estimated that the company ranked seventh in sales among the general line houses.

A general line candy can best be described as a commodity candy such as the orange jelly slices, chocolated covered nuts, etc., sold in bulk. These candies can also be found in supermarkets where they are packaged in cellophane or polyethylene bags.

The entire confectionery industry included bar candy houses, such as Hershey and Peter Paul Mound, as well as specialty houses, and had total sales of several billion dollars in 1985. Management believed that the company was in competition with all the industry, because "if a woman buys a package of Hershey bars, Hartford has lost a sale." However, general candy lines were subject to great price competition, unlike bar candy houses which had a relatively high base of constant demand and strong consumer preferences. Sales in all candy lines were affected strongly by seasonal peak demands during the spring (Valentine's Day and Easter) and fall (Christmas and Halloween).

The company sold its products to a variety of wholesalers and chains in New England, New York, Pennsylvania, and New Jersey. Most sales were arranged by 16 candy brokers, acting as agents for Hartford, and earning 3–5% commissions on their sales. The exact amount of the commission varied between these

This case was prepared by E.D. Bennett. Copyright© by the President and Fellows of Harvard College. Harvard Business School case 9-159-002.

figures, and averaged about $3\frac{1}{2}$% on all sales. Commissions of 4–5% were granted only on a few lines which management believed were especially profitable.

The company operated on a very informal basis, managed by the founders, Messrs. Graham, Williams, and Johnson. Few records were maintained to analyze performance. Foremen had been with the company many years and exercised a great deal of freedom in scheduling and controlling production. Management did not want to install control procedures which required additional expense or would "annoy" employees.

Manufacturing

Candy at the Hartford Confectioners was made in seven departments as follows:

- *Mogul, or Starch Department.* In this department, sugar syrup, dye, and corn syrup were heated in steam kettles and poured into molds of starch powder on large machines called "moguls," producing jelly centers, marshmallows, and cream centers. In addition, facilities were available to sand (cover with sugar) certain types of jellies such as orange slices and gumdrops.
- *Nougat or Caramel Department.* Sugar syrup, egg whip, dyes, and butter were heated in steam kettles to the desired consistency and poured into large flat pans to cool to taffy-like "cakes" of nougat or caramel. Jelly centers from the Mogul department were added to make "Spanish" nougats.
- *Hard Candy Department.* Hard candies such as "jawbreakers," as well as hard centers for chocolate covering were made here.
- *Wafer Department.* Wafers were made of sugar and small amounts of dye and gelatin. These ingredients were mixed into a "dough," which was then rolled into a thin sheet and punched to form "Necco"-like wafers.
- *Enrobing, or Chocolate Department.* Enrobing machines sprayed chocolate coatings on centers arriving from the Mogul or the Hard Candy departments.
- *Pan Room.* Sugar syrup and dye were added to jelly egg centers from the Mogul department or to nuts to "build up" coatings. This build-up took place in large pans, which were similar in design to small cement mixers. The candy to be coated was forced to the periphery of the spinning pan and the rising and falling of these centers caused a rapid and uniform build-up of the sugar coat.
- *Jelly Packing.* This department was equipped with polyethylene and cellophane packaging and boxing machines and was used to package the output of the Mogul, Enrobing, and Pan Room departments. (The Hard Candy, Nougat, and Wafer departments packaged their own finished goods.) All packed candy was sent finally to the shipping area before shipment.

Cost System

Prior to 1975 the only financial or cost records were the semiannual reports presented to the company by a public accounting firm. These reports consisted of a balance sheet and an abbreviated income statement. However, management had developed, from years of experience in the candy business, some "rules of thumb" for estimating costs. For example, the weights of the ingredients of the different items were estimated along with the cost of the ingredients to arrive at an estimated material cost. Then members of management would estimate the direct labor cost of making the item from observations of workers performing the required operations. Finally, an allocation for factory overhead would be added to the estimated direct labor and material costs for the candy. This amount was based upon a percentage (derived from past experience) of the combined direct labor and material cost of the item. The same percentage was used for each item of candy in the line.

Development of New Cost Procedures

In 1984, the management retained the services of a new accountant to help develop more cost information and to determine, if possible, why the company was not making greater profits (see Exhibit 1). Management told the accountant that if a new system were installed the cost of maintaining it would have to be kept to a minimum.

While reviewing the company's operations the accountant concluded that two basic changes in estimating the cost of manufacturing the candy were necessary. First, he wanted factory overhead to be apportioned as a percentage of direct labor cost only since overhead costs seemed to have no relationship to the material costs. Second, he wished to develop an overhead rate for each department to be used in costing the different candy items, rather than using a plant-wide rate. The reasons for the second change were based upon the following facts: (a) no item went through all departments, (b) the volume of production in one department did not necessarily vary directly with the volume in other departments, and (c) costs generally varied from department to department because different candy was being made, different machines were being utilized, and different methods were being employed.

Before going any further in developing a new system for estimating costs, the accountant tried to persuade management of the need for these two changes. After much discussion he convinced them of the need for the first change by giving an illustration showing how the company could make a wrong decision based upon their old method. Having won acceptance for the first change, the accountant showed management the merits of the second change and was authorized to establish overhead rates for each department.

In establishing these overhead rates, his first step was to select bases for distributing factory overhead among the seven producing departments. For example, certain expenses such as foremen's pay could be collected by departments. Expenses such as general factory, real estate taxes, and building insurance were allocated to each department on the basis of area. Workmen's compensation, vacation pay, payroll taxes, etc., were allocated on the basis of direct labor dollars. The costs of operating the receiving and shipping "department" were allocated to the producing departments on the basis of pounds produced. Exhibit

EXHIBIT 1   Hartford Confectioners, Inc.

Operating Statement for Ten Months

	ACTUAL	BUDGET	GAIN (LOSS)
Sales	$5,177,872	$5,183,961	$ 6,089L
Deductions:			
Freight	261,395	262,358	963
Discounts	99,805	102,150	2,345
Total deductions	$ 361,200	$ 364,508	$ 3,308
Net sales	$4,816,672	$4,819,453	$ 2,781
Costs:			
Material	$2,880,314	$2,883,053	$ 2,739
Direct labor	522,432	525,730	3,298
Overhead	722,116	693,979	28,137L
Total costs	$4,124,862	$4,102,762	$22,100L
Gross profit	$ 691,810	$ 716,691	$24,881L
Selling and other expenses:			
Salesmen	183,666	183,610	56L
Selling, general and administrative	367,274	351,551	15,723L
Total selling and other expenses	$ 550,940	$ 535,161	$15,779L
Operating profit	$ 140,870	$ 181,530	$40,660L
Interest expense	(49,938)	(59,334)	9,396
Markdowns	(49,197)	—	49,197L
Total interest and markdowns	(99,135)	(59,334)	(58,593)L
Total profit	$ 41,735	$ 122,196	$80,461L
Taxes	(19,051)		
Profit after taxes	$ 22,684		

This ten-month period was the result of the change in the company's fiscal year. The fiscal year now ends October 31 instead of December 31.

2 lists the complete breakdown of factory overhead expenses and the bases for distribution.

The accountant then estimated sales by product line in order to determine the direct labor cost that could be expected in each department. These sales estimates were based upon management's feelings about the future and their past experience. Next, he estimated the percentage of direct labor dollars to sales dollars by department, based upon the historical relationships between these factors. These percentages were applied against the departmental sales estimated for 1985 to obtain a budgeted direct labor cost for each department.

After this, a budget was drawn up for factory overhead expenses, based upon the previous year's expenses and management's sales expectations for the coming year. These budgeted overhead costs were then distributed to each of the seven departments. The departmental overhead budgets were divided by the

EXHIBIT 2 Hartford Confectioners, Inc.

Burden Allocation

ITEM	BASIS OF ALLOCATION TO THE PRODUCING DEPARTMENTS
Supervisory salaries and wages:	
Foremen	Estimated
Factory administration	Direct labor dollars
General factory expenses	Area
Maintenance and repairs:	
Machinery (83%)	Machinery investment
Buildings (17%)	Area
Receiving	Pounds produced
Rent	Area
Heat, light, and power:	
Electricity—Refrigeration 40%	Estimated
General 60%	HP—Connected load
Steam—Process 80%	Pounds produced and/or estimated
Heating 20%	Area
Gas	Estimated
Insurance:	
Workmen's compensation	Direct labor dollars
Employee group insurance	Direct labor dollars
Other insurance	Area
Real estate taxes	Area
Depreciation:	
Machinery and equipment	Machinery investment
Buildings and improvements	Area
Purchasing expenses	Direct labor dollars
Factory supplies	Direct labor dollars
Factory services	Pounds produced
Trucking	Direct labor dollars
Vacations, holidays, etc.	Direct labor dollars
Overtime and shift premiums	Direct labor dollars
Pensions and severance	Direct labor dollars
Payroll taxes	Direct labor dollars
Other	Direct labor dollars

expected direct labor cost within each department to get departmental overhead rates. A plant-wide rate was also established by dividing total budgeted factory overhead by total estimates of direct labor cost. The plant-wide rate was used in preparing monthly income statements.

A selling and administrative expense budget was also prepared (see Exhibits 3 and 4 for 1985 comparisons of budgeted and actual overheads). Estimated total annual sales were divided into the total budget for selling and administrative costs (excepting commissions) to obtain average selling and administrative cost as a per cent of sales dollars. This per cent was calculated as 7% for 1985. The accountant planned to add the actual commission (3–5%) for each item to the

EXHIBIT 3 Hartford Confectioners, Inc.

Selling and General Expenses for Ten Months, to October 31, 1985

ITEM	ACTUAL	BUDGET	GAIN (LOSS)
SELLING			
Payroll:			
Sales Office	$ 13,151	$ 15,200	$ 2,049
Shipping and traffic	39,655	39,000	655*L*
Bonus	4,000	2,600	1,400*L*
Packaging and merchandising	11,538	6,300	5,238*L*
Advertising	4,869	3,400	1,469*L*
Trucking (1/2)	10,685	11,800	1,115
Samples	282	800	518
Conventions	2,999	3,300	301
Payroll taxes	1,900	1,700	200*L*
Other	2,372	4,551	2,179
Total selling	$ 91,451	$ 88,651	$ 2,800*L*
GENERAL			
Executives and office payroll	$154,046	$168,600	$14,554
Office bonus	3,000	1,100	1,900*L*
Professional fees	27,257	20,000	7,257*L*
Travel and promotion	25,861	21,200	4,661*L*
Executive autos	9,112	8,300	812*L*
Telephone and telegraph	7,146	6,700	446*L*
Research and development	10,473	5,000	5,473*L*
Payroll taxes	3,500	2,700	800*L*
Executive group insurance	3,548	3,300	248*L*
Office services	3,155	3,300	145
Postage	2,689	3,400	711
Depreciation	3,151	3,300	149
Consulting fees	4,167	4,200	33
Credit and collections	322	600	278
Dues and subscriptions	1,767	800	967*L*
Office supplies and expenses	5,417	4,200	1,217*L*
Bad debts	7,394	4,200	3,194*L*
Contributions	439	800	361
Miscellaneous taxes	268	800	532
Other	3,111	400	2,711*L*
Total general expenses	$275,823	$262,900	$12,923*L*
TOTAL SELLING AND GENERAL EXPENSES	$367,274	$351,551	$15,723*L*

This ten-month period was the result of the change in the company's fiscal year. The fiscal year now ends October 31 instead of December 31.

7% figure, convert the total to dollars, and deduct the latter figure from the item's sales price to obtain net after selling and general administrative expense.

Material costs by product line were calculated by pricing standard quantities per item at prevailing prices. The company chemist provided formulas

EXHIBIT 4 Hartford Confectioners, Inc.

Factory Overhead Expenses for Ten Months, to October 31, 1985

ITEM	*ACTUAL*	*BUDGET*	*GAIN (LOSS)*
INDIRECT PAYROLL			
Superintendence and product supervision	$ 82,637	$ 89,600	$ 6,963
Maintenance	74,791	71,700	3,091L
Power plant	10,547	12,500	1,953
Receiving and handling	38,763	30,200	8,563L
Pensions and severance	11,292	8,300	2,992L
General factory	43,090	37,600	5,490L
Bonus	21,000	15,000	6,000L
Vacations and holidays	62,962	63,300	338
Overtime and shift premiums	9,294	8,200	1,094L
Total indirect payroll	$354,376	$336,400	$17,976L
FACTORY EXPENSES			
Electricity	$ 22,610	$ 24,500	$ 1,890
Oil	7,800	16,300	8,500
Gas	11,041	4,100	6,941L
Water	1,578	2,100	522
Repairs and maintenance	74,665	40,800	33,865L
Real estate taxes	17,464	16,700	764L
Insurance:			
Workmen's Compensation	11,755	14,600	2,845
Group	23,572	15,800	7,772L
General	6,781	7,500	719
Depreciation	84,725	83,300	1,425L
Payroll taxes	33,098	31,000	2,098L
Supplies	49,469	43,588	5,881L
Laundry and other services	9,390	9,200	190L
Trucking (1/2)	10,685	11,400	715
Consulting fees	2,042	—	2,042
General	3,107	2,500	607L
Rental income	(2,042)	(2,100)	58L
Total factory expense	$356,582	$310,400	$46,452L
Total factory overhead	$722,116	$657,688	$64,428L
Direct labor	$522,432	$525,730	
Overhead as a percent of direct labor	138.2	125.1	

This ten-month period was the result of the change in the company's fiscal year. The fiscal year now ends October 31 instead of December 31.

which indicated the exact proportions of ingredients for each line and estimated yield data.

The Cost Book

The accountant prepared a "cost book," based on the preceding cost collection procedures. This book contained material, labor, and overhead costs for each item produced. Selling prices, freight charges, and profit or loss figures were also calculated for each item by sales areas, because shipping costs and selling prices often varied by sales area. Direct labor costs were estimated by operation, and manufacturing overhead was charged at departmental rates. Selling and administrative costs were computed at 7% plus the commission applying to the particular item. (Exhibit 5 is a page from this cost book for one item. Selling and administrative costs are charged at 12% since this item carried a 5% commission.) Standard formulas for ingredients, yield, and overweight were established for each item by the chemist as illustrated. Overweight was included to ensure that every Hartford candy item would pass weight inspection by Federal Pure Food and Drug inspectors.

The cost book along with the expense budgets were designed to provide more than simply an accurate estimate of the costs of making candy. The accountant expected that these data would enable managment to measure company performance because they could compare actual direct costs (material and direct labor) incurred during each quarter with the material and direct labor costs of goods sold based upon the cost book; and factory overhead budgeted expenses as well as budgeted general, administrative, and selling expenses could be compared with actual expenses during the quarter.

Monthly Profit and Loss Statements

The cost book along with the budgets were used in the monthly preparation of profit and loss statements. (Exhibit 6.) The person making up this statement would get a record of shipments for the month from the controller's department. This record showed the breakdown by item for each salesman and gave gross sales, returns, allowances, net sales, and salesmen's commissions. From the net sales the following items were subtracted:

1. *Cash discounts at 2% of net sales.* The company allowed 2% cash discount if the customer paid within ten days. It was estimated that more than 95% of Hartford's customers took the cash discount.
2. *Freight.* Actual freight paid on the shipments made during the month per invoices in the controller's office.
3. *Material.* The estimated material cost of all items shipped during the month based on figures in the cost book.
4. *Labor.* The estimated direct labor cost, based on figures in the cost book, of all items shipped during the month.
5. *Overhead.* Factory overhead was calculated by multiplying the direct labor cost found in 4, above, by the plant-wide rate of 132%.

The items were then totaled and subtracted from net sales. Then general administrative and selling expenses were deducted at 7% of net sales. Next sales commissions were deducted at actual cost. The estimated profit and loss was then adjusted for "general administrative selling expense over-or-under-run." General

EXHIBIT 5 Hartford Confectioners, Inc.

Eggs # 1 (Page from Cost Book)

	MATERIALS	*COST*	*MATERIAL*	*D.L.*	*O/H*
CENTERS					
400#	Sugar	at $.093/#	$37.20		
680	Corn syrup	at .065	44.20		
208	Thin boiling starch	at .060	12.00		
1,288#	Yield		$93.40		
	Ingredients/# (93.40 ÷ 1,288)		.0725		
	Labor cost to cook and cast			$ .01	$ .012
	Total cost—centers/#		$ .0725	$ .01	$ .012
COATING					
125#	Above centers	at $.073/.01/.012	$ 9.13	$1.25	$1.50
25	Syrup	at .078	1.95		
50	Fruit fine sugar	at .093	4.65		
50	Fine granular sugar	at .093	4.65		
	Color and flavor		1.00		
250#	Yield		$21.38	$1.25	$1.50
	Stock/# (21.38/1.25/1.50 ÷ 250)		$ .086	$ .005	$ .006
	Labor cost to build and shine			.006	.012
	Total cost/#		$ .086	$ .011	$ .018
PACKING					
24—1#	Eggs (allow ½ oz. for each pound)				
	Stock	at $.086/.011/.018	$ 2.13	$ .27	$0.45
	Cost of bag	at .87/#	.11		
	Cost of carton	at 148.70/M	.15		
	Labor cost to pack			.12	.16
	per 24		$ 2.39	$ .39	$ .61
	per dozen		1.195	.195	.305

TOTAL COST PER DOZEN FOR MATERIAL, LABOR, OVERHEAD $1.695

	A	B	C	D
Selling price (per dozen)	$2.16	$2.16	$2.16	$2.16
Net after selling, general, and administrative expense (88%)	1.90	1.90	1.90	1.90
Less: materials, labor, and overhead	1.695	1.695	1.695	1.695
Margin for freight and profit	$ .205	$ .205	$ .205	$ .205
Less: freight and shipping charges	.19	.22	.35	.45
Profit or (loss)	$ .015	$(.015)	$(.145)	$(.245)

Note: The letters A,B,C,D represent different areas served by the company; # represents pounds.

EXHIBIT 6 Monthly Estimated Profit and Loss Statement as of October, 1985

Gross sales (per Billing Dept.)		$485,658.98
Less: Returns and allowances		4,011.24
Net sales and prepaid freight		$481,647.74
Less:		
Cash discounts, 2%	$ 9,632.95	
Freight	21,588.83	
Material	285,294.66	
Labor	42,359.71	
Overhead (132% Labor)	55,914.82	
		414,790.97
		$ 66,856.77
Less: General and administration expenses 7%		33,715.34
		$ 33,141.43
Less: Sales commissions		16,824.71
Estimated Profit		$ 16,316.72
General and administration expense adjustment[a] (Underrun)		(1,284.66)
Actual profit		$ 15,032.06

[a]General and Administration expenses average out to 7% of net sales per year. However these expenses are fairly constant from month to month and do not vary directly with sales. Therefore the above correction factor of $1,284.66 is used to make G and A expenses for the month equal $35,000.

administrative and selling expenses were expected to total about 7% of net sales at year's end and to remain fairly constant from month to month. Therefore, an amount equal to the difference between the month's budgeted general administrative and selling expenses, $35,000, and the amount listed on the profit and loss statement was added or subtracted from the estimated profit and loss to make the total cost for the month equal to $35,000. The final result was then called "actual" profit for the month.

The accountant also helped prepare quarterly statements of profit and loss showing actual and budgeted results. In these statements actual results were computed using actual costs for the quarter, accumulated by natural expense classification; except for materials costs which had to be estimated based on purchases and beginning and ending inventories. (Exhibit 1 illustrates the form of these reports, but is for a ten-month period rather than one quarter.)

Installation of New Procedures

After this preliminary systems work had been accomplished, two questions remained as far as the accountant was concerned. First, who in the company would keep the cost book and make out the monthly profit and loss statements? Second, would the company, in fact, believe in and use the system?

The accountant felt that the logical place for this work was in the controller's office. However, when the controller made the suggestion that he ought to go out into the plant to study the production processes in order to better understand and better operate the cost system, other members of management vetoed the idea. They claimed he was needed in the controller's office and that the company just could not afford having him spend much time outside the office. The decision was then made by company officials that the secretary of Mr. Smith, the vice president in charge of promotion and purchasing, would have the responsibility for keeping the cost book up to date and for publishing the monthly profit and loss statements. His secretary had the necessary information for keeping the cost book current in terms of the latest market prices of raw materials and was located on the first floor within the area used by the executives. The controller's office was located on the second floor. Mr. Smith believed that the cost book should be on the first floor where the executive group was located.

The accountant kept management informed as to what he was doing at each step and tried to enlist their help in developing the system as he went along. For example, under the old method three members of management, Mr. Williams (the treasurer), Mr. James (the factory superintendent), and Mr. Smith (in charge of purchasing) estimated the direct labor cost involved in manufacturing any item. In developing data for the cost book these same men estimated the cost of direct labor. Further, the company chemist who had made up the formulas for all the items in the Hartford line also made up the formulas used in the cost book. The accountant proceeded in this way so management would be more likely to accept and use the new system. Despite these precautions, management still had doubts about its usefulness. After the first quarter's results these doubts were intensified.

The first quarter's results showed a large discrepancy between actual costs of materials used in production and estimated material costs, based upon the cost book, of good shipped during that period. When this happened the accountant discussed the matter with the company management. The company immediately thought that the estimates were incorrect. The accountant, on the other hand, felt the trouble lay elsewhere. He offered suggestions as to what might have caused the discrepancy. For instance, was it possible that either raw materials or finished goods had been taken from the plant without management's knowledge? Company officials believed, however, that they had been in the candy business long enough to know if anything like that were going on. "No," they said, "it must be the estimates." The accountant and the chemist rechecked the formulas but these appeared to be correct; however, the discrepancy occurred again at the end of the second quarter.

For three days the accountant and the firm's officials discussed the second quarter results without finding a satisfactory explanation for the discrepany. Finally, Mr. Smith went into the plant, picked up some finished packages, and brought them back to the conference room. The packages were weighed and found to be 10 to 15% overweight. It was estimated that these overweights had been costing the company more than $100,000 per year. Because of this dramatic confirmation of its utility, the new system immediately gained widespread acceptance.

Mr. Johnson, executive vice president, was strongly convinced of the system's usefulness. He believed that the quarterly statements were extremely worthwhile in measuring company performance. Mr. Johnson, Mr. Graham, the president, and Mr. Williams, the treasurer, discussed each quarterly statement in considerable detail. If there were large discrepancies between estimated results and actual results they called in the man concerned for an explanation. Mr. Johnson believed that now management had a very accurate estimate of the cost of its items. He also thought that they now had good month to month information on profit performance. All this was accomplished under the new system, with little additional expense, since Mr. Smith's secretary kept the cost book current and developed the monthly statements along with her regular work.

Required

1. Evaluate Hartford's new cost accounting system. How, if at all, would you change it?

2. Explain how the new cost accounting system, with the changes you propose in Question 1, will result in improving Hartford's profits.

CASE 3.2   AMERICAN ASPHALT AND PAPER PRODUCTS CO., INC.

Introduction

In 1984, American Asphalt witnessed several major organizational changes. The president, moving to the position of chairman of the board, was replaced by Mr. Wylie. Shortly afterwards, Mr. Berry, the treasurer-controller, retired, and two new officers were named to operate the treasurer's and controller's functions separately.

This division of the financial function was accomplished because Mr. Wylie and other top management believed that the company's extensive cost accounting department should have a full-time controller to permit a more thorough review of cost collection procedures. Some members of management had viewed Mr. Berry as "old fashioned" and believed that this new organization would be useful in determining and implementing any improvements in accounting procedures deemed necessary, as well as reducing the costs of accounting functions.

Following this reorganization of the accounting and financial offices, Mr. Wylie established an Accounting Review Committee which was to analyze the existing accounting system. This committee consisted of Mr. Jamison, the new controller and former assistant treasurer-controller; Mr. Wentworth, the general

This case was prepared by E.D. Bennett. Copyright© by the President and Fellows of Harvard College. Harvard Business School case 9-103-003.

manager of manufacturing; and Mr. McNally, executive vice president and secretary. The organization after the above changes is presented in Exhibit 1.

Company Background

American Asphalt and Paper Products Company is a large producer of building materials with 1986 sales of about $50 million. The company's principal products are asphalt shingles, roll roofings, sidings, tars, adhesives, and cement, which are produced in three plants in the United States. American Asphalt has maintained a good earnings record during the last ten years of rapidly expanding sales. (For the company's financial statements see Exhibit 2.)

The production process for shingles and roll products consists of "converting" purchased felt paper by applying tars and asphalt, a coating of grit, and then cutting the processed felt into strips and shingles. The entire process is operated continuously with the raw felt passing first through a bath of asphalt saturant; then under a thick spray of asphalt which coats one side of the felt; under a hopper which sprinkles grit on the coated surface; through a roller to compress the grit into the heavy coating; and finally, through cutters to packaging machinery. The products' physical properties were easily varied by altering the

EXHIBIT 1   American Asphalt and Paper Products Co., Inc.

Partial Organization Chart—1986

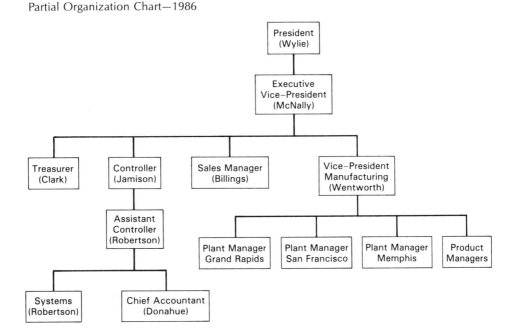

EXHIBIT 2   American Asphalt and Paper Products Co., Inc.

Financial Statements as of December 31, 1986

BALANCE SHEET

ASSETS		*LIABILITIES AND NET WORTH*	
Cash	$ 3,134,243	Accounts payable	$ 3,467,285
Government securities	5,496,573	Accrued taxes	2,395,287
Accounts receivable	5,392,298	Other current liabilities	1,187,562
Notes receivable	168,396	Total current liabilies	$ 7,050,134
Inventories	4,673,587		
Total current assets	$18,865,097	Fixed liabilities	8,342,571
Plant and equipment (net)	20,385,496	Capital stock	10,000,000
Other fixed assets	542,386	Earned surplus	14,400,274
	$39,792,979		$39,792,979

INCOME STATEMENT, YEAR ENDING DECEMBER 31, 1986

Net sales	$51,246,871
Cost of goods sold	39,341,892
Gross profit	$11,904,979
Selling, administrative, and general expense	5,742,356
Operating profit	$ 6,162,623
Other income	635,482
	$ 6,798,105
Other expenses	978,495
Net profit before taxes	$ 5,819,610
Federal taxes	3,025,682
	$ 2,793,928

SOURCE: Company records.

type of felt or saturant used, the type and quantity of the heavy coating, and the color, amount and type of grit spread on the surface.

At American Asphalt's main plant and home office, in Grand Rapids, there were three converting machines which could produce a variety of shingles and roll roofings. Additional machinery was placed at the end of the converting machines to package finished products. Roll roofings were wrapped or headed, in roll form, and shingles were packed in wired cardboard wrappers.

Cost Accounting System

American Asphalt's plants were segregated for accounting purposes, into product departments. At Grand Rapids these product departments were asphalt roofing, siding, asbestos cement products, and liquid products. Each product department was in turn divided into several cost centers. For example, the asphalt roofing department consisted of five cost centers: each of three converting machines was considered as a cost center, and the heading and packing facilities were treated as two separate cost centers.

Each plant collected actual expenses by cost center where possible, as in the cases of direct wages and depreciation, and developed from these figures total departmental costs. All other costs were collected by cost center, as in the case of supervision costs, or allocated to departments from plant totals, as in the case of property taxes which were allocated to departments on a square foot basis. This collection and allocation of costs was made not only for each product department, but also by service departments.

Exhibit 3 illustrates the summary of expenses for each product and service department in the Grand Rapids plant. This summary includes all costs except materials and was prepared monthly for each plant. It can be seen in this exhibit that the costs of two service departments (steam plant and tractor pool) and general factory expenses are accumulated separately and then allocated to the other departments. The end result is total costs for each product department.

The tractor pool consisted of a separate service department which maintained and operated all tractors, fork lifts, and loaders. Departmental shares in the pool's costs were determined from records of actual hourly usage. The general factory expenses represented the plant's share in total central office administrative, staff, research, and engineering costs; as well as three groups of plant expense which were not allocated separately to departments (general administration, telephone, and travel expenses).

Expenses were also determined for each cost center within product departments. In Exhibit 4, Analysis of Manufacturing Expense—Asphalt Roofing Department, the department's total cost (from Exhibit 3) is distributed among the five cost centers. As noted earlier, some of these expenses (such as labor and depreciation) are originally collected by cost center: all other expenses are allocated to each cost center on the basis of square feet, units produced, direct labor hours employed, or some other basis.

Product costs were developed by distributing total costs of each cost center to products, roughly in proportion to each product's share in that center's total machine hours or labor cost. For example, in the asphalt roofing departments, the costs of the converting machine cost centers were distributed to product in the following manner: A normal minimum direct labor "line-up" was known for most operations on these machines. This "standard" labor line-up consisted of 12 people for two of the machines and 11 people for the other. The production of every other product required one to three extra workers: A "standard excess

EXHIBIT 3 American Asphalt and Paper Products Company, Inc.

Summary of Manufacturing and Other Expenses—Grand Rapids, Period Ending April 30, 1987

DEPARTMENTS	ASPHALT ROOFING	SIDING	CEMENT PRODUCTS	LIQUID PRODUCTS	STEAM PLANT	TRACTOR POOL	GENERAL FACTORY	TOTAL	BASIS OF ALLOCATION
Supervision	$ 1,965	$ 876	$ 1,652	$ 1,123	—	—	$ 2,428	$ 8,044	Collected by cost centers
General clerical	541	386	295	493	—	—	4,173	5,888	Allocated in transportation to direct labor hours
Laboratory	471	214	998	1,127	—	—	3,141	5,951	Allocated by estimate of usage
General administration	—	—	—	—	—	—	8,644	8,644	
Depreciation	6,572	2,199	5,272	1,419	$ 896	$ 2,418	4,967	23,743	Collected by cost centers
Insurance	260	120	237	89	24	135	214	1,079	Allocated in proportion to insurance value/dept.
Taxes	1,097	221	346	117	52	213	512	2,558	Allocated in proportion to square feet
Finishing materials	5,136	1,492	896	432	—	—	—	7,956	Collected by cost centers
Labor	49,567	7,491	12,344	7,182	2,516	10,982	3,961	94,043	Collected by cost center and dept.
Supplies	1,431	675	1,193	651	192	877	2,498	7,517	Direct supplies collected by center, other in general factory
Repair labor	12,443	896	193	496	372	1,510	1,736	17,646	Collected by department and cost center
Repair material	11,971	965	3,498	819	255	1,816	3,959	23,263	Collected by center
Waste removal	2,694	396	1,171	652	25	—	4,382	9,320	Collected by center
Inspection	1,215	196	359	—	—	—	—	1,770	Collected by center
Telephone and telegraph	—	—	—	—	—	—	821	821	Collected by center
Purchased power	3,149	412	1,916	637	396	872	96	7,478	Allocation based on usage
Fuel	2,496	31	865	259	10,596	—	—	14,247	Collected by department at actual
Travel and miscellaneous	—	—	—	—	—	—	1,929	1,929	
Receiving and shipping	1,364	829	762	391	—	—	1,436	4,782	Collected by departments
TOTAL	$102,372	$17,399	$31,997	$15,887	$15,324	$18,823	$44,877	$246,679	
Distribution of:									
Steam plant	9,496	932	2,601	876	(15,324)	—	1,419	—	Allocated in proportion to usage
General factory	26,437	5,829	7,212	2,092	—	4,726	(46,296)	—	Allocated in proportion to direct labor hrs.
Tractor pool	11,192	6,752	5,238	367	—	(23,549)	—	—	Collected by cost center
TOTAL	$149,497	$30,912	$47,048	$19,222	$ —	$ —	$ —	$246,679	

EXHIBIT 4 American Asphalt and Paper Products Co., Inc.

Analysis of Manufacturing Expenses—Asphalt Roofing Department, Grand Rapids

	MACHINE #1	MACHINE #2	MACHINE #3	HEADING	PACKING	TOTAL	BASIS OF ALLOCATION
Supervision	$ 196	$ 317	$ 769	$ 141	$ 542	$ 1,965	Collected by cost centers
General, clerical	36	106	186	58	155	541	Allocated in proportion to direct labor hours
Laboratory	43	89	135	92	112	471	Allocated by estimate of usage
Depreciation	362	1,651	2,657	1,138	764	6,572	Collected by cost center
Insurance	25	65	93	57	20	260	Allocated in proportion to appraised values
Taxes	59	368	505	89	76	1,097	Allocated in proportion to square ft
Finishing materials	—	—	—	1,312	3,824	5,136	Collected by cost centers
Labor	5,875	9,783	13,673	3,997	16,239	49,567	Collected by cost centers
Supplies	194	276	319	249	393	1,431	Allocated in proportion to direct supplies per center
Repair labor	862	3,597	7,361	389	234	12,443	Collected by cost centers
Repair material	789	3,735	6,876	246	325	11,971	Collected by cost center
Waste removal	286	514	972	477	445	2,694	Allocated in proportion to wastage per center
Inspection	84	184	263	317	367	1,215	Collected by cost center
Purchased power	721	793	852	356	427	3,149	Allocation based on usage
Fuel	584	752	796	158	206	2,496	Allocation based on usage
Receiving and shipping	227	267	294	295	281	1,364	Allocated in proportion to pounds produced
TOTAL MANUFACTURING EXPENSE	$10,343	$22,497	$35,751	$ 9,371	$24,410	$102,372	
Distribution of:							
Steam plant	1,293	2,317	2,439	1,594	1,853	9,496	Allocation based on usage
General factory	2,674	5,816	9,233	2,422	6,292	26,437	Allocated in proportion to total manufacturing expense
Tractor pool	1,036	2,871	3,396	1,472	2,417	11,192	Collected by center
TOTAL COSTS	$15,346	$33,501	$50,819	$14,859	$34,972	$149,497	

over standard." By multiplying average wage rates times standard line-ups, standard hourly direct labor rates were established for the production of most products. The average labor cost of "standard excess over standards" was also determined to reflect the extra cost of other products requiring extra workers.

These "standard" labor costs were used to allocate actual costs. The hourly "excess over standard" rates were applied against the actual production of products to which they pertained in each center, to determine the standard "extra" direct labor cost required for these products. These "extra costs" were then deducted from each center's total direct labor cost. With this extra removed, all remaining direct labor and manufacturing expenses in each center (as in Exhibit 4) were distributed among all products in proportion to each product's share in the total machine hours utilized during the period.

In the heading and packing cost centers a standard hourly direct labor cost was determined, based upon the number of people needed to operate the center and their average hourly wages. This standard hourly labor rate was applied to the total hours devoted to each product during an accounting period to obtain standard labor per product. The total actual labor and manufacturing expenses (as in Exhibit 4) incurred by the center were allocated to each product in proportion to the share of total standard labor cost applied to each product.

The total manufacturing expenses as listed in Exhibit 4 for each cost center were distributed to products in the above manner. Then, these costs were divided by the quantity of each product that had been produced to obtain per unit costs for each product. Exhibit 5 indicates the conversion and heading or packaging costs which each product in the roofing department at Grand Rapids incurred during a recent month. It should be noted that these costs include all expenses other than materials, as listed in Exhibit 4; and that if material cost were not included in Exhibit 5, the extensions of unit costs would total $149,497, the total costs from Exhibit 4.

Materials. The accounting system for materials was based upon standard formula weights; a finished square of shingles of any particular grade or style had specifications as to the weight of felt, saturant, asphalt coating and grit content. Production was based upon these specifications and finished products were examined closely for deviations from standard weight because industry advertising and contract specifications were based upon formula weights.

American Asphalt kept records of production (in pounds) for each grade or style of asphalt roofing by converting machine monthly. A "standard usage" of each component material was calculated by applying the formula proportions against actual production pounds. Actual usage of component materials was determined by product department by adding purchases and beginning inventory in pounds and subtracting an ending inventory figure determined by a physical count. Actual costs of beginning inventories and purchases were added to monthly handling costs, collected at actual cost for each material, and the sums divided by total pounds to get an average cost per pound for costing actual usage

EXHIBIT 5 American Asphalt and Paper Products Co., Inc.

Products Costs—Roofing Department, Grand Rapids

PRODUCT	UNITS PRODUCED	MATERIALS COST PER UNIT	CONVERSION COST PER UNIT	HEADING ON PACKING UNIT	COST PER UNIT	TOTAL COST
FLEX-EASE STRIP SHINGLES						
10″ Regular	33,596	$2.76	$0.46	$0.45	$3.67	$123,297.32
10″ Grade A	21,274	3.00	.63	.61	4.24	90,201.76
10″ Architect	22,436	3.16	.71	.72	4.59	102,981.24
SPECIALTY STRIP SHINGLES						
11″ Tapered	6,792	3.89	.68	.76	5.33	36,201.36
11″ Tapered-Regular	7,711	3.94	.75	.82	5.51	42,487.61
11″ Strip "A"	2,496	4.16	.84	.99	5.99	14,951.04
INDIVIDUAL ASPHALT SHINGLES						
Double coverage	4,965	2.12	.68	.72	3.52	17,476.80
Standard—Tite	3,471	2.34	.37	.37	3.08	10,690.68
Regular—Tite	1,915	3.12	.71	.65	4.48	8,579.20
Straight Lap "A"	2,158	2.96	.86	.91	4.73	10,207.34
ASPHALT SIDINGS						
14″ Straight Grain	836	1.87	.31	.38	2.56	2,140.16
14″ Regular	747	1.72	.35	.38	2.45	1,830.15
ASPHALT ROLL ROOFING						
#70 Mineral Surface	1,476	1.33	.46	.29	2.08	3,070.08
#90 Mineral Surface	8,596	1.12	.37	.61	2.10	18,051.60
14″ First Roll	876	1.66	.26	.36	2.28	1,997.28
20″ Regular	932	.72	.51	.29	1.52	1,416.64
SMOOTH SURFACE ROOFING						
30″ Safety	1,496	1.10	.31	.26	1.67	2,498.32
28″ Grade A	2,386	.91	.42	.34	1.67	3,984.62
26″ Superior	1,917	.65	.36	.29	1.30	2,492.10
SATURATED FELTS						
#60 Felt	2,496	1.10	.21	.00	1.31	3,269.76
#30 Felt	876	1.36	.38	.42	2.16	1,892.16
30″ Standard	1,172	.73	.27	.57	1.57	1,840.04
	130,620					$501,557.26

and ending inventory. Then the actual usage was allocated to individual roofing products in proportion to each product's share in the total standard usage figure.

In the heading center, additional materials entered production in the form of wrapping paper. Since each roll of roofing products was approximately the same size, the total cost of wrapping materials used by heading was distributed evenly to all rolls headed during the period. The actual cost of heading materials was the difference between purchases and beginning inventory and a physical count of ending inventory, all valued at average cost. A material cost rate per roll was determined by dividing total cost of heading materials used by the number of rolls headed.

In the packing center a standard quantity of wire and wrappers used to package a square of each shingle style had been established. Total standard packaging costs for each grade of shingle was determined by applying this standard rate by quantity produced. Actual packaging material costs, collected as in the heading center, were then distributed to products in proportion to each product's share in the total standard packaging materials cost.

Accounting Reports. In the above section the collection of costs for one plant, a department, and for the department's cost centers and products has been reviewed. This procedure was employed with few variations for the various departments in all plants, using cost summaries similar to those illustrated in Exhibits 3, 4, and 5.

Many additional reports were prepared by the accounting offices, such as production summaries, analyses of conversion costs (Exhibit 6), and raw materials reports. Such monthly cost reports (about 100 per plant) were issued to top management about the eighth day of the succeeding month at all American plants. Central accounting consolidated most of these reports and issued comparative statements about the 15th day of the month. These statements included summaries of total unit costs by product at each plant (Exhibit 7); manufacturing cost per unit at each plant; summaries of average actual weight for finished shingles; average unit production of each product per hour at all plants; and many others, all permitting detailed comprehension of production and costs for all products for different periods at each plant.

Because of the week delay in mailing out comparative cost reports by the central accounting department, this department issued a "flyer" on the 9th day of each month giving unit costs of key items per plant for the preceding month, the previous period, and the corresponding period a year before. A typical "flyer" can be seen (Exhibit 8) illustrating major cost comparisons.

The central accounting department also prepared over 150 financial statements quarterly. These consisted chiefly of profit and loss statements by plants, products and sales divisions; and consolidated and divisional expense summaries of selling, research, and general administrative expenses. Approximately 35 members of management received more than 30 of these reports each and about

EXHIBIT 6 American Asphalt and Paper Products Co., Inc.

Comparative Analysis of Conversion Costs[a]—Roofing Machine Products, Grand Rapids   Period Ending April 30, 1987

	CURRENT PERIOD		LAST PERIOD		YEAR TO DATE		LAST YEAR TO DATE	
	Costs	Per unit	Costs	Per unit	Costs	Per unit	Costs	Per unit
FACTORY UNITS PRODUCED	130,620		162,450		581,732		621,342	
Supervision	$ 1,965	$0.0151	$ 2,469	$0.0152	$ 9,482	$0.0163	$ 9,072	$0.0146
General clerical	541	.0041	634	.0039	2,443	.0042	2,361	.0038
Laboratory	471	.0036	520	.0032	1,920	.0033	2,547	.0041
Depreciation	6,572	.0503	6,709	.0413	28,272	.0486	24,729	.0398
Insurance	260	.0020	341	.0021	1,105	.0019	1,118	.0018
Taxes	1,097	.0084	1,088	.0067	4,188	.0072	3,790	.0061
Finishing materials	5,136	.0393	6,319	.0389	23,386	.0402	23,673	.0381
Labor	49,567	.3795	61,097	.3761	214,368	.3685	218,340	.3514
Supplies	1,431	.0110	845	.0052	5,992	.0103	5,405	.0087
Repair labor	12,443	.0953	13,272	.0817	46,248	.0795	47,284	.0761
Repair material	11,971	.0916	14,556	.0896	49,273	.0847	54,119	.0871
Waste removal	2,694	.0206	3,493	.0215	12,740	.0219	9,693	.0156
Inspection	1,215	.0093	1,397	.0086	5,294	.0091	4,474	.0072
Purchased power	3,149	.0241	3,931	.0242	14,136	.0243	14,229	.0229
Fuel	2,496	.0191	3,298	.0203	10,355	.0178	13,297	.0214
Receiving and shipping	1,364	.0104	1,901	.0117	5,526	.0095	5,344	.0086
TOTAL	$102,372	$0.7837	$121,870	$0.7502	$434,728	$0.7473	$439,475	$0.7073
Distribution of:								
Steam plant	9,496	.0727	10,608	.0653	40,256	.0692	40,077	.0645
General factory	26,437	.2024	28,120	.1731	112,216	.1929	97,799	.1574
Tractor pool	11,192	.0857	11,599	.0714	41,477	.0713	42,997	.0692
TOTAL	$149,497	$1.1445	$172,197	$1.0600	$628,677	$1.0807	$620,348	$0.9984

[a]Includes heading and packing costs.

EXHIBIT 7 American Asphalt and Paper Products Co., Inc.

Comparative Statement of Product Costs—Roofing Departments, All Plants

Period Ending April 30, 1987

	GRAND RAPIDS				SAN FRANCISCO				MEMPHIS			
	This period	Last period	(Increase) Decrease	Year 1986	This period	Last period	(Increase) Decrease	Year 1986	This period	Last period	(Increase) Decrease	Year 1986
FLEX-EASE STRIP SHINGLES												
10" Regular	$3.67	$3.51	$(0.16)	$3.41	$3.52	$3.46	$(0.06)	$3.29	$3.46	$3.51	$ 0.05	$3.24
10" Grade A	4.24	4.19	(.05)	4.06	4.16	4.09	(.07)	3.94	4.12	4.16	.04	3.89
10" Architect	4.59	4.62	.03	4.47	4.42	4.41	(.01)	4.38	4.38	4.35	(.03)	4.32
SPECIALTY STRIP SHINGLES												
11" Tapered	5.33	5.31	(.02)	5.18	5.17	5.11	(.06)	5.12	5.15	5.17	.02	5.14
11" Tapered—Regular	5.51	5.67	.16	5.26	5.34	5.32	(.02)	5.16	5.26	5.21	(.05)	5.29
11" Strip "A"	5.99	5.68	(.31)	5.37	5.76	5.74	(.02)	5.33	5.68	5.59	(.09)	5.30
INDIVIDUAL ASPHALT SHINGLES												
Double coverage	3.52	3.34	(.18)	3.36	3.37	3.38	.01	3.31	3.31	3.28	(.03)	3.28
Standard—Tite	3.08	2.86	(.22)	2.75	2.94	2.98	.04	2.71	2.88	2.91	.03	2.66
Regular—Tite	4.48	4.41	(.07)	4.23	4.46	4.41	(.05)	4.18	4.44	4.48	.04	4.19
Straight lap A	4.73	4.82	.09	4.46	4.63	4.58	(.05)	4.42	4.58	4.61	.03	4.44

ASPHALT SIDINGS												
14" Straight Grain	2.56	2.41	(.15)	2.34	2.51	2.49	(.02)	2.33	2.43	2.41	(.02)	2.29
14" Regular	2.45	2.27	(.18)	2.16	2.42	2.37	(.05)	2.12	2.38	2.36	(.02)	2.10
ASPHALT ROLL ROOFING												
#70 Mineral Surface	2.08	2.12	.04	2.13	1.88	1.78	(.10)	2.05	2.02	1.96	(.06)	2.09
#90 Mineral Surface	2.10	2.07	(.03)	2.15	1.94	1.83	(.11)	1.76	2.05	1.98	(.07)	1.81
14" First Roll	2.28	2.25	(.03)	2.22	2.22	2.16	(.06)	2.19	2.31	2.27	(.04)	2.22
20" Regular	1.52	1.46	(.06)	1.38	1.47	1.41	(.06)	1.34	1.54	1.52	(.02)	1.34
SMOOTH SURFACE ROOFING												
30" Safety	1.67	1.52	(.15)	1.45	1.68	1.70	.02	1.47	1.72	1.69	(.03)	1.45
28" Grade A	1.67	1.46	(.21)	1.38	1.70	1.72	.02	1.40	1.74	1.76	.02	1.41
26" Superior	1.30	1.24	(.06)	1.13	1.35	1.34	(.01)	1.16	1.33	1.36	.03	1.17
SATURATED FELTS												
#60 Felt	1.31	1.37	.06	1.22	1.27	1.26	(.01)	1.13	1.21	1.25	.04	1.08
#30 Felt	2.16	2.19	.03	2.04	1.96	2.02	.06	1.88	1.86	1.84	(.02)	1.77
30" Standard	1.57	1.54	(.03)	1.39	1.35	1.37	.02	1.25	1.31	1.28	(.03)	1.15

EXHIBIT 8 American Asphalt and Paper Products Co., Inc.

"Flyer" (Issued May 9)

Period Ending April 30, 1987

	GRAND RAPIDS			SAN FRANCISCO			MEMPHIS		
	April 1987	March 1987	Year 1986	April 1987	March 1987	Year 1986	April 1987	March 1987	Year 1986
ASPHALT ROOFING									
10" Regular	$3.67	$3.51	$3.41	$3.52	$3.46	$3.29	$3.46	$3.51	$3.24
10" Grade A	4.24	4.19	4.06	4.16	4.09	3.94	4.12	4.16	3.89
10" Architect	4.59	4.62	4.47	4.42	4.41	4.38	4.38	4.35	4.32
11" Tapered—Regular	5.51	5.67	5.26	5.34	5.32	5.16	5.26	5.21	5.29
#90 Mineral Surface	2.10	2.07	2.15	1.94	1.83	1.76	2.05	1.98	1.81
Units produced	130,620	162,450		88,592	86,437		114,591	102,594	
SIDING									
Superior Wall—Red	$8.64	$8.14	$8.26	$8.36	$8.21	$8.28	$7.97	$7.82	$7.88
#5 Panel	7.39	7.41	7.54	7.09	7.12	6.95	6.84	6.81	6.67
Units produced	23,542	18,436		16,594	13,343		33,478	27,746	
LIQUID									
#9 Pitch	$1.33	$1.42	$1.26	$1.12	$1.18	$1.09	$1.41	$1.18	$1.11
#8 Tar	1.46	1.53	1.39	1.37	1.28	1.32	1.31	1.36	1.38
Units produced	5,493	6,482		3,295	2,971		8,572	7,637	

nine persons (including Messrs. Wylie, Jamison, Wentworth, and McNally) received all of them.

The treasurer's and controller's departments, in addition to cost accounting and the preparation of cost reports, were responsible for all ordering, billing, credit work, insurance, salary administration payroll, and general accounting, tax and systems work, and office work throughout the company. These departments employed about 100 persons, with an aggregate compensation of $914,600 in 1986. Mr. Wylie and Mr. McNally recognized that their organization and the nature of their production processes required extensive cost collection work, but were particularly interested in reducing the cost of the accounting functions. They agreed that it would be desirable to have a general review of their system, with such cost reduction as the major objective.

The accounting review committee had been studying this question during the last few months of 1987 and both Mr. Jamison and Mr. Wentworth were quite satisfied with the existing system and its results. However, Mr. McNally did not believe that the committee had made a very thorough and critical review of the system and suggested that American's auditors, (Watson, Henson, and Bean) be asked to review the accounting procedures.

In late 1987, Mr. Wylie requested, during a routine meeting with Mr. Watson, that the accounting firm's system service staff make a general appraisal of American's accounting system.

Required

1. Evaluate American Asphalt's cost accounting system with respect to its adequacy in inventory valuation, cost control, and marketing decisions.

2. What changes, if any, would you recommend be made? Explain how these changes would overcome the limitations described in Question 1.

chapter 4

ASSIGNING OVERHEAD COSTS TO PRODUCTS

Chapters 2 and 3 described the flow of information through the books of account for the different types of cost accounting systems. All these systems required the assignment of overhead to product. Since this is the most difficult technical problem in product cost accounting and one in which the manager has a vital concern, this topic has been covered in a separate chapter.

Direct material and direct labor can, by definition, be identified with a unit of finished product; consequently, there are no theoretical problems with assigning material and labor costs accurately to the products to which they apply. (Occasionally, there can be practical problems connected with keeping a record of how much was used on a particular product.) In nearly every case where cost accounting systems generate inaccurate (and, consequently, misleading) product cost information, the fault is in the methods used for assigning overhead costs to product. The purpose of this chapter is to describe and evaluate these methods.

The problems of assigning overhead costs to products can be divided into three types, as follows:

1. The assignment of product costs to productive department.
2. The assignment of productive department costs to the products produced.
3. The determination of the volume to be used in calculating unit costs.

This chapter is divided into three sections, covering each of these types of problems.

ASSIGNMENT TO PRODUCTIVE DEPARTMENT

Overhead costs are collected and classified in several different ways. First, they are identified by expense classification. For example, indirect labor, supplies, expense tools, utilities, depreciation, and so forth. These major expense categories are subdivided to the extent that management needs the information. For example, there could be 20 or 30 subclassifications of indirect labor—such as clerks, inspectors, sweepers, and so forth. Next these costs are assigned to cost centers (a department or other organizational unit to which costs are charged.) In general, there are three types of cost centers. First, there are productive departments. These are departments that contribute directly to the manufacture of the product. In a textile factory, the picking, carding, spinning, and weaving departments are examples of productive departments. Second, there are service departments. These departments, as the name implies, provide service to the productive departments but have no physical output. Maintenance, quality control, cafeteria, and industrial engineering are examples of service departments. Third, there are cost accounting centers that accumulate certain plant-wide costs. Water, electricity, and building costs are examples of cost centers of this type. These are not formal departments but are record-keeping classifications.

Before costs can be assigned to product, they must all be assigned eventually to some productive department because the productive departments are the only ones for which bases for assigning costs directly to product are available. The first step in this process is to assign all costs to some department or cost center. As much as possible, cost should be assigned directly. For example, the wages of people working in a department, the supplies issued, and the depreciation on equipment used by the department would be assigned directly. The second step is to allocate to the productive departments the costs of the service departments and the cost accounting centers. The principle in allocating costs is *fair share*. That is to say, each department should be assigned its fair share of the service and general costs. Fair share is generally interpreted to mean the costs for which the department is responsible or which were generated on its behalf. This is sometimes called *effort expended* because it is based on the effort expended by the service department for the benefit of the productive department. Where there is no basis for effort expended, the allocations are made on the basis of *benefits received*. This is usually relative size, on the assumption that the larger the department, the greater the potential benefit from a particular service. Clearly, this principle is given rather broad interpretation.

Allocation Techniques

Allocation techniques can be divided into five general categories: floor space, services received, service base, size, or special study. Each of these is described next:

1. *Floor space.* Heat, light, building costs, and so forth are usually allocated on the basis of the relative amounts of floor space occupied by the department.

2. *Services received.* In some cost accounting systems, a record is kept of the services rendered. For example, maintenance departments often keep records of the time spent in each department and the cost of maintenance is allocated according to the relative amounts of time spent. If utilities are metered by department, the cost is allocated on the relative amount of utilities consumed.

3. *Service base.* Where records of services rendered are not maintained, some costs can be allocated on the relative size of the service base. For example, maintenance can be assigned on the basis of the relative value of equipment, industrial relations on the relative number of people, or electricity on the relative potential usage based on the type and amount of equipment.

4. *Size.* There are some costs (chiefly general administrative) for which it is difficult to find any really rational base for allocation. These costs are usually allocated on the basis of relative size. Relative size can be measured by such means as total labor, or total labor and overhead. Relative size is used only when better measures of fair share are not available.

5. *Special Study.* In some instances special studies are conducted to see the relative usage of a particular cost during a specific period of time, say a month. These usages are translated into percentages and the percentages used to allocate the cost to department. For example, the actual cost of grinding wheels used by each productive department is calculated for one month. This becomes the basis for allocating total grinding wheel costs in subsequent periods.

Common Bases of Allocation. Following is a list of general plant costs and service departments with some common basis for allocation.

Cost or Department	*Allocation Basis*
Building depreciation	Relative floor space occupied
Building maintenance and repairs	Relative floor space occupied
Rent	Relative floor space occupied
Heat and light	Relative floor space occupied
Property taxes and insurance	Relative floor space occupied
Power (if not metered to department)	Relative horsepower of equipment
Taxes and insurance on machinery	Relative book value of machinery and equipment
Maintenance	Time spent by maintenance people or value of equipment in department

Cost or Department	Allocation Basis
Water and steam (if not metered to department)	Analysis of departmental requirement (i.e., special studies of usage)
Laboratory	Relative number of jobs performed or relative time spent on jobs for each department
Industrial relations department	Relative number of people
Plant superintendent	Relative direct labor dollars
Miscellaneous plant costs	Relative direct labor dollars
Payroll department	Relative number of people
Accounting department	Relative value of production

Deciding Which Base to Use

In deciding which base of allocation to use, it is useful to separate the costs to be allocated into three groups, as follows.

1. Those costs that can be controlled by the department manager using the service.
2. Those costs that, although not directly controllable by the department manager, are more or less variable with the level of production.
3. Those costs that are neither controllable by the department manager nor variable with the level of production.

Where department managers can control levels of an expense, it is important to use an allocation method that will motivate them to keep these expenses under careful control. Perhaps the best example of this occurs with respect to maintenance cost. A department supervisor frequently can exercise considerable control over the level of this expense. If maintenance cost is allocated on, for example, the book value of the machinery and equipment in the department, the manager has little incentive to schedule maintenance efficiently because the charge is approximately the same amount no matter how much maintenance is incurred. If, however, maintenance costs are allocated on the basis of the hours of maintenance time actually devoted to a department, the supervisor would be motivated to use the maintenance people judiciously.

The second category contains those allocated costs that vary with the volume of production. It is important to allocate this category of expenses as precisely as possible so that the variable product cost can be determined with a reasonable degree of accuracy. For example, a considerable part of power expense usually varies with the volume of production. In calculating product cost, it is important that this expense be reflected as a variable cost. If power is allocated to the department on some arbitrary basis (such as rated horsepower of equipment), the cost would not vary with volume at the department level. If Department A, for instance, had 30% of the total rated horsepower in the plant, it would be allocated 30% of the power costs. If, however, Department A worked at 50% of capacity during a particular month and the rest of the plant worked at 100%, 30% of the total power bill would not be a reasonable allocation.

Usually, where an allocated cost varies with volume, it is quite easy to find a basis for determining a department's fair share. (In the case of power, water, or steam, for example, it is the actual amount used.) It is, however, sometimes a problem to find an inexpensive method for measuring this share. It may not be practical, for example, to meter water, steam, or power by department. If the total amount of the expense is relatively small, a more or less fixed allocation will do no harm. It is important, however, to recognize this situation so that the departmental overhead rates will reflect these costs as variable.

In allocating costs that are neither variable nor controllable it is not necessary to consider the impact of the allocation on cost control or variability. The method to use is the one that provides the best measure of fair share.

One method to test the reasonableness of a particular system of allocation is to try several combinations. All reasonable combinations should give approximately the same answers. To decide which of the possible combinations gives the most reliable results, ask, "Which method provides differences in unit costs between the products that best reflect the differentials that might exist if each product were produced in its own plant? Unit cost differentials should result from differences in such things as design, quality, or production techniques rather than from the vagaries of the cost allocation system.

Allocating Service Department Costs to Productive Departments

There are two principal procedures for allocating service department costs to productive departments: (1) Allocate the service department cost to productive departments only; (2) allocate the service department cost to other service departments as well as to productive departments.

Under the first procedure: (1) decide on a basis for allocating the costs of each service department (as described in the previous section); (2) allocate the costs of each service department directly to the productive departments on these bases.

Under the second procedure, service department costs are allocated as follows:

1. Decide on a method for allocating the cost of each service department to the other departments.
2. Place the service departments in the order that they are to be closed out.
3. Close the service departments to the productive departments.

The close-out order is based on the amount of service that a department renders to other service departments as compared to the amount of services that it receives. The first department to be closed out is the one with the greatest net amount of services rendered to other service departments. The next department to be closed will be the one rendering the second greatest net amount of service to other service departments, and so on, until the last service department, which will be the one providing the least service to other service departments. (A general approximation of this order is all that is required.)

The first service department on the list of departments will be closed to all of the other departments, service as well as productive. The second department on the list will be closed to all departments except the first one (and, of course, the department being closed). This will be continued until all service departments have been closed to the productive departments. The bases for allocating the service departments' costs will usually be the same as if the service departments were allocated directly to productive departments. In some cases, however, the fact that the service departments' costs are being allocated to other service departments may require a change in allocation base. For example, the plant manager's office cannot be allocated on the basis of relative direct labor costs because the service departments have no direct labor; therefore, the allocation base could be, for example, total labor dollars.

Example of Allocation. The following is a simplified example of the techniques and procedures described in this part of the chapter. Expenses directly assigned are as follows.

	PRODUCTIVE DEPARTMENTS		SERVICE DEPARTMENTS		COST CENTERS	
Type of expenses	A	B	Plant manager	Maintenance	Building	Electricity
				(000's)		
Direct labor	$100	$200				
Indirect labor	50	75	$20	$60		
Indirect material	10	10	—	70	$10	
Utilities	—	—	—	—	—	$30
Expense tools	5	15	—	20	—	—
Depreciation	40	70	—	10	30	—
Total	$205	$370	$20	$160	$40	$30

It has been decided to allocate service department and cost accounting centers in the following order: Building, Electricity, Maintenance, and Plant Manager. It has further been decided to use the following techniques of allocation.

Building:	relative floor space
Electricity:	relative kilowatt hours used last year
Maintenance:	book value of equipment
Plant Manager:	total direct charges (labor and overhead)

The statistics on these items are as follows:

	FLOOR SPACE (SQ. FT)	RELATIVE KILOWATT HOURS IN 1986	BOOK VALUE OF EQUIPMENT
Department A	100,000	40%	$400,000
Department B	150,000	50	200,000
Plant manager	2,500	2	—
Maintenance	40,000	8	100,000
Building	—	—	10,000
Total	292,500	100%	$710,000

The allocation of costs (in thousands of dollars) to productive department is as follows:

DEPARTMENT OR COST CENTER		ALLOCATIONS				
Name	Direct amount	Building[a]	Electricity	Maintenance[b]	Plant manager[c]	Total amount
			(000's)			
Building	$ 40	$(40)				
Electricity	30	—	$(30)			
Maintenance	160	6	2	$(168)		
Plant manager	20	—	1	2	$(23)	
Department A	205	14	12	55	8	$294
Department B	370	20	15	111	15	531
Total	$825	—	—	—	—	$825

[a]Floor space: 34%, Dept. A; 51%, Dept. B; 1% Plant Manager; 14% Maintenance.
[b]Relative volume of equipment (excluding maintenance and building equipment): Dept. A, 66%; Dept. B, 33%, Plant Manager, 1%.
[c]Dept. A, 205/575 or 36%; Dept. B, 370/575 or 64%.

Summary of Allocation to Department

All overhead costs must be assigned to some production department.[1] Costs are assigned directly to productive department to the extent that this is practical. Those costs that cannot be assigned directly are accumulated in service departments and cost accounting centers. These are then allocated to productive department. The principle of allocation is to give each department its fair share. Although cost allocation is a technical problem generally left to the cost accountant, it is important that the student of management have some understanding of these techniques. Note, also, that the decision on the allocation base to be used

---

[1]Note that some overhead costs may be treated as period costs and thus would not be assigned to a product.

is *not* an accounting problem but a management problem. Often managers have a much better concept of how costs should be allocated than the cost accountant because they are more familiar with the circumstances of cost generation.

ALLOCATION OF OVERHEAD TO PRODUCT

When all overhead costs have been allocated to productive departments, the next step is to allocate these costs to the products produced. If there is only a single product produced in a department, the problem is easy. Simply divide the total overhead costs for the period by the units produced. This will provide an over-head amount per unit that can be added to the direct material and direct labor costs. The one-product department is rare, however. It is not unusual to have one thousand different products produced in a single productive department. It is important, therefore, to find a technique for assigning a fair share of the department overhead costs to each product produced in that department.

The most common way of allocating overhead costs to product is on the basis of direct labor, either dollars or hours. In the example given in the previous section, Department A had direct labor of $100,000 and overhead (after the allocation of service departments) of $194,000. Dividing 194,000 by 100,000 we get a rate of 194%. (This is called an *overhead* or *burden* rate.) For each product produced in Department A, 194% of direct labor would be added as the overhead amount. Suppose, for example, the following products were produced in Department A: Product 1 with a direct labor cost of $2.00 per unit and Product 2 with a direct labor cost of $0.50 per unit. Labor and overhead costs for these products would be calculated as follows:

	PRODUCT 1	PRODUCT 2
Direct labor	$2.00	$0.50
Overhead (194% of DL)	3.88	0.97
Total	$5.88	$1.47

Note that direct labor is used to assign a fair share of the overhead to each product, not because direct labor *generates* the overhead but because it measures approximately the relative amount of overhead required to produce it. In the example above, Product 1 has four times as much labor cost as Product 2. Consequently, it is assumed that Product 1 used four times as much machine capacity, four times as many supplies, four times as many utilities, and so forth.

Homogeneous Cost Centers

When direct labor (or, for that matter, any other base) is used to allocate overhead, the method will provide useful costs only if the cost center is homogeneous. A homogeneous cost center is one in which the equipment and the degree of automation are comparable. If the cost center is not homogeneous, a dollar (or an hour) of direct labor will not give a reasonable approximation of the fair share of the overhead cost. Two examples are given next.

EXAMPLE 1. MACHINING AND ASSEMBLY.   A productive department contains automatic lathes in one part of the department and hand assembly in another. The average overhead rate is 300%. If the department was divided into two cost centers, the automatic lathes would have an overhead rate of 500% because of the relatively low labor and the high cost of depreciation of the equipment. The assembly center would have an overhead rate of 100% because of the high labor content and low depreciation cost. To combine these two into a single cost center could give significantly misleading costs. Products with high assembly labor would be incorrectly charged with the high overhead costs of the automatic lathes.[2]

EXAMPLE 2. DIFFERENT DEGREE OF AUTOMATION.   A stamping department has a highly automatic line to make parts on a nearly continuous basis. It has another line with little automation to make small volume parts. The two lines together have an average overhead rate of 500%. If each line were made into a separate cost center, the automatic line would have an overhead rate of 1000%, whereas the hand-operated line would have an overhead rate of 200%. To combine these the lines into a single cost center would result in overcosting the products of the hand-operated line and undercosting the products of the automatic line.

Although the determination of cost centers is a technical cost accounting problem, it is vital that the student of management understand it. First, it is a problem that exists in every type of cost accounting system except in the very simplest. Second, it is in this area that most cost accounting systems are deficient. It has been my experience that a large number of cost accounting systems generate incorrect and misleading information to mangement because the cost centers are not homogeneous. One reason is that, the greater the number of cost centers, the more complex and expensive the cost accounting system becomes. In a misguided attempt at economy, some cost accountants limit the number of cost centers. (Some companies have a *single* cost center for an entire factory.) The information generated by a cost accounting system that has an inadequate number of cost centers is often worthless, or worse, misleading to management. As a consequence, economy can never be used to rationalize a cost accounting system that allocates overhead to product from nonhomogeneous cost centers.

---

[2]An exception to this generalization occurs when all the parts spend the same proportion of time in each operation. For example, if the direct labor on all parts going through the department were 40% in machining and 60% in assembly, the costs would be the same with either one cost center or two cost centers.

Cost Allocation on Machine Hours.   Machine hours also form a common base for the allocation of overhead to products. Essentially each machine or group of comparable machines is a cost center. All costs are assigned to the various machines or groups of machines and a cost per machine hour is calculated. (Usually, this cost will include both direct labor and overhead.) Then the product costs are calculated by multiplying the number of machine hours required to produce each part by the cost per hour. For example, suppose that Product 3 was produced as follows:

MACHINE	NUMBER OF HOURS
Milling	.50
Grinding	.25
Assembly	.25
Total	1.00

If the machine hour rates for direct labor and overhead were as indicated next, the costs would be calculated as follows:

		LABOR AND OVERHEAD COST OF PRODUCT 3	
Type of operation	Number of hours	Cost per hour	Total cost
Milling	.50	$5.24	$2.620
Grinding	.25	4.60	1.150
Assembly	.25	3.10	.875
Total	1.00		$4.645

Although the use of machine hours is currently unusual, it is being increasingly used. In the future, it will be used almost exclusively in complex manufacturing operations. This is described in the last part of this chapter.

Multiple Rates.   Another means of allocating overhead costs to product is to use several rates. For example, material handling costs might be allocated on the basis of the weight of materials, labor generated costs such as fringe benefits and indirect labor on the basis of direct labor, and machine generated costs such as depreciation and fuel on the basis of machine hours. As might be expected, methods such as these are more expensive, although they can result in greater accuracy.

Criterion for Evaluating Allocation Methods

The decision that cost accountants face in cost determination is to trade off the cost of obtaining the data against the accuracy obtained. The question, therefore, is how complex should the cost allocation be and how many cost centers (or costing rates) should be used. One fact overrides all other considerations. *The cost data should be as accurate as management requires to support its decisions.* If it is not, it is worse than useless. The degree of accuracy will differ in different situations and each case must be decided separately. It is necessary to find out, first, how management uses the cost accounting data, then estimate the degree of error in the data that can be allowed.

The allocation methods can be tested by trying out more and more complex (and presumably accurate) techniques. Stop at the point where the degree of accuracy required by management is obtained. For example, try a gradual increase in the number of cost centers. Continue to increase the number of cost centers as long as the change in product costs between two sets of cost centers is great enough for management to make different decisions using the two sets of costs. The optimum number of cost centers is reached when management decisions are the same for either set of cost centers. Note that all this assumes that *more accurate* costs result from increasing the sophistication of the system. Although this assumption is generally true, there are exceptions and judgment will always be required.

The evaluation of the accuracy of cost data is a technical accounting task. The student of management, however, should be assured that there has been some attempt to consider this problem. Some cost accountants allocate overhead to product by the least expensive techniques and are completely oblivious to the potential inaccuracies of the data that they generate. Managers should always be sure that the cost accounting system is providing them with data that are accurate enough to allow them to make correct decisions. If it is not, they should either insist on accurate data or discontinue the generation of inaccurate data and thus at least save the cost of compiling these data.

VOLUME

As described in Chapter 1, overhead costs may be variable or fixed. The amount of a variable cost will vary directly and proportionately with the volume of production. Conversely, variable costs will be the same for each unit of production. Fixed costs, on the other hand, will remain the same in total within wide ranges of production volumes. Consequently, the higher the volume the smaller the fixed cost per unit will be. For example, if the fixed costs of operating a department are $100,000 a month, the cost per unit will be $1.00 if 100,000 units are produced and $0.50 if 200,000 units are produced. This means that unit costs will rise as volume falls and fall as volume rises, if costs are calculated at the actual volume of production. What is actually happening when volume drops below normal is that there is a greater amount of idle capacity and the cost of this idle capacity is being assigned to the products that are being produced.

The volume that is used to calculate unit costs can have a significant impact on the level of the cost. It is most important, therefore, that careful consideration be given to the volume used in a cost accounting system. The purpose of this part of the chapter is to describe the different types of volumes that are used in cost accounting and explain how they affect unit costs.

The volumes used by cost accountants to calculate unit costs can be classi-fied into four general types: actual, forecast, capacity, and standard; each is de-scribed in detail next.

Actual Volume

As the name implies, the *actual volume method* means that unit costs are calcu-lated using the actual volume of production for the period. The usual method is to divide the total actual departmental overhead by the total actual departmental direct labor to obtain an overhead rate. This overhead rate is then applied to the actual unit direct labor for each product to obtain the overhead cost per unit. (Obviously, the actual volume method can only be used with a historical cost system).

As explained in Chapter 3 the use of actual volume is quite limited because unit costs are low in periods of high volume and high in periods of low volume; this makes it difficult for management to use unit costs for any purpose. Only in the most unusual circumstances could costs that fluctuate with volume be used as a guide for pricing action or other marketing decisions. The use of unit costs for even the most primitive cost control is impaired by the fact that changes in volume affect these costs. It is nearly impossible to compare the unit costs of one period with those of another and make any sensible evaluation of the changes. Even costs for inventory valuation can be badly distorted. When volume is low, costs can be seriously overstated.

Another disadvantage is that unit costs cannot be calculated until after the end of the period. This can be a disadvantage when customers are charged on a basis of the actual work performed. It is not possible to bill them until after the books are closed. Furthermore, when billing is based on actual costs, it is difficult to explain that volume is the reason for the same job costing a different amount in two different periods.

About the only time that unit costs based on actual volume appear to be useful is when capacity has been set aside for only one purchaser. The smaller the volume of purchases, the more each unit will cost the buyer. This may exist in certain cost plus fixed fee contracts. A company agrees to maintain a facility to supply whatever is demanded by the purchaser. The purchaser agrees to pay the actual cost of the products produced. The less the purchaser orders, the more it will cost per unit under this kind of agreement. (Even then, it would probably be better to charge a total fee for the capacity plus a variable cost for the units produced.) Such a contract is unusual in most businesses, occurring only in a few types of special contracts.

Annual Forecast

A variation of the actual volume method is to forecast the coming year's production volume and to calculate a standard overhead rate at this volume. The annual forecast is widely used and the unsatisfactory effects associated with actual volume are considerably lessened.

The principal problem with using actual volume is caused by the fluctuations in costs as a result of the fluctuations in volume. Monthly volumes tend to fluctuate relatively more widely than annual volumes, particularly where there is a seasonal trend. The use of an annual volume, therefore, is one factor that tends to lessen the period-to-period fluctuations. (Using actual volume, it is impractical in most cases to use annual volume because this requires waiting until the end of the year before unit costs are calculated.)

Even more important than the time period is the fact that the volumes are forecast. People rarely forecast extreme volume levels, either high or low. Thus, even though the actual volume fluctuates significantly from year to year, costs are calculated at a more constant level. In many cases, forecast volume will be very similar to the standard volume described later.

The use of an annual forecast is generally a much more satisfactory basis for calculating unit costs than actual volume. Nevertheless, it has the same problems created by fluctuations in volume. Unit costs will be high in periods of low volume and low in periods of high volume forecasts. This can lead management to take precisely the wrong action if unit costs are used as a basis for establishing prices or influencing product mix. Meaningful comparisons of year-to-year unit costs are also difficult.

The reason that annual forecasts usually prove satisfactory is that forecast volumes tend to be reasonably constant from year to year. Since this is the case, it might be better to recognize this fact and use a volume that is designed to be constant.

Capacity Costing

There are two types of capacity used in cost accounting: theoretical and practical. It is important to distinguish between them because they affect unit costs differently.

Theoretical Capacity.   *Theoretical capacity* is defined as the maximum output of a plant or other production unit. There is usually no allowance for down time due to repairs or any loss in production caused by such factors as inefficient scheduling or offstandard labor performance. There are, however, two important assumptions that can affect the volume significantly: one is the number of shifts per week; the other is the assumptions with respect to product mix. A three-shift, seven-day weekly operation will result in more than four times the capacity of a one-shift, five-day operation. Also, the mix of products will affect the machine utilization. An ideal mix may make it possible to keep all machines operating at rated capacity all the time. Anything less than an ideal mix will result in some machines operating at less than their rated capacity. In a complex manufacturing operation is it unlikely that the total theoretical capacity of the plant will equal the sum of the rated capacities of all of the equipment in the plant. When theoretical capacity is discussed, therefore, the term must be defined precisely.

For purposes of this discussion, theoretical capacity will mean the maximum that a plant can produce during the standard work week, assuming "normal" mix of products, but allowing for no loss from inefficient production procedures or down time for repairs. In other words, this would be the production volume if everything went absolutely right.

One school of thought recommends using theoretical capacity to calculate unit costs. The principal reasons given are as follows:

1. Theoretical capacity is a constant volume and will eliminate unit cost fluctuations because of volume changes. (This will generally be true. If capacity is increased, it usually means that an increase in equipment has taken place, thereby increasing fixed costs. Because both the numerator and the denominator will be increased, the overhead rate will tend to remain constant.)

2. Other methods of costing include the cost of idle capacity in the unit cost. Costing at theoretical capacity eliminates the cost of idle capacity and thus values inventories on a conservative basis. (A similar argument is that idle capacity is a "loss" and not a "cost" and should not be included in inventory.)

3. The cost of idle capacity is clearly identified in the overhead variance.

The overriding disadvantage in using theoretical capacity is that the resulting unit costs cannot be used in decision-support systems without adding something for those idle capacity costs that are a necessary part of being in business. Costs calculated at theoretical capacity are unattainable and cannot be used by management to determine the adequacy of the pricing structure, the profitability of the various products, or the desirability to expand or contract any of the product lines.

The decision as to whether to use theoretical capacity as a basis for calculating unit cost depends on the information that management needs. If isolating all costs that result from operations at less than theoretical capacity provides the information that management finds most useful, then theoretical capacity should be used (assuming that management understands the limitations of the resulting unit cost figures). If, however, management needs unit costs as a basis for pricing and product decisions, the use of theoretical capacity will usually not be justified.

Practical Capacity. *Practical capacity* is also defined in various ways. In most cases, practical capacity allows for necessary down time for repairs and for normal restrictions in available capacity for such factors as line balancing and scheduling.

In other words, it represents the possible production that a plant could attain if there were no shortage of orders and if the plant were being operated at normal efficiency. (Note that there are several areas where individual judgment can affect the figures.) A frequent modification of the definition allows for a margin of capacity to provide for seasonal peaks and normal growth. The implications of this are: (1) it is necessary to maintain some idle capacity to meet seasonal peaks; and (2) some idle capacity is normally expected when a facility is first built to allow for the subsequent growth of sales volume.

Theoretical versus Practical Capacity. Although both theoretical and practical capacity are used in describing *capacity costing*, there is a wide difference in these two concepts. At theoretical capacity, unit costs contain no allowance for idle capacity and must be adjusted before these cost figures can be used by management for decisions in the pricing or product areas. On the other hand, unit costs calculated at practical capacity exclude from unit costs only the cost of abnormal idle capacity. (Abnormal idle capacity is that resulting from an insufficient sales volume or an inefficient production performance. This will differ somewhat depending on how practical capacity is defined. The purpose in all cases, however, is to allow for necessary down time in calculating unit costs.) In general, unit costs calculated on the basis of practical capacity are much more useful to management in making pricing and product decisions. They represent more nearly the costs for which the customer should pay. If some idle capacity is required (and it almost always is) as part of an efficient production and marketing plan, it is to be expected that the cost of this idle capacity will be passed on to the customer. Also, unit costs based on practical capacity are much more realistic for forward planning purposes, than cost based on theoretical capacity. The latter costs, by definition, are unattainable because theoretical capacity is unattainable except for limited periods of time.

There can be no categorical statement that practical capacity is better than theoretical capacity for calculating unit costs. Each method will result in different information; the correct method is the one that provides the most meaningful information to management. Of the two methods, practical capacity will be the more useful method in most business situations. When using theoretical capacity, therefore, the requirements of the particular situation should be analyzed to make sure that the method is justified in terms of more useful information to management.

Standard Volume

Standard volume is ususally defined as the average volume expected over the next five to ten years. The General Motors Corporation has used the concept of standard volume as a guide to pricing, product, and making facility decisions for more than 60 years. Albert Bradley's description of the concept of standard volume and its use as a guide to management in making pricing decisions is still a classic in the field.[3]

One of the principal purposes of standard volume is for facility planning.

The usual method is to determine how much practical capacity is required to meet standard volume, taking into account seasonal fluctuations, cyclical fluctuations and secular growth. Plants are then built to provide this capacity. For example, in the early postwar years, General Motors estimated that practical capacity would have to equal 125% of standard volume. The excess capacity was necessary to meet peak sales requirements.

Which Volume to Use?

In cases where a company has established a standard volume and built facilities in line with this volume, standard volume is the most useful for calculating unit costs. When a company does not have a formal standard volume, should it establish such a volume for calculating unit costs?

In most business situations, the best volume for calculating unit costs requires two conditions: (1) the volume represents a realistic average expected volume of sales; and (2) practical capacity is (or will be) consistent with this volume. In other words, the facilities should be such that practical capacity is in line with standard volume. Under this condition, no problem exists in deciding which volume to use. Where the two differ, there are three possible actions:

1. *Use standard volume.* This could have the disadvantage of either overstating unit costs (if excess capacity exists) or understating them (if there is insufficient capacity).
2. *Use practical capacity.* This could have the disadvantage of distorting unit costs if the capacity was significantly different from the standard volume. For instance, practical capacity is 100,000 units a year and fixed costs equal $100,000 annually. If, however, the expected sales volume is only 50,000 units, there is a large amount of excess capacity which should not be reflected in the unit costs. If unit costs are calculated at practical capacity, the fixed cost per unit will be $1.00. If, however, the capacity was in line with the expected sales, a plant with an annual practical capacity of 50,000 units might reflect entirely different fixed costs. Fixed costs for a plant to produce 50,000 units might equal $75,000 annually, for a unit fixed cost of $1.50.
3. *Use standard volume but eliminate the cost of idle capacity* from the product cost (or add costs if the capacity is inadequate). This means that fixed costs will be adjusted to reflect the amount that would have been incurred if practical capacity were in line with standard volume.

Of the three courses of action, the third is the most accurate. In most cases, however, the distortion in unit costs may not be large enough to warrant the

---

[3]*N.A.C.A. Bulletin,* January 1927.

extra work involved. In addition, the theoretical justification for eliminating the costs of excess capacity (or, worse, adding fixed costs that do not exist) may be difficult to explain to management.

Summary of Discussion of Volume

Because the volume that is used in calculating unit costs can have a significant effect on the absolute amount of the cost, it is an important consideration in any cost accounting system. The volume to be used depends on the use to which the cost figures are to be put. If unit costs are to be used principally to guide management in pricing and product decisions, the volumes in order of preference are as follows.

1. Standard volume when the practical capacity of the facilities is approximately in line with this volume.
2. Standard volume with fixed costs adjusted to reflect what they would be if capacity were in line with standard volume.
3. Practical capacity if there is no standard volume.
4. Standard volume when capacity figures are not available.

The objectives are to: (1) use a volume that will be reasonably constant (or have constant relationship to capacity) so that costs between periods will not be affected by random changes in the level of production; (2) exclude from unit cost the cost of excess capacity that results from inefficiency, poor planning, or lower than projected sales volume; (3) include in unit cost the cost of capacity required to meet normal down time, product mix, seasonal fluctuations and secular growth.

In some cases, it may be necessary to use annual sales estimates. When a company has many products and changing conditions (such as a rapid growth), estimating either standard volume or capacity may be impractical because both are changing each year. In cases such as this, annual sales estimates provide the best volume.

FUTURE COST ACCOUNTING SYSTEMS

As described earlier in this chapter, the critical problem in cost accounting has been assigning overhead, particularly fixed overhead, to product. The solution is the homogeneous cost center. Since the end of World War II, factories have been introducing complex new equipment with increasing amounts of automation. This has increased the number of cost centers that are required for reasonable homogeneity. Because of the increased cost of operating a cost accounting system with an increasing number of cost centers, many—if not most—cost ac-

counting systems have not kept up with the physical changes in plant and equipment.

A second important development since World War II has been the increase
in the amount of overhead cost relative to direct labor. First, of course, automation decreases direct labor and increases overhead. In addition, there has been an
increase in the number and size of service departments, for example, scheduling,
industrial engineering, accounting, and industrial relations, to name a few. As a
result, overhead has become a much greater element of cost than direct labor.
Even in the 1950s, an overhead to direct labor ratio of four or five to one was not
uncommon in mass production plants. Currently, this ratio can be much higher.

Developments in computer technology are now making the problem of assigning overhead to products even more critical. These developments, unlike
early automation, are not solely applicable to large, mass-production factories.
The effect of these changes is to make the allocation of overhead costs to product
on the basis of direct labor increasingly questionable, even in smaller factories.

Direct labor has been used as a basis for allocation not because labor generated most of the overhead, but because it was a surrogate for the amount of
capacity dedicated to producing a particular product. With current developments in automation, direct labor is fast becoming an unsatisfactory basis for
allocating overhead to product. As long as a single direct laborer operated a
single machine, direct labor hours equaled machine hours. When a single direct
laborer tends several machines, however, direct labor hours may no longer accurately substitute for machine hours. The solution, therefore, is to use machine
hours.

When machine hours are used to allocate overhead and direct labor costs
to product, each type of machine must become a cost center. This can increase
the number of cost centers dramatically. This, in turn, greatly increases the number of calculations required to assign overhead to products. The number and
complexity of these calculations require a complex computer model.

In all likelihood, future cost accounting systems will assign costs to products
on the basis of machine hours. Each type of machine will be a separate cost center
(an exception may be where two or more types of machine have approximately
the same cost configuration). Normally, these costs will be developed once a year
on the basis of standard costs and overhead budgets at standard volume.

The principal problem with developing the new systems will be developing
an appropriate computer model. Computer models have already been developed
to perform these allocations and we can expect software companies to develop
improved models in the future. It is probable that in the next few years, the
majority of companies will adopt cost systems that assign cost to product on the
basis of machine hours, using a complex computer model to make the calculations.[4]

---

[4]An example of such a model is demonstrated in the Mayers Tap series of cases (6-185-024
through 6-125-027). These cases, together with a computer disc, are available from Case Services,
Harvard Business School, Soldiers Field, Boston, Mass., 02163.

QUESTIONS

4.1 Why should it be easier to assign variable overhead costs to product than it is to assign fixed overhead costs?

4.2 Explain why service department costs cannot be assigned directly to a product? Can you think of any exceptions to this generalization?

4.3 What allocated overhead costs, other than maintenance, would a supervisor be able to control? How should these costs be allocated to departments?

4.4 How can you tell whether a cost center is sufficiently homogeneous?

4.5 Describe a procedure that could be used to test whether a cost accounting system is providing sufficiently accurate costs.

4.6 Explain why it is important to eliminate the costs of excess capacity from the unit costs. How would you go about doing this?

4.7 Describe a procedure for calculating (a) the theoretical and (b) the practical capacity of a plant.

4.8 How would you go about developing a standard volume for a company?

4.9 What are the advantages of allocating nonmanufacturing period costs to product where there is a reasonable method for doing it?

4.10 As president of a company you ask for an analysis of product profitability. You are provided with a report that shows revenue, variable costs, contribution, fixed costs, and profit, both unit and total, for all major products. Before making any decision on the basis of this information, what are some of the questions you should ask the cost accountant concerning these data?

PROBLEMS

4.1 Following are selected data for the Slide Company for January 1986 expressed in thousands.

	PRODUCTIVE DEPARTMENTS		SERVICE DEPARTMENTS	
	A	B	1	2
Direct labor	$ 250	$ 680	—	—
Indirect labor	200	300	$150	$300
Supplies	50	75	50	75
Maintenance	350	100	25	75
Depreciation	1000	300	50	100
Utilities	500	150	400	300
	$2350	$1605	$675	$850

Service Department 1 is to be allocated on the relative amount of floor space. Service Department 2 is to be allocated on the basis of total labor and overhead cost before allocation. Relative floor space is as follows: Department A, 10,000 ft²; Department B 15,000 ft²; Department 1, 3000 ft²; and Department 2, 2000 ft².

Required

Calculate burden rates for Departments A and B, assigning service department costs directly to productive department.

4.2 Calculate overhead rates for the Slide Company for January 1986, allocating Department 1 costs both to Productive Departments and Department 2 first. Then allocate Department 2 to Productive Department.

4.3 The direct labor costs for January on four selected parts are as follows:

PART	DEPT. A	DEPT. B
W	$1.00	$2.00
X	2.00	1.00
Y	1.00	1.00
Z	4.00	5.00

Calculate the overhead costs for each part based on the information developed in Problem 4.1, on the following bases:
- **(a)** Using the burden rates developed in 4.1
- **(b)** Using the burden rates developed in 4.2.
- **(c)** Using a single burden rate for the entire plant.

4.4 Below are selected data taken from the 1986 budget of the Rule Textile Company, expressed in thousands.

Productive Departments

DIRECT EXPENSES	PICKING	CARDING	SPINNING	WEAVING
		(000s)		
Direct labor	$100	$150	$200	$130
Indirect labor	10	30	40	50
Supplies	20	30	30	40
Expense tools	5	10	10	15
Depreciation	40	80	100	110
Miscellaneous	10	10	10	10

Service Departments

	MAINTENANCE	PLANT MANAGER'S OFFICE	INDUSTRIAL ENGINEERING	ACCOUNTING
		(000s)		
Indirect labor	$100	$30	$40	$50
Supplies	20	2	5	10
Expense tools	50	—	5	—
Depreciation	50	2	2	3
Miscellaneous	10	6	10	2

Cost Accounting Centers

TYPE	AMOUNT BUDGETED
	(000's)
Building maintenance and depreciation	$50
Utilities	20

Operating Statistics

DEPARTMENT	RELATIVE FLOOR SPACE OCCUPIED	ESTIMATED RELATIVE UTILITY USAGE	NO. OF EMPLOYEES		ESTIMATED RELATIVE MAINTENANCE
			Direct	Indirect	
Picking	20%	15%	23	2	10%
Carding	25	22	25	5	25
Spinning	25	25	35	6	30
Weaving	17	30	30	8	35
Maintenance	5	5	—	20	—
Plant manager	2[a]	1	—	3	—
Industrial engineering	3[a]	1	—	5	—
Accounting	3[a]	1	—	10	—

[a]Office space. This is considered to be twice as valuable as factory space.

Required

Develop budgeted overhead rates for each of the productive departments. Close out the cost accounting centers first; then, the service departments in the following order: plant manager's office (relative number of employees); accounting (relative amounts of labor and overhead); industrial engineering (relative number of direct labor employees); and maintenance (estimated usage).

4.5 Given are several products of the Rule Textile Company, together with their budgeted direct labor dollars. Calculate the budgeted overhead cost per yard for each of these products:
  (a) Using the overhead rates that you developed in Problem 4.4.
  (b) Using a single company-wide overhead rate.
  (c) Calculate the percentage difference between the two estimates.

Budgeted Direct Labor Cost per 10,000 yd

PRODUCT	PICKING	CARDING	SPINNING	WEAVING
101	$250	$500	$400	$300
102	200	200	200	200
103	300	200	100	50
104	100	150	200	250
105	300	250	200	200

4.6 A plant has been using a single cost center to cost out its products. A proposal has been made to use multiple cost centers. The problem is to find the minimum number of cost centers necessary to provide accurate costs. From the data provided below develop a system of cost centers. Cost centers must be within the departments. An accuracy of ±3% is desired. You can assume that the accuracy increases with the number of centers. You can also assume that product X-6 is representative of all of the products in the plant.

	TOTAL STANDARD DIRECT LABOR	TOTAL BUDGETED OVERHEAD	STANDARD LABOR PER UNIT FOR PRODUCT X-6
	(000s)	*(000s)*	
GRINDING:			
Cost Center G-1	$ 10	$ 25	$ .25
Cost Center G-2	15	30	.40
Cost Center G-3	20	42	.20
MACHINING:			
Cost Center M-1	30	90	.90
Cost Center M-2	30	150	.05
Cost Center M-3	30	900	.15
WELDING:			
Cost Center W-1	20	40	.30
Cost Center W-2	40	90	.10
Cost Center W-3	10	25	.20
Assembly	60	60	.30
Total	$265	$1452	$2.05

4.7 Following are some operating statistics of the Faber Corporation for November, 1986.

	OVERHEAD COSTS	
PRODUCTIVE DEPARTMENT	*Variable (per DLH)*	*Fixed (000s)*
A	$1.00	$200
B	1.25	500
C	1.50	400
D	0.75	50

Volume in Direct Labor Hours (000s)

PRODUCTIVE DEPARTMENT	THEORETICAL CAPACITY	PRACTICAL CAPACITY	STANDARD VOLUME	ACTUAL VOLUME IN NOVEMBER
A	260	220	200	180
B	360	330	300	200
C	800	750	600	500
D	480	440	400	440
Total	1900	1740	1500	1320

Standard volume in all departments is about 90% of practical capacity except Department C. (90% is considered to be the normal relationship.) In Department C, standard volume is only 80% of capacity.

Required

(1) Calculate the overhead rates per direct labor hour for each department and for the entire plant at each of the volumes.

(2) Adjust Department C's overhead rate at standard volume for the fact that standard volume is out of line with practical capacity.

4.8 Given are the direct labor hours for three representative products of the Faber Corporation.

	DIRECT LABOR HOURS REQUIRED TO MANUFACTURE PRODUCTS		
DEPARTMENT	1	2	3
A	1.00	3.00	1.00
B	1.50	1.50	1.00
C	2.00	1.00	1.00
D	3.00	1.00	1.00
Total	7.50	6.50	4.00

Required

Calculate the overhead cost for each product at each of the volumes given in Problem 4.7.

(1) Using departmental rates,

(2) Using average rates.

4.9 Given a product line profitability analysis of the Jones Candy Company. How would you rank the product lines (from most profitable to least profitable) for management?

	PRODUCT LINES ($000's)									
	A		B		C		D		Total	
	Amt.	%	Amt.	%	Amt.	%	Amt.	%	Amt.	%
Revenue	$100	100	$200	100	$50	100	$250	100	$600	100
Var. manufacturing cost	50	50	150	75	20	40	175	70	395	66
Contribution	$ 50	50	$ 50	25	$30	60	$ 75	30	$205	34
Depreciation	10	10	5	3	10	20	15	6	40	7
	$ 40	40	$ 45	22	$20	40	$ 60	24	$165	27
Delivery	15	15	5	3	10	20	5	2	35	6
Direct selling[a]	10	10	5	3	5	10	5	2	25	4
Net after direct costs	15	15	35	17	5	10	50	20	105	17
Indirect selling and administration[b]	6	6	19	9	3	6	22	9	50	8
Net profit	$ 9	9	$ 16	8	$ 2	4	$ 28	11	$ 55	9

[a]These costs were the amounts spent specifically on selling the indicated product line.
[b]Allocated on the basis of direct manufacturing costs.

CASES

SVENSON MANUFACTURING COMPANY

The Svenson Manufacturing Company, a medium-sized manufacturer of plumbing and pipe-fitting equipment, was located in Telleberg, a small city in the southern part of Sweden. The company was started at the end of World War II by Olaf Svenson and enjoyed a steady growth in both sales and profits since that time.

In the fall of 1979, Mr. Svenson's son Jan joined the company. Jan Svenson had recently graduated from the University of Stockholm with a degree in economics and business. The first assignment given to Jan was to investigate the possibility of instituting new methods of cost control. Mr. Svenson felt the need for better cost control keenly because his firm competed on a price basis with large corporations that were firmly entrenched in the market.

Jan Svenson decided to start his investigation in the company's valve department, because this department produced almost one-third of the company's total volume of sales. The valve department contained drilling and grinding machines, lathes, welding equipment, and assembly space. In this department all the operations necessary to produce and assembly valves were performed.

The valve department occupied almost one-half the total floor space in the Svenson Company's three-story plant. Section 1, the welding section, was located on the first floor of the plant and occupied about one-sixth of the space on that floor. Sections 2, 3, and 4 as well as the office, toolroom, and stock room were all located on the third floor. None of these sections occupied more than one-fifth of the third floor's space. Section 5, the assembly section, occupied about one-half of the second floor and one-sixth of the third floor. Exhibit 1 describes

EXHIBIT 1   Svenson Manufacturing Company

Functions Performed in Valve Department

Section 1 Welding	This section repairs casting defects, welds special fittings to valve bodies, and performs other welding operations required in fabrication of valve parts.
Section 2 Grinding	Grinding is done to prepare castings for further machining. Also, various parts that make up valves are ground for precision fit.
Section 3 Machining	All the necessary machining operations to produce various standard valves are done in this section.
Section 4 Special Work	Here, the layout, drilling, tapping, and special machining needed on valves other than the standard line are done.
Section 5 Assembly	This section is responsible for the assembly and testing of all valves produced in the department.

This case was prepared by John Dearden. Copyright © by the President and Fellows of Harvard College. Harvard Business School case 9-180-160.

the functions of these sections, each of which was under the supervision of an assistant supervisor.

Exhibit 2 indicates the flow of production through the various sections of the valve department. Valves in the standard line went through Sections 1, 2, 3, and 5. Special valves (i.e., valves not in the standard line) went through all five sections. Pieces produced for spare parts inventory went through only the first three sections. In addition, any section of the valve department might perform some operations on products for other departments of the Svenson Manufacturing Company.

Jan Svenson's investigation showed that all factory costing in the valve de-

EXHIBIT 2 Svenson Manufacturing Company

Production Flow Through Valve Department

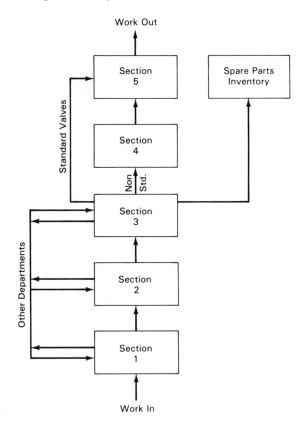

EXHIBIT 3 Svenson Manufacturing Company

Calculation of Manufacturing Cost per Direct Labor Hour in
the Valve Department: (August)

SECTION	LABOR CHARGE PER MONTH KR.	BURDEN KR.	TOTAL KR.
1	48,388		
2	24,070		
3	168,200		
4	64,332		
5	274,296		
Total	579,286	944,074	1,523,360

Total number of hours worked: 16,970/month
Average hourly charge: 1,523,360 ÷ 16,970 = 89.77

Does not include materials.

partment (except material costs) was done on a department-wide, direct labor–
hour basis; that is, each lot of products going through the department was costed
at a certain rate for each direct labor hour actually spent on the lot. Exhibit 3
shows the computation made to arrive at the cost figure of Kr. 89.77, which was
the rate per labor hour in the whole department in August. Costs were accumulated and allocated to jobs each month.

Jan Svenson did not feel that this method of obtaining and apportioning
costs was accurate enough. He believed that problems could arise in trying to
judge performance and in obtaining the true cost of different products by following this method. He proposed, therefore, that costs be collected monthly for each
section of the department and that these costs be apportioned to jobs according
to the amount of time spent in each section.

In order to study the effect of this proposal, Mr. Svenson recomputed the
costs for August so as to show the cost applicable to each section. Since direct
labor charges were already being collected by sections, no change in procedures
was necessary for the collection of labor costs. Some overhead items, such as
leadman wages, could be charged directly to the section in which they were incurred. Other overhead charges, such as heating and lighting, were allocated on
bases that seemed to Jan Svenson to be reasonable. He divided the total overhead
costs charged to each section by the number of labor hours worked in the section,
and arrived at costing rates for each section. These are shown in Exhibit 4.

Jan Svenson made the following calculations in support of his proposal for
revising the costing rates. One of the items produced in largest volume by the

EXHIBIT 4   Svenson Manufacturing Company

Proposed Cost per Direct Labor Hour for Each Section
of the Valve Department: (August)

SECTION	TOTAL HOURS	LABOR CHARGE PER HOUR KR.	BURDEN CHARGE PER HOUR KR.	TOTAL COST PER HOUR KR
1	1,370	35.32	52.34	87.66
2	1,000	24.07	40.12	64.19
3	4,000	42.05	102.93	144.98
4	1,800	35.74	65.84	101.58
5	8,800	31.17	34.32	65.49
Total	16,970			

Does not include materials.

department was Valve 301. During August, a standard production run of Valve 301 required the following hours in the different sections of the department:

SECTION	HOURS
1	15
2	10
3	65
5	40

Jan Svenson said that there obviously was a wide difference between the cost for this valve as figured under the present system and the cost as figured under his proposed system. His contention was that the present method led to a false conclusion as to the profitability of a line.

Jan Svenson also saw problems in the valuation of the spare parts inventory produced by the valve department. The company produced a wide line of valves, and it was necessary to maintain an inventory of spare parts in order to be able promptly to supply repair parts to customers. The following amounts of time were spent on producing parts for inventory during August.

SECTION	HOURS
1	160
2	145
3	560

When Jan Svenson's proposal was explained to the heads of the operating departments, it met with immediate and strong opposition. First to voice disapproval were heads of other departments, which had work totaling the following amounts done by the valve department during August.

	HOURS
Welding (Section 1)	350
Grinding (Section 2)	250
Machining (Section 3)	1,100

These supervsiors thought that it was unfair to change a sizable part of their departments' costs, especially since they had no control over the costs incurred in the valve department.

Mr. Johnson, the head of the pipe fixture department, was very much against the proposal: "The valve department does the machining work on all the work that my department can't handle. If you raise my costs on this work, I'll never be able to stay within my budget, because the valve department is already charging me more than I could do the work for in my own department if I had the capacity."

The sales manager was also against the proposal: "If you start monkeying around with our cost system, we'll have to start changing our prices, and we're having enough trouble with price competition from the major companies as it is. After all, our complete valve line is showing a profit. You have to carry some items for sales reasons regardless of their profitability, so why worry about the very small variation in cost between different items."

The head of the valve department also opposed the change: "I'm too busy to fool with more paperwork. It takes all my time to get the production out without trying to keep up with this stuff, section by section. And my leadmen in the sections don't have time for it either. The department is carrying all its costs now, so why put in an extra gimmick?"

Mr. Olaf Svenson remained neutral on the question. He was most interested in whether or not the added cost and trouble of the proposed system would be justified by the benefits the system would give.

Required

1. How was the Kr. 89.77 rate developed?

2. How were the five rates developed?

3. Calculate the cost of valve 301, spare parts, and work done for other departments during August using: (a) the present system, and (b) the proposed system.

4. Are the cost differences between the present and the proposed system significant?

5. Why is the proposed system better than the present system?

6. If five cost centers are better than one, how do you know that you have gone far enough?

7. Why do you think that everyone is really opposed to the proposed system?

CASE 4.2   THE THORNDYKE MANUFACTURING COMPANY

The Thorndyke Manufacturing Company is a medium-sized (1985 sales of $75 million) producer of small metal parts and assemblies located in Wyandotte, Michigan. It was founded in 1982 to supply one of the large Detroit Automobile Companies with small stamped parts. It remained essentially an automobile stamped parts producer until the end of World War II. In 1947, it moved to its present location and added die castings and machined parts. (The machined parts are produced from purchased gray iron castings.) At the same time, the company expanded its marketing activities to include household appliances and a variety of other products requiring small stamped or machined parts and assemblies. All of Thorndyke sales were to other manufacturers; the company sold no parts directly to the ultimate consumer. Exhibit 1 is an organization chart of the company.

Profit Position

Although volume had been increasing over the past few years (from $8 million annual sales in 1956 to $75 million in 1985), profits had not kept pace with the increase in sales volume. In 1985, Thorndyke's profit after taxes was a little less than $1,500,000, or 2% on sales. This represented a return of a little over 4% on invested capital. At least part of the poor profit could be attributed to the tightening of profit margins in the automobile industry over the past few years.

The declining profit margin was, of course, of considerable concern to Mr. Hoover, President of Thorndyke. It was partially because of this that he hired a new assistant, Young. Hoover felt that the present executives might be a little too ingrown, since all had been with Thorndyke for twenty years or more. (Hoover considered all of his top executives extremely capable, however.) After graduating from a large midwest college, Young had worked for three years in the financial analysis department of a large Detroit automotive manufacturer. At the end of this time, he had resigned and had attended an eastern business school. Upon graduation, he was hired by Hoover as assistant to the president.

One of the things Hoover asked Young to do was to try to find out the

This case was prepared by John Dearden. Copyright © by the President and Fellows of Harvard College. Harvard Business School case 9-113-069.

EXHIBIT 1   The Thorndyke Manufacturing Company, Organization Chart,
January 1, 1986

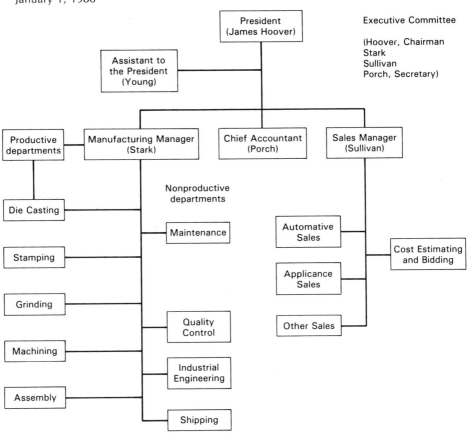

reasons for Thorndyke's poor profits. While working on this assignment, Young developed a proposal for changing the cost accounting system.

The Present Cost Accounting System

Production was scheduled in job lots for most of the products manufactured at Thorndyke. Each job lot was given a number and the amount of material requisitioned was entered against the job for which it was required. The amount of time that each worker spent on each job was recorded on a time card. Each month the cost department would calculate costs as follows:

1. A labor rate was calculated by dividing the total direct labor cost by the total direct labor hours worked during the month.

2. An overhead rate was calculated by dividing the total manufacturing overhead incurred by the total direct labor hours for the month.

3. These two rates were used to calculate the direct labor and overhead costs on the jobs that were worked on during the month. That is, the labor rate was multiplied by the hours worked to get the direct labor cost, and the overhead rate was multiplied by the hours worked to obtain the overhead costs.

4. When a job was completed, all of the costs (material, labor, and overhead) were added and this amount was divided by the number of units produced to get the unit cost. Generally, unit costs were shown as "cost per 1000 items."

Unit costs calculated in this way were used for three purposes:

1. To value the work-in-process and finished goods inventories.

2. To prepare a monthly unit cost report, showing the material, labor, and overhead costs for all products produced during the month. This report went to the president, the manufacturing manager, and the sales manager.

3. To prepare a monthly report comparing the unit cost, by cost element, for major volume parts for the past six months. This report also went to the president, the manufacturing manager, and the sales manager.

Proposed System

When Young studied the cost system, he was concerned with the fact that Thorndyke used only one cost center for the entire plant. He knew that his former employer (the large automobile manufacturer) made each department a cost center. He believed it would be worthwhile to try a multiple cost center system and see how costs would be affected. Consequently, with the aid of one of the cost accountants, he took the January 1986 cost data and charged or allocated these costs to productive department. For example, direct labor, indirect labor, supplies, and depreciation of machinery were charged directly to each department. Building depreciation, building repairs, heat and light were allocated on the basis of floor space. Power was allocated on the basis of the relative power requirements of the machinery. Plant supervision was allocated on the basis of departmental head count. Maintenance was distributed on the basis of time spent. For each indirect expense Young found some means for allocating a fair share to each department involved.

Young thus obtained a separate rate for direct labor and overhead for each of the five productive departments; using these five rates he costed out four representative products. The results are shown on Exhibit 2.

After calculating the costs shown in Exhibit 2, Young was convinced that the cost system needed changing. He prepared a memorandum to Hoover telling him this. Hoover then asked Young to make a presentation of his proposal to the Executive Committee. Young did this and the results of this presentation are on pages 128–29.

EXHIBIT 2   The Thorndyke Manufacturing Company
Comparison of Present and Proposed Costing System

Present Method

PRODUCT	STANDARD DIRECT LABOR HOURS PER 1000 UNITS	JANUARY 1986 COST PER HOUR	TOTAL LABOR AND OVERHEAD COSTS
A	.42	$23.85	$10.02
B	.46	23.85	10.97
C	1.30	23.85	31.01
D	.91	23.85	21.70

Proposed Method

DEPARTMENT	STANDARD DIRECT LABOR HOURS PER 1000 UNITS	JANUARY 1986 COST PER HOUR	TOTAL LABOR AND OVERHEAD COST
PRODUCT A			
Stamping	.12	$23.85	$ 2.86
Assembly	.30	13.74	4.13
Total	.42		$ 6.99
PRODUCT B			
Die casting	.25	$40.58	$10.13
Machining	.21	28.71	6.03
Total	.46		$16.16
PRODUCT C			
Grinding	.65	$24.21	$15.74
Machining	.30	28.71	8.61
Assembly	.35	13.74	4.81
Total	1.30		$29.16
PRODUCT D			
Die casting	.20	$48.53	$ 8.11
Stamping	.25	23.85	5.86
Machining	.33	28.71	9.47
Assembly	.13	13.74	1.79
Total	.91		$25.23

Comparison of Costs Using Present and Proposed System

	PRODUCT A	PRODUCT B	PRODUCT C	PRODUCT D
Present cost system	$10.02	$10.97	$31.01	$21.70
Proposed cost system	6.99	16.16	29.16	25.33
Present under/(over) proposed				
Amount	$ 3.03	$(5.19)	$ 1.85	$(3.63)
Percent	30%	47%	6%	(17%)

The Executive Committee Discussion

The following is an edited manuscript of the discussion of the proposed cost accounting system by the members of the Executive Committee.

HOOVER: Well what do you think of Young's proposed new system? Maybe we had better start with Tom (Thomas Porch, Chief Accountant), since it involves the accounting system.

PORCH: Frankly, I think it's just another of these big company ideas that Young learned at that business school he attended. In a big company it may make sense to have 5, 10, or even 30 cost centers. I don't think it applies to us; we know what's going on without all of these cost centers and allocations.

One of the main points that bothers me is: "When do we stop?" Young has set up five cost centers because as he says they are more "homogeneous." "Homogeneous" my foot! We all know that they use both virgin steel and offal (pieces of metal left as scrap when sheets of virgin steel are cut) in the stamping department and that the offal requires a lot more handling than virgin steel. Also, in the machining department, there are a lot of differences among those machines. We'd end up needing one accountant for every production worker if we carried this system to its logical conclusion.

I have run an economical cost accounting system so far and everybody seems to be satisfied. Why complicate it and increase our costs just because General Motors does it that way? I vote that we reject the proposal.

SULLIVAN: (Fred Sullivan, Sales Manager): I agree with Tom. According to Young's figures here, I'd have to raise the price of Product B by nearly two dollars to maintain my profit margin and Product D by two and a half dollars. That's silly: I can't get that kind of an increase. In fact, his new system would just upset our whole pricing structure. As Tom points out, the new system doesn't give better costs than the old. It just gives different costs. The present system gives us approximate costs and we are used to working with it. The new system wouldn't be any better and it would cost more to run it.

HOOVER: But if Young's right that present costs are inaccurate, doesn't that give you problems in setting selling prices?

SULLIVAN: I don't set selling prices; competition does.

HOOVER: But most of our products, especially in the automobile business, are unique. You don't have a competitive price when you bid. You must use a cost buildup.

SULLIVAN: That's right. We do estimate costs. If it's a new part, we estimate the amount of material and the direct labor hours. Then, we use the latest material prices to get the material cost and the latest labor and overhead rates per hour to get the direct labor and overhead. We than add a 10% markup for selling expense, administrative costs, and profit. If it's a part that we are currently making, we use the latest monthly unit cost plus 10%. However, that's only the indicated price. We see what the part, or a similar part was sold for before. If our indicated price is out of line we change it. Also, we talk to the buyer to get an idea of the price he has in mind. We try to get a feel of what competition might be bidding and go a little lower. So, for our purpose Tom's cost system is good enough.

HOOVER: Thanks Fred. What do you think about the proposed system, John (John Stark, Manufacturing Manager)?

STARK: I agree with Tom and Fred. The present system is good enough for me. I don't want an accountant standing behind each of my production workers.

HOOVER: But, John, don't you think the proposed system will give you more accurate costs so that we'll be able to tell when your costs are getting out of line? You know that every time I ask you about costs going up you tell me that it is caused by volume going down; or, if volume has gone up, you say the increase is caused by the mix changing to the more expensive products. Wouldn't this new system allow us to pinpoint the reasons for cost changes?

STARK: No, it wouldn't. As Tom pointed out, the new system is no better than the old. It's just different. I'm satisfied with the present system. Anyway, I don't control my costs through accounting reports. I'm in the plant every day and I can see what's going on there. For the items that need special controls, I have reports, like my daily scrap report.

HOOVER: Well, I guess that settles that. If none of you want Young's systems, there's no sense in spending the money. I'll tell Young that he's struck out again.

Required

In spite of the unanimous disapproval by the Executive Committee, Hoover still had some misgivings about the present cost accounting system. Consequently, he talked it over with the firm's outside auditor. The auditor recommended that a management service's consultant be assigned to look over Young's proposal and give Hoover a confidential opinion.[1] Suppose you were that consultant. What would you recommend that Hoover do? In preparing your recommendation, be sure to answer the following questions:

1. Is the difference between the present and proposed system significant? Why?

2. If it is significant, which one is right? Why?

3. If the proposed system is better than the present one, how do you know that you have enough cost centers?

4. Are there other changes you would incorporate in the proposed system?

5. If you decide the present system is inadequate, how do you account for the Executive Committee's position?

---

[1]This is exactly what Hoover did in the actual situation. When the consultant prepared his **report**, he knew essentially the facts given in the case.

CASE 4.3   A/S DANSK MINOX, COPENHAGEN

"Costing the Cabbage"

A/S Dansk Minox in Copenhagen, specializing in branded vacuum-packed meat and other food products, has for many years sold vacuum-packed sliced pork in gravy, a very popular dish in Denmark. In 1965 the product represented about 15% of the firm's total sales in the country in a product range which comprises 30 products. The Danish housewife very often serves this dish together with a red cabbage salad. This salad is rather time-consuming to prepare at home and certain competitors of A/S Dansk Minox had recently introduced red cabbage salad in either vacuum-packed, canned, or frozen form. However, A/S Dansk Minox estimated that the major part of the red cabbage sold was still prepared at home, and although sales of ready-made red cabbage salad expanded rapidly, it was felt—and consumer research confirmed this—that there was still a great untapped potential for such a product.

At the end of 1985 A/S Dansk Minox had not marketed vacuum-packed red cabbage salad, but in view of existing market potential, and since it was so often eaten together with sliced pork, the company management considered producing red cabbage salad also. A/S Dansk Minox had during the last year considered introducing a speciality line of complete meals, which were to be sold in an attractive carton containing vacuum-sealed bags with the different ingredients for the meal. The management decided that the first product in this specialty line was to be "sliced pork in gravy with red cabbage" and the product was to be packed in a carton containing the standard vacuum-sealed bag with sliced pork plus another bag with the red cabbage. Cost allocation problems arose in this connection, leading to long discussions between the marketing and finance departments of the Danish company.

The standard product "sliced pork in gravy" was sold in a 450-g bag at a consumer price of D.Kr. 4.85. This was the "ideal" quantity for an average family, giving between 3 and 4 servings. Therefore, when considering the "complete meal" product, the marketing department did not wish to change the quantity of sliced pork in gravy. Extensive testing showed that the average family consumed between 500 and 600 g of red cabbage salad with 450 g of sliced pork in gravy. It was therefore decided to sell the "complete meal" product in a 1 kg pack, containing the standard 450-g bag with sliced pork in gravy plus another vacuum-sealed bag with 550 g of red cabbage salad.

The marketing department received the following preliminary selling price calculation from the finance department, based on the assumption that the new

The case was prepared by an IMEDE participant, edited by Homer A. Black, and revised by Professor G. Shillinglaw as a basis for class discussion rather than to illustrate either effective or ineffective handling of an administrative situation. Copyright by IMEDE (International Management Development Institute), Lausanne, Switzerland. Reproduced by permission.

product should produce approximately the same profit per kilogram as the standard sliced pork in gravy. For comparison, the selling price calculation for standard sliced pork in gravy is also given, both for 1 kg and for 450 g, to show that the raw material costs and labor costs for sliced pork in gravy are exactly the same in both the existing standard pack of this product and in the new 1-kg "complete meal" pack.

The difference in consumer price between the two packs as proposed by the finance department meant that the consumer would have to pay D.Kr. 3.35 (8.20–4.85) for the red cabbage salad, since the sliced pork in gravy content of the two packs was the same. The marketing department protested that this price difference was prohibitive, since the ingredients for making the red cabbage salad at home could be bought for approximately 1.10 and the labor costs at home (if counted at all) would not amount to more than approximately 0.70.

	"COMPLETE MEAL" 1 KG	SLICED PORK IN GRAVY 1 KG	SLICED PORK IN GRAVY 450 G
	(All amounts are in D. Kr.)		
Consumer price	8.20	10.78	4.85
Less turnover tax (12.5% of consumer price before tax)	.91	1.20	.54
Consumer price before tax	7.29	9.58	4.31
Retailer's margin (27.5% of price to retailer	1.57	2.07	.93
Price to retailer	5.72	7.51	3.38
Raw material, sliced pork	1.67	3.71	1.67
Raw material, red cabbage	.50	—	—
Labor, sliced pork	.25	.56	.25
Labor, red cabbage	.25	—	—
Packaging material	.26	.24	.11
Transport and storage	.20	.20	.09
Margins and discounts to wholesalers (8% of price to retailer)	.46	.60	.27
Sundry variable costs	.10	.10	.04
Total variable costs	3.69	5.41	2.43
Marginal contribution	2.03	2.10	.95
Production fixed expenses	1.20	1.20	.54
Other product-related fixed expenses	.30	.30	.14
General selling and administrative expense and overhead (4% of price to retailer).	.23	.30	.14
Total fixed expenses	1.73	1.80	.82
Net operating profit	.30	.30	.13

The marketing department argued that A/S Dansk Minox could not expect the consumer to pay more than D.Kr. 2.00 at the most for the red cabbage salad and added convenience, thus leaving a consumer price for the new pack of 4.85 + 2.00 or 6.85. The marketing department contended, furthermore, that the selling price calculation showed that the raw material and labor costs amounted to only 0.75 for the red cabbage salad and that it was unreasonable that the other cost elements should result in a consumer price difference of 3.35.

Since the only difference between the standard pack and the "complete meal" pack was the red cabbage and a more elaborate package, the marketing and finance departments listed those cost elements which varied between the 1000-g "complete meal" pack and the 450-g standard pack with sliced pork in gravy. These elements were the following:

	"COMPLETE MEAL" 1 KG	*SLICED PORK IN GRAVY 450 G*	*DIFFERENCE*
Raw material, red cabbage salad	.50	—	.50
Labor, red cabbage salad	.25	—	.25
Packaging material	.26	.11	.15
Transport and storage	.20	.09	.11
Margins and discounts	.46	.27	.19
Sundry variable costs	.10	.04	.06
Production fixed expense	1.20	.54	.66
Other product-related fixed expenses	.30	.14	.16
General overhead	.23	.14	.09
Totals	3.50	1.33	2.17

The retail margin and the turnover tax were added to the cost difference of D.Kr. 2.17 plus the difference in operating profit of D.Kr. 0.17 to arrive at the previously mentioned selling price difference of D.Kr. 3.35. As an approximation, the consumer price is computed by multiplying the retail price by 1.45. This means that if the marketing department wished a new price of D.Kr. 6.85 for the "Complete meal" pack (D.KR. 2.00 more than the standard pack with sliced pork in gravy), the difference in the price to the retailer could not exceed approximately D.Kr. 1.38 (D.Kr. 2.00 divided by 1.45). Thus, with a consumer price of D.Kr. 6.85 and an unchanged net operating profit per pack, the difference in the cost elements in the selling price calculation would have to be reduced from D.Kr. 2.17 to 1.38 (a reduction of 0.79).

There was no disagreement between the marketing and finance departments with regard to the raw material, labor, packaging material, transport and storage, and sundry variable costs. The item "Other product-related fixed expenses" covered mainly advertising; consequently, the marketing department could not argue with the finance department about this item, either, since it was under the control of the marketing department. The two items "Margins and discounts" and "General overheads" are, as a standard rule in the company, cal-culated as fixed percentages of the price to the retailer (8% and 4%, respectively). Although this procedure might be open to question, the marketing department was satisfied that the costs would decrease automatically if a lower selling price could be agreed upon.

The main discussion, therefore, centered upon the item "Production fixed expenses." After internal agreement on the sales budget every year, the total pro-duction fixed expenses were divided by the total sales quantity, expressed in kg. This computation resulted in a rate of D.Kr 1.20 per kg for the year under consid-eration. This rate was then applied to all products from the company's factory. There was no need to buy any new equipment for making the red cabbage salad and there was spare capacity available for the estimated production of the new "complete meal" product. The estimated sales of the new product were included in the budgeted sales quantity.

The finance department claimed that any departure downwards from the rate of D.Kr. 1.20 per kg for production fixed expenses would result in an under-coverage of fixed expenses. The marketing department replied that a strict appli-cation of this rule would lead to unreasonable consequences in this case, where a relatively cheap component (red cabbage) is added to an expensive component (sliced pork in gravy), and where the cheap component more than doubles the weight of the new pack and thus also doubles the fixed burden charged to the product. The finance department stated that it would be impractical to use differ-ent burden rates per kg for different products. It was supported in this view by the managing director, who said that the product should not be introduced if a normal selling price calculation did not show an operating profit.

The marketing department responded that selling the new product at D.Kr. 8.20 per pack was out of the question; therefore, only two alternatives remained:

1. Abandon the whole project.
2. Establish a consumer price of D.Kr. 6.85 and a price to the retailer of D.Kr. 4.78. The 8% margins and discounts to wholesalers and the 4% general overhead would then amount to 0.38 + 0.19 instead of 0.46 + 0.23, a reduction of 0.12. If the production fixed expense were then reduced from 1.20 to 0.54, the same amount as for one standard pack of sliced pork in gravy, expenses in the selling price calculation would then be reduced by a total of 0.78. This is almost exactly the necessary reduction of 0.79 mentioned earlier.

The managing director decided in spite of the marketing department's ar-guments that the new product should not be introduced without full coverage of fixed expenses. It was introduced at a consumer price of D.Kr. 8.20, and the sales budget was set at 85 metric tons. (A metric ton is equal to 1000 kg.) This was about 45% of the budgeted sales of the standard pack of sliced pork in gravy, which reflected the assumption that the upward sales trend of recent years would continue. In other words, the company did not expect that the new "complete meal" product would steal sales from the standard pack. Some customers would certainly switch over from the old product to the new, but these losses would be offset by the added sales resulting from greater consumer awareness of Minox products due to the planned advertising campaigns for the "complete meal" item.

In the months that followed, a number of complaints about the high price of the new product were received from retailers and consumers, and sales for the first year amounted to only 30 tons in contrast to the budgeted 85 tons. Sales of the standard pack, on the other hand, exceeded the budgeted amount by a small percentage.

Required

1. Comment on the method used for allocating production fixed expenses to units of product.

2. Comment on any other cost assignment procedures which you think are subject to question.

3. How much would the company's net operating profit have differed from the actual results (assuming that all costs behaved as expected) if:

    (a) The proposal to sell the "complete meal" pack had been abandoned?

    (b) The consumer price had been D.Kr. 6.85 and the budgeted volume of sales had been achieved?

4. At what sales level would a consumer price of D.Kr. 6.85 give the same total net operating profit as 30 tons at a consumer price of D.Kr. 8.20?

5. Try to suggest an alternative pricing formula for A/S Dansk Minox to use in situations of this kind. Would your alternative be better than the one used in this case?

6. What other facts would you like to have before making a decision on what consumer price to charge for a kilogram of sliced pork in gravy with red cabbage salad? How would these facts enter into your decision?

chapter 5

MISCELLANEOUS TOPICS IN COST ACCOUNTING

The purpose of this chapter is to take up two topics: (1) joint and by-product costing and (2) direct costing systems. Each of these topics, while important, does not warrant a full chapter in a book of this size. They are, therefore, discussed in a single chapter, even though they are not directly related to each other.

JOINT AND BY-PRODUCT COSTING

When two or more products *must* be produced together, they are called *joint products*. The purpose of this part of the chapter is to describe the accounting techniques for costing joint products.

Joint Products Defined

Joint production occurs whenever two or more products must result from the same production process. The key word in this definition is *must*. The crucial characteristic of joint products is that *the production of one automatically results in the production of the others*. It is often possible, of course, to eliminate one of the joint products; it may not be economic to do so if the product has a sales value greater than the unique costs of completing and marketing. For example, in marble quarrying, it is possible to leave all the marble except the best grade at the quarry site. If other grades must be quarried to obtain the best grade, it may not be economic to leave the other grades at the quarry, as long as their sales value exceeds the unique costs of finishing and selling. In this case, the quarrying of marble is a joint production process because, in quarrying pure white marble, it is necessary (from an economic point of view) to quarry other grades.

The fact that joint products *must* be produced together is of major importance to the cost accountant because it means that all *cost allocations among joint products are entirely arbitrary.* If two products must result from a single production process, one product cannot be had without the other. If it is not possible to have one product without both, the cost of producing only one cannot be logically isolated. The fact is that it costs a certain sum of money to produce a certain amount of each of two or more products. If part of the joint production cost is assigned to one of the products, it is a meaningless allocation. This is the most important point to remember about joint cost accounting because it is this characteristic that makes it necessary to modify traditional cost accounting techniques.

Joint Costs and Common Costs

There is an important difference between joint costs and common costs. Common costs occur when two products, which may be produced separately, are produced together. For example, when several products are made in different departments of the same plant, the plant costs (such as plant maintenance and depreciation) are common. Common costs differ from joint costs, however, in that the *production of common parts can be undertaken separately.* Because the production of one product does not mean that the other product must be produced, the cost accountant is able to estimate the costs of producing any of the products individually. Depending on the degree of accuracy required, the cost determination may include several allocations. Nevertheless, it is at least theoretically possible to allocate costs in such a way that the costs of each of the common products will approximate the relative costs of these products if they were produced separately or in other combinations. This is not true of joint products, since they cannot be produced separately and can be produced only in limited (and frequently noncontrollable) other combinations.

The unit costs of common products are useful in making pricing decisions or in determining product-line profitability; however, in joint products, unit costs are meaningless for determining the adequacy of price levels or the profitability of product lines. The relevant figures for decision making are the total price and the total profit of all of the joint products.

Methods of Allocating Joint Costs

If it were not for inventories, there would be no reason for estimating the costs of each of the joint products at all. On the income statement the total cost of the joint products would be subtracted from the total revenue without regard to individual products. Inventories do exist in most companies, however, and a value must be placed on these inventories. Inventory values are generally obtained by allocating the joint costs of production to the joint products. In allocating these costs, the overriding consideration is that they should be allocated in such a way that management, using the information, will not be led into making incorrect decisions. The incorrect decisions can take two forms:

1. Management may discontinue producing and marketing a joint product that should be retained; or
2. Management may continue to produce and market a joint product that should be discontinued.

The first mistake can occur if management is given information on profits by product. A joint product may show a loss and, unless the nature of joint costs are known, management may wish to discontinue selling the unprofitable product. Profits by product should, therefore, never be reported because at best they are meaningless and, at worst, they could lead to incorrect decisions. The second mistake occurs when a company sells a joint product for a price that is less than the unique costs of completing and selling it.

In deciding on a procedure for allocating the joint cost of production, it is important to consider the effect that this procedure will have on the cost and financial statements and, consequently, on management decisions. The most common mistake accountants make is to show profit by product line, somewhat as follows:

| | JOINT PRODUCT | | | |
	A	B	C	Total
Sales	$10,000	$5,000	$4,000	$19,000
Joint cost of production[a]	7,000	3,500	2,800	13,300
Gross profit	$ 3,000	$1,500	$1,200	$ 5,700
Unique costs of production	2,000	1,000	300	3,300
Selling and administration expense	1,000	800	200	2,000
Net profit	$ 0	$ (300)	$ 700	$ 400

[a]Calculated in accordance with the market price method described in the next section.

Management, receiving a statement such as this, would be justified in believing that Product A earned no profit, Product B sustained a loss of $300, and

Product C earned $700. *This is not the case at all.* The only profit fact that the accountant possesses is that the total profit of all joint products is $400. Nothing is accomplished by breaking down profits further.

In evaluating a method for allocating the joint costs of production to the joint products, the question to ask is, How will the financial statements be affected by this method? A satisfactory method should result in no incorrect or misleading information appearing on the financial statements or accounting reports. Two methods for allocating joint costs are described in the following pages. In each case, these methods will be evaluated in terms of their effects upon the financial statements of the company.

Average Method

The average method, as the name implies, involves assigning the same average cost to each unit produced. The unit is usually a quantity such as a pound, ton, gallon, board foot, or cubic foot. For example, in petroleum refining, the total joint costs of "cracking" the petroleum can be assigned to the joint products by dividing the joint costs by the number of gallons in the yield. Each of the products will then be valued for inventory purposes at the average joint cost per gallon plus unique costs, if any. Or in the marble quarrying, the cost of quarrying the marble can be divided by the cubic feet of marble quarried. The inventory would then be valued at the average cost per cubic foot of marble.

The average method of joint costing can only be used when the selling prices of each of the joint products are about equal after adjusting for the unique costs. If it is used where there are significant differences in the selling prices of the finished product, the income statement can be seriously distorted by difference in the sales mix of the joint products.

An extreme example could occur if a meat packer valued all the products from a steer at the average cost. If a 2000-pound steer is bought for $200, the average cost per pound would be $0.10. Thus a pound of steak would be valued at $0.10 and a pound of bone would have the same value. If there were no inventory or if the inventory were always perfectly balanced (that is, production was equal to the sales) the total income would not be distorted. If, however, the inventory varied from month to month, income could be distorted. If a steer were purchased and butchered in January and all the steak (but none of the other products) were sold that month, January profits would be very high because the selling price of the steak would be offset by a cost of only $0.10 a pound. In February, however, when the bones and other waste products were sold, the income statement would show a loss. Thus, even though product-line profits are not shown separately on the income statement, the arbitrary differences in profits (resulting from the average method of allocating joint costs) are reflected in the income statement. *The possible effect on profits from changes in product mix is an important consideration in deciding which method of allocation to use.*

In addition to the possibility of profit distortion, the average method of valuing joint products is also questionable accounting practice. On the "lower of cost or market" rule the value of the inventories of the lower priced products will be overstated and, consequently, it will be necessary to write them down. This will result in a significant undervaluation of inventory because the high price products will continue to be understated.

The only advantage of the average method is ease of calculation. Even here, other more satisfactory methods are not a great deal more work. As a rule of thumb, any time the average method is used, the possible undesirable effect on the cost and income statements should be considered carefully.

Market Price Method

The market price method of allocating costs is computed as follows:

1. Calculate the total cost of the joint production up to the point that the products are *separated*. (This includes labor and overhead as well as material.)
2. Calculate the total sales value of the joint products.
3. Divide the amount in (1) by the amount in (2). This is the percentage of cost to selling price.
4. To find the joint cost of any product, multiply the unit selling price by the percentage in (3).
5. Add any unique production costs to the joint costs calculated in (4).

Example of Joint Cost
    Calculation

JOINT COSTS OF PRODUCTION	
Material	$50,000
Labor	10,000
Overhead	20,000
Total	$80,000

	UNITS PRODUCED AND SELLING PRICES		
Product	Number of units produced	Selling price	Units in ending inventory
A	10,000	$10.00	100
B	25,000	1.00	500
C	80,000	.10	10,000

Required

Calculate the value of the ending inventory.

1. Total costs of production = $80,000.
2. Total sales value = 10,000 × $10.00 = $100,000
   25,000 × $ 1.00 =   25,000
   80,000 × $ 0.10 =   8,000

   Total $133,000

3. The percentage of cost of sales = $\dfrac{80,000}{133,000}$ = 60%

4. The value of the ending inventory is calculated as follows:

PRODUCT	COST	VOLUME	TOTAL VALUE
A	$6.00	100	$ 600
B	0.60	500	300
C	0.06	10,000	600
Total			$1,500

The principal advantage of the market price method from a management accounting point of view is that gross profit as a percent of the sales dollar is the same for all products. This minimizes the effect on the monthly income statements of changes in the sales mix of the joint products. In the meat-packing example, the gross profit of all products will be the same percentage of sales, using the market price method. The monthly income statement will not, therefore, show high profits when the steaks are sold and losses when other products are sold.

Another advantage of the market price method is that it provides inventory values that are generally acceptable to the public accountant. For this reason, probably more than any other, the market price method is the one most commonly used.

It should be noted, however, that the market price method does not provide product costs for determining product-line profits. It is useful only to value inventories. The method is recommended because it minimizes distortion in the income statements. The costs have no further significance and product costs calculated using this method are as arbitrary as the product costs obtained using the average method.

Opportunity Costs

In some instances, it might be possible to assign a useful cost to a joint product. This occurs when there is a valid market price at which the joint product can be sold. If the joint product is not sold but processed into a final product, the opportunity cost of the joint product is the market price, less the cost of disposal. This is the amount of economic resources given up for the opportunity of producing the finished product. For example, suppose that A and B are joint products that have a total joint cost of $6.00 per lb. If B can be sold after the joint products are separated for a net price of $2.00 per pound, this cost could be assigned to product B. Product A therefore will have a cost of $4.00 per pound. If all the joint products have market prices, these costs can be assigned at the point where the joint products separate. In this way, it is possible to separate the profit obtained by producing the joint products from the profit obtained from finishing the products. For example, consider the following:

	JOINT PRODUCTS		
	A	*B*	*C*
Selling price at point of separation	$1.00	$2.00	$3.00
Selling price of finished product	4.00	4.00	6.00
Variable cost of finishing	2.00	2.00	2.00
Volume	1000	500	100

The profits position could be analyzed as follows:

	PRODUCT A	*PRODUCT B*	*PRODUCT C*	*TOTAL*
Sales of joint products	$4000	$2000	$ 600	$6600
Cost of joint products	1000	1000	300	2300
Profit from manufacturing	$3000	$1000	$ 300	$4300
Cost of finishing	2000	1000	200	3200
Profit from finishing	$1000	$ 0	$ 100	$1100

This is a meaningful analysis. For example, it would be economically better not to finish a product that shows a loss. This type of breakdown, however, is only valid where there is the genuine option of selling the joint products before finishing.

Variable Output

The discussion so far in this chapter has assumed that the relative quantities of the joint products were not controllable. In some instances, however, the relative quantities of the different joint products can be changed through the manufacturing methods as, for example, in petroleum cracking. The problem is to determine which combination of joint products provides the maximum total contribution. In some instances, it is quite easy because the contribution from each of the joint products is easily ascertained. In other instances it can be very complicated, particularly when the unit contribution of a particular product changes with the amount available or where there are complex interrelationships in finishing and selling the joint products. In many instances, computer simulation models or linear programming models are required to deal effectively with this problem. (Oil companies have developed large-scale computer models to calculate the optimum output from their refineries.) The problem of deciding optimum outputs is essentially a production decision and, consequently, is outside of the scope of this book. The accountant assists in these decisions by providing cost and revenue data to be included in the models.

By-Products

A by-product is merely a joint product that is treated in a special way because it has relatively little value. The usual method is to subtract the net revenue from the joint costs. For example, suppose Products A, B, and X resulted from a given process. The sales value of A and B accounted for most of the value of three products. X was of small value and was produced only because it is automatic. Product X might then be a by-product. This means that instead of allocating to it a share of the joint costs, it would be treated as having no value until it is sold. Then, the net revenue would be subtracted from the total joint costs. There are several similar methods for handling by-product costs but they all boil down to pretty much the same treatment. This is really all there is to by-product accounting. There is no mysterious system that says one product is a joint product and another is a by-product. It depends entirely on the accounting treatment, and this is based on relative value.

DIRECT COSTING

Direct costing is a term applied to a cost accounting system that assigns only *variable manufacturing costs* to the product. The theory is that the variable costs are really the cost of production, because the fixed costs will be incurred whether a product is produced or not. To put it another way, the variable costs represent the cost of *doing* business; the fixed costs represent the costs of *being* in business.

A direct cost system values work-in-process and finished goods inventories at variable costs. Fixed costs are treated as period costs and written off each month. It is important to understand that a direct cost system separates fixed and variable costs in the *books of account*. In a full cost system it is necessary to calculate variable costs outside of the books. On the other hand, in a direct cost system total product costs should be calculated outside of the books of account. Consequently, a full cost system does not mean that management will not be provided with variable costs; neither does a direct cost system mean that management will not be provided with full costs. In most businesses, management needs both types of costs, and a good cost accounting system will provide this information. A direct cost system, therefore, does not provide any information that cannot be available under a full cost system. The reverse is also true. Any arguments for or against direct costing based on the contention that more information is available are spurious.

Mechanics of Direct Costing

Most of direct costing systems are standard cost systems, so the mechanics of a standard direct cost system will be described. Material and labor are handled in an identical manner with a full standard cost system, as described in Chapter 2. Overhead, of course, is handled differently and the purpose of this part of the chapter is to explain the mechanics for handling overhead costs in a direct cost system.

Standard Overhead Rate. The overhead rate is calculated in exactly the same way for a direct cost system as for a full cost system except that it includes only variable overhead costs. The budgeted fixed and variable overhead costs are segregated. The variable overhead costs are divided by the direct labor dollars or hours at standard volume to obtain a standard overhead rate.[1] This rate is then used to cost the products produced.

For example, suppose the following monthly overhead costs were budgeted:

	DEPT. A	DEPT. B	DEPT. C	TOTAL
Indirect labor	$ 4,500	$ 6,000	$ 8,000	$18,500
Supplies	2,000	1,600	2,000	5,600
Utilities	1,500	2,000	2,000	5,500
Depreciation of equipment	4,000	5,000	6,000	15,000
Rent of building	500	500	500	1,500
Total	$12,500	$15,100	$18,500	$46,100
Standard direct labor hours at standard volume	5,000	6,000	7,000	

Assume that indirect labor, supplies, and utilities are considered to be variable costs; depreciation and rent are considered to be fixed. The standard overhead would be calculated as follows:

Product A   8,000/5,000   or $1.60/h
Product B   9,600/6,000   or $1.60/h
Product C   12,000/7,000   or $1.714/h

---

[1]The more sophisticated methods of assigning overhead to products, described in Chapter 4, also are applicable to direct cost accounting systems.

Journal Entries. Assume that the following actual costs were incurred in January:

	DEPT. A	DEPT. B	DEPT. C	TOTAL
Indirect labor	$ 4,700	$ 6,400	$ 8,000	$19,100
Supplies	2,100	1,000	1,800	4,900
Utilities	1,400	2,000	2,000	5,400
Depreciation	4,000	5,000	6,200	15,200
Rent	500	500	500	1,500
Total	$12,700	$14,900	$18,500	$46,100
Standard direct labor hours at actual volume	5,000	6,000	7,000	

There was no work-in-process inventory at either the beginning or end of the the period.

Following are the journal entries reflecting these transactions.

(1)

Indirect labor—Dept. A	$4,700	
Supplies Dept. A	2,100	
Utilities Dept. A	1,400	
Depreciation Dept. A	4,000	
Rent Dept. A	500	
Accrued wages payable		
Accounts payable		$12,700
Cash		
Allowance for depreciation		

(2)

Indirect labor—Dept. B	$6,400	
Supplies Dept. B	1,000	
Utilities Dept. B	2,000	
Depreciation Dept. B	5,000	
Rent Dept. B	500	
Accrued wages payable		
Accounts payable		$14,900
Cash		
Allowance for depreciation		

(3)

Indirect labor—	Dept. C	$8,000
Supplies	Dept. C	1,800
Utilities	Dept. C	2,000
Depreciation	Dept. C	6,200
Rent	Dept. C	500

Accrued wages payable ⎫	
Accounts payable ⎬	$18,500
Cash ⎪	
Allowance for depreciation ⎭	

Note: Entries (1) through (3) record the actual overhead expenses in the depart-ments where they are incurred.

(4)

Work-in-process inventory: Overhead—Dept. A	$ 8,200	
Indirect labor—Dept. A		$ 4,700
Supplies—Dept. A		2,100
Utilities—Dept. A		1,400

(5)

Work-in-process inventory: Overhead—Dept. B	$ 9,400	
Indirect labor—Dept. B		$ 6,400
Supplies—Dept. B		1,000
Utilities—Dept. B		2,000

(6)

Work-in-process inventory: Overhead—Dept. C	$11,800	
Indirect labor—Dept. C		$ 8,000
Supplies—Dept. C		1,800
Utilities—Dept. C		2,000

Note: Entries (4) through (6) transfer the actual variable overhead costs to the work-in-process inventory.

(7)

Finished goods inventory	$29,600	
Work-in-process inventory: Overhead—Dept. A		$ 8,000
Work-in-process inventory: Overhead—Dept. B		9,600
Work-in-process inventory: Overhead—Dept. C		12,000

This transfers the overhead costs to the finished goods inventory at standard cost.

(8)

Work-in-process inventory: Overhead—Dept. B	$200	
Work-in-process inventory: Overhead—Dept. C	200	
Work-in-process inventory: Overhead—Dept. A		$200
Overhead spending variance		200

This entry transfers the difference between standard and actual variable overhead cost to a variance account.

Depreciation and rent are treated as period costs and are handled in the same way as selling and administrative expenses.

Advantages of Direct Costing

1. *Eliminates profit fluctuations caused by differences between sales and production volume.* The major advantage of a direct costing system to many managers and controllers is that it eliminates fluctuations in profits resulting from differences between the volume of sales and the volume of production within an accounting period. Management tends to think of profits directly related to the volume of sales. It is, therefore, frequently confusing to management when this month's sales are higher than last month's and yet profits are lower because of overhead volume variances. It often is very difficult for the controller to explain this situation to the nonaccounting-oriented manager.

2. *Product costs approximate differential costs.* A second advantage of direct costing is that the product costs generated through the accounting system tend to approximate differential costs. This helps to eliminate confusion when the accounting costs differ from those used in making product decisions.

For example, a study showed that a product could be modified to make it more acceptable to the customer for an increase in costs of $0.50 in direct labor and $0.50 in variable overhead. Under a full absorption system, this cost increase might show up on the books at $1.50 if the overhead rate were 200% of direct labor. To be sure, the overhead on other products would be reduced so that the overall costs were the same as stated in the study. The fact remains, however, that under a full cost system, the new cost of the part will not reflect this fact. The same conditions will be true when adding a new product to the line or substituting a new product for an old one.

Whether this advantage applies in any particular company will depend on the nature of the business and, again, on how well management understands the system. In a business that characteristically makes frequent changes in design or product mix to gain short run market advantages, direct costing will usually provide the best monthly accounting information.

In some cases, product design or mix changes may be infrequent and, when made, may be expected to continue for a period of years. In such cases, total costs may be closer than variable costs to the differential costs of the decision. The longer the period of time involved, the closer will be differential and total costs.

3. *Fewer allocations are required.* A third advantage of a direct costing system is that fewer allocations are required. For example, it is not necessary to allocate fixed costs to department and product each month. This advantage will apply to companies that do not need to know total unit costs or to have product line profits beyond the contribution amount. This situation is unusual, however, and the question becomes: "Is there an advantage to allocating fixed costs to products outside the books of account?" (Remember, when management needs an approximation of total costs, it must be done *outside* of the accounting system when direct costing is used.) In many cases there is an advantage to allocating fixed costs to products outside of the books of account. Running these allocations through the books of account makes them no more accurate and sometimes gives an unwarranted appearance of precision. When fixed costs are allocated to products outside the books of account, there is often greater flexibility. There is no problem in crossing departmental lines. For example, where one department has old equipment and another has new equipment, it is possible to average the total fixed costs of both departments and assign an average amount per unit to each product produced (assuming the products require comparable manufacturing processes). Also, it is less of a problem to use depreciation based on replacement cost.

Once fixed costs have been allocated to product lines, it is often unnecessary to change them more than once a year. Fixed costs, by definition, should not change much from month to month and accounting for minor monthly fluctuations does not add accuracy to figures that are already approximations.

4. *Contribution is reflected on the books of account.* A fourth advantage that is frequently cited for direct costing is that contribution is reflected in the books of account. Management must know contribution to make many product decisions; if it is not calculated on the books of account, it will have to be done outside of the accounting system. The only question here is, What is the advantage of having contribution reflected in the books of account? Since management will be provided with the contribution amount involved in any product decision, the principal difference between a full absorption system and a direct costing system is the profit breakdown on the monthly or quarterly financial statements. Under direct costing, management will be shown monthly contribution; under a full cost system, management will see gross profit. In any particular system, this advantage will apply only if there appears to be any reason for showing management the contribution amounts on the monthly (or quarterly) profit statements.

5. *Provides better control over fixed costs.* A final advantage proposed by direct costing advocates is that it provides better control over fixed costs. The argument is that fixed costs can be controlled better in total and that direct costing treats fixed costs in total. The control of fixed costs does not appear to be a compelling reason for adopting direct costing. These costs can be controlled in total under either a full costing or a direct costing system. The only advantage of a direct costing system is that fixed costs are shown in one place, in total, on the monthly income statement. Under a budgetary control system, however, management can compare actual fixed cost in total to budget, even though these figures will not appear on the income statement. If there is no budgetary control system in a company, there may be some advantage to showing fixed costs in total on the income statement. Again, whether this advantage will apply depends on the nature of the business and the cost control system in operation. (If fixed costs were essentially uncontrollable from month to month, for example, there is little advantage to showing them separately.)

Disadvantage of Direct Costing

Under certain conditions, some of the advantages listed in the previous section can be considered disadvantages. If, for example, the management of a company were prone to make all decisions, both short and long term, on the basis of contribution, it might be a disadvantage to have the monthly accounting statements reflect contribution. In addition to those disadvantages that may apply in particular cases, there are other disadvantages to direct costing.

1. *Internal financial statements differ from published reports.* The primary disadvantage is that the internal financial statements will differ from the published reports. This results because most direct costing methods are not considered acceptable by the public accounting profession for external financial statements. (Also, most of these methods are not considered acceptable by the Internal Revenue Service for income tax purposes.) Consequently, when a company uses direct costing, it is necessary to increase the value of the inventory to reflect full costs. This adjustment may cause confusion because the internal profit figure will be different from that included in the annual report.

The calculation to adjust the inventories to full cost is usually not a serious problem, with respect to either the public accountant or the Internal Revenue Service. Acceptable methods are available that can be applied to the entire inventory value so that it is not necessary to recalculate the cost of each item. The clerical cost of making this calculation is relatively small.

2. *It is difficult to calculate variable costs.* A second disadvantage, offered by proponents of full costing, is the inability of some companies to calculate variable costs, or even to agree on a definition. Management must make decisions based on differential costs and, consequently, these costs must be estimated. The objection refers to having these variable costs reflected on the books of account. Since the variability of costs differs under different circumstances, the usefulness of a single calculation of the variability of overhead costs is questioned.

3. *Inventories are undervalued.* A third disadvantage of direct costing is that inventories are undervalued. There is no question that inventories will have a lower value under a direct costing system than under a full absorption system and, in this respect, could be considered undervalued. Whether this disadvantage applies to any situation will depend on what effect this lower inventory value has. (The same disadvantage applies to the last-in, first-out, or LIFO, method of inventory valuation.) To the extent that in direct costing inventories are smaller than in full absorption costing, internal statements will show a lower profit (in the year of the changeover) and lower retainer earnings. Since external statements, however, will not be changed, the ability to borrow money or pay dividends will be unaffected. If there are positive reasons for adopting a direct costing system, it is questionable whether lower inventory value is really a disadvantage.

Management Consideration of Direct Costing

The question to be answered with respect to direct costing is *not* whether direct costing is better than full absorption costing. The question *is* whether direct costing is better in a particular situation. The way to decide whether to adopt a direct costing system is to study the advantages and disadvantages that will apply to each specific case. If the advantages do not outweigh the disadvantages, direct costing should not be adopted. For cost accounting purposes, the advantages and disadvantages are those related to the value of the information that mangement will receive rather than those applicable to theoretical accounting principles. Because of the increasing complexity of cost accounting systems described in Chapter 4, it is probable that direct cost systems will become increasingly popular. For example, fixed costs could be assigned to a product once a year by means of a computer model; then, variable overhead costs only would be assigned to the productive departments. This would result in considerable simplification of the cost accounting system with no decrease in the information available to managers.

QUESTIONS

5.1 Name as many examples of joint product industries as you can. Name some examples of common cost industries. How do the two differ?

5.2 Give an example of how a manager can make a wrong decision from receiving a report that shows product profitability figures for a joint product.

5.3 If you have joint products, what information do you use to diagnose unprofitable situations or to guide you in setting selling prices?

5.4 Explain how the market price method of joint costing overcomes the problems that are experienced when average costs are used.

5.5 Explain why an available market makes it possible to establish a useful joint cost. In what way is such a cost useful to management?

5.6 What do you think is the most important advantage of direct costing to the typical mass-production industry in the United States? Why?

5.7 What do you think is the most important disadvantage of direct costing to the typical mass-production industry in the United States? Why?

5.8 In what kind of business do you think direct costing is most useful? In what kind of business do you think full costing is most useful?

PROBLEMS

5.1 The following financial statistics apply to a meat packing plant:

- Cost of steers purchased during the month: $36,000
- Amount of product obtained (in pounds):

Steaks	10,000
Roasts	20,000
Hamburger	25,000
Waste products	5,000
Total	60,000

The average selling price per pound of each of the products sold during the month was:

Steaks	$1.75
Roasts	1.25
Hamburger	0.75
Waste	0.05

There was no beginning or ending in inventory of beef.

Required

Calculate the gross profit of each of the products using: (a) the average cost method and (b) the market price method of assigning joint costs.

5.2 The Mercred Glue Company produces glue. The manufacturing process results in various grades of glue, in addition to certain by-products (grease and tankage) that are sold for whatever they will bring. Following are the operating and financial statistics for the Mercred Glue Company for January 1986.

Production
(in tons)

Grade A	1,100
Grade B	600
Grade C	300
Grade D	300
Grease	40
Tankage	10

Cost of Production

Material	$25,400
Direct labor	10,500
Indirect labor	10,000
Indirect material	4,200
Utilities	8,500
Depreciation	14,500
	$73,100

Beginning Finished Goods Inventory

PRODUCT	UNITS (TONS)	VALUE PER UNIT	TOTAL
A	900	$45	$40,500
B	400	40	16,000
C	200	30	6,000
D	100	25	2,500
Grease	50	0	0
Tankage	575	0	0
	2,225		$65,000

Sales

PRODUCT	TONS	AVERAGE SELLING PRICE	TOTAL SALES
A	1,000	$60	$60,000
B	500	50	25,000
C	200	40	8,000
D	300	30	9,000
Grease	60	20	1,200
Tankage	300	5	1,500
	2,360		$104,700

Inventories

There was no work-in-process inventory at the beginning nor at the end of the month. Finished goods inventory is valued at average costs. That is, the value of the beginning inventory is added to the costs of production and the total is divided by the sum of the number of tons in the beginning inventory and the number of tons produced.

Other Costs

Costs of disposing of grease and tankage	$ 1,000
Selling expenses	15,000
Administrative expenses	10,000

Required

(1) Prepare an income statement for January on the following assumptions:

  (a) Products A, B, C, and D are treated as joint products and are costed using the market price method.

  (b) Grease and tankage are treated as by-products and are given no value. The net sales revenue is subtracted from the total joint costs.

(2) Calculate the value of the ending finished goods inventory.

5.3 Make the journal entries to record the financial transaction described in Problem 5.2.

5.4 How would the profits and the value of the ending inventory differ in Problem 5.2 if tankage and grease were treated as joint products and their value in the beginning finished goods inventory were: tankage, $805; grease, $652?

5.5 The Western Quarries Company has developed the following plan for valuing inventories of marble blocks. Each block is given two grades from 4 to 1: First they are graded on color and second on soundness. For example, a block classified as 4–4 would be best in color and best in soundness; a block classified 4–1 would be best in color but poor in soundness. A block classified as 1–1 would be poor in both color and soundness. There are, therefore, ten different classifications. Blocks are valued proportional to the square of the sum of the two numbers with 1–1 blocks the common denominator. For example, 4–4 blocks are 16 times as valuable per ton as 1–1 blocks.

$$\left[\frac{(4 + 4)^2}{(1 + 1)^2} = 16 \right]$$

Listed below is an inventory of blocks of each classification. Given that the total value of the inventory is $1,500,000, place an inventory value on each type of block.

CLASSIFICATION	NUMBER OF TONS IN INVENTORY
4–4	1,000
4–3	2,000
3–4	5,000
3–3	6,000
3–2	8,000
2–3	7,000
2–2	4,000
1–2	3,000
2–1	2,000
1–1	1,000
Total	39,000

5.6 The Jeudi Company produces three grades of raw plastic. The proportional yield of each grade differs with each mix as a result of several factors such as raw material input, length of processing, and so forth. Each grade of raw plastic can be sold immediately after being produced or it can be manufactured into finished plastic parts. Listed below are some financial data for the Jeudi Company for January 1986. From this data, prepare a report of gross profit by product line.
(*Hint:* separate the profits from the production and sale of raw plastic from the profits arising from the production and sales of finished plastic parts.)

Selling Price of Raw Plastic

Grade A	$1.00 per pound
Grade B	0.70 per pound
Grade C	0.50 per pound

Cost of selling raw plastic: 10% of sales price

Raw Plastic

Production costs $70,000

PRODUCTION:

Grade A	25,000 lb
Grade B	50,000 lb
Grade C	60,000 lb

Finished Products

	PER UNIT		
MATERIAL CONTENT	*Product X*	*Product Y*	*Product Z*
RAW PLASTICS USED *(in pounds):*			
Grade A	1	1	—
Grade B	—	1	2
Grade C	2	—	2
Direct labor	$1.00	$1.50	$2.00
Overhead	2.00	2.50	3.50

Sales

PRODUCT	*UNITS*	*SELLING PRICE*
X	10,000	$6.00
Y	12,000	6.50
Z	15,000	8.00

RAW PLASTICS	*POUNDS*	*SELLING PRICE*
Grade A	3,000	$1.00
Grade B	8,000	.70
Grade C	10,000	.50

Selling costs of raw plastic during January: $1,360
All raw plastic must be sold or used; it cannot be stored except for a short while.

5.7 Listed next are some financial data for the Novem Company.

Budget Data

	JAN.	*FEB.*	*MAR.*	*APR.*	*MAY*	*JUNE*
Sales (units)	10,000	9,000	8,000	11,000	12,000	15,000
Production (units)	20,000	10,000	8,000	10,000	8,000	6,000
Selling price	$ 3.00 per unit					
Standard variable cost	$ 1.00 per unit					
Standard fixed cost	$15,000 per month					
Standard volume	10,000 units per month					

Required

Calculate the budgeted gross profit for January through June, assuming:

(1) A standard direct cost system is used.

(2) A standard full cost system is used, with under- or overabsorbed overhead written off each month.

(3) A standard full cost system is used, with under- or overabsorbed overhead deferred until the end of the year.

5.8 The Vend Company uses a standard direct cost accounting system. Listed next are financial transactions for January 1986.

(1) Prepare the journal entries to record these financial transactions.

(2) Prepare an income statement for the month of January 1986.

(3) Prepare an analysis of variances from standard.

Standard Cost Data

	PROD. A	*PROD. B*	*PROD. C*
Material	$1.00	$1.25	$1.50
Direct labor	0.50	1.00	1.50
Variable overhead	1.00	1.50	1.50
Standard volume (units)	10,000	20,000	15,000

ACTUAL FINANCIAL DATA FOR JANUARY

Volume of sales (units)	12,000	20,000	20,000
Selling price per unit	$4.00	$5.00	$6.00
Volume of production (units)	15,000	15,000	15,000

COSTS INCURRED

Variable costs:	
Material (at standard prices)	$55,000
Direct labor	46,000
Indirect labor—variable	38,000
Indirect material	20,000
Utilities	11,500
Fixed costs:	
Indirect labor—fixed	$22,000
Depreciation	29,000
Selling expense	6,000
Administrative expense	8,000

There was no beginning or ending work-in-process inventory.

CASES

CASE 5.1   THE WILLIAMSON CHOCOLATE CO., LTD

The Williamson Chocolate Co., Ltd which has its headquarters and principal factory in Leicester, England, has been engaged in the production of chocolate and cocoa products since the beginning of this century. Subsidiary companies have been established in Canada, Australia and South Africa, and each of the subsidi-

This case was prepared by Professor David Solomons as a basis for class discussion rather than to illustrate either effective or ineffective handling of an administrative situation. Copyright by IMEDE (International Management Development Institute), Lausanne, Switzerland. Reproduced by permission.

aries manufactures the more important of the company's products and markets them in its home market.

The Australian company is located in Melbourne, where all of its manufacturing activities take place, and warehouses for local distribution are also maintained in Sydney, Adelaide and Perth. The main output at the factory is chocolate in bars. Cocoa beans, the principal raw material for the manufacture of chocolate, are imported from abroad. As a rule, the beans are cleaned, roasted, ground and passed through a press. In the press, cocoa butter is separated from cocoa powder, which comes out of the press in the form of cocoa cake. The cocoa butter leaves the press in liquid form because of the heat that is generated from the press operations. The cocoa butter is then stored in large tanks, ready for use in the current production of chocolate.

The Melbourne factory was a net user of cocoa butter, i.e., its chocolate production called for more cocoa butter than could be obtained from the pressing of cocoa beans for powder manufacture. This extra butter could have been imported but it was subject to a heavy import duty, and the local management believed it was cheaper to import beans and extract the cocoa butter from them. As a result of implementing this policy, the factory found itself with a steadily mounting stock of cocoa powder. The following figures show how the stock of cocoa powder increased during the period 1983–85:

		NUMBER OF POUNDS
Stock at January 1, 1983		30,500
Output of press		416,975
		447,475
LESS:		
Usage in 1983		324,500
Stock at December 31, 1983		122,975
Output of press		638,750
		761,725
LESS:		
Usage in 1984	506,420	
Sales in 1984	35,500	
		541,920
Stock at December 31, 1984		219,805
Output of press		792,125
		1,011,930
LESS:		
Usage in 1985	641,600	
Sales in 1985	43,385	
		684,985
Stock of cocoa powder, December 31, 1985		326,945

These large stocks of cocoa powder held at the factory caused a serious storage problem and the local management made continuous efforts to find prof- itable outlets for the excess cocoa powder. However, the sale of this powder on the Australian market raised a question as to its proper valuation. In accordance with accounting instructions issued by the head office in London some time be- fore the last war, the cost of the cocoa beans purchased together with the labor and overhead costs of the pressing process had to be allocated between the cocoa butter and the cocoa cakes on the basis of the fat content remaining in these two products after the pressing operations. This gave a cost for cocoa powder of about 23d a pound, or about 50% above its current market price at the end of 1985.[1] The company was therefore unable to dispose of its excess stock of cocoa cakes without incurring a considerable loss. For balance sheet purposes, however, the company made a provision in its accounts in order to bring the book value of its stock of cocoa down to the market value.

During 1986, cocoa prices fell further and the subsidiary was unable to sell any large quantities of its excess stocks, because its costs were too high. There was practically no internal market for cocoa cakes. It did succeed, however, in exchanging 13,000 lb of cake against 2000 lb of cocoa butter with another manufacturer.

In the middle of 1986, Mr. Cannon, the marketing manager, brought forward a scheme to market a new cocoa preparation for making a hot chocolate drink. The marketing prospects seemed good so long as the selling price could be kept low enough. This new product offered a promising means of disposing of the excess stocks of cocoa powder but only if they were costed out at sub- stantially less than the cost allocated to them in the books.

The production manager, Mr. Parker, supported this proposal with enthusi- asm. He had drawn the attention of the subsidiary's managing director, Mr. Woodstock, repeatedly to the storage problem created by the cocoa stocks, and he welcomed the possibily which now opened up of dealing with this problem once and for all. Besides, he said, he had never been able to see the logic of basing the cost of cocoa powder on its fat content. It was its flavor which was important, and fat content had little to do with flavor.

Both Cannon and Parker were surprised to find that Mr. Woodstock was not unreservedly enthusiastic about Cannon's proposal. He pointed out that if cocoa powder were charged to the new product at present cost levels, the product would never show a profit; and without a drop in the price of cocoa beans greater than anyone could at present foresee, the only way to reduce the cost of cocoa powder would be to change the basis of cost allocation betwen cocoa powder and cocoa butter. This could not be done without permission from London and he was by no means certain that such permission would be given unless some basis of cost allocation which was clearly better than the present one could be pro-

---

[1] The Australian pound stands at a discount in relation to the English pound. All values men- tioned in this case are expressed in Australian currency.

posed. It was all very well to attack the present basis of allocation, as Mr. Parker had done. But unless he or somebody else could suggest a better one, why should London agree to a change?

Mr. Woodstock went on to point out that there was another aspect of the matter which made him reluctant to approach London. If the allocation of costs to cocoa powder were reduced, with a consequent increase in the cost of cocoa butter, the calculation which had been supplied to London in 1986 to support the expenditure of £A40,000 on a new cocoa press would be completely undermined. Only on the basis of the present cost of producing cocoa butter as compared with the cost of importing it could investment in the press be justified. If more cost were to be allocated to cocoa butter, it might be shown that it ought to be imported after all, and the investment in the press would be shown to have been misguided.

Required

Would you

1. Decline to ask the London office for new instructions? If so, defend this position.

2. Decide to ask for new instructions? If so, precisely what would you request from the London office?

CASE 5.2   AB SUNDQVIST

Pricing In An Export Market

"You just can't do it," said Mr. Erik Berggren, controller to AB Sundqvist. "Our policy has always been to bill our distributors at cost and that doesn't mean variable cost. We just can't afford to sell below cost."

AB Sundqvist is a medium-sized manufacturer of cough medicines, headache pills, and similar products. It has three factories and a large sales force, all in Sweden, and a chain of general agents, one in each country in Western Europe. These general agents buy products from Sundqvist "at cost" and sell them to pharmacies for distribution to the ultimate consumer. The general agents, in addition to the cost price of the products themselves, pay Sundqvist a royalty equal to 5% of the amounts they bill their customers for Sundqvist products.

Sundqvist had been very fortunate in obtaining large, well-managed and

The case was prepared by Professor Gordon Shillinglaw as a basis for class discussion rather than to illustrate either effective or ineffective handling of an administrative situation. Copyright by IMEDE (International Management Development Institute), Lausanne, Switzerland, Reproduced by permission.

well-financed companies as its general agents. Its general agent in Britain, Edwards Enterprises, Ltd., was a subsidiary of a large Belgian company engaged in the manufacture and distribution of a wide variety of pharmaceutical and cosmetic products. Although Edwards Enterprises did no manufacturing itself, its parent company had manufacturing plants to supply it with products representing approximately 30% of its annual sales volume. Edwards Enterprises regarded itself as a marketing organization and was reluctant to get into manufacturing, although the issue had come up from time to time as the company encountered difficulties in obtaining adequate supplies of a specific kind of product as profitable prices.

Edwards Enterprises, like Sundqvist's other general agents, represented several manufacturers, but did not carry directly competing merchandise. In other words, if it obtained a line of face creams from one manufacturer, it would not handle another line of face creams.

The statement quoted at the beginning of this case was made by Mr. Berggren in the course of a conversation with Mr. Nils Lindstrom, the company's manager for foreign markets. Mr. Lindstrom was anxious to build up sales volume abroad, particularly in view of the recent plant expansion program which for the first time had provided enough capacity to supply all the company's markets. Although some operations were still subcontracted during peak seasons, the company's plant was operating at about 85% of its annual capacity.

The Sundqvist Company had just developed a new liquid headache remedy which it had introduced on the Swedish market with considerable initial success. Mr. Frank Keeling, president of Edwards Enterprises, was very interested in marketing this new item in Britain. Although his parent company had a somewhat similar product, Mr. Keeling regarded it as inferior in quality to the Sundqvist product and much more difficult to market. The British public had recently shown a preference for Swedish-made products in this field, at least partly because of an intensive advertising campaign carried out by Edwards Enterprises itself.

Mr. Keeling was anxious to capitalize on this preference by offering the Sundqvist product. He was not happy, however, with the price quoted him by Mr. Lindstrom, a price of 10 Swedish crowns for a case of 12 bottles. "Let's face it," he said, "your direct costs of manufacturing this product are probably about 6 crowns per case. We make approximately the same product in Belgium and your cost can't be very different from ours. This means that you're adding four crowns a case to cover your overhead cost. I think this just isn't warranted here, particularly because you get a royalty of 5% on our gross sales volume anyway. We would sell this to retailers at about four times the price we pay you. At 6 crowns a case, our price would be 24 crowns and your royalty alone would be about 1.20 crowns. We'd be willing to pay you a little more than your direct cost, but this is just too much to ask."

The accounting system used by AB Sundqvist was a "direct costing" system.

In this system, product cost included only labor and material cost, and was bro-ken down into four categories:

1. The materials required for the manufacture of the product itself.
2. Containers, packages and packing materials.
3. Direct manufacturing labor.
4. Filling and packaging labor.

The labor charges included a provision for social benefits of 20%, which was almost exactly the cost of these benefits to the Sundvqvist Company. The salaries of the foremen in the direct production departments were not included in direct cost.

For pricing purposes, Mr. Berggren included in product cost an allowance of 175% of direct cost to allow for factory, sales, technical and administrative overhead costs. This was based on the breakdown shown in Exhibit 1. The 175% rate was computed as follows:

$$\frac{\text{Overhead cost}}{\text{Direct cost of goods sold}} = \frac{\text{Kr. } 5700}{\text{Kr. } 3260} = 175\%.$$

The company's accounts included no provision for depreciation on plant and equipment. The original cost of the factory buildings amounted to Kr. 1,400,000, while factory re-equipment had cost Kr. 350,000. As far as the building was concerned, one company official stated that increases in the market value of the land were expected to exceed any depreciation on the building itself and that depreciation was therefore unnecessary. Comparable buildings in Sweden were likely to remain in productive use for fifty years or even longer. The equipment was a different matter. On the average, it was likely to last for 5–7 years, but this was such an uncertain figure that Mr. Berggren was unwilling to reflect it in the accounts.

Mr. Lindstrom persisted in his argument with Mr. Berggren. "After all," he said, "if we can increase our sales, only the variable costs will increase; the fixed costs will remain constant. Besides, it is a fact that we can make money on the royalties we get on the added sales."

Mr. Berggren was unimpressed. "If your sales expand by as much as you hope they will," he said, "we'll have to add another shift in at least one factory and make some additional investments in mixing machinery. If you're really suc-cessful, we'll even have to expand one of the plants earlier than we now plan. Your variable cost figures ignore these facts. I'm perfectly willing to work out some figures on the profitability of the added volume that might come from price reductions, but don't try to get me to support your bid to sell the product at direct cost. Cost is cost, and that's all there is to it."

EXHIBIT 1 AB Sundqvist

Budgeted Income Statement

Sales		Kr. 10,390
Direct cost of goods sold		3,260
Direct margin		Kr. 7,130
Overheads:		
Top management	Kr. 160	
Staff (finance, tax, purchasing)	230	
Routine clerical	1,060	
Selling expense—Sweden	3,080	
Warehousing and shipping	550	
Export sales expense	60	
Factory overhead (see Schedule A)	430	
Research and testing	130	
Total overheads		5,700
Net income before taxes		Kr. 1,430

Schedule A: Budgeted Factory Overhead Costs

Materials control	Kr.	100
Engineering		105
Supervision		15
Indirect labor		30
Outside services		30
Maintenance		35
Utilities		20
Work clothes		15
Other		80
Total factory overhead costs	Kr.	430

Required

1. Would you have supported Mr. Lindstrom or Mr. Berggren? Does it appear that a price equal to direct product cost plus a royalty of 5% of the agents' billing price would be profitable or unprofitable for the Sundqvist company?

2. What changes in this company's accounting system, if any, would yield data that are more relevant to decisions of this type?

3. Would your answer to (1) differ in any way if there were a one-time order for a single shipment of a product made to a customer's specifications?

4. Would you describe Sundqvist's direct cost system as a variable costing system? How different is it?

5. The company's contracts with its general agents call for billing the latter "at cost." Because of the controversy that arose in this case, the company planned to revise its contract forms to provide a more specific definition of cost. What items do you think should be included as "cost"?

chapter 6

DECISION SUPPORT SYSTEMS: TACTICAL MARKETING DECISIONS

Managers need to know, on a systematic basis, the profitability of the products that are being sold. The product is the smallest segment of the business about which profitability information is available. It is also the smallest segment of the business about which managers make decisions that affect the volume or direction of sales. For example, managers make decisions on advertising expenditures, sales efforts, and price changes. They make decisions to drop products and to market new products. They make decisions to enter new markets and to withdraw from existing markets. All the decisions must be supported by an appropriate cost accounting decision-support system.

A cost accounting decision-support system requires two steps. First, past performance must be measured and evaluated. Second, the economic impact of any proposed courses of action must be forecast. The first step identifies problems or opportunities; the second step projects the financial impact of specific product decisions. The usual procedure is to move from step 1 to step 2. However, often nothing further is done as a result of measuring the profitability of a product. On the other hand, specific product proposals may come from a number of sources other than the measurement process. The separation of these two steps is important, however, because different techniques are required for forecasting than for diagnosing and confusion between these steps, which is not uncommon, can result in managers using incorrect information.

Cost accounting decision-support systems are required to help management to (1) make tactical marketing decisions; (2) make disinvestment decisions; and (3) decide on the extent and direction of expansion.

In these chapters, systems for supporting management decisions in these three areas are described.

Managers need to make tactical marketing decisions on a day-to-day basis. These decisions do not usually involve a change in the total resources nor a permanent change in the deployment of these resources. Tactical marketing decisions have two characteristics: First, the decision is expected to have an immediate impact on the volume of sales. Second, the effect of the decision is expected to last a year or less.

Examples of tactical marketing decisions are:

- Establishing and redeploying the advertising and sales promotion budgets.
- Deciding which products to promote most aggressively.
- Deciding the amount to bid on a proposal.
- Deciding whether and by how much to change the price of an existing product.
- Deciding whether to make or buy a product.

In other words, these are decisions that marketing managers must make continually for existing products in existing markets.

INFORMATION REQUIREMENTS

In order to make any decision that is expected to influence the volume of the sales of an existing product in an existing market, the manager must have a reliable estimate of the financial impact of that decision. What is needed is an estimate of the *differential cash flow* that will result from the decision.

As stated in Chapter 1, differential cash flow has two characteristics. First, it includes all the cash flows and *only* the cash flows that are expected to change as a result of a decision. Second, it includes the cash flows that are expected to exist during the period of the decision. In short, it means *future* cash flows.

Differential Cash Flow

The *differential cash flows* of tactical marketing decisions are the differences in the revenues and the costs that have been triggered by a specific decision affecting the volume of sales. Once the change in volume is estimated, differential revenues are quite straightforward and generally offer no serious problem in calculation. Differential costs, however, can be more difficult to identify.

The concept of differential cost may be clearer if we take the example of a person with an automobile that is to be leased (that is, the person is the lessor). A hypothetical example of the cost of operating this automobile is as follows:

Hypothetical Example: Costs of Operating
   an Automobile

	PER MILE	ANNUAL TOTAL
Miles driven per year		10,000
Gas, oil, grease, tires, repairs	$0.12	$1,200
Depreciation	0.10	1,000
Insurance	0.04	400
Total	$0.26	$2,600

Let us assume that the car whose operating costs are shown is owned by person A. Now, let us assume that B wishes to lease the car to make a short trip and that A is to supply all the gas. Suppose B offers to pay A $0.10 a mile. What are the differential costs to A in deciding whether or not to accept this offer? Obviously, the cost of such factors as gasoline, oil, and tires would be differential because these costs will increase directly and proportionately with the number of miles B drives. All the revenue will be differential because it also will increase proportionately with the miles driven. The job of the cost accountant is to provide A with an estimate of the financial impact of renting the car to B. This is as follows:

Financial Impact to A of Renting an Automobile to B at $0.10 per Mile

	LENGTH OF B'S TRIP					
	200 Miles		400 Miles		600 Miles	
	Per Mile	Total	Per Mile	Total	Per Mile	Total
Revenue	$0.10	$20	$0.10	$40	$0.10	$60
Costs	0.12	24	0.12	48	0.12	72
Profit/Loss	$(0.02)	$(4)	$(0.02)	$(8)	$(0.02)	$(12)

First, note that the only differential costs for this particular decision are the costs of gasoline, oil, and so on. These are differential because they are the costs that will change as a result of leasing the automobile. Insurance and depreciation will stay the same regardless of whether or not A rents the automobile to B. Note that the differential revenue of $0.10 a mile is $0.02 less than the differential costs. Consequently, at $0.10 a mile, A will lose $0.02 for each mile that the lessee drives the car. A will have to pay $4 more than was received from B if B takes a 200-mile trip. Furthermore, the longer B's trip, the more money A will lose. Clearly, on this basis, A would not lease the automobile to B.

Suppose, however, that B offers to pay $0.17 a mile. Let us look at the economics of this example.

Financial Impact to A of Renting an Automobile to B at $0.17 per Mile

	LENGTH OF B'S TRIP					
	200 Miles		400 Miles		600 Miles	
	Per Mile	Total	Per Mile	Total	Per Mile	Total
Revenue	$0.17	$34	$0.17	$68	$0.17	$102
Costs	0.12	24	0.12	48	0.12	$ 72
Profit	$0.05	$10	$0.05	$20	$0.05	$ 30

In this case, A's cash flow would increase because the differential revenue received would be greater than the differential costs incurred. This tells A that there would be an increase in cash flow by renting the automobile, and the further that B travels, the more the cash will increase. A may be in a dilemma, however. Although A's cash balance will increase by renting the car to B, the rental will still not cover the cost of insurance or depreciation. A may decide not to rent the car unless more than $0.26 per mile is paid. This, however, is a managerial decision. A knows that cash flow will be increased by renting the automobile, but other considerations, such as not wishing to set a precedent of low rental, could influence the decision. Also note, that if this decision required purchasing a car for the purpose of leasing it, even $0.26 a mile would not be satisfactory.

Summary

To summarize, the accountant must provide managers making tactical marketing decisions with financial information that will allow these managers to estimate the financial impact of these decisions. Since the differential revenue is usually readily available, the accountant must estimate the differential costs.

MEASURING DIFFERENTIAL COSTS

Differential costs, by definition, are those that will change as the result of a specific decision. Since there can be many kinds of decisions that affect the volume or mix of sales, it can be difficult for a cost accounting system to provide differential costs on a systematic and routine basis. The alternative, however, would require a special analysis each time a decision had to be made. In many instances this could be impractical for tactical marketing decisions because often hundreds of such decisions must be made quickly during any period of time. It has been necessary, therefore, to develop a surrogate that approximates the differential costs resulting from tactical marketing decisions. This surrogate is called *variable costs.*

Variable Costs

Conditions.   The objective is to develop a system that can be used to calculate differential costs in tactical marketing decisions. It is necessary, therefore, first to develop a set of conditions that characterize these decisions and, second, to develop a cost accounting system consistent with these conditions. These conditions are as follows:

1. Adequate capacity exists to produce all products involved in the analyses.
2. The product will continue to be produced and sold during the time period involved.
3. The volume of production and sales will be in the "normal" range.
4. The volume change, whether up or down, will not be permanent.

Variable Costs Defined.   Variable costs are those costs that vary directly with and are approximately proportional to volume under the conditions described above. They include direct material, direct labor, variable overhead, and variable selling and administrative costs. Variable overhead includes such costs as supplies, power, some indirect labor, and some maintenance. Variable marketing and administration includes certain costs incurred *after the point of sale,* such as commissions, picking and packing orders, shipping (if not paid by the customer), billing, and collections.

Calculating Variable Costs.   For each accounting location, it is necessary to decide which costs are variable. Note that this will differ with different companies, with different management policies, and, particularly, in different countries. In the United States, direct labor is usually considered variable unless management's policy is to maintain the work force regardless of the level of activity. This may not be true, however, in many countries where the dismissal of workers is so expensive that it is impractical in the short run.

The usual technique is to identify each expense classification as either fixed or variable and code them as such. Some expenses, particularly indirect labor and maintenance, are usually partially variable and partially fixed. It is usually possible to identify the fixed portion of these semivariable costs by observing the movements of these costs at different volumes. (This subject is discussed in detail in Chapter 10.)

Some points to consider in identifying variable costs are as follows:

1. Few costs are entirely variable over even the normal range of production volume. Perfection is not necessary, however. It is sufficient that they be approximately variable.
2. In some instances, direct labor may appear to be fixed because of restrictions on hiring and firing. It should normally be treated as variable, however. With good production scheduling, there should be little idle direct labor, even if it involves producing for inventory.

3. When in doubt, treat an expense as variable.
4. The decisions about which costs are variable should be reviewed each year.
5. Fixed costs are irrelevant in calculating the differential cash flow from tactical marketing decisions since, by definition, the cost will not be affected by such a decision.

Of all cost accounting terms, the term *variable costs* is most subject to differences in interpretation, and hence it is important to define the term. For example, the expression "in the long run, all the costs are variable" is sometimes made. The author of this statement has a different concept of variable costs from the one just defined. The definition provided in this chapter is probably the most useful. To consider as variable those costs that vary in any way with volume means that there is no definition at all, because what is variable can be determined only in the context of the specific situation.

Contribution

Contribution is the difference between the revenue of a product (or group of products) and the variable cost. Contribution is the cash flow from producing and selling a product, given the constraints listed earlier. The term contribution is a contraction of the expression contribution to overhead and profit. Management should be provided with contribution by product on a systematic basis. Such information can trigger managerial actions such as raising the price of a product earning a low contribution or placing increasing sales emphasis on a product earning a high contribution. The systematic analysis of individual product contributions is the basis for many tactical marketing decisions.

CAUTION

There are two areas in which the user of variable cost data must be cautious. First, the decision being considered must be consistent with the conditions assumed in defining variable cost. Second, the information must not be based on historical costs that have become out of date. Each is discussed in this part of this chapter.

Consistent Conditions

Variable costs will not approximate differential costs if the conditions surrounding a decision are not consistent with the conditions described earlier. For example, consider the following:

1. If insufficient capacity exists, the differential costs may be radically different from the variable cost. Overtime might be incurred or parts of an assembly might be purchased from an outside source rather than being manufactured internally.

2. If the decision is to drop a product, many costs can be eliminated that must be incurred as long as the product is produced in any volume.
3. When the production volume of a product becomes very low, cost patterns tend to change, and so the differential costs may vary from the variable costs when production is outside the "normal" range.
4. A permanent change in volume will often cause a change in those costs that remain fixed when the change in volume is temporary.

It is the responsibility of the user of cost information to avoid using variable cost information for decisions that do not conform to the conditions upon which the costs were developed. Where deviations from these conditions exist, a special study is usually required to determine the differential cash flow.

Up-To-Date Information

Cost accounting systems measure *past* performance. This is consistent with the accountant's responsibility to measure past financial events. However, if cost information is to be used to predict the economic effect of specific product decisions, future costs rather than past costs are required. This can be a serious problem in countries experiencing significant inflation. It is particularly important that the cost information used for tactical marketing decisions be current.

QUESTIONS

6.1   What problems would you expect in calculating differential revenue?

6.2   Why are automobile depreciation and insurance not differential costs? Can you think of some instances where they might be?

6.3   In the example given in the text, what reason could A have for not accepting the $0.17 per mile price? For rejecting it? Would it make a difference if A was in the car rental business?

6.4   Explain why variable costs should be defined in terms of specific conditions.

6.5   What is contribution? Where is it used in decision-support systems?

PROBLEMS

6.1   Fred Smith estimates that the costs to run his automobile are as follows:

Gas, oil, grease, and so on	$0.08 per mile
Tires and repairs	$0.05 per mile
Depreciation	$1500
Insurance	$900

Approximate mileage driven per year: 10,000

(a)   What is Smith's total cost per year for running his car?

(b) What is Smith's cost per mile?

(c) If Smith were to rent his car for $0.30 a mile, for how many miles would he have to rent it before he would break even?

(d) Assume Smith has an investment of $10,000 in his car. For how many miles would he have to rent it in order to earn 10% on his investment?

(e) Smith estimates he can rent his car for 12,000 miles next year. What price per mile must be charge (1) to break even? (2) To earn 10% on his investment?

6.2 Product costs for the ABC Company are budgeted as follows:

	BUDGETED COSTS AT STANDARD VOLUME, 1986			
	A	*B*	*C*	*Total*
Direct material	$ 6,000	$ 7,500	$1,000	$14,500
Direct labor	3,000	4,500	1,500	9,000
Variable overhead	2,000	6,000	1,500	9,500
Fixed overhead	2,000	4,500	3,000	9,500
	$13,000	$22,500	$7,000	$42,500
Standard volume units	1,000	1,500	500	

Assume that you have an opportunity to sell an additional 100 units of either Product A, B, or C. You have ample capacity and you expect to be able to produce at budgeted cost. Which product would you sell under the following price assumptions:

	SELLING PRICE PER UNIT		
	A	*B*	*C*
Assumption 1	$16.00	$16.00	$16.00
Assumption 2	18.00	16.00	14.00
Assumption 3	13.10	14.10	10.00

6.3 Make the same assumption as in Problem 6.2, except that the alternative action is to sell $1000 worth of any of the three products. Which products would you sell under the three pricing assumptions?

6.4 Indicate the action that you would take under the following conditions. It is expected that actual costs of the ABC Company will be equal to budget and that ample capacity will exist to produce any of the columns indicated.

(a) The present price of Product A is $16 a unit. At that volume, you expect to sell 1000 units a year. The price of your principal competitor drops to $14 a unit. If you do not reduce your price, you can expect to sell only 750 units. If you reduce your price you can expect to sell 1000 units. What action would you take?

(b) Product B is currently selling for $14 a unit. Your competitor's price is raised to $15 a unit. If you keep your price at $14, you could sell 3000 units. If you raise your price to $15 you can expect to sell only 1500 units. What should you do?

6.5 In one of the plants of the Castell Corporation, there is a machine that produces five different products, A through E. Listed are some financial facts about these products.

PRODUCT	PRICE	VARIABLE COST	UNITS PRODUCED PER MACHINE HOUR
A	$1.00	$0.50	1000
B	1.50	0.90	700
C	2.00	1.00	300
D	2.75	2.00	1000
E	5.00	3.50	350

(a) If the machine has sufficient capacity to produce all the products that can be sold, rank the products in the order in which you would prefer to sell them.
(b) If the machine does not have the capacity to produce all the products that you can sell, rank the products in the order in which you would prefer to produce them.

CASES

CASE 6.1 HANSON MANUFACTURING COMPANY

In February 1974, Herbert Wessling was appointed general manager by Paul Hanson, president of Hanson Manufacturing Company. Wessling, age 56, had wide executive experience in manufacturing products similar to those of the Hanson Company. The appointment of Wessling resulted from management problems arising from the death of Richard Hanson, founder and—until his death in early 1973—president of the company. Paul Hanson had only four years' experience with the company, and in early 1974 he was 34 years old. His father had hoped to train Paul over a 10-year period, but the father's untimely death had cut this seasoning period short. The younger Hanson became president after his father's death, and he had exercised full control until he hired Wessling.

Paul Hanson knew that he had made several poor decisions during 1973 and that the morale of the organization had suffered, apparently through lack of confidence in him. When he received the income statement for 1973 (Exhibit 1), the loss of over $100,000 during a good business year convinced him that he needed help. He attracted Wessling from a competitor by offering a stock option incentive in addition to salary, knowing that Wessling wanted to acquire financial security for his retirement. The two men came to a clear understanding that Wessling, as general manager, had full authority to execute any changes he desired. In addition, Wessling would explain the reasons for his decisions to Hanson and thereby train him for successful leadership upon Wessling's retirement.

This case was prepared by R. N. Anthony. Copyright © by the President and Fellows of Harvard College. Harvard Business School case 9-156-004.

EXHIBIT 1   Income Statement—Year Ended December 31, 1973

Gross sales		$21,178,810
Cash discounts		313,156
Net sales		20,865,654
Cost of goods sold		13,022,076
Gross margin		7,843,578
Less: Selling expense	$3,676,476	
General administration	1,306,040	
Depreciation	2,716,880	7,699,396
Operating income		144,182
Other income		42,130
Income before interest		186,312
Less: Interest expense		290,166
Income (loss)		$ (103,854)

Hanson Manufacturing Company made only three industrial products—101, 102, and 103. These were sold by the company sales force for use in the processes of other manufacturers. All of the sales force, on a salary basis, sold the three products but in varying proportions. Hanson Co. sold throughout New England and was one of eight companies with similar products. Several of its competitors were larger and manufactured a larger variety of products. The dominant company was Samra Company, which operated a plant in Hanson's market area. Customarily, Samra announced prices annually and the other producers followed suit.

Price cutting was rare; the only variance from quoted selling prices took the form of cash discounts. In the past, attempts at price cutting had followed a consistent pattern: all competitors met the price reduction, and the industry as a whole sold about the same quantity but at the lower prices. This continued until Samra, with its strong financial position, again stabilized the situation following a general recognition of the failure of price cutting. Furthermore, because sales were to industrial buyers and because the products of different manufacturers were very similar, Hanson Co. was convinced it could not individually raise prices without suffering volume declines.

During 1973, Hanson Co.'s share of industry sales was 12% for Product 101, 8% for 102, and 10% for 103. The industrywide quoted selling prices were $4.90, $5.16, and $5.50, respectively.

Upon taking office in February 1974, Wessling decided against immediate major changes; he chose instead to analyze 1973 operations and to wait for the results of the first half of 1974. He instructed the accounting department to provide detailed expenses and earnings statements by products for 1973 (see Exhibit 2). In addition, he requested an explanation of the nature of the costs including their expected future behavior (see Exhibit 3).

To familiarize Paul Hanson with his methods, Wessling sent copies of these exhibits to Hanson and they discussed them. Hanson stated that he thought Product 103 should be dropped immediately, as it would be impossible to lower ex-

EXHIBIT 2 Analysis of Profit and Loss by Product—Year Ended December 31, 1973

	PRODUCT 101		PRODUCT 102		PRODUCT 103		Total
	$ thousands	*$ per cwt.*	*$ thousands*	*$ per cwt.*	*$ thousands*	*$ per cwt.*	*$ thousands*
Rent	376	.1762	314	.3050	374	.3788	1,064
Property taxes	125	.0586	100	.0970	80	.0810	305
Property insurance	104	.0490	80	.0774	105	.1066	289
Compensation insurance	165	.0774	87	.0844	90	.0910	342
Direct labor	2,585	1.2126	1,220	1.1844	1,375	1.3930	5,180
Indirect labor	882	.4136	424	.4116	460	.4660	1,766
Power	45	.0210	50	.0484	60	.0610	155
Light and heat	30	.0140	25	.0246	20	.0204	75
Building service	20	.0094	15	.0150	15	.0150	50
Materials	1,529	.7170	942	.9152	970	.9824	3,441
Supplies	104	.0490	95	.0924	70	.0710	269
Repairs	35	.0166	30	.0290	20	.0206	85
Total	6,001	2.8144	3,382	3.2844	3,639	3.6868	13,022
Selling expense	1,821	.8540	915	.8890	940	.9524	3,676
General administrative	690	.3234	260	.2526	355	.3596	1,306
Depreciation	1,130	.5298	856	.8310	731	.7408	2,717
Interest	104	.0490	80	.0776	105	.1064	290
Total cost	9,745	4.5706	5,493	5.3346	5,770	5.8460	21,011
Less other income	20	.0096	10	.0100	10	.0100	42
	9,725	4.5610	5,482	5.3246	5,760	5.8360	20,969
Sales (net)	10,335	4.8470	5,195	5.0456	5,335	5.4054	20,866
Profit (loss)	610	.2860	(287)	(.2790)	(425)	(.4306)	(103)
Unit sales (cwt.)	2,132,191		1,029,654		986,974		
Quoted selling price	$4.90		$5.16		$5.50		
Cash discounts taken, percent of selling price	1.08%		2.22%		1.72%		

Note: Figures may not add exactly because of rounding.

penses on Product 103 as much as 43 cents per cwt. In addition, he stressed the need for economies on Product 102.

Wessling relied on the authority arrangement Hanson had agreed to earlier and continued production of the three products. For control purposes, he had the accounting department prepare monthly statements using as standard costs the costs per cwt. from the analytical profit and loss statement for 1973 (Exhibit 2). These monthly statements were his basis for making minor marketing and production changes during the spring of 1974. Late in July 1974, Wessling received the six months' statement of cumulative standard costs from the accounting department including variances of actual costs from standard (see Exhibit 4). They showed that the first half of 1974 was a successful period.

During the latter half of 1974 the sales of the entire industry weakened. Even though Hanson Co. retained its share of the market, its profit for the last six months was small. In January 1975, Samra announced a price reduction on Product 101 from $4.90 to $4.50 per cwt. This created an immediate pricing problem for its competitors. Wessling forecast that if Hanson Co. held to the $4.90

EXHIBIT 3   Accounting Department's Commentary on Costs

Direct Labor: Variable. Union shop at going community rates of $3.20/h (including social security taxes). No abnormal demands foreseen. It may be assumed that direct labor dollars is an adequate measure of capacity utilization.

Compensation Insurance: Variable. 5% of direct and indirect labor is an accurate estimate.

Materials: Variable. Exhibit 2 figures are accurate. Includes waste allowances. Purchases are at market prices.

Power: Variable. Rates are fixed. Use varies with activity. Averages per Exhibit 2 are accurate.

Supplies: Variable. Exhibit 2 figures are accurate. Supplies bought at market prices.

Repairs: Variable. Varies as volume changes within normal operation range. Lower and upper limits are fixed.

General Administrative, Selling Expense, Indirect Labor, Interest, and Other Income: These items are almost nonvariable. They can be changed, of course, by management decision.

Cash Discount: Almost nonvariable. Average cash discounts taken are consistent from year to year. Percentages in Exhibit 2 are accurate.

Light and Heat: Almost nonvariable. Heat varies slightly with fuel cost changes. Light a fixed item regardless of level of production.

Property Taxes: Almost nonvariable. Under the lease terms Hanson Company pays the taxes; assessed valuation has been constant; the rate has risen slowly. Any change in the near future will be small and independent of production volume.

Rent: Nonvariable. Lease has 12 years to run.

Building Service: Nonvariable. At normal business level variances are small.

Property Insurance: Nonvariable. Three-year policy with fixed premium.

Depreciation: Nonvariable. Fixed dollar total.

---

price during the first six months of 1975, unit sales would be 750,000 cwt. He felt that if the price were dropped to $4.50 per cwt., the six months' volume would be 1,000,000 cwt. Wessling knew that competing managements anticipated a further decline in activity. He thought a general decline in prices was quite probable.

The accounting department reported that the standard costs in use would probably apply during 1975, with two exceptions: materials and supplies would be about 5% below standard; and light and heat would decline about one-third of 1%.

Wessling and Hanson discussed the pricing problem. Hanson observed that even with the anticipated decline in material and supply costs, a sales price of $4.50 would be below cost. He wanted the $4.90 to be continued, therefore, since he felt the company could not be profitable while selling a key product below cost.

Required

1. If the company had dropped Product 103 as of January 1, 1974, what effect would that action have had on the $160,000 profit for the first six months of 1974?

EXHIBIT 4 Profit and Loss by Product, at Standard, Showing Variations from January 1 to June 30, 1974

Item	PRODUCT 101		PRODUCT 102		PRODUCT 103		Total Standard ($ thousands)	Total Actual ($ thousands)	Variations + = Favorable − = Unfavorable
	Standard per cwt.	Total at Standard	Standard per cwt.	Total at Standard	Standard per cwt.	Total at Standard			
Rent	.1762	176	.3050	217	.3788	190	583	522	+ 61
Property taxes	.0586	58	.0970	69	.0810	41	168	154	+ 14
Property insurance	.0490	49	.0774	55	.1066	53	157	146	+ 11
Compensation insurance	.0774	77	.0844	60	.0910	46	183	184	− 1
Direct labor	1.2126	1,209	1.1844	843	1.3930	698	2,750	2,764	− 14
Indirect labor	.4136	412	.4116	293	.4660	234	939	896	+ 43
Power	.0210	21	.0484	34	.0610	31	86	84	+ 2
Light and heat	.0140	14	.0246	18	.0204	10	42	40	+ 2
Building service	.0094	9	.0150	11	.0150	8	28	20	+ 8
Materials	.7170	715	.9152	652	.9824	492	1,859	1,856	+ 3
Supplies	.0490	49	.0924	66	.0710	36	150	150	—
Repairs	.0166	17	.0290	21	.0206	10	48	50	− 2
Total	2.8144	2,806	3.2844	2,339	3.6868	1,848	6,992	6,866	+126
Selling expense	.8540	851	.8890	633	.9524	477	1,962	1,966	− 4
General administrative	.3234	322	.2526	180	.3596	180	683	656	+ 27
Depreciation	.5298	528	.8310	592	.7408	371	1,491	1,362	+129
Interest	.0490	49	.0776	55	.1064	53	157	146	+ 11
Total cost	4.5706	4,556	5.3346	3,799	5.8460	2,930	11,285	10,996	+289
Less other income	.0096	10	.0100	7	.0100	5	22	22	—
	4.5610	4,547	5.3246	3,792	5.8360	2,925	11,264	10,974	+290
Actual sales (net)	4.8470	4,832	5.0456	3,593	5.4054	2,710	11,134	11,134	+289
Profit or loss	.2860	285	(.2790)	(199)	(.4306)	(216)	(129)	160	+289
Unit sales (cwt.)	996,859		712,102		501,276				

Note: Some numbers in these columns may appear to be ±1 on error; this occurs due to rounding.

175

2. In January 1975, should the company have reduced the price of Product 101 from $4.90 to $4.50?

3. What is Hanson's most profitable product?

4. What appears to have caused the return to profitable operations in the first six months of 1974?

CASE 6.2   ATHERTON COMPANY

Early in January 1975, the sales manager and the controller of the Atherton Company met to prepare a joint pricing recommendation for Item 345. After the president approved their recommendation, the price would be announced in letters to retail customers. In accordance with company and industry practice, announced prices were adhered to for the year unless radical changes in market conditions occurred.

The Atherton Company was the largest in its segment of the textile industry; its 1974 sales had exceeded $12 million. Company salespersons were on a straight salary basis, and each salesperson sold the full line. Most of Atherton's competitors were small; they usually waited for the Atherton Company to announce prices before mailing out their own price lists.

Item 345, an expensive yet competitive fabric, was the sole product of a department whose facilities could not be utilized for other items in the product line. In January 1973, the Atherton Company raised its price from $3 to $4 a yard. This had been done to bring the profit per yard on Item 345 up to that of other products in that line. Although the company was in a strong position financially, it would require considerable capital in the next few years to finance a recently approved long-term modernization and expansion program. The 1973 pricing decision had been one of several changes advocated by the directors in an attempt to strengthen the company's working capital position, thus insuring that adequate funds would be available for this program.

Competitors of the Atherton Company had held their prices on products similar to Item 345 at $3 during 1973 and 1974. The industry and Atherton Company volumes for Item 345 for the years 1969–1974, as estimated by the sales manager, are shown in Exhibit 1. As shown by this exhibit, the Atherton Company had lost a significant portion of its former market position. In the sales manager's opinion, a reasonable forecast of industry volume for 1975 was 700,000 yards. He was certain that the company could sell 25% of the 1975 industry total if it adopted the $3 price. He feared a further volume decline if it did not meet the competitive price. Since many consumers were convinced of the

---

This case was prepared by R. N. Anthony. Copyright © by the President and Fellows of Harvard College. Harvard Business School case 9-156-002.

EXHIBIT 1 Item 345, Prices and Production, 1969–1974

	PRODUCTION VOLUME (IN YARDS)		PRICE PER YARD	
YEAR	*Industry Total*	*Atherton*	*Most Competitors*	*Atherton*
1969	610,000	213,000	$4.00	$4.00
1970	575,000	200,000	4.00	4.00
1971	430,000	150,000	3.00	3.00
1972	475,000	165,000	3.00	3.00
1973	500,000	150,000	3.00	4.00
1974	625,000	125,000	3.00	4.00

Atherton product's superiority, the sales manager reasoned that sales of Item 345 would probably not fall below 75,000 yards, even at a $4 price.

During the pricing dicussions, the controller and sales manager considered two other aspects of the problem. The controller was concerned about the possibility that competitors would reduce their prices below $3 if the Atherton Company announced a $3 price for Item 345. The sales manager was confident that competitors would not go below $3 because they all had higher costs to cover, and several of them were in tight financial straits. He believed that action taken on Item 345 would not have any substantial repercussions on other items in the line.

The controller prepared estimated costs of Item 345 at various volumes of production (see Exhibit 2). These estimated costs reflected current labor and material costs. They were based on past experience, except for the estimates of 75,000 and 100,000 yards. The company had produced more than 100,000 yards

EXHIBIT 2 Estimated Cost per Yard of Item 345 at Various Production Volumes

	75,000[a]	100,000	125,000	150,000	175,000	200,000
Direct labor	$ .800	$ .780	$ .760	$ .740	$ .760	$ .800
Material	.400	.400	.400	.400	.400	.400
Material spoilage	.040	.040	.038	.038	.038	.040
Department expense						
Direct[b]	.120	.112	.100	.100	.100	.100
Indirect[c]	.800	.600	.480	.400	.343	.300
General overhead[d]	.240	.234	.228	.222	.228	.240
Factory cost	2.400	2.166	2.006	1.900	1.869	1.880
Selling & administrative expense[e]	1.560	1.408	1.304	1.236	1.215	1.222
Total Cost	$3.960	$3.574	$3.310	$3.136	$3.084	$3.102

[a]Production volume in yards.

[b]Indirect labor, supplies, repairs, power, and so forth.

[c]Depreciation, supervision, and so forth.

[d]30% of direct labor.

[e]65% of factory cost.

in each of the last 10 years, and earlier experience was not applicable because of equipment changes and increases in labor productivity

Required

1. Should $3 or $4 have been the recommended price? (Assume no intermediate prices are being considered.)

2. How, if at all, did the company's financial condition relate to the pricing decision?

3. If you were the manager of the department that produced Item 345, would it be to your economic advantage to reduce the price to $3.00?

CASE 6.3   INDUSTRIAL GRINDERS N.V.

In late May, 1984, Mr. Bridgeman, the general manager of the German plant of Industrial Grinders (I.G.), N.V., was considering what he should do at a meeting he was to attend that afternoon with his sales manager, accountant, and development engineer. The meeting was to discuss the introduction by Henri Poulenc, a French competitor, of a plastic ring to take the place of a steel ring presently used in certain machines sold by the company. The new ring, which had been put on the market recently, not only had a much longer life than the I.G. steel ring but also apparently had a much lower cost. Mr. Bridgeman's problem stemmed from the fact that I.G. had a large quantity of the steel rings on hand and had a substantial inventory of special steel for their manufacture. After a thorough survey, he had found that the special steel could not be sold even for scrap. The total book value of these inventories was in excess of $93,000.

For nearly 70 years Industrial Grinders had manufactured industrial machines, which it sold in a number of countries. The particular machine involved in Mr. Bridgeman's decision was made only at the German plant situated in Cologne, which employed several thousand people. The different models were priced between $4,500 and $6,820 and were sold by a separate sales organization. Parts which in total accounted for a substantial part of the company's business were sold separately. As in the case of the steel rings, these parts could often also be used on similar machines manufactured by competitors. The company's head office was in Holland. In general the separate plants were allowed considerable leeway in administering their own affairs. However, the executives in Holland could be approached easily for advice either by correspondence and telephone or during their visits to the individual plants.

In recent years, competition had become fairly strong. Japanese manufac-

This case was prepared by M. E. Barrett. Copyright © by the President and Fellows of Harvard University. Harvard Business School case 9-175-246.

turers had had more than a little success in entering the field with low-priced spare parts. Other comanies had appeared with lower-quality and lower-priced machines. There was little doubt but that in the future, competition would become more intense.

The steel ring manufactured by I.G. had a normal life of about two months, depending upon the extent to which the machine was used. A worn-out ring could be replaced in a few seconds and, although different models of the machine required from two to six rings, the rings were usually replaced individually as they wore out.

The sales manager, Mr. Greiner, had learned of the new plastic ring shortly after its appearance and had immediately asked when I.G. would be able to supply them, particularly for sale to customers in France where Henri Poulenc was providing the strongest competition faced by Industrial Grinders. Mr. Ericsson, the development engineer, estimated that the plastic rings could be produced by mid-September. The additional tools and equipment necessary could be obtained for about $1,800. At this point Mr. Ericsson had raised the question about the investment in steel ring inventories which would not be used up by September. Mr. Greiner said that if the new ring could be produced at a substantially lower cost than the steel ones, the inventory problem was irrelevant. It should be sold for whatever could be obtained or even thrown away if it could not be sold. However, the size of the inventory caused Mr. Bridgeman to question this suggestion. He recalled that the size of the inventory was the result of having to order the higher specialized steel in large amounts in order to find a mill willing to handle the order.

Mr. Greiner emphasized that as Henri Poulenc was said to be selling the plastic ring at about the same price as the I.G. steel ring, and as the cost of the former would be much less than the latter, the company was refusing profits as well. Finally, it was decided that the company should prepare to manufacture the new ring as soon as possible but that they would only be sold in those markets where they were offered by competitors until the inventories of the old model and the steel were exhausted. No one expected that the new rings would be produced by any company other than Henri Poulenc for some time. This meant that no more than 10% of the company's markets would be affected.

Shortly after this, Mr. Van Boetzalaer of the parent company in Holland visited Cologne. During a review of company problems the plastic ring case was discussed. Although the ring was a small part of the finished machines, Mr. Van Boetzalaer was interested in the problem because the company wanted to establish policies for the production and pricing of all such parts which, in total, amounted to a substantial portion of I.G.'s revenues. Mr. Van Boetzalaer agreed that the company should proceed with plans for its production and try to find some other use for the steel. He then said, "If this does not seem possible, I would, of course, expect you to use this material and produce the steel rings."

Within a few days after Mr. Van Boetzalaer's visit, both Mr. Ericsson and Mr.

Greiner came in to see Mr. Bridgeman. The former came because he felt that the plastic ring would completely destroy demand for the steel ring as tests had indicated that it had at least four times the wearing properties. However, because he understood that the price of the competitive ring was very high (perhaps even higher than the I.G. steel ring) he felt that the decision to sell the plastic ring only in the market areas where difficulties existed was a good one. "In this way we would probably be able to continue supplying the steel ring until stocks at least of processed parts were used up."

Mr. Greiner, the sales manager, was still strongly against selling any steel rings after the new ones became available. If steel rings were sold in some areas while plastic rings were being sold elsewhere, customers in the former would eventually find out. The result would affect the sale of machines, the selling price of which was many times that of the rings. He produced figures to show that if the selling price of both rings remained at $320.40 per hundred, the additional profit from the plastic rings, which would cost $66.60 per hundred as contrasted with $263.85 per hundred for the steel, would more than cover the "so-called" investment in the steel inventory within less than a year at present volume levels. Mr. Bridgeman refused to change his decision of the previous meeting but agreed to have another discussion within a week.

In anticipation of the meeting and also having in mind Mr. Van Boetzalaer's concern, Mr. Bridgeman obtained the following data from the cost department on the cost of plastic and steel rings:

	PLASTIC RINGS	*STEEL RINGS*
Material	$ 4.20	$ 76.65
Direct labor	15.60	46.80
Overhead[a]		
Departmental	31.20	93.60
Administrative	15.60	46.80
Total (per 100 rings)	$66.60	$263.85

[a]Overhead was allocated on the basis of direct labor dollars. It was estimated that the variable overhead costs included in this summary were largely fringe benefits related to direct labor and amounted to about 40% of the departmental amounts.

Mr. Bridgeman also learned that the inventory of special steel had cost $26,400. This steel consisted of a large-enough quantity to produce approximately 34,500 rings. Assuming that sales continued at the current rate of 690 rings per week, some 15,100 finished rings would be left on hand by mid-September without any further production taking place. It then occurred to him that during the next two or three months the plant would not be operating at capacity. The company had a policy of employing its excess labor during slack periods at about 70% of regular wages on various make-work projects rather than laying the men off. He wondered if it would be a good idea to convert the steel inventory into rings during this period and use some of this labor productively.

Required

What action should Mr. Bridgeman take? Why?

CASE 6.4   ROANOKE STAMPING PLANT

The Roanoke Stamping Plant, completed in the late summer of 1985, was one of the largest and most modern stamping plants in the United States. It began producing parts for Excelsior's 1986 model cars in the autumn of 1985. It had ten major stamping lines and fifteen minor ones.

A stamping line consisted of a series of presses. The first press cut sheets of metal to the desired size. Each subsequent press performed bending, punching, or shaping operations. After the metal was passed through the last press in the line, it was bonderized and shipped to the different Excelsior assembly plants.

The major lines were used to produce the stampings where the volume was sufficiently large to keep the line operating continuously for the entire model year. Major lines produced such items as body sides, fenders, deck lids, floor panels, and so forth. The major lines contained a great deal of automatic handling equipment, such as air ejection and iron hands. The minor lines were used to produce lower volume parts such as past model service parts, convertible body sides, and so forth. Minor lines would be set up for each run which could last from an hour or two to several days depending on the size of the run. The minor lines contained much less automation and the metal was generally placed in the press and removed by hand.

The cutting, shaping, bending, and punching operations were accomplished by exerting great pressure on a piece of steel which was placed in a pair of dies. Depending on the size of the part and the complexity of the operation, these dies varied in size from a few pounds to hundreds of pounds. The dies were all carefully made to Excelsior's specifications and were manufactured from hard tool steel. Every time a part changed, new dies were required. Since the automobile companies change models frequently, every year hundreds of new dies were made or purchased.

The Toolroom

The Roanoke Stamping Plant had a large toolroom capable of producing smaller dies and many of the other tools and specially designed jigs and fixtures required by the extensive production equipment used in the plant. In the early

---

This case was prepared by John Dearden. Copyright © by the President and Fellows of Harvard University. Harvard Business School case 9-113-071.

part of 1986, the toolroom was operating at considerably less than capacity and this was a source of concern to the plant manager.

The Make-or-Buy Conference

In February 1986, Mr John Secrest, the plant manager, called a meeting to discuss what should be done about the toolroom. Attending the meeting were Smith, the Controller, Harding, the Manager of Purchasing, and Walker, the Toolroom Manager.

Following is an edited version of the meeting.

SECREST: It seems to me we have to develop a policy for deciding what tools and dies we should make ourselves and which ones we should buy. At the present time, we are making decisions by the seat of our pants and, as a result, we have a lot of excess capacity in the toolroom.

HARDING: It seems to me that we should make those tools and dies on which we can make an adequate profit, say 10% over cost. If the purchase price of a die or tool is less than our cost plus 10%, we should buy it. Otherwise, we should make it, if we have capacity.

WALKER: Wait a minute. If I had to meet the overhead costs in this plant, I'd never make anything. The independent die makers don't have the overhead that we have. They don't have our training program, company newspapers, engineers, and accountants. Also, their pay scales are considerably less than ours. As a result, they can outbid me every time. I think we should make any tool or die as long as my variable costs are less than the purchase price.

SMITH: I can't agree with that position. Walker, you can't hire and fire these tool and die makers. They are too hard to get. Consequently, *all* of your costs, except material, are fixed. If we follow your policy, we would decide all make-or-buy decisions in favor of making. We could fill the toolroom with parts on which we would be losing our shirts. It seems to me that we should produce nothing unless our total costs are less than the purchase price.

SECREST: I would be a little worried about Walker's suggestion too. How do we know that we are making the most profitable items? Also, what do we do when the toolroom reaches capacity? Do we just fill the toolroom with everything until we use up its capacity and then buy everything else? If we did this, the decision as to whether we should make or buy an item would depend on the timing of the purchase order. Today we have capacity, so we make it; tomorrow, our capacity is committed, so we buy it. How do we know that today's part isn't a lot more profitable than yesterday's? Also, it seems to me that there should be a different policy when we have a lot of excess capacity than when we are close to full capacity operations.

HARDING: I certainly disagree with Walker. I have to keep our vendors reasonably happy; otherwise, we'll be in trouble when we need them. I don't see how we can expect to have them compete against Walker, if he gets to produce everything that sells for more than his material costs.

SECREST: We aren't getting anywhere here. We need to utilize our toolroom capacity. We need to produce the parts that earn us the most money. Smith, why don't you come up with a proposed policy that will meet these two objectives and we'll discuss it again next week.

Required

Recommend a make-or-buy policy for the Roanoke Stamping Plant. In this recommendation, be sure to include the following:

(a) The policy to be followed where excess capacity exists in the toolroom.

(b) The policy to be followed when there is no excess capacity.

(c) A workable definition of capacity—that is to say, if the policies for (a) and (b) are different, how can the Manager of Purchasing know whether capacity exists or not?

(d) Details as to what should be included in costs if the policy includes the use of cost data.

(e) An explantion telling why your policy will not result in filling the toolroom with unprofitable parts.

chapter 7

DECISION SUPPORT SYSTEMS: DISINVESTMENT DECISIONS

Chapter 6 described the decision support systems required to help managers make tactical marketing decisions. Managers also need to know the total amount of net resources either generated or used by each product. Note that contribution over variable costs will not provide this information because there are many non-variable costs that are required to produce and sell a product. Sometimes, therefore, a product earning a large contribution over the short run may in the long run be using more resources than it is generating. Consequently, we need a system that will, on a systematic basis, provide managers with the resources generated and used in producing current products. This is called *product profitability analysis*.

Product profitability analysis has two principal uses for managers. First, it is a means of identifying segments of the business that require attention. Second, it is used in profit budgeting and financial planning. This chapter is concerned with decision-support systems that identify problem areas within a business, with particular emphasis on identifying products that should be discontinued.

IDENTIFICATION OF PROBLEM AREAS

The profitability of a business is the weighted average of the profits of all segments. These segments or subsegments can vary widely with respect to profitability, and so, even when a business is profitable, there may be areas of low or nonexisting profitability. Subsegments will vary in profitability and a profitable segment is no guarantee that everything is satisfactory. For this reason, it is important that profitability be calculated for the lowest level of operations where meaningful profit information can be calculated.

There are two steps in product profitability analysis. First, there must be a cost acounting system that calculates product profitability on a systematic basis. Second, there must be a procedure for taking action where products earn unsatisfactory profits. These correspond to the two steps required by all cost accounting decision-support systems: diagnosis and forecasting.

Measuring Product Profitability

Managers need to know the extent to which individual products are generating or using resources. Ideally, managers would be supplied with a list of products ranked in order of their net resource usage. Those with the greatest excess of resources used over resources supplied would be given the most immediate attention.

Resources Used.   As with tactical marketing decisions, we need a method for calculating the profitability (resources generated minus resources used) that can be applied to all products on a systematic basis. The result is the product ranking just described.

Since the measurement of resources generated (revenue) is usually quite straightforward, the problem in profitability analysis is to identify the resources used by each product. This requires a definition of resources used, such as the following: *Resources used are all costs that would have been saved had the product not been produced.* In short, they are the costs that could have been *avoided* had the product not been produced.

We therefore require a means for calculating avoidable costs on a systematic basis. Avoidable costs, however, will differ among different products and in different circumstances. For example, there may be limited capacity for producing one product and excess capacity for producing another. Or, there may be excess capacity at one time and a capacity shortage at another time. Consequently, we need a surrogate that best approximates avoidable costs. This surrogate is *unique* cost.

Unique Costs.   Unique costs are costs that can be uniquely identified with particular products. In principle, if a cost can be identified with a particular product, this cost can be avoided if the product is not produced. By definition, all variable costs are unique. The problem, then, is to identify those nonvariable costs that were incurred specifically for particular products. All other nonvariable costs are called *joint costs*, because they are incurred for a group of products; these costs are unaffected if one of the products in the group is discontinued. Joint costs are irrelevant to product profitability analysis for the same reason that fixed costs are irrelevant to tactical marketing decisions.

The problems of identifying unique costs can be separated into two parts: manufacturing costs and period costs.

MANUFACTURING COSTS.   There are two areas in manufacturing that present problems in separating unique costs from joint costs. First, there is the question of how physical facilities would be affected if the product using these facilities were not produced. Would these facilities have been used to produce other products, or would they have remained idle? The second problem occurs with respect to general factory administration and occupancy costs. To what extent could they have been avoided if a particular product had not been produced? One way to consider a manufacturing facility is that it is a finite amount of available capacity. Any product produced by a manufacturing facility uses a portion of that capacity and should be charged for that use. This charge would be in the nature of an *opportunity* cost. That is, if a particular product had not been produced, capacity would be available for other products. Thus it could be argued that every product should be charged with its share of the full manufacturing costs as representative of its share of the capacity that has been used to produce it. Under this concept, it is unnecessary to distinguish between unique and joint costs in a manufacturing facility.

The following reasons support this viewpoint:

1. In most instances available capacity has alternative uses. Most companies discontinue the production of many products during a typical year. Yet this, in itself, does not appear to create excess capacity. New products use the available capacity.
2. Under normal circumstances, the revenue from a product should be able to cover full manufacturing costs. If it cannot cover these costs, there is considerable question about its economic viability.
3. Full manufacturing costs are calculated on a systematic basis by all good cost accounting systems. Consequently, this information should be readily available.
4. This is the first of two steps in the product profitability analysis process. Before a product is dropped, consideration will be given to other factors such as the alternative uses of the capacity that would be made available.

Manufacturing costs normally account for a significant percentage of the total costs of a product. If the cost accounting system is not identifying product cost accurately, the entire product profitability analysis procedure will be supplying misleading information to managers. The usefulness of the entire cost accounting decision-support information system rests on the quality of the man-ufacturing cost accounting system.

PERIOD COSTS.   It is necessary to analyze the distribution, warehousing, marketing, and administration costs to determine which cost classification can be identified with specific products. A system is then developed to allocate these costs to the appropriate products. The following points should be considered in doing this:

1. The distinction between unique cost and a joint cost does not have to be com-pletely precise. As with the separation of fixed and variable costs, if an item of cost is largely unique, treat the entire cost classification as unique, and vice versa.

2. Warehousing should be treated as entirely unique because, as with manufactur-ing facilities, a warehouse represents available capacity, and products should be charged an opportunity cost for the capacity that they use.

3. Marketing cost incurred before the point of sale may be unique—for example, specific product advertising and sales promotion.

4. A test of whether a cost is unique or not is the ease with which a reasonable way to allocate that cost can be found. A unique cost represents the resources actually used in producing or selling a product. It should be practical, therefore, to measure the amount of these resources used. If you cannot do this, it is prob-ably a joint cost.

5. Product profitability analysis normally is done only once a year. It may be done more frequently for a limited number of products. (This is in contrast to vari-able costs, which are normally calculated and published monthly.)

Summary.   To summarize, product profitability analysis is designed to provide managers with the long-run profitability of each product. The long-run profitabil-ity is the difference between the resources generated and the resources used to produce and sell the product. The resources used are the opportunity costs of using manufacturing capacity plus the unique period costs. Unique costs are sur-rogates for those costs that would not have been incurred had the product not been produced. All period costs that are not unique are joint. A joint cost has no economic significance in calculating resources used and, consequently, is irrel-evant to product profitability analysis.

SCREENING AND ACTION

The second step in product profitability analysis is to develop procedures for processing the information and taking appropriate action. There are two steps in this procedure. First, a minimum standard must be set, below which the prod-uct is evaluated further. (This is called a *screen*.) Second, a procedure for evaluat-ing and acting on products with substandard profitability must be instituted. Each of these steps is discussed in this part of the chapter.

Screening

There are several methods of establishing the *minimum standard*, or *screen*. Some companies use a minimum monetary amount of profit. Other companies use a minimum rate of return on investment. There are problems with both of these measures. An absolute minimum profit does not take into account the size of the investment required to support a product. A specific level of profit could be minuscule for some products and large for other products with a smaller investment. Return on investment does take into account the size of the investment. It does not, however, take into account the size and importance of the product being measured. A high rate of return could be earned by a product of little importance, and vice versa. Neither system seems to be effective in ranking products properly.

Management needs a procedure that ranks products proportionately to the net amount of resources used. Ranking products according to the amount of profit or loss may be one system. However, this system does not take into account the resources tied up in producing and selling a product. For example, if a product were discontinued, an amount of working capital would be released and manufacturing capacity would be made available and these should be considered in the ranking process.

The most satisfactory way to rank products is to subtract from the profit (revenue minus unique costs) an implicit interest charge for the working capital and facilities being used. This method measures the entire resources that have been devoted to a product. A product with a heavy investment in resources that earns a small profit may be a more serious problem than a product that is losing money but does not tie up significant amounts of investment. This method also provides a standard for screening products experiencing problems. Any product that has a negative amount after subtracting an implicit interest charge may be assumed to be using more resources than it is generating and is, therefore, an appropriate product for further evaluation.

The question arises as to what implicit interest rate should be used. The long-term borrowing rate seems most appropriate, but other rates may be equally satisfactory. The important point is that some charge be made for the investment in working capital and facilities.

Evaluation and Action. At this point, we have an accounting system that provides management with a list of products that have used more resources in the past 12 months than they have generated, ranked according to the size of this deficit. Some method must be developed to evaluate this information and take appropriate action on specific products. Clearly, this is a management problem, not an accounting problem. Consequently, procedures that some companies have used successfully are simply outlined. There are two appropriate observations, however. First, if arrangements are not made to take appropriate action, the entire product profitability analysis is a fruitless exercise. Second, there are few activities more important in the typical manufacturing company than a systematic approach to product profitability. Without such an approach, it is almost certain that products are being carried and will continue to be carried that are draining resources from the company.

One method of evaluation and action is to assign a team to analyze unprofitable products and make appropriate recommendations. (This is similar to the process of *value analysis* that was so popular a few years ago.) For example, the team might consist of representatives from manufacturing, marketing, product development, and accounting. Each product is evaluated to see what steps, if any, could be taken to improve the profitability. These might include raising prices, lowering costs, increasing volume, or changing design. If nothing of this nature can be done, the next step is to see what the effect of dropping the product would be by estimating the amount of costs (i.e., the differential costs) that would be saved if the product were dropped. If there were a large amount of excess capacity, if the product were necessary for some non-economic reason, or if it were a new product, the decision might be to leave the product in the line. Otherwise, the recommendation would be to discontinue the product.

Note that the decision to keep a product is a temporary decision, since it can be reversed at any time. However, the decision to drop a product is a permanent decision, since its reversal may be difficult and expensive. If there is doubt, therefore, about the economic desirability of dropping a product, it may be prudent to leave it in the product line, with appropriate follow-up procedure. However, all products have a finite economic life. It is as costly to drop them too late as too soon. One of the principal purposes of product profitability analysis is to help management make that decision at the right time. Inflation has made this type of decision even more imperative than it has been in the past.

DIFFERENCES BETWEEN VARIABLE COSTS AND UNIQUE COSTS

First, *variable costs* are used for tactical marketing decisions. *Unique costs* are used to identify net resource users. If variable costs are used for product profitability analysis or unique costs are used for tactical marketing decisions, management will almost certainly be misled.

Second, the principal use of unique costs is to identify unprofitable products. Variable costs are not usually satisfactory for the purpose because revenues will normally exceed variable costs.

Third, unique costs are used as a first step in product profitability analysis. Specific action is taken on the basis of a second evaluation of the costs that are relevant to the particular decision being made, whereas variable costs are used by managers as a basis for taking specific actions.

Fourth, variable costs are calculated monthly and often include forecasted amounts, particularly for material costs. Unique costs are normally calculated annually and are based on the costs that were actually incurred.

Note that unique costs are used to decide whether or not to keep a product. Once the decision is made to keep it, tactical marketing decisions concerning this product are made on the basis of variable costs.

JOINT COSTS

As described earlier, joint costs are those costs that do not change if a product is discontinued. There are several points about joints costs to consider.

First, which costs are joint and which costs are unique changes as the business segment being analyzed becomes smaller. For example, all the costs incurred by a company are unique. If divisional performance is being analyzed, all the divisional costs are unique but most of the headquarter costs are joint. If plant performance is being analyzed, most divisional costs are joint but all the plant costs are unique. Within a plant, the larger the product line, the more plant costs that are unique to that product line. (However, for reasons stated earlier, *all* plant costs should be treated as unique.) The implication of this situation is that it is often better to consider a number of products together when making disinvestment decisions.

Second, an argument for including joint costs in product profitability analysis is that they must be covered somehow. To omit them is to understate costs. Although joint costs must be covered, they need not be covered proportionally by all products. Some will cover more joint costs than others. Unique costs, however, are the only economic reality, and to include joint costs in the product profitability analyses will only result in misstating the amount of net resources either provided or used.

There is only one instance where joint costs should be allocated to a product, and there is one instance where they should be allocated to a larger segment. If a company is working on a cost-plus-fixed-fee type of contract, joint costs must be assigned to that contract because the costs are legitimate costs of doing business for which the buyer should be expected to pay. The second exception occurs where a company wishes to compare the profitability of a segment of the business (such as a division) with the profitability of outside companies. Outside companies incur headquarter costs, and a portion of the company's headquarter costs, therefore, should be charged to the division to make the profits comparable with the outside companies.

INFLATION

Product profitability analysis and appropriate action with respect to unprofitable products are even more important in countries experiencing significant inflation (10% or more a year) than in countries with more stable price levels. Consider the following.

First, the high cost of money in inflationary economies makes it important that products creating a financial drain be identified accurately and that corrective action be taken quickly. Second, the availability of funds in an inflationary economy, rather than manufacturing capacity, may be the limiting factor in the ability to produce and sell. Consequently, there may no longer be the luxury of maintaining product lines simply because they earn a contribution. It may be necessary to eliminate profitable products simply because there are more profitable products that require the available funds. It is vital, therefore, that profitability studies differentiate between degrees of profitability—in particular, those products generating the greatest amounts of resources.

Third, it is important that both depreciation and cost of sales be calculated at replacement costs and that the implicit interest charges be made on the basis of the replacement cost of fixed assets and inventories. Historical costs, under high inflation, simply do not identify accurately the degree that resources are being used. Since inflation affects different products differently, a ranking based on historical costs could be misleading.

Incidentally, there are several companies in Europe that use replacement costs for internal accounting purposes. (Phillips has done this for years.) There appear to be no insurmountable problems in doing this. In fact, once an internal replacement cost system has been installed, it seems to present no special problems.

SUMMARY

It is important to keep in mind that this chapter described a two-step procedure. The first is the calculation of profitability for a period of time in the past. This would be included in Square I of the Accounting and Control Matrix. As with all information included in Square I, these calculations are made in accordance with accounting principles and practices and are intended to measure past economic events. The second step is to decide what to do about products generating insufficient profits. It is included in Square II and, like all calculations in Square II, it involves differential cash flow.

It is important to understand this two-step procedure because a great deal of the confusion about cost accounting is caused by confusion over these two types of information. For example, some economists appear to believe that traditional product cost information is useless, if not misleading, because it does not approximate marginal costs, which provide the information managers need to make forward decisions.

Traditional product costs are used to diagnose potentially undesirable situations. Managerial action is based on a study of the effect on differential costs of making a particular decision, such as discontinuing a product. Both steps are necessary. If a manager looked only at the contribution of each product independently, almost no product would ever be discontinued. A product is in very poor economic condition if the potential selling price is less than the variable costs.

Not only is it necessary to look at long-run cost savings for discontinuing a product, but such an evaluation should consider discontinuing a number of unprofitable products or product lines. In other words, it is necessary not to look at each unprofitable product separately. Although the differential costs might be relatively small for each product individually, they might be considerably greater for a number of products taken together. For example, it might be practical to close an entire plant, thus saving almost all the manufacturing costs.

QUESTIONS

7.1 Explain the difference between variable costs, differential costs, and marginal costs.

7.2 Can you think of some period costs other than those stated in the text that would normally be unique?

7.3 Exactly what is a screen for identifying products that need attention? Can you think of measures other than the three described in the text for implementing such a screen?

7.4 Give examples where contribution alone would not be useful in identifying products that need attention. Can you think of types of manufacturing plants where contribution would be sufficient?

7.5 What are some typical joint costs that might occur in a typical manufacturing company?

PROBLEMS

Exhibit 1 provides financial information on five products manufactured by the XYZ Company.

7.1 Rank each product on the following bases:
- **(a)** Unit contribution
- **(b)** Total contribution
- **(c)** Revenue over unique costs
- **(d)** Revenue over total costs
- **(e)** Return on contribution (contribution divided by total investment)
- **(f)** Return on revenue over unique costs
- **(g)** Return on investment
- **(h)** Net resources earned (use a 10% rate of return as the cost of money)

7.2 Which product do you consider to be the most profitable? Which product do you consider to be the least profitable?

7.3 Which products do you think should be analyzed further to see if they should be discontinued?

7.4 Which of the criteria used in 7.1, should be used as a screen for disinvestment analysis? Why? At what level would you establish this screen?

EXHIBIT 1 XYZ Company

	A	*B*	*C*	*D*	*E*
Volume	10,000	20,000	500	1,000	5,000
Unit Information					
Price	$1.00	$2.00	$1.00	$2.00	$1.00
Variable manufacturing cost	0.50	0.75	0.30	1.50	0.50
Variable period cost	0.05	0.10	0.04	0.15	0.10
Total Information					
Nonvariable manufacturing cost	$ 1,000	$ 5,000	$100	$200	$ 5,000
Nonvariable unique cost	500	2,000	100	100	2,000
Joint period cost[a]	500	2,000	25	100	250
Working capital	10,000	30,000	400	400	500
Property, plant and equipment	15,000	75,000	400	40	10,000
	$25,000	$105,000	$800	$440	$10,500

[a]Allocated to product at 5% of total revenue.

CASES

CASE 7.1   SHAW CONFECTIONERS, LTD.

A year after the adoption in 1986 of the so-called direct costing method of accounting by Shaw Confectioners, Ltd., its accounting director, Mr. Butterworth, was in general satisfied with the way the system was working out. He was convinced that the new accounting system, by providing useful information needed for overall profit planning and control, had helped 'he management greatly in its effort to pull the company out of the recent period of approximately level annual sales and low or nonexistent profits.

Introduction of Direct Costing

Shaw Confectioners, Ltd., was a long-established medium-sized manufacturer of candy products. It was located in Shaw, a small town about 12 miles from Manchester, England. In 1985, a new management team was organized to revitalize the company under the leadership of Mr. Smyth, the newly elected chairman and managing director. Mr. Butterworth was brought in as a member of this team. He recognized immediately the inadequacy and even misleading nature of the existing accounting system. In his opinion, any accounting system ought to serve at least three purposes: (1) to facilitate cost control, (2) to supply management with quantitative data timely and relevant for intelligent profit planning, and (3) to produce reports to stockholders, government, and other outside agencies. The old Shaw Confectioners' system had done reasonable justice

This case was prepared by John Dearden. Copyright © by the President and Fellows of Harvard College. Harvard Business School case 9-180-163.

only to the third. In order to serve the other two purposes effectively, he believed, the whole accounting system had to be reorganized around the concept of direct costing. With encouragement from Mr. Jones, deputy managing director, and upon approval by Mr. Larson, treasurer, Mr. Butterworth put the new system into effect in the summer of 1986. The following sections of the case are based on his explanation of the procedures and his appraisal as to how the system met the needs of management.

Direct Costing Procedure

Direct costing is a method of recording and reporting cost data which distinguishes between "period" and "direct" elements of cost. Period costs are those costs which tend to remain constant over a given period of time independent of fluctuations in production or sales volume within the period. Insurance, depreciation, administrative expenses, factory supervisory salaries, and property taxes are of this nature. Direct costs, on the other hand, are those costs which tend to increase or decrease as production or sales volume moves up or down. Costs of raw materials, operating labor, certain factory overhead, and sales commissions vary directly with volume and belong to this category.

Under the new procedure of direct costing, Shaw Confectioners classified all its costs and expense items into these two categories, as they were initially collected for various cost centers; the segregation was maintained in the preparation of reports for internal control. Products were charged only with direct costs, and all period costs, whether manufacturing or not, were written off in the period incurred. No attempt was made to allocate period costs to products as under the old system, except for the preparation of external reports.

Exhibits 1 and 2 are sample forms of reports prepared for internal purposes under the direct costing system. Exhibit 1, "Product Family Report," showed, in total and for each of the four product families, revenue, direct costs, and merchandising contribution or margin which was the difference between them. No period costs appeared on this report. Exhibit 2 showed a consolidated income statement for all products. From the "total merchandising contribution" of all product families, all period costs were deducted to arrive at the net operating income of the company.

Benefit in Cost Control

In Mr. Butterworth's opinion, period costs are the responsibility of top management, while the responsibility for control of direct costs rests at a lower level of management, principally supervisors. Thus, the distinction between period costs and direct costs corresponded closely to that between "controllable" and "noncontrollable" cost, which was essential for effective cost control. Assuming no change in selling price, the amount and percentage of the merchandising contribution for an individual product was a direct indication of efficiency with which the product was manufactured, since changes in merchandising contribu-

EXHIBIT 1 Shaw Confectioners, Ltd.

Product Family Report for June 1987

| | TOTAL | | PRODUCT FAMILIES | | | | | | | |
| | | | A | | B | | C | | D | |
	Amount	%	Amount	%	Amount	%	Amount	%	Amount	%
Gross sales	£1,199,800	100.0	£540,100	100.0	£143,800	100.0	£407,600	100.0	£108,300	100.0
Less allowances										
Freight	84,800	7.0	37,800	7.0	9,900	6.9	29,400	7.2	7,700	7.1
Cash discount	21,400	1.8	10,200	1.9	2,200	1.5	7,400	1.8	1,600	1.5
Returns	5,700	0.5	1,100	0.2	2,200	1.5	2,000	0.5	400	0.4
General	6,900	0.6	3,800	0.7	800	0.6	1,600	0.4	700	0.6
Total allowances	£ 118,800	9.9	£ 52,900	9.8	£ 15,100	10.5	£ 40,400	9.9	£ 10,400	9.6
Net sales	£1,081,000	90.1	£487,200	90.2	£128,700	89.5	£367,200	90.1	£ 97,900	90.4
Less direct cost of sales										
Standard manufacturing costs	£ 706,200	58.9	£308,900	57.2	£ 81,000	56.3	£251,500	61.7	£ 64,800	59.8
Material variances	(5,700)	(0.5)	(4,800)	(0.9)	1,500	(1.1)	(2,000)	(0.5)	(400)	(0.3)
Labor and burden variances	11,000	0.9	3,800	0.7	3,600	2.5	3,600	0.9	—	—
Total direct manufacturing costs	£ 711,500	59.3	£307,900	57.0	£ 86,100	59.9	£253,100	62.1	£ 64,400	59.5
Direct warehouse and shipping costs	7,100	0.6	3,200	0.6	1,300	0.9	2,000	0.5	600	0.5
Direct selling costs	39,200	3.3	18,900	3.5	6,200	4.3	11,000	2.7	3,100	2.9
Total direct costs	£ 757,800	63.2	£330,000	61.1	£ 93,600	65.1	£266,100	65.3	£ 68,100	62.9
Merchandising contribution	£ 323,200	26.9	£157,200	29.1	£ 35,100	24.4	£101,100	24.8	£ 29,800	27.5

EXHIBIT 2   Shaw Confectioners, Ltd.

Consolidated Income Statement for June 1987

ITEM	BUDGET Amount	%	PERFORMANCE Amount	%
Gross Sales	£1,386,000	100.0	£1,199,800	100.0
Less allowances				
Freight	81,800	5.9	84,800	7.0
Cash discount	22,200	1.6	21,400	1.8
Returns	5,500	0.4	5,700	0.5
General	8,300	0.6	6,900	0.6
Total allowances	£ 117,800	8.5	£ 118,800	9.9
Net sales	£1,268,200	91.5	£1,081,000	90.1
Less direct cost of sales				
Standard manufacturing costs	805,300	58.1	706,200	58.9
Material variances	—	—	(5,700)	(0.5)
Labor and burden variances	6,900	0.5	11,000	0.9
Total direct manufacturing costs	£ 812,200	58.6	£ 711,500	59.3
Direct warehouse and shipping costs	12,500	0.9	7,100	0.6
Direct selling costs	43,000	3.1	39,200	3.3
Total direct costs	£ 867,700	62.6	£ 757,800	63.2
Merchandising contribution	400,500	28.9	323,200	26.9
Less period costs				
Manufacturing division	62,000		58,700	
Marketing division	53,600		52,000	
Financial division	27,800		27,100	
Purchasing division	4,100		4,000	
Personnel division	5,300		6,200	
President's office	11,000		10,400	
Advertising	89,300		92,500	
Depreciation	54,700		54,100	
State and local taxes	7,800		6,100	
Interest	5,000		4,400	
Total period costs	£ 320,600	23.1	£ 315,500	26.3
Net Operating Income	£ 79,900	5.8	£ 7,700	0.6
Other Income or (Expense)	600	—	1,800	0.2
Total Net Income	£ 80,500	5.8	£ 9,500	0.8

tion reflected changes in controllable costs. The isolation of period costs in the reports to top management stressed the nature and importance of the "fixity" of these costs and thus facilitated their control. Budgeting was the primary tool for controlling these period costs.

Benefits in Profit Planning

In Mr. Butterworth's opinion, better understanding of the distinctly different behavior of direct and period costs in response to changes in sales and production volume made it easier to prepare reasonably accurate budgets of costs and profits. The analysis of "profit-cost-volume" relationships was no longer obscured or confused by the fluctuating unit-product cost, which was unavoidable under the old absorption-accounting system.

At the time direct costing was introduced, Shaw Confectioners had about 700 individual items in production, grouped into four broad product families. Although management suspected that some items were not profitable enough to justify their continued production, the old accounting reports, which included an arbitrary allocation of fixed costs to products, did not provide a ready basis for deciding which items to drop or, conversely, which items warranted special selling effort because of their attractive margins. The new procedure enabled management to identify a number of low-profit items; consequently, in the first year the line was reduced to 400 items. The practice was that any item with a low merchandising contribution was investigated. "Low" was defined as a merchandising contribution of less than £4,000 per annum and/or less than 25 percent of turnover. Such items were referred to the Product Line Committee, consisting of the deputy managing director, treasurer, production director, marketing director, purchasing director, and accounting director, who decided whether their continued production was warranted. Unless the selling price could be raised without much anticipated sacrifice in sales volume or unless direct costs could be reduced substantially through increased efficiency or changes in raw material composition, there was thought to be little justification for keeping them in the line, except possibly for items that brought some sales benefits to other products in the line.

When considering the addition of a new product, a calculation of its expected merchandising contribution in pounds and percentage gave a starting point for an intelligent decision. Here also the £4,000 or 25 percent merchandising contribution was the minimum requirement.

Theoretically, since any merchandising contribution, however small, represented a contribution to the recovery of period costs, the minimum acceptable selling price for an item was equal to an amount slightly above its direct cost. It could therefore be argued that with such a low minimum, sales people would be tempted to set selling prices too low. Mr. Butterworth thought that this danger was avoided by entrusting the authority for establishing and changing prices to the product line committee. Prices were set only after a careful consideration of all relevant factors, such as cost, demand, competition, customer relations, and so on. In addition, the "£4,000 or 25 percent" minimum rule was a safeguard against setting prices too low.

The "£4,000 or 25 percent" criterion was admittedly somewhat arbitrary. It was considered as furnishing an adequate cushion for any one, or combination, of the following factors:

1. The classification of direct and period costs was not exactly "black and white"; some arbitrary demarcation was unavoidable, particularly in classifying so-called semivariable costs. Conservatism and long-run considerations therefore dictated that, for deciding which items to drop or which items to add, the ac-

ceptable minimum should be adjusted upward from the bare minimum of direct costs.

2. Adding or dropping a product item involved increase or decrease in certain period costs such as promotion and product design and engineering costs. No product could be said to be "on its own feet" until such costs were covered. The "£4,000 or 25 percent" adjusted for this factor.

3. Most important of all, since management-supervision capacity was limited, management's attention was not without an element of opportunity cost. Products unable to meet the requirement were regarded as not deserving of management's attention.

A specific example of how the new accounting aided management was in connection with the establishment of the sales promotion policy for 1987, which was that effort for additional sales be concentrated more on Product Family A than on Product Family C. The logic of the policy was obvious to the management once it concluded that the significant difference between merchandising contributions of the two product families in 1986 would be continued in 1987. Exhibit 3 shows a 29 percent contribution for A and 25 percent for C for the month of June 1980. A pound increase in sales of A would therefore contribute four pence more to the recovery of period costs than would the same increase in the sales of C.

External Reporting

The new system did not apply to external reports. For reports to stockholders, tax authorities and other governmental agencies, inventory values were adjusted to include fixed manufacturing costs. As a matter of fact, the board of directors periodically received from the treasurer a condensed income statement in the form of Exhibit 4, which showed this inventory adjustment and the net income calculated under the conventional system of absorption accounting.

EXHIBIT 3 Shaw Confectioners, Ltd.

Summary of Sales and Contributions by Product Families for June 1987

PRODUCT FAMILY	POUND SALES	PERCENT OF TOTAL	MERCHANDISING MARGIN (£)	MERCHANDISING MARGIN (%)
A	£ 540,100	45.0%	£157,200	29.1%
B	143,800	12.0	35,100	24.4
C	407,600	34.0	101,100	24.8
D	108,300	9.0	29,800	27.5
Total	£1,199,800	100.0	323,200	26.9

EXHIBIT 4   Shaw Confectioners, Ltd.

Condensed Income Statement for June 1987

Gross Sales	£1,199,800	100.0%
Less allowances	118,800	9.9
Net sales	£1,081,000	90.1
Less direct cost of sales	757,800	63.2
Merchandising contribution	£ 323,200	26.9
Less period costs	315,500	26.3
Net operating income	£ 7,700	0.6
Other income or (expense)	1,800	0.2
Net income — direct cost basis	£ 9,500	0.8
Inventory adjustment to absorption costing basis	2,000	
Net income before taxes	£ 7,500	
Provision for taxes	4,100	
Net income after taxes	£ 3,400	—

Summary of Controller's Appraisal

Pleased as he was with Shaw Confectioners' new accounting system, Mr. Butterworth did not regard it as a cure-all. He recognized that direct costing did not eliminate the necessity of exercising sound judgment in using accounting data; it merely reflected more closely the thinking of management in planning and control, and making reports easier to understand to their users. He also admitted that an intelligently designed and utilized conventional absorption accounting system could serve the same purposes as direct costing, in that supplementary analyses for specific purposes could always be prepared from the accounting data. However, he thought that many people, including even accountants, were often puzzled by the fluctuations of unit cost with changing volume and the fluctuations of income when sales and production volumes of a period did not coincide, which was characteristic of conventional accounting.

Trouble

By the summer of 1987, Mr. Butterworth was almost sure that everyone in the organization was happy with the direct cost system. In August 1987, however, he had a long discussion with Mr. Larson, the treasurer, which raised some doubts in his mind. Mr. Larson had been with the company for over 30 years; his opinions were therefore based on long experience.

Mr. Larson suggested that the product line committee reexamine the policy that promotion of Product Family A be given priority over that of Product Family C. The substance of his reasoning is given below:

"June 1987 was typical in that Product Family A had a substantially greater merchandising contribution than Product Family C (see Exhibit 3). Apparently, for the same pound sales, A is more profitable than C. This inference, however, is incorrect; for ultimate profitability cannot be determined until meaningfully allocable fixed costs are taken into account. Under the old accounting procedure, depreciation of roughly £50,000 for the month of June 1987 would have been allocated to the four product families as follows:

	ALLOCATION OF DEPRECIATION			
Product Family	*A*	*B*	*C*	*D*
Sales	£540,000	£144,000	£408,000	£108,000
Merchandising margin	157,000 29%	35,000	101,000 25%	30,000
Depreciation	27,000	7,000	9,000	7,000
Margin after depreciation	£130,000 24%	£ 28,000	£ 92,000 23%	£ 23,000

Apportionment of depreciation shifts the relative profitability of A and C; A is now only one percentage point ahead of C. This shift occurs because the ratio of direct cost to equipment use is different between the product families; in other words, because the manufacturing process is more mechanized for A than for C.

"Depreciation of equipment is a fixed cost in the short run but becomes variable if enough time is allowed. This fact becomes obvious when volume increases: Owing to the concentrated promotion, the turnover of A has been increasing at such a rate that soon the present equipment capacity for the production of A will become inadequate. Either additional equipment must be acquired or a new shift added, and either alternative will entail a jump in fixed costs.

"The promotional cost itself, which we treat as a period cost, must also be taken into account. In June 1987, out of the total advertising cost of £92,500, £66,000 was directly identifiable with product families, and can be charged to them as follows:

	ALLOCATION OF ADVERTISING AND PROMOTION COSTS			
Product Family	*A*	*B*	*C*	*D*
Margin after depreciation	£130,000 24%	£28,000	£92,000 23%	£23,000
Advertising & production	37,000	4,000	19,000	6,000
Margin	93,000 17%	24,000	73,000 18%	17,000
Sales per promotion pound	£15		£22	

The adjusted margin of C becomes superior to that of A, after charging each with its direct advertising and other promotional expenses. Note also that a pound expended on promotion of A brings in £15 of sales, while for C one pound generates £22. This suggests that greater and greater effort is needed to obtain a dollar increase in sales as the level of sales moves up, and that A has possibly reached a saturation point. Talk with the sales people convinces me that an incremental advertising dollar spent for C will induce more sales than for A.

"On the basis of the above analysis, I think we should reverse the present policy, and this leads me to wonder whether the direct costing system is causing us to make mistakes that we could avoid by returning to conventional absorption costing."

Required

1. Which cost system, the accounting director's or the treasurer's (or neither) should be used to help management decide which product line to give priority to in 1987?

2. If £1 of additional advertising was expected to produce £10 of additional sales of either product line A or product line C, which product should be given priority, assuming that there was adequate capacity to satisfy all expected demand? Would the answer be different if £1 of advertising produced £15 of sales for product C?

3. How can management use the "sales per promotion pound" shown on page 200 in their decision-making process?

4. Which cost system should be used in the screening process: the accounting director's? the treasurer's? both? neither?

5. If you decide that the answer to Question 4 is not to use the direct cost system for the screen, which nondirect costs would you assign to product families?

CASE 7.2   STALCUP PAPER COMPANY

In March 1985, the president of the Stalcup Paper Company, while examining a group of charts regarding unit costs submitted to him by the cost department, noted that the unit costs of sorting rags had been rising for approximately two years. In order to determine the reason for this increase, he invited the manager of the rag-sorting department and the head of the cost department to his office to discuss the matter. The head of the cost department submitted three exhibits, as shown in Exhibits 1, 2, and 3, giving the details of the upward trend in costs shown in the charts. The manager of the rag-sorting department said that his costs were lower rather than higher than they had been in past years, and that

This case was prepared by A. Brimshaw. Copyright © by the President and Fellows of Harvard College. Harvard Business School case 9-186-297.

EXHIBIT 1   Stalcup Paper Company

Output of Rag-Sorting Department in Pounds

	1982	*1984*	*CHANGE*
Old rags	3,220,000	2,460,000	− 23.6%
New rags	810,000	2,520,000	+211.1%
	4,030,000	4,980,000	+ 23.6%
Percent of old rags	79.9%	49.4%	
Percent of new rags	20.1%	50.6%	

the basis of the cost department's estimates was unsound. He submitted Exhibit 4 in support of this contention.

The Stalcup Paper Company used old rags, new rags, and pulp in manufacturing its papers. The proportions in which these materials were mixed were varied in accordance with the requirements for different grades and types of paper. The new rags, which were purchased from textile converters, cost substantially more than old rags, which were purchased through junk dealers. The old rags were usually received in the form of garments, from which it was necessary to remove carefully all foreign materials such as buttons, rubber, and metal. New rags were largely remnants containing only a small percentage of foreign matter requiring removal and as a result could be sorted much more rapidly than old rags.

The sorters sat at benches. Their task was to remove all foreign matter from the material placed before them and to distribute the usable cloth, according to

EXHIBIT 2   Stalcup Paper Company

Expenses of Rag-Sorting Department

	1982		*% of Direct Labor*	*1984*		*% of Direct Labor*
Direct labor		$314,475			$257,775	
Rag-sorting department burden						
Indirect labor	$127,995			$143,100		
Repair labor	9,150			7,620		
Repair materials	1,845			4,065		
Supplies	2,340			2,400		
Power	9,180			8,295		
Investment	233,235			228,060		
		383,745	122%		393,540	153%
General overhead		286,920	91%		227,790	88%
		$985,140			$879,105	

EXHIBIT 3 Stalcup Paper Company

Rag-Sorting Department Costs of Sorting Old and New Rags (as shown
in cost records)

	1982		1984	
	Dollars	Cents per Pound	Dollars	Cents per Pound
Old rags				
Wages	307,188	9.54	234,684	9.54
Department overhead	374,808[a]	11.64	359,160[b]	14.60
General overhead	280,140	8.70	207,378	8.43
	962,136	29.88	801,222	35.57
Increase				2.69
New rags				
Wages	7,371	0.91	23,184	0.92
Department overhead	8,991[a]	1.11	35,532[b]	1.41
General overhead	6,723	0.83	20,412	0.81
	23,085	2.85	79,128	3.13
Increase				0.28

[a]122% of wages

[b]153% of wages

EXHIBIT 4 Stalcup Paper Company

Rag-Sorting Department Costs of Sorting Old and New Rags (as
estimated by manager)

	1982		1984	
	Dollars	Cents per Pound	Dollars	Cents per Pound
Old rags				
Wages	307,188	9.54	234,684	9.54
Department overhead	306,544	9.52	194,340	7.90
General overhead	229,264	7.12	112,442	4.57
	842,996	26.18	541,466	22.01
Decrease				4.17
New rags				
Wages	7,371	0.91	23,184	0.91
Department overhead	77,112	9.52	199,080	7.90
General overhead	57,672	7.12	115,164	4.57
	142,155	17.55	337,428	13.38
Decrease				4.18

quality, into containers placed beside them. The sorters inspected and graded, on the average, 55 pounds of old rags or 575 pounds of new rags per hour. They were paid on a day-rate basis, the management having discovered by experience that payment on a piece-rate basis resulted in picking over rags less carefully.

Between 1982 and 1984 the composition of rags purchased by the Stalcup Paper Company changed considerably, as shown in Exhibit 1. The percentage of old rags to the total dropped from approximately 80% to approximately 50%. During the same interval the amount of rags handled increased nearly 25%. In spite of the large increase in total volume, labor costs declined over the period because of the smaller amount of old rags handled.

Costs charged to the rag-sorting department were of three types: first, those incurred for direct labor in the department; second, overhead burden charged directly to the department; and third, general factory overhead. It was the practice of the cost department to charge all burden incurred directly by each department to all products processed within it as a uniform percentage of direct labor. This percentage was obtained by dividing the total department burden by total department direct labor. The amount of general overhead charged to a department was obtained by multiplying the direct labor in the department by the ratio of total general overhead to total direct labor in the plant.

The items included in rag-sorting department burden were as shown in Exhibit 2. The most important of these were indirect labor, including the salary of the manager and wages of employees engaged in taking material to and from the sorters, and investment, which included the charge against the department for taxes, depreciation, and insurance on the premises and equipment it used. General overhead included factory-wide waste collection, miscellaneous labor, building repair labor and materials, manufacturing executive salaries, and expenses of functional departments, such as planning, costing, and research.

The head of the cost department pointed out to the president that between 1982 and 1984 the rag-sorting department burden charge had increased from 122% of direct labor to 153% and that the difference in cost of sorting in the two years was, as shown in Exhibit 3, almost entirely attributable to this increase.

The manager differed with the cost department's estimated unit costs and pointed out that it was hard to conceive of unit costs increasing while total costs were diminishing and volume of output was rising. He stated that the cost department was not charging the proper proportion of overhead charges to the new rags and that therefore old rags were taking more than their share of total department burden. He said that, in his opinion, a much sounder method of allocating burden charges would be on a per-pound basis rather than on the percentage-of-direct-labor basis previously used, and he recommended that costs in the rag department in the future should be calculated on the basis shown in Exhibit 4.

The unit cost for old and new rag sorting, as calculated by the cost department, were used in setting up standard costs. These standard costs, however, were only rarely used in setting prices of finished paper, since most of the company's paper was sold in a competitive market at prices established by competition. The company used the standard costs mostly as a check on the profit and loss in-curred on the various lines of paper manufactured in order to determine which were relatively more profitable. When the plant was being operated at capacity, and orders were being refused, the relative profitability of lines was a factor in determining what lines should be discontinued. In 1985, the Stalcup Paper Com-pany was operating at about 55% of capacity.

Questions

1. The existing cost system and the one proposed by the manager will result in different product costs. Discuss the implications to the firm of changing from the existing system to the manager's.

2. How useful are the per-pound costs collected by the cost system to man-agement? In particular, how useful are they

  (a) For setting prices or selecting among products, under current market conditions and at full capacity?

  (b) For making purchasing decisions?

3. How useful are Exhibits 3 and 4 in evaluating the manager's perform-ance?

4. Explain why the cost system shows that the unit costs of both old and new rags have increased, whereas the manager shows that they have decreased.

5. How well did the manager perform in 1984 as compared to 1982?

6. What changes would you propose to the cost system? Why?

chapter 8

DECISION SUPPORT SYSTEMS: CAPITAL INVESTMENT DECISIONS

This chapter describes decision support systems for helping managers make capital investment decisions. A capital investment decision is one that involves the commitment of resources for capital assets, that is, assets that will be capitalized and written off over a future time period.

Most companies have procedures requiring all executives to obtain formal approval before investing in new capital assets in excess of a minimum amount. These procedures involve the preparation of a capital investment proposal; the submission of that proposal to a specified executive or a committee of executives for approval; after approval, the control of the expenditures that were authorized; and, subsequently, some form of follow-up, comparing what actually occurred with the proposal.

This chapter is divided into four parts:

- Part 1: Measuring profitability
- Part 2: Estimating cash flows
- Part 3: Follow-up procedures
- Part 4: Some theoretical considerations

Although this chapter considers only capital projects, the same principles of measurement and analysis apply to proposals involving all types of long-run commitment of resources.

PART 1: MEASURING PROFITABILITY

Capital investments affect cash flows over a number of years. Typically, there is an initial investment that generates subsequent positive cash flows. It is necessary to measure the expected profitability of each proposed project in order to assess its desirability.[1] This measure may be used to rank projects in order of their desirability or to compare the profitability with a minimum acceptable level.

In this part of the chapter, four measures of profitability are described: payback, the accounting rate of return, the internal rate of return (IRR), and net present value (NPV).

Payback

Although strictly speaking not a measure of profitability, *payback* is the simplest and earliest-used technique for measuring the relative economic desirability of investment proposals. Payback is simply the length of time for the positive cash flows to equal the negative cash flows. In other words, payback is the estimated time it will take to recover the investment.

The payback method is of limited use because it does not distinguish accurately between the profitability of alternative investments. For instance, take the following example:

	INVESTMENT 1	*INVESTMENT 2*
Investment	$10,000	$10,000
Annual Earnings	5,000	3,000
Life	2 years	10 years
Payback	2 years	$3\frac{1}{3}$ years

In this example, Investment 1 has the shortest payback in spite of the fact that there is *no* profit on the investment. The example is exaggerated, of course, and no one would be so foolish as to take Investment 1 over Investment 2. Sup-

---

[1] In many capital investment projects, profitability is not an issue—for example, investments required by law, such as antipollution devices. This chapter is concerned only with those proposals where profitability is an issue.

pose, however, that Investment 1 had a life of 3 years instead of 2 years. Which one would be the better investment? The payback method does not measure this. Since the entire purpose of these techniques is to help select among alternative investments, the payback method is of very limited value. Today, this method is used exclusively only where a quick return of capital is of primary importance, although it is often calculated as supplementary information.

The Accounting Method

The *accounting method* (also called the unadjusted rate of return method) is calculated as follows:[2]

$$\frac{\text{Average annual cash flow } - \text{ average annual depreciation}}{\text{Investment}}$$

or

$$\frac{\text{Average annual cash flow } - \text{ average annual depreciation}}{\frac{1}{2} \text{ investment}}$$

The investment is sometimes divided by two on the theory that over the life of the investment, there will be a gradual return of the initial investment through depreciation. Consequently, the average amount of investment outstanding over the period of time is one-half of the initial outlay.

The advantages of the accounting method are as follows:

1. It has been commonly used in the past.
2. It is easy to understand (although not as simple as the payback method).
3. It distinguishes accurately between investments where the timing of the cash flows is approximately the same.

The disadvantage of the accounting method is that it treats a dollar received in the future as equal in value to a dollar received today. Consider the following example:

---

[2]Average annual cash flow is the total cash flow to be generated by the proposed investment divided by the number of years it is expected to continue.

	INVESTMENT 1	*INVESTMENT 2*
Amount of investment	$10,000	$10,000
Earnings	3,000 a year for 10 years	30,000 at the end of 10 years
Life	10 years	10 years
Rate of return equation	$\dfrac{\$3{,}000 - \$1{,}000}{\$10{,}000}$	$\dfrac{\$3{,}000 - \$1{,}000}{\$10{,}000}$
Amount	20%	20%

Both of these investments earn the same average rate of return; yet clearly it is better to have the money returned evenly during the life of the investment than at the end of the period.

To summarize, the accounting method is more accurate than the payback. In fact, if all alternative investments have a similar pattern of profits, it will distinguish between them with reasonable accuracy. For this reason, this method was used by many businesses until a few years ago. However, *all* investments will never have the same cash flow patterns. Consequently, the accounting method alone is rarely used by large corporations today.

The Internal Rate of Return Method

The *internal rate of return* (IRR) method corrects the basic problem with the accounting method. It takes into account the time value of money.

The Concept of Present Value. Present value is based on the mathematics of compound interest. For example, suppose that $1000 is invested in a bank that pays 6% interest, compounded annually. (This means that interest is *calculated* annually and added to the account.) If both principal and interest are left in the bank, the growth will be as follows:

END OF:	*AMOUNT IN BANK*	*AMOUNT OF INTEREST EARNED*
Year 1	$1060.00	$60.00
2	1123.60	63.60
3	1191.02	67.42

The equation for calculating compound interest on $1 is as follows:

$$(1 + i)^n,$$

where

$$i = \text{the interest rate per period}$$

$$n = \text{the number of periods the money is left in the bank}$$

In the preceding example, $1000 today is worth $1,191.02 at the end of three years. Consequently, if money earned 6%, one would be more or less indifferent to receiving either $1000 today or $1191 three years from now. This is the concept of present value. We say the present value of $1191 to be received in three years is $1000 if money is worth 6%. (Notice that present value cannot be expressed without stating both a time period and an interest rate.) The equation for the present value of $1 is

$$\frac{1}{(1 + i)^n},$$

or the reciprocal of the compound interest equation. This formula is the basis for present-value tables.

Present value is critical in capital investment analysis because an investment always involves a payment *now* in return for cash flow in the *future*. The profitability of a capital investment proposal is determined by the present value of these future cash flows.

PRESENT-VALUE TABLES.   There are two present-value tables at the end of this chapter on pages 250–51.

TABLE A.   Table A on page 250 shows the present value of $1 at various periods in future and at various interest rates. For example, the present value of $1 received ten years from now is $0.386 if money is worth 10%; it is $0.247 if money is worth 15%. The present value of $1 twenty years from now is $0.026 if money is worth 20%.

TABLE B.   Table B on page 251 is the present value of a stream of dollars ($1 per year) received annually for various numbers of years at various interest rates. For example, $1 a year for five years ($5 in all) is worth $3.791 if money is worth 10%. Table B is a cumulation of the amounts shown in Table A.

For example:

	10%		
	Table A	*Table B*	*Difference*
Year 1	0.909	0.909	—
2	0.826	1.736	0.827[a]
3	0.751	2.487	0.751
4	0.683	3.170	0.683
5	0.621	3.791	0.621

[a]Discrepancy due to rounding.

The purpose of Table B is to simplify calculations. Since some capital investments may provide for equal annual cash flows, it is more convenient to use Table B than to calculate the present value for each year and then find the sum. For example, suppose the savings from an investment were $10,000 a year for 10 years and that money is worth 10%. To find the present value of this amount, it is easier to look it up on Table B (10,000 X 6.145 = $61,450) than to calculate the present value for each year and sum these amounts.

CALCULATION OF THE INTERNAL RATE OF RETURN. Assume that the amount of proposed investment, the amount of anticipated cash flow from this investment, and the timing of these cash flows are known. From this information, it is possible to calculate the rate of return (time-adjusted) that is expected on the investment. Suppose that the proposed investment was $3000 and the anticipated cash flows were $1000 a year for five years. (In this instance, assume that the cash is received at the end of the year.) One way to find the rate of return is to discount the earnings (find their present value) at various rates until a rate was found that would equate the present value of the earnings to the amount of the investment. For example:

	10%	*20%*	*30%*
Year 1	$ 909	$ 833	$ 769
2	826	694	592
3	751	579	455
4	683	482	350
5	621	402	269
	$3790	$2990	$2435

This shows that cash flows of $1000 a year for five years on an investment of $3000 will earn slightly less than 20%. It may be more meaningful to look at it this way. The process of discounting (i.e., finding present value) means that the amount of cash flow is reduced by the interest; the remainder, therefore, is the return or principal. If the discounted cash flow adds up to the principal, this means that the investment is earning the interest rate that was used to calculate the discounted cash flow. In the preceding example, at the 10% rate, the return of principal was $3790. This means that 10% + $790 was earned; this is obviously more than 10%. However, when the cash flows were discounted at 30%, the return of principal was only $2435, or $565 *less* than the $3000 investment. This means that 30% minus $565, or less than 30%, was earned.

If the cash flows are equal for all years, there is a shortcut for obtaining the internal rate of return. This method is as follows:

1. Divide the annual cash flows into the investment (investment ÷ cash flow).
2. Pick (from Table B) the line for the number of years the cash will be received.
3. Move across the line to the figure most nearly equal to the amount calculated in 1. The rate indicated by this column is the time-adjusted rate of return.

In the preceding example, 3000 ÷ 1000 = 3.000. Looking at Table B and moving across the five-year line, it can be seen that 2.991 is the closest to 3.000. This is the 20% column of Table B; consequently, the rate of return is about 20%. If the cash flows are uneven, the only way to determine the internal rate of return is by trial and error. Since, in actual business situations, the cash flows are rarely even, the method just described can be used only infrequently. However, with modern computers and calculators, calculating the internal rate of return is no problem.

ADVANTAGES AND DISADVANTAGES OF IRR METHOD. The IRR method takes into account the fact that money in the future is worth less than an equal amount today. It is, therefore, a much more precise way of ranking investment proposals than either the payback or the accounting method. Money has a time value and, if this value is not considered in the analysis, an important factor has been omitted. Specifically, the advantages of the internal rate of return in capital investment analysis are as follows:

1. The timing of cash flows can be taken into account. Consequently, important factors that cannot be handled adequately by the accounting method can be included in the analysis of the internal rate of return. For example, the timing of income taxes may influence a decision. The accounting method cannot take this into account. Also, the timing of a capital investment may be important. For example, a project may call for using currently idle facilities. If the use of these facilities would require the purchase of new facilities in, say, five years, this fact can be taken into consideration in the internal rate of return. The accounting method will not take into account the fact that the investment has been deferred five years.

2. The internal rate of return is consistent with the rate of return on bonds, the interest paid on borrowings, or the yield from common stocks. The accounting rate of return is not. In the accounting method, if one-half of the investment is used as the denominator, the rate of return will be overstated. If the entire investment is used in the denominator, the rate of return will be understated. For example, an investment of $10,000 that yields $2,000 a year for 10 has a internal rate of return of 15%. The accounting method shows a return of 20% on half of the investment [(2000 − 1000) ÷ 10,000] or 10% on the full investment [(2000 − 1000) ÷ 5000].

3. When the internal rate of return is used, the more distant the time of an event, the less impact it will have on the decision. This improves the quality of the estimate because the more distant an event, the greater is its uncertainty. For example, assume that the estimated scrap value of a piece of equipment is $1000 at the end of ten years. Under the accounting method, this would be reflected as a reduction in the net investment of $1000. If the estimate were in error by 50%, the investment would be overstated by $500. If the time-adjusted rate return were 10%, the impact of this estimate on the decision would be only $386. (This is the present value of $1000.) Thus if it were 50% in error, it would affect the present value analysis by only $193.

   The internal rate of return has the disadvantage, however, of not distinguishing between alternative investments with complete accuracy in some instances because implicit in the calculation is the assumption that the incoming cash can be invested at the indicated rate of return. For example, a 30% return on a one-year investment may not be better than at 25% return on a two-year investment. It all depends upon the investment opportunities that will be available in the next two years.

Net Present Value

Net present value is a type of present-value calculation that is designed to overcome the disadvantage attributable to the internal rate of return. Under this method, *all* cash flows are discounted at some desired rate of return. Pluses and minuses are then added algebraically. If this results in a plus figure, the investment will earn the desired rate in addition to the amount of the plus figure. If it results in a minus figure, the investment has failed to earn the desired rate by the amount of the minus figure. In the example given earlier, suppose that the desired rate of return (called *cutoff* or *hurdle* rate) was 10%. The analysis is as follows:

ITEM	UNADJUSTED CASH FLOW	PERIOD	DISCOUNT FACTOR	DISCOUNTED CASH FLOW
Investment	− 3000	0	1.000[b]	− 3,000
Cash Flows	+ 1000	0–5[a]	3.791[c]	+ 3,791
				+ 791

[a]From the present (0) to the end of the fifth year.
[b]The present value of the $3,000 investment is $3,000; consequently the discount factor is 1.
[c]Table B: $1 a year for five years at 10%.

This analysis shows that 10% will be earned on the investment plus $791.

The net present-value method overcomes the disadvantage of the internal rate of return because the cutoff rate represents the rate of return that can normally be expected from the cash being generated by the proposed investment.

Profitability Index. One adaptation of the net present method that provides a ranking of alternative investments is the profitability index (PI). PI is a ratio. The numerator is the total net present value of the earnings from the investment; the denominator is the amount of the investment. The higher the profitability ratio, the more desirable the investment. If the ratio is less than 1, it means that the earnings are less than the hurdle rate.

PART 2: ESTIMATING CASH FLOWS

A capital investment decision is a specific decision that may have an impact on cash flows over a considerable period of time. As with all such decisions, managers need an estimate of the *differential cash flow* that will result from the decision.

This is the same concept that was discussed earlier under tactical marketing decisions and disinvestment decisions. That is, the concern is with those cash flows that will change as the result of the decision. The second consideration is that these should be *future* cash flows. Although the concept is the same as previously described, the calculation of differential cash flows in capital investment analysis has several unique features. These unique features are discussed in this part of the chapter.

Income Taxes

Income taxes must always be considered when calculating cash flows from new investments. The income tax rate, however, is not applied to the full amount of the cash flow because depreciation is deductible for tax purposes. Consequently, the depreciation should be subtracted from the cash flows and the tax applied to the difference (taxable income).

In the example cited earlier, the before-tax earnings were $1000 a year. The depreciation would be $3000 ÷ 5, or $600, a year, assuming straight-line depreciation. If the tax rate were 46%, the cash flow would be calculated as follows:

a.	Before-tax cash flow	$1000
b.	Depreciation	600
c.	Taxable income	$ 400
d.	Tax (46%)	184
e.	After-tax cash flow	
	[(a) − (d)]	$ 816

(Note that if some other method, such as accelerated depreciation, were used, it would be necessary to calculate a different cash flow for each year.) Where tax depreciation is different from the depreciation used in the accounting method, the tax depreciation should always be used.

Selling or Scrapping Old Equipment

When, as the result of purchasing new equipment, old equipment will be scrapped, there may be an immediate savings in income taxes. This results when the equipment has a book value. This immediate reduction in income taxes is offset by the fact that future tax savings are given up. This is an important point to remember. When a tax loss is taken from scrapping a piece of equipment, the advantage is only one of timing. The advantage is that there is an immediate tax reduction instead of one in the future.

Scrapping Old Equipment. Take the following example:

- Investment in new equipment = $5,000
- Earnings = $1000 a year for 10 years
- Old equipment scrapped: cost = $3,000; age, 3 years; accumulated depreciation $1,500; remaining life 3 years

- Tax rate = 50%
- Hurdle rate = 10%

The analysis of this investment is as follows:

ITEM	UNADJUSTED CASH FLOW	TIME PERIOD	DISCOUNT FACTOR	DISCOUNTED CASH FLOW
Investment	− 5,000	0	1.000	− 5000
Earnings (AT)	+ 750[a]	0–10	6.145[b]	+ 4609
Tax reduction on scrapping of old equipment	+ 750[c]	0	1.000	+ 750
Taxes on depreciation given up	− 250[d]	0–3	2.487	− 622
Total				− 263

[a]Before-tax earnings — 1,000
Depreciation (5000 ÷ 10) — 500
Taxable income — 500
Tax — 250
After-tax earnings — $ 750

[b]Table B, 10% for 10 years.

[c]1,500 book value × 0.50 = 750.

[d]Depreciation given up is $500 a year for 3 years. This means an increase of 500 × 0.50, or $250, a year in taxes. This example shows that the investment will not earn the desired 10%.

Sale of Old Equipment. Sometimes old equipment is sold and either a profit or a loss is earned on the sale of this equipment.[3] In these cases, the principle is exactly the same as in the example above; calculate the after-tax cash flows and then be sure to take into account the tax increase from the fact that future depreciation was given up. In the last example, assume that the old equipment could be sold for $1000. The analysis would be as follows:

ITEM	UNADJUSTED CASH FLOW	TIME PERIOD	DISCOUNT FACTOR	DISCOUNTED CASH FLOW
Investment	− 5000	0	1.000	− 5000
Earnings	+ 750	0–10	6.145	+ 4609
Sale of old equipment	+ 1000	0	1.000	+ 1000
Tax savings on sale of old equipment	+ 250[a]	0	1.000	+ 250
Tax payments on depreciation given up	− 250	0–3	2.487	− 622
				+ 237

[a]Book value — 1,500
Sales price — 1,000
Tax loss — 500
Tax savings — 250

---

[3]A profit on the sale of capital equipment is not always taxed in exactly the same way as other profits. For the purposes of this chapter, however, no tax rate distinctions will be made.

The analysis shows that the investment is expected to earn 10% after taxes plus $237.

Working Capital. Frequently, an investment in capital equipment will also in-volve an additional investment in working capital. For example, if a piece of equipment is purchased to manufacture a new product, it will probably be neces-sary to increase the inventory. The characteristic of working capital, however, is that the money will be returned at the end of the period; for example, the inven-tory can be sold when the product is discontinued.

To demonstrate this, take the following example:

Investment in new equipment	$5000
Additional working capital required	1000
Cash flows = $1000 a year for 10 years	
Tax rate 50%	
Hurdle rate 10%	

The analysis is as follows:

ITEM	UNADJUSTED CASH FLOW	TIME PERIOD	DISCOUNT FACTOR	DISCOUNTED CASH FLOW
Investment	−5000	0	1.000	−5000
Working capital invested	−1000	0	1.000	−1000
Cash flows (after tax)	+750[a]	0–10	6.145	+4609
Working capital returned	+1000	10	0.386[b]	+386
Total				−1005

[a]1000 − [(1000 − 500) 0.5] = 750.
[b]Table A, present value of $1 ten years from now at a 10% discount rate.

This analysis shows that the proposed investment is expected to earn less than 10% after taxes by $1005.

An alternative treatment of working capital is to reduce the cash flows by an interest rate equal to the cost of borrowing. The rationale for this is that the additional inventories and receivables provide a basis for borrowing additional money. Consequently, the cost of the additional working capital is the cost of borrowing the money required to support the investment in working capital.

Changes in Price Level of Proposed Investment. Occasionally, it might be expected that the cost of a capital asset will be reduced in the next year. The question to be answered, then, is whether or not the investment should be deferred for a year. This can be answered by making two calculations: The first calculation as-sumes the equipment is purchased now; the second calculation assumes that the equipment will be purchased one year from now. A comparison of the discounted cash flows will indicate the most profitable alternative. Consider the following example:

- Proposed investment: $10,000
- Cash flows: $4000 a year for five years
- Tax rate: 50%
- Hurdle rate: 10%

By waiting a year, it is expected that the price of the equipment will be reduced to $8,500. (The life of the new equipment will be only five years from the present time regardless of when it is purchased because it is expected that the demand for the product that the equipment makes will be replaced by a substitute product at the end of five years.)

The analysis is as follows:

1. Assuming immediate purchase:

ITEM	UNADJUSTED CASH FLOW	TIME PERIOD	DISCOUNT RATE	DISCOUNTED CASH FLOW
Investment	− 10,000	0	1.000	− 10,000
Cash flows (after taxes)	+ 3,000[a]	0–5	3.791[b]	+ 11,373
				+ 1,373

[a] $4000 - \dfrac{(10,000)}{5} = 2,000$ taxable earnings;

$2000 \times 0.50 = 1000$ tax; $4000 - 1000 = 3000$ after-tax cash flow.

[b] Table B, five years at 10%

2. Assuming purchase one year from now:

ITEM	UNADJUSTED CASH FLOW	TIME PERIOD	DISCOUNT RATE	DISCOUNTED CASH FLOW
Investment	− 8500	1	0.909[a]	− 7,727
Cash flows (after taxes)	+ 3062.50[c]	1–5	2.882[b]	+ 8,826
				+ 1,099

[a] Table A, the present value of $1 to be invested at the end of one year at 10%.

[b] Table B Years 0–5 at 10% = 3.791

Year 1   at 10% = 0.909

Years 1–5   = 2.882

[c] $4000 - 8500/4 = 1875$ taxable earnings $\times 0.50 = \$937.50$ tax;

$4000 - 937.50 = 3062.50$ after-tax earnings.

The analysis shows that in spite of the expected price reduction, it is better to invest immediately.

Accelerated Depreciation. Almost all profitable companies use some form of accelerated depreciation for tax purposes. This means that the after-tax earnings on an investment will be greater in the earlier years because the tax will be smaller. In the example given in the previous section, the after-tax earnings, assuming the use of sum of the years' digits depreciation, are shown in the following table:

YEAR	BEFORE TAX CASH FLOWS	DEPRECIATION	TAXABLE INCOME	TAX (50%)	AFTER-TAX CASH FLOWS
1	$1,000	$ 909	$ 91	$ 46	$ 954
2	1,000	818	182	91	909
3	1,000	727	273	136	864
4	1,000	636	364	182	818
5	1,000	545	455	228	772
6	1,000	455	545	272	728
7	1,000	364	636	318	682
8	1,000	273	727	364	636
9	1,000	182	818	409	591
10	1,000	91	909	454	546
	$10,000	$5,000	$5,000	$2,500	$7,500

The analysis of the investment is now as follows:

ITEM	UNADJUSTED CASH FLOW	TIME PERIOD	DISCOUNT FACTOR	DISCOUNTED CASH FLOW
Investment Cash flow	− 5000	0	1.000	− 5000
Year: 1	+ 954	1	0.909	+ 867
2	+ 909	2	0.826	+ 751
3	+ 864	3	0.751	+ 649
4	+ 818	4	0.683	+ 559
5	+ 772	5	0.621	+ 479
6	+ 728	6	0.564	+ 411
7	+ 682	7	0.513	+ 350
8	+ 636	8	0.467	+ 297
9	+ 591	9	0.424	+ 251
10	+ 546	10	0.386	+ 211
				− 175

If the annual earnings are even, there are tables available that will allow you to calculate the present value of these savings, using the sum of the years' digits depreciation for tax purposes. It would not be necessary, therefore, to calculate each year separately.

Note that if a business uses accelerated depreciation for income tax purposes, it must also use accelerated depreciation in its capital investment analyses. Otherwise, the profitability of proposed investments would be understated. Since most businesses use accelerated depreciation for tax purposes, most capital investment analyses should be developed using accelerated depreciation. Straight-line depreciation has been used exclusively in this chapter only because it somewhat simplifies the calculations.

Investment Versus Financing. It is important to separate the calculation of the profitability of a proposed capital investment from the financing of that investment. The reason for this is that completely inconsistent results occur if this is not done. As long as the interest rate is less than the internal rate of return, any capital expenditure proposal will show an infinite return if all of the money to finance it is borrowed. There is simply a zero investment. The inconsistency of this extreme situation is, of course, obvious. Not so obvious, however, is that partial borrowing will make an investment look better than an alternative investment with exactly the same internal cash flows. For example:

	PROPOSAL A	PROPOSAL B	PROPOSAL C
1. Gross investment	$100,000	$100,000	$100,000
2. Annual cash flows	15,000	15,000	15,000
3. Life	10 years	10 years	10 years
4. Borrowings	0	50,000	90,000
5. Annual interest payment (5%)	0	2,500	4,500
6. Net investment (1 − 4)	100,000	50,000	10,000
7. Net cash flow (2 − 5)	15,000	12,500	10,500
8. Time-adjusted rate of return	8%	21%	Nearly infinite return

This means that if the financing is not separated from the calculation of profitability, the project with the greatest amount of borrowing will tend to show the highest return. Clearly, this could give a completely wrong ranking of projects. It is particularly important to be careful of leasing agreements that are included in investment proposals. Most long-term leases are really financing arrangements.

On all project analyses, the assumption that the project will be financed from internal funds and that all leased assets will be purchased should be made. (This means that all interest payments are also eliminated.) Then, if the project seems to be sufficiently profitable, the decision can be made on the best way to finance it. In other words, there are two questions to be answered: First, is the capital investment sufficiently profitable? Second, what is the best way to finance it? These two decisions should be separated. About the only exception to this generalization that comes to mind is in real-estate operations. In this case, the financing conditions are so much a part of the operations that it may not be useful to separate the financing decisions.

PART 3: FOLLOW-UP PROCEDURES

Project Control

Once a project has been authorized it is necessary to make sure that funds in excess of those authorized are not spent on the project without prior authorization. (It is usual to allow a small overrun, say 5% or 10%, without additional authorization.) The control over project expenditure is, for the most part, routine. Funds are released as required and a record of expenditures on each project is maintained. There is one feature of project control, however, that is important and not so routine. It is necessary to have a periodic cost-to-complete estimate for each project. This is added to the amount spent and any indicated over- or underruns explained. Without this feature, the project status report is not useful in warning of possible problems. The cost-to-complete feature, if done correctly, warns management of possible future overruns as soon as it becomes likely that they will occur.

Follow-Up After Project Completion

It is often difficult to compare actual cash flow with those included in the investment proposal. The following are some of the reasons for this difficulty:

1. In a replacement investment, the old equipment is scrapped. Consequently, it is impossible to check on the accuracy of any assumptions concerning this equipment. For example, suppose that the purchase of a new truck was justified on the basis of expected repair costs on the old truck. If the truck has been scrapped, there is no way of knowing what the repair costs would have been.
2. Most accounting systems are not designed to keep track of revenues and expenses by capital investment project. Consequently, it is often not possible to determine from the accounting records the profits or savings from many of the capital investment projects.
3. Actual conditions can change so radically from those assumed in the investment proposal that it is impossible to determine whether the actual performance is better or worse than the proposal.

Many companies try to handle the problem by having two follow-up studies: one at the end of the first year after the project has been completed and a second at the end of five years. These follow-up studies simply take whatever information is available and try to evaluate how closely the actual situation compared to the proposal. This method is far from completely satisfactory, but better techniques are usually not available.

The important point that management should remember is that precise evaluation of performance on capital investment projects can be quite difficult and often impossible. In spite of the difficulties, however, some formal follow-up system should be used.

PART 4: SOME THEORETICAL CONSIDERATIONS

The Hurdle Rate

The theory behind the determination of the rate of return that a company should use to determine the minimum level of profitability required for an investment is complex and outside of the scope of this book. Nevertheless, some consideration must be given to this problem, since managers must decide, either implicitly or explicitly, on an acceptable rate of return for a capital investment.

The basic theory is that the hurdle rate should not be less than the company's "cost of capital." There are two problems with implementing this theory. First, there is no agreement among theorists as to how cost of capital should be calculated—in particular, the cost of equity capital. Second, the cost of capital can change dramatically over time. Consequently, it is necessary to forecast the cost of capital over the time period of the investment. As a result of these difficulties, most businesses determine their hurdle rate more or less by intuition. Fortunately, businesspeople tend to have a sense of capital costs and priorities.

One consideration, however, should be noted. A high hurdle rate, in itself, does not assure optimum allocation of resources and, in fact, could cause the opposite to happen. If the hurdle rate is too high, desirable investments might be rejected while an unnecessary amount of cash is accumulated.

Inflation

In projecting earnings, many companies simply assume that the value of money will remain constant in the future. One should be very careful about using this assumption because continued inflation in the future is the most likely prospect. If the earnings come from increased sales, it is not illogical to assume that increases in prices will offset increases in costs, and thus the earnings will remain constant. If the earnings are to come from savings in costs, particularly in direct labor, the earnings might well be understated if the analysis does not take into account the fact that labor costs are almost certain to be higher in the future. Inflation tends to cause interest rates to rise. Consequently, the hurdle rates also tend to rise, thus discouraging investments. If the impact of future increases in costs is not taken into account, capital expenditures might be decreased at a time when they should be increased.

Risk

The treatment of risk is a complex as well as controversial subject and is generally beyond the scope of this book. Businesspeople, however, cannot wait until the theoreticians have decided how to treat risk, because risk is a fact of their business existence and they must deal with it every day. From a practical point of view, the greatest danger is often overreaction to apparent risk, resulting in hurdle rates that are too high. It is important not to confuse uncertainty with undesirability. For instance, investment A might have an expected rate of return of 10%, with a high probability of not earning less than 8% or more than 12%. Investment B might have an expected return of 12% with a 30% probability of earning only 5% but a 30% probability of earning 15%. Since B has greater expected earnings than A, B should not be rejected simply because it had a wider range of possible earnings.[1]

---

[1]For those interested in a formal method for treating risks in capital investment analysis, see David B. Hertz, "Risk Analysis in Capital Investment," *Harvard Business Review,* January-February, 1964.

Uncertainty

As with all management decisions, the financial analysis is only one of several inputs in the decision process. In capital investment analysis, however, the importance of the analysis can vary greatly depending on two factors: first, the reliability of the financial analysis; second, the strategic considerations involved in the capital investment proposal.

Reliability. Capital investment proposals vary from routine replacement investments to major strategic investments. Clearly the degree of the reliability of the financial forecast will vary with length of the forecast, the controllability of the variables, the availability of information, and the uncertainty of the environment, to name a few. The reliability of a financial estimate can be thought of as a continuum. At one end is the routine replacement investment and the other is a major strategic investment in a new product or market. The importance of the financial analysis as part of the final decision decreases from the routine replacement investment, where it is a very important factor in the management decision, to the strategic investment, where it may be much less important. Consequently, the concept of ranking investments in the order of their profitability may be of limited use in many growing businesses.

Strategic Investments. Many strategic investments must be undertaken without reference to the immediate profitability effects. For example, the decision might involve additional investments or abandoning a market or product. In these instances, the decision is often made on the belief that the investment will result in better long-run profitability, without reference to specific profitability analysis. In the United States, automobile companies regularly invest hundreds of millions in model changes on the assumption that those changes are necessary to remain competitive.

Sometimes accounting departments place excessive constraints on capital investment proposals on the assumption that (1) the proposals are accurate and (2) that financial considerations dominate—in fact, even exclusively determine—the decision. Since this is, at best only true for those investments on the replacement side of the continuum, rigid procedures can interfere with optimum resource allocation. All capital investment analysis procedures should be flexible enough to take into account the inherent limitation in the financial anslysis.[5]

QUESTIONS

8.1 Can you think of any examples other than those described in the text in which important alternatives may have been omitted when analyzing a proposed capital expenditure?

---

[5]For further consideration of this topic, see Bela Gold, "The Shaky Foundations of Capital Budgeting," *Califiornia Business Review*, Vol. XIX, no. 2, pp. 51–60.

8.2 Describe some circumstances in which the payback method of analysis would be useful.

8.3 How would you explain the concept of present value to someone who had no background in business?

8.4 Explain why the accounting method (unadjusted return) gives a rate of return that is inconsistent with the real financial return.

8.5 Explain how an investment with a time-adjusted return of 30% could really be less desirable than one with a time-adjusted return of 25%, if resulting cash flow from the investment could be reinvested at only 10%.

8.6 If a company uses straight-line depreciation in its accounting statements and accelerated depreciation for its tax reports, which method should be used for calculating capital investment proposals? Why?

8.7 A company plans to borrow $1,000,000 to build a plant. It expects to give the bank a first mortgage on the plant. Interest is to be paid at 6% per year. How would you treat these facts in your capital investment proposal?

8.8 Explain why an investment with an uncertain return is not necessarily worse than an investment with a relatively certain return. Give an example to support your explanation.

8.9 Explain how a company would go about determining a hurdle rate.

8.10 What is the value of a postcompletion audit? How does it affect management actions?

PROBLEMS

For all the problems and cases in this chapter, use the following assumptions unless otherwise indicated:

(a) The hurdle rate is 10% after taxes.
(b) The income tax rate is 50%.
(c) Capital gains are taxed at the 50% rate and capital losses will reduce taxes by 50% of the loss.
(d) Straight-line depreciation is used.

8.1 Calculate the present value of the following.

	AMOUNT TO BE RECEIVED	NUMBER OF YEARS IN THE FUTURE	RATE OF INVESTMENT
(a)	$ 1,000	2	4%
(b)	500	3	6%
(c)	200	4	20%
(d)	5,000	6	15%
(e)	10,000	8	12%
(f)	100	7	8%
(g)	400	3	10%
(h)	600	9	14%
(i)	20,000	5	20%
(j)	30,000	11	25%

8.2 **(a)** At what rate of return must money be invested for one to be indifferent to receiving $1000 10 years from now or $160 now?

(b) At what rate of return must money be invested for one to be indifferent to receiving $1000 in 15 years or $120 now?

(c) You are offered your choice of $350 now or $1000 at some future date. You can earn 10% on your money. How many years in the future would you have to receive the $1000 to make either alternative equally acceptable?

(d) You are offered your choice of $140 now or $1000 at some future date. You can earn 15% on your money. How many years in the future would you have to receive the $1000 to make either alternative equally acceptable?

8.3 Decide which of the proposed investments listed below should be approved.

	PROPOSED INVESTMENT	*ANNUAL CASH FLOW FROM INVESTMENT*	*NUMBER OF YEARS OF CASH FLOW*	*HURDLE RATE*
(a)	100	$ 30	5	6%
(b)	1,000	400	3	10%
(c)	10,000	3,300	4	8%
(d)	20,000	8,000	6	15%
(e)	50,000	15,000	5	12%
(f)	100,000	60,000	2	10%

8.4 An investment proposal given to the management of the Defer Company provides the following data.

PROPOSED NEW MACHINE—TYPE B	
Amount of investment	$200,000
Annual savings	35,000
Life	10 years
OLD MACHINE—TYPE A	
Cost	$150,000
Accumulated depreciation	60,000
Remaining depreciable life	6 years
Scrap value	0

(a) Should the Defer Company buy the New Type B machine?

(b) Assume the same facts as in (a), except that the old machine has a sales value of $50,000. Should the Defer Company buy the new Type B machine?

(c) Assume the same facts as in (a), except that the old machine has a sales value of $110,000. Should the Defer Company buy the new Type B machine?

(d) The management of the Defer Company decided to buy the new Type B machine as described in (c). Two years later a new machine, Type C, was developed to replace the Type B machine. The Type C machine sells for $300,000 and will give operating savings of $70,000 a year over the Type B machine. The life of the Type C machine is projected at 10 years. The Type B machine has no salvage value.

Should the Defer Company buy the new Type C machine? Was a mistake made in buying the Type B machine?

8.5 Assume the facts are the same as those stated in Problem 8.4(a), except that the annual savings are as follows:

Years 1 and 2	$ 10,000 a year
Years 3 through 6	$ 70,000 a year
Years 7 through 10	$100,000 a year.

Should the Defer Company purchase the Type B machine?

8.6 Assume the facts are the same as stated in Problem 8.5, except that the company will use the sum of the years' digits method for depreciating the new machine. Should the Defer Company purchase the Type C machine under these circumstances?

8.7 The GHI Company is considering the purchase of some new equipment to produce a new product (X). The new equipment will cost $500,000. Product X is expected to sell for $2.00 a unit. Out-of-pocket costs of production (material, labor, variable overhead, and variable selling expenses) are expected to be $1.50 a unit. The anticipated sales volume is as follows:

Year 1	200,000 units
Year 2	300,000 units
Year 3	400,000 units
Years 4 and 5	500,000 units

After year five it is estimated that the product sales will drop off to the point where it will be uneconomical to produce it.

If the GHI company waits one year, they believe that they will be able to buy the equipment for $400,000. Anticipated sales are as follows:

Year of purchase	$200,000
Year 2	$400,000
Years 3 and 4	$500,000

Should the GHI company buy the new equipment? If so, should they buy it now or one year from now?

8.8 Assume the same facts as in Problem 8.7, except that it is necessary to carry additional inventory as follows:

	BEGINNING-OF-YEAR INVENTORY LEVELS	
	"Buy now" assumption	*"Buy one year from now"* assumption
Year 1	$ 75,000	—
Year 2	100,000	$ 75,000
Year 3	125,000	125,000
Year 4	200,000	200,000
Year 5	200,000	200,000

(a) Does this make any difference to the decision reached in Problem 8.7?

(b) Suppose that the added inventory allows you to obtain additional loans from the bank at a 5% interest rate. Does this make any difference to your decision?

8.9 The Wallis Company is considering buying a new machine to replace some existing equipment. The new machine is an automatic one that can be run by a single man instead of the four men required on the present equipment, which runs two shifts, five days a week. The new equipment is expected to run about the same number of hours. Current wage costs, including fringe benefits, are $4.00 per hour. Currently, the cost of scrapped parts is $50.00 a day in excess material costs. The automatic machine is expected to reduce this scrap by one-half. The new automatic machine will cost $300,000 installed and is expected to have a life of ten years.

Required

(a) Should the Wallis Company buy the new machine, assuming that price levels remain constant?

(b) Should the Wallis Company buy the new machine, assuming that:

(1) Wages and fringe benefits will increase on an average of 5% per year from the present level (not compounded)?

(2) Material will increase on an average of 3% per year from the present level?

8.10 Listed are three alternative investments together with the amount of financing that is available for each. Calculate the rate of return that each will earn:

(a) Without considering the financing arrangements.

(b) Combining the financial with the investment decision.

	PROJECT A	PROJECT B	PROJECT C
Amount of investment	$100,000	$225,000	$300,000
Earnings before tax	20,000	35,000	70,000
Life	10 years	15 years	6 years
Available financing	0	$100,000	$200,000
Interest rate		6%	5%

CASES

CASE 8.1   CAROB COMPANY

In March 1972, the Carob Company was considering a proposal to replace four hand-loaded transmission case milling machines with an automatic machine. The company operated a large machine shop that did machine work on a subcontract basis for local industries in the Detroit area. One of the contracts was to machine transmission cases for truck engines for the Avida Automobile Company. The Carob Company had negotiated such a contract with the Avida Automobile Company for each of the previous ten years. For the last few years, the contract had been 60,000 transmission cases annually.

This case was prepared by M. E. Barrett. Copyright © by the President and Fellows of Harvard College. Harvard Business School case 9-174-056.

The unfinished cases were supplied by Avida. With a hand-loaded machine, all the faces could not be machined at the same time. Each machine required the constant attention of one skilled machine operator.

The machines used by Carob were only three years old. Each machine had an annual output of approximately 15,000 cases on a two-shift, five-day-week basis; therefore, four machines had been purchased at a total cost of $295,000.

The useful life of a hand-loaded machine on a two-shift, five-day-week basis was estimated to be fifteen years. Its salvage value at the end of its useful life was estimated to be $2,500. Depreciation of $57,000 has been built up for the four machines, representing three years' accumulation. The purchase of the machines had been financed by an 8 percent bank loan, and $90,000 of this loan had not yet been repaid. It was estimated that the four machines could be sold in their present condition for a total of $120,000 net, after dismantling and removal costs. The book loss resulting from the sale would be a deductible expense for income tax purposes and would therefore result in a tax saving of 46 percent of the loss.

The machine being considered in 1972 was a fully automatic transfer-type machine, equipped with four machining stations. Automatic transfer equipment on this machine moved the part progressively from one station to the next and indexed at each station, finishing a complete case with each cycle of the machine. One skilled machine operator was required to observe the functioning of the machine and make any necessary adjustments.

An automatic transfer-type machine with an annual output of 60,000 transmission cases on a two-shift basis would be specially built by a machine tool manufacturer, and it was estimated that such a machine would cost $340,000, delivered and installed. The new machine would be eligible for an investment tax credit of 10% of its cost. The useful life of this machine was estimated to be twelve years. No reliable estimate of scrap value could be made; a rough estimate was that scrap value would approximate the removal costs.

Automatic transfer-type machines similar to the one being considered had first been offered for sale in 1971 at a price of approximately $390,000. It was expected that the price would continue to drop somewhat over the next several years.

The Carob Company's engineering department was asked to prepare a study for use by the executives of the company in deciding what action to take. The direct labor rate for milling machine operators was $5.00 an hour, including provision for social security taxes and fringe benefits, which varied with the payroll. There would also be a saving in floor space. This saving would amount to $800 annually on the basis of the charge made in 1972 for each square foot of floor space used, although the factory layout was such that it would be difficult to use this freed space for some other purpose, and no other use was planned. Out-of-pocket savings of $10,000 per year for other costs items were estimated if the automatic machine was purchased.

The Carob Company planned to finance any new equipment purchase with a bank loan at a rate of 8 percent. Some selected financial data for the company

EXHIBIT 1 Carob Company

Selected Financial Information

CONDENSED INCOME STATEMENT, 1971

Net sales	$10,728,426
Less: All costs and expenses	8,277,294
Profit before taxes	$2,451,132
Provision for income taxes	1,245,430
Net Income	$1,205,702

CONDENSED BALANCED SHEET, DECEMBER 31, 1971

Current assets	$6,102,698	Current liabilities	$1,860,654
Fixed assets (net)	8,478,420	6% mortgage bonds	1,000,000
Other assets	302,982	Capital stock	2,000,000
		Surplus	10,023,446
	$14,884,100		$14,884,100

are shown in Exhibit 1. The company considered the picture given by these statistics to be normal and expected the same general pattern to prevail in the foreseeable future.

Required

1. Calculate the net present value of the proposed investment on the assumption that the company's hurdle rate is 20%.

2. What are the uncertainties with this estimate?

CASE 8.2   THE SUPER PROJECT

In March 1967, Crosby Sanberg, manager-financial analyst at General Foods Corporation, told a casewriter, "What I learned about incremental analysis at the Business School doesn't always work." He was convinced that under some circumstances sunk costs were relevant to capital project evaluations. He was also concerned that financial and accounting systems did not provide an accurate estimate of incremental costs and revenues, and that this was one of the most difficult problems in measuring the value of capital investment proposals. Sanberg used the Super project[1] as an example.

This case was written by Harold E. Wyman. Copyright © by the President and Fellows of Harvard College. Harvard Business School Case 9-112-034.

[1]The name and nature of this new product have been disguised to avoid the disclosure of confidential information.

Super was a new instant dessert, based on a flavored, water-soluable, ag-glomerated[2] powder. Although four flavors would be offered, it was estimated that chocolate would account for 80% of total sales.

General Foods was organized along product lines in the United States, with foreign operations under a separate division. Major U.S. product divisions included Post, Kool-Aid, Maxwell House, Jell-O, and Birds Eye. Financial data for General Foods are given in Exhibits 1, 2, and 3.

The $200,000 capital investment project request for Super involved $80,000 for building modifications and $120,000 for machinery and equipment. Modifications would be made to an existing building, where Jell-O was manufactured. Since available capacity of a Jell-O agglomerator would be used in the manufacture of Super, no cost for the key machine was included in the project. The $120,000 machinery and equipment item represented packaging machinery.

The Market

A Nielsen survey indicated that powdered desserts constituted a significant and growing segment of the total dessert market, as shown in Table A on page 232. On the basis of test market experience, General Foods expected Super to capture a 10% share of the total dessert market. Eighty percent of this expected Super volume would come from growth in total market share or growth in the powders segment, and 20% would come from erosion of Jell-O sales.

Production Facilities

Test market volume was packaged on an existing line, inadequate to handle long-run requirements. Filling and packaging equipment to be purchased had a capacity of 1.9 million units on a two-shift, five-day workweek basis. This represented considerable excess capacity, since 1968 requirements were expected to reach 1.1 million units, and the national potential was regarded as 1.6 million units. However, the extra capacity resulted from purchasing standard equipment, and a more economical alternative did not exist.

Capital Budgeting Procedure

The General Foods Accounting and Financial Manual identified four categories of capital investment project proposals: (1) safety and convenience; (2) quality; (3) increase profit; and (4) other. Proposal procedures and criteria for

---

[2]Agglomeration is a process by which the processed powder is passed through a steam bath and then dried. This fluffs up the powder particles and increases solubility.

EXHIBIT 1 Consolidated Balance Sheet of General Foods
Corporation, Fiscal Year Ended April 1, 1967 ($ millions)

ASSETS

Cash	$ 20
Marketable securities	89
Receivables	180
Inventories	261
Prepaid expenses	14
Current assets	564
Land, buildings, equipment (at cost, less depreciation)	332
Long-term receivables and sundry assets	7
Goodwill	26
Total	$929

LIABILITIES AND STOCKHOLDERS' EQUITY

Notes payable	$ 22
Accounts payable	86
Accrued liabilities	73
Accrued income taxes	57
Current liabilities	238
Long-term notes	39
$3\frac{3}{8}$% debentures	22
Other noncurrent liabilities	10
Deferred investment tax credit	9
Stockholders' equity	
Common stock issued	164
Retained earnings	449
Common stock held in treasury, at cost	(2)
Stockholders' equity	611
Total	$929
Common stock—shares outstanding at year-end	25,127,007

EXHIBIT 2 Common Stock
Prices of General Foods
Corporation, 1958–1967

YEAR	*LOW*	*HIGH*
1958	$24	$ 39¾
1959	37⅛	53⅞
1960	49⅛	75½
1961	68⅝	107¾
1962	57¾	96
1963	77⅝	90½
1964	78¼	93¼
1965	77½	89⅞
1966	62¾	83
1967	65¼	81¾

EXHIBIT 3 Summary of Statistical Data of General Foods Corporation, Fiscal Years 1958–1967
($ millions, except assets per employee and figures on a share basis)

	1958	1959	1960	1961	1962	1963	1964	1965	1966	1967
EARNINGS										
Sales to customers (net)	$1,009	$1,053	$1,087	$1,160	$1,189	$1,216	$1,338	$1,478	$1,555	$1,652
Cost of sales	724	734	725	764	769	769	838	937	965	1,012
Marketing, admin., and general expenses	181	205	236	261	267	274	322	362	406	449
Earnings before income taxes	105	115	130	138	156	170	179	177	185	193
Taxes on income	57	61	69	71	84	91	95	91	91	94
Net earnings	$48	$54	$61	$67	$72	$79	$84	$86	$94	$99
Dividends on common shares	24	28	32	35	40	45	50	50	53	55
Retained earnings—current year	24	26	29	32	32	34	34	36	41	44
Net earnings per common share[a]	$1.99	$2.21	$2.48	$2.69	$2.90	$3.14	$3.33	$3.44	$3.73	$3.93
Dividends per common share[a]	1.00	1.15	1.30	1.40	1.60	1.80	2.00	2.00	2.10	2.20
ASSETS, LIABILITIES, AND STOCKHOLDERS' EQUITY										
Inventories	169	149	157	189	183	205	256	214	261	261
Other current assets	144	180	200	171	204	206	180	230	266	303
Current liabilities	107	107	126	123	142	162	202	173	219	238
Working capital	206	222	230	237	245	249	234	271	308	326
Land, buildings, equipment, gross	203	221	247	289	328	375	436	477	517	569
Land, buildings, equipment, net	125	132	148	173	193	233	264	283	308	332
Long-term debt	49	44	40	37	35	34	23	37	54	61
Stockholders' equity	287	315	347	384	419	454	490	527	569	611
Stockholders' equity per common share[a]	11.78	12.87	14.07	15.46	16.80	18.17	19.53	20.99	22.64	24.32
CAPITAL PROGRAM										
Capital additions	28	24	35	40	42	57	70	54	65	59
Depreciation	11	14	15	18	21	24	26	29	32	34
EMPLOYMENT DATA										
Wages, salaries, and benefits	$128	$138	$147	$162	$171	$180	$195	$204	$218	$237
Number of employees (in thousands)	21	22	22	25	28	28	30	30	30	32
Assets per employee ($ thousands)	$21	$22	$23	$22	$22	$23	$24	$25	$29	$29

[a] Per share figures calculated on shares outstanding at year-end and adjusted for 2-for-1 stock split in August 1960.

TABLE A
Dessert Market, August–September 1966 Compared with August–September 1965

	MARKET SHARE (%) AUG.–SEPT. 1966	% CHANGE FROM AUG.–SEPT. 1965	
		Share	Volume
Jell-O	19.0%	3.6	40.0
Tasty	4.0	4.0	(new)
Total powders	25.3	7.6	62.0
Pie fillings and cake mixes	32.0	−3.9	(no change)
Ice cream	42.7	−3.4	5.0
Total market	100.0%		13.0

accepting projects varied according to category (Exhibit 4). In discussing these criteria, Sanberg noted that the payback and return guidelines were not used as cutoff measures and added:

> Payback and return on investment are rarely the only measure of acceptability. Criteria vary significantly by type of project. A relatively high return might be required for a new product in a new business category. On the other hand, a much lower return might be acceptable for a new product entry which represented a continuing effort to maintain leadership in an existing business by, for example, filling out the product line.

Super fell into the third category, as a profit-increasing project. Estimates of payback and return on funds employed were required for each such project requiring $50,000 or more of new capital funds and expense before taxes. The payback period was the length of time required for the project to repay the investment from the date the project became operational. In calculating the repayment period, only incremental income and expenses related to the project were used.

Return on funds employed (ROFE) was calculated by dividing 10-year average profit before taxes by the 10-year average funds employed. Funds employed included incremental net fixed assets plus or minus related working capital. Start-up costs and any profits or losses incurred before the project became operational were included in the first profit and loss period in the financial evaluation calculation.

Capital Budgeting Atmosphere

A General Foods accounting executive commented on the atmosphere within which capital projects were reviewed:

> Our problem is not one of capital rationing. Our problem is to find enough good solid projects to employ capital at an attractive return on investment. Of course,

The basic criteria to be applied in evaluating projects within each of the classifications are set forth in the following schedule:

| Purpose of Project | Payback and ROFE Criteria |

a. SAFETY AND CONVENIENCE:

1. Projects required for reasons of safety, sanitation, health, public convenience, or other over-riding reason with no reasonable alternatives. Examples: sprinkler systems, elevators, fire escapes, smoke control, waste disposal, treatment of water pollution, etc.

Payback - return on funds projections not required but the request must clearly demonstrate the immediate need for the project and the lack or inadequacy of alternative solutions.

2. Additional nonproductive space requirements for which there are no financial criteria. Examples: office space, laboratories, service areas (kitchens, rest rooms, etc.)

Requests for nonproductive facilities, such as warehouses, laboratories, and offices should indicate the advantages of owning rather than leasing, unless no possibility to lease exists. In those cases where the company owns a group of integrated facilities and wherein the introduction of rented or leased properties might complicate the long-range planning or development of the area, owning rather than leasing is recommended. If the project is designed to improve customer service (such as market centered warehouses) this factor is to be noted on the project request.

b. QUALITY:

Projects designed primarily to improve quality.

c. INCREASE PROFIT:

1. Projects that are justified primarily by reduced costs.

If Payback and ROFE cannot be computed, it must be clearly demonstrated that the improvement is identifiable and desirable. Projects with a Payback period up to ten years and a ten-year return on funds as low as 20% PBT are considered worthy of consideration, provided (1) the end product involved is believed to be a reasonably permanent part of our line or (2) the facilities involved are so flexible that they may be usable for successor products.

2. Projects that are designed primarily to increase production capacity for an existing product.

Projects for a proven product where the risk of mortality is small, such as coffee, Jell-O Gelatin, and cereals, should assure a payback in no more than ten years and a ten-year PBT return on funds of no less than 20%

3. Projects designed to provide facilities to manufacture and distribute a new product or product line.

Because of the greater risk involved such projects should show a high potential return on funds (not less than a ten-year PBT return of 40%) Payback period, however, might be as much as ten years because of losses incurred during the market development period.*

*These criteria apply to the United States and Canada only. Profit-increasing capital projects in other areas in categories c1 and c2 should offer at least a ten-year PBT return of 24% to compensate for the greater risk involved. Likewise, foreign operation projects in the c3 category should offer a ten-year PBT return of at least 48%.

d. OTHER:

This category includes projects which by definition are excluded from the three preceding categories. Examples: standby facilities intended to insure uninterrupted production, additional equipment not expected to improve profits or product quality and not required for reasons of safety and convenience, equipment to satisfy marketing requirements, etc.

While standards of return may be difficult to set, some calculation of financial benefits should be made where possible.

Source: The General Foods Accounting and Financial Manual

EXHIBIT 4 Criteria for Evaluating Projects by General Foods Corporation

the rate of capital inputs must be balanced against a steady growth in earnings per share. The short-term impact of capital investments is usually an increase in the capital base without an immediate realization of profit potential. This is particularly true in the case of new products.

The food industry should show a continuous growth. A cyclical industry can afford to let its profits vary. We want to expand faster than the gross national product. The key to our capital budgeting is to integrate the plans of our eight divisions into a balanced company plan which meets our overall growth objectives. Most new products show a loss in the first two or three years, but our divisions are big enough to introduce new products without showing a loss.

Documentation for the Super Project

Exhibits 5 and 6 document the financial evaluation of the Super project. Exhibit 5 is the summary appropriation request prepared to justify the project to management and to secure management's authorization to expend funds on a capital project. Exhibit 6 presents the backup detail. Cost of the market test was included as "Other" expense in the first period because a new product had to pay for its test market expense, even though this might be a sunk cost at the time capital funds were requested. The "Adjustments" item represented erosion of the Jell-O market and was calculated by multiplying the volume of erosion times a variable profit contribution. In the preparation of this financial evaluation form, costs of acquiring packaging machinery were included but no cost was attributed to Jell-O agglomerator capacity to be used for the Super project because the General Foods Accounting and Financial Manual specified that capital project requests be prepared on an incremental basis:

> The incremental concept requires that project requests, profit projections, and funds-employed statements include only items of income and expense and investment in assets which will be realized, incurred, or made directly as a result of, or are attributed to, the new project.

Exchange of Memos on the Super Project

After receiving the paper work on the Super project, Sanberg studied the situation and wrote a memorandum arguing that the incremental approach advocated by the manual should not be applied to the Super project. His superior agreed with the memorandum and forwarded it to the corporate controller with the covering note contained in Appendix A on pages 241–244. The controller's reply is given in Appendix B on page 245.

NY 1292-A 12-63
PTD. IN U.S.A.

"Super" Facilities   66-42
Project Title & Number

New Request ☒   Supplement ☐

Jell-O Division - St. Louis
Division & Location

Expansion-New Product   ☒ A
Purpose   ☐ R

PROJECT DESCRIPTION

To provide facilities for production of Super, chocolate dessert. This project included finishing a packing room in addition to filling and packaging equipment.

· SUMMARY OF INVESTMENT	
NEW CAPITAL FUNDS REQUIRED	$ 200M
EXPENSE BEFORE TAXES	--
LESS: TRADE-IN OR SALVAGE, IF ANY	--
Total This Request	$ 200M
PREVIOUSLY APPROPRIATED	--
Total Project Cost	$ 200M

FINANCIAL JUSTIFICATION*		
ROFE (PBT BASIS) - 10 YR. AVERAGE	62.9	%
PAYBACK PERIOD April F'68 Feb. F'75 *FROM* *TO*		6.83 YRS.
NOT REQUIRED		☐
* BASED ON TOTAL PROJECT COST AND WORKING FUNDS OF		$ 510M

ESTIMATED EXPENDITURE RATE			
QUARTER ENDING Mar.	F19	67	$ 160M
QUARTER ENDING June	F19	68	40M
QUARTER ENDING	F19		
QUARTER ENDING	F19		
REMAINDER			

OTHER INFORMATION		
MAJOR ☐ SPECIFIC ☐ ORDINARY		BLANKET ☐
INCLUDED IN ANNUAL PROGRAM YES ☐	NO ☐	
PER CENT OF ENGINEERING COMPLETED		80 %
ESTIMATED START-UP COSTS	$	15M
ESTIMATED START-UP DATE		April

LEVEL OF APPROVAL REQUIRED			
☐ BOARD ☐ CHAIRMAN ☐ EXEC. V.P. ☐ GEN. MGR.			

SIGNATURES		DATE
DIRECTOR CORP. ENG.		
DIRECTOR B & A		
GENERAL MANAGER		
VICE PRESIDENT		
EXEC. VICE PRESIDENT		
PRESIDENT		
CHAIRMAN		

For Division Use - Signatures	
NAME AND TITLE	DATE

EXHIBIT 5 Capital-Project Request Form of General Foods Corporation

INSTRUCTIONS FOR CAPITAL PROJECT REQUEST FORM NY 1292-A

The purpose of this form is to secure management's authorization to commit or expend funds on a capital project. Refer to Accounting and Financial Manual Statement No. 19 for information regarding projects to which this form applies.

NEW REQUEST - SUPPLEMENT - Check the appropriate box.

PURPOSE - Identify the primary purpose of the project in accordance with the classifications established in Accounting and Financial Statement No. 19, i.e., Sanitation, Health and Public Convenience, Non-Productive Space, Safety, Quality, Reduce Cost, Expansion - Existing Products, Expansion - New Products, Other (specify). Also indicate in the appropriate box whether the equipment represents an addition or a replacement.

PROJECT DESCRIPTION - Comments should be in sufficient detail to enable Corporate Management to appraise the benefits of the project. Where necessary, supplemental data should be attached to provide complete background for project evaluation.

SUMMARY OF INVESTMENT

New Capital Funds Required - Show gross cost of assets to be acquired.

Expense Before Taxes - Show incremental expense resulting from project.

Trade-in or Salvage - Show the amount expected to be realized on trade-in or sale of a replaced asset.

Previously Appropriated - When requesting a supplement to an approved project, show the amount previously appropriated even though authorization was given in a prior year.

FINANCIAL JUSTIFICATION

ROFE - Show the return on funds employed (PBT basis) as calculated on Financial Evaluation Form NY 1292-C or 1292-F. The appropriate Financial Evaluation Form is to be attached to this form.

Not Required - Where financial benefits are not applicable or required or are not expected, check the box provided. The non-financial benefits should be explained in the comments.

In the space provided, show the sum of The Total Project Cost plus Total Working Funds (line 20, Form NY 1292-C or line 5, Form NY 1292-F) in either of the first three periods, whichever is higher.

ESTIMATED EXPENDITURE RATE - Expenditures are to be reported in accordance with accounting treatment of the asset and related expense portion of the project. Insert estimated quarterly expenditures beginning with the quarter in which the first expenditure will be made. The balance of authorized funds unspent after the fourth quarter should be reported in total.

OTHER INFORMATION - Check whether the project is a major, specific ordinary, or blanket, and whether or not the project was included in the Annual Program. Show estimated percentage of engineering completed; this is intended to give management an indication of the degree of reliability of the funds requested. Indicate the estimated start-up costs as shown on line 32 of Financial Evaluation Form NY 1292-C. Insert anticipated start-up date for the project; if start-up is to be staggered, explain in comments.

LEVEL OF APPROVAL REQUIRED - Check the appropriate box.

Source: General Foods

EXHIBIT 5 (continued)

EXHIBIT 6 Financial Evaluation Form of General Foods Corporation ($ in thousands)

NY 125-2-C
PTD. IN U.S.A.

Division: **Jell-O** Location: **St. Louis** **The Super Project** (Project Title) Project No. **67-89** Date _____ Supplement To. _____

PROJECT REQUEST DETAIL

PROJECT REQUEST DETAIL	1ST PER.
1. LAND	$
2. BUILDINGS	80
3. MACHINERY & EQUIPMENT	120
4. ENGINEERING	
5. OTHER (EXPLAIN)	
6. EXPENSE PORTION (BEFORE TAX)	
7. SUB-TOTAL	$200
8. LESS: SALVAGE VALUE (OLD ASSET)	
9. TOTAL PROJECT COST*	$200
10. LESS: TAXES ON EXP. PORTION	
11. NET PROJECT COST	$200

* Same as Project Request

RETURN ON NEW FUNDS EMPLOYED - 10-YR. AVG.

	PAT (C ÷ A)	PBT (B ÷ A)
A - NEW FUNDS EMPLOYED (LINE 21)	$380	$380
B - PROFIT BEFORE TAXES (LINE 35)		239
C - NET PROFIT (LINE 37)	115	
D - CALCULATED RETURN	30.2 %	62.0 %

PAYBACK YEARS FROM OPERATIONAL DATE

PART YEAR CALCULATION FOR FIRST PERIOD	— Yrs.
NUMBER OF FULL YEARS TO PAY BACK	6.00 Yrs.
PART YEAR CALCULATION FOR LAST PERIOD	0.83 Yrs.
TOTAL YEARS TO PAY BACK	6.83 Yrs.

FUNDS EMPLOYED / PROFIT AND LOSS

	1ST PER. F 68	2ND PER. F 69	3RD PER. F 70	4TH PER. F 71	5TH PER. F 72	6TH PER. F 73	7TH PER. F 74	8TH PER. F 75	9TH PER. F 76	10TH PER. F 77	11TH PER.	10-YR. AVG.
12. NET PROJECT COST (LINE 11)	$200	200	200	200	200	200	200	200	200	200		
13. DEDUCT DEPRECIATION (CUM.)	19	37	54	70	85	98	110	121	131	140		
14. CAPITAL FUNDS EMPLOYED	$181	163	146	130	115	102	90	79	69	60		113
15. CASH												
16. RECEIVABLES	124	134	142	157	160	160	169	169	178	178		157
17. INVENTORIES	207	222	237	251	266	266	281	281	296	296		260
18. PREPAID & DEFERRED EXP.												
19. LESS CURRENT LIABILITIES	(2)	(82)	(108)	(138)	(185)	(184)	(195)	(195)	(207)	(207)		(150)
20. TOTAL WORKING FUNDS (15 THRU 19)	329	274	271	264	241	242	255	255	267	267		267
21. TOTAL NEW FUNDS EMPLOYED (14 + 20)	$510	437	417	394	356	344	345	334	336	327		380
22. UNIT VOLUME (in thousands)	1100	1200	1300	1400	1500	1500	1600	1600	1700	1700	1700	1460
23. GROSS SALES	$2200	2400	2600	2800	3000	3000	3200	3200	3400	3400	3400	2920
24. DEDUCTIONS	88	96	104	112	120	120	128	128	136	136	136	117
25. NET SALES	2112	2304	2496	2688	2880	2880	3072	3072	3264	3264	3264	2803
26. COST OF GOODS SOLD	1100	1200	1300	1400	1500	1500	1600	1600	1700	1700	1700	1460
27. GROSS PROFIT	1012	1104	1196	1288	1380	1380	1472	1472	1564	1564	1564	1343
GROSS PROFIT % NET SALES	%											
28. ADVERTISING EXPENSE	1100	1050	1000	900	700	700	730	730	750	750	750	841
29. SELLING EXPENSE												
30. GEN. AND ADMIN. COSTS												
31. RESEARCH EXPENSE												
32. START-UP COSTS	15											
33. OTHER (EXPLAIN) Post Mkt. Cost	360											
34. ADJUSTMENTS (EXPLAIN) Erosion	180	200	210	220	230	230	240	240	250	250	250	225
35. PROFIT BEFORE TAXES	$(643)	(146)	(14)	168	450	450	502	502	564	564	564	239
36. TAXES	(334)	(76)	(7)	87	234	234	261	261	293	293	293	125
36A. ADD: INVESTMENT CREDIT	(1)	(1)	(1)	(1)	(1)	(1)	(1)	(1)	(1)	(1)	(1)	(1)
37. NET PROFIT	$(308)	(69)	(6)	82	217	217	242	242	271	271	271	115
38. CUMULATIVE NET PROFIT	(308)	(377)	(383)	(301)	(84)	133	375	617	888	1159		
39. NEW FUNDS TO REPAY (21 LESS 38)	$818	814	800	695	440	211	(30)	(283)	(552)	(832)		

EXHIBIT 6 (continued)

INSTRUCTIONS FOR PREPARATION OF FORM NY 1292-C

FINANCIAL EVALUATION

This form is to be submitted to Corporate Budget and Analysis with each profit-increasing capital project request requiring $50,000 or more of capital funds and expense before taxes.

Note that the ten-year term has been divided into eleven periods. The first period is to end on the March 31st following the operational date of the project, and the P & L projection may thereby encompass any number of months from one to twelve, e.g. If the project becomes operational on November 1, 1964, the first period for P & L purposes would be 5 months (November 1, 1964 through March 31, 1965). The next nine periods would be fiscal years (F'66, F'67, etc.) and the eleventh period would be 7 months (April 1, 1974 through October 30, 1974). This has been done primarily to facilitate reporting of projected and actual P & L data by providing for fiscal years. See categorized instructions below for more specific details.

PROJECT REQUEST DETAIL - Lines 1 through 11 show the breakdown of the Net Project Cost to be used in the financial evaluation. Line 8 is to show the amount expected to be realized on trade-in or sale of a replaced asset. Line 9 should be the same as the "Total Project Cost" shown on Form NY 1292-A, Capital Project Request. Space has been provided for capital expenditures related to this project which are projected to take place subsequent to the first period. Indicate in such space the additional costs only; do not accumulate them.

FUNDS EMPLOYED

Capital Funds Employed - Line 12 will show the net project cost appearing on line 11 as a constant for the first ten periods except in any period in which additional expenditures are incurred; in that event show the accumulated amounts of line 11 in such period and in all future periods.

Deduct cumulative depreciation on line 13. Depreciation is to be computed on an incremental basis, i.e., the net increase in depreciation over present depreciation on assets being replaced. In the first period depreciation will be computed at one half of the first year's annual rate; no depreciation is to be taken in the eleventh period. Depreciation rates are to be the same as those used for accounting purposes. Exception: When the depreciation rate used for accounting purposes differs materially from the rate for tax purposes, the higher rate should be used. A variation will be considered material when the first full year's depreciation on a book basis varies 20% or more from the first full year's depreciation on a tax basis.

The ten-year average of Capital Funds Employed shall be computed by adding line 14 in each of the first ten periods and dividing the total by ten.

Total Working Funds - Refer to Financial Policy NO. 21 as a guide in computing new working fund requirements. Items which are not on a formula basis and which are normally computed on a five-quarter average shall be handled proportionately in the first period. For example, since the period involved may be less than 12 months, the average would be computed on the number of quarters involved. Generally, the balances should be approximately the same as they would be if the first period were a full year.

Cash, based on a formula which theorizes a two weeks' supply (2/52nds), should follow the same theory. If the first period is for three months, two-thirteenths (2/13ths) should be used; if it is for 6 months, two-twenty-firsts (2/21sts) should be used, and so forth.

Current liabilities are to include one half of the tax expense as the tax liability. The ten-year averages of Working Funds shall be computed by adding each line across 'or the first ten periods and dividing each total by ten.

PROFIT AND LOSS PROJECTION

P & L Categories (Lines 22 through 32) - Reflect only the incremental amounts which will result from the proposed project; exclude all allocated charges. Include the P & L results expected in the individual periods comprising the first ten years of the life of the project. Refer to the second paragraph of these instructions regarding the fractional years' calculations during the first and eleventh periods.

Any loss or gain on the sale of a replaced asset (see line 8) shall be included in line 33.

As indicated in the caption Capital Funds Employed, no depreciation is to be taken in the eleventh period.

The ten-year averages of the P & L items shall be computed by adding each line across for the eleven periods (10 full years from the operational date) and dividing the total by ten.

Adjustments (line 34) - Show the adjustment necessary, on a before-tax basis, to indicate any adverse or favorable incremental effect the proposed project will have on any other products currently being produced by the corporation.

Investment Credit is to be included on Line 36-A. The Investment Credit will be spread over 8 years, or fractions thereof, as an addition to PAT.

RETURN ON NEW FUNDS EMPLOYED - Ten-year average returns are to be calculated for PAT (projects requiring Board approval only) and PBT. The PAT return is calculated by dividing average PAT (line 37) by average new funds employed (line 36); the PBT return is derived by dividing average PBT (line 37) by average new funds employed (line 21).

PAYBACK YEARS FROM OPERATIONAL DATE

Part Year Calculation for First Period - Divide number of months in the first period by twelve. If five months are involved, the calculation is 5/12 = .4 years.

Number of Full Years to Pay Back - Determined by the last period, excluding the first period, in which an amount is shown on line 39.

Part Year Calculation for Last Period - Divide amount still to be repaid at the end of the last full period (line 39) by net profit plus the annual depreciation in the following year when payback is completed.

Total Years to Pay Back - Sum of full and part years.

To: J. C. Kresslin, Corporate Controller

From: J. E. Hooting, Director, Corporate Budgets and Analysis

March 2, 1967

Super Project

At the time we reviewed the Super project, I indicated to you that the return on investment looked significantly different if an allocation of the agglomerator and building, originally justified as a Jell-O project, were included in the Super investment. The pro rata allocation of these facilities, based on the share of capacity used, triples the initial gross investment in Super facilities from $200,000 to about $672,000.

I am forwarding a memorandum from Crosby Sanberg summarizing the results of three analyses evaluating the project on an:

     I. Incremental basis
    II. Facilities-used basis
  III. Fully allocated facilities and costs basis

Crosby has calculated a 10-year average ROFE using these techniques. Please read Crosby's memo before continuing with my note.

*   *   *   *   *

Crosby concludes that the fully allocated basis, or some variation of it, is necessary to understand the long-range potential of the project.

I agree. We launch a new project because of its potential to increase our sales and earning power for many years into the future. We must be mindful of short-term consequences, as indicated by an incremental analysis, but we must also have a long-range frame of reference if we are to really understand what we are committing ourselves to. This long-range frame of reference is best approximated by looking at fully allocated investment and "accounted" profits, which recognize fully allocated costs because, in fact, over the long run all costs are variable unless some major change occurs in the structure of the business.

Our current GF preoccupation with only the incremental costs and investment causes some real anomalies that confuse our decision making. Super is a good example. On an incremental basis the project looks particularly attractive because by using a share of the excess capacity built on the coattails of the lucrative Jell-O project, the incremental investment in Super is low. If the excess Jell-O capacity did not exist, would the project be any less attractive? In the short term, perhaps yes because it would entail higher initial risk, but in the long term it is not a better project just because it fits a facility that is temporarily unused.

Looking at this point from a different angle, if the project exceeded our investment hurdle rate on a short-term basis but fell below it on a long-term basis (and Super comes close to doing this), should we reject the project? I say yes because over the long run, as "fixed" costs become variable and as we have to commit new capital to support the business, the continuing ROFE will go under water.

In sum, we have to look at new project proposals from both the long-range and the short-term point of view. We plan to refine our techniques of using a fully allocated basis as a long-term point of reference and will hammer out a policy recommendation for your consideration. We would appreciate any comments you may have.

APPENDIX A Memos to Controller

To: J. E. Hooting, Director, Corporate Budgets and Analysis

From: C. Sanberg, Manager, Financial Analysis

February 17, 1967

Super Project: A Case Example of Investment Evaluation Techniques

This will review the merits of alternative techniques of evaluating capital investment decisions using the Super project as an example. The purpose of the review is to provide an illustration of the problems and limitations inherent in using incremental ROFE and payback and thereby provide a rationale for adopting new techniques.

Alternative Techniques

The alternative techniques to be reviewed are differentiated by the level of revenue and investment charged to the Super project in figuring a payback and ROFE, starting with incremental revenues and investment. Data related to the alternative techniques outlined below are summarized [at the end of this memo].

Alternative I. Incremental Basis

Method — The Super project as originally evaluated considered only incremental revenue and investment, which could be directly identified with the decision to produce Super. Incremental fixed capital ($200M) basically included packaging equipment.

Result — On this basis the project paid back in 7 years with a ROFE of 63%.

Discussion — Although it is General Foods' current policy to evaluate capital projects on an incremental basis, this technique does not apply to the Super project. The reason is that Super extensively utilizes existing facilities, which are readily adaptable to known future alternative uses.

Super should be charged with the "opportunity loss" of agglomerating capacity and building space. Because of Super the opportunity is lost to use a portion of agglomerating capacity for Jell-O and other products that could potentially be agglomerated. In addition, the opportunity is lost to use the building space for existing or new product volume expansion. To the extent there is an opportunity loss of existing facilities, new facilities must be built to accommodate future expansion. In other words, because the business is expanding Super utilizes facilities that are adaptable to predictable alternative uses.

Alternative II. Facilities-Used Basis

Method — Recognizing that Super will use half of an existing agglomerator and two-thirds of an existing building, which were justified earlier in the Jell-O project, we added Super's pro rata share of these facilities ($453M) to the incremental capital. Overhead costs directly related to these existing facilities were also subtracted from incremental revenue on a shared basis.

Result — ROFE 34%

Discussion — Although the existing facilities utilized by Super are not incremental to this project, they are relevant to the evaluation of the project because potentially they can be put to alternative uses. Despite a high return on an incremental basis, if the ROFE on a project was unattractive after consideration of the shared use of existing facilities, the project would be questionable. Under these circumstances, we might look for a more profitable product for the facilities.

APPENDIX A (continued)

240

In summary, the facilities-used basis is a useful way of putting various projects on a common ground for purposes of *relative* evaluation. One product using existing capacity should not necessarily be judged to be more attractive than another practically identical product which necessitates an investment in additional facilities.

Alternative III. Fully Allocated Basis

Method — Further recognizing that individual decisions to expand inevitably add to a higher overhead base, we increased the costs and investment base developed in Alternative II by a provision for overhead expenses and overhead capital. These increases were made in year five of the 10-year evaluation period, on the theory that at this point a number of decisions would result in more fixed costs and facilities. Overhead expenses included manufacturing costs, plus selling and general and administrative costs on a per unit basis equivalent to Jell-O. Overhead capital included a share of the distribution system assets ($40M).

Result — ROFE 25%

Discussion — Charging Super with an overhead burden recognizes that overhead costs in the long run increase in proportion to the level of business activity, even though decisions to spend more overhead dollars are made separately from decisions to increase volume and provide the incremental facilities to support the higher volume level. To illustrate, the Division–F1968 Financial Plan budgets about a 75% increase in headquarters' overhead spending in F1968 over F1964. A contributing factor was the decision to increase the sales force by 50% to meet the demands of a growing and increasingly complex business. To further illustrate, about half the capital projects in the F1968 three-year Financial Plan are in the "non-payback" category. This group of projects comprised largely "overhead facilities" (warehouses, utilities, etc.), which are not directly related to the manufacture of products but are necessary components of the total business activity as a result of the cumulative effect of many decisions taken in the past.

The Super project is a significant decision which will most likely add to more overhead dollars as illustrated above. Super volume doubles the powdered dessert business category; it increases the Division businesses by 10%. Furthermore, Super requires a new production technology: agglomeration and packaging on a high-speed line.

Conclusions

1. The incremental basis for evaluating a project is an inadequate measure of a project's worth when existing facilities with a known future use will be utilized extensively.

2. A fully allocated basis of reviewing major new product proposals recognizes that overheads increase in proportion to the size and complexity of the business and provides the best long-range projection of the financial consequences.

APPENDIX A (continued)

APPENDIX A (continued)

Alternative Evaluations of Super Project ($ in thousands)

	I. INCREMENTAL BASIS	II. FACILITIES-USED BASIS	III. FULLY ALLOCATED BASIS
INVESTMENT			
Working capital	$267	$267	$267
Fixed capital			
Gross	200	653	672
Net	113	358	367
Total net investment	380	625	634
PROFIT BEFORE TAXES[a]	239	211	157
ROFE	63%	34%	25%

JELL-O PROJECT

$$\text{Building} \qquad \$200 \times \tfrac{2}{3} = \$133$$

$$\text{Agglomerator} \qquad \underline{640 \times \tfrac{1}{2} = \ 320}$$

$$\$453$$

Note: Figures based on 10-year averages

[a]Assumes 20% of Super volume will replace existing Jell-O business

To: Mr. J. E. Hooting, Director, Corporate Budgets and Analysis

From: Mr. J. C. Kresslin, Corporate Controller

Subject: Super Project

March 7, 1967

On March 2 you sent me a note describing Crosby Sanberg's and your thoughts about evaluating the Super project. In this memo you suggest that the project should be appraised on the basis of fully allocated facilities and production costs.

In order to continue the dialogue, I am raising a couple of questions below.

It seems to me that in a situation such as you describe for Super, the real question is a *management decision* as to whether to go ahead with the Super project or not go ahead. Or to put it another way, are we better off in the aggregate if we use half the agglomerator and two-thirds of an existing building for Super, or are we not, on the basis of our current knowledge?

It might be assumed that, for example, half of the agglomerator is being used and half is not and that a minimum economical size agglomerator was necessary for Jell-O and, consequently, should be justified by the Jell-O project itself. If we find a way to utilize it sooner by producing Super on it, aren't we better off in the aggregate, and the different ROFE figure for the Super project by itself becomes somewhat irrelevant? A similar point of view might be applied to the portion of the building. Or if we charge the Super project with half an agglomerator and two-thirds of an existing building, should we then go back and relieve the Jell-O projects of these costs in evaluating the management's original proposal?

To put it another way, since we are faced with making decisions at a certain time on the basis of what we then know, I see very little value in looking at the Super project all by itself. Better we should look at the total situation before and after to see how we fare.

As to allocated production costs, the point is not so clear. Undoubtedly, over the long haul, the selling prices will need to be determined on the basis of a satisfactory margin over fully allocated costs. Perhaps this should be an additional requirement in the course of evaluating capital projects, since we seem to have been surprised at the low margins for "Tasty" after allocating all costs to the product.

I look forward to discussing this subject with you and with Crosby at some length.

APPENDIX B Controller's Reply

Questions:

1. How would you handle the following items in the capital investment proposal?

(a)   Market testing.

(b)   The share of the Jell-O building and the agglomerator that Super Project would use.

(c)   The general overhead.

(d)   The erosion.

2. Calculate the internal rate of return that you think the project will earn using whatever figures you believe are appropriate.

3. On a marginal basis, General Foods calculates an FOFE of 63%. What are the reasons for the difference between your calculation on Question 2 and the 63%?

4. How do you evaluate GF's system of capital investment analysis?

CASE 8.3   LAKESIDE OIL COMPANY

Mr. Karsten, treasurer of the Lakeside Oil Company, received a memorandum from Mr. Bocatelli, manager of the service station division. A few days earlier Mr. Bocatelli had submitted an appraisal of a plan to lease and operate a chain of service stations and restaurants. The Capital Investment Committee, of which Mr. Karsten was a member, had rejected this proposal on the ground that it did not show an adequate return on the investment. In his memorandum Mr. Bocatelli set out to explain and support his belief that the proposal did in fact show an adequate return.

The proposal referred to was the operation of a chain of ten service stations and four restaurants that were to be built on a new automobile turnpike. When the proposition first came to Lakeside's attention, Mr. Bocatelli had proposed that Lakeside lease the properties from the Turnpike Authority for 25 years, agreeing to pay a flat minimum annual rental of $782,300, plus an additional annual rental based on sales of gasoline and food. In the course of negotiations the flat minmum rental was increased by a supplemental annual amount of $474,800 to be paid during the first five years only. The supplemental amount was occasioned by an unexpected increase in the estimated costs of building the properties.

The case was prepared by Donald Hutchinson under the supervision of Professor Robert N. Anthony as a basis for class discussion rather than to illustrate either effective or ineffective handling of an administrative situation. Copyright IMEDE (International Management Development Institute), Lausanne, Switzerland. Reproduced by permission.

These minimum rental figures were equal to the level repayment schedule needed to amortize loans of $10 million and $2 million over 25 and 5 years, respectively, both including interest at 6%. The Turnpike Authority, which was the corporation set up by the State to borrow funds and construct and operate the toll highway, intended to borrow these amounts.

The calculations originally made by Mr. Bocatelli to evaluate this proposal are summarized in Exhibit 1. He considered that from Lakeside's standpoint the lease was a form of investment, since it committed the company to a fixed financial burden over a number of years in the future, and he calculated the amount of the investment by taking the present value of all the flat annual payments guaranteed by Lakeside. For this calculation he used a discount rate of $2\frac{1}{4}\%$ which was the after-tax cost of long-term borrowing to Lakeside. Lakeside had recently successfully sold $215 million of its 25-year bonds at $4\frac{1}{2}\%$. The effective cost of this money, after allowance for income taxes at 50%, was therefore $2\frac{1}{4}\%$.

The revenue from the investment, from Lakeside's viewpoint, was the profit expected to be derived from sales of gasoline and food, less the additional rental based on sales volume. Past experience was similar projects had shown the profit ratios and operating costs that might be expected. Mr. Bocatelli applied these estimates to traffic forecasts supplied by the Turnpike Authority. These forecasts indicated that Lakeside could conservatively expect to sell an average of 40,000,000 gallons of motor fuel per year. He thus calculated average annual income after taxes to be $921,000.

Mr. Bocatelli then calculated the discount factor which made this stream of earnings over 25 years equal the original investment. This was approximately 10%, and therefore he concluded that the project had a rate of return of 10%.

On the basis of some informal discussion, Mr. Bocatelli gathered the impression that at least one or two members of the capital investment committee would approve this method of treating the investment costs and rate of return calculations.

However, before any formal action could be taken on the matter, an unexpected problem arose. In the original plan, the Turnpike Authority intended to borrow the funds needed for the construction of the property from the Trowton National Bank, using the long-term lease from Lakeside as security. In December, however, the Authority's legal counsel ruled that such a loan would be illegal. By State legislation the Authority had been set up as a special corporation, wholly owned by the State. The legislation clearly defined limits on the type and amount of the funds the Authority could borrow. In December 1970, the top limit on bank loans had been reached, and a further extension of credit was therefore not possible.

Mr. Bocatelli thereupon conceived the idea of creating a special corporation which would act as an arms-length intermediary, thereby overcoming the legal restrictions on financing. This corporation, temporarily called X company, would lease the properties directly from the Turnpike Authority, and immediately sublease them to Lakeside. Using the sublease as security, X Company would

EXHIBIT 1   Lakeside Oil Company

Summary of Mr. Bocatelli's First Appraisal

CAPITAL INVESTMENT

Annual flat rental, $782,300
Capitalized at a discount rate of $2\frac{1}{4}\%$ over 25 years and after taxes of 50% on the rental
($782,300 \times 50\% \times 18.47$) $7,224,500
Annual supplemental rental, $474,800
Capitalized at a discount rate of $2\frac{1}{4}\%$ over 5 years, after taxes
($474,800 \times 50 \times 4.68$)   1,111,000

Total present value of future minimum flat rental	$8,335,500
Equipment and fittings	150,000
Total capital investment	$8,485,500

PROFIT

	¢ PER GALLON OF MOTOR FUEL	$ PER YEAR AT 40 MILLION GALLONS OF MOTOR FUEL
Gross margins:		
Motor fuel	11.1	4,440,000
Motor oil	1.5	600,000
Service and labor	.6	240,000
Miscellaneous sales	1.1	440,000
Restaurant sales	3.7	1,480,000
Total gross margin	18.0	$7,200,000
Less variable expense	5.2	2,080,000
Pretax profit before fixed expense	12.8	$5,120,000
Less fixed expense	—	454,000
Pretax profit before gallonage sales rental		$4,666,000

GALLONAGE SALES RENTAL

	RENTAL BASE	$ PER YEAR
Motor fuel, 40,000,000 gallons	4.4¢/gal.	1,760,000
Motor oil (sales of $2,000,000)	4%	80,000
Service and labor (sales of $400,000)	4%	16,000
Miscellaneous sales (sales of $1,800,000)	4%	72,000
Restaurant sales (sales of $8,960,000)	10%	896,000
Total		$2,824,000
Pretax profit before capitalized minimum flat rent		1,842,000
Income taxes at 50%		921,000
After-tax income for *appraisal* purposes (does not include lease expense)		$ 921,000

CALCULATION OF RATE OF RETURN

Present value of $1 per year for 25 years at 10% (from published discount table)	$ 9,077
Present value of $921,000 annual payment for 25 years ($921,000 $\times$ 9.077)	$8,360,000

Since $8,360,000 is approximately equal to the investment of $8,485,000, the rate of return is approximately 10%.

246

borrow the funds needed, which it would then advance to the Turnpike Authority. The money would be borrowed by X Company from the Trowton National Bank under exactly the same conditions as had been previously arranged for the Turnpike Authority. Two separate loans, for $10 million and for $2 million, each at 6%, were to be made. The former would be repaid over each of the next 25 years, including interest, by equal annual payments of $474,800. Lakeside would pay exactly the same annual rent as previously arranged; but in this case payments would be made to X Corporation instead of to the Turnpike Authority.

The only change that Mr. Bocatelli made in the new study, which is summarized in Exhibit 2, was to use a different discount rate in calculating the present value of the lease. In his opinion all other costs were identical with those in his original study. He used a rate of 3% because this was the after-tax cost of this particular piece of credit. The use of this new rate changed the total investment cost to $8,054,800, and consequently resulted in a higher rate of return, that is, $10\frac{1}{2}\%$.

However, when this second report was submitted to the Capital Investment Committee, it was rejected. In particular the Committee did not accept Mr. Bocatelli's figure for the cost of the investment. Its argument was that as X Company was a wholly owned subsidiary its borrowing placed just as much of a strain on Lakeside's credit as borrowing made by Lakeside itself. Thus the net investment should be $12 million, the face amount of the loan. On such an investment the indicated rate of return was only $5\frac{1}{2}\%$, as shown in Exhibit 3. The Committee felt that this was too low a return, and they therefore recommended rejection of the scheme.

EXHIBIT 2 Lakeside Oil Company

Summary of Mr. Bocatelli's Second Appraisal

CAPITAL INVESTMENT

Annual flat rental, $782,300	
(Amortizes $10 million 6% bank loan over 25 years)	
Capitalized at 3% and after taxes of 50% on the rental (783,300 × 17.413 × 50%)	$6,819,800
Annual supplemental rental, $474,800	
(Amortizes $2 million 6% bank loan over 5 years)	
Capitalized at 3% and after taxes at 50% (474,800 × 4.570 × 50%)	1,085,000
Equipment and fittings	150,000
Total capital investment	$8,054,800
After-tax income for appraisal purposes	$921,000
(As calculated in Exhibit 1)	

CALCULATED OF RATE OF RETURN

Present value of $1 per year for 25 years at $10\frac{1}{2}\%$ (from published discount table)	$8.75
Present value of $921,000 annual payments for 25 years	
($921,000 × 8.75)	$8,058,700
Since $8,058,700 is approximately equal to the investment of $7,236,000, the rate	
of return is approximately $10\frac{1}{2}\%$	

EXHIBIT 3   Lakeside Oil Company

Capital Investment Committee's Appraisal

CAPITAL INVESTMENT

X Corporation's $10,000,000 loan at 6%	$10,000,000
X Corporation's $ 2,000,000 loan at 6%	2,000,000
Equipment and fittings	150,000
Total investment	$12,150,000

CALCULATION OF RATE OF RETURN

Present value of $1 per year for 25 years at $5\frac{1}{2}\%$
(from published discount table) $13.15

Present value of $921,000 annual payments for 25 years
($921,000 × 13.15) $12,111,000

Since $12,111,000 is approximately equal to the investment of $12,150,000,
the rate of return is approximately $5\frac{1}{2}\%$.

In his memorandum, asking for a reconsideration, Mr. Bocatelli disagreed with the attitude expressed by the committee, and explained his viewpoint as follows.

> "I reasoned that under this financing agreement, the proper measure of the effect on Lakeside's credit would be the present value of Lakeside's 25 flat annual after-tax rental payments discounted at either:
> (a) 8%, the weighted after-tax cost of capital to Lakeside[1]
> (b) $2\frac{1}{4}\%$, the after-tax cost of long-term borrowing to Lakeside
> (c) 3%, the after-tax cost of this specific piece of Lakeside's credit.
> "I chose the 3% rate as being the most logical in the belief that prospective lenders evaluate the effect of long-term lease commitments on our credit as something less than the long-term borrowing rate.... I do not agree that Lakeside's investment, under such circumstances, is the face amount of X Company's debts. ...It seems to me that such an evaluation departs completely from the discounted cash flow appraisal technique officially recognized by Lakeside.
> "Nonetheless I shall of course defer to the judgment of the Investment Committee."

Mr. Karsten considered this memorandum carefully. More and more of the company's investments were taking the form of leases. It was important that there should not be such a wide difference of opinion among the senior executives of the company on such a basic matter. He wondered what position he should take at the following day's meeting of the Capital Investment Committee.

---

[1]The 8% figure for the weighted after-tax cost of capital included the cost of equity. The latter item was considerably higher than that of debt.

Required

1. Which of the analyses, if any, shows the correct rate of return for the proposed project?

2. If none of the analyses given in the case is correct, what is the correct rate of return on the proposed project?

TABLE A
Present Value of $1

YEARS HENCE	1%	2%	4%	6%	8%	10%	12%	14%	15%	16%	18%	20%	22%	24%	25%	26%	28%	30%	35%	40%	45%	50%
1	.990	.980	.962	.943	.926	.909	.893	.877	.870	.862	.847	.833	.820	.806	.800	.794	.781	.769	.741	.714	.690	.667
2	.980	.961	.925	.890	.857	.826	.797	.769	.756	.743	.718	.694	.672	.650	.640	.630	.610	.592	.549	.510	.476	.444
3	.971	.942	.889	.840	.794	.751	.712	.675	.658	.641	.609	.579	.551	.524	.512	.500	.477	.455	.406	.364	.328	.296
4	.961	.924	.855	.792	.735	.683	.636	.592	.572	.552	.516	.482	.451	.423	.410	.397	.373	.350	.301	.260	.226	.198
5	.951	.906	.822	.747	.681	.621	.567	.519	.497	.476	.437	.402	.370	.341	.328	.315	.291	.269	.223	.186	.156	.132
6	.942	.888	.790	.705	.630	.564	.507	.456	.432	.410	.370	.335	.303	.275	.262	.250	.227	.207	.165	.133	.108	.088
7	.933	.871	.760	.665	.583	.513	.452	.400	.376	.354	.314	.279	.249	.222	.210	.198	.178	.159	.122	.095	.074	.059
8	.923	.853	.731	.627	.540	.467	.404	.351	.327	.305	.266	.233	.204	.179	.168	.157	.139	.123	.091	.068	.051	.039
9	.914	.837	.703	.592	.500	.424	.361	.308	.284	.263	.225	.194	.167	.144	.134	.125	.108	.094	.067	.048	.035	.026
10	.905	.820	.676	.558	.463	.386	.322	.270	.247	.227	.191	.162	.137	.116	.107	.099	.085	.073	.050	.035	.024	.017
11	.896	.804	.650	.527	.429	.350	.287	.237	.215	.195	.162	.135	.112	.094	.086	.079	.066	.056	.037	.025	.017	.012
12	.887	.788	.625	.497	.397	.319	.257	.208	.187	.168	.137	.112	.092	.076	.069	.062	.052	.043	.027	.018	.012	.008
13	.879	.773	.601	.469	.368	.290	.229	.182	.163	.145	.116	.093	.075	.061	.055	.050	.040	.033	.020	.013	.008	.005
14	.870	.758	.577	.442	.340	.263	.205	.160	.141	.125	.099	.078	.062	.049	.044	.039	.032	.025	.015	.009	.006	.003
15	.861	.743	.555	.417	.315	.239	.183	.140	.123	.108	.084	.065	.051	.040	.035	.031	.025	.020	.011	.006	.004	.002
16	.853	.728	.534	.394	.292	.218	.163	.123	.107	.093	.071	.054	.042	.032	.028	.025	.019	.015	.008	.005	.003	.002
17	.844	.714	.513	.371	.270	.198	.146	.108	.093	.080	.060	.045	.034	.026	.023	.020	.015	.012	.006	.003	.002	.001
18	.836	.700	.494	.350	.250	.180	.130	.095	.081	.069	.051	.038	.028	.021	.018	.016	.012	.009	.005	.002	.001	.001
19	.828	.686	.475	.331	.232	.164	.116	.083	.070	.060	.043	.031	.023	.017	.014	.012	.009	.007	.003	.002	.001	
20	.820	.673	.456	.312	.215	.149	.104	.073	.061	.051	.037	.026	.019	.014	.012	.010	.007	.005	.002	.001	.001	
21	.811	.660	.439	.294	.199	.135	.093	.064	.053	.044	.031	.022	.015	.011	.009	.008	.006	.004	.002	.001		
22	.803	.647	.422	.278	.184	.123	.083	.056	.046	.038	.026	.018	.013	.009	.007	.006	.004	.003	.001	.001		
23	.795	.634	.406	.262	.170	.112	.074	.049	.040	.033	.022	.015	.010	.007	.006	.005	.003	.002	.001			
24	.788	.622	.390	.247	.158	.102	.066	.043	.035	.028	.019	.013	.008	.006	.005	.004	.003	.002	.001			
25	.780	.610	.375	.233	.146	.092	.059	.038	.030	.024	.016	.010	.007	.005	.004	.003	.002	.001	.001			
26	.772	.598	.361	.220	.135	.084	.053	.033	.026	.021	.014	.009	.006	.004	.003	.002	.002	.001				
27	.764	.586	.347	.207	.125	.076	.047	.029	.023	.018	.011	.007	.005	.003	.002	.002	.001	.001				
28	.757	.574	.333	.196	.116	.069	.042	.026	.020	.016	.010	.006	.004	.002	.002	.002	.001	.001				
29	.749	.563	.321	.185	.107	.063	.037	.022	.017	.014	.008	.005	.003	.002	.002	.001	.001	.001				
30	.742	.552	.308	.174	.099	.057	.033	.020	.015	.012	.007	.004	.003	.002	.001	.001	.001	.001				
40	.672	.453	.208	.097	.046	.022	.011	.005	.004	.003	.001	.001										
50	.608	.372	.141	.054	.021	.009	.003	.001	.001	.001												

TABLE B
Present Value of $1 Received Annually for N Years

YEARS (N)	1%	2%	4%	6%	8%	10%	12%	14%	15%	16%	18%	20%	22%	24%	25%	26%	28%	30%	35%	40%	45%	50%
1	990	980	962	943	926	909	893	877	870	862	847	833	820	806	800	794	781	769	741	714	690	667
2	1 970	1 942	1 886	1 833	1 783	1 736	1 690	1 647	1 626	1 605	1 566	1 528	1 492	1 457	1 440	1 424	1 392	1 361	1 289	1 224	1 165	1 111
3	2 941	2 884	2 775	2 673	2 577	2 487	2 402	2 322	2 283	2 246	2 174	2 106	2 042	1 981	1 952	1 923	1 868	1 816	1 696	1 589	1 493	1 407
4	3 902	3 808	3 630	3 465	3 312	3 170	3 037	2 914	2 855	2 798	2 690	2 589	2 494	2 404	2 362	2 320	2 241	2 166	1 997	1 849	1 720	1 605
5	4 853	4 713	4 452	4 212	3 993	3 791	3 605	3 433	3 352	3 274	3 127	2 991	2 864	2 745	2 689	2 635	2 532	2 436	2 220	2 035	1 876	1 737
6	5 795	5 601	5 242	4 917	4 623	4 355	4 111	3 889	3 784	3 685	3 498	3 326	3 167	3 020	2 951	2 885	2 759	2 643	2 385	2 168	1 983	1 824
7	6 728	6 472	6 002	5 582	5 206	4 868	4 564	4 288	4 160	4 039	3 812	3 605	3 416	3 242	3 161	3 083	2 937	2 802	2 508	2 263	2 057	1 883
8	7 652	7 325	6 733	6 210	5 747	5 335	4 968	4 639	4 487	4 344	4 078	3 837	3 619	3 421	3 329	3 241	3 076	2 925	2 598	2 331	2 108	1 922
9	8 566	8 162	7 435	6 802	6 247	5 769	5 328	4 946	4 772	4 607	4 303	4 031	3 786	3 566	3 463	3 366	3 184	3 019	2 665	2 379	2 144	1 948
10	9 471	8 983	8 111	7 360	6 710	6 145	5 650	5 216	5 019	4 833	4 494	4 192	3 923	3 682	3 571	3 465	3 269	3 092	2 715	2 414	2 168	1 965
11	10 368	9 787	8 760	7 887	7 139	6 495	5 988	5 453	5 234	5 029	4 656	4 327	4 035	3 776	3 656	3 544	3 335	3 147	2 752	2 438	2 185	1 977
12	11 255	10 575	9 385	8 384	7 536	6 814	6 194	5 660	5 421	5 197	4 793	4 439	4 127	3 851	3 725	3 606	3 387	3 190	2 779	2 456	2 196	1 985
13	12 134	11 348	9 986	8 853	7 904	7 103	6 424	5 842	5 583	5 342	4 910	4 533	4 203	3 912	3 780	3 656	3 427	3 223	2 799	2 468	2 204	1 990
14	13 004	12 106	10 563	9 295	8 244	7 367	6 628	6 002	5 724	5 468	5 008	4 611	4 265	3 962	3 824	3 695	3 459	3 249	2 814	2 477	2 210	1 993
15	13 865	12 849	11 118	9 712	8 559	7 606	6 811	6 142	5 847	5 575	5 092	4 675	4 315	4 001	3 859	3 726	3 483	3 268	2 825	2 484	2 214	1 995
16	14 718	13 578	11 652	10 106	8 851	7 824	6 974	6 265	5 954	5 669	5 162	4 730	4 357	4 033	3 887	3 751	3 503	3 283	2 834	2 489	2 216	1 997
17	15 562	14 292	12 166	10 477	9 122	8 022	7 120	6 373	6 047	5 749	5 222	4 775	4 391	4 059	3 910	3 771	3 518	3 295	2 840	2 492	2 218	1 998
18	16 398	14 992	12 659	10 828	9 372	8 201	7 250	6 467	6 128	5 818	5 273	4 812	4 419	4 080	3 928	3 786	3 529	3 304	2 844	2 494	2 219	1 999
19	17 226	15 678	13 134	11 158	9 604	8 365	7 366	6 550	6 198	5 877	5 316	4 844	4 442	4 097	3 942	3 799	3 539	3 311	2 848	2 496	2 220	1 999
20	18 046	16 351	13 590	11 470	9 818	8 514	7 469	6 623	6 259	5 929	5 353	4 870	4 460	4 110	3 954	3 803	3 546	3 316	2 850	2 497	2 221	1 999
21	18 857	17 011	14 029	11 764	10 017	8 649	7 562	6 687	6 312	5 973	5 384	4 891	4 476	4 121	3 963	3 816	3 551	3 320	2 852	2 498	2 221	2 000
22	19 660	17 658	14 451	12 042	10 201	8 772	7 645	6 743	6 359	6 011	5 410	4 909	4 488	4 130	3 970	3 822	3 556	3 323	2 853	2 498	2 222	2 000
23	20 456	18 292	14 857	12 303	10 371	8 883	7 718	6 792	6 399	6 044	5 432	4 925	4 499	4 137	3 976	3 827	3 559	3 325	2 854	2 499	2 222	2 000
24	21 243	18 914	15 247	12 550	10 529	8 985	7 784	6 835	6 434	6 073	5 451	4 937	4 507	4 143	3 981	3 831	3 562	3 327	2 855	2 499	2 222	2 000
25	22 023	19 523	15 622	12 783	10 675	9 077	7 843	6 873	6 464	6 097	5 467	4 948	4 514	4 147	3 985	3 834	3 564	3 329	2 856	2 499	2 222	2 000
26	22 795	20 121	15 983	13 003	10 810	9 161	7 896	6 906	6 491	6 118	5 480	4 956	4 520	4 151	3 988	3 837	3 566	3 330	2 856	2 500	2 222	2 000
27	23 560	20 707	16 330	13 211	10 935	9 237	7 943	6 935	6 514	6 136	5 492	4 964	4 524	4 154	3 990	3 839	3 567	3 331	2 856	2 500	2 222	2 000
28	24 316	21 281	16 663	13 406	11 051	9 307	7 984	6 961	6 534	6 152	5 502	4 970	4 528	4 157	3 992	3 840	3 568	3 331	2 857	2 500	2 222	2 000
29	25 066	21 844	16 984	13 591	11 158	9 370	8 022	6 983	6 551	6 166	5 510	4 975	4 531	4 159	3 994	3 841	3 569	3 332	2 857	2 500	2 222	2 000
30	25 808	22 396	17 292	13 765	11 258	9 427	8 055	7 003	6 566	6 177	5 517	4 979	4 534	4 160	3 995	3 842	3 569	3 332	2 857	2 500	2 222	2 000
40	32 835	27 355	19 793	15 046	11 925	9 779	8 244	7 105	6 642	6 234	5 548	4 997	4 544	4 166	3 999	3 846	3 571	3 333	2 857	2 500	2 222	2 000
50	39 196	31 424	21 482	15 762	12 234	9 915	8 304	7 133	6 661	6 246	5 554	4 999	4 545	4 167	4 000	3 846	3 571	3 333	2 857	2 500	2 222	2 000

chapter 9

MANUFACTURING COST VARIANCE ANALYSIS

Financial Control is exercised by management through the process of financial planning and variance analysis. Formal financial plans are submitted to senior management, usually annually, for review and approval. After approval, actual results are compared to the plan or budget and variances are analyzed and explained. This part of the book is concerned primarily with the procedural aspects of financial control, while Part IV of the book is concerned primarily with the managerial aspects of financial control.

One of the most important functions of a standard cost system is to help managers control manufacturing costs. Standard cost system are designed to compare systematically the actual cost with the appropriate standards. This part of a standard cost system is called *variance analysis*. This chapter describes manufacturing cost variance analysis.

Chapter 2 described standard cost accounting procedures. (It might be useful to review this chapter before proceeding.) In Chapter 2, the generation of four variances in a typical cost accounting system was described. These variances are material price, material usage, direct labor, and overhead. These variances were generated *within* the books of account. It is almost always necessary, however, to disaggregate these variances further *outside* of the books of account.

REQUIREMENTS OF GOOD VARIANCE ANALYSIS

A variance analysis system has two principal uses. First, it is a system of *management by exception*. A variance analysis system is designed to provide management with information only when conditions vary from what they should be. Under ideal conditions, a variance should appear *only* where management attention is required. Conversely, where management attention is required, a variance should *always* appear. The second use of variances by management is to evaluate the performance of the operating manager. In short, variance analysis provides a means of control and evaluation. Five criteria are necessary, however, before a standard cost system can be used effectively for control and evaluation.

1. There must be accurate standards.
2. It must be possible to control the production variables.
3. It must be possible to measure performance accurately.
4. Responsibility for variances must be pinpointed.
5. Performance variances should be separated from forecast variances.

Good Standards of Performance

First, the variances must be based on accurate standards of performance. This is self-evident. For a variance to be a meaningful measure of performance, it must be a variance from a meaningful standard of performace. If the standard is unattainable, unfavorable variance will be indicated when no management attention is required. Conversely, if the standard does not represent satisfactory performance, no variance will be indicated in instances where the performance is not satisfactory.

Control of Production Variables

Second, the production variables must be controllable. (Production variables include such things as the quality and availability of raw material, the availability of necessary equipment with the right tools in good condition, and so forth.) To the extent that the production variables cannot be controlled by the operating manager, unfavorable variances will not necessarily reflect unsatisfactory performance.

Measurement of Performance

Third, both output and input must be measured accurately. This means that the quality of the production output must be defined and measured and an accurate record and classification of costs maintained.

Indicate Responsibility for Variances

Fourth, the system should pinpoint the responsibility for the variance. This means that the variances should be shown by "responsibility" center. There is usually no serious problem with assigning responsibility for variances. The standard cost system can be designed so that standard cost variances are accumulated by each area of management responsibility. This, of course, requires more clerical work than having a single variance analysis for an entire plant. The procedure, however, is exactly the same. If, for example, there were six productive departments and it was decided to make each manager responsible for meeting standard costs, standards would be developed and output measured for each department.

Separation of Performance and Forecast Variables

Fifth, the system should separate the variances caused by performance from the variances caused by errors in forecasting. For example, material price variances (forecast errors) should be clearly segregated from material usage variances (performance variances). This is necessary if the standard cost system is to be used for performance evaluation. Operating managers should be evaluated on their abilities to manage, not their abilities to forecast economic levels. No system, of course, meets all of these five criteria perfectly. Consequently, even the best variance analysis system requires considerable judgment in evaluating management performance.

DISAGGREGATION OF MANUFACTURING VARIANCES

There are several things to note about standard costs. First, all the standard manufacturing costs are capitalized in work-in-process and finished goods inventories. The standard costs are not subtracted from revenue until the goods are sold. Then the finished goods inventory is credited and cost of sales debited for the *standard cost of the goods sold.*

Second, the variances are written off against income usually in the period in which they were incurred but in any event by the end of the year. Thus the cost of sales consists of the standard cost of the goods sold plus or minus the net amount of variance incurred during the period.

Third, the variance calculations are based on the volume of goods *produced.* It is important to keep this in mind because in Chapter 12 the analysis of variance from the profit budget is described. All profit budget variances, except for manufacturing costs, are based on the volume of *sales.*

Material Cost Variances

Purchase Price Variance. The purchase price variance is the difference in material costs that occur because actual purchase prices differed from standard prices. Purchase price variances are usually segregated at the time of the purchase for reasons previously stated.

A purchase price variance is not an efficiency variance. Standard purchase prices are the best forecast of actual price levels at the time the standards are set. When actual prices differ from these forecasts, it does not mean that the purchasing department has been buying inefficiently. In many instances, the purchasing department has little control over price levels. In other words, prices could increase 5% for example, showing an unfavorable variance. Yet, this could represent an effective buying job because competitive material costs may have gone up even more.

An unfavorable purchase price variance will generally trigger a management decision to examine selling prices. If purchased material costs are rising faster than expected, as shown by unfavorable purchase price variances, the usual answer is to try to recover these increased costs in the selling price.

The formula for calculating *purchase price variance* is:

$$(\text{Standard price} - \text{actual price}) \times \text{actual quantity purchased}$$

A negative variance is unfavorable; a positive variance is favorable. For example:

PRODUCT	STANDARD PRICE	ACTUAL PRICE	QUANTITY PURCHASED
A	1.00	1.25	10,000 units
B	1.50	1.40	5,000 units

Applying the formula for purchase price variance, we get

$$
\begin{aligned}
\text{For A:} \quad (1.00 - 1.25) \times 10,000 &= -\$2500 \\
\text{For B:} \quad (1.50 - 1.40) \times 5,000 &= +\ \underline{\ \ 500} \\
&= -\$2000 \quad \text{(unfavorable variance)}
\end{aligned}
$$

Material Usage Variance. A material usage variance results from using more or less than the standard amount of material. Material usage variance is an efficiency variance and is the responsibility of the manager of the plant or department producing the finished product. Material usage variances are caused principally by excess spoilage.

The formula for *material usage variance* is:

(Standard amount of material − actual amount of material) × standard price

A negative amount is unfavorable; a positive amount is favorable.

For example, assume that a finished product requires $1\frac{1}{2}$ pounds of material for each finished unit. During the month, 50,000 units of this product were completed. The actual amount of the material consumed was 80,000 pounds and the standard cost of the material was $1 per unit. The material usage variance would be calculated as follows:

$$50,000 \text{ units} \times 1.5 \text{ lb} = 75,000 \text{ lb standard usage}$$
$$(75,000 - 80,000) \times \$1 = \$5000 \quad \text{(unfavorable variance)}$$

Direct Labor Variances

A direct labor variance is the difference between the standard direct labor cost and the actual direct labor cost. A direct labor cost variance is an efficiency variance and is the responsibility of the plant or department manager. This variance is caused by a worker's taking either more or less than the standard time, being paid more or less than the standard rate of pay, or both. The formula for calculating direct labor variance is as follows:

$$\text{Direct labor variance} = \left[\begin{array}{c} \text{(standard} \\ \text{hours} \end{array} \times \begin{array}{c} \text{standard rate} \\ \text{per hour)} \end{array} \times \begin{array}{c} \text{(number of} \\ \text{units produced)} \end{array} \right] - \text{actual labor cost}$$

For example, assume that 10,000 units of a product were manufactured for a direct labor cost of $72,000. The standard direct labor hours for the product were 1.5 hours per unit, and the standard rate per hour was $5.00. The standard cost of producing 10,000 units of product would be

$$(1.5 \times \$5) \ (10,000) = \$75,000.$$
$$\$75,000 \ \text{(standard)} - \$72,000 \ \text{(actual)} = \$3000 \ \text{variance} \quad \text{(favorable)}.$$

It is sometimes useful to subdivide further the labor cost variance between that caused by labor hours being different from standard and that caused by the labor rate being different from standard. This is done on the theory that the plant manager is responsible for the hours taken to produce a part but someone else is responsible for the labor rate per hour. This is not true in many cases because the labor costs are usually based on union-management agreement and standards are changed when the level of wages is changed. Thus actual labor rates will differ from standard labor rates only in the case where persons are working out of their wage classification, as when a worker with a skilled classification is doing a job that calls for a semiskilled worker. The assignment of worker to job is the responsibility of the plant manager. Consequently, the entire labor variance is the plant manager's responsibility in this instance.

Rate and Efficiency Variances

Where it is decided that it is useful to separate the labor cost variances into rate variance and efficiency variance, the formula for doing this is as follows:

$$\text{Rate variance} = \text{(actual hours} \times \text{[(standard rate)} - \text{(actual rate)]}$$
$$\text{Efficiency variance} = \text{(total labor variance)} - \text{(rate variance)}$$

$$\text{Efficiency variance} = \left[\left(\begin{array}{c} \text{standard hours for} \\ \text{actual production} \end{array} \right) - \left(\begin{array}{c} \text{actual} \\ \text{hours} \end{array} \right) \right] \times \text{actual rates}$$

$$\text{Rate variance} = \text{(total labor variance)} - \text{(efficiency variance)}.$$

This is an example of a *joint variance*, which is explained next.

Joint Variances

In analyzing variances, a condition known as a *joint variance* occurs when the actual results of two or more elements of cost differ from the standard. This can be illustrated by the following diagram. Assume that a labor standard for producing a unit is 0.5 hours at a rate of $10.20 per hour. The actual results were 0.8 hours per unit at a rate of $10.50 per hour. Diagrammatically this can be shown as follows:

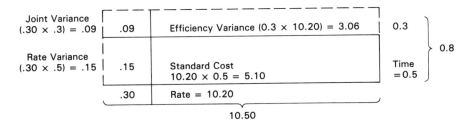

Note that both the time and the rate exceeded standard. There is, therefore, a variance of $0.09 that is attributable to *both* rate and efficiency. This is the *joint* variance. It could be analyzed in at least three ways as follows. The total variance per unit is:

$$5.10 - (10.50 \times 0.8) = 5.10 - 8.40 = -3.30.$$

First, the joint variance can be assigned to rate:

$$\text{Rate variance} = [0.8 \, (-0.3)] = -.24$$
$$\text{Efficiency variance} = (-3.30 + 0.24) = \underline{-3.06}$$
$$-3.30$$

Second, the joint variance can be assigned to efficiency. Thus the variance analysis would be as follows:

$$\text{Efficiency variance} = [(0.5 - 0.8) \times 10.5 = -3.15$$
$$\text{Rate variance} = (-3.30 + 3.15) = \underline{-0.15}$$
$$-3.30$$

Third, the joint variance could be reported separately. The variances per unit would be as follows:

Efficiency variance	-3.06
Rate variance	$- .15$
Joint variance	$\underline{- .09}$
	-3.30

The concept of joint variance is somewhat complex. The manager, however, need not be concerned with joint variances for the following reasons:

1. There is no logical way to divide the joint variance among the elements that caused it. It can occur only when both actual elements differ from standard. Consequently, the only mathematically correct way is to show it separately.
2. It is impractical to show the joint variance separately. It is confusing to managers and is generally so small as to be insignificant. Further, if there are *more* than two elements to the variance, the mathematics becomes increasingly complex. In any event, it is most unlikely the accounting treatment of a joint variance will affect a manager's decisions.
3. From a practical point of view, therefore, the joint variance is almost always assigned to one or the other variance. In the examples in this chapter, the joint labor variances are assigned to the rate variance.

Overhead Variances

To be meaningful, the *overhead variance* must be divided into at least two categories: overhead spending variance and overhead volume variance. This part of the chapter describes the mathematical procedure for calculating these variances.

As described in previous chapters, overhead expense consists of two types of cost: fixed and variable. A standard overhead budget is prepared at standard volume because the total overhead cost is dependent upon the volume of production. For example, assume a plant produces only one product, Y. The plant has a standard fixed overhead cost of $10,000 and a standard variable overhead cost of $1 per unit. If the standard volume is 5000 units, the *total standard overhead cost at standard volume* is calculated as follows:

$$\text{Fixed cost} + (\text{standard volume} \times \text{standard variable cost per unit})$$

or

$$\$10,000 + (5,000 \times \$1) = \$15,000.$$

The standard overhead cost per unit at standard volume is:

$$\frac{\$15,000,}{5,000} \quad \text{or} \quad \$3 \text{ per unit.}$$

The work-in-process overhead account will be debited for the actual overhead costs. For every unit completed, the finished goods inventory account will be debited for $3 and the work-in-process inventory account will be credited. (This is called *absorbed overhead* because the standard cost is absorbed into finished goods inventory.) For example, suppose that 6000 units were produced in the first period and the actual cost of overhead was $17,000. The accounts would look somewhat as follows:

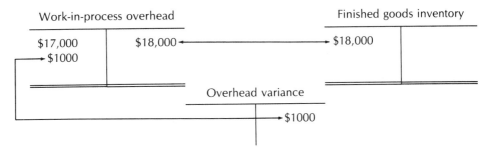

Thus there is a favorable variance of $1000. However, two things have happened. First, the actual volume differed from standard; second, the actual expenditures differed from standard. For the variances to be meaningful, we must separate these two.

Spending Variance.   First, let us look at the spending variance. If the manager had spent according to the standard, he or she would have spent $10,000 plus $1 for each unit produced, or $16,000. Since $17,000 was spent, this is $1,000 *more* than should have been spent. Consequently, there is an unfavorable variance of $1000. The spending variance is the responsibility of the plant manager.

Volume Variance.   There is, however, a net favorable variance of $1000. How does this come about? It is because the actual volume of production was 1000 units *more* than standard. In setting the overhead cost per unit, we assumed a fixed cost of $10,000 and a standard volume of 5000 units, or $2 fixed costs per unit. When production reached 5000 units, we had already debited finished goods inventory with $10,000, or the full amount of the fixed costs. We continued to debit finished goods inventory, however, and to credit work-in-process inventory $2 per unit for an additional 1000 units. Consequently, we removed from work-in-process $2000 *more* than was incurred in fixed cost. This is called the *volume variance* because it is the part of the variance that is caused by the volume being different from standard. This variance is not usually the responsibility of the plant manager. Volume variance can be demonstrated graphically as shown in the accompanying figure.

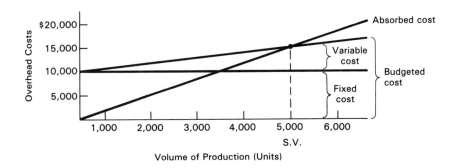

Formulas.   The formulas for calculating overhead variances are as follows:

Absorbed overhead = (standard cost per unit × actual units produced)

Budgeted overhead = (Standard fixed cost)
  + (standard variable cost per unit × actual units produced)

Total variance   = absorbed overhead − actual overhead

Spending variance = budgeted overhead − actual overhead

Volume variance = absorbed overhead − budgeted overhead

A *negative figure* is unfavorable; a *positive figure* is favorable. For example, assume the following:

Standard volume units	1000
Standard variable cost per unit	$ 5
Total standard fixed cost	$10,000

The total standard overhead cost at standard volume is

$$\$10,000 + \$5(1000) = \$15,000.$$

The standard cost per unit is

$$
\begin{array}{lr}
\text{Fixed } \$10,000/1000 = & \$10 \\
\text{Variable} & \underline{5} \\
& \$15 \\
\end{array}
$$

During the first period, the actual volume of production was 1,200 units and the actual overhead cost was \$16,500. The analysis of variance is as follows:

$$
\begin{aligned}
\text{Total variance} &= (\$15 \times 1200) - \$16,500 \\
&= \$18,000 - \$16,500 = \$1,500 \quad \text{(favorable)} \\
\text{Spending variance} &= \$10,000 + (\$5 \times 1200) - \$16,500 \\
&= \$16,000 - \$16,500 = -\$500 \quad \text{(unfavorable)} \\
\text{Volume variance} &= (\$18,000 - \$16,000) = \$2000 \quad \text{(favorable)}
\end{aligned}
$$

We see, then, that the overhead spending variance was \$500 (unfavorable), but the overhead volume variance was \$2000 (favorable). It is evident why a breakdown of the total overhead variance is necessary if management is to be provided with meaningful data.

Chapter 10 describes techniques for controlling overhead costs in more detail.

Summary of Manufacturing Variance Analysis

TYPE OF VARIANCE	RESPONSIBILITY	INDICATED ACTION
Material price	Purchasing	Review selling prices
Material usage	Plant or	Improve efficiency
Labor cost	Department	
Overhead spending	Manager	
Volume variance	Sales	Review sales position

ACCOUNTING FOR VARIANCES

Variances are treated in two ways in accounting. First, they can be written off each month to cost of sales. Second, they can be treated as a deferred expense (unfavorable variance) or a deferred credit (favorable variance) on the balance sheet during the year and the net amount written off to cost of sales at the end of the year. (It is only rarely that standard cost variances are carried over the year end.) The reason for deferring the write-off of a variance is that it is assumed that it will level off over the year and that an unfavorable variance at the beginning of the year will be offset by a corresponding favorable variance later in the year. In general, variances that have a seasonal pattern are deferred. Those that do not have a seasonal pattern are written off monthly.

Material and labor variances are generally written off monthly unless they have a significant seasonal pattern. Overhead volume variances, on the other hand, are usually written off annually, but overhead spending variances are generally written off monthly. In the problems and cases, all variances are written off (i.e., included in cost of sales) in the period that they are incurred.

Where variances are deferred, it is customary to analyze them periodically to make sure that there will not be large unfavorable balances remaining at the end of the year. Where it is evident that a significant deferred variance will not be offset before the end of the year, it is usual to write off the balance over the remaining months. For example, assume that the overhead volume variance was $30,000 at the end of October, with little prospect of it being reduced in November and December. It would be written off at the rate of $10,000 a month for October, November, and December.

In some instances, public accountants may require that part of the variances be allocated to the inventory for financial statement purposes. This is often the case where the variances are significant, particularly if they are favorable.

QUESTIONS

9.1 Explain the concept of management by exception. Give some examples of how standard cost variances make it possible for management to operate on an exception basis.

9.2 What types of action would operating management take when unfavorable variances occur? What types of action would top management take?

9.3 How do standard cost variances help the plant manager when, typically, they might be published several days after the end of the month?

9.4 How does standard cost variance analysis help the supervisor to control costs?

9.5 Explain why it is important to establish objective quality standards where standard cost accounting systems are used.

9.6 How would you go about deciding whether a particular type of variance was useful, neutral, or confusing?

9.7 Why would a purchase price variance suggest that management should review the selling prices of the finished product?

9.8 How can a direct labor "rate" variance occur when standard rates are up to date? What type of management action would such a variance trigger?

9.9 Explain the term *absorbed overhead*. Can you think of why the term *absorbed* is used?

9.10 To what extent do you think that the overhead spending variance should be broken down and analyzed?

PROBLEMS

9.1 Refer to the standard material costs for the Soennecken Company in Problem 2.1. The actual operating information for April 1986 is provided here. Calculate the material price and usage variance for April.

	PRICE PER POUND	AMOUNT USED[a]	MATERIAL COST
Material 1	$ .11	8,400 lb	$ 924
Material 2	.48	15,000	7,200
Material 3	5.25	4,900	25,725
Total			$33,849

Production Volume: A, 1000 units; B, 1200 units; C, 1600 units.

[a]This was also the amount purchased.

9.2 Refer to the standard direct labor costs for the Soennecken Company in Problem 2.1. The actual operating information for April is provided here. Calculate the direct labor efficiency and rate variance for April.

	AVERAGE LABOR RATE	TOTAL HOURS WORKED	ACTUAL LABOR COST
Forging	$3.75	5,000	$18,750
Machining	3.90	4,000	15,600
Assembly	2.10	2,000	4,200
Total			$38,550

Production Volume: A, 1000 units; B, 1200 units; C, 1600 units.

9.3 Refer to the standard overhead costs for the Soennecken Company in Problem 2.1. The actual operating information for April is provided here. Calculate the overhead volume and spending variances for April.

	ACTUAL OVERHEAD	ABSORBED OVERHEAD
Forging	$46,000	$64,800
Machining	60,000	73,800
Assembly	12,000	5,700
Total	$118,000	$144,300

Production Volume: A, 1000 units; B, 1200 units; C, 1600 units.

9.4 The standard labor cost for Product XYZ is as follows:

Department	Direct labor hours	Rate per hour	Direct labor cost per unit
1	6.40	$3.00	$19.20
2	8.12	3.50	28.42
3	4.30	4.00	17.20
4	3.10	2.50	7.75
Total	21.92		$72.57

UNIT DIRECT LABOR COST FOR PRODUCT XYZ

In January, the actual production volume was 10,000 units, and the actual direct labor costs were as follows:

DEPARTMENT	DIRECT LABOR HOURS	DIRECT LABOR RATE	DIRECT LABOR COSTS
1	6,500	$3.10	$20,150
2	8,230	3.20	26,336
3	4,500	4.30	19,350
4	3,000	2.30	6,900
Total	22,230		$72,736

Required

Analyze the labor cost variance in terms of efficiency and rate.

9.5 through 9.7 Fill in the blank spaces.

	PROBLEMS		
	9.5	9.6	9.7
Standard volume (units)	10,000	—	50,000
Variable overhead at S.V.	$10,000	$50,000	—
Fixed overhead costs	10,000	20,000	$25,000
Actual volume (units)	10,000	25,000	40,000
Actual overhead costs	$22,000	$75,000	$43,000
Budgeted costs	—	$82,500	—
Absorbed costs	—	—	$40,000
Total variance	—	—	—
Volume variance	—	—	—
Spending variance	—	—	—

9.8 From the information provided, prepare an analysis of overhead costs compared to budget for the year 1986.

	1986 DEPARTMENTAL BUDGETS			
	Forging	*Machining*	*Assembly*	*Total*
STANDARD DIRECT LABOR AT S.V.	$75,000	$100,000	$100,000	$275,000
VARIABLE OVERHEAD AT S.V.				
Indirect labor—variable	$22,500	$ 40,000	$ 20,000	$ 82,500
Indirect materials	7,500	20,000	10,000	37,500
Utilities	15,000	10,000	10,000	35,000
Subtotal	$45,000	$ 70,000	$ 40,000	$155,000
FIXED OVERHEAD				
Indirect labor—fixed	$15,000	$ 30,000	$ 10,000	$ 55,000
Depreciation	30,000	50,000	10,000	90,000
Subtotal	$45,000	$ 80,000	$ 20,000	$145,000
Total budget S.V.	$90,000	$150,000	$ 60,000	$300,000

	1986 ACTUAL OVERHEAD COSTS			
	Forging	*Machining*	*Assembly*	*Total*
STANDARD DIRECT LABOR AT ACTUAL VOLUME	$100,000	$ 90,000	$110,00	$300,000
ACTUAL DIRECT LABOR COSTS	105,000	93,000	106,000	304,000
OVERHEAD COSTS				
Indirect labor—variable	$ 30,000	$ 38,000	$ 23,000	$ 91,000
Indirect materials	10,000	19,000	10,500	39,500
Utilities	20,000	7,000	11,000	38,000
Indirect labor—fixed	16,000	30,000	11,000	57,000
Depreciation	29,000	51,000	10,000	90,000
Total	$105,000	$145,000	$ 65,500	$315,500

CASES

CASE 9.1   BROADSIDE BOAT BUILDERS, INC.

Located in Cornish, New Hampshire, Broadside Boat Builders provided boaters using the New England lake, river, and coastal waters with a small, lightweight fiberglass sailboat capable of being carried on the roof of a Volkswagen. While the firm could hardly be considered one of the nation's industrial giants, its burgeoning business required it to institute a formal system of cost control.

Mr. Decatur, Broadside's president, explained that "our seasonal demand opposed to a need for regular and level production means that we must keep a good line of credit at the Windsor banks. Modern cost-control methods and consistent inventory-valuation procedures enhance our credibility with the bankers and more importantly have enabled us to improve our methods and procedures. Our foremen have realized the value of good cost accounting and the main office has, in turn, become more aware of problems in the barn."

Broadside's manufacturing and warehouse facilities consisted of three historic New England barns, where 11-foot *Silver Streak* sailboats for "fun and adventure" were made. The company's plans for the near-term future included the addition of 15- and 18-foot sailboats to its present line. Longer-term plans called for adding additional sizes and styles in the hope of becoming a major factor in the regional boat market.

The *Silver Streak* was an open-cockpit day sailer sporting a mainsail and small jib on a telescoping 17-foot aluminum mast. It was ideally suited to the many small lakes and ponds of the region, and after three years it had become quite popular. It was priced at $450 complete.

Manufacturing consisted basically of three processes: molding, finishing, and assembly. Molding included mixing all ingredients to make the fiberglass hull, performing the actual molding, and removing the hull from the mold. Finishing included hand additions to the hull for the running and standard rigging, reinforcement of the mast and tiller steps, and general sanding of rough spots. Assembly consisted of the attachment of cleats, turnbuckles, drain plugs, tiller, and so on, and the inspection of the boat with mast, halyards, and sails in place. The assembly department also prepared the boat for storage or shipment.

All masts, sails, tillers, and hardware were purchased from outside. The molds were good for 250 hulls each and were easily attached to the injection-type equipment used in production.

Mixing and molding fiberglass hulls, while manually simple, required a great deal of expertise or "eyeball," as it was known in the trade. Addition of too much or too little catalyst, use of too much or too little heat, or failure to allow proper time for curing could each cause a hull to be discarded. Conversely, spending too much time on adjustments to mixing or molding equipment or on "personalized" supervision of each hull could cause severe underproduction problems. Once a "batch" of fiberglass was mixed, there was no time to waste being overcautious or it was likely to "freeze" in its kettle.

With such a situation, and the company's announced intent of expanding its product line, it became obvious that a standard cost system would be necessary to help control costs and to provide some reference for evaluating performance.

After lengthy discussion, Davey Jones, the molding foreman, and Rick Ober, chief accountant, agreed to the following standard costs:

MATERIALS

Glass cloth (120 ft² @ $0.40)	$48.00
Glass mix (40 lb @ $0.75)	30.00

DIRECT LABOR

Mixing (0.5 hr @$4.00)	2.00
Molding (1.0 hr @ $4.00)	4.00

INDIRECT COSTS

Absorb @ $3 per hull[a]	3.00
Total Cost to Mold Hull	$87.00

[a]The normal volume of operations for overhead derivation purposes was assumed to be 450 hulls per month. The estimated indirect-cost equation was budget = $1.44 × hulls + $702.

Analysis of Operations

After several additional months of operations, Mr. Ober expressed some disappointment about the apparent lack of attention being paid to the standard costs. He observed that although standards existed, they were infrequently met. Molders tended to have a cautious outlook toward mixing too little or "cooking" too long. No one wanted to end up throwing away one-half of a hull because of too little glass mix.

In reviewing the most recent month's production results, Mr. Ober noted the actual costs for production of 430 hulls:

MATERIALS

Purchased	60,000 ft² glass cloth @ $0.39/ft²
	20,000 lb glass mix @ $0.76/lb
Used	54,000 ft² glass cloth
	19,000 lb glass mix

DIRECT LABOR

	Mixing 210 h @ $4.10/h
	Molding 480 h @ $4.00/h

OVERHEAD

	Incurred $1,400

Before proceeding with further analysis, Ober called Jones to arrange a discussion of variances. He also told President Decatur, "Maybe we should look into an automated molding operation. Although I haven't finished my analysis, it looks like there will be unfavorable variances again. Jones insists that the standards are reasonable, then never meets them!"

Decatur seemed disturbed and answered, "Well, some variances are inevitable. Why don't you analyze them in some meaningful manner and discuss your ideas with Jones? He is a molding expert whose opinion I respect. Then the two of you meet with me to discuss the whole matter."

Required

1. Determine the direct cost and overhead variances. Why do you think they occur?

2. Do you think Broadside's standards are meaningful? How would you improve them?

3. Are the direct-cost variances in mixing a significant matter for Decatur's concern? Why?

CASE 9.2 BEALE COMPANY

Early in November 1986 the new president of the Beale Company was eagerly awaiting the completion of the profit and loss statement for October. He knew that October sales had exceeded those for September by more than $50,000, and he was anxious to see how much of this increased sales volume was reflected as extra profit. When the report came in, however, it showed an overall loss of $5,015 compared with a September profit of $3,509 (see Exhibit 1). The president immediately thought a mistake had been made and called in the controller for an explanation. The controller said the figures were correct, but that in October the company had not produced anywhere near its usual volume, hence the charge for unabsorbed burden had decreased the profit more than added sales had increased it. He said that if the rate of sales was always the same as the rate of factory production, the kind of distortion that was bothering the president would not appear. When the factory operations were out of phase with sales operations, however, such distortions were almost certain to result as long as the company followed the common accounting convention of charging or crediting periodic over- or underabsorbed factory overhead to the current profit and loss account.

The president reacted strongly to the controller's explanations: "I don't care a hoot for your accounting conventions. But I do know this: when our sales go up, with other things reasonably equal, I am going to expect my profit to show an increase. If your reports can't show so simple a thing as that, why do we spend so much money on your department?"

The controller had been thinking about the same problem that disturbed the president, but from a slightly different angle. Accordingly, he seized the op-

---

This case was prepared by C. A. Bliss. Copyright © by the President and Fellows of Harvard University. Harvard Business School case 9-152-001.

EXHIBIT 1   Condensed Income Statement

October 1986

Sales	$336,903	
Cost of sales at standard	178,168	
Gross margin above standard costs		$158,735
Less manufacturing variances		
Labor	4,321[a]	
Material	3,972	
Overhead		
Volume	26,870	
Spending	1,347	
		27,868
Gross profit		130,867
SELLING COSTS:		
Selling expenses	84,514	
Sales taxes	3,236	
Freight allowed	7,195	
Total selling costs		94,945
Operating profit before admin. costs		35,922
ADMINISTRATION COSTS:		
General administrative expenses	20,640	
Research expenses	5,879	
Total administration costs		26,519
Operating profit		9,403
Other income or charges		14,418
Loss, current month		$ 5,015

[a]Credit variance

portunity to propose a radically different approach to the problem of overhead: *charge the fixed overhead costs for the month to the current operating statement in a lump sum* just as is commonly done in the case of selling and administrative expenses. Thus there would be no problem of heavy over- or underabsorbed overhead as the volume of operations changed. Cost of goods sold, of course, now would reflect only the nonfixed factory costs—that is, variable costs, which the controller called direct costs.

As an illustration, the controller reworked the company's figures for October, with the startling result that the former loss of $5,015 was turned into a profit of $11,028 (see Exhibit 2). When this figure was shown to the president he first exclaimed, "That's more like it." Then he hesitated and started to speculate: "But this means more taxes and more demands for wage increases and dividends and what-all. Maybe your idea isn't so good after all."

The controller was in favor of the new plan, largely because of its simplified accounting procedures. For one thing, there would be no fixed overhead costs in

EXHIBIT 2 Condensed Income Statement (proposed style)

October 1986

Sales		$336,903	
Standard "variable" cost of sales		123,133	
Gross margin above variable costs			213,770
SELLING EXPENSES:			
Selling expenses		84,514	
Sales taxes		3,236	
Freight allowed		7,195	
Total selling expenses			94,945
Merchandising margin			118,825
ADMINISTRATIVE EXPENSES:			
General administrative expenses		20,640	
Research expenses		5,879	
Total			26,519
ADDITIONAL FACTORY EXPENSES:			
Fixed factory overhead		65,862	
Manufacturing variances			
Labor variance	4,321[a]		
Material variance	3,972		
Overhead variance (spending)	1,347	998	66,860
Operating margin			25,446
Other income or charges			14,418
Profit, current month			$ 11,028

[a]Credit variance

the standard cost figures for different products, but only the three classes of direct costs:

1. The cost of raw materials;
2. direct labor; and
3. the portion of the outlay for manufacturing expenses that varies directly or closely in proportion to productive activity.

Omission of fixed overhead costs from the individual product costs would mean that the vexing and expensive task of working out an acceptable allocation of overhead to each product would be unnecesasry. Inasmuch as many of these prorations had in fact become out of date, the controller was further attracted to this plan by the possibility that the expense of overhauling the figures might be avoided.

The controller also believed the proposed system would greatly sharpen the focus of management on the *controllable* portion of costs by spotlighting the variable elements. Standards for the variable costs incurred by the different departments at different levels of output could be worked out by engineering methods. Since the fixed costs pertaining to factory operations tend to fall into quite a different category from that of the variable costs, they should be segregated anyway. By way of analogy he suggested that, like a retail store, a manufacturing company "purchases" its product for a known direct cost. Consequently, the chief difference between the two kinds of business is that to make a profit the manufacturing company has to pay the fixed factory costs in addition to the selling salaries, administration costs, storage, and so forth. Furthermore, the fixed factory costs are like the occupancy costs (rent, maintenance, etc.) of the retail store. (On such a basis, the factory's direct costs, i.e., variable costs, are similar to the retail store's "cost of purchase.")

The controller argued that a further advantage of his proposal would be the provision of a more satisfactory basis for making the usual monthly comparison of margin figures in the company's product-by-product *Gross Margin Statement*. When recast in the new form (with fixed costs excluded), the figures would be much more meaningful than at present. The new margin figures would be much higher all down the line, of course, but once management adjusted its thinking to the new basis, the controller was confident that the value of knowing how much each product was contributing to the fixed costs and profit would be greatly appreciated.

One of the sales executives supported the controller's argument on the usefulness of the new margin figures. He pointed out, for example, that if there were two products sold by one of his divisions, Products A and B, and if the situation was as described in the following example, Product B, in general, would clearly appear to be the more desirable item to sell.

PRODUCT	STANDARD FACTORY COST PER LB.	SELLING PRICE	MARGIN	% OF SALES
A	$0.897	$1.55	$0.653	42.1
B	1.015	1.80	0.785	43.6

But if the new margin figures were to work out something as follows, then the company's selling effort really should be concentrated on Product A.

PRODUCT	VARIABLE FACTORY COST	SELLING PRICE	NEW MARGIN	% OF SALES
A	$0.413	$1.55	$1.137	73.6
B	0.809	1.80	0.991	55.6

The controller's proposed method of keeping records, the sales executive reasoned, would thus reveal the true opportunities for profit. He cited one company he knew that had so redirected its selling effort that in less than eight months it had shifted from an operating loss to an operating profit and had maintained good profits ever since.

At this point in the discussion the treasurer entered the argument. He observed cynically that if the example cited was typical of the Beale Company, the sales department—in its efforts to get business—would be selling at its usual markup over the new standard cost figures (variable costs only). "When that time comes," he snorted, "how are we going to cover the fixed costs? Where do we get our capital replacements? We'll have to pay the piper sooner or later."

Turning to the controller, who had talked of the desired focus of the new system on variable costs, the treasurer gave his opinion—based on long experience—that it was the lack of control of the long-run costs that really wrecked a

EXHIBIT 3   Condensed Balance Sheets as Actually Prepared

	AS OF SEPTEMBER 30, 1986	*AS OF OCTOBER 31, 1986*
ASSETS		
Current assets	$ 80,560	$ 95,553
Cash	80,560	95,553
Accounts receivable	150,428	178,610
Inventory	573,630	521,822
Total current assets	804,618	795,985
Plant and equipment (net)	2,120,450	2,108,788
Total assets	$2,925,068	$2,904,773
LIABILITIES AND NET WORTH		
Current liabilities	$ 397,480	$ 382,200
Mortgage payable	560,000	560,000
Total liabilities	957,480	942,200
Net worth		
Capital stock	1,000,000	1,000,000
Retained earnings	967,588	962,573
Total net worth	1,967,588	1,962,573
Total liabilities and new worth	$2,925,068	$2,904,773

EFFECT OF DIRECT COST METHOD

If the Beale Company had used the direct cost method, its balance sheets would appear as above except for the inventory and retained earnings items; these would appear as shown below:

	AS OF SEPTEMBER 30, 1986	*AS OF OCTOBER 31, 1986*
Inventory	$401,541	$365,776
Retained earnings	795,499	806,527

Note: In both present and proposed statements, the effect of income taxes is not shown. The Beale Company record estimated income tax expense only at the end of the calendar year.

company. "You can make mistakes on the direct costs," he said, "but because things in this area are constantly changing and because one never makes much of a commitment anyway, the life of the company is really not prejudiced. If necessary, a new management can quickly reverse the trend. But once a company lets the long-run costs get out of control, then the fat really is in the fire. I'm opposed to anything that leads us to take a shortsighted view of cost." To this argument the controller had little to say, except that it was a matter of emphasis, and that he still thought variable costs were most important. (Variable costs were 67% of total costs in 1986.)

All of those discussing the proposal were aware of the effect of the controller's scheme on the inventory items in the balance sheet. The treasurer and the president were worried about this effect, and both wondered if the possible improvement of the operating statement was worth the price of distorting the balance sheet. The controller proposed that a footnote be carried in the balance sheet calling attention to the matter, thus perhaps indicating the extent of the distortion. Balance sheets for Beale as of September 30 and October 31, 1986, are shown in Exhibit 3, with an indication of how the balance sheet figures would appear if the company had used the direct-cost method. Income statements for September, under both the present and proposed methods, are shown in Exhibit 4. The nomenclature and arrangement in Exhibit 4 have been changed somewhat in order to facilitate comparison between the present and proposed systems.

EXHIBIT 4   Condensed Income Statement, September 1986

	AS ACTUALLY PREPARED	UNDER PROPOSED METHOD
Sales	$283,028	$283,028
Cost of sales at standard	152,604	104,662
Gross margin	130,424	178,366
Less manufacturing variances		
Labor	5,426[a]	5,426[a]
Material	5,081	5,081
Overhead		
Volume	447[a]	—
Spending	2,173	2,173
Fixed factory overhead	—	65,862
Subtotal overhead and variances	1,381	67,690
Profit before administrative & selling expenses	129,043	110,676
Selling expenses (total)	85,482	85,482
Administrative expenses (total)	26,026	26,026
Total administrative & selling expenses	111,508	111,508
Operating profit	17,535	(832)
Other income or charges	14,026	14,026
Net profit or loss, current month	$ 3,509	$(14,858)

[a]Credit variance

When one of the officials asked about the federal income tax implications, the controller pointed out that the tax return was a special report, and that it already differed from the company's operating reports in several respects. The reports he was suggesting were monthly profit estimates largely for internal use and were not annual reports. Furthermore, if the company wished to do so, the annual reports could be computed on a more orthodox basis. "But," he insisted, "let's make these monthly reports so that they help us, not handicap us."

Required

1. What do you recommend?

2. What would be the effects of the controller's proposal on the balance sheet?

3. Approximately how busy (relative to normal volume) was the factory in October?

4. Could the problem in the case ever arise with respect to *annual* statements of profit?

CASE 9.3 DAWKINS MANUFACTURING COMPANY

Early in January 1976, the cost report shown in Exhibit 1 was submitted to Mr. Peter Dawkins, president of the Dawkins Manufacturing Company. This report was for the frame department which was one of the primary producing departments in the company. Mr. Dawkins was alarmed by the report because of the

EXHIBIT 1 Comparison of Manufacturing Costs

	METAL FRAME DEPARTMENT		
	1974	*1975*	*Variance, 1975 over 1974*
Raw materials	$535,000	$616,000	$81,000
Direct labor	130,000	135,000	5,000
Deparment overhead:			
Indirect labor	50,000	10,000	(40,000)
Supervision	10,000	10,000	—
Power	4,100	4,750	650
Depreciation	15,000	50,000	35,000
General burden	116,000	132,250	16,250
Total	$860,100	$958,000	$97,900

This case was prepared by N. E. Harlan. Copyright © by the President and Fellows of Harvard University. Harvard Business School case 9-161-002.

increase in cost. He commented that the only area of efficiency seemed to be in the use of indirect labor. Mr. Dawkins requested an investigation of the situation, which produced the following additional information.

The department made two types of metal frames which were used in the construction industry. The primary difference in the types was their size. The larger size of frame, called the J frame, required more material than the small frame (S frame), but less direct labor time was required because of an automatic assembly process which had not yet been adapted to the small frames. The department supervisor said that the J frame required about two units of raw material (primarily metal stripping), whereas the S frame required only one unit. The supervisor indicated that these quantities were based on normal operating efficiency. An investigation of the store room records showed that 560,000 units of raw materials had been issued during 1975, whereas 535,000 units had been issued during 1974.

The direct labor requirement was the opposite of the raw material. A J frame required about one-half the amount of labor time as did the S frame. The foreman estimated that, under normal working conditions, the department should produce about ten J framers per labor hour. The direct labor in the department was about the same insofar as the level of skill required, and the average wage rate per hour was $2.50. Failure to schedule work properly and failure to provide adequately for absenteeism (primarily the responsibility of the personnel department) sometimes resulted in a night shift which was paid a 10% premium. The policy of the company was to avoid night shift work if at all possible.

Late in 1974, the raw material supplier announced that his prices would go up by 10% on January 1, 1975, from $1.00 to $1.10 per unit. The direct labor rate for 1975 was expected to continue at $2.50 per hour. An investigation of the payroll showed that about 52,000 direct labor hours were actually paid for during 1985, while about 50,500 hours had been paid in 1974. The actual direct labor rate did vary from the $2.50 rate because of some night shift work and also because in February 1975, some workers were transferred into the frame department to cover excess absenteeism due to a mild influenza epidemic. These transferred workers received a wage rate somewhat higher than the average for the frame department.

An investigation of the general burden revealed that this cost was an assigned cost. The company's practice was to assign the general administration burden (the cost of such departments as accounting, personnel, general factory management, engineering, etc.) to producing departments on the basis of total direct and indirect labor dollars (excluding supervision). The total general burden for the company was $575,000 in 1975 and $580,000 in 1974. The total direct and indirect labor cost for all producing departments was $900,000 in 1974 and $630,000 in 1975.

During 1975, the company purchased and installed some portable conveyers which made it possible to release several material handlers who made up the largest element of indirect labor. The desirability of the equipment had been assessed by using a ten-year economic life, and this period was chosen for depreciation purposes. A full year's depreciation had been included for 1975.

The power cost was assigned to the frame department by using the unit cost of power as determined by the power service department. In 1974, this cost was 0.8 cents ($0.008) per kilowatt-hour, whereas the rate went up to 0.9 cents ($0.009) in 1975 because of an increase in the cost of fuel used to make the power. The foremen of the power department and the frame department agreed that power consumption was highly dependent on direct labor hours. The frame department foreman said that a fairly good rule of thumb that had been used in the past was 10 kWh of power for every hour of direct labor. He said that if power were used efficiently that this rate of consumption should be attainable.

A check of the production reports showed that production of completed frames for each of the two years was as follows:

	1974	1975
S Frames	150,000	150,000
J Frames	180,000	200,000

Required

1. Explain, insofar as possible, the significance of and reasons for the increase in costs.

2. In general, how would you rate the efficiency of the metal frame department in 1975?

3. Can you suggest a better way of reporting costs for the department in the future?

chapter 10

FINANCIAL CONTROL OF MANUFACTURING OVERHEAD EXPENSES

A standard cost system provides financial control of material and direct labor. Many standard cost systems, however, provide only elementary control over manufacturing overhead. This is because the control of overhead presents two problems not present in the control of material and labor. First, it is much more difficult to set a standard for overhead than for material or direct labor, which can usually be measured with a fair degree of precision. Second, overhead contains variable, semivariable, and fixed costs. Consequently, it is necessary to develop a system that will provide an equitable standard at any level of operation. It should also be noted that overhead can amount to a large proportion of controllable costs, and this is becoming increasingly true. It is vital, therefore, to have a good financial control system for overhead costs. The technique for controlling overhead costs is called *flexible budgeting* or sometimes *overhead expense budgeting*. A complete financial control system for manufacturing costs usually requires a flexible budgeting system as part of the standard cost system. The purpose of this chapter is to describe such systems.

FLEXIBLE OVERHEAD BUDGETING

As indicated in the preceding section, the development of overhead budgets involves two special problems that do not occur to the same degree in controlling other manufacturing costs. First, it is more difficult to establish a standard of performance for overhead than for material and direct labor, which can usually be measured precisely. Second, overhead is partly fixed, partly variable, and partly semivariable, while material and labor costs are, for practical purposes, variable. Consequently, the development of an effective system for controlling overhead costs involves dealing with these two problems.

Cost-Volume Relationship

The problem with the volume of operations occurs, of course, because manufacturing overhead costs are not entirely variable. If the overhead budget is established on a dollar-per-unit basis (as standard costs are), standard volume is the only volume where the amount of budgeted overhead will represent a fair task. For example:

Standard volume	100,000 units
Variable overhead costs	$200,000
Fixed overhead costs	100,000
Total budgeted overhead	$300,000
Standard overhead cost per unit =	$\dfrac{\$300,000}{100,000}$ or $3.00 per unit

If the overhead authorization were based on $3 per unit, at 80,000 units of production the overhead authorization would be 80,000 × $3, or $240,000. If, however, the department was operating at budgeted efficiency, the actual costs would be $100,000 (fixed expense) + $2 (variable cost per unit) × 80,000, or $260,000. The budget performance report would show that the department had spent $20,000 *more than budget*, even though the level of efficiency was exactly at budgeted levels. The reason for this is that $100,000 of overhead costs is fixed any volume. It is clearly more appropriate to have a budget allowance based on the fixed cost plus the variable cost per unit multiplied by the units produced. Budgets employing this principle are known as flexible or variable budgets. This was explained briefly in Chapter 9, and the following diagram was used to explain over- or underabsorbed overhead.

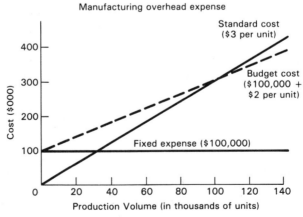

The diagram used to explain under- or overabsorbed overhead also demonstrated the flexible budget. The budgeted line provides the authorization at any volume. The lower the volume, the less the authorization, but only by the amount of the variable cost. In this way, the budget authorization is adjusted to the amount that *should* have been spent at the actual volume of production; the difference between actual and budget is the result of efficiency or inefficiency.

The Flexible Budget Equation. The standard technique for budget authorization under a flexible budget system is expressed by the equation for a straight line, as follows:

$$y = a + bx, \text{ where}$$

$$y = \text{the total budget authorization at volume } x,$$

$$a = \text{total fixed costs,}$$

$$b = \text{variable costs per unit,}$$

$$x = \text{volume in units.}$$

(This is the same equation used in Chapter 9 to separate volume and spending variances.)

Although the mathematics of authorizing budget expenditures on a fixed and variable basis are quite straightforward, few overhead expenses will vary with volume on a straight-line basis in actual business situations. The rate of variability of these expenses is different at different volumes. For example, the rate of scrap expense often tends to increase as volume icnreases. At 80% of standard volume, the scrap rate may be 1 bad item in 100; at 130% of standard volume it may be 3 bad items in 100. Conversely, some expenses tend to level off at higher volumes. The increase in indirect labor between 80% and 100% of standard volume may be greater than the increase between 100% and 120%. Another complication in many production processes is that some expenses tend to increase in steps. For example, it may be necessary to add one foreman with each 10% increase from standard volume. Between 100% and 109% of standard volume, therefore, no increase in the cost of indirect labor occurs, but at 110% of standard volume it is necessary to add one person. In summary, then, manufacturing overhead expense, as experienced in most industries, does not fit into a simple straight-line mathematical function. It is important to remember this when analyzing budget performance. The best that can be done is to *approximate a linear relationship between cost and volume over a limited range of volume.*

Procedure for separating fixed and variable overhead. The *first step* in establishing a flexible budget is to classify all manufacturing overhead accounts into fixed, variable, and semivariable categories. This is done analytically by examining each expense to see which it should be. For example, depreciation, property taxes, property insurance, building maintenance, and the plant manager's office are generally considered completely fixed; whereas supplies and scrap are usually considered completely variable. (In general, only a small number of overhead accounts are completely variable.)

The *second step* is to examine each of the semivariable accounts to see whether the fixed and variable portion of any of these can be separated by inspection. For example, the demand charge for power may be treated as fixed and the remainder of power expense as variable. Or the estimated cost of heating the building may be treated as fixed and the other steam costs treated as variable. In making this analysis, it is not necessary to establish exact relationships between fixed and variable because this is usually not possible. It is sufficient to have approximate relationships. Particularly in accounts with small values the most practical course is to classify the account as either entirely fixed or entirely variable.

The *third step* is to segregate the fixed and variable elements of those semivariable accounts that cannot be segregated readily by inspection. (These usually include most of the indirect labor, maintenance, and fringe benefits.) There are several methods for separating the fixed and variable elements in a semivariable cost. Before discussing these methods, however, the measurement of volume must be considered.

Measurement of Volume.   The task of separating the fixed and variable elements of an expense account involves calculating: (1) the fixed expense at zero volume; and (2) the variable cost per unit of volume. If a department manufactured only one product, there would be no problem in expressing the volume—it is in units produced. Since a one-product department is unusual, some other measure of volume must be used. If a department makes only a limited number of comparable products, it is possible to express volume in terms of standard units. For example, if unit A were considered standard, unit B 80% of standard, and unit C 110% of standard, production could be estimated as follows:

	ACTUAL UNITS PRODUCED	PRODUCTION IN STANDARD UNITS
A	100,000	100,000
B	100,000	80,000
C	100,000	110,000
Total	300,000	290,000

In most instances, even this method is not practical because of the number and diversity of parts produced in the typical department. In these cases, it is usual to use direct labor (either dollars or hours) as a measure of volume. In using direct labor, two things should be noted.

1. Standard direct labor should be used. If not, inefficient direct labor can result in excess overhead authorization.
2. Because volume is measured in terms of direct labor, it does not follow that direct labor creates the overhead costs. Production creates overhead costs and the direct labor is merely a measure of production.

In the examples used throughout the remainder of this chapter, standard direct labor dollars will be used as a measure of the volume of production.

Calculating the Fixed and Variable Components of a Semivariable Expense

The methods for separating semivariable expenses into their fixed and variable components are as follows.

Method 1. Estimate the fixed cost at zero volume and the total cost at standard volume. The slope of the line drawn between these two points represents the variable cost per unit of volume.

For example, the cost of supervision is $200,000 at a standard volume of $1,000,000 standard direct labor; $100,000 of this is considered to be fixed, in that this amount of expense is incurred at zero volume. The variable cost rate would be

$$\frac{\$100,000}{\$1,000,000} \quad \text{or} \quad 10\%$$

The budget authorization equation would be

$$y = 100,000 + 0.10x,$$

that is, total supervisory cost at any volume (*x*) is $100,000 + 10% of standard direct labor at volume *x*.

This method has the advantage of simplicity. It also has the advantage of having a fixed cost that is meaningful to the operating personnel. (In some of the other methods, the fixed expense is determined by a mathematical equation and is not directly related to expected levels of overhead costs at zero volume.)

The main disadvantage of this method is that the variable expense rate represents the *average* variability over a wide range of volume whereas most of the time, the equation is used to authorize overhead at a volume close to standard. As already explained, most overhead costs are not linear from zero volume to capacity. This means that the degree of variability is different at different volumes. The limitations of this method are evident from the fact that the variable expense authorization, when actual volume is in excess of standard volume, depends on the definition of fixed costs at zero volume. One company defined fixed costs as those that would continue through a six months' shutdown. This results in a different equation than if fixed costs were defined as those that would continue for a week after shutdown. (Both definitions are for fixed costs at zero volume.) Clearly, the definition of fixed costs at zero volume has no effect on the expected variability at standard volume.

Method 2. Another method is to estimate the total cost at two volumes, for example, 80% and 120% of standard volume. A line is drawn through these points and extended to zero volume. The point at which this line intercepts the cost line at zero volume (the y-intercept) is the fixed cost. The slope of the line is the variable cost per unit.

For example, assume that standard direct labor is $1,000,000 at standard volume. At 80% of standard volume ($800,000 standard direct labor), it is estimated that supervision should be $450,000. At 120% of standard volume ($1,200,000 standard direct labor), supervision should be $500,000. The variable cost rate is calculated as follows:

	SUPERVISION	*DIRECT LABOR*
Cost of 120% of S.V.	$500,000	$1,200,000
Cost of 80% of S.V.	450,000	800,000
Difference	$ 50,000	$ 400,000

$$\text{Variable cost rate} = \frac{\$50,000}{\$400,000} = 0.125, \text{ or } 12.5\%$$

of standard direct labor dollars. Fixed cost = total cost at 80% of standard volume minus variable cost at 80% of standard volume or $450,000 - (800,000 \times 0.125) = \$350,000$. (The calculation can also be made using 120% of standard volume.) The budget equation then is

$$y = \$350,000 + 0.125x,$$

that is, budgeted cost at volume x is $350,000 + 12.5% of the standard direct labor cost at volume x.

This equation can also be developed by plotting the two points on a graph and drawing a straight line between them. The fixed cost and variable cost rate can then be read directly from the graph.

This method has the advantage of calculating the rate of variability over the range of volume most likely to occur. It has the disadvantage of having a fixed cost that has been developed mathematically. It is only a coincidence if this is the cost that would be incurred at zero volume. The fixed cost is merely the extrapolation of the line drawn between the two estimated costs. It is required only for the budget equation and it is not supposed to represent the cost at zero volume. This fact is sometimes difficult for operating personnel to understand and, because they do not understand it, they tend to suspect its accuracy.

Method 3. A third method is to plot the actual expenses for some previous period and fit a straight line to the points either by inspection or mathematically (e.g., the method of least squares[1]). The usual procedure is to use monthly data for the past 12 to 24 months. Frequently, unusual months are either eliminated or adjusted. Also, periods of either extremely high or low volumes are sometimes excluded.

One advantage of this method is that it provides a measure of the *validity* of the equation. If there is a good linear relationship between the level of costs and the volume, it is immediately evident in the fit of line. (Usually, visual inspection of the fit is all that is required. It is possible, however, to calculate goodness of fit mathematically.) Conversely, if the fit is not good, this is also evident. A second advantage of this method is that the slope of the line is determined by many points instead of just two. The effect of a distortion in any plot point is reduced proportionately to the number of points that have been plotted.

A disadvantage of Method 3 is that it provides only historical data with respect to variability of the cost. One of the main advantages of a flexible budgetary control system is that it makes operating supervisors aware of the necessity of reducing costs quickly as volume is reduced. Usually, the adoption of a flexible budget will result in better cost control with resulting lower costs. (If it did not, what would be the point of installing it?) Historical variability, before the installation of a flexible budget, may not represent a desirable relationship between cost level and volume.

Not only may the historical relationship of cost to volume be undesirable but the absolute level of historical overhead cost may not represent an adequate degree of efficiency. These two points should be kept in mind when using this method for calculating the budget equation.

Method 4. There are several other methods that are combinations of these three. For example, some companies estimate the overhead costs at several production volumes and fit a line to the data. This method is very good (although more costly) because it eliminates the danger of basing the equation on only two points.

Another method that is sometimes used is to estimate the variability of each expense from historical data and then develop a total budgeted cost at standard volume. The line is drawn through the total cost at standard volume and extended to zero volume to obtain the fixed expense part of the equation. For example, an historical study of cost levels reveals that supervision expense varies $0.05 for every dollar change in standard direct labor, that is, a variable rate of 5%. It is further estimated that at a standard volume ($1,000,000 standard direct labor dollars) the supervision expense should be $150,000. At zero volume, the supervision will be $150,000 - ($1,000,000 × 0.05), or $100,000. The equation, therefore, is $y = \$100,000 + 0.05x$. This equation can be developed from a graph

---

[1]The least-squares method for fitting a line is described in the appendix to this chapter.

by drawing a line with a slope of 0.05 for each $1.00 change in standard direct labor through the $150,000 point at standard volume. This line intercepts the *y*-axis at $100,000.

Nonlinear Methods. The flexible budget assumes a linear relationship between cost and volume over the entire range of production. Clearly, this linear relationship does not usually exist, particularly at volumes that are significantly different from standard. In fact, it is generally true that the further the actual volume is from standard, the less accurate will be the adjustment of the budgeted cost to the actual volume of operations. There are several methods that are used to overcome this situation.

First, some companies use a step budget. A *step budget*, as the name implies, is one that is developed at several levels of operation, say 70%, 80%, 90%, 100%, 110% and 120% of standard volume. If done correctly, a step budget should provide a more accurate basis for the volume adjustment.

A second method is to use step budgets for indirect labor, and to use the budget equation for the other costs. A third method is to use step budgets at the supervisor level only. The supervisors' budget would include only the expenses over which they have control and these would be developed on a step basis. Above the supervisory level, a regular flexible budget would be used. This method can be very effective because the step function is most pronounced at the department level. The larger the operation, the more likely it will be that these step functions will be smoothed out. Consequently, a linear approximation may be quite accurate for a plant but quite inaccurate for a given department.

A fourth method is to use a higher-degree function, such as a quadratic equation. This could take into account the curvilinear nature of some cost functions. If a better approximation can be obtained with a quadratic function (and it often can), the only objections would be as follows:

1. It is more complex and harder for the manager to understand;
2. The variable costs would be different at different volumes and, consequently, may not tie into a direct costing system.

Probably, for the above reasons, quadratic formulas are rarely used in budgeting.

In summary, most companies that have a standard cost system and an overhead budgeting system use a linear flexible budget, although often they do not extend the flexible budget down to the supervisor level. It is very important, however, to understand that there are limitations to the accuracy of even the best flexible budget formula.

Determining Levels of Cost

Because the operating budget is used to evaluate the line manager, it must represent a reasonable "task." A budget that can be met by an inefficient manager is hardly a satisfactory basis for evaluating the efficiency of cost performance. Furthermore, performance is frequently measured on a relative basis; that is, even though the budget is supposed to be a more or less absolute goal, there is always a tendency to evaluate the budget performance of a department manager in relation to what others in the group have done. If a budget performance report is to be an effective evaluation tool, the budget must not only represent a reasonable task but the degree of task should be comparable for all departments. Frequently one of the most difficult problems in administering an overhead budget system is establishing a reasonable and equal task among the departments.

In general, the determination of an "adequate task" in a manufacturing plant is a serious problem only in manufacturing overhead budgets. Direct material and direct labor are subject to objective measures, but exact techniques for measuring the efficiency of overhead costs are generally not readily available. Unfortunately, however, overhead costs are frequently the most important segment of controllable manufacturing cost, often four or more times as large as direct labor. The problems associated with establishing an "adequate task" for manufacturing overhead budgets are considered in this section.

The principal reason for the difficulty in establishing an "adequate task" is that a conflict of interests exists between the plant manager and the supervisors (or the divisional manager and the plant manager). It is sometimes perceived to be to the benefit of the plant manager to have as loose a budget as possible. Precisely the same condition applies to the department manager: the easier the budget, the better will be the performance. *It is important in budget administration to recognize that this conflict of interest exists and to take appropriate safeguards.*

The appropriate safeguard is the budget review. Although the budget must be prepared by the managers and approved by their superiors between the preparation and approval there must be some independent group who analyzes the budget and otherwise provides staff assistance to management in evaluating the adequacy of the proposed budget. This function usually comes under the controller, except where there is a separate budget department not reporting to the controller.

The following techniques are used by budget departments (frequently with the help of the industrial engineering department) to insure an adequate and equal task for each budget.

1. **Engineering standards**. For indirect labor, this requires a study of the specific people needed at each volume, using industrial engineering "manning" charts. Through these charts, the precise number of people required for each function is established. For other costs, the actual level is determined, to the extent practical, by industrial engineering studies.

2. **Comparison among departments or plants**. It is sometimes possible to compare directly specific kinds of overhead costs among departments or plants. This usually requires using a common denominator such as direct labor hours. For example, Plant A may have budgeted maintenance expense of $1.00 per direct labor hour; Plant B, $1.10; Plant C, $1.20; and Plant D, $2.00. This comparison does not mean that Plant D's budget is inefficient; it does mean, however, that

the level of expense should be justified by unique circumstances. Comparisons of this kind are used to isolate the questionable areas of the budget. The budget analyst, then, goes back to the plant and either obtains a good reason for the difference or tries to get the plant personnel to change the budget.

This method, although commonly used, has three limitations.

(a)   It can be used only where there are a number of roughly comparable budget units.

(b)   In almost all cases, each budget unit has unique conditions that make comparison in some area of expense meaningless.

(c)   It does not expose a situation in which one plant, because of a unique condition, should have a significantly lower cost than others.

3. **Comparison with past performance**. The most commonly used method for evaluating a budget is to compare the proposed budget with the expense level actually experienced during some previous period (usually the past year). In making this comparison, it is necessary to adjust the previous year's costs to reflect the current year's conditions. For example, adjustments are made for increases in direct labor rates or prices of indirect materials and supplies; the previous year's actual costs are adjusted to standard volume; sometimes adjustments are also made for unusual changes in operating conditions that have occurred since the previous year (for example, changes in the products manufactured).

The principal weaknesses of this method of evaluation are the following:

(a)   It shows only whether the proposed budget represents cost levels that are different from the previous year's. It does not indicate that the absolute level of costs is efficient. The most efficient manager will frequently end up with the most difficult budget.

(b)   The correctness of the adjustment to bring the previous year's expenses up to present conditions is sometimes difficult to evaluate, particularly when technical production or design changes are involved. (These adjustments cannot be eliminated because, in most cases, comparisons are meaningless, without them.)

4. **Best past performance**. An adaptation of Method 3 is to make the proposed budget levels equal to the best cost performance for some previous period of time, for example, the best three months of last year. There are many variations of this method. For example, a different "best" period of each account series could be used. That is, if the "best three months of last year," is chosen, this test could be applied independently for each account series so that indirect labor might have one three-month period as a base and supplies another three-month period. Another adaptation is to use the three best months, rather than the best three-month period. In using this method, it is necessary to use a sufficiently long period. A one-month period can be most unrepresentative.

The best performance method, of course, has some of the disadvantages of using last year's performance. The period selected must be adjusted for changes in conditions that have occurred and this is often difficult to do correctly. Moreover, it tends to penalize the more efficient managers. The best past performance method can be quite useful, however, in isolating those areas of a proposed budget that are seriously out of line. The new budget should not show drastic changes from the best performance of last year without good reasons.

5. **Arbitrary reductions**. A method sometimes used to try to reach an efficient cost level is to make it mandatory each year that the budget level be a designated percentage lower than the previous year's actual cost. The principle is that by constantly tightening the task, the line managers will be forced to use maximum ingenuity and effort in controlling costs.

This method has some obvious disadvantages and should be used with great care. For example, it tends to favor the department that was most inefficient at the time the budget system was installed. The most important drawback, however, is that it can give the line manager an incentive to hold back cost-saving plans. If the expected reduction is 5% a year, it is to a manager's interest to hold back, until the following year, further cost savings as soon as he knows he can attain his present budget.

In general, this method is not satisfactory and should be used only under unusual circumstances. For example, it may be useful for the first year or two after a budget system has been installed until more objective techniques can be developed.

In actual business situations, a good budget analyst uses parts of all the first four methods in analyzing overhead budgets. The important point to remember is that all these methods have some weaknesses and should be used with judgment.

Budget Performance Reporting

The purpose of this part of the chapter is to describe a typical manufacturing overhead expense budget performance report and to explain the general principles of expense budget reporting. The reporting of direct material or direct labor are not considered here because these reports were covered as part of standard cost variance analysis.

Preparation of the Budget Performance.   The preparation of a budget performance report can probably be best explained by an example. The approved budget for Department X in Plant Y of the ABC Company is as follows.

ABC Company
Plant Y, Department X—Overhead Expense Budget at Standard Volume for 1986

| | ACCOUNT SERIES | | | | Variable authorization rate |
		Fixed costs	Variable costs	Total costs	(Variable cost ÷ standard direct labor)
No.	Name				
100	Indirect labor	$ 60,000	$ 60,000	$120,000	$ .500
200	Supplies	1,200	6,000	7,200	.050
300	Tools	3,600	3,000	6,600	.025
400	Utilities	4,800	12,000	16,800	.100
500	Maintenance	12,000	24,000	36,000	.200
600	Fringe benefits	12,000	36,000	48,000	.300
700	Scrap	—	24,000	24,000	.200
800	Depreciation and property taxes	30,000	—	30,000	—
	Total overhead	$123,600	$165,000	$288,600	$1.375
	Standard direct labor at standard volume			$120,000	

In January of 1986, the standard direct labor cost of the products produced in department X was $12,000. Actual costs were as follows: direct labor, $12,500; indirect labor, $12,000; supplies, $750; tools, $500; utilities, $1750; maintenance, $2000; fringe benefits, $4900; scrap, $2500; depreciation and property taxes, $2500.

The budgeted authorization for each expense series is calculated by adding $\frac{1}{12}$ of the annual fixed expense to the variable overhead authorization. The latter is calculated by multiplying the variable authorization rate by the *standard* direct labor at actual volume. (Using the actual direct labor would provide the inefficient manager with additional overhead authorization.)

A typical budget performance report is similar to the following exhibit.

ABC Company
Plant Y, Department X—Direct Labor and Overhead Performance for January 1986

				BUDGET OVER/ (UNDER) ACTUAL	
	ACCOUNT SERIES				
No.	*Name*	*Budget*	*Actual*	*Amount*	*%*
100	Indirect labor	$11,000	$12,000	$(1,000)	(9)%
200	Supplies	700	750	(50)	(7)
300	Tools	600	500	100	17
400	Utilities	1,600	1,750	(150)	(9)
500	Maintenance	3,400	2,000	1,400	40
600	Fringe benefits	4,600	4,900	(300)	(7)
700	Scrap	2,400	2,500	(100)	(4)
800	Depreciation and property taxes	2,500	2,500	—	—
		$26,800	$26,900	$ (100)	—
	Direct labor	12,000	12,500	(500)	(4)
	Total overhead and labor	$38,800	$39,400	$ (600)	(2)%

Timing of Budget Performance Reports

The timing of budget performance reports depends, of course, on management's uses of these reports. A typical report schedule is as follows:

- Daily—Direct labor performance by productive department.
- Weekly—Estimated direct labor and overhead performance reports for all departments.
- Monthly—A preliminary direct labor and overhead performance report for the month by department and for the total plant. (This would be prepared before the books are closed and would be partially forecast.) Final monthly and year-to-date performance report for the plant.

All these reports are not always necessary. A common fallacy is that the department manager depends on his performance report to know what has happened and, consequently, what action must be taken. Usually, the department managers know daily approximately what their cost performance will be because they keep a rough estimate. The performance report only makes the rough estimate more precise. The manager, therefore, does not need to get daily or even weekly reports because he or she does not use these reports as a basis for action. The performance report is used to evaluate performance, after the fact, and to let the manager's superior know when something is going wrong. (If things are going very wrong, it would be very surprising if the department manager's superiors did not already know about it.)

A method that makes it possible to publish a report shortly after the end of the month is to forecast the last few days of the month and publish a preliminary report. A final report is subsequently published, based on the actual data. In most cases, the advantage in timing far offsets the decrease in accuracy resulting from forecasting part of the cost performance.

Some General Principles for Performance Reporting

1. *Include an annual forecast.* A monthly budget performance report is almost always improved by including a forecast of what is expected to happen during the remainder of the year. This forecast indicates to management whether or not action should be taken about the off-standard conditions. If the off-standard results from a seasonal factor, for example, the annual forecast will probably show that by the end of the year the expenses will be at budget levels. This indicates to management that it need not be concerned about a monthly off-standard. The annual forecast also indicates to management *when* to be concerned. If an off-standard condition is expected to become significantly worse before the end of the year, management is forewarned.

2. *Include an explanation of variance.* All budget reports should be accompanied by a letter explaining the reasons for the variances from budget and the corrective actions being taken as well as answering any other questions that the report is likely to raise.

3. *Relate the current month's variances to past performances.* A month is usually too short a time period for any kind of reasonable evaluation. The monthly performance reports can be made much more meaningful, therefore, by analyzing the variances over a longer period of time and classifying them according to their characteristics over this period. For example, variances can be classified between new and chronic (those appearing for a given number of months). Chronic variances can be further classified into those showing trends and those remaining static, and so forth. In this way, it is possible to extend considerably the effective time span of the reporting system.

4. *Review the budget performance reports regularly.* The principal purpose of the expense budget is to motivate the line manager to maintain an efficient operation. The budget will be effective in motivating managers only if they believe that it is being used by their superiors. The budget performance report should, therefore, be reviewed regularly with the people involved. Monthly cost meetings have proved to be a very effective device in many companies. At such meetings, the cost performance of each department is reviewed by the entire group (headed, of course, by the plant manager).

MANAGEMENT CONSIDERATIONS OF MANUFACTURING COST CONTROL SYSTEMS

1. Standard costs and overhead budgeting are not usually systems for direct action. It is very important to understand that often little direct action can be taken on the basis of a budget or standard cost variance report. The reason is that all accounting reports are cumulative and, even if a report is published the day after the month end, an event could have occurred over 30 days ago that needed correction. Even weekly reports are not frequent enough when immediate corrective action must be taken. This situation has three basic implications:

   (a) The person who must take direct action must have other types of control reports and these control reports should be given priority in the timing of their preparation. For example, a department manager may need a scrap report, possibly on an hourly basis and perhaps even more often. Managers need reports on direct labor efficiency, product output, down time of equipment, and so forth. Almost all these reports will be in physical units and will be timed to allow managers to take action as quickly as possible. Many of these reports will be on an exception basis. It is important for the accountant to realize that these are the reports required by the manager in running the department. A delay in these reports could be expensive.

   (b) The standard cost and budget reports are often useful more to the person managing than the person being managed. The budget report usually tells the line manager little that was not already known. On the other hand, it tells the senior manager, who is not intimately familiar with the plant operation, what has happened during the month.

   (c) Two separate systems of control are necessary: one, mostly in nonmonetary units, for direct action and two, a financial control system for directing, motivating, and evaluating line personnel. Combining them into a single system can result in a system that satisfies neither requirement.

2. Many of the benefits of a manufacturing cost control system come from motivating the line manager.

   The managers are motivated to meet cost objectives because they will be evaluated on the basis of performance and will have to explain why they have failed. The senior manager rarely takes any direct action on the basis of a budget performance report. On occasion a line manager may be replaced. Only rarely can senior managers give positive advice because they are usually not close enough to the problem. Manufacturing cost control reports often result in long-term action such as changing personnel, reorganizing a plant or department, or adding new equipment. On a day-to-day basis, however, the positive results of a manufacturing cost control system pretty well boil down to the motivating effect. This has the following implications:

   (a) It is important that the standards and budgets be accepted by the line managers as a fair goal.

   (b) Senior managers should review the budget performance reports regularly and ask for reasons for significant variances. If management does not treat budget performance as an important matter, it will lose much of its motivational impact.

   (c) Senior management must be aware of the motivational impact of standards and budgets and act accordingly. For example, care must be taken not to blame line managers for events that are clearly out of their control. On the other hand, it is necessary that a careful evaluation of variances be made so that line managers can be assigned responsibility where they have control.

3. *Performance reports are only approximations and should not be taken as exact.* There are several reasons for this:

   (a) The standard or budget goal is only an approximation.

   (b) The adjustment of the budget overhead to actual volume will contain some degree of error.

   (c) The measurement of cost, particularly in a short period, can be somewhat inexact. For instance, supplies are usually charged to expense when they are requisitioned, rather than when they are used. As a result, the supply expense in one period could be high because supplies were requisitioned but unused and low in the next because the supplies that were used had been requisitioned during the previous period. As a general rule, the shorter the time period, the less exact are accounting data.

CHAPTER 10 APPENDIX: LINE FITTING

Fitting by Inspection

One of the simplest and often the most effective ways of determining a relationship is simply to plot a number of points on a graph and to fit a line by inspection. This means that you take a ruler and move it around until it is in a position that seems to be closest to the plotted points. When it seems that the fit is good, draw a line to the *y*-axis. Then, the *a*-value for the equation can be obtained by reading it directly from the graph. (That is the point where the line touches the *y* axis.) The *b* can be obtained by subtracting the *a*-value from the total value at any point and dividing by the value of *x* at that point.

For example, suppose that the relationships between the volume of production and the cost of production are required. The costs and production volumes are known for each month of last year and it is believed that this relationship will continue. The historical data are as follows.

MONTH	TOTAL COST	UNITS PRODUCED
January	110	50
February	110	60
March	120	70
April	140	80
May	130	80
June	130	70
July	140	90
August	120	50
September	110	40
October	130	60
November	140	70
December	140	80

One way to determine the fixed and variable costs of production is to plot the points, draw a line through them, and read the information directly from the chart. This has been done in the accompanying figure.

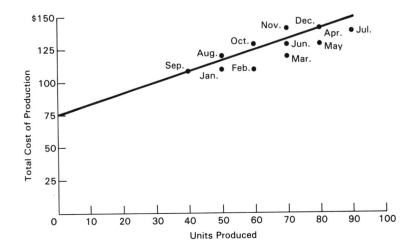

The line drawn through the plot points intersects the y-axis at $75. Therefore, the fixed costs are $75. At a production volume of 90, the line shows the total cost to be $150. The variable cost of production, then is $75. (150 total cost minus 75 fixed) and the variable cost per unit is 75/90 = $0.833 per unit. This calculation can be made from any point on the graph and the answer will be the same. For example, the total cost of 40 units is something over $105, say $107. The total variable cost, therefore is 32/40 = $0.80. (The difference is caused by the inaccuracy of the readings.) Try several other points on the graph.

Method of Least Squares

The objective in fitting a line to historical data is to draw the line in such a way that the differences between the plotted point and the values indicated by the line are at a minimum. The best-fitting line is the one that results in the smallest total difference when the differences between the plotted points and the line are summed. The deviations will, of course, be both negative and positive. If actual values of the deviations are used and added algebraically, they might net to a small amount even though the fit of the line were poor. One alternative is to use the absolute values (the value ignoring the signs) of the deviations. Absolute values, however, are inconvenient to work with mathematically. All the actual deviations can be converted mathematically to a positive sign by squaring them. If the squares of the deviations are used, this eliminates the problem of different signs and, at the same time, provides a more convenient mathematical method. For this reason the most common method for fitting a line is one that results in a line that minimizes the sum of the *squares* of the deviations. This is called the *least-squares* method of line fitting. The purpose of this part of the appendix is to describe this method.

The least-squares method of fitting a line is accomplished as follows:

1. Calculate the values for the sum of the
   (a) *y*-values (Σy),
   (b) *x*-values (Σx),
   (c) *x*-values multiplied by *y*-values (Σxy),
   (d) *x*-values squared (Σx^2).

2. Substitute the values calculated in (1) in the following two equations:

$$\Sigma y = na + b\Sigma x$$

$$\Sigma xy = a\Sigma x + b\Sigma x^2$$

(The value of *n* is the number of observations or points in your data.)

3. Solve these equations like any other system of simultaneous linear equations for *a* and *b*. Substitute these values in the equation $y = a + bx$, and you will obtain the equation for the line that will minimize the squares of the deviations of actual data from the line.

Take the example given in the previous section and fit a line using the least-squares method. First, the following computations are made:

(1) y	(2) x	(3) xy	(4) x^2
(Total cost)	*(Volume of production)*	*(1 × 2)*	*(2 × 2)*
110	50	5,500	2,500
110	60	6,600	3,600
120	70	8,400	4,900
140	80	11,200	6,400
130	80	10,400	6,400
130	70	9,100	4,900
140	90	12,600	8,100
120	50	6,000	2,500
110	40	4,400	1,600
130	60	7,800	3,600
140	70	9,800	4,900
140	80	11,200	6,400
1,520	800	103,000	55,800

We find then that

$$\Sigma y = 1{,}520,$$

$$\Sigma x = 800,$$

$$\Sigma xy = 103{,}000,$$

$$\Sigma x^2 = 55{,}800,$$

$$n = 12.$$

Substituting these values in the normal equations, we get

$$1{,}520 = 12a + 800b, \tag{1}$$

$$103{,}000 = 800a + 55{,}800b. \tag{2}$$

Multiplying Eq. (1) by 200. and Eq. (2) by 3, and subtracting, we find that

$$
\begin{array}{rl}
(2)\ \ 309{,}000 = & 2400a = 167{,}400b \\
(1)\ \ \underline{304{,}000 = 2400a + 160{,}000b} \\
5{,}000 = & 7{,}400b \\
7{,}400b = & 5{,}000 \\
b = \dfrac{5{,}000}{7{,}400} = & 0.676.
\end{array}
$$

Substituting .676 for *b* in Eq. (1), we have

$$304{,}000 = 2400a + 108{,}160,$$

$$2400a = 195.840,$$

$$a = 81.6.$$

The equation, then, is

$$y = 81.6 + .676x$$

There are a number of short cut methods for calculating a least-squares fit. There are also computer and calculator programs available to do this.

QUESTIONS

10.1 Explain why standard direct labor hours can be used as a measure of the actual volume of production in adjusting overhead budgets, if many expenses (e.g., utilities, supplies, or maintenance) are not affected significantly by the level of direct labor.

10.2 How are changes in the mix of products taken in account in a flexible budget system where standard direct labor hours are used as the measure of volume?

10.3 Explain why a budget developed from two points—budgeted fixed costs at zero volume and budgeted total costs at standard volume—result in an "average" variability. Why is this a problem?

10.4 Explain why, the larger the production unit, the better approximation of variability is provided by the flexible budget. Can you think of any exceptions to this generalization?

10.5 In order to determine whether a proposed budget represents a greater or lesser efficiency than the previous year, it is necessary to adjust the actual results to present conditions. What would some of these adjustments be? How would you calculate them?

10.6 Under a flexible budgeting system, why would line managers not be better off to hold back the implementation of cost-saving projects once they are sure of meeting their budget? How could this be prevented?

10.7 In what ways can a monthly budget performance report help a plant manager to control cost directly? How can a supervisor use an overhead budget report to control costs?

10.8 How does a budget performance report motivate the operating managers? That is, what actions would they take as a result of these reports that they would not take in any event?

10.9 How do you decide when a variance represents submarginal performance and when it results from the inaccuracies of the system?

10.10 What type of action would top management be likely to take when faced with an unfavorable variance for a given month? If the variance continued for three months?

PROBLEMS

10.1 Express the relationship between cost and volume algebraically in each of the cases described:

    (a) A company has fixed costs of $10,000 and variable costs of $5 per unit.

    (b) The total cost of 1000 units is $5000; the cost of 2000 units is $8000.

    (c) The total cost of 10,000 units is $20,000; the total cost of 15,000 units is $25,000.

    (d) The fixed costs of producing a product are $500. The total cost of producing 1000 units is $700.

    (e) The total cost of producing 5000 units of a product is $10,000. The variable cost per unit is $1.50.

10.2   **(a)** In each of the following cases, calculate the flexible budget equation.

	A	*B*	*C*	*D*
Fixed cost at zero volume	$ 1,000	$10,000	$ 50,000	$100,000
Cost at standard volume	10,000	50,000	200,000	500,000
Standard volume (standard direct labor hours)	10,000	40,000	100,000	200,000

(b) If it has been decided that the fixed costs at zero volume are too low and should be doubled, what effect will this have on the budget equations calculated in (a) above?

(c) What will be the impact of the change described in (b) on budgeted cost at 125% of standard volume?

10.3 Calculate the budget equation for each of the examples listed below.

	A	*B*	*C*	*D*
Standard volume (units)	10,000	20,000	30,000	40,000
Budget cost at:				
80% of S.V.	$20,000	$40,000	$100,000	$540,000
120% of S.V.	30,000	45,000	112,000	700,000

10.4 Calculate the budget equation for each of the examples listed.

	A	*B*	*C*	*D*
Budget cost at S.V.	$10,000	$100,000	$600,000	$400,000
Variable cost per unit	$1.00	$1.50	$.75	$4.00
Standard volume (units)	5,000	50,000	400,000	80,000

10.5 For the following problems: (a) plot the data and fit a line by inspection: (b) calculate the equation for this line: (c) calculate the equation for the line fitted by the method of least squares.

A		B	
x	*y*	*x*	*y*
10	20	4	12
15	32	6	19
11	20	8	27
20	46	10	33
6	9	12	30
25	48	14	32

10.6 At a monthly standard volume of 600,000 units, the budgeted overhead cost is $48,400. It has been determined that the best approximation of the relationship of variable cost to volume is the following quadratic equation:

$$Y = 10,000 + 100X - 0.06X^2,$$

where
Y = the total budgeted cost at volume X, and
X = the number of units produced in thousands of units.

The operating statistics for the final six months of 1987 are as follows.

MONTH	PRODUCTION VOLUME (thousands of units)	TOTAL OVERHEAD COST (in thousands)
January	300	$40.8
February	400	44.1
March	500	46.0
April	600	47.1
May	700	49.2
June	800	55.3

Required

Calculate the under- or overabsorbed overhead for each month and separate it into spending and volume variance.

10.7 The Tri-Ply Company uses a step budget. The budget for Department X for 1987 was as follows:

	PERCENT OF CAPACITY (thousands)				
Expense series	60	70	80	90	100
Indirect labor	$10	$15	$20	$22	$23
Indirect material	5	6	7	8	9
Utilities	7	9	11	12	13
Depreciation	10	10	10	10	10
Maintenance	8	8	8	9	12
Total	$40	$48	$56	$61	$67

The actual results for the first three months were as follows.

EXPENSE SERIES	JANUARY	FEBRUARY	MARCH
Indirect labor	$16	$22	$22
Indirect material	6	8	9
Utilities	11	11	12
Depreciation	11	11	11
Maintenance	8	8	14
Total	$52	$60	$68
Percent of capacity	75%	85%	92%

Required

Analyze the cost perforamnce for January through March. (The budget allowance is calculated by interpolating between the steps. For example, at 75% of capacity, the budget allowance would be halfway between the budget at 70% and the budget at 80% of capacity.)

10.8 Given are the variances from standard, expressed as a percentage of the standard cost for six months. What conclusions can you draw from this information?

		VARIANCE FROM BUDGET: PERCENT OF STANDARD COST				
Indirect Labor:	*Jan.*	*Feb.*	*Mar.*	*Apr.*	*May*	*June*
Supervision	2%	2%	(5)%	(5)%	(5)%	(5)%
Clerical	3	(2)	(2)	3	4	(1)
Inspection	(5)	(5)	(15)	(15)	(5)	—
Sweepers	1	(1)	1	2	1	(1)
Maintenance	5	10	5	(5)	(10)	(5)
Indirect Material:						
Supplies	3	3	3	—	—	—
Maintenance material	5	10	(15)	(20)	20	10
Utilities:						
Electricity	(10)	(7)	(6)	(5)	(4)	(3)
Water	2	3	5	(4)	(3)	5
Steam	(10)	(12)	(18)	(5)	5	10
Depreciation	—	—	—	(10)	(10)	(10)

10.9 From the following data, estimate the budget equation by plotting the data and fitting a line by inspection.

	PROBLEM A		**PROBLEM B**	
Month	*Total budgeted overhead cost*	*Standard direct labor*	*Total budgeted overhead cost*	*Standard direct labor*
Jan.–Feb.	$25,460	$12,500	$435,000	$224,000
Mar.–Apr.	30,920	16,430	526,000	275,000
May–June	40,140	35,690	639,000	352,000
July–Aug.	24,170	12,960	782,000	455,000
Sept.–Oct.	20,190	8,540	843,000	582,000
Nov.–Dec.	18,640	6,420	915,000	625,000

10.10 Listed below are the actual standard direct labor hours and overhead costs incurred during 1985 by month for the Heavy Machining Department of the Weldon Company. The management of Weldon believes that this department was operated in a reasonably efficient manner in 1985.

The Weldon Company—Heavy Machining Department
Actual Standard Direct Labor Hours and Overhead Expenses for 1985

MONTH	STANDARD DIRECT LABOR (hours)	INDIRECT LABOR	INDIRECT MATERIAL	UTILITIES	MAINTE-NANCE	LOSSES AND SCRAP	DEPRECIA-TION AND PROPERTY TAXES
Jan.	10,400	$ 20,980	$ 6,240	$ 6,160	$ 8,100	$ 5,206	$ 10,631
Feb.	11,820	21,763	6,864	6,721	9,430	5,990	10,849
Mar.	12,690	21,897	7,589	6,983	10,150	6,422	11,362
April	14,420	24,460	8,640	7,762	14,605	7,225	11,498
May	15,030	25,190	9,092	8,190	12,782	7,341	10,843
June	10,940	23,465	6,543	6,481	9,745	8,683	10,496
July	9,860	21,841	5,950	5,963	9,440	4,936	10,320
Aug.	8,420	19,360	5,042	5,420	17,105	4,528	10,506
Sept.	8,380	18,398	5,100	5,582	8,095	5,682	10,708
Oct.	9,620	18,243	5,763	5,848	11,405	4,823	11,100
Nov.	10,560	19,624	6,333	6,290	8,640	5,948	10,870
Dec.	9,390	19,041	5,645	5,762	8,450	4,642	10,562
	131,530	$254,262	$78,801	$77,162	$127,947	$71,426	$129,745

Required

1. Prepare what you believe to be a reasonable budget for this department for 1986, assuming that there will be no changes in the general level of wages or material prices. It is also expected that the 1986 volume of activity will be about the same as 1985. The budget should be expressed in terms of monthly fixed cost plus a variable cost per standard direct labor hour for each expense classification.

2. Prepare the January 1986 budget allowances by expense category for the Heavy Machining Department, assuming that there were 10,000 standard direct labor hours in that month.

CASES

CASE 10.1   MALONE MANUFACTURING CORPORATION

Malone Manufacturing Corporation, located in Birmingham, Michigan, was founded in 1965 by George W. Malone. Mr. Malone held both a Bachelor of Science degree in mechanical engineering and a Master of Business Administra-

This case was prepared by John Dearden. Copyright © by the President and Fellows of Harvard University. Harvard Business School case 9-161-014.

tion. After his graduation from the university, Mr. Malone held a series of responsible jobs in engineering and business administration. In 1965 he founded the company that bears his name to supply the automobile companies located in the area with small and medium-sized machined parts.

The company prospered from the start and, by 1980 the company had grown to a size where Mr. Malone could no longer control costs through personal observation. Consequently, he employed a controller, Ms. Helen Bennett. One of the first things Ms. Bennett did after taking over her new job was to establish a variable budgetary control system.

The company continued to grow and by 1985 it contained four major departments: foundry department, heavy machining department, light machining department, and assembly department.

Exhibit 1 is a summary of the 1986 overhead expense budget for the Light Machining Department. This department machined light ferrous castings (up to five pounds). These castings were made by the Foundry Department; the machined castings were then transferred to the Assembly Department.

Manufacturing overhead costs were controlled through a variable budgetary control system. Under this system, the budget authorization was adjusted to the actual volume of production. Authorized costs were the fixed costs plus the variable rate per standard direct labor dollar multiplied by the standard direct labor dollars applicable ῳ the actual production.

The variable rates were calculated each year from the budget. For example,

EXHIBIT 1 Malone Manufacturing Corporation—Light Machining Department

1986 Overhead Budget Summary

Account series number	Account series name	ANNUAL BUDGETED AMOUNT AT STANDARD VOLUME		
		Fixed	Variable	Total
100	Indirect labor	$ 72,000	$ 78,000	$150,000
200	Supplies	1,200	23,800	25,000
300	Utilities	6,000	44,000	50,000
400	Maintenance—material	6,000	9,000	15,000
	Maintenance—labor	6,000	14,000	20,000
500	Scrap	—	15,000	15,000
600	Fringe benefits	12,000	60,000	72,000
700	Depreciation and taxes	36,000	—	36,000
800	Miscellaneous	6,000	4,000	10,000
	Total	$145,200	$247,800	$393,000
Standard direct labor at standard volume				$130,000

the variable rate for indirect labor in the Light Machining Department would be calculated from the data in Exhibit 1 as follows:

Authorized variable cost at standard volume	$ 78,000
Standard direct labor dollars at standard volume	130,000
Authorized cost per dollar of standard direct labor	0.60

For example, if during the month of January, 1986, the standard direct labor at actual volume was $12,000, the authorized budget for indirect labor would be $6000 (the monthly fixed expense) + $7200 [the authorized variable cost (12,000 × .60)] or $13,200. This amount would be compared to the actual cost to determine the efficiency of the department superintendent in this area of overhead expense.

The same procedure was followed for each expense account series except fringe benefits. The variable portion of this account series was 20% of total authorized labor.

Exhibit 2 is a partially completed budget performance report for the month of January.

Required

1. Complete Exhibit 2.

2. What are some of the possible reasons for the variances shown on Exhibit 2?

EXHIBIT 2   Malone Manufacturing Corporation—Light Machining Department

Direct Labor and Manufacturing Overhead Performance Report

ACCOUNT SERIES NUMBER	ACCOUNT SERIES NAME	ACTUAL	BUDGET	ACTUAL UNDER/(OVER) BUDGET Amount	ACTUAL UNDER/(OVER) BUDGET Percent
100	Indirect labor	$13,500	_____	_____	_____
200	Supplies	2,200	_____	_____	_____
300	Utilities	4,400	_____	_____	_____
400	Maintenance—material	560	_____	_____	_____
	Maintenance—labor	600	_____	_____	_____
500	Scrap	1,000	_____	_____	_____
600	Fringe benefits	6,020	_____	_____	_____
700	Depreciation and taxes	3,200	_____	_____	_____
800	Miscellaneous	700	_____	_____	_____
	Total	$32,180	_____	_____	_____

Direct Labor—Actual		$11,000
—Standard		10,000
—Actual under/(over) standard		_____

CASE 10.2   SOCIETÀ RIGAZIO

Flexible Budgets for Cost Control

Società Rigazio manufactures a wide variety of metal products for industrial users in Italy and other European countries. Its head office is located in Milan and its mills in northern Italy provide about 80% of the company's production volume. The remaining 20% is produced in two factories, one in Lyon, France, and the other in Linz, Austria, both serving local markets exclusively through their own sales organizations.

Until recently, the methods used by the Milan headquarters to review subsidiary operations were highly informal. The managing director of each subsidiary visited Milan twice a year, in October and in April, to review his subsidiary's performance and discuss his plans for the future. At other times the managing director would call or visit Milan to report on current developments or to request funds for specified purposes. These latter requests were usually submitted as a group, however, as part of the October meeting in Milan. By and large, if sales showed an increase over those of the previous year and if local profit margins did not decline, the directors in Milan were satisfied and did nothing to interfere with the subsidiary manager's freedom to manage his business as he saw fit.

Società Rigazio found itself for the first time in twelve years with falling sales volume, excess production capacity, rising costs, and a shortage of funds to finance new investments. In analyzing this situation, the Milan top management decided that one thing that was needed was a more detailed system of cost control in its mills, including flexible budgets for the overhead costs of each factory.

The Lyon mill was selected as a "pilot plant" for the development of the new system. Because the Lyon mill produced a wide variety of products in many production departments, it was not possible to prepare a single flexible budget for the entire mill. In fact, Mr. Spreafico, the company's comptroller, found that the work done in most of the production departments was so varied that useful cost volume relationships coud not even be developed on a departmental basis. He began, therefore, by dividing many of the departments into cost centers so that a valid single measure of work performed could be found for each one. Thus a department with both automatic and hand-fed cutting machines might be divided into two cost centers, each with a group of highly similar machines doing approximately the same kind of work.

The establishment of the cost centers did not change the responsibility pattern in the factory. Each department had a foreman who reported to one of two production supervisors; the latter were responsible directly to Mr. Forclas, the plant manager. Each foreman continued to be responsible for the operations of

This case was prepared by Professor G. Shillinglaw. Copyright © by IMEDE (Institut pour l'Etude des Methodes de l'Entreprise, Lausuanne, Switzerland).

EXHIBIT 1

Overhead Cost Summary—Cost Center 2122 (in francs)   September

	STANDARD ALLOWANCE AT NORMAL VOLUME (500 H 25 TONS)	*BUDGETED AT ACTUAL VOLUME (430 H, 23 TONS)*	*ACTUAL MONTH OF SEPTEMBER*	*OVER/ (UNDER) BUDGET*
Supervision	180	180	145	(35)
Indirect labor	1,500	1,360	1,610	250
Waiting time	105	90	177	87
Hourly wage guarantee	70	60	30	(30)
Payroll taxes, etc.	1,614	1,416	1,504	88
Materials and supplies	150	129	141	12
Tools	750	645	638	(7)
Maintenance	1,600	1,536	1,876	340
Scrap loss	2,110	1,941	2,456	515
Allocated costs	5,260	5,260	5,305	45
Total	13,339	12,617	13,882	1,265
Per ton	533.56	548.57	603.57	55.00

all the cost centers in his department. In some cases a cost center embraced an entire department, but most departments contained between two and five cost centers.

Once he had completed this task, Mr. Spreafico turned to the development of flexible budgets. For each cost center he selected the measure or measures of volume that seemed most closely related to cost (e.g., machine hours) and decided what volume was normal for that cost center (e.g., 1000 machine hours per month). The budget allowance at the normal level of operations was to be used later as an element of standard product costs, but the budget allowance against which the foremen's performance was to be judged each month was to be the allowance for the volume actually achieved during that particular month.

Under the new system, a detailed report of overhead cost variances would be prepared in Lyon for the foreman in charge of a particular cost center and for his immediate superior, the production supervisor; a summary report, giving the total overhead variance for each cost center would be sent to the plant manager and to Mr. Duclos, the managing director of Rigazio France, S.A., Lyon. The Milan top management would not recieve copies of any of these reports, but would receive a monthly profit and loss summary, with comments explaining major deviations from the subsidiary's planned profit for the period.

The preparation of the budget formulas had progressed far enough by mid-1986 to persuade Mr. Spreafico to try them out on the September cost data. A top management meeting was then scheduled in Milan to discuss the new system on the basis of the September reports. Mr. Duclos and Mr. Forclas flew to Milan to attend this meeting, accompanied by the comptroller of Rigazio France and a

EXHIBIT 2

Flexible Budget Formula—Cost Center 2122 (figures in francs)

ALLOWANCE FACTORS

	Fixed amount per month	Variable rate	Remarks
Supervision	180	—	% of foreman's time spent in cost center
Indirect labor	500	2.00/DLh	—
Waiting time	—	0.21/DLh	Wages of direct labor workers for time spent waiting for work
Hourly wage guarantee	—	0.14/DLh	Supplement to wages of workers paid by the piece to give them guaranteed minimum hourly wage
Payroll taxes, etc.	204	2.82/DLh	Payroll taxes and allowances at 30% of total payroll excluding direct labor payroll[a]
Materials and supplies	—	0.30/DLh	—
Tools	—	1.50/DLh	—
Maintenance	800	32.00/ton	Actual maintenance hours used at predetermined rate per hour, plus maintenance materials used
Scrap loss	—	84.40/ton	Actual scrap multiplied by difference between materials cost and estimated scrap value per kg
Allocated costs	5260	—	Actual cost per month, allocated on basis of floor space occupied

[a]Budgeted direct labor at standard volume, 500 hr at fr. 7.00 per hr, actual direct labor cost for September was 3053 francs.

production supervisor responsible for some thirty cost centers in the Lyon factory.

Mr. Enrico Montevani, Società Rigazio's managing director, opened the meeting by asking Mr. Spreafico to explain how the budget allowances were prepared. Mr. Spreafico began by saying that the new system was just in its trial stages and that many changes would undoubtedly be necessary before everyone was satisfied with it. "We started with the idea that the standard had to be adjusted each month to reflect the actual volume of production," he continued, "even though that might mean that we would tell the factory they were doing all right when in fact we had large amounts of underabsorbed burden. In that case the problem would be that we had failed to provide enough volume to keep the plant busy, and you can't blame the foremen for that. When you have fixed costs, you just can't use a single standard cost per hour or per ton or per unit, because that would be too high when we're operating near capacity and too low when we're underutilized. Our problem, then, was to find out how overhead cost varies with volume so that we could get more accurate budget allowances for overhead costs at different production volumes.

"To get answers to this question, we first made some preliminary estimates at headquarters, based on historical data in the accounting records both here and in Lyon. We used data on wage rates and purchase prices from the personnel and purchasing departments to adjust our data to current conditions. Whenever we could, we used a mathematical formula known as a "least squares" formula to get an accurate measure of cost variability in relation to changing volume, but sometimes we just had to use our judgment and decide whether to classify a cost as fixed or variable. I might add that in picking our formulas we tried various measures of volume and generally took the one that seemed to match up most closely with cost. In some cost centers we actually used two different measures of volume, such as direct labor hours and product tonnage, and based some of our budget allowances on one and some on the other. These estimates were then discussed with Mr. Forclas and his people at Lyon.

"Although you have a complete set of the cost center reports, perhaps we might focus on the one for cost center 2122, labeled Exhibit 1. You can see that we have used two measures of volume in this cost center, direct labor hours and product tonnage. During September we were operating at less than standard volume, which meant that we had to reduce the budget allowance to fr.12.617, which averaged out at fr.548.57 per ton. Our actual costs were almost exactly 10% higher than this, giving us an overall unfavorable performance variance of fr.1265, or fr.55 per ton.

"I know that Mr. Duclos and Mr. Forclas will want to comment on this, but I'll be glad to answer any questions that any of you may have. Incidentally, I have brought along some extra copies of the formulas I used in figuring the September overhead allowances for cost center 2122, just in case you'd like to look them over."

Required

1. Do you agree with Mr. Spreafico that fr.548.57 per ton (see Exhibit 1) is a more meaningful standard for cost control than the "normal" cost of fr.533.56?

2. Comment on the variances in Exhibit 1. Which of these are likely to be controllable by the foreman? What do you think the production supervisor should have done on the basis of this report?

3. What changes, if any, would you make in the format of this report or in the basis on which the budget allowances are computed?

4. In developing the budget allowances, did Mr. Spreafico make any mistakes that you think he could have avoided? Does his system contain any features that you particularly like?

CASE 10.3   MAMMOTH MANUFACTURING COMPANY

The Mammoth Manufacturing Company is a large producer of manufactured metal parts. It produces stampings, machined castings, and assemblies of stamped and machined parts for the automobile industry, the appliance industry, the tractors and implements business and several other types of manufacturers and assemblers all over the United States. The company produces few parts for direct sale to the consumer. Instead, the parts are included in the final assembly of a consumer product such as an automobile or a home appliance sold by Mammoth's customers.

The Mammoth Manufacturing Company has 41 manufacturing plants spread throughout the country. Total sales are in excess of one-half billion dollars.

The Cost Control System

For many years, Mammoth had no cost control system worthy of the name. The plants had an historical cost system and reports were submitted monthly to the central office in Cleveland, Ohio. Nothing much was done with these reports and, as long as the plant managers met their production commitments, no one bothered much about costs. By mid-1980's however, competition became quite severe in the type of products Mammoth produced. As a consequence, profit margins were reduced drastically and the management of the company began looking around for means of improving their competitive position. Manufacturing cost control was an obvious area. The management decided that they must install a system of control over their manufacturing costs.

Several people with experience in standard costing and budgeting were hired to develop and install a cost control system in the manufacturing plants. Each manufacturing plant was considered to be a cost responsibility center, with plant managers responsible for meeting their cost targets.

At each plant, industrial engineering departments were established and labor standards were set for each part. The accounting department at each plant was expanded to include a budgeting section. This section was responsible for developing flexible budgets to cover manufacturing overhead costs in accordance with instructions from the corporate controller's staff.[1]

The Budget Analysis Department.   Under the corporate controller, at the central staff in Cleveland, was the Budget Analysis Department. It was the responsbility of this department to establish time tables for budget submission; to provide

This case was prepared by John Dearden. Copyright © by the President and Fellows of Harvard University. Harvard Business School case 9-113-072.

[1]Material costs were controlled by a different system and will not be considered in this case.

forms and instructions so that the budgets would be prepared in a uniform manner; to analyze the budget proposals and recommend whether they should be
accepted or not. This was to insure a uniform "task" in each budget. The Budget
Analysis Department also had responsibility for prescribing the budget performance reports. Each month the direct labor and overhead cost performance of
each plant was analyzed and the results summarized for management.

Results of the Control System. Almost from the beginning the effect of the new
control system was to reduce manufacturing costs significantly. Part of these savings came from the industrial engineering studies required to set the labor standards. Part of the savings resulted from the analysis of overhead costs that was
required to prepare the budgets. Often, it became evident on analysis that certain
costs were seriously out of line. Much of the savings came because the system
made the plant managers and the line supervisors cost conscious. The system,
however, was not installed without problems and the purpose of this case is to
describe three situations that occurred during the initial period of installation.

Situation 1: Definition of Fixed Expense. Several of the people in the Budget Analysis Department came from a large automobile company where the flexible budget
equation was calculated by using the budgeted costs at two volumes: zero and
standard volume. The budget expense at zero volume was defined as the "level
of costs that would be required with a six months' shut down." This resulted in
a low fixed cost and, consequently, a high variable cost. Since the variable cost
per unit was relatively high using this method, the reduction in budgeted cost
for each unit below standard volume was also high. This meant that when a plant
was operating below standard volume, the budget allowance was squeezed. On
the other hand, when volume exceeded standard, the budget authorization would
be relatively high. This relationship is shown below.

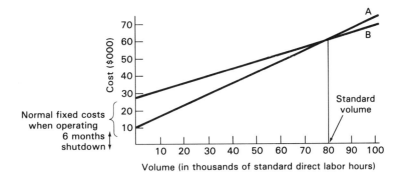

Line A shows the relation of budgeted expenses to volume assuming that
there is a fixed cost at zero volume of $10,000. This is the estimated fixed cost
that would be incurred after a six months' shutdown.

Line B shows the relation of budgeted expenses to volume assuming that there is a fixed cost at zero volume of $30,000. This is the estimated normal fixed cost incurred when the plant is operating.

At a standard volume of 80,000 hours, the total budgeted expense is estimated to be $70,000. Note that at less than SV, Line B gives the greater budget authorization. At more than SV, Line A provides the higher budget.

The argument for using this method is that it forces costs down when volume drops and the company really needs the cost savings, whereas, when volume is above standard, the company can afford to be a little more liberal about expenditures because it is earning increased profits from the additional volume.

Required

1. What do you think of the method of determining the budget equation used by the automobile company?

2. How do you think the budget equation should be calculated at Mammoth?

Situation 2: Reasonable and Consistent "Task."   The Budget Analysis Department is responsible for analyzing the proposed budget from each plant and recommending to top management whether it should be accepted as proposed, accepted with adjustment, or rejected. The ideal budget is one that can be attained if plant management is consistently efficient. The variance from budget, then, represents the extent of the plant's inefficiency.

It was important not only that the approved budget represent an efficient "task" but that the degree of "task" be consistent among the divisions. Although each plant's budget performance was analyzed individually, comparison among the plants was inevitable. If the budget levels did not represent a consistent task, some managers would be judged unfairly.

One of the principal problems facing the Budget Analysis Department was how to ensure that the approved budgets include a reasonable task and that the degree of task was consistent among the divisions. This problem was made particularly difficult because the plants realized that it was to their benefit to have a "loose" budget since they were being evaluated against it. Furthermore, no absolute standards existed. Overhead rates differed because of differences in automation, in facilities, in location, and so forth. Also, it was not possible to compare plants directly. No two plants produced exactly the same product line. Even where production processes were similar, there were enough differences because of geographic location, type of equipment, and mix of products that direct comparisons may not be meaningful.

Required

How would you solve the problem described above if you were the manager of the budget Analysis Department? The contraints within which you must work are as follows:

(a) The Budget Analysis Department consists of thirty analysts, varying in experience from one to ten years.

(b) Each Plant Budget Department consists of a supervisor and three to five analysts. The budgeting people, however, tend to identify themselves with the plant rather than the central controller's office.

Situation 3: The Oak Park Plant. The Oak Park Plant produced machined parts and assemblies almost exclusively for the automobile industry.

At the time that the budget system was first being introduced, a new plant manager, Mr. L. Hart, was placed in charged of the Oak Park Plant. Hart came from one of the large automotive manufacturers where he had developed a reputation as a "cost cutter."

Hart went to work on cost cutting at Oak Park with vigor. His first budget proposal was 15% less than the previous year's actual expense, adjusted to a comparable volume of production. Although the budget represented substantial reduction in all areas of cost, Hart's proposal represented a 25% reduction in indirect labor.

The Oak Park Plant's actual costs for the first year of the budget system (also Hart's first year with the company) was 10% *less than budget*! In other words, Hart's actual overhead costs, for his first year as manager of the Oak Park Plant were about 25% less than the preceding year's, at comparable volumes. Because of this performance Hart was given a special award by the President of Mammoth.

Hart's proposed budget for his second year was 10% less than his first year's actual costs. The proposed indirect labor budget was now about one-half of the amount being spent when Hart first took over the Oak Park Plant. Hart's actual costs continued to be better than budget until the autumn of his second year.

The Oak Park Plant had been producing the same parts, with only slight modifications, for the past several years. During Hart's second year at Oak Park, almost all of the automobile companies made drastic changes in the design of the parts that were being produced at the Oak Park Plant. Hart was faced with the necessity of changing over nearly every production line in the plant. This process was made particularly difficult because one of the automobile producers failed to finalize several designs until very close to the time that production on the parts was supposed to begin. Hart had reduced his staff so drastically that he did not have nearly enough manufacturing and industrial engineers to handle the changeover. Furthermore, his supervision was spread so thin that, even where the changeover was accomplished, trouble developed on several lines and production was severely curtailed. As a result, Hart failed to meet production schedules on several major parts, and consequently, the business was given to competitors. By the time the production had been straightened out, the Oak Park Plant had lost nearly half of its business. Needless to say, Hart was replaced.

Required

How do you make sure that a budget system does not motivate a manager to take too drastic cost-cutting action?

CASE 10.4   REED PAINT COMPANY

Standards For Selling Expense Control

In August 1982, C. H. Macrae was elected president of the Reed Paint Company to fill the vacancy created by the retirement from active business life of the former chief executive. Mr. Macrae had been with the company for 15 years, and for the preceding 6 years he had been vice-president in charge of manufacturing. Shortly after taking over his new position, Mr. Macrae held a series of conferences with the controller in which the general subject under discussion was budgetary control technique. The new president thought that the existing method of planning and checking on selling costs was particularly unsatisfactory, and he requested the controller to devise a system which would provide better control over these costs.

The Reed Paint Company manufactured a complete line of paints which it sold through branch offices to wholesalers, retailers, builders, and industrial users. Most of the products carried the Reed branch name, which was nationally advertised. The company was one of the largest in the industry.

Under the procedure then being used, selling expenses were budgeted on a "fixed" or "appropriation" basis. Each October the accounting department sent to branch managers and to other executives in charge of selling departments a detailed record of the actual expenses of their departments for the preceding year and for the current year to date. Guided by this record, by estimates of the succeeding year's sales and by his own judgment, each department head drew up and submitted an estimate of the expenses of his department for the succeeding year, detailed as to main items of expense. The estimates made by the branch managers were sent to the sales manager, who was in charge of all branch sales. He determined whether or not they were reasonable and cleared up any questionable items by correspondence. Upon approval by the sales manager, the estimates of branch expenses were submitted to the manager of distribution, Mr. Campbell, who was in charge of all selling, promotional, and warehousing activities.

The manager of distribution discussed these figures and the expense estimates furnished by the other department heads with the executives concerned, and after differences were reconciled, he combined the estimates of all the selling

This case was prepared by R. G. Walker. Copyright © by the President and Fellows of Harvard University. Harvard Business School case 9-147-002.

departments into a selling expense budget. This budget was submitted to the budget committee for final approval. For control purposes, the annual budget was divided into twelve equal amounts, and actual expenses were compared each month with the budgeted figures. Exhibit 1 shows the form in which these monthly comparisons were made.

Mr. Macrae believed that there were two important weaknesses in this method of setting the selling expense budget.

1. It was impossible for anyone to ascertain with any feeling of certainty the reasonableness of the estimates made by the various department heads. Clearly, the expenses of the preceding year did not constitute adequate standards against which these expense estimates could be judged, since selling conditions were never the same in two different years. One obvious cause of variation in selling expenses was the variation in the "job to be done," as defined in the sales budget.

2. Selling conditions often changed substantially after the budget was adopted, but there was no provision for making the proper corresponding changes in the selling expense budget. Neither was there a logical basis for relating selling expenses to the actual sales volume obtained or to any other measure of sales effort. The chief executive believed that it was reasonable to expect that sales

EXHIBIT 1   Reed Paint Company: Budget Report

Branch Sales and Expense Performance
Date: October, 1982   Branch A   Manager: H. C. Obermeyer

	THIS MONTH				YEAR TO DATE
	Budget[a]	Actual	Over* Under	% of Sales	Over*· Under
Net Sales	1,900,000	1,600,000			
Executive salaries	20,000	20,000	—	1.25	—
Office salaries	11,500	11,340	160	0.71	12,030
Salespeople's compensation	114,000	96,000	18,000	6.00	28,020*
Traveling expense	34,200	31,270	2,930	1.95	10,120*
Stationery, office supplies and expense	10,420	8,900	1,520	0.56	3,600
Postage	2,300	2,620	320*	0.16	210
Light and heat	1,340	870	470	0.05	1,280
Subscriptions and dues	1,500	1,120	380	0.07	260
Donations	1,250	—	1,250	0.00	1,300
Advertising expense (local)	19,000	18,000	1,000	1.12	12,000*
Social security taxes	2,910	2,050	860	0.13	270*
Rental	9,750	9,750	—	0.61	—
Depreciation	7,620	7,620	—	0.48	—
Other branch expense	25,510	24,260	1,250	1.52	2,470*
	261,300	233,800	27,500	14.61	34,200*

[a] $\frac{1}{12}$ of annual budget

expenses would increase, though not proportionately, if actual sales volume were greater than the forecasted volume; but that with the existing method of control it was impossible to determine how large the increase in expenses should be.

As a means of overcoming these weaknesses the president suggested the possibility of setting selling cost budget standards on a fixed and variable basis, a method similar to the techniques used in the control of manufacturing expenses. The controller agreed that this manner of approach seemed to offer the most feasible solution to the problem, and he therefore undertook with the cooperation of the sales department a study of selling expenses for the purpose of devising a method of setting reasonable standards. Over a period of several years, the accounting department had made many analyses of selling costs, the results of which had been used in determining the proper bases for allocating costs to products, customers, functions, and territories and in assisting in the solution of certain special problems, such as the problem of determining how large an individual order had to be in order to be profitable to the company. Many of the data which had been accumulated for these purposes were helpful in the controller's current study.

The controller was convinced that the fixed portion of selling expenses— in other words, the portion which was independent of any fluctuation in volume—could be established by determining the amount of expenses which had to be incurred at the minimum sales volume at which the company was likely to operate. He therefore asked Mr. Campbell, the manager of distribution, to suggest a minimum volume figure and the amount of expenses which would have to be incurred at this volume level. A staff assistant was assigned the task of studying the past sales records of the company over several business cycles, the long-term outlook for sales and sales trends in other companies in the industry. From the report prepared by his assistant Mr. Campbell concluded that sales volume would not drop below 45% of the current capacity of the factory.

Mr. Campbell then attempted to determine the selling expenses which would be incurred at the minimum volume. With the help of his staff assistant, he worked out a hypothetical selling organization which in his opinion would be required to sell merchandise equivalent to 45% of factory capacity, complete as to the number of persons needed to staff each branch office and the other selling departments, including the advertising, merchandise and sales administration departments. Using current salary and commission figures, the assistant calculated the amount of money which would be required to pay salaries for such an organization. The manager of distribution also estimated the other expenses, such as advertising, branch office upkeep, supplies and travel, which he thought would be incurred by each branch and staff department at the minimum sales volume.

The controller decided that the variable portion of the selling expense standard should be expressed as a certain amount per sales dollar. He realized that the use of the sales dollar as a measuring stick had certain disadvantages in that it would not reflect such important influences on costs as the size of the order, the selling difficulty of certain territories, changes in buyer psychology, etc. The sales dollar, however, was the measuring stick most convenient to use, the only figure readily available from the records then being kept, and also a figure which all the individuals concerned thoroughly understood. The controller believed that a budget which varied with sales would certainly be better than a budget which did not vary at all. He planned to devise a more accurate measure of causes of variation in selling expenses after he had had an opportunity to study the nature of these factors over a longer period of time.

As a basis for setting the initial variable expense standards, the controller prepared a series of charts on which the actual annual expenditures for the principal groups of expense items for several preceding years were correlated with sales volume for the year. Using these charts, which showed to what extent the principal expense items had fluctuated with sales volume in the past, and modifying them in accordance with his own judgment, the controller determined a rate of variation for the variable portion of each item of selling expense. The controller thought that after the new system had been tested in practice, it would be possible to refine these rates, perhaps by the use of a technique analogous to the time-study technique which was employed to determine certain expense standards in the factory.

At this point the controller had both a rate of variation and one point (i.e., at 45% capacity) on the selling expense curve for each expense item. He was therefore able to construct a formula for each item by extending a line through the known point at the slope represented by the rate of variation. He determined the height of this line at zero volume and called this amount the fixed portion of the selling expense formula. The diagram in Exhibit 2 illustrates the procedure, although the actual computations were mathematical rather than graphic.

The selling expense budget for 1982 was determined by adding to the new standards for the various fixed components the indicated flexible allowances for the 1982 estimated sales volume. This budget was submitted to the budget committee, which studied the fixed amounts and the variable rates underlying the final figures, making only minor changes before passing final approval.

The controller planned to issue each month reports showing for each department actual expenses compared with budgeted expenses. The variable portion of the budgeted allowances would be adjusted to correspond to the actual volume of sales obtained during the month. Exhibit 3 shows the budget report which he planned to send to branch managers.

One sales executive privately belittled the controller's proposal. "Anyone in the selling game," he asserted, "knows that sometimes customers fall all over each other in their hurry to buy, and other times, no matter what we do, they won't even nibble. It's a waste of time to make fancy formulas for selling cost budgets under conditions like that."

Required

1. From the information given in Exhibits 2 and 3, determine, insofar as you can, whether each item of expense is (a) nonvariable, (b) partly variable

EXHIBIT 2 Reed Paint Company

Budget for "Other Branch Expense," Branch A

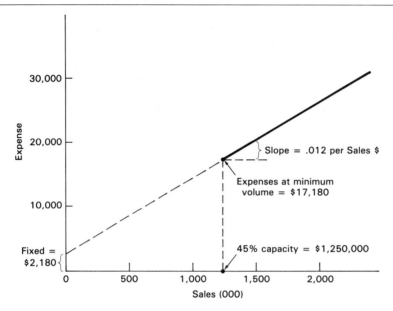

with sales volume, (c) variable with sales volume, or (d) variable with some other factor.

2. Should the proposed sales expense budget be adopted?

3. If a variable budget is used, should dollar sales be used as the measure of variation?

CASE 10.5   UNCLE GRUMPS TOYS

One morning, John Worby, President of Uncle Grumps Toys, sat down with Anne McMullen, the Executive Vice-President, to discuss year-end performance evaluations of the management group. These discussions were important because the company had traditionally given managers a sizeable bonus based on their evaluation. To the extent that it was possible, John and Anne preferred to base their evaluation on objective measures of performance with an emphasis on achievement of budgeted goals.

The budget process began in late August and by mid-November the manage-

This case was written for an examination in the first-year Control course.

EXHIBIT 3 Reed Paint Company: Budget Report Proposed by Controller

Expense Budget Report

Branch: A
Manager: H. C. Obermeyer
Date: October

	BUDGET FACTORS		THIS MONTH			YEAR TO DATE
	Fixed	*Variable*	*Budget*	*Actual*	*Over* Under*	*Over* Under* (a)
Net Sales				1,600,000		
Executive salaries	20,000	—	20,000	20,000	—	
Office salaries	1,100	0.0051	9,260	11,340	2,080*	
Salespeople's compensation	—	0.0600	96,000	96,000	—	
Traveling expense	5,680	0.0142	28,400	31,270	2,870*	
Stationery, office supplies and expense	2,820	0.0042	9,540	8,900	640	
Postage	470	0.0010	2,070	2,620	550*	
Light and heat	1,340	—	1,340	870	470	
Subscriptions and dues	100	0.0008	1,380	1,120	260	
Donations	200	0.0005	1,000	—	1,000	
Advertising expense (local)	1,500	0.0100	17,500	18,000	500*	
Social security taxes	420	0.0013	2,500	2,050	450	
Rental	9,750	—	9,750	9,750	—	
Depreciation	7,620	—	7,620	7,620	—	
Other branch expense	2,180	0.0120	21,380	24,260	2,880*	
	53,180	0.1091	227,740	233,800	6,060*	

ᵃThe controller had not recalculated budgets for previous months, and figures were therefore not available for this column.

315

ment team supplied the Board of Directors with a complete budget outlining monthly sales estimates, production cost estimates, and capital spending requirements. The directors then discussed the implications of the budget and, upon acceptance, authorized it. The firm's progress throughout the year was monitored against this budget every six months at the board meetings which were held on the 15th of January and July each year. At the January meeting the board also voted on the management bonuses for the prior year.

Uncle Grumps Toys was a Boston-based company which manufactured a very successful line of foam rubber toys called "Uncle Grumps." These were cuddly Hobbit-like dolls with large noses, a discerning smile, and enormous feet, which sold for $20 wholesale. From the moment of introduction, they had been a runaway success. Plans to expand the line were on the drawing board and a smaller baby version was to be introduced in the spring of 1987.

The business was highly seasonal with over half of the sales occurring from mid-August to early November. This was followed by a two-month trough before birthday and occasional gift sales picked up again. Sales were then fairly static until the next Christmas rush began. Budgeted sales for 1986 were $40 million with a standard gross margin, on full cost, of 33%.

Management had decided that even though sales were highly seasonal, production would be level throughout the year. This enabled Uncle Grumps Toys to stabilize employment and to sell a greater number of toys during the Christmas period than would have been possible if a shift approach had been used. Current production was at full capacity using one shift a day, five days a week. In 1985, sales were considerably greater than expectation and had almost resulted in orders being rejected due to a lack of inventory. In fact, by the end of the year, only 44,000 toys were left in stock.

John and Anne decided to discuss the production manager's performance first. The production manager, Holly Frost, had been with the firm for just over a year and this was to be her first bonus. John and Anne admired Holly and felt she had been very innovative and had substantially improved the production process. One improvement, which was introduced at the beginning of the third quarter, resulted in the average material content of each toy being reduced from 5 lbs. to 4.5 lb—a substantial savings.

In measuring Holly's managerial performance, John and Anne felt that some adjustment was necessary because the year 1986 had been rather turbulent. The factory had been closed from February 5 to March 3 (20 working days) due to a blizzard. During the time that that factory was closed, the factory roof collapsed under the weight of three feet of snow. During this period, employees did not work but were given half pay.

To make up for lost production, a four-hour Saturday morning shift was introduced from March 3 until the end of the year. Employees were paid time-and-a-half for this work. Additional overtime was required in the fourth quarter when the sales department managed to gain a $750,000 order from a catalog sales company for an extra 50,000 toys. The order was placed in the middle of October and, along with other orders, required that overtime be increased to 16 hours per weekend, at time-and-a-half, for six weekends (this includes the Saturday morning time already planned). Sales for 1986 were 2,094,000 units.

John and Anne started with the budgeted and actual figures reported in Exhibit 1. The company had not implemented a standard cost system. Because unit costs were relatively stable, direct materials were tracked in pounds, direct labor in hours, and actual usage was compared with budget. Before they could adequately judge Holly's performance, however, John and Anne decided they needed additional information. John spoke with the raw material inventory clerk and came back with an inventory listing (Exhibit 2) and a reminder that the company used FIFO inventory costing. Anne spoke with the payroll clerk and was given a summary of monthly payroll listings (Exhibit 3).

Looking at the pile of information they had collected, John and Anne settled down to the process of evaluating Holly's performance. After several hours, John and Anne took a break. They felt they had made progress but still were not certain that they knew how Holly had performed.

Over coffee, Anne remarked to John, "Well, now we have a lot of facts but it's not clear to me how we can use these figures to analyze Holly's performance."

"I have the same concern," replied John. "There are so many numbers and only some are relevant to Holly."

"I know, but which ones? That's the question."

"That's first on the agenda, when we finish coffee, but there is something else that is bothering me and that is a comment Holly made about those catalog sales," said John.

EXHIBIT 1 Uncle Grumps Toys

Quarterly Production Report (All figures in thousands)

VARIABLE COSTS	QUARTERLY BUDGET	ACTUAL				TOTAL 1986
		1	2	3	4	
Raw Materials	$1,800[a]	$1,410	$1,775	$2,190	$1,880	$ 7,255
Direct Labor	3,848[b]	3,205	4,406	4,466	5,453	17,530
Indirect Labor	300	250	350	356	410	1,366
Supplies	75	50	100	50	90	290
Power	375	270	420	410	450	1,550
FIXED COSTS						
Repair & Maintenance	300	130	120	500	280	1,030
Depreciation	700	700	700	700	700	2,800
Insurance	250	252	231	260	260	1,003
	$7,648	$6,267	$8,102	$8,932	$9,523	$32,824
Units Produced	500	350	550	550	600	2,050

[a]Budget based on 5 lb/toy.
[b]Budget based on 0.962 h/toy.

EXHIBIT 2 Uncle Grumps Toys

Summary of Raw Material Inventory Movements
(All figures in thousands)

	POUNDS	*DOLLARS*
Opening Balance (Dec. 1, 1985)	718	$ 500
Purchases (Dec. 1, 1985 – Dec. 1, 1986)	10,000	7,255
Usage (Dec. 1, 1985 – Dec. 1, 1986)	9,570	6,891
Closing Balance (Dec. 1, 1986)	1,148	864

"What was that?" asked Anne.

"Well, Holly thinks we lost out on the deal because we sold them below cost."

"Didn't you explain to her about contribution analysis?" asked Anne.

"Well, yes, but she said she understood that, and we were still losing out. Unfortunately, she was called away before she could explain to me what she meant."

Required

1. How well did Holly Frost perform as production manager in 1986? Explain.

2. Was the special deal made with the catalog company a good idea? Explain.

EXHIBIT 3 Uncle Grumps Toys

Summary of Direct Labor Expenses (All figures except employees in thousands)

	AVERAGE NUMBER OF EMPLOYEES	*REGULAR HOURS*	*OVERTIME HOURS*	*COST*[b]
First Quarter (ending 3/8/86)	960	494[a]	0	$3,205
Second Quarter (ending 6/2/86)	970	500	52	4,406
Third Quarter (ending 9/1/86)	980	505	54	4,466
Fourth Quarter (ending 12/1/86)	990	510	135	5,453
Total		2,009	241	$17,530

[a]Includes the 153,000 hours when factory was closed for 20 days during which time employees received half pay.

[b]Holly was responsible for negotiating all labor contracts.

chapter 11

FINANCIAL CONTROL OF DISCRETIONARY EXPENSES

Discretionary expenses (also called *managed* costs) are those expenses that, within a reasonable degree, are subject to management's discretion. Discretionary expenses can be divided into three main categories: administrative, research, and marketing. Although each of these three types of expenses is different and, to some extent, requires different financial control techniques, they have one characteristic in common. It is almost never practicable to set financial standards and measure performance against these standards because the output of these activities cannot usually be measured in financial terms.[1] The inability to set cost standards and measure performance against these standards makes budgeting techniques for discretionary expense of limited use in indicating the efficiency of an activity.

---

[1]There are activities within each of these categories for which financial standards may be set, such as the handling of accounts receivable within the accounting department. These activities tend to be those with repetitive operations where the variables of performance can be controlled. Where this type of activity constitutes an important proportion of the total staff cost, it should be controlled by comparing actual costs against performance standards. In every case, however, there will be important discretionary costs for which standards cannot be established.

CHARACTERISTICS OF DISCRETIONARY EXPENSE BUDGETS

The Budget Proposal

The decision that management must make with respect to a discretionary expense budget is different from the decision that it must make with respect to an operating expense budget. In the latter, management must decide whether the proposed operating budget represents a reasonable and efficient task for the coming year. Management is not so much concerned with the magnitude of the task because this is largely determined by the sales budget. In the former, however, management's principal decision is the magnitude of the job to be done in each area of discretionary expense. Therefore, when a budget proposal is presented, management should be provided with all available information useful in making the decision on the magnitude of the job to be performed.

In general, financial information indicating the level of efficiency (such as cost standards) is not applicable. Evaluating the efficiency of a discretionary expense budget is usually a difficult task because it is not possible to measure the output with any degree of accuracy. Only in the exceptional circumstance is management in a position to evaluate the efficiency of, for example, the research department, the legal department, or the finance staff.[2] Management must rely on the director of each of these activities, therefore, to get the most for each dollar spent.

In preparing a budget proposal for management, one should be very careful not to include irrelevant data that might obscure the important information. For example, some budget proposals include a breakdown of the number of people by classification, the expense by each account, and a history of these costs for several years, all in great detail. At the same time, there may be little information that will aid management in making an intelligent decision, such as the costs classified by the tasks to be accomplished. As a result, management must either rubber-stamp its approval or try to question individual expense items. The latter is usually a hopeless task. If the budget proposal has been prepared carefully, any individual expense can be justified (whether or not it is really justifiable). Furthermore, if management reduces a budget arbitrarily in one year, it can expect to receive a budget proposal the following year that contains sufficient "water" so that a reduction creates no hardship. The following questions should be asked with respect to a discretionary expense budget proposal.

1. What are the precise decisions that management should make?
2. Does the proposal include all the available information pertinent to making these decisions?

---

[2]This statement refers to financial measures of efficiency, similar to standard cost analysis. Clearly there are other indications of efficiency or inefficiency that management may be able to use. At best, however, it is difficult for someone outside a staff department to judge its efficiency.

3. Does the proposal include irrelevant information which, at best, tends to obscure the real issues?

The Method of Cost Control

The financial control exercised through a discretionary expense budget is quite different from the financial control exercised through an operating expense budget. The latter attempts to minimize operating costs by setting a standard and reporting actual costs against this standard. Costs are minimized by *motivating* line managers to maintain maximum efficiency and by giving higher management a means of *evaluating* the efficiency of line management. The main purpose of a discretionary expense budget, on the other hand, is to allow management to control costs by *participating in the planning*. Costs are controlled by deciding what projects should be undertaken.[3]

There is one school of thought in budgeting philosophy that believes categorically that a tight budget is a good budget. The theory behind this philosophy is that a tight budget will result in more pressure to reduce costs than one that is more easily attainable. While this philosophy may be correct for an operating budget, it is certainly of questionable validity when applied to a discretionary expense budget. It is easy to reduce costs in a discretionary expense budget by reducing the magnitude of the job to be done. In this case, the individual responsible for spending the money, instead of management, is making the decision as to the job to be done. This is correct procedure *only* if management explicitly delegates this decision.

The general rule, then, is that discretionary expense budgets should reflect as closely as possible the *actual costs of doing the job*. A deviation from this rule should be backed by adequate reasons and this condition should be known to management when the budget is presented for approval.

Budget Reports

In discretionary expense budgets, the performance report is used to insure that the budget commitment will not be exceeded without management's knowledge. It is not a means for evaluating the efficiency of the manager. (This is in complete contrast to the operating expense budget, which is designed to be a tool to help higher management evaluate the efficiency of manufacturing management in cost control.) Because the two types of budgets are sometimes confused, management may treat a discretionary expense budget report as an indication of efficiency. If this is done, the people responsible for the budget may be motivated to spend less than budgeted. This can be accomplished either by pro-

---

[3]Management may, of course, set certain kinds of standards to be used company-wide, for exmple, the ratio of secretaries to professionals or the relative amounts to be spent on professional societies, and so forth.

posing a budget that can be bettered or by subsequently reducing the size of the job to be done. This is, of course, undesirable for the reasons given in the preceding section. This pressure toward lower costs may possibly result in the same job being done for less money, either by increasing productivity or eliminating unnecessary operations, but management cannot depend on this. In an operating expense budget, this is about the only way to better the budget. In a discretionary expense budget, it is the most difficult way. In any event, since management can so rarely gauge the efficiency of the discretionary expense budget, there is little point in trying to increase the efficiency by such indirect methods as rewarding executives who spend less than budget.

Control over the actual expenses can be exercised by requiring that management approval be obtained before the budget can be overrun. Sometimes, a certain percentage (say, 5%) is allowed without additional approval. If the budget includes the best estimate of actual costs, there is an even chance that it will be overrun somewhat. If approval is required before any overrun, the budget proposals will come in on the high side.

In summary, then, the budget reports for a discretionary budget should be used to follow up on the original estimates. Control is exercised by requiring additional approval if the original budget is to be overrun by more than a given percentage.

TYPES OF DISCRETIONARY EXPENSE BUDGETS

In this part of the chapter, the problems of controlling and the techniques for budgeting each of the three main types of discretionary expense are described.

Administrative Expense

Administrative expense includes the top management of the company and all of the central staff operations except for marketing and research and development. In divisionalized companies, the divisional manager and his staff are also classified as administrative expense.[4] Because the problems of controlling administrative expenses are most intensive in the area of the administrative staff, this part of the chapter focuses on administrative staff expense budgets.

Problems of Controlling Administrative Staff Expense. There are two problems that make the control of administrative staff expense difficult.

---

[1]Many factory administrative costs are also discretionary. These expenses are traditionally included under the factory overhead budget and will not be considered specifically here. It should be noted, however, that they have the same general characteristics as higher-level administrative expenses.

1. As stated earlier, it is almost impossible to measure the output of an administrative staff office.
2. Often, it is in the best interests of the staff manager to take action that is not in the best interests of the company. In other words, there is frequently a lack of congruence between the goals of the staff department and the goals of the company. Each of these problems is discussed in this part of the chapter.

Measurement of Output. Most of the output of a staff office is advice and service. There are no realistic means of measuring the value or even the amount of this output for most administrative staff activities. If output cannot be measured, it is not possible to set cost standards and measure financial performance against these standards. A budget variance, therefore, cannot be interpreted as representing either efficient or inefficient performance. Even where the budget is subdivided into tasks, the results cannot be interpreted in terms of efficiency or inefficiency. For instance, suppose the finance staff was given a budget allowance to "develop a standard cost system." When the system has been completely installed, a comparison of actual cost to budget in no way measures how effectively and efficiently this system was installed. A poor job of development and installation could have been accomplished for less than budget. The important consideration is the quality of the system, and this could be far more important than meeting a budget commitment; yet, the budget report does not in any way indicate the quality of the system.

Lack of goal congruence. The problem with many administrative staff offices is that it is to the benefit of the manager to have as excellent a department as it is possible to have. On the surface, this sounds as though it should be beneficial. A great deal depends, however, on how you define an "excellent department." For example:

1. It is to the benefit of the controller to be able to answer immediately any question involving accounting data that he is asked by management. The cost of a system to do this, however, might far exceed the benefits it provides.
2. It is to the benefit of the legal staff never to have the slightest flaws in any contract that it approves. It can be very costly to review all proposed contracts so intensively that one will be completely sure that nothing will happen that might be construed as a mistake by the legal staff. The potential loss may be much less than the cost of ensuring perfection.
3. It is to the benefit of the manager of training to have the most complete and up-to-date visual aid devices. Yet the benefits received may not be worth the cost.

What these points boil down to is that, at best, the staff office may want to develop the "ideal" system, program, or function. However, the ideal can be too costly in terms of additional profits that it generates. At worst, there can be a tendency to "empire build" or to "safeguard one's position," without regard for its value to the company.

The severity of these two problems is related fairly directly to the size and prosperity of the company. In small- to medium-sized businesses, the operating executives use their staffs daily and can determine from personal observations what they are doing and whether it is worth the expense. Also, in a business with low earnings, discretionary expenses are often kept under tight control. In a large business, top management cannot possibly know and evaluate all the staff activities, and, where a company is profitable, there is a temptation to go along with staff requests for constantly increasing budgets.

Budgeting Techniques. From a purely accounting point of view, the administrative budget presents no serious problems. A budget is approved each year. The approved budget should contain at least as much detail as is needed for reporting purposes. Subsequently, actual costs are accumulated and reported periodically to the people involved. Each person responsible for a spending unit is given a report of actual expenses against the budget. These reports are summarized for the different levels of management concerned.

For each staff department, a complete administrative budget proposal ideally consists of the following.

1. A section covering the basic costs of the department. This includes the costs of "being in business" plus the costs of all activities which *must* be undertaken and for which no general management decisions are required.
2. A section covering all other activities of the department. This includes a description of the purposes and the marginal costs of each activity. The quantity of detail depends on the amount of money involved and the ability of management to make a decision about the activity. For example, a limited amount of detail may be enough for a financial analysis department because management does not need to review its functions each year.
3. A section explaining fully all proposed increases in budget.
4. A section explaining the activities that would be curtailed or canceled if the budget were reduced 5% and 10%.
5. A section explaining the activities that would be increased or started if the budget could be increased 5% and 10%.

Clearly, all five sections will be required only where the departmental budget is large and where management wishes to decide on the extent of the activities of the department. For other departments, the amount of detail depends on the importance of the expenses and the desire of managment. The important point, however, is that *if* management is expected to decide the level of administrative activity, the presentation should be aimed at providing the information needed for an intelligent decision. Although items 4 and 5 are not prepared in most budget analyses, they can be of primary importance to the management decision. In effect, they indicate to management the costs of the marginal activities.

A monthly report of actual expenses against budget is usually prepared once an administrative budget has been approved. As indicated earlier, this report is not desigend to measure efficiency, but rather to keep management informed about any possible under- or overruns. There are few accounting problems associated with administrative budget reporting. The actual costs are kept in at least the same detail as that required for reporting purposes. The budget reports are designed for the most part to help the staff executives control their costs. Top management usually needs only totals by department.

Management Considerations. The problem for management is that even under the best circumstances, the budgeting and accounting systems are of limited help in determining the optimum level of expenses. Consequently, the budget decision must be based largely on executive judgment. These decisions become more difficult as staff offices become more numerous and specialized. It is not unusual to have a dozen staff groups reporting to the president, such as legal, treasury, controllership, systems and operations research, industrial relations, community relations, government relations, and so forth. The president often has neither the time nor the specialized knowledge to exercise more than cursory control over these activities. As a result, many of the larger companies have appointed an "executive" or an "administrative" vice president, to whom all or most of these staff functions report. This should assure an independent review and an appraisal by an executive with the time and expertise required to exercise the necessary control over these staff activities.

Research and Development Expense

Problems With Controlling Research and Development Expense. The purpose of this part of the chapter is to describe the problems of controlling research and development expenses. These are as follows:

1. *Results are difficult to measure quantitatively.* Most research, as contrasted to administration, has at least a semitangible output in terms of patents, new products, new processes, and so forth. Research and development expenses, however, cannot be controlled in the same way as operating costs for three reasons: (a) The output of a research group can take a long time to be realized. Consequently, the input in terms of an annual budget may be completely unrelated to the output. (b) Even where output can be determined, it is often impossible to place a precise value on it. (c) Even where the value of the output can be calculated, it is usually not possible for management to evaluate the efficiency of the research effort because of its technical nature. The *causal connection* between the input and the output often cannot be established. A brilliant effort may fail and a mediocre effort may, by luck, result in a bonanza. As a result of these conditions, a research budget must be treated like an administration budget. Management uses the budget to participate in the planning, not to evaluate efficiency.

2. *The goal congruence problem in research is similar to that in administration.* It is often to the benefit of the research manager to build the best research organization that money can buy, even though this might be undesirable from the total company point of view. A further problem that sometimes exists in a research organization is that the research people often do not have sufficient knowledge of

(or interest in) the business to determine the direction of the research efforts in an optimal manner.

3. *Research cannot be controlled effectively on an annual basis.* Not only can research be years in reaching fruition, but the organization often must be built up slowly over a long period of time. The principal cost is for labor. Scientific labor is scarce, and people working on a given project often cannot be efficiently replaced because only they have sufficient knowledge of the project. This means that it is inefficient to have short-term fluctuations in costs and, consequently, in labor. It is not reasonable, therefore, to reduce research costs in years when profits are low and increase them in years when profits are high. Research must be looked at as a long-term investment, not a speculation to be manipulated with the short-term prosperity of the company.

Techniques for controlling research costs.   Management must make three decisions concerning research cost:

1. Decide on the amount of financial commitment in research over the next several years.
2. Decide on the direction of the research expenditure.
3. Evaluate the effectiveness of the research group.

None of these decisions is related to the calendar year; consequently, the annual budget is not particularly useful in making any of these decisions. The purpose of this part of the chapter is to describe a system for controlling research and to show how the annual research budget fits into this decision pattern.

A decision must be made by top management as to the amount of funds that will be made available for research over a period of years. This plan can, of course, be reviewed periodically and changed. The advantage of a long-range plan is that the change will be made in the *entire plan* and the total effect of these changes can be evaluated. When a research budget is approved on an annual basis, it is very difficult to make intelligent changes because the impact of any change is not restricted to a single year.

This long-range plan can be used for two purposes:

1. As a guide to approving specific projects.[5]
2. As a guide to approving the annual budget.

Specific Projects.   Except in the most unusual circumstances, management must decide on the direction of research expenditures. This is often best accomplished by having a research committee review and approve the individual project (or group of projects) before they are undertaken by the research staff.[6] This makes

---

[5] A project is a specific research task with a definite end or accomplishment. There can be wide variances in the size and type of task, but this is a technical problem. For our purposes, think of a project as a specific job to be done.

[6] The research committee is usually composed of either the president or executive vice president, the director of research, the director of marketing plus other executives who are likely to use the research results.

it possible for management to *control the direction of expenditures.* Funds for the proposed projects should have been included in the long-range plan. That is, all proposed projects should be able to be accomplished within the funds available in the long-range plan. The research committee, therefore, does not have to concern itself with the availability of funds each time that it approves a specific project. Its concern is whether the amount of money requested should be spent on the particular research proposed. If the number of projects increases to the point where the long-range plan will not provide enough funds, the plan should be reviewed and revised if this is appropriate.

The periodic reporting of actual costs against approved costs by project is an important control devivce for research costs. Actual costs to date, however, considered separately, are not very useful because one does not know how much has been accomplished. Consequently, project performance reports should emphasize the *total expected cost.* This tells management how present estimates differ from original ones and how much more or less is the latest expectation. This information can be used by management or the research committee to change the direction of expenditure if that appears desirable. Note that variances from original project estimates do not represent efficiency or inefficiency. Depending on the type of research undertaken, the variances can be caused by many factors other than the ability of the researcher.

Annual Budgets.   If a company has systematically developed a long-range research expenditure plan and implemented this plan with a system of project approval similar to that described in the previous section, preparation of the annual research and development budget becomes a fairly simple matter. The annual budget is the calendarization of the expected expenses for the budget period. If the annual budget is in line with the long-range plan and the approved projects (as it should be), the budget approval is routine and its main function is in cash planning. It does, of course, give management an opportunity for another look. Management can ask the question: "Is this the best way to use our resources next year?" Also the annual budget ensures that actual costs will not exceed budget without management knowledge. Significant variances from budget must be approved by management *before they are incurred.*

The reporting for research expense is like that for administrative expense. Monthly or quarterly, actual expenses are shown compared to budget for all spending units. These are summarized progressively for each executive who controls a spending unit. The purpose of these reports is to assist the managers of each spending unit to plan their expenses and to assure management that expenses are within approved plans.

To summarize, then, the accounting function provides two types of reports to management. The first type of report compares the latest forecast of total cost with the approved project, for each active project. This is prepared periodically and given to the executive or group of executives that approve the research projects. The main purpose of this report is to see whether changes should be made in approved projects. The second is a report of actual expenses agains budget. Neither report informs management about the efficiency of the research effort.

Evaluation.   Not much evaluation can be done using financial control techniques. The entire future of the company, however, could depend on the ability of the research group. Although there are no mathematical or accounting techniques that provide this evaluation automatically, we believe that the research staff should be explicitly evaluated by top management periodically, using whatever relevant data are available.[7]

Managment Considerations of Control of Research Expense.   There are five important points to keep in mind.

Point 1. Where a company depends on research for its future products (and certainly most large companies do), it is vital that the right amount of money be spent for the right things and that the research effort be staffed by highly competent people. The accounting function can be of only limited help in making these decisions. The important point is that the accounting function should provide all the relevant information that is available. It should be recognized, however, that, at best, this is of limited value. As in the control of administrative expense, the lack of relevant data does not mean that irrelevant data should be provided instead. Always the question should be answered as to what decision has to be made and what information is relevant to that decision.

Point 2. Research and development expenses are more similar to capital investments than to most other types of discretionary expenses. Consequently, the annual budget is almost always an unsatisfactory vehicle for making basic decisions with respect to research and development. Instead, these decisions should be made without the time constraints inherent in an annual budget. Subsequently, the impact of these decisions on the timing of expenses can be incorporated into the annual budget. The budget, however, is for cash and expense control, *not* for otherwise controlling research and development expenses.

Point 3. Research and development expenses are controlled in terms of projects. Consequently, it is vital to have a system of project approval and review. The accounting function is responsible for maintaining a record of actual costs by project and presenting these results. The projection of the cost of completion of each project in process must be made by the research staff and included in any presentation to the executive or group of executives responsible for approving and controlling the research effort.

---

[7]See "How to Evaluation Research Expenditure" by James B. Quinn in the March-April 1960 issue of the *Harvard Business Review,* for some techniques on estimating the value of certain types of research.

Point 4. The impact of an error in judgment concerning either the amount or direction of expenditures can be much greater in research than in administration. For one thing, it may take a much longer time to correct the effects of an error in research expenditures. For another, the impact on profits can be much greater, even where it can be corrected quickly.

Point 5. The problems described in this part of the chapter apply more to research than to development. If research and development are thought of as a time spectrum, the closer a development project is to the production stage, the more practical it is to use, at least to some degree, industrial engineering measures of efficiency.

Marketing Expenses

Marketing expenses include selling, advertising and sales promotion, and warehousing. Marketing activities are much more heterogeneous in their nature than either administration or research and development activities. As a result, it is necessary to use several techniques. Marketing expenses can be subdivided into three types for control purposes:

1. Expenses incurred *after* the time of sale, called *order-filling costs*
2. Administrative-type expenses
3. Expenses incurred *before* the point of sale, called *order-getting costs*.

Each of these is discussed in this part of the chapter.

Expenses Incurred After the Time of Sale. One of the features of the marketing expense control is that *operating-type budgets may apply to costs incurred after the sale has been made*. For example, shipping and delivery expense, salesmen's commissions, and collection costs all occur after the sale has been made and, in many instances, can be controlled through budgets that are adjusted to reflect the costs at different levels of operation (i.e., flexible budgets).

The failure to realize that flexible budget techniques are applicable only to costs incurred after the time of sale has caused much confusion in sales budgeting. It arises as follows: A manager or controller realizes that fixed budgets result in inequitable situations because, for example, a sales manager overruns his or her budget for sales commissions when a higher than budgeted sales volume was achieved. The entire sales budget therefore, is developed on a variable basis. A reasonably good correlation may often be found between volume of sales and the level of sales promotion and advertising (and even the cost of sales staff). This is taken to mean that sales expenses vary with sales volume. Consequently, a flexible budget is established, using manufacturing overhead budget techniques. Flexible budgets, however, cannot be used to control selling expenses that are incurred *before* the time of sale. Advertising or sales promotion expense, for example, should *not* be authorized on the basis of a flexible budget.[8] The correlation between sales volume and advertising costs results either from the mutual growth of both expenses as a result of the growth of the company or because advertising costs have *caused* the increase in sales. It does not make sense to turn this around and act as though the sales volume *caused* the advertising expenditures. A flexible budget, however, may be useful for controlling expenses that are incurred *after* the sale has been made. In these cases, the job to be done is determined by the volume of sales.

Administrative-Type Costs.   Most marketing budgets include administrative-type costs. There is usually a basic staff plus other peripheral activities (for example, marketing research). The former is necessary if one is to stay in business, but the latter can be changed by management decree. This part of the sales budget should be handled like any other administrative staff budget.

Order-Getting Costs.   There are two features about order-getting costs that are unique. They are:

1.   The output of a marketing organization can be measured. Except at fairly low levels, however, it is often difficult to evaluate the effectiveness of the marketing effort because the environment cannot be controlled. The marketing effort is undertaken in an environment subject to changes in economic conditions, competitive action, and customer tastes, to name a few. As a result, it is often very difficult to evaluate the efficiency of the organization.

2.   Meeting the budgetary commitment (particularly in selling expense) is normally just a small part of the evaluation of marketing performance. For example, if a marketing group sells twice as much as its quota, no one is going to worry too much if they exceeded their budget by 10%. The impact of sales on profits is so great that it tends to overshadow completely the cost performance. Few companies evaluate a marketing organization on its ability to meet its cost targets. The sales target is the critical factor in evaluation.

Management Considerations of Marketing Expense Control.

1.   In spending money for order getting, the objective is to spend a dollar for this type of expense as long as it returns more than a dollar in contribution from additional sales. In advertising, for example, one of the principal decisions that management must make is *when to stop* advertising. This can be particularly complicated beause there are many such decisions that need to be made. For example, there are optimum points for media, for geographic locations, and for products. As in research, these are not decisions for which accounting data can provide much relevant information. The point is, however, that as much relevant information as possible should be provided (for instance, marginal contri-

---

[8]Unless, of course, management wishes to base its advertising expenses on the volume of sales, on the theory that the higher the sales volume, the more the company can afford to spend on advertising.

bution of products) and, where sufficient relevant information is not available, irrelevant data should not be substituted.

2. It should be possible to change planned order-getting expenses rapidly. (This is just the opposite of research expenses.) The reason is that environmental conditions can change rapidly. Consequently, it is necessary that the sales and advertising plans be flexible enough to change with changing conditions. It is unwise to use a plan based on certain assumptions after these assumptions are no longer valid. For example, assume that it were possible to decide the exact point at which the marginal costs of advertising equaled the marginal revenue that was earned and a budget was prepared on this basis. If, three months later, the economy changed or a competitor took some unanticipated action, it would be unwise to stay with the original budget if there were a more profitable pattern of expenses. It is vital, therefore, that the marketing budget not be a straitjacket that hampers necessary management action.

QUESTIONS

11.1 List as many staff activities as you can that might be controlled through operating-type budgets. Explain how you would go about establishing the budget and measuring the output.

11.2 Can you give some examples of irrelevant financial information that might be included in the staff budget proposal?

11.3 Give some specific examples, other than those cited in the text, where the goals of a staff manager might not be congruent with the overall goals of the company.

11.4 Several experts in staff budgeting have recommended a technique called *zero-base budgets*. This technique is based on the concept that all staff budgets should be completely justified each year. In other words, the budget proposal starts out from a zero base, with no expenditure taken for granted. Can you comment on the advantages and disadvantages of this technique? Where would it be most useful? Where would it be least useful?

11.5 It is certainly true that research expenditures tend to be relatively fixed in the short run. Where this is the case, an overrun on one project must cause a deferment or curtailment of other projects equal to the amount of the overrun. How should the research committee control this process?

11.6 If you were presindent of a company, how would you go about evaluating the research staff?

11.7 Can you explain how research expenditures are more similar to capital investments than other types of programmed costs?

11.8 Name some marketing costs, other than those given in the text, that are incurred after the point of sale. How would you go about setting up an operating-type budget for these costs?

11.9 What kind of financial information would be valuable in determining the effectiveness of advertising and sales promotion expenses?

11.10 The text stated that some of the large companies in the United States have been appointing an administrative vice president, to which many of these staff offices report. What type of an executive would be best for this job? In what ways would he improve the overall profitability of the company?

CASES

CASE 11.1   CURWEN CHEMICAL COMPANY

The Curwen Chemical Company produces a standard line of chemical products with annual sales between $50 million and $60 million. It had 200 persons in the research department. About half these were directly connected with the research effort; the other half were clerical and executive. Over 90% of the work done by the research department is on product development. About three-quarters of this is spent on developing new products. Last year's expenditures for research totaled a little over $2 million. About 10% of the sales each year comes from products that were not produced in the previous year.

The Research Committee

Curwen Chemical has a permanent committee, the Research Committee. This Committee is responsible for controlling the entire research effort of the company. The committee is composed of the President, the Executive Vice President, the Marketing Vice President, and the Director of Research. The Committee usually meets five times a year. At the first meeting of the year, the annual research budget is reviewed and approved. In the four subsequent meetings, the committee reviews the budget performance of the Research Division for the quarter preceding the meeting.

Budget Development

The budgets are developed by the department managers in the Research Department. They are helped in this task by the accounting personnel. For each department, the budget costs are broken down by section, by project, and by account classification (e.g., salaries, supplies, depreciation).

Essentially the annual budget consists of the following:

1. The cost to complete those projects, in process at the beginning of the year, that are expected to be completed during the year;
2. The coming year's expenditure for projects that are in process at the beginning of the year but which will *not* be completed during the year;
3. The coming year's expenditures for new projects that are expected to be started during the year.

This case was prepared by John Dearden. Copyright © by the President and Fellows of Harvard University. Harvard Business School case 9-109-032.

The Director of Research reviews the proposed budget of each of his managers and makes changes where he believes it is appropriate. During the past few years, the general guideline to total allowable expenditures has been that research costs should not exceed 3% of projected annual sales. Accordingly, when the proposed departmental budgets have totaled more than 3% of the coming year's projected sales, the Director of Research has generally eliminated some projects, reduced the scope of others, and slowed down expenditure on still others, until the total proposed research budget was about 3% of the sales projection for the coming year.

After adjustment by the Director of Research, the budgets are summarized by department, by project, and by expense classification and presented to the Research Committee for review and approval. After review, and occasional adjustments, the committee approves the annual budget. Once approved, the budget is the basis for controlling actual expenditures.

There is no formal approval of a total project if the money is spent in more than one calendar year; however, authorization to begin a project at the time of budget approval has been considered to be approval of the entire project.

The Accounting System

All direct costs are accumulated by department, by project, and by detailed expense classification. Indirect costs are allocated to department and project monthly. Each month, a report is prepared that compares actual expenditures to budget[1] in total, by project, and by department. Variances from budget are explained in an accompanying letter. Each department manager receives a copy of his own departmental figures. Each member of the Research Committee receives copies of the entire report.

The monthly reports are consolidated each quarter and become the basis for the quarterly review to the Research Committee. The review is made by the Director of Research in a formal presentation. Actual expenditures are projected on a screen and compared in detail (project, department, and expense classification) to budget and the variances are explained orally by the Director of Research.

In addition to the budget performance reports, each quarter a report of all projects completed during the quarter is provided to the Research Committee. The reports show the actual costs compared to the amount budgeted for the entire project. Where the project has covered more than one calendar year, the budgeted costs are the sum of the costs budgeted for each year.

---

[1]The approved annual budget is broken down by month at the beginning of the year.

Summary

In summary, then, the Research Committee approves an annual budget and reviews the status of expenditures on a formal basis once a quarter. Each month the committee members are provided with detailed information on the current status of expenditures and can, therefore, take action during the quarter if it is appropriate.

Required

1. Evaluate Curwen's system for controlling research costs.
   (a) What are the good practices?
   (b) What are the poor practices?
2. Describe the system that you think should be used by Curwen.

CASE 11.2   BUILT-RITE APPLIANCE CORPORATION

The Built-Rite Appliance Corporation, with headquarters in Chicago, is a major producer of all types of electrical home appliances—washers, dryers, ironers, freezers, refrigerators, vacuum cleaners, dishwashers, mixers, and so forth. The Corporation has twenty-five manufacturing plants located throughout the country. The country is divided into six sales regions, and within region, into districts. There is a district sales office in every major city in the country. There are twelve warehouses located strategically throughout the country. There is at least one warehouse in each sales region.

Sales have increased each year since 1970. The expected sales volume for 1987 is more than a billion dollars.

The Sales Organization

Exhibit 1 is a chart of Built-Rite's sales organization. At the corporate level, the responsibility for product design, advertising and sales promotion is by product line, each line is in charge of a product manager who is also a vice president of the Corporation. The Vice President (Distribution) is responsible for the actual distribution of all appliances. Appliances are sold to the consumer by independent retail dealers. These dealers are serviced by company-owned distributors. Each sales district is controlled by one or more distributors. The distributor orders appliances through the regional office, either for inventory or for direct delivery to a dealer. The appliances are delivered from the closest warehouse where they are available. The warehouses are the direct responsibility of the Re-

---

This case was prepared by John Dearden. It has not been previously copyrighted.

EXHIBIT 1 Organization of Sales Function

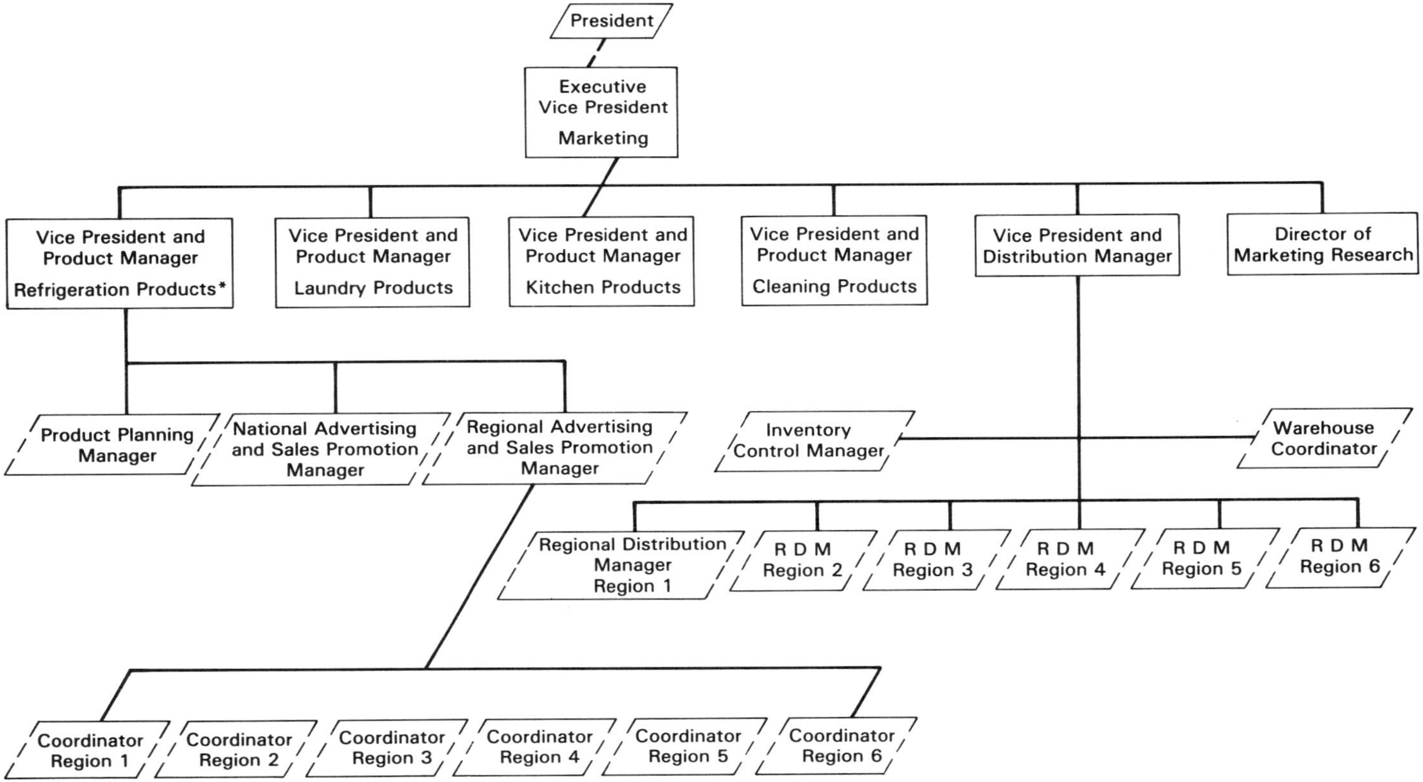

*All product managers had organizations similar to that of the refrigeration products division.

gional Distribution Manager in whose region they are physically located. Shipments across regional lines are, of course, common where products are unavailable at the warehouse where the order was originally placed.

Regional Distribution Managers are responsible for the distribution of all product lines. They order appliances through the warehouse coordinator and prescribe inventory levels for both the warehouses and distributors in their region. They are also responsible for the hiring, training, promoting, and so forth, of all of the distributors in their regions. They are responsible for recruiting, training, and maintaining a dealership organization within their regions. They are not responsible for either product design or for advertising and sales promotion. This is the responsibility of the Product Managers.

The Product Manager

As indicated on Exhibit 1, there are four vice presidents who are Product Managers. These product managers are responsible for all of the product planning, advertising, and sales promotion for their appliances. Product planning is essentially a central staff operation, although individual product planners spend varying amounts of time in the field. Advertising and sales promotion, on the other hand, require a great deal of field coordination. As a result, each Product Manager has advertising and sales promotion personnel at each of the six regional offices. These people are responsible for: (a) communicating the advertising plans to the Regional Distribution Manager so that the availability of appliances will be coordinated with the advertising; (b) coordinating the advertising plans with the other appliance lines; (c) conducting local advertising campaigns; and (d) providing feedback to the central group on sales promotion and advertising.

Evaluation of Product Manager.   Each of the Product Managers is evaluated informally by the Marketing Vice President. Important factors in his evaluation are growth in the market share, new product development, meeting sales volume commitments, customer acceptance of his products, and meeting cost and budget goals.

Each year the Finance Committee President, Executive Vice President (Marketing), Executive Vice President (Administration) and Vice President (Finance) review and either adjust or approve the budget for each Product Manager. The budget is a fixed amount, divided into the three major functions: product planning, national advertising and sales promotion, and regional advertising and sales promotion. Product Managers are expected to keep expenditures within budget both in total and by activity. They are allowed to come back to the Finance Committee and ask for a budget revision if one becomes necessary. This is done, however, only where serious emergencies develop. The attitude of the Finance Committee generally discourages revisions. This attitude, together with the time and expense of preparing and justifying an increase in budget, makes most managers reluctant to go back for a revision of their budgets. The rigidity of the advertising and sales promotion budget has created problems for the Product Managers. To solve these problems, Larry Semple, Vice President and Product Manager (Laundry Products), proposed a technique for making the advertising and sales promotion budgets more flexible. He called this method the "ever-filling granary" technique.

The Ever-Filling Granary Technique

As explained by Larry Semple, the ever-filling granary technique operates as follows:

> Suppose we were to start with my technique in 1987. I would be allowed an advertising and sales promotion fund based on last year's sales for each product multiplied by the advertising expenses charged against that product. In other words, my beginning fund would equal my last year's recovery of advertising expense. For instance, our deluxe dryer is charged $10 a unit by the accounting department for advertising. If I sold 1000 units last year, I would receive $10,000 in my advertising fund. The sum of all products sold last year multiplied by the accounted advertising charge would be my total beginning fund. Once my fund is established, I would not go back for any more money.
>
> You can think of it as a granary and the money in the fund is the grain to fill my granary initially. I reduce the amount of funds (or grain) in my granary as I spend money on advertising. I refill the granary by selling products because the sales price includes a charge for advertising. In this way, I get my money back and so my granary will constantly be filling itself. As long as I do not deplete my fund, I do not need to get further approval to spend money on advertising.
>
> This method has several advantages:

> 1. It gives me flexibility on how much and when to spend my advertising funds. The fixed budget does not give me enough latitude to take optimum action and it is too difficult and slow to get revisions.
> 2. The control over my expenditures is automatic. The Finance Committee is taken off the hook completely. If I do not get the money from my customers, I cannot spend it. When my sales are high, then we can afford to spend more.
> 3. If I need more money for advertising, I must get it from my customers, or I cannot spend it. In this way, advertising is practically free. The customers pay for it in the price of the product and all I do is collect it from them and then spend it.

Required

1. Evaluate the "ever-filling granary" proposal. Should it be adopted as proposed? When modifications? Not at all?

2. If you believe it should not be adopted, what alternative, if any, do you propose?

CASE 11.3 **WESTPORT ELECTRIC CORPORATION**

On a day in the late autumn of 1986, Peter Ensign, the Controller of Westport Electric; Michael Kelly, the Manager of the Budgeting Department (reporting to Ensign); and James King, the Supervisor of the Administrative Staff Budget Section (reporting to Kelly) were discussing a problem raised by King. In reviewing the proposed 1987 budgets of the various administrative staff offices, King was disturbed by the increases in expenses that were being proposed. He believed that, in particular, the proposed increases in two offices were not justified. King's main concern, however, was with the entire process of reviewing and approving the administrative staff budgets. The purpose of the meeting was to discuss what should be done about the two budgets in questions and to consider what revisions should be made in the approval procedure for administrative staff budgets.

Organization of Westport

Westport Electric is one of the giant United States Corporations that manufactures and sells electric and electronic products. Sales in 1985 were in excess of $30 billion and profits after taxes were over $1.25 billion. The operating activities of the corporation are divided into four groups, each headed by a group vice president. These groups are: the Elecrical Generating and Transmission Group; the Home Appliance Group; the Military and Space Group; and the Electronics Group. Each of these groups is comprised of a number of relatively independent divisions, each headed by a divisional manager. The division is the basic operating unit of the corporation and each is a profit center. The divisional manager is responsible for earning an adequate profit on his investment. There are twenty-five divisions in the corporation.

At the corporate level there is a Research and Development Staff and six administrative staff offices, each headed by a vice president as follows: Finance; Industrial Relations; Legal; Marketing; Manufacturing; and Public Relations. The responsibilities of the administrative staff offices, although they vary depending upon their nature, can be divided into the following categories:

1. *Top management advice*: Each of the staff offices is responsible for providing advice to the top management of the corporation in the area of its speciality. Also, all of the staff vice presidents are members of the Policy Committee, the top decision-making body of the corporation.

2. *Advice to operating divisions and other staff offices*: Each staff office gives advice to operating divisions and, in some instances, to other staff offices. (An example of the latter is the advice the Legal Staff might give to the Finance Staff with respect to a contract.) In theory, at least, the operating divisions can accept or

This case was prepared by John Dearden. Copyright © by the President and Fellows of Harvard University. Harvard Business School case 9-113-073.

reject the advice as they see fit. In most cases, there is no formal requirement that the operating divisions even seek advice from the central staff. In fact, however, the advice of the staff office usually carries considerable weight and divisional managers rarely ignore it.

3. *Coordination among the divisions*: The staff offices have the responsibility for coordinating their areas of activities among the divisions. The extent of this coordination varies considerably, depending upon the nature of the activity. For example, the Finance Staff has the greatest amount of this coordination to do because it is necessary to establish and maintain a consistent accounting and budgetary control system. On the other hand, the Legal and Public Relations Staffs have no direct representation in the activities of the divisions.

Exhibit 1 is an organization chart of the Westport Electric Corporation.

The Budgeting Organization

Exhibit 2 provides a partial organization chart of the Finance Staff. As you can see from the chart, Ensign, the Controller, reports to the Finance Vice President. Reporting to him is Kelly, who is in charge of the Budgeting Department. Reporting to Kelly is King, who is in charge of the Administrative Staff Budget Section.

EXHIBIT 1 Organization Chart

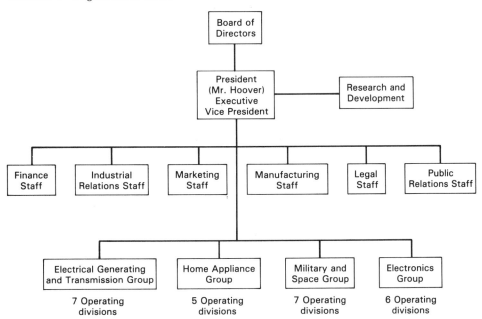

EXHIBIT 2 Finance Staff

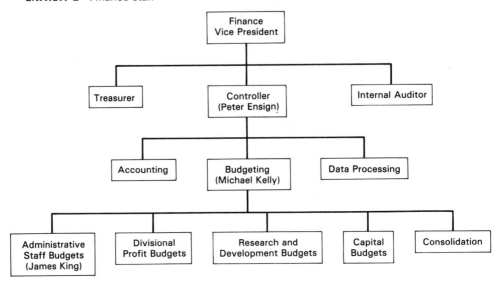

Approval Procedure. Information is submitted in the following way:

In the early autumn of each year, the Budgeting Department issues instructions and time-tables for the preparation, submission, and approval of the budgets for the coming year. Since we are concerned in this case with the administrative staff budgets, we will limit our description to the nature of the information submitted by each administrative staff office.

Each staff office completes the following schedule:

BUDGET BY EXPENSE CLASSIFICATION. This schedule shows the proposed budget, last year's budget, and the current year's expected actual costs, by expense classification (professional salaries, clerical salaries, supplies, consulting services, utilities, and so forth). The purpose of this schedule is to compare the new budget with the current year's budget and the current year's expected actual by expense categories.

BUDGET BY ACTIVITY. This schedule shows the same information as the previous schedule except that the information is classified by organizational component. The purpose of this schedule is to show which activities are being increased, which decreased, and which new activities are being proposed.

EXPLANATION OF CHANGES. This schedule is really a letter that accompanies the budget proposal and explains the reasons for the proposed budget. Explanations are divided into the following categories: economic changes (i.e., changes in the general level of wages and materials); increases or decreases in existing activities; new activities added and old activities dropped.

These reports are submitted by each administrative staff office to the Budgeting Department two weeks before the office is to present its proposed budget. The Budget proposal is then presented:

Each administrative staff office budget was approved by the President and the Executive Vice President in a "budget review meeting." The Finance Vice President sat in on all the budget presentations but had no official power to approve or disapprove.

On the day scheduled for presentation, the vice president of the administrative staff office whose budget was to be approved would make a presentation to the President and Executive Vice President. The presentation would be based on the budget schedules previously submitted, but the explanations justifying the proposals might go into much greater detail. For example, last year the Marketing Vice President used three-dimensional colored slides to describe a new activity that he was proposing to organize.

Attending these meetings were the President, the Executive Vice President, the administrative staff office vice president and his principal executives, the Finance Vice President, the Controller, the Budgeting Manager, and the particular budget supervisor involved.

Typically, a budget meeting would proceed as follows: The presentation would be made by the administrative staff vice president. During the presentation, questions would be raised by the President and the Executive Vice President. These would be answered by the administrative staff vice president or one of his executives. At the end of the presentation, the President and Executive Vice President would decide whether to approve the budget or whether to curtail some of the proposed activities. Before the final decision, the Finance Vice President would be asked to comment. In almost every case, he would agree with the decision of the President and the Executive Vice President.

Once approved, the budget became authorization to undertake the budgeted activity for the coming year.

The functions of the Budgeting Department with respect to administrative staff budgets has been to prescribe the schedules to be submitted and timetable for their submission and to "keep the presentations honest." In fulfilling the last function, the Budgeting Department analyzed the proposed budgets and made sure that the facts were correctly stated. For instance, they checked to make sure that the increases due to economic changes were accurate; or, if some present activity were to be dropped, they made sure that the cost of this activity was shown as a reduction, so that the cost savings could not be used to hide an increase in another activity. The details of the presentation were worked out beforehand between James King and the administrative assistant to the administrative staff vice president involved. When the presentation was made, the Budgeting Department would be asked to concur with the financial information being presented. The Budgeting Department, however, took no position on the appropriateness of the proposed budget or the efficiency of the activity. It was this situation that bothered James King.

Budget Evaluation

This was James King's second year as Supervisor of the Administrative Staff Budget Section. Prior to that, he had been the Budget Manager in the Electric Stove Division. At the divisional level, the budget analysts exercised considerable influence over the level of efficiency represented in the operating budgets. For example, in the Electric Stove Division, the Divisional Controller attended every divisional budget meeting and argued long and hard for rejecting any budget that he believed was not sufficiently "tight." Because he had had a considerable amount of experience in the operations of that division, he was usually success-ful. King found it hard to reconcile the attitude of the Finance Vice President (who never seemed to raise any objections to the proposed budgets) with his former boss, the Controller of the Electric Stove Division. Consequently he asked to meet with Ensign and Kelly to see if something could not be done to improve the evaluation techniques for administrative staff budgets. Below is an edited version of the meeting between Ensign, Kelly and King on this problem.

KING: All we do about these budgets is to make sure that the accounting figures are correct. We don't do anything about the efficiency represented by the fig-ures and I know for a fact that it is lousy in at least two cases and I have my suspicions about some of the others.

KELLY: Tell Peter about Legal.

KING: Earlier this year, you remember, we hired a consultant to work with our Data Processing Group. We gave the contract to the Legal Staff to look over and it took them three months before they approved it. They had all kinds of nit-picking changes that didn't amount to a hill of beans, but which took up everybody's time.

Shortly after the contract was approved, I had a college friend of mine visiting who's a lawyer in one of the biggest New York firms. We discussed the matter and he looked over the original contract and the revised one and was astounded at the time that it had taken to get it approved. He said that a simple contract like that would be handled in a day or two by an outside lawyer. Since then, I find that everyone in the organization seems to feel the same about Legal. They take forever to do a five-minute job and they never stick their necks out in the slightest.

To add insult to injury, this year the Legal Staff is asking for a 30% in-crease in their budget to take care of the added cost resulting from the expan-sion of their work load. The trouble is that unless we do something, they will get this increase.

ENSIGN: If everyone feels that the Legal Staff is so inefficient, why should Mr. Hoover (the president) approve their budget?

KING: I think that Mr. Hoover has neither the time nor the knowledge to evaluate the Legal Staff. Any time Mr. Hoover asks for anything from them, he gets superdeluxe treatment. Since none of us are lawyers we have a hard time proving inefficiency, but we know it is there.

ENSIGN: What is the other budget that you think is out of line?

KING: Industrial Relations—especially management training: We are spending more money on senseless training than you can shake a stick at. It's not only costing us money, but it is wasting management's time. For instance, last month we all had to take a course in quality control. It was the most simple-minded course I have ever seen. They gave us a test at the end to see how much progress we had made. I gave a copy of the test to my secretary and she got 100% without taking the course, or really even knowing what quality control is. Out in the division, the training was even worse. At one time they had a slide film that was supposed to teach us economics in three lessons! The film consisted of "Doc Dollar" explaining to "Jim Foreman" about money markets, capitalism, and so forth. We all felt that it was an insult to our intelligence. In their new budget, Industrial Relations is proposing to increase training by nearly 50% and, because the general profit picture is so good, it will probably be approved.

ENSIGN: If the training program is so bad, why don't we hear more complaints?

KING: I will have to admit that I feel more strongly than most of the other people, a lot of managers and supervisors just go along with these programs because to be against management training is like being against motherhood. Also, the personnel evaluation forms that Industrial Relations prescribes have a section on the performance of the individual in these courses. I guess people are afraid to rebel against them because it might hurt their chances of promotion. The point is, at best, they are not worth the money that they cost. No one seems to get much out of them as far as I can see, so we certainly don't want to *increase* the training budget.

The conversation continued for some time. Although he did not express it in exactly these terms, King's other concern was a lack of goal congruence between the activities of the administrative staff office and the earnings for the corporation. It seemed to him that each administrative staff officer, at best wanted to have the "best" operation in the country and, at worst, was simply interested in building an empire. Even, the "best" operation, however, might cost much more than it was worth in terms of increasing profits. He was also concerned about the ability of the President and the Executive Vice President to evaluate the efficiency and the effectiveness of the staff offices or even to decide whether additional activities were really worthwhile. King, therefore, believed it was necessary for someone to evaluate the budget proposals critically as they did at the divisional level.

The meeting closed with Ensign asking Kelly and King to prepare a proposal that would solve the issue raised at the meeting.

Required

What should Westport Electric do about the evaluation problem raised in the case?

CASE 11.5   TYLER MANUFACTURING CORPORATION

Planning and Implementing the Establishment of a Research Laboratory in a Large Industrial Organization

Tyler was a large industrial manufacturer of fasteners. In 1965 the company's sales exceeded $100 million, and net profits were in excess of $6 million. The company produced no end products; all its products were supplied to manufacturers for use as components in final products. Tyler's fasteners were used in a variety of products including home appliances, office equipment, automobiles, aircraft, communications equipment, and clothing. Perhaps the company's best known trademark in this field was "Lok"; Lok fasteners were common on golf bags, clothing, and the like.

In recent years Tyler had been steadily diversifying its product line. In addition to fasteners and connectors the company manufactured and sold pilot lights and switches, printed circuits, semiconductor headers, and heat sinks. These new items were compatible with the company's traditional product lines in two ways; both the manufacturing skills required for their production and the marketing channels used for their distribution were related.

Since the war the company had experienced considerable growth in sales and in earnings. Many of the industries which Tyler supplied, however, were sensitive to general economic conditions, and consequently Tyler's sales were adversely affected by a recession.

Prior to 1957 management had tended to rely upon the company's strengths in manufacturing and marketing to produce satisfactory results. New electronic products had usually been acquired on a royalty basis from sources external to the company. Apart from industrial and product engineering, the company had virtually no research and development capabilities.

In 1957 Mr. Fowler became president of Tyler. He decided that the company should begin an aggressive program of new product development, and part of his plans included the establishment of a research laboratory. He began preparing the way for this innovation by bringing on to the board of directors two men who knew the research field and could provide support and advice. These men were Mr. Estill Green, Executive Vice President of the Bell Telephone Laboratories, and Mr. Gordon Brown, Dean of Engineering at M.I.T.

This case was prepared by J. R. Yeager. Copyright © by the President and Fellows of Harvard University. Harvard Business School case 9-113-092.

In 1962 Mr. Walter Martin, a physicist, joined the company to plan and lead the establishment of the laboratory. He soon realized that a major part of his initial work would be involved with convincing the operating management that research could in fact be a valuable addition to the company's capabilities.

The company was organized on a divisional basis. Divisions were judged as profit centers, and the division managers were compensated to a large extent upon their profit showings. There was considerable pressure on the division managers to produce as much profit as possible from their divisions on a yearly basis. Thus, long-term product development projects tended to be of secondary importance to these men.

In the current organization, the domestic divisions were classified by the industries which they supplied into industrial products and electronics. An executive vice president was responsible for each of the groups, and the division managers reported to their respective vice presidents. A third executive vice president was responsible for the company's six overseas subsidiaries. Mr. Martin was given the title of vice president in charge of research and development and he reported directly to the president. Mr. Martin was, therefore, at a level of authority in the organizational structure of the company comparable with the three executive vice presidents.

Establishing Objectives. In 1962 a research committee was formed to plan the work of the laboratory. This committee comprised four men: Mr. Martin, Mr. Fowler, and the two outside directors, Mr. Green and Mr. Brown. Once the laboratory had been organized and had begun operations the two executive vice presidents of the domestic divisions attended the meetings of the committee in the capacity of observers. It was the intention from the outset that the laboratory should operate independently of the manufacturing divisions, and should not be affected by the pressures generated by short-run profit considerations. Nevertheless, it was recognized that some degree of communication and cooperation between the laboratory and the divisions was both desirable and essential.

Mr. Martin, with the advice of the others on the research committee, developed a number of objectives for the laboratory. An examination of the company's manufacturing and markcting capabilties isolated four areas of interest where development work could properly be pursued. These were chemistry, physics, metallurgy and engineering. It was in these areas that a capability was to be developed, and the organization of the laboratory was to follow the same lines.

The emphasis here was on scientific disciplines rather than on specific projects. The reason for this was that an organization oriented towards a project might face severe difficulties should the project, for some reason, have to be terminated. Further, it was thought that the selection of personnel should be balanced by discipline, and that men should not be hired for specific projects.

The initial program was chosen with two purposes in mind. Comparatively simple projects were selected so that the newly formed group could gain confidence in itself, and also allow the rest of the company to gain confidence in the laboratory. Mr. Brown isolated a number of possible projects which would be aimed at developing products suited to the competences of the company, and the final selection was made by the committee.

It was recognized that the initial year's program would probably be too elementary for the laboratory to pursue after a few years. The question arose as to the type of projects which the laboratory would undertake. As an initial guideline in this area it was decided that a three-day, three-month rule of thumb should be adopted. That is to say, the laboratory would only take on projects which were estimated to require less than three days of work or more than three months. Development work not meeting these contraints was to be performed by the divisions each of which already had its own product engineering capabilities.

Finally a budget had to be estimated for the laboratory. Mr. Martin was aware that the decision on how much should be spent on research was always somewhat arbitrary. Nonetheless it was important to come to grips with the problem and to come up with a reasonable figure, because all capital appropriations in Tyler had to be approved by the operating committee. This committee was composed of the executive vice presidents and the division managers. While it was expected that Mr. Fowler's backing of the project would minimize the objections which the operating committee might raise, it was also considered important that the value of research should be accepted by the operating men.

Mr. Brown first turned to an industry comparison of research expenditures. The National Science Foundation publishes annually a booklet entitled "Funds for Research and Development in Industry." This publication summarizes research and development expenditures as a percentage of sales by industry, and also gives a variety of information such as the sources of funds and the cost of maintaining one scientist or engineer for a year.

Broadly speaking, Tyler's sales could be categorized into two industries; fabricated metal products and electronic components. The percentages of research and development to sales (company financed) for these industries were 0.9 and 3.4, respectively. In 1962 Tyler's total sales of $75 million came from $40 million sales of fabricated metal products and $35 million sales of electronic components. Weighing the industry percentages, these figures gave a total of $1.55 million.

The fabricated metal products industry percentage was composed of 32% basic and applied research, and 68% development. For the electronic components industry the figures were 17% and 83%, respectively. Since it was not intended that a great deal of development work was to be done by the laboratory two-thirds of the development percentages were excluded from the total. This was done on the assumption that about 70% of Tyler's development work would be done by the various divisions. From this a final total of approximately $.73 million was developed, or 1% of Tyler's sales. This was accepted by the research committee as a target rate of expenditure for the future. It was also agreed that the expenditures would be built up to this level over a five-year period, and Mr. Martin made the projection of expenditures for the laboratory shown in Exhibit 1.

EXHIBIT 1 Tyler Manufacturing Corporation

Projected Total Budget for the Exploratory Development Laboratory

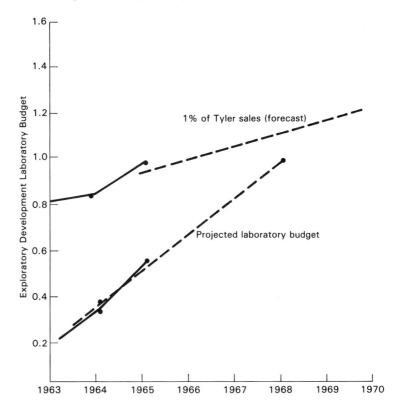

It was planned that the laboratory should seek an equal amount of federal funds to support additional related work. A one-to-one ratio of federal to company funds was actually substantially below the average of the two industries examined, but it was proposed that greater control of the research program and better patent protection on developments emerging from the program would result.

Finally, the planned level of expenditures was translated into terms of the size of professional staff it would support. The industry average figure for the electronic components industry for the support of one research professional was $34,000 per year. On this basis forty research workers could be supported by a budget of $1.5 million. Mr. Martin made a projection of the size of the laboratory staff, similar to the projected budget shown in Exhibit 1. He also made supporting projections such as, for example, the floor area of laboratory which would be required.

Having finalized his plans, Mr. Martin made a presentation to the operating committee. He pointed out that, while the company's sales had been growing, the rate of growth was not keeping up with the growth of the served industries. In particular, Tyler could not match the economic pace of the electronics industry without a substantial corporate research organization. Mr. Martin suggested that if the research activity could produce "true growth" for the company, that is, the company's share of the value added to end products could be increased, then the return on the money invested in research would be considerable. This analysis was greeted with a certain skepticism, but the plans were accepted and the laboratory was establshed and began operations early in 1963.

The expenditures incurred by the laboratory were included in the company's G. & A. expenses. They were allocated to divisions on a basis on the division's total sales.

The Laboratory in Operation.　By early 1966 the laboratory was employing twenty-one professional men. The solid line in Exhibit 1 shows the actual expenditures incurred by the laboratory during 1964 and 1965.

Ideas for work to be done in the laboratory had come from several sources including the research committee, the laboratory staff, and outside consultants. Some of the operating divisions had offered suggestions for routine engineering work but after being turned down they learned that their requests for work to be done were not being sought after. The exception to this was the request for help on a short-term basis (less than three days, in theory). When a division was faced with a problem which required the special talents of the laboratory staff for its solution, and the problem was estimated to require less than three days of work, the laboratory would accept the assignment. No direct charge was made for these short-term consulting jobs. It was considered important that the divisions be encouraged to seek some contact with the laboratory in order that a working relationship be developed. This relationship would become important once products started to be passed from the laboratory to the various divisions.

Essentially Mr. Martin emphasized the selection of people rather than projects. The research committee met every so often to plan ahead, and to outline the directions in which the company should expand. The selection of people followed from this, in that men were hired who had training in the direction in which expansion was sought. Direction, in this context, was defined in terms of scientific disciplines, and areas within disciplines, rather than in terms of projects.

As yet no clear organizational structure had emerged within the laboratory. Mr. Martin's concept of the structure was that of four departments, based on the four scientific disciplines, each with a department head reporting directly to Mr. Martin. However, no department heads had yet been appointed, and Mr. Martin found that he was able to maintain close personal contact with all of his professional men.

The professional men were divided into senior staff members and staff members. Promotions to senior staff were made by Mr. Martin. In 1966 there were eight senior staff, and most of these men were of the order of ten years older than staff members. Promotion to senior staff was not, however, intended to be based upon age. In fact one senior staff member, a recent graduate of Harvard Business School, was younger than some of the staff members.

Financial Reports.   Each year Mr. Martin compiled a budget for his operations, and submitted it for approval by the operating committee. Costs incurred were collected and reported by function, correspondoing to the breakdown in the budget. Monthly Mr. Martin received a report showing actual expenditures, comparing them with the budget, and also a summary of the expenditures for the year to date. Exhibit 2 shows the report for March 1966.

For control purposes Mr. Martin compared actual expenditures with budget and investigated any significant variances. He also paid close attention to the total number of people employed compared with his budget. Other indictors which he used to keep himself informed were the cost per scientist (compared with National Science Foundation figures), overhead as a ratio of direct labor, and direct to indirect labor ratios. The last measure tended to be very volatile. Direct labor personnel (e.g., scientists) charged their time to an overhead account whenever they were not working on a project. These charges might include such things as time spent on cleaning up the laboratory, writing proposals for new work, and recruiting.

EXHIBIT 2 Tyler Manufacturing Corporation

Corporate Office Exploratory Development Laboratory—Actual
  Versus Budgeted Expenditures

YEAR TO DATE			MONTH OF MARCH, 1966	
Actual	*Variable budget*		*Actual*	*Variable budget*
$ 61,985	$ 65,920	Executive and supervisory salaries	$20,762	$22,520
8,949	9,450	Clerical salaries—general	3,025	3,150
15,809	12,200	technical	5,615	4,400
16,514	12,337	Other payroll costs	5,945	3,849
$103,257	$ 99,907	Total payroll costs	$35,347	$33,919
8,284	8,250	Outside and professional services—general	2,270	2,750
5,529	3,900	Contract consulting services—direct	1,878	1,300
11,861	16,170	Supplies, stationery and postage—general	4,064	6,390
2,893	4,200	Material—direct	766	1,400
2,478	2,128	Telephone and telegraph	462	376
1,454	2,700	Travel expense	688	900
2,040	1,900	Other direct expense	281	300
13,650	11,500	Depreciation and building costs	3,230	3,500
$151,446	$150,655	Total expense	$48,986	$50,835

Cost Collection by Project. In addition to collecting costs by function, costs were also collected by project. Each week a project review was held, in which all of the workers on a project met with Mr. Martin to discuss progress and current problems. There were no project budgets. In effect the actual expenditures on projects were compared qualitatively with progress being made, and with estimated future

EXHIBIT 3 Tyler Manufacturing Corporation

Monthly Review, Project Recap—March, 1966

PROJECT		HOURS	COST
1	002	124	$ 146,456
1	003	23	8,278
1	004	3	2,184
1	005	291	110,077
1	006	38	27,384
1	008	32	12,128
1	100	31	70,861
		542	$ 377,368
2	001	946	$452,581
2	004	552	325,326
2	009	206	82,248
2	010	680	259,181
2	012	28	6,720
2	013	8	3,520
2	014	520	283,290
2	016	199	119,084
2	017	302	388,938
2	018	75	250,893
2	019	76	24,696
2	106	26	10,140
2	210	108	40,932
		3726	$2,247,549
3	102	78	£36,972
3	302	186	116,842
3	401	399	255,090
3	402	9	2,529
3	403	20	8,800
3	501	42	20,046
3	502	3	3,150
3	504	16	12,640
3	506	94	38,574
3	508	13	9,464
3	509	24	10,560
		884	$ 514,667
5	001	48	20,388
		48	20,388
		5200	$3,159,972

benefit of the line of investigation. As experience and judgment dicated, Mr. Martin would make changes in the level of effort devoted to specific projects. From time to time a project would be discontinued when it appeared that there was a diminished likelihood of economic benefit deriving from it.

To aid him in keeping in touch with the projects Mr. Martin was given a monthly project report, an example of which is shown in Exhibit 3. The source documents for this report were the weekly time sheets which each man filled in. The sheet was signed by the project leaders concerned. In the case of senior staff Mr. Martin signed their time sheets.

Each project had a code number, shown in the left-hand column. The first figure of the code number indicated the class of project. In fact, the first class of project in the report (code number starting with a 1) was overhead, and 1 005 referred to sick leave. A detailed breakdown of each project (and overhead accounts) was also prepared, and the monthly sick leave report is shown in Exhibit 4. Direct labor charges were collected under 2000, and 3000 series numbers. The detailed breakdown for project 2 014 is shown in Exhibit 5. The second column of the monthly reports showed the direct labor hours spent on the project, and the third column showed the direct labor dollars spent for the corresponding hours. For example, 753 direct labor hours, at a direct cost of $3,737.91, were expended on project 2 014 during March 1966.

Each project was headed by a project leader, and he received a copy of the monthly project report except that dollar amounts were excluded so that salary comparisons could not be made. The project leader was then able to compare the reported hours with his tally of the actual hours, and investigate any discrepancies.

At year end a summary by project was made. Exhibit 6 shows the report for 1965. Mr. Martin discussed progress with his staff at the year end and compared expenditures with progress. This aided in the planning of future efforts. The

EXHIBIT 4 Tyler Manufacturing Corporation

Monthly Review, Sick Leave Report—March 1966

NAME	PROJECT	HOURS	COST
C. F. Johnson	1 005	19	$ 12,293
A. R. Lee	1 005	8	3,872
A. McGregor	1 005	32	12,128
B. J. Fleming	1 005	24	11,232
M. Young	1 005	12	8,736
J. J. McDonough	1 005	8	3,520
A. S. Bennet	1 005	56	17,696
B. S. Mancuso	1 005	24	13,800
G. P. Gross	1 005	88	22,000
A. M. Ludwick	1 005	20	4,800
		291	$110,007

EXHIBIT 5   Tyler Manufacturing Corporation

Monthly Review, Project 2014, March 1966

NAME	PROJECT		HOURS	COST
D. M. Thomas	2	014	178	102,350
I. N. Jacobs	2	014	168	132,720
A. S. Bennet	2	014	37	9,805
A. M. Ludwick	2	014	135	37,935
R. F. Madera	2	014	2	480
			520	283,290

EXHIBIT 6   Tyler Manufacturing Corporation

Project Cost Summary, 1965

LABORATORY PROJECTS

Thin film resistors (2001, 2012)		$102,492
Coaxial cable and connectors:		
Pilot production (2010)	$137,464	
Coaxial connectors (2013)	29,213	
Coaxial plant construction (3401)	29,936	
Other coax projects (2011, 3402, 3403, 5001)	5,709	
		202,322
Adhesive formulation and testing (2003, 4, 5)		64,240
Metallurgy studies (2015, 16)		30,387
Magnetic thin films (2014)		37,737
Catalytic burner (2017)		12,962
Heat motor (2018)		19,969
		$470,109

DIVISION PROJECTS

Expoxy molding compound (2009, 3302)	30,730
Printed circuit drill (3102)	39,570
	$ 70,300

DIVISION CONSULTING

Marlin	1,075
Speedlok	938
Trimcon	270
Tabset	5,788
Circuit boards, Inc.	2,075
Alloy Metals	937
Corporate Office	762
Longacre Products	392
Hycon	1,090
	$ 13,327
Total project cost	$553,736

yearly summary was presented to the operating committee, along with Mr. Martin's report on progress.

Evaluation of Personnel. Mr. Martin kept in close contact with his professional staff and was thus able to form a sound opinion of each man's abilities. Once each year, on his anniversary of joining the company, a man was thoroughly evaluated. Senior staff were evaluated by Mr. Martin. A staff member was evaluated by Mr. Martin and by the senior staff members with whom he had worked during the year. On the basis of the evaluation the man was given a salary increase.

In setting salaries Mr. Martin was guided by the Los Alamos National Salary Survey of Professional Scientific Salaries. These figures gave the salaries of people in industry with scientific degrees, broken down by the number of years out of college. They also gave the low, median and high salaries in each year group. In his evaluation of an employee Mr. Martin judged where the employee's salary should be in relation to contemporaries, and adjusted the salary accordingly.

Each month Mr. Martin received a report showing him the way in which each employee had spent time. Part of this report is shown in Exhibit 7. From this Mr. Martin could see how much time an employee was charging to overhead accounts, and how many projects the man had been working on. In general, a man was not encouarged to work on a large number of projects for fear that he might spread his effort too thinly. In effect, the project leaders judged the latter point, because they invited men to work on their projects. If a man, because of other commitments, could spend only a short time on a certain project, and thus might be ineffective, the project leader would probably not invite or allow him to work on the project.

Up to a point employees were encouraged to travel to professional conferences. Mr. Martin considered that each employee should attend at least two conferences a year, but not more than three. Employees were also encouraged to study for advanced degrees. On the successful completion of courses the company would reimburse the employee 75% of the expenses.

Conclusion. In 1966 the laboratory was still expanding. Mr. Martin was well satisfied with progress to date, but he was aware that further expansion would probably generate some problems of control. He felt that the time had come to review thoroughly the laboratory's system of reporting and control, and to isolate areas for improvement. He was also concerned about the way in which any changes should be implemented.

Required

1. Appraise the approach taken to setting objectives for the laboratory.
2. Would project control be more useful? Why or why not?
3. Evaluate Tyler's control system. What changes, if any, would you make?

EXHIBIT 7

Monthly Review—Employee Analysis   March, 1966

NAME	*PROJECT*		*HOURS*	*COST*
A. M. McGregor	1	006	24	$ 22,416
	2	010	9	8,406
	3	401	151	141,034
			184	$171,856
C. V. Watson	2	010	104	$ 62,296
	3	401	80	47,920
			184	$110,216
A. S. Bennet	1	002	24	$ 25,200
	2	004	121	127,050
	2	017	4	4,200
	3	302	24	25,200
	3	401	8	8,400
	3	502.	3	3,150
			184	$193,200
B. S. Mancuso	2	014	178	$102,350
	3	401	6	3,450
			184	$105,800
G. P. Gross	1	005	19	$ 12,293
	2	009	43	27,821
	3	302	122	78,934
			184	$119,048
P. F. Wright	2	001	184	$176,272
			184	$176,272
R. S. Franklin	1	002	8	$ 3,000
	1	006	8	3,000
	2	010	128	48,000
	3	401	40	15,000
			184	$ 69,000
B. F. Meyer	1	005	8	$ 3,872
	1	006	2	968
	2	004	135	65,340
	3	501	39	18,876
			184	$ 89,056

chapter 12
PROFIT ANALYSIS

This chapter is concerned with the analysis of profitability. The major emphasis is placed on profit budgeting and the analysis of variance from budget, because this is the major type of profitability analysis used in business. The same techniques, however, are used to analyze differences in profitability between one year and the next in the same organizational unit and, to some extent, to analyze differences in profitability between two organization units.

Break-even analysis is also covered in this chapter because, next to profit budget analysis, it is probably the most widely used technique in profitability analysis.

THE PROFIT BUDGET

A *profit budget* is an annual profit plan. It consists of a set of projected financial statements for the coming year with appropriate supporting schedules. A profit budget, sometimes called a *master budget*, has the following uses:

1. In centralized companies or divisions of decentralized companies, it is used as follows:

(a) For planning and coordinating the overall activities of the company or divisions. For instance, the profit budget can be the basis for ensuring that production facilities are in line with sales forecasts or that cash availability is in line with proposed capital expenditures.

(b) As a final gauge in evaluating the adequacy of the expense budgets, particularly discretionary expenses. For example, management may have reviewed and tentatively approved all the expense budgets. After the profit budget is prepared, however, it may become evident that the expense budgets are too high because the projected profit is too low. A further review and revision of the expense budgets will then be made to bring them into line with projected revenues.

(c) For assigning to managers the responsibility for their shares of the financial performance of the company or division. For example, the marketing activity will be assigned responsibility for the revenue budget. This budget can be further subdivided into regions and districts. The responsibility for meeting cost standards is assigned to the plants and, within plants, to departments. In this way, each manager will know exactly what is expected. Subsequently, actual financial performance can be compared to each share of the overall plan.

2. In decentralized companies, divisional profit budgets are used by top management for the following purposes:

(a) To review expected total company financial performance for the coming year and to take action where this performance is not satisfactory.

(b) To plan and coordinate the overall activities of the company.

(c) To participate in divisional planning.

(d) To set a financial goal for the divisional manager.

(e) To exercise financial control over the divisions.

PROFIT BUDGET VARIANCE ANALYSIS

Profit budgets are used almost universally in companies having a number of profit-responsible units. Variance reports provide management with feedback on how the plans are being executed and this assists top managers in evaluating the performance of divisional managers. It will, of course, also help divisional managers by identifying specific areas that require attention.

A good profit budget analysis system will do the following:

1. *Separate revenue variances.* The profit effect of variances in sales volume and price should be segregated from other variances because the effect of revenue changes is likely to be so large that they obscure other smaller, yet more controllable, variances.

2. *Separate noncontrollable revenue and cost variances, if possible.* In some circumstances, certain revenue variances are, for practical purposes, uncontrollable by the responsible manager. In these cases, it is helpful to separate these variances clearly. For example, in the automobile industry, statistics are available that show the total industry volume and the market share of each car line. If the sales volume of an automobile model is different from budget, it is possible to segregate this difference between industry volume (the result of the level of economics activity) and market share (the responsibility of the manager).

EXHIBIT 1

Profit Budget Variance Disaggregation

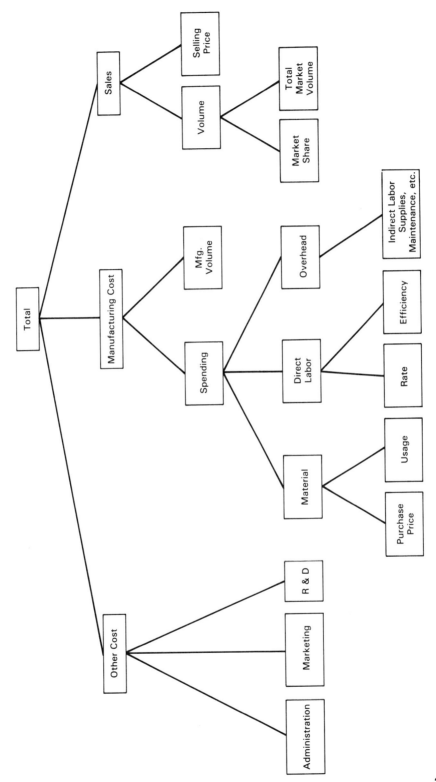

3. *Include an annual forecast.* All profit budget reports should include an annual forecast. This forecast may not mean too much in the early months of the year. In the later months, however, it gives top managment information about the probable annual profitability, which is often of vital interest. Also, it shows the extent to which unfavorable variances are expected to be corrected. In this way, the annual profit forecast might be an early warning of some expected problems.

Disaggregation

A profit budget variance is the difference between a budgeted financial item and the actual results achieved for that item. The process of variance analysis is hierarchical in that it begins with the total variance between the budgeted profit and the actual profit and progressively subdivides the variance until the point where further subdivision is not worth the cost.

Disaggregation is necessary for the following reasons:

1. As profit variance information moves down through an organization, more detail is required. This means that, at each lower level, managers require more information about a smaller segment of the total performance. For example, a plant manager requires more information about a plant's cost performance than a divisional manager and a divisional manager requires more detail about plant cost performance than senior management.
2. Variances are both negative and positive. Consequently, large offsetting variances could cover up serious problems.

The Total Variance

Profit budget analysis begins with the total variance between the original budget and the actual performance. This is simply the difference between the amount of profit included in the approved budget for the period and the actual profit recorded on the income statement for the period. The term *original budget* will be used to distinguish this budget from the adjusted budget that is required to calculate variances. The first level of disaggregation is to divide the total variance into three parts: the revenue variance; the manfucturing cost variance; and the nonmanufacturing cost variance. The next three parts of this chapter describe the methods for calculating each of these variances.

THE REVENUE VARIANCE

The *revenue variance* is the difference in *profit* because the actual sales were different from those projected in the original budget. The revenue variance is divided into sales volume variance and price variance.[1] Each is discussed in this part of the chapter.

The Sales Volume Variance

We need to know the impact on the profit that resulted from the actual sales volume being more or less than the original budgeted sales volume. An adjustment for volume is also necessary because direct comparisons of budgeted variable costs with actual variable costs are not meaningful when the budgeted and actual volumes are different. Consequently, the first step in profit budget variance disaggregation is to calculte a sales volume adjusted (SVA) budget. This is sometimes called a *flexed* budget.

The SVA budget is the original budget adjusted to the actual volume of sales. Note that the original budget is adjusted for—and *only* for—the volume of sales.

1. The difference between the original budgeted profit and the SVA budgeted profit is the *sales volume variance*. This will always be so because the only difference between the original budget and the SVA budget is the volume of sales.

2. The sales volume variance is the *profit* effect of the difference in volume, *not* the revenue effect.

3. The only use of the original budget in variance analysis is to calculate the sales volume variance. All other variances are calculated from the SVA budget.

Market Penetration and Industry Volume Variance

If possible, the sales volume variance should be separated into the profit effect of the difference between actual and budgeted market share and actual and forecast industry volume. The reason for this is that market share is a performance factor and is the responsibility of the manager, whereas the industry volume is a forecast factor over which the manager may have little or no control. This is very important because sales volume variance often accounts for a large proportion of the total variance and yet it may be a variance over which the manager has little control.

Assume for example, that a budget was prepared at a projected level of sales of 1,000 units, calculated as follows:

---

[1] A third variance, mix, is sometimes calculated. For example, the actual number of units sold could equal the budgeted number but the mix of these units might be more or less profitable than the budgeted mix. For example, an automobile division might sell the budgeted number of vehicles but the vehicles sold could be less profitable (such as subcompacts) than the type of vehicle included in the budget (full-sized cars). In many instances, however, volume and mix variances are so interrelated that separating them is not meaningful. In this chapter, it is assumed that the sales volume variance also includes any mix variance that may exist.

Projected industry volume	20,000 units
Budgeted market share	5%
Budgeted volume	1,000 units

Assume that the actual sales volume turned out to be 1320 units based on an industry volume of 22,000 units and a market share of 6%. Assume also that the total volume variance was $640 favorable, or $2 a unit ($640 ÷ 320 units variance). Volume variance can be segregated between industry volume and market share as follows.

Market Share Variance.   The formula is (actual industry volume × the difference between actual and budget market share) × profit per unit, or (22,000 × 0.01) ($2) = $440. A positive variance is favorable; a negative variance is unfavorable.

Industry Volume Variance.   The formula is (actual industry volume − budgeted industry volume) × budgeted market share × profit per unit, or (22,000 − 20,000) × 0.05 × $2 = $200. A positive variance is favorable; a negative variance is unfavorable.

Note that in this case there can be joint variances. As with manufacturing costs, we put the entire joint variance in the first variance that we calculate, which, in this case, is the market share variance.

Selling Price Variance

The different between the SVA revenue and the actual revenue is the *selling price variance*. This must be so because both the SVA budget and the actual revenue are calculated using the same unit sales volume. The difference, then, can be only in the selling price.

COST VARIANCES

The different between the SVA budget costs and the actual costs represent the first level of *cost variance* disaggregation.

Manufacturing Cost Variances

Manufaucturing cost variances are analyzed using techniques described in Chapters 9 and 10. Manufacturing cost variances are calculated using *production volumes rather than sales volumes*. The difference between the production and the sales volume is the increase or decrease in finished goods inventory. As explained in Chapter 9, manufacturing cost variances are actually recorded in the books of account and thus affect the reported earnings. Consequently, the actual cost of sales consists of the actual units *sold* multiplied by the standard cost per unit plus or minus the net amount of the manufacturing variance. (A favorable variance reduces the cost of sales; an unfavorable variance increases it.) A further breakdown of these variances are made outside the books of account as described in Chapter 9.

Nonmanufacturing Costs

Most of the nonmanufacturing costs (for instance, marketing, administration, and research and development) are fixed and need no adjustment for differences between the actual sales volume and the original budgeted sales volume. However, there can be elements of variable cost in distribution and selling. These costs are adjusted for differences in *sales volume* as part of preparing the SVA budget. Variances, then, are obtained by subtracting the SVA budgeted amounts from the actual costs. Note that nonmanufacturing variable costs are adjusted to the actual volume of *sales*. The reason for this is that nonmanufacturing variable costs will vary with the level of *sales* (sales commissions).

EXAMPLE 1.   The Midwest Division of the Continental Glass Company manufactures and sells glass bottles in the Midwest Sales Region.

The 1986 approved profit budget for the Midwest Division was as follows:

Sales	$720,000[a]
Cost of sales	480,000[b]
Gross margin	$240,000
Selling expenses	104,000[c]
Administrative expense	64,000[d]
Net profit before taxes	$ 72,000

[a]Budgeted revenue was 120,000 units at $6 per unit. A unit is 100 bottles. The 120,000 units represented a 10% market share on an estimated 1,200,000 industry volume.

[b]The cost of sales projection was based on the standard costs shown at the top of page 362.

[c]Selling expense consists of 0.40/unit variable cost (such as commissions and delivery) and $56,000 fixed costs (such as advertising and administration).

[d]Administrative cost is entirely fixed.

	VARIABLE	**FIXED**	**TOTAL FOR 120,000 UNITS**
Direct material	$2/unit*	—	$240,000
Direct labor	0.5/unit**	—	60,000
Overhead			
Indirect labor	0.2/unit	36,000	60,000
Indirect material	0.1/unit	—	12,000
Utilities	0.1/unit	1,000	13,000
Maintenance	0.2/unit	21,000	45,000
Depreciation	—	40,000	40,000
Taxes	—	10,000	10,000
	3.1/unit	108,000	$480,000†

*Consists of 40 lbs. of material at $0.05/lb.

**Consists of .05 of an hour at $10/h.

†The company uses a full absorption system. The standard cost per unit is $4.00 (480,000 ÷ 120,000).

The actual results of operations for the first quarter of 1986 were as follows:

Sales	$215,000[a]
Standard cost of sales	140,000
Manufacturing cost variances	(5,815)[b]
Gross margin	$ 80,815
Selling expense	30,000[c]
Administrative expense	20,000
Net profit after tax	$ 30,815

[a]35,000 units were sold and 36,000 units were produced. Industry volume was 437,500. Market share was 8%.

[b]Actual Manufacturing Costs

Direct material*	$ 67,760
Direct labor**	19,425
Indirect labor	16,750
Indirect material	2,650
Utilities	3,200
Maintenance	15,400
Depreciation	11,000
Taxes	2,000
Total	$138,185
Standard cost (36,000 × 4)	144,000
Variance from standard	$ (5,815)

* Consists of 1,540,000 lb at average price of 0.044/lb.

**Consists of 1,850 h at $10.50/h.

[c]Consists of $15,750 in variable costs and $14,250 in fixed costs.

SOLUTION. The first step is to calculate the quarterly budget at budget volume and the quarterly budget at actual volume. Then compare this with the actual results of operation.

| | QUARTERLY BUDGET AT | | | |
	Budgeted Volume	Actual Volume	Actual	Variance Favorable/ (Unfavorable)
Units	30,000	35,000	35,000	5,000
Sales	$180,000	$210,000	$215,000	$ 5,000
Cost of sales	120,000	140,000	140,000	—
Manufacturing variances	—	—	(5,815)	(5,815)
Gross margin	$ 60,000	$ 70,000	$ 80,815	$10,815
Selling expense	26,000	28,000	30,000	(2,000)
Administrative expense	16,000	16,000	20,000	(4,000)
Net profit before taxes	$ 18,000	$ 26,000	30,815	4,815

NOTES

1. The quarterly budget at budget volume is one-fourth of the annual budget. This has been done for simplicity. In most instances, the annual budget will be calendarized, that is, prepared by month or quarter.
2. Since the company has a full absorption cost accounting system, the cost of sales is the standard cost per unit multiplied by the number of units sold.

ANALYSIS OF VARIANCES: REVENUE. *Sales volume variance* is the difference between the budgeted profit at budgeted volume and the budgeted profit at actual volume, which is $18,000 − $26,000, or $8000 unfavorable. Sales volume variance is further broken down between *industry volume* and *market share* as follows.

Market share variance is 437,500 × (0.08 − 0.10) = 8750 units unfavorable. This simply says that if the Continental Glass Co. had a market peneration of 10% (the budgeted market penetration) instead of 8%, it would have sold 8570 more units.

Industry volume variance is (437,500 − 300,000) × (0.10) = 137,500 × 0.10 = 13,750 units favorable variance. This indicates that 13,750 more units were sold because industry volume exceeded expectations.

Profit effect. The 5000 additional units resulted in an additional budgeted profit of $8000. This is $1.60 a unit. Therefore, the market penetration variance of 8750 units is $14,000 unfavorable; the industry volume variance of 13,750 is $22,000 favorable; the net variance is $8000 favorable.

Selling price variance is the difference between the budgeted sales at actual volume and the actual sales. This is $5000 favorable.

Manufacturing Costs

DIRECT MATERIAL

Standard: 36,000 units × \$2 =	\$72,000
Actual	67,760
Variance	\$ 4,240 favorable

Price Variance: 1,540,000 lb × (0.050 − 0.044)	
= 1,540,000 × 0.006 =	\$ 9,240 favorable

Usage variance: [(36,000 × 40) − 1,540,000] (0.05)	
= (−100,000) (0.05) =	\$ 5,000 unfavorable

DIRECT LABOR

Standard: 36,000 × 0.5 = \$18,000	
Actual	19,425
Variance	\$ 1,425 unfavorable

Rate variance = (1850) (10.50 − 10.00) =	\$ 925	unfavorable
Efficiency variance = (1850 − 1800) (10) =	500	unfavorable
	\$1,425	unfavorable

OVERHEAD

Absorbed overhead (36,000 × 1.50)	\$54,000	
Budgeted overhead (27,000 + 0.6 (36,000)	48,600	
Actual overhead	51,000	
Volume variance (54,000 − 48,600	5,400	favorable
Spending variance (48,600 − 51,000)	2,400	unfavorable
Net overhead variance (54,000 − 51,000)	3,000	favorable

The spending variance of \$2400 is further subdivided as follows:

Manufacturing Overhead Budget Performance

	FIRST QUARTER, 1986		*Favorable/ (Unfavorable) Variance*
	Budget	*Actual*	
Indirect labor	\$16,200	\$16,750	\$ (550)
Indirect material	3,600	2,650	950
Utilities	3,850	3,200	650
Maintenance	12,450	15,400	(2,950)
Depreciation	10,000	11,000	(1,000)
Taxes	2,500	2,000	500
Total	\$48,600	\$51,000	\$(2,400)

OTHER COSTS

Selling

Budget (0.4) (\$35,000) + $\dfrac{56,000}{4}$		
14,000 + 14,000) =	28,000	
Actual	30,000	
Variance	2,000	unfavorable

This could be further subdivided as follows:

	BUDGET	ACTUAL	FAVORABLE/ (UNFAVORABLE) VARIANCE
Variable selling expense	$14,000	$15,750	$(1,750)
Fixed selling expense	14,000	14,250	(250)
Total	$28,000	$30,000	$(2,000)

Administrative

Budget	$16,000
Actual	20,000
Variance	$ (4,000)

Budget Performance Report

FIRST QUARTER, 1986

Actual profits	$30,815
Budgeted profits	18,000
Variance favorable/(unfavorable)	$12,815

ANALYSIS OF VARIANCE	FAVORABLE/ (UNFAVORABLE)
REVENUE VARIANCES	
Volume variances—Market share	$(14,000)
Industry volume	22,000
Net	$ 8,000
Price variance	5,000
Total revenue variance	$ 13,000
MANUFACTURING COSTS	
Direct material—Purchase price	$ 9,240
Usage	(5,000)
Direct labor—Rate	(925)
Efficiency	(500)
Manufacturing overhead—Spending	(2,400)
Volume	5,400
Net manufacturing cost variance	$ 5,815
Selling expense	(2,000)
Administrative expense	(4,000)
Net variances	$ 12,815

This report demonstrates the necessity for analyzing variances. Although there was a favorable variance of $12,815, it was entirely due to conditions being better than forecast, that is, a *forecast* variance rather than a *performance* variance. For example, the industry volume variance was $22,000 favorable and material purchase price variance was $9240 favorable. These are largely due to incorrect forecasts. However, there was a market share variance of $14,000 unfavorable and a material usage variance of $5000 unfavorable. These two, together with the other cost variances, are largely performance variances.

EXAMPLE 2. The Midwest Division's financial results for the second quarter of 1986 were as follows:

Sales	$148,000[a]
Standard cost of sales	100,000
Manufacturing costs variances	12,795[b]
Gross margin	$ 32,205
Selling expense	24,000[c]
Administrative expense	18,000
Loss before taxes	$ (6,795)

[a]25,000 units were sold; 24,000 produced; industry volume was 200,000 units.

[b]Actual Manufacturing Costs

Direct material*	$ 51,700*
Direct labor**	10,807**
Indirect labor	15,400
Indirect material	2,300
Utilities	2,900
Maintenance	11,688
Depreciation	11,000
Taxes	3,000
Total	$108,795
Standard cost (24,000 × 4)	96,000
Variance from standard	$ 12,795

* Consists of 940,000 lb at 0.055/lb.

**Consists of 1070 h at 10.10/h.

[c]Consists of $9500 variable selling expense and $14,500 fixed selling expense.

Prepare a variance analysis report for the second quarter and check it with the solution in the appendix to this chapter.

SOME OTHER CONSIDERATIONS. The profit budget variance procedures described in this chapter are a necessary but not a sufficient condition to insure an effective profit control system.

First, a profit budget variance analysis is only as good as the budget upon which it is based. Good profit budgets are not a matter of chance. A system of review and analysis that precedes the approval of a budget is needed and management participation in this process is essential.

Second, profit budget variance analysis typically tells you three things and only three things:

1. It identifies the responsibility center where a deviation has occurred.
2. It identifies the income statement element affected.
3. It provides the amount of the deviation and, to some extent, its cause.

What it does not tell you is what has happened, why it has happened, and what is being done to correct it. It is necessary to know all of these things before a judgment can be made on what, if any, action to take. Consequently, all profit budget reports should include, on a systematic basis, the answers to the above questions.

Third, only the effect of events that have already transpired are identified. Many managerial actions, for good or bad, may not affect the financial reports until long after the action has been taken. This situation can be partly mitigated by requiring a forecast of the entire year to accompany the profit budget report. The profit budget performance report, in itself, however, will never be a completely reliable early warning system.

Fourth, a profit reporting system must be used regularly by management if it is to be effective.

In actual practice, of course, profit budget systems are much more complex than those described in this chapter. First, instead of one product, there may be hundreds. Second, there may be multiple factories with different cost accounting systems. Third, there will almost always be changes in both beginning and ending work in process and finished goods inventories. Nevertheless, although these systems are much more complex clerically and employ more sophisticated techniques, they provide information of a nature similar to that described. An understanding of the simpler systems provides an understanding of more complex systems. The outputs are similar. It is only the inputs and processing that are more complex.

BREAK-EVEN AND PROFIT-VOLUME ANALYSIS

The Break-Even and Profit-Volume Equations

Break-even is the point at which the total revenues equal the total costs. Mathematically, it is the intersection of two lines: the revenue and the total cost line. The equation for the revenue line is

$$Y^r = Px, \tag{1}$$

where

Y^r = total revenue when x number of units are sold,

P = the price per unit (a constant),

x = the number of units sold.

The equation for the cost line is

$$Y^c = a + bx, \tag{2}$$

where

Y^c = total cost when x number of units are sold,

a = total fixed cost,

b = variable cost per unit,

x = the number of units sold.

Note that (2) is the same equation as the flexible budget equation. The fixed cost in (2), however, includes the *total* fixed cost of the company and the variable costs per unit is the total cost (including variable marketing costs where applicable).

By definition *break-even is the point at which the total costs are equal to the total revenues* or at the point when Eq. (1) is equal to Eq. (2). Thus we have

$$Px = a + bx.$$

By transferring bx to the left-hand side of the equation, we get

$$Px - bx = a.$$

Then

$$x(P - b) = a \text{ and } x = \frac{a}{P - b}$$

$$\text{Break-even volume} = \frac{\text{total fixed cost}}{\text{price} - \text{variable cost per unit}}.$$

But (price–variable cost) is contribution. Therefore,

$$\text{Break-even volume} = \frac{\text{total fixed cost}}{\text{contribution per unit}}.$$

For example, let us assume that the price of a product is \$2.00, the variable cost per unit is \$1.00, and the fixed costs are \$5000. What is the break-even point?

$$BE = \frac{FC}{P - VC} = \frac{5000}{2.00 - 1.00} = \frac{5000}{1} = 5000 \text{ units.}$$

The break-even volume is 5000 units. If more than 5000 units are sold, the company will earn a profit of \$1 for each unit in excess of 5000. If fewer than 5000 units are sold, it will have an accounted loss of $1 for each unit it sells less than 5000.

The break-even equation just described was for a single product. To calculate break-even for multiple products, the sales revenue is expressed in dollars and the variable cost is expressed as the number of cents per dollar of sales. For example, suppose that a company had variable costs equal to $0.60 for each dollar of sales and fixed costs of $120,000. What is the break-even?

Let x = the number of dollars of sales at volume x,

$0.60x$ = the variable cost at volume x,

$120,000$ = the fixed costs.

The break-even point is:

$$x - 0.60x = \text{the fixed cost at volume } x,$$

$$0.40x = 120,000,$$

$$x = \frac{120,000}{.40} = \$300,000.$$

When sales equal $300,000 the company will just break even. [$300,000 \times 0.40$ (the contribution per dollar of sales)] = $120,000, the total fixed cost. The formula for calculating the break-even point when using sales dollars is:

$$BE = \frac{\text{fixed cost}}{\text{contribution per dollar of sales}}.$$

This indicates one of the potential inaccuracies of the break-even calculation. To obtain contribution per dollar of sales, a given product mix must be assumed because different products contribute different amounts per dollar of sales. Consequently, if the mix of products changes from that assumed in developing the break-even point, the break-even volume will change.

The profit-volume line is another way of expressing the break-even equation. Profit, of course, is the revenue line minus the cost line. Mathematically it is developed as follows:

$$Y_r = Px, \, Y_c = a + bx,$$

$$Y_r - Y_c = Px - a - bx = x(P - b) - a,$$

but

$$P - b = \text{contribution per unit.}$$

Therefore,

$$Y_r - Y_c = xc - a,$$

or

> The profit at any volume x = (the contribution per unit × the number of units) − the fixed costs.

For example, assume that the price of a product is $3.00 per unit, the variable cost is $2.50, and the fixed costs are $5000. The profit-volume equation is:

$$P(x) = 0.50x - 5000.$$

The profit at volume x = $0.50 for each unit sold minus $5000. If 20,000 units are sold,

$$P = (20,000 \times .50) - 5000$$
$$= 10,000 - 5000 = \$5000.$$

The same equation is used to express the profit-volume relationship for a multiproduct company. As in the case of the break-even equation, the contribution is expressed as a number of cents per dollar of sales. For example, assume that contribution is equal to $0.25 per dollar of sales (i.e., variable costs equal $0.75 per dollar of sale) and fixed costs equal $100,000. The profit-volume equation is:

$$P(x) = .25x - 100,000.$$

If sales are equal to $500,000, the profit is

$$P = (500,000 \times 0.25) - 100,000$$
$$= 125,000 - 100,000 = \$25,000.$$

To convert the profit-volume equation into a break-even equation, simply place the contribution figure on one side of the equation and the fixed costs on the other. In the preceding example,

$$P(x) = 0.25x - 100,000.$$

At break-even $P(x)$ will equal zero. Hence

$$0.25x - 100,000 = 0$$

$$0.25x = 100,000$$

$$x = \frac{100,000}{.25} = \$400,000.$$

Preparing Break-Even and Profit-Volume Charts

Break-even and profit-volume charts are used to show graphically the relationship of profit and cost data to volume. Profits and costs are plotted on the vertical axis and volumes are plotted on the horizontal axis. The purpose of this part of the chapter is to describe how these charts are prepared.

Using the Profit Budget Relationship. Where a company has already prepared a profit budget that separates the fixed and variable costs, a break-even chart and profit-volume chart is very easy to develop (see the accompanying figure). Plot

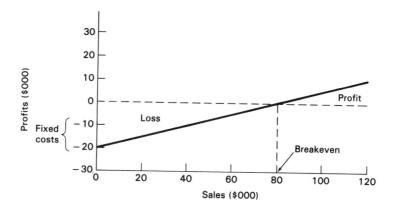

budgeted profits at any two volumes (usually zero and standard volume) on a chart and connect them with a straight line. This is the company's profit-volume line. A break-even chart is equally easy except that it is necessary to plot three lines: fixed cost, variable costs and revenues (see the accompanying figure).

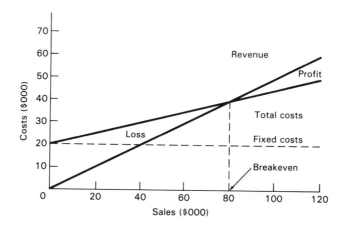

The fixed cost line is, of course, a horizontal line. (Remember that it includes *all* fixed costs, not just fixed overhead.) The variable cost line and the revenue line can be determined by plotting the total revenue and total variable cost at standard volume; the revenue line is drawn from the zero point (the intersection of the *x*- and *y*-axes) through the plotted point at standard volume; the variable cost line is drawn from the point at which the fixed cost line intersects the *y*-axis to the plotted point of total cost at standard volume.

Using Other Relationships

If there is no profit budget (or if the profit budget does not separate the fixed and variable costs), the following methods can be used for constructing a profit-volume or break-even chart.

Fitting a Line to Historical Data. This method is basically the same as that used to determine the variability of manufacturing overhead costs. Actual profits are plotted against volumes on the chart and a line is fitted to the plot points either by sight or by the method of least squares. A break-even chart can be made by plotting total costs against volume and adding a revenue line. For example, the monthly income statements for the ABC Company are shown next.

(000's) MONTH	SALES	COSTS	PROFITS/ (LOSS)
January	$1000	$ 900	$ 100
February	1300	1100	200
March	1400	1200	200
April	500	650	(150)
May	600	700	(100)
June	1200	1000	200
July	900	900	—
August	800	850	(50)
September	1400	1100	300
October	700	650	50
November	1200	1100	100
December	700	700	—

A profit-volume chart can be developed as shown in the accompanying figure (the line is fitted by sight).

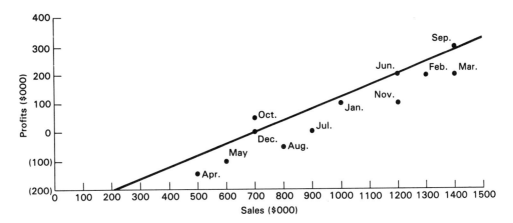

A break-even chart is developed as follows.

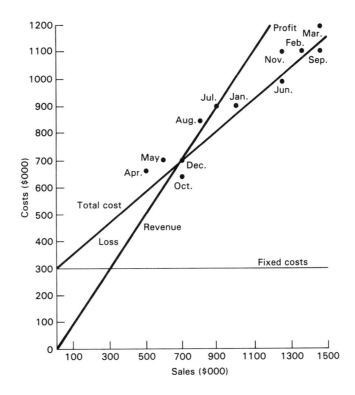

In using historical data to develop a break-even or profit-volume chart, two possible distortions must be avoided.

1. The shorter the period of time covered by the profit amount, the relatively greater will be the random fluctuations resulting from the inherent inaccuracies of profit measurement. For example, the amount of inventory is an important factor in profit determination. In a monthly income statement, inventories are frequently only roughly approximated; yet an error in the amount of inventory has twelve times the relative effect on monthly profits as the same mistake has on the annual profits. (Usually, also, the annual inventory is much more carefully calculated.)

2. If the historical information covers a relatively long period of time, significant changes in the break-even point may be occurring during the period. Fitting a line to these data does not give the current profit-volume line. For example, if annual profits are plotted over a period of five years during which a company was expanding, it might show an excellent fit on a profit-volume chart. This does not mean, however, that profits will drop along this line when volume drops. (Facilities and fixed costs may have increased proportionately with sales volume.) This point can be demonstrated by a simple though extreme example. Suppose a company employs a chemical processing technique that is characterized by having costs that are 100% fixed. A plant costs $100,000 a year to operate and could produce a maximum of 100,000 pounds, selling at $1.50 per pound. As sales demand increases beyond the capacity of the current plant, additional plants are added. Assume that sales, costs, and profits are as shown next.

| | SALES | | | | NUMBER OF PLANTS IN |
YEAR	Pounds	Dollars	COSTS	PROFITS	OPERATION
1964	75,000	112,500	$100,000	$12,500	1
1965	100,000	150,000	100,000	50,000	1
1966	150,000	225,000	200,000	25,000	2
1967	220,000	330,000	300,000	30,000	3
1968	250,000	375,000	300,000	75,000	3

A profit-volume chart would look somewhat as follows.

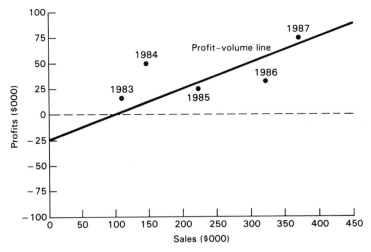

Although there are several other possible ways to fit the line (including one that shows no fixed costs at zero volume) all will include some variability. In fact, the fixed costs are $300,000 and, since there are no variable costs, the break-even point is at a $300,000 sales volume. This conclusion would never be drawn from the profit-volume chart just given because this chart reflects the changes in fixed costs over the years. Although the example is extreme, there will be the same type of distortion (although less in magnitude) any time profit-volume data are plotted covering a period of time when the company has been changing in size.

Plotting Two Points.   Other methods for developing a break-even or profit-volume chart are similar to those described in Chapter 10 for developing flexible budget equations. Consequently, these methods will be described only briefly here. The methods involve obtaining two points on the chart and drawing a line between them. The two points may be derived from analysis or from historical data. A frequent method is to calculate profit at zero volume and standard volume and connect these two points with a line.

Another common method is to calculate profits at 90% and 110% (or some other levels such as 80% and 120%) of standard volume and connect these points with a line. Another method is to take the profits at the highest and lowest volumes experienced during the past year and connect these points with a line. (When this is done, it is usual to adjust both profit amounts for unusual items.) The principal disadvantage of using only two points is that a distortion in either point can affect the line seriously.

Uses of Break-Even and Profit-Volume Charts

The break-even and profit-volume charts are simple graphic presentations of the relationship of profit to volume. These charts are easy for management to understand and use. Their principal advantages are as follows:

1. They furnish a simple evaluation of current profit levels. Actual profits are plotted on the profit-volume chart and management can see at a glance whether the level is better or worse than expected at the actual volume of operations. In other words, they show the profit performance adjusted for volume.
2. They provide management with a handy tool for calculating the effect of planned volume changes quickly.
3. They demonstrate graphically the approximate sales volume at which the company will lose money. If several break-even points for different periods of time are plotted on the same chart, it shows graphically the changes in the break-even points, the changes in the fixed costs, and the changes in contribution per sales dollar.

Limitations of Break-Even and Profit-Volume Charts

Although break-even and profit-volume charts are useful tools to management, they by no means solve problems in themselves. The best they can do is to help management diagnose a problem. All the information shown on a profit-volume chart is usually available in tabular form on an accounting report. The profit-volume chart merely presents this information graphically. These charts have several weaknesses, of which the user should be aware. Their principal limitations are as follows.

1. Unless the chart includes only one product, the profit-volume chart assumes a constant mix. Actual profits can vary from the profit-volume line because proportionately more of one product was sold than was assumed in developing the profit-volume chart. (This can also be a problem in developing a profit-volume chart from historical data.)

2. The profit-volume line is a linear approximation of a curvilinear function. The further away actual volume is from the volumes used to develop the line, the less accurate is this approximation.

3. Many factors can cause actual profits to be different from that indicated by the profit-volume line, yet the chart does not show the reasons for variance. For example, actual profits can be different from those indicated in the chart because prices changed, mix changed, or cost changed. Differences also occur because the profit-volume line only approximates the profit-volume relationship. The chart does not indicate in any way what caused the variances; worse, offsetting variances are left undetected.

4. Like all charts, the profit-volume chart shows a limited amount of information. All the information shown on a profit-volume chart usually occupies only a portion of an $8\frac{1}{2}$-inch × 11-inch report.

5. In actual business situations, if the volume of sales should drop to the point indicated on the break-even chart, there is a good chance that fixed costs would be reduced. This is because many fixed costs are discretionary in nature and, when volume drops to low levels, these expenses are arbitrarily reduced. Thus the break-even point is often overstated.

Management Implications of Break-Even Analysis

One of the most serious misconceptions about break-even analysis is that an increase in the break-even point of a company is bad. If this were true, all our industrial giants would be in bad shape indeed. How can production capacity be increased without increasing break-even? It may be possible, but it is usually difficult and uneconomic.

The important comparison is break-even as a percentage of capacity. If the break-even point is increasing as a percentage of capacity, it could indicate some highly unfavorable conditions. For example, if the contribution per dollar of sales is reduced because of lower prices or higher variable costs, the break-even increases both absolutely and as a percentage of capacity. This condition is usually unfavorable. An increase in the break-even because of the addition of new facilities that expand production capacity, however, is not unfavorable. This was expected when the purchase of the new facilities was approved.

CHAPTER 12 APPENDIX

Continental Glass Company—Midwest Division
   Profit Budget Analysis

SECOND QUARTER, 1986	
Actual profit/(loss)	$ (6,795)
Budgeted profit	18,000
Variance Favorable/(Unfavorable)	$(24,795)

ANALYSIS OF VARIANCE

Revenue Variances Favorable/(Unfavorable)

Market share	$ 8,000
Industry volume	(16,000)
Selling price	(2,000)
Net revenue variance	$(10,000)

Manufacturing Cost Variances

Material price	$ (4,700)
Material usage	1,000
Direct labor efficiency	1,300
Direct labor rate	(107)
Manufacturing overhead spending	(4,888)
Manufacturing overhead volume	(5,400)
	$(12,795)

Other Costs

Selling expense	—
Administrative expense	$ (2,000)
Total variance	$(24,795)

	QUARTERLY BUDGET AT			
	Budgeted Volume	*Actual Volume*	*Actual*	*Variance Favorable/ (Unfavorable)*
Units	30,000	25,000	25,000	(5,000)
Sales	$180,000	$150,000	$148,000	$ (2,000)
Cost of sales	120,000	100,000	100,000	—
Variances	—	—	12,795	(12,795)
Gross margin	$ 60,000	$ 50,000	$ 35,205	$(14,795)
Selling expense	26,000	24,000	24,000	—
Administrative expense	16,000	16,000	18,000	(2,000)
Profit/(Loss)	$ 18,000	$ 10,000	$ (6,795)	$(16,795)

Revenue Variances

- Sales volume variance = $8000 unfavorable, or $1.60/unit.
- *Market penetration* (200,000)(12.5 − 10.0) = 5000 units favorable.
- *Industry volume* (300,000 − 200,000)(0.10) = 10,000 unfavorable.
- 5,000 × 1.60 = $8,000 favorable market penetration
- 10,000 × 1.60 = $16,000 unfavorable industry volume variance

Manufacturing Cost Variance

	BUDGET	ACTUAL	FAVORABLE/ (UNFAVORABLE) VARIANCE
Direct material	$ 48,000	$ 51,700	$(3,700)
Direct labor	12,000	10,807	1,193
Manufacturing overhead			
Indirect labor	13,800	15,400	(1,600)
Indirect material	2,400	2,300	100
Utilities	2,650	2,900	(250)
Maintenance	10,050	11,688	(1,638)
Depreciation	10,000	11,000	(1,000)
Taxes	2,500	3,000	(500)
Total manufacturing overhead	$ 41,400	$ 46,288	$(4,888)
Total manufacturing cost	$101,400	$108,795	$(7,395)

Material Variances:

$$\text{Material Price Variance} = (940,000)(0.050 - 0.055)$$
$$= 940,000 \times 0.005 = \qquad \$4,700 \quad \text{unfavorable}$$
$$\text{Material Usage Variance} = (960,000 - 940,000)(.05)$$
$$= 20,000 \times 0.05 = \qquad 1,000 \quad \text{favorable}$$
$$\text{Net Variance} \qquad\qquad\qquad \$3,700 \quad \text{unfavorable}$$

Direct Labor Variances:

$$\text{Rate variance} = (1070)(10.00 - 10.10) = \quad 107 \quad \text{unfavorable}$$
$$\text{Efficiency variance} = (1200 - 1070)(10) = 1,300 \quad \text{favorable}$$
$$\qquad\qquad\qquad\qquad\qquad\qquad 1,193 \quad \text{favorable}$$

Manufacturing Overhead Variance:

Absorbed overhead	$= 24{,}000 \times 1.5^2$	$= \$36{,}000$	
Budgeted overhead	$= 27{,}000 + (24{,}000 \times 0.6)$	$= 41{,}400$	
Actual overhead		$46{,}288$	
Spending variance	$= (41{,}400 - 46{,}288$	$= 4{,}888$	unfavorable
Volume variance	$= 36{,}000 - 41{,}400$	$= 5{,}400$	unfavorable
Total overhead variances		$10{,}288$	unfavorable

QUESTIONS

12.1 Why do you think that a profit budget is sometimes called a *master* budget?

12.2 Top management has received and approved all the elements of the profit budget—marketing, production, research, administrative staff, and so forth. When these elements are combined, the total budgeted profits are less than was earned during the current year. This is a situation that management considers unsatisfactory. What actions can management take?

12.3 In analyzing changes in profitability between the current year and the proposed profit budget, the text states that it is important to separate changes that are not controllable by the manager from changes that result from management action. Give some examples of noncontrollable changes, and of controllable changes.

12.4 Explain why a *difference* between the sales volume and the production volume causes profits calculated using a full cost system to vary from profits calculated using a direct costing system. Give a formula for calculating this difference.

12.5 Can you think of any factors other than inventory valuation that make monthly profit calculations relatively unreliable?

12.6 Can you think of any factors, other than the increased facility acquisitions, that distort profit-volume comparisons over a period of years?

12.7 Both flexible budgets and break-even charts provide a linear approximation of what is often a curvilinear function. Would you say that this situation is more significant in break-even charts or in flexible budgets? Why?

12.8 Name some causes of increases in break-even that would reflect adverse situations. Name some causes of increases in break-even that may reflect favorable situations.

12.9 Name some causes of decreases in break-even that would reflect adverse situations. Name some causes of decreases in break-even that would reflect favorable situations.

---

[2]180,000 budgeted annual overhead divided by 1,200,000 units.

PROBLEMS

The annual profit budget of the XYZ Company is as follows:

	AMOUNT (000's)
Sales	$12,000
Material	1,200
Labor	2,400
Overhead—variable	3,600
Overhead—fixed	1,800
Selling expense (nonvariable)	1,200
Administrative expense	600
Budgeted profit	$ 1,200

Prepare a profit budget performance report, given the data described in the following problems. (In all cases, assume that the actual sales mix was the same as in the budget.)

12.1   The actual income statement for January is:

	AMOUNT (000's)
Sales	$1200
Material	105
Labor	220
Overhead—variable	310
Overhead—fixed	160
Selling expense	100
Advertising expense	50
Net profit	$ 255

There was a favorable selling price variance of $110,000 in January.

12.2   The actual income statement for February is:

	AMOUNT (000's)
Sales	$900
Material	95
Labor	200
Overhead—variable	275
Overhead—fixed	160
Selling expense	105
Administrative expense	45
	$ 20

There was no sales price variance in February.

12.3 The actual income statement for March is:

	AMOUNT (000's)
Sales	$1500
Material	190
Labor	410
Overhead—variable	642
Overhead—fixed	140
Selling expense	125
Administrative expense	60
Net profit	$ (67)

There was a $500,000 unfavorable selling price variance in March.

12.4 The actual income statement for April is:

	AMOUNT (000's)
Sales	$600
Material	45
Labor	95
Overhead—variable	140
Overhead—fixed	140
Selling expense	90
Administrative expense	50
Net profit	$ 40

There was a favorable sales variance of $100,000 in April.

12.5 Given are certain sales and profit data for the Fetmo Corporation for 1986.

MONTHS	SALES	PROFITS
Jan. and Feb.	$110,000	$ 7,000
Mar. and Apr.	130,000	15,000
May and June	150,000	20,000
July and Aug.	140,000	14,000
Sept. and Oct.	160,000	25,000
Nov. and Dec.	190,000	30,000

(a) Plot the data on a profit-volume chart.
(b) Fit a line to this data by the method of least squares.
(c) Calculate the profit-volume equation and the break-even point.

12.6 Given are the sales and profit data for the Gemo Company for 1986.

MONTHS	SALES	PROFITS
Jan. and Feb.	90,000	$ 10,000
Mar. and Apr.	110,000	28,000
May and June	80,000	(9,000)
July and Aug.	100,000	21,000
Sept. and Oct.	60,000	(17,000)
Nov. and Dec.	120,000	33,000

(a) Plot the data on a profit-volume chart.
(b) Fit a line by the method of least squares.
(c) Calculate the profit-volume equation and the break-even point.

CASES

CASE 12.1   WEBSTER COMPANY

The annual sales and net profit data of the Webster Company over an eleven-year period are shown in Exhibit 1.

EXHIBIT 1

	(IN MILLIONS)	
YEAR	SALES	NET PROFIT
1976	$48	$ 8.0
1977	52	9.4
1978	58	11.3
1979	64	9.5
1980	70	10.0
1981	75	11.8
1982	78	8.6
1983	80	6.6
1984	70	4.1
1985	62	.8
1986	55	(1.7)

Required

Plot this data on a profit-volume chart and see if you can come to any conclusions about what has been happening to the profit over the past few years.

CASE 12.2   BILL FRENCH, ACCOUNTANT— DUO-PRODUCTS CORPORATION

Bill French picked up the phone and called his boss, Wes Davidson, controller of Duo-Products Corporation, "Say, Wes, I'm all set for the meeting this afternoon. I've put together a set of break-even statements that should really make the boys sit up and take notice—and I think they'll be able to understand them, too." After a brief conversation about other matters, the call was concluded and French turned to his charts for one last check-out before the meeting.

French had been hired six months earlier as a staff accountant. He was directly responsible to Davidson and, up to the time of this case, had been doing routine types of analysis work. French was an alumnus of a liberal arts undergraduate school and graduate business school, and was considered by his associates to be quite capable and unusually conscientious. It was this latter characteristic that had apparently caused him to "rub some of the working guys the wrong way," as one of his coworkers put it. French was well aware of his capabilities and took advantage of every opportunity that arose to try to educate those around him. Wes Davidson's invitation for French to attend an informal manager's meeting had come as some surprise to others in the accounting group. However, when French requested permission to make a presentation of some break-even data, Davidson acquiesced. The Duo-Products Corporation had not been making use of this type of analysis in its review or planning programs.

Basically, what French had done was to determine the level of operation at which the company must operate in order to break even. As he phrased it, "The company must be able to at least sell a sufficient volume of goods that it will cover all of the variable costs of producing and selling the goods; further, it will not make a profit unless it covers the fixed, or nonvariable, costs as well. The level of operation at which total costs (that is, variable plus nonvariable) are just covered is the break-even volume. This should be the lower limit in all of our planning."

The accounting records had provided the following information which French used in constructing his chart:

Plant capacity	2,000,000 units
Past year's level of operations	1,500,000 units
Average unit selling price	$1.20
Total fixed costs	$520,000
Average variable unit cost	$0.75

This case was prepared by N. E. Harlan. Copyright © by the President and Fellows of Harvard University. Harvard Business School case 9-104-039.

From this information, he observed that each unit contributed $0.45 to fixed overhead after covering the variable costs. Given total fixed costs of $520,000, he calculated that 1,155,556 units must be sold in order to break even. He verified this conclusion by calculating the dollar sales volume that was required to break even. Since the variable costs per unit were 62.5% of the selling price, French reasoned that 37.5% of every sales dollar was left available to cover fixed costs. Thus fixed costs of $520,000 require sales of $1,386,667 in order to break even.

When he constructed a break-even chart to present the information graphically, his conclusions were further verified. The chart also made it clear that the firm was operating at a fair margin over the break-even requirements, and that the profits accruing (at the rate of 37.5% of every sales dollar over break-even) increased rapidly as volume increased (see Exhibit 1).

Shortly after lunch, French and Davidson left for the meeting. Several representatives of the manufacturing departments were present, as well as the general sales manager, two assistant sales managers, the purchasing officer, and two men from the product engineering office. Davidson introduced French to the few men that he had not already met and then the meeting got under way. French's presentation was the last item on Davidson's agenda, and in due time the controller introduced French, explaining his interest in cost control and analysis.

French had prepared enough copies of his chart and supporting calcula-

EXHIBIT 1

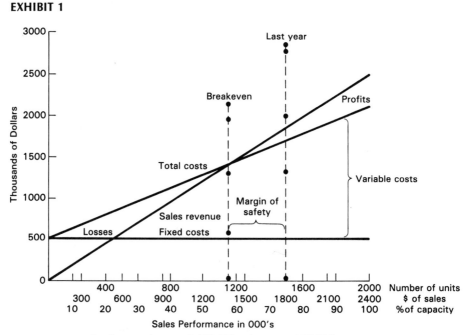

Breakeven volume = 1,156,000 units, or $1,387,000

tions so that they could be distributed to everyone at the meeting. He described carefully what he had done and explained how the chart pointed to a profitable year, dependent on meeting the volume of sales activity that had been maintained in the past. It soon became apparent that some of the participants had known in advance what French planned to discuss; they had come prepared to challenge him and soon had taken control of the meeting. The following exchange ensued (see Exhibit 2 for a checklist of participants with their titles).

COOPER: (Production Control) You know, Bill, I'm really concerned that you haven't allowed for our planned changes in volume next year. It seems to me that you should have allowed for the sales department's guess that we'll boost sales by 20% unitwise. We'll be pushing 90% of what we call capacity then. It sure seems that this would make quite a difference in your figuring.

FRENCH: That might be true, but as you can see, all you have to do is read the cost and profit relationship right off the chart for the new volume. Let's see— at a million-eight units we'd . . .

WILLIAMS: (Manufacturing) Wait a minute, now! If you're going to talk in terms of 90% of capacity, and it looks like that's what it will be, you damn well better note that we'll be shelling out some more for the plant. We've already got okays on investment money that will boost your fixed costs by ten thousand dollars a month, easy. And that may not be all. We may call it 90% of plant capacity, but there are a lot of places where we're just full up and we can't pull things up any tighter.

COOPER: See, Bill? Fred Williams is right, but I'm not finished on this bit about volume changes. According to the information that I've got here—and it came from your office—I'm not sure that your break-even chart can really be used even if there were to be no changes next year. Looks to me like you've got

EXHIBIT 2 Duo-Products Corporation

Product Class Cost Analysis (Normal Year)

	AGGREGATE	*A*	*B*	*C*
Sales at full capacity (units)	2,000,000			
Actual sales volume (units)	1,500,000	600,000	400,000	500,000
Unit sales price	$1.20	$1.67	$1.50	$0.40
Total sales revenue	$1,800,000	$1,000,000	$600,000	$200,000
Variable cost per unit	$0.75	$1.25	$0.625	$0.25
Total variable cost	$1,125,000	$750,000	$250,000	$125,000
Fixed costs	$ 520,000	$ 170,000	$275,000	$ 75,000
Net profit	$ 155,000	$ 80,000	$ 75,000	0
Ratios:				
Variable cost to sales	0.63	0.75	0.42	0.63
Variable income to sales	0.37	0.25	0.58	0.37
Utilization of capacity	75%	30%	20%	25%

average figures that don't allow for the fact that we're dealing with three basic products. Your report here (see Exhibit 3) on costs, according to product lines, for last year makes it pretty clear that the "average" is way out of line. How would the break-even point look if we took this on an individual product basis?

FRENCH: Well. I'm not sure. Seems to me that there is only one break-even point for the firm. Whether we take it product by product or in total, we've got to hit that point. I'll be glad to check for you if you want, but . . .

BRADSHAW: (Assistant Sales Manager) Guess I may as well get in on this one, Bill. If you're going to do anything with individual products, you ought to know that we're looking for a big swing in our product mix. Might even start before we get into the new season. The "A" line is really losing out and I imagine that we'll be lucky to hold two-thirds of the volume there next year. Wouldn't you buy that Arnie? [Agreement from the General Sales Manager.] That's not too bad, though, because we expect that we should pick up the 200,000 that we lose, and about a quarter million units more, over in "C" production. We don't see anything that shows much of a change in "B." That's been solid for years and shouldn't change much now.

WINETKI: (General Sales Manager) Bradshaw's called it about as we figure it, but there's something else here too. We've talked about our pricing on "C" enough, and now I'm really going to push our side of it. Ray's estimate of maybe half a million—four hundred fifty thousand I guess it was—up on "C" for next year is on the basis of doubling the price with no change in cost. We've been priced so low on this item that it's been a crime—we've got to raise, but good, for two reasons. First, for our reputation; the price is out of line class-wise and is completely inconsistent with our quality reputation. Second, if we don't raise the price, we'll be swamped and we can't handle it. You heard what Williams said about capacity. The way the whole "C" field is exploding, we'll have to answer to another half million units in unsatisfied orders if we don't jack that price up. We can't afford to expand that much for this product.

EXHIBIT 3 Duo-Products Corporation

List of Participants in the Meeting

Bill French	Staff Accountant
Wes Davidson	Controller
John Cooper	Production Control
Fred Williams	Manufacturing
Ray Bradshaw	Assistant Sales Manager
Arnie Winetki	General Sales Manager
Hugh Fraser	Administrative Assisitant to President

At this point, Hugh Fraser, administrative assistant to the president, walked up toward the front of the room from where he had been standing near the rear door. The discussion broke for a minute, and he took advantage of the lull to interject a few comments.

FRASER: This has certaintly been enlightening. Looks like you fellows are pretty well up on this whole operation. As long as you're going to try to get all of the things together that you ought to pin down for next year, let's see what I can add to help you.

Number One: Let's remember that everything that shows in the profit area here on Bill's chart is divided just about evenly between the government and us. Now, for last year we can read a profit of about $150,000. Well, that's right. But we were left with half of that, and then paid out dividends of $50,000 to the stockholders. Since we've got an anniversary year coming up, we'd like to put out a special dividend about 50% extra. We ought to hold $25,000 in for the business, too. This means that we'd like to hit $100,000 *after* the costs of being governed.

Number Two: From where I sit, it looks like we're going to have to talk with the union again and this time it's liable to cost us. All the indications are—and this isn't public—that we may have to meet demands that will boost our production costs—what do you call them here, Bill—variable costs—by 10% across the board. This may kill the bonus-dividend plans, but we've got to hold the line on past profits. This means that we can give that much to the union only if we can make it in added revenues. I guess you'd say that that raises your break-even point, Bill—and for that one I'd consider the company's profit to be a fixed cost.

Number Three: Maybe this is the time to think about switching our product emphasis. Arnie Winetki may know better than I which of the products is more profitable. You check me out on this Arnie—and it might be a good idea for you and Bill French to get together on this one, too. These figures that I have (Exhibit 2) make it look like the percentage contribution on line "A" is the lowest of the bunch. If we're losing volume there as rapidly as you sales folks say, and if we're as hard pressed for space as Fred Wiliams has indicated, may be we'd be better off grabbing some of that big demand for "C" by shifting some of the facilities over there from "A."

That's all I've got to say. Looks to me like you've all got plenty to think about.

DAVIDSON: Thanks, Hugh. I sort of figured that we'd get wound up here as soon as Bill brought out his charts. This is an approach that we've barely touched, but, as you can see, you've all got ideas that have got to be made to fit here somewhere. I'll tell you what we'll do. Bill, suppose you rework your chart and try to bring into it some of the points that were made here today. I'll see if I can summarize what everyone seems to be looking for.

First of all, I have the idea buzzing around in the back of my mind that your presentation is based on a rather important series of assumptions. Most of the questions that were raised were really about those assumptions; it might help us all if you try to set the assumptions down in black and white so that we can see just how they influence the analysis.

Then, I think that Cooper would like to see the unit sales increase taken up, and he'd also like to see whether there's any difference if you base the calculations on an analysis of individual product lines. Also, as Bradshaw suggested, since the product mix is bound to change, why not see how things look if the shift materializes as Sales has forecast?

Arnie Winetki would like to see the influence of a price increase in the "C" line, Fred Williams looks toward an increase in fixed manufacturing costs of ten thousand a month, and Hugh Fraser has suggested that we should consider taxes, dividends, expected union demands, and the question of product emphasis.

I think that ties it all together. Let's hold off on our next meeting, fellows, until Bill has time to work this all into shape.

With that, the participants broke off into small groups and the meeting disbanded. French and Wes Davidson headed back to their offices and French, in a tone of concern, asked Davidson, "Why didn't you warn me about the hornet's next I was walking into?"

"Bill, you didn't ask!"

Required

1. What are the assumptions implicit in Bill French's determination of his company's break-even point?

2. On the basis of French's revised information, what does next year look like:

   (a) What is the break-even point?

   (b) What level of operations must be achieved to pay the extra dividend, ignoring union demands?

   (c) What level of operations must be achieved to meet the union demands, ignoring bonus dividends?

   (d) What level of operations must be achieved to meet both dividend and expected union requirements?

3. Can the break-even analysis help the company decide whether to alter the existing product emphasis? How much can the company afford to invest for additional "C" capacity?

4. Is this type of analysis of any value? For what can it be used?

CASE 12.3 NORTH AMERICAN CAN (A): THE KOKOMO DIVISION

The Kokomo division of the North American Can Company produced a single product: a 12-ounce beer can. Exhibit 1 provides financial information about the revenues and costs that were projected for 1986 for the Kokomo division. The total market volume is expected to be 60,000 units for the year. The volume of production and sales for the Kokomo division is projected to be 12,000 units for the year. A unit is 400 cases. Each case contains 24 of the 12-ounce cans.

Required

Prepare a 1986 profit plan for the Kokomo division (the profit plan is before income taxes). The Kokomo division's budgeted sales and production volumes are equal.

EXHIBIT 1 North American Can (A): The Kokomo Division

1986 Annual Budget Data

ITEM OF REVENUE OR COST[a]	*1984 EXPECTED AMOUNT*[b]
Price	$85.20 per unit
Direct Material	$28.80 per unit
Direct Labor	$5.10 per unit
Manufacturing overhead:	
Indirect Labor	$69,000 per year
	+ $3.10 per unit
Indirect Material	$1.84 per unit
Utilities	$1.54 per unit
Maintenance	$30,800 per year
	+ $1.25 per unit
Depreciation	$92,500 per year
Property Taxes	$30,900 per year
Marketing Expense:	
Sales Commissions	$4.25 per unit
Salaries	$92,000 per year
Distribution	$0.82 per unit
Administrative Costs	$106,000 per year

[a]All numbers have been disguised and, therefore, may not be representative of actual revenues or costs experienced in a typical can-manufacturing plant.

[b]Expected manufacturing costs are standard costs.

This case was prepared by John Dearden. Copyright © by the President and Fellows of Harvard University. Harvard Business School case 9-182-006.

CASE 12.4 NORTH AMERICAN CAN (B): THE KOKOMO DIVISION

Exhibit 1 provides the actual results of operations for the Kokomo division for the first quarter of 1986. Kokomo employed a standard full-cost system.

Required

1. Compare the actual results with the budgeted amounts prepared in the (A) case. (The budget for the first quarter is one-fourth of the annual budget).

2. What conclusions can you draw about the first quarter financial performance of the Kokomo division?

3. What managerial actions would you take as a result of your analysis?

EXHIBIT 1 North American Can (B):
The Kokomo Plant

Results of Operations—First Quarter, 1986

Sales	$275,400
Standard cost of sales	195,145
Variances	(12,147)
Cost of goods sold	182,998
Gross profit	$ 92,402
Marketing expense (Schedule B)	40,000
Administrative expense	26,474
Profit before taxes	$ 25,928
Volume of sales (units)	3240
Volume of production (units)	3500

SCHEDULE A—COST OF GOODS MANUFACTURED

Direct material	$ 87,500
Direct labor	28,000
Indirect labor	28,350
Indirect materials	5,662
Utilities	5,584
Maintenance	12,712
Depreciation	23,125
Property tax	7,725
Total	$198,658

SCHEDULE B—MARKETING EXPENSE

Commissions	$ 13,770
Salaries	23,476
Distribution	2,754
Total marketing expense	$ 40,000

This case was prepared by John Dearden. Copyright © by the President and Fellows of Harvard University. Harvard Business School case 9-182-007.

CASE 12.5   NORTH AMERICAN CAN (C): THE KOKOMO DIVISION

Exhibit 1 provides a more detailed description of both budgeted and actual results of operations for the Kokomo division for the first quarter of 1986.

Required

1. Analyze the causes of the variances from budget and evaluate the first quarter's financial performance of the Kokomo division.

2. Separate the variances into three classifications:

   (a) Largely controllable by management.

   (b) Largely uncontrollable by management.

   (c) Semicontrollable by management.

3. What managerial actions would you take on the basis of your analysis?

EXHIBIT 1

	BUDGETED	*ACTUAL*
Direct Material	6 cents per square foot	5 cents per square foot
	480 square feet per unit	500 square feet per unit
Direct Labor	$10.20 per hour	$10.00 per hour
	0.5 hours per unit	0.8 hours per unit
Total market (first quarter)	15,000 units	18,000 units
Sales Volume (first quarter)	3,000 units	3,240 units
Production Volume (first quarter)	3,000 units	3,500 units

This case was prepared by John Dearden. Copyright © by the President and Fellows of Harvard University. Harvard Business School case 9-182-008.

CASE 12.6   MARWICK & COMPANY

In preparing its profit plan for 1983, the management of Marwick & Company realized that its sales were subject to monthly seasonal variations but expected that for the year as a whole the profit before taxes would total $972,000.

1983 Budget

	AMOUNT	PERCENT OF SALES
Sales	$5,400,000	100%
Standard cost of goods sold:		
Prime costs	$1,890,000	35%
Factory overhead	1,890,000	35%
Total standard cost	$3,780,000	70%
Gross profit	$1,620,000	30%
Selling and general overhead	648,000	12%
Profit before taxes	$ 972,000	18%

Management defined "prime costs" as those costs for labor and materials which were strictly variable with the quantity of production in the factory. The overhead in the factory included both fixed and variable costs; management estimates that the variable factory overhead would be equal to 30% of prime costs. Thus the total factory overhead budgeted for 1983 consisted of $567,000 of variable costs (30% of $1,890,000) and $1,323,000 of fixed costs. All the selling and general overhead was fixed, except for commissions on sales equal to 5% of the selling price.

Mr. Marwick, the president of the company, approved the budget, stating that, "A profit of $81,000 a month isn't bad for a little company in this business." During January, however, sales suffered the normal seasonal dips, and production in the factory was also cut back. The result, which came as some surprise to the president, was that January showed a loss of $7155.

Operating Statement, January 1983

Sales		$270,000
Standard cost of goods sold		189,000
Standard gross profit		$ 81,000
Manufacturing variances:		fav/(unfav)
Prime cost variance	$(7,680)	
Factory overhead:		
Spending variance	$ 1,500	
Volume variance	$(33,075)	(39,255)
Actual gross profit		$ 41,745
Selling and general overhead		48,900
Loss before taxes		$ (7,155)

This case was prepared as a first-year Control examination.

Required

Note: Selling prices in January were the same as the budgeted prices.

1. What was Marwick's January production level compared to average budgeted monthly production?

2. What were actual manufacturing overhead costs in January?

3. Explain, as best you can with the data available, why the January profit was $88,155 less than the average monthly profit expected by the president.

4. By how much did finished goods inventory change in January?

5. What would the January profits have been if Marwick had used a direct costing system? What accounts for the difference?

6. At what annual dollar volume will Marwick have a budgeted profit of zero, assuming sales and production were equal?

CASE 12.7 MATTEL MANUFACTURING COMPANY

The Mattel Manufacturing Company manufactures and sells a single product. The Company employs a full absorption standard cost accounting system. Each year a budget is prepared for the coming year and actual results are compared with budget semiannually. The budget for a semiannual period is one-half of the annual budget. The four exhibits at the end of the case provide the results of operations for 1984, together with relevant details on standard and actual manufacturing costs.

Required

1. Explain as far as possible why actual profits for the first six months of 1984 were different from budget.

2. Explain as far as possible why the profits in the second six months of 1984 increased by $2,420,000 over the first six months.

3. Show the income statement for the first six months of 1984 as it would have been had Mattel used a direct cost system.

_____

This case was prepared as a first-year Control examini ion.

EXHIBIT 1 Mattel Manufacturing Company

Comparative Income Statement ($000)

	ANNUAL BUDGET 1984	ACTUAL RESULTS — 1984	
		First 6 months	*Second 6 months*
Sales	$56,000	$29,680	$27,072
Cost of Sales[a]	46,280	25,732	20,704
Gross margin	9,720	3,948	6,368
Selling and Administrative expense[b]	8,000	4,000	4,000
Operating income	1,720	(52)	2,368

[a]All manufacturing cost variances are closed to the cost of sales account every six months.
[b]Selling and administrative costs are all fixed.

EXHIBIT 2

Sales, Production and Inventory Statistics

	1984	
	First 6 months	*Second 6 months*
Budgeted sales	400,000 units	400,000 units
Actual sales	424,000 units	376,000 units
Budget production	400,000 units	400,000 units
Actual production	376,000 units	424,000 units
Beginning finished goods inventory	200,000 units at a standard cost of $57.85 per unit	152,000 units at a standard cost of $57.85 per unit

EXHIBIT 3

Actual Manufacturing Costs ($000)

	1984	
	First 6 months	*Second 6 months*
Direct material	$ 3,422	$ 3,648
Direct labor	6,800	7,438
Factory overhead—variable	3,760	3,990
Factory overhead—fixed	8,974	8,404
Total	$22,956	$23,480

EXHIBIT 4

Standard Cost Sheet
    (Based on normal production
    volume of 400,000 units every
    six months)

COST PER UNIT	
Raw materials	$ 9.00
Direct labor	17.00
Variable Overhead	9.40
Fixed overhead	22.45
	$57.85

CASE 12.8   BONDSVILLE MANUFACTURING COMPANY

"Let's face it," said William Haywood, Controller of the Bondsville Manufacturing Company, to Frederick Strong, the Manager of the Budget Department, "Our budgetary control program is considerably less than a roaring success. As far as I can tell, no one in top management takes any action from our monthly analyses of actual profit performance against budget. Jim [James Smith, Bondville's president] told me this afternoon that he really cannot use these reports to control the divisions. He said that the variance from budgeted profits always seem to be large, but there always appear to be reasonable explanations. Further, he pointed out that once a division starts to miss its budget, the variances seem to get larger each month. And Jim wasn't concerned only with unfavorable variances. He said that some divisions are showing favorable variances when he knows darn well that they are doing a poor job."

Frederick Strong was crestfallen. He had come to the Bondsville Manufacturing Company three years before from a large automobile manufacturer where he had been a budget analyst in one of the divisions. He was responsible for developing and installing the present profit budget system. The system had gone into effect 18 months ago. For the first year, it was considered experimental. Beginning with the current year (1986) the profit budget was officially installed as the basic tool of management control. Now, after six months, the President of Bondsville was questioning the utility of the budgetary control system and the Controller was evidently agreeing.

"I don't understand it," said Strong to Haywood. "The system is similar to the one we used at Universal Motors and they sure paid attention to it. If we missed our budget, we were called on the carpet to explain—and the explanation had to be good."

"Well, it may have worked at Universal," said Haywood, "but it isn't working here. I'll arrange for you to talk with Jim about it. Then, I want you to go over the system and either modify it so that it will work or scrap it and develop something that will." With this last comment, Strong was dismissed to ponder his problems.

History of the Company

The Bondsville Manufacturing Company started during World War I as a family-owned manufacturer of cotton textiles for the United States Army. The original plant was located in the town of Bondsville, a small village in western Massachusetts. The company's early growth was slow and it remained a one-plant manufacturer of cotton textiles until the outbreak of World War II. (With difficulty, Bondsville had managed to weather the economic shoals of the Depression.)

By the beginning of World War II, the company was taken over from the original family by a group of investors. This group renovated the Bondsville plant, built a knitting plant in nearby Ware, Massachusetts, and purchased a woolen plant in Monson, Massachusetts. During the War, the company prospered and grew until, at the cessation of hostilities, its annual profit was $3 million on a sales volume of nearly $28 million. After World War II, the company again went into somewhat of a decline. Sales increased very slowly and profits declined. By 1976, the stockholders (who had changed from the group who bought out the original family business) together with a Springfield, Massachusetts bank that held a large loan forced out the incumbent president and appointd James Smith to the post. Smith had been marketing vice president of a large southern textile company where he had developed a reputation for "getting things done."

Since 1976 the company had continued to expand. Sales in the three current lines (cotton, knitted goods, and woolens) grew and by 1981 the company had added two new lines of goods: artificial fiber products (dacron and nylon hosiery, underwear, blouses, etc.) in a plant in Dedham, Massachusetts, and artificial leather in a plant in Milton, Massachusetts. These plants were both acquired by buying the companies that had been operating them. In each case the acquisition was made by a combination of exchange of stock and cash.

By mid-1986 (the date of the events described earlier in the case), Bondsville's sales were approaching $100 million a year. The profits, however, still were only about $3 million.

Products

The Bondsville Manufacturing Company has five product lines. Each line is produced in a separate plant and is marketed by a separate organization. A description of each line follows:

- *Cotton textiles*: The Bondsville plant produces gray goods that are sold directly to jobbers and converters (about 50% of the volume) and printed cotton fabrics that are sold to jobbers and also directly to clothes manufacturers.
- *Knitted goods*: The Ware plant produces knitted fabrics and converts these fabrics into clothes. Part of the production is such standard items as underwear and pajamas. Over 50% of the production is in women's clothes, which are style items and seasonal. These are sold directly to department stores by company salesmen.
- *Artificial fibers*: The Dedham plant produces products made of artificial fibers (principally dacron and nylon). The yarn is purchased but the plant weaves the cloth and manufactures the garments. These are sold to jobbers and also directly to buyers from large department stores.
- *Woolen goods*: The Monson plant produces woolen cloth of various types. About three-quarters of the cloth is sold to finishers by company salesmen. The company finishes (dyes) the remaining one-quarter of its production and sells this cloth to manufacturers of clothes.
- *Artificial leather*: The Milton plant produces artificial leather for automobile and furniture upholstery. About 50% of the production is for automobiles; the remainder is used in a variety of furniture. Artificial leather is sold exclusively by company salesmen directly to manufacturers.

Exhibit 1 shows the 1986 sales and gross profits (sales minus manufacturing costs) of each of the product lines (in thousands of dollars).

Organization

Exhibit 2 is an organization chart of the Bondsville Manufacturing Company. Each of the five operating divisions is headed by a divisional manager who is responsible for the profits that the division earns. Theoretically, the staff is responsible only for helping the divisions when needed and to coordinate the functional activities. In fact, the sales staff vice president and the manufacturing staff vice president had been senior operating people before taking up staff positions. Consequently, they exercise considerable direct control over their functional areas in the divisions. The president also spends several days a month visiting the divisional offices and counseling the managers on their various problems. Exhibit 3 shows the organization of the cotton textiles division: this is typical of the other divisions.

EXHIBIT 1

	SALES	GROSS PROFIT
Cotton textiles	$42,581	$ 463
Knitted goods	27,862	4,068
Artificial fiber	13,733	716
Woolen goods	10,429	(28)
Artificial leather	5,216	1,582
	$99,866	$6,801

EXHIBIT 2

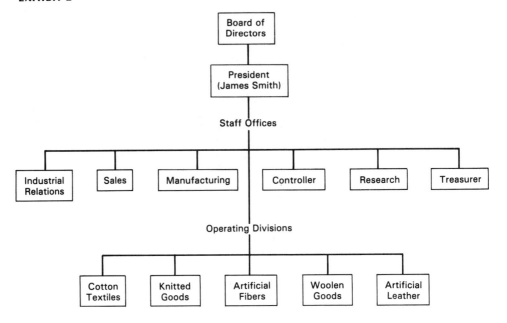

EXHIBIT 3

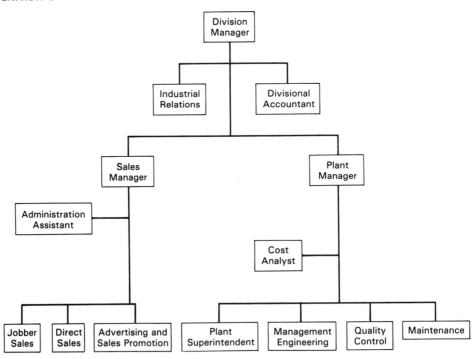

The company's research efforts have been quite modest (about $500,000 a year) and all formal research is done at the central office level. Some informal research is done at the divisional level.

The president and all the staff are located in a two-story office building and laboratory in Worcester, Massachusetts. This location is very close to the geographic center of the operating plants.

The Controller's Office

Exhibit 4 is the organization chart for the Controller's office, showing the Budgeting Deparatment organization through the second level.

The basic accounting records are maintained at the divisional offices. Each month the divisional balance sheet and profit and loss accounts are submitted to the central office. The central office's Accounting Department prescribes the company's accounting systems, maintains the central office accounting records, consolidates monthly all of the accounts, and publishes a companywide balance sheet and profit and loss statement on the tenth working day after the end of the month.

Each division has its own accounting department. Reporting to the divisional accountant, the divisional budget manager is responsible for the budget reports in the division. Each plant manager has a cost analyst who reports directly to him and whose job is to assist the manager by interpreting budget and cost reports and obtaining any cost information that he needs. In addition, the cost analyst is responsible for providing the analysis of budget variances to the divisional budget manager.

At the plant level, the company uses a standard cost system to control material and labor and a flexible budget to control manufacturing overhead.

EXHIBIT 4

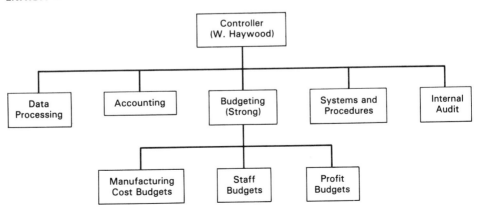

The Budgetary Control System

Divisional Profit Budgets.   Each divisional manager is responsible for preparing and submitting a profit budget in December to cover the succeeding year. The sales department first prepares an estimate of annual sales. This is reviewed and approved by the divisional manager. After sales volume approval, everyone reporting to the divisional manager is responsible for preparing his or her budget, based on the indicated volume of sales. The plant budget is based on standard costs for material and direct labor and the flexible budget for manufacturing overhead. Other departments budget in accordance with their estimated requirements for the coming year. The divisional manager reviews each budget and approves or adjusts it if he thinks the proposed budget is out of line.

The divisional manager next meets with the president, the manufacturing staff vice president, the sales staff vice president, and the controller. (This is the Budget Approval Committee.) The divisional manager presents his proposed budget. In evaluating the proposed budget, differences from the current year's actual performance are carefully explained. (Since the current year's results are not usually known at the time of budget submission, 10 months' actual and two months' forecast is used as the basis of comparison.) The committee discusses the proposed budget with the divisional manager and either approves it, adjusts it, or sends it back to be partially redone.

After final approval, the budget becomes the basis for evaluating actual profit performance.

Staff Budgets.   Each staff vice president also presents his budget for the coming year to the president. After discussion, the budget is either approved or adjusted.

Company Budget.   The Controller's office combines the divisional and staff budgets into a companywide profit budget which is presented to the president for final approval. (The president could call for a change in previously approved budgets if the total company profits were not satisfactory.)

Budget Reports.   Each month a report is prepared for each division showing actual profits compared to budget. Exhibit 5 is an example of a budget performance report.

These budget performance reports are prepared by the divisions and submitted to the central staff on the twelfth working day after the end of the month. After review by the Central Budget Department, copies are distributed to the president, the sales staff vice president, and the manufacturing staff vice president. The Central Budget Department prepares a brief analysis of each report, indicating points that should be brought to management's attention.

The Central Budget Department prepares a "Company Profit Budget Report" on the fifteenth working day after the end of the month. This is a consolidation of the five operating divisions and the six staff offices. Copies of this go to the three executives indicated above.

EXHIBIT 5

Woolen Goods Division:
 Profit Budget Performance Report (000's) April 1986

	MONTH OF APRIL	*YEAR TO DATE*
Actual profit	$(12)	$ (43)
Budgeted profit	42	150
Actual over/(under) budget	$(54)	$(193)
Analysis of variance	favorable/(unfavorable)	
REVENUE ITEMS:		
Sales volume	$(65)	$(240)
Selling prices	15	(25)
Product mix	2	10
COST ITEMS:		
Material prices	4	10
Material usage	(3)	6
Direct labor	10	45
Variable overhead	5	30
Advertising and sales promotion	(16)	(35)
Other selling	(1)	(9)
Administration	(5)	15
	$(54)	$(193)

NOTE: This exhibit was backed up with schedules showing the details of the variances and explanations of the reasons for the variances. The explanations were provided by the various operating executives responsible for these variances.

Discussion with Smith

Strong made an appointment to talk to the president, James Smith, about the profit budget system. Following is a partial transcript of Smith's statements to Strong:

"Frankly, your profit budget performance reports are just about worthless to me. For one thing, we just cannot budget sales revenue with any degree of certainty. All of the budgets show large variances, but what do I do with them? The big variances are almost always in revenue. Either volume has been higher or lower than budget or prices have gone up or down. Furthermore, once a division starts having problems with sales or prices, it might take several months to change the situation. You might have to change your product line, wait until your competitors get tired of losing money and raise prices, or wait until the economy improves. In other words, I look at the budget performance report and say 'so what?'

"Another thing, I really get no surprises from the budget reports because I know when something has happened long before the budget report reaches me. I get weekly sales reports from each division and I can easily see those divisions that are having trouble with volume or prices. Costs do not usually vary much from month to month. The few times that our costs have gone to hell temporarily, I have known it ahead of time. What I need is a report that will tell me what is going to happen, not one that tells me what I have known for several weeks.

"There's a third thing that bothers me, but I'd like you to keep this under your hat. I know for a fact that John Bennett (the manager of the Artificial Leather Division) has been doing a poor job with that division this year, even though his budget performance is the best of the five divisions. Because of quality problems in his plant, he lost one of our best customers in the furniture business. Yet, because automobiles are selling far better than we anticipated, Bennett shows a large favorable sales volume variance. On the other hand, the most capable manager that I have shows the poorest budget performance.

"There you are, Fred—three complaints: I can't do anything with the reports: They contain no important information that I did not already know; they do not reflect the true performance of the managers. I had hopes of using profit budget performance as a basis for paying bonuses to the managers. You can see that I can't do this with your system.

"You will have to do something about these complaints or discontinue this fancy profit budget system. As it is now, it may have been all right for the big automobile firms, but it's no good for us."

Required

1. What do you think should be done about Bondsville's profit budgeting system?

2. If you believe it should be discontinued, what are company characteristics that have made it unworkable? With what should the system be replaced?

3. In what type of company does a profit budget system work effectively?

chapter 13

PROFIT CENTERS

Management control is the process by which management assures that an organization carries out its strategies effectively and efficiently. Effectively means doing the right things: Efficiently means doing them well, i.e., maximizing output while minimizing input.

CHARACTERISTICS OF MANAGEMENT CONTROL

The management control process begins after *strategies* and *goals* have been established. Management control involves the allocation of resources to accomplish the strategies and, subsequently, the follow-up to ascertain that either the strategies are being accomplished or modifications ae being approved.

    Management control is a very broad concept that involves all interrelationships between managers and their subordinates. The assurance that subordinates are acting efficiently and effectively in carrying out strategies involves three types of action by a manager with respect to the subordinate:

1. It is necessary to *communicate* to subordinates what is expected of them. They must know the organization strategies and their part in carrying out these strategies.
2. The subordinates must be *motivated* to act efficiently and effectively.
3. It is necessary to *measure* the performance of subordinates and *evaluate* them.

A logical question is "What does all this have to do with accounting and control?" The answer is that, although no precise distinctions are made in the literature, management accountants are involved professionally principally with a subset of the management control process. That subset is concerned with financial resources. We are concerned with assisting top managers in making the financial resource allocation decisions, and, subsequently, measuring how effectively and efficiently these financial resources are being used. This process could more accurately be called "financial control."

FINANCIAL CONTROL VERSUS MANAGEMENT CONTROL

Although financial control is a subset of any management control relationship, it is much more important in some relationships than in others. For example, a management control relationship exists between a controller and, say, the chief cost accountant. While it is true that the controller does exercise some financial control over the cost accountant, e.g., approving the departmental budgets, the financial performance is not generally important in the overall communication, motivation, and evaluation of this subordinate. At the other extreme, however, is the relationship between the controller and the manager of a foreign subsidiary. In this instance, the predominant means of communication, motivation, and evaluation is through the financial control system.

The relative importance of financial control as a subset of management control is determined by two factors:

1. The amount of financial resources that the subordinate controls.
2. The degree of delegation extended to the subordinate to deploy those resources.

The importance of a financial control system should not be underestimated. The ability to delegate safely financial responsibility is dependent upon the ability to measure financial results. For example, the decentralization of Du Pont and General Motors in the 1920s may not have been practical if Donaldson Brown (GM financial manager) had not developed the concept of measuring financial performance on the basis of return on investment. *The approval of the budget by top management represents an allocation of financial resources and the delegation of authority to the budgetee to deploy those resources.* This is the first step in implementing strategy. The accounting function is to provide relevant financial information to help management make the financial resource allocation decision. *After the budget has been approved, it is necessary to monitor the results of operations.* This is the second step in implementing financial strategy. The accountant's responsibility is to compare the actual results of operation against the budget and analyze the causes of variance. On the basis of this feedback, together with any other information concerning the financial performance that is available, top management takes whatever action it deems appropriate. Thus the accounting function plays an important part in the management control process, as well as in the financial control systems described in Part III.

The management accountant's impact comes through:

1. Profit center designation.
2. Transfer pricing.
3. Performance measurement.

PROFIT CENTER VERSUS FUNCTIONAL ORGANIZATION

A *functional* organization is one that is organized by functions. That is, the responsibility for the line functions—marketing, manufacturing, and product development—goes from the top to the bottom of the organization scale. The divisionalized company is at the opposite end of the organization scale. Such a company is organized by units, each of which has responsibility for all of its line functions. The difference between the two types of organizations is the locus of profit responsibility. In a functional organization, profit responsibility remains principally at the top. With a divisionalized company, profit responsibility is delegated to the operating units. We say, therefore, that a divsionalized company has *decentralized* profit responsibility.

The following are some generalizations to keep in mind about organizations:

1. All companies are organized functionally at some level.
2. The difference between a functional organization and a divisionalized organization is a continuum. Between the extremes of the entirely functional organization and the entirely divisionalized organization are all types of combinations of functional and divisional organizations.
3. Complete authority for generating profits is rarely, if ever, delegated to a segment of the business, and the degree of delegation differs among businesses.

This chapter is concerned with delegation of profit responsibility to segments of a business. These segments are called *division,* or *profit centers,* to indicate that they have profit responsibility.

DELEGATION OF RESPONSIBILITY

As a general rule, responsibility should be delegated down to the lowest point in an organization where all of the relevant information is available.[1] There are several advantages in doing this. First, a decision may be made more quickly by the person closest to the activity. Another advantage is that much information about a particular situation may be known only to the person close to that activity. It is often difficult to communicate adequately such things as environmental or cultural conditions to higher authorities. A third advantage is that most decisions are not made on the basis of a precise analysis of data. Precise data are frequently not available. Often only the person near the activity has a sufficient intuitive "feel" for a situation. The last two advantages can be very important in a business segment that operates in a different culture, such as a foreign subsidiary.

Conditions for Delegating Profit Responsibility

Profit, of course, is the difference between costs and revenues. Many day-to-day management decisions involve making an optimum trade-off between costs and revenues. For example, a marketing manager may have to decide how much to spend on promoting a particular product. This involves comparing the estimated contribution from additional sales against the costs of obtaining these sales. Before a decision of this sort can be delegated safely to a lower level manager, two conditions must exist:

1. The manager should have all of the *relevant information* that is available.
2. There must be some way to measure how effectively the trade-off decisions are being made.

These two conditions limit the delegation of authority for profit responsibility. To the extent that these conditions cannot be met, profit responsibility cannot be safely delegated. Since cost-revenue trade-off decisions are so prevalent, the inability to delegate this type of decision means that a much higher degree of centralized decision-making is required. The problem, then, is to determine the lowest point in an organization where these two conditions prevail.

Large companies form a continuum based on their degrees of diversification. Such companies as ITT and Textron are at one extreme and integrated companies such as General Motors and International Paper are at the other extreme. Between these two extremes are all degrees of integration and diversification.

---

[1]There are, of course, many exceptions to this generalization. For example, some decisions may be so important that they should be checked by a higher authority. Or, it may be felt that a higher authority has more ability to make a decision even though that authority has no additional information.

For example, dominant product companies such as General Electric and Du Pont tend to be somewhere in the middle of the continuum. Some points to consider about this continuum are these:

1. The closer a company is to the diversified extreme, the easier it is to divisionalize because these companies tend to be divided into groups, each responsible for unique products, manufacturing facilities, and markets. Managers of these unique activities have the relevant information to optimize profits and can be measured on how well they are performing.

2. Conversely, the closer a company is to the integrated extreme of the continuum, the more difficult it is to divisionalize because the responsibility for profits of a single product line tends to be divided among several organization units. It is necessary, therefore, to develop methods for assigning the total profits among the units that contributed to those profits in proportion to their contribution. This is the function of the transfer price system.

3. One critical factor, therefore, in divisionalization is the ability of a company to develop a satisfactory transfer price system. A satisfactory transfer price system is one that will assign revenues to the participating divisions in such a way that: (a) divisional managers will be provided with all the available relevant information required for the decisions they must make, and (b) the measurement of divisional profits must reflect how well these decisions are being made.

In integrated companies, the transfer price system is critical to divisionalization. Transfer pricing is discussed in Chapter 14.

PSEUDOPROFIT CENTERS

Marketing

Any marketing activity can be made into a profit center by charging the cost of the products sold to the responsible marketing manager.[2] The assignment of manufacturing costs provides the marketing manager with the relevant information to make the optimum revenue-cost trade-offs. Since the manager is measured on profitability, there is a check on how well these decisions are being made. Also, since managers are being evaluated on profitability, they will be motivated to maximize profits. Note that the marketing manager should be charged with a *standard* cost, not an actual cost. This separates manufacturing cost performance from the marketing performance. The former is affected by changes in the levels of efficiency that are outside of the control of the marketing manager.

When should a marketing activity be delegated profit responsibility? This should occur when the marketing activity is in the best position to make the

---

[2] Note that this charge may be made outside of the books of account. A profit report that shows the revenues generated and the costs of these products is prepared. There may be no transfer of costs (in the form of prices) between organization units as there is in divisionalized profit centers.

principal cost-revenue trade-offs. For practical purposes, this most often occurs where different conditions exist in different geographical areas, for example, a foreign marketing activity. In this instance, it may be difficult to control centrally such decisions as how to market a product; how much to spend on sales promotion, when to spend it, and on which media; how to train salespeople or dealers, and where and when to establish new dealers.

To summarize, it is relatively easy to make a marketing activity into a profit center. All that is necessary is to charge the activity with the relevant product costs. The decision about whether to do this or not is determined by the point in the organization where the relevant marketing information is available. Delegation of profit responsibility can be made only to this point.

Manufacturing

The manufacturing activity is usually a cost center, and the management of such activities is judged on the basis of standard costs and overhead budgets as described in Chapters 9 and 10. Problems can occur because standard cost performance may not measure all of the responsibilities of the manufacturing manager:

1. Quality control may be inadequate. Put another way, products of inferior quality may be shipped in order to obtain standard cost credit.
2. Manufacturing managers may be reluctant to interrupt production schedules in order to produce an emergency order to accommodate a customer.
3. When a manager is measured against standard, there is no incentive to manufacture products that are difficult to produce or even to expand production.
4. There may be little incentive to improve standards.

As a consequence, where the performance of the manufacturing activities are measured against standards, it is necessary that quality control, production scheduling, make-or-buy decisions, and the setting of standards be controlled by someone outside of the plant. Where this is not practical, some companies measure manufacturing activities on profitability.

A common way of measuring a manufacturing activity on profitability is to give the activity credit for the selling price of the products minus the estimated cost of sales and distribution. Note that there are many factors that influence the volume of sales that are outside of the control of the manufacturing manager. The purpose of measuring managers on profitability is to provide an incentive to maximize profits rather than minimize costs. Although such an arrangement is often far from perfect, it seems to work better in some cases than simply holding the manufacturing operation responsible only for costs. Note that even where a manufacturing activity is measured as a pseudoprofit center, cost performance is also measured and reported, and this will normally be the most important financial measurement of the manufacturing manager.

CONSTRAINTS TO DIVISIONAL AUTHORITY

A divisional manager must be able to exercise a significant amount of influence over the factors that affect the profitability of the division. Even in diversified companies, however, complete authority is neither feasible nor necessary. It is not feasible because divisional managers may not have the necessary information to make some decisions. It is not necessary because managers can be measured only on the factors that they can influence. Some examples where divisional managers do not have the necessary information are as follows.

Resource allocation is a top management function because it is only at this level that information on the amount of resources available and the potential uses for these resources is known. Consequently, divisional managers are always constrained in the amount and direction of resources they can use. Resource allocations are made through capital and profit budgets.

Industrial relations are normally controlled by top management. This is necessary where there are company-wide unions and almost always desirable even where union representation is local. It is only at the corporate level that information required for company-wide employee policies are available.

Accounting policies are controlled by top management. Consistent accounting systems are required for consolidation, both for external and internal purposes. In addition, control systems are prescribed from the top. Again, it is only at the corporate level that the information required to develop a company-wide accounting and control system is available.

Divisional managers in integrated companies tend to be subject to much greater constraints than managers in diversified companies. In addition to the constraints described earlier, divisional managers in an integrated company may be limited in the sources from whom they purchase and the customers to whom they sell.

SUMMARY

It is generally desirable to delegate responsibility for decisions down to the lowest point in an organization where all of the relevant information is available. Many management decisions at all levels, however, involve maximizing profits through trade-offs between cost and revenues. Thus a constraint on delegation is the ability (1) to provide lower-level managers with the necessary cost and revenue information and (2) to measure how well cost-revenue decisions are being made. In almost no instance can this be done perfectly. All activities fit on a continuum ranging between those activities that clearly should be profit centers to those that clearly should not. The problems occur as activities approach the end of the continuum. Management must decide where the advantages of giving profit responsibility offset the disadvantages. As with all management control systems problems, there is no clear line of demarcation. Sometimes it is necessary to pick the least worst alternative.

QUESTIONS

14.1 Explain why managers are in a position to make optimum trade-offs between revenues and costs only when they have profit responsibility. Give some examples of suboptimum trade-offs that may occur in a company where profit responsibility is centralized. How can such suboptimization be prevented in a centralized company?

14.2 Explain why every business organization must be functionally organized at some level.

14.3 What are some instances where the lack of relevant information at the divisional level would require that certain decisions be made by higher management?

14.4 Describe some specific instances where a marketing activity might be better controlled as a pseudoprofit center rather than a revenue center.

14.5 Describe some specific circumstances where a manufacturing activity might be better controlled as a pseudoprofit center.

14.6 Why would it be necessary also to measure standard cost performance where a manufacturing activity is measured as a pseudoprofit center?

14.7 In a typical profit center, what are some income statement items over which the profit center manager might have little or no influence?

CASES

CASE 13.1   THUNDERBOLT MANUFACTURING COMPANY

Early in 1986, Mr. Ray Alexander, recently elected president of the Thunderbolt Manufacturing Company, was reflecting on the progress the company had made since 1978. That was the year in which his predecessor, Mr. Earl Goodwin, became president. Annual sales had increased from about $30 million to nearly $80 million during this period and profits had risen from $1 million to about $3 million. The company had become a leading supplier in the automotive parts industry.

In Mr. Alexander's view, however, current operation practices were not satisfactory in several areas. For example, there were an excessive number of disagreements between the plant managers and those in charge of marketing. There also were disagreements between plant managers and corporate management. The disputes centered upon transfer prices, out-of-stock position, and production mix. Many of the problems seemed to arise from the fact that performance was

This case was prepared by R. H. Caplan. Copyright © by the President and Fellows of Harvard University. Harvard Business School case 9-113-036.

measured by profit and loss statements for three plants in the manufacturing group (excluding the OEM plant at Ironville) and for the marketing group.

Profit centers had been introduced in 1978. Thunderbolt had only two plants at that time, and each had its own product lines. Even though they both sold through a common sales force, it was relatively easy to think of each plant manager as the president of his own small company.

But circumstances had changed. Now there were four plants, and product lines were no longer associated with particular plants. Also the company now had six profit centers, instead of just two.

It seemed to Mr. Alexander that, under the present organization, the managers of the various profit centers had relatively little control over the factors that influenced the profitability of their operations. He wondered whether conditions had changed enough since 1978 to call for reconsideration of the use of profit centers.

Mr. Alexander decided that this problem needed attention. Also, he thought it should be studied by someone not associated with the company, someone with an objective viewpoint. Consequently, he called in an acquaintance, Mr. James Smith. Mr. Smith was a management consultant, recognized as an authority on organization and management control.

Mr. Smith began his assignment by familiarizing himself with the company in general terms—its environment, its history, and its present organization. His notes from this familiarization phase are attached as Appendix A.

As his second major step, Mr. Smith interviewed several members of Thunderbolt management to obtain their views on the company's use of profit centers. He started his interviewing with Mr. Charles Campbell, vice president and treasurer (see organization chart, Exhibit 1).

CAMPBELL: We've discovered that there are a number of problems with making profit centers work well, now that our company is quite a bit different from the way it used to be. In fact it makes you wonder sometimes if the whole thing is still worthwhile, and if it might not be better to drop the profit center idea completely.

SMITH: Mr. Campbell, can you tell me about some of the problems you have encountered?

CAMPBELL: Yes, One of them is caused by the fact that measurement of performance tends to be unfair. A plant manager really has little control over some of the major factors that influence his profitability. Product mix, production volume, transfer price, all things he does not control, can make a plant manager show a low profit. Thus, a poor plant P&L may not necessarily mean poor performance. Of course, we try to recognize all this, because we compare profits to budget. But somehow, performance measurement always seems to get back to the profit figure alone. Even though a plant manager may be doing a tremendous job, he'll get discouraged if his profit is low for period after period. He figures that no matter how hard he tries he just can't improve

EXHIBIT 1 Thunderbolt Manufacturing Company

Organization Chart

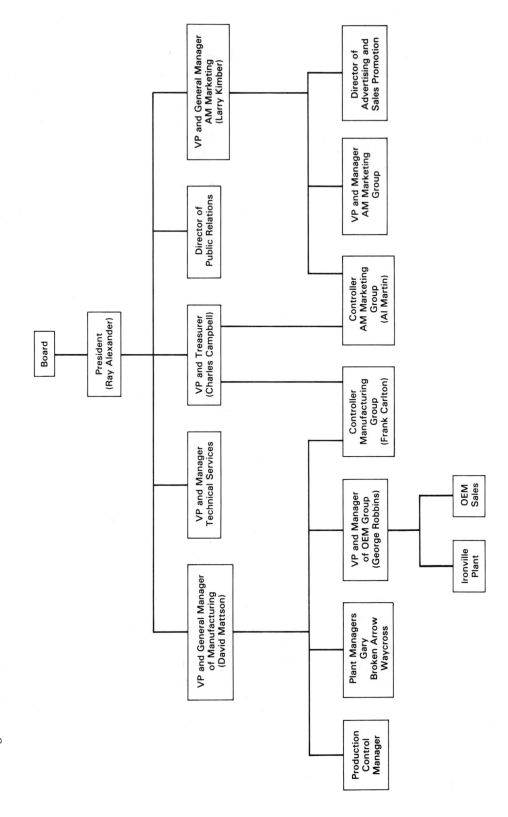

profits. Worse yet is the opposite case, where a manager is not doing a good job but has a high profit figure. Whenever we try to question this guy on some of his variances from budgeted figures, the first thing he'll say is: "Yeah, but look at the profits I brought in." And it becomes somewhat difficult to motivate him to improve his performance because he is unwilling to give up this crutch.

Another problem we've found is that some managers tend to spend too much time worrying about the wrong things. For example, they'll often argue about the product mix assigned to them by the production scheduling group, or they'll grumble about transfer prices not being fair, or they'll complain that their assigned production volume is too low.

Of course, it is good to have some tension in an organization; it motivates people to produce. But it has to be aimed in the proper direction; that is, it should make managers worry about matters that they have some control over, not about things they can't change.

Also, while it is good to have some tension, there should not be too much tension. If there is, then people become frustrated and their output suffers.

Now, in our case, we somtimes get the feeling that we have too much tension, and tension aimed in the wrong direction. And that both are the result of profit centers.

There is another disadvantage to profit centers. As you know, we have a considerable number of product transfers between profit centers. But in order to figure out how the company as a whole is doing, we have to eliminate profits on these transfers from corporate financial statements. And this makes an awful lot of extra work for the accounting department. So, if we did away with profit centers, we probably would save a nice bundle of cash.

SMITH: Mr. Campbell, so far you've told me about the disadvantages of profit centers. Can you tell me about some advantages that apply to them?

CAMPBELL: You're right, I have. I didn't mean to paint such a bleak picture. If there were only disadvantages, we would have done away with profit centers some time ago.

Earlier I mentioned two advantages that existed in 1978, when profit centers were installed. [See the Appendix for a more complete discussion of these points.] One was that managers received valuable training for top management jobs; the other was that they tended to become more profit conscious. These advantages still hold today.

There is another advantage, related to this greater profit consciousness. As we see it, the alternative to using profit centers is expense centers controlled by budgets. But holding a manager responsible only for variances from expense budgets is nit-picking; such an approach doesn't look at the major economic factors that make or break a business. Thus, despite all the problems I mentioned earlier, I feel that control by means of expense centers would not be as effective as with profit centers.

And then, I think we also should consider how the managers feel about profit centers before making a decision to drop them. Now that our managers are used to being measured on the basis of their profit contribution, they might not want to change to something else, despite the fact that this measurement by profits may not be fair to them. I think that they get quite a bit of satisfaction out of being held responsible for running their own show.

Mr. Smith next interviewed Mr. Frank Carlton, manufacturing group controller. As his title indicates, Mr. Carlton was mainly responsible for control functions within the manufacturing group. He reported directly to Mr. David Mattson, vice president and general manager of manufacturing. Because of his position, Carlton was described by other members of Thunderbolt management as being "able to present the plant managers' side of the situation." Since some of his comments were similar to those made by Mr. Campbell, only selected remarks representing additional points are reported here.

CARLTON: . . . And since there is no real market price for transfers between the plants and marketing, transfer prices are fictitious. Therefore, management is just playing games, and the managers know this. . . .

. . . If you are going to judge a man on the profits of his group, he's going to try to maximize these profits, even if this may not be in the best interest of the whole company. Let me give you a few example of this here at Thunderbolt. Sometimes a plant manager will make production runs that are longer than scheduled, because this reduces his set-up costs. Now, you can't really blame him for doing this, because it increases his profits. But it also increases the finished goods inventory. And by deviating from his production schedule in order to have longer production runs, he may even increase the out-of-stock position of other items, a situation clearly not in the best interest of the company.

Another example, when it comes to new products, the marketing people like to include just about everything. As long as they can get even a small contribution from an item, they're willing to add it to their line, regardless of the volume they can get, because it will increase their profit figure. On the other hand, the boys in manufacturing lean in the opposite direction. Since there are start-up and capital costs associated with a new product, they need a certain volume before they reach the breakeven point. The net result is that marketing tends to over-estimate demand for new products, just to increase the chance that these will be added to the line. On the other hand, manufacturing tends to overestimate their costs, just to make sure that marginal products are not authorized by headquarters for production.

Actually, there's another reason why the boys in manufacturing tend to overestimate their costs. Cost estimates are used in setting the initial transfer prices, and, of course, the higher the transfer prices, the better their chance of showing a profit of any items added. . . . It is obvious, of course, that this, too, can lead to decisions that are contrary to the best interests of the company.

Another problem we have encountered with profit centers is that feelings between manufacturing and marketing run pretty high sometimes. Arguments may result over transfer prices, out-of-stock position, or whatever. And the result is that these two groups then become antagonistic, don't communicate well, and withhold information from each other....

Despite all I've said against profit centers, I'm still not sure that we should do away with them. We haven't really got anything that is *better* for management control purposes than our present profit center P&L reports.

And then, there's the fact that our managers don't want to do away with the profit center approach, despite all their complaints. And they feel quite strongly about this. In fact, one of our managers told me that he would quit if we eliminated profit centers at the plant level. And he may very well mean it. You know, there's quite a bit of prestige in being responsible for the whole operation.... If we replace profit centers with expense centers, we're reducing our plant managers to mere supervisors, mere foremen....

Mr. Smith also asked Mr. Al Martin, marketing group controller, for his views on profit centers. Mr. Martin was responsible for control functions within the AM marketing group. He reported to Mr. Larry Kimber, vice president and general manager of AM marketing. (See the Appendix for explanation of the term AM.)

MARTIN: When you measure a manager's performance by profits, he's going to try to maximize this measure. And that may not always be the best thing for the company. Let me give you an example. You're aware that marketing is permitted to obtain products either from our plants or from the outside. But when they do buy outside, it usually turns out that they are not making a good decision from the company's standpoint. Of course, they're only looking at their own profits, so they don't recognize this. Now, even though my associates and I report to Mr. Kimber, we are also members of the treasurer's staff. Consequently, we have some information on our manufacturing costs, too, and we can usually figure out which way such decision should go. And we've had to intervene time after time in situations like this, trying to convince marketing to buy from our plants.

Now you may say that we could easily eliminate this problem by setting transfer prices in such a way that we would have "goal congruence," or whatever you call this animal. But before you do, let me tell you that it is impossible to set goal congruent prices on over 3000 different items when manufacturing costs, and even selling prices, are constantly changing. About the only way we can eliminate this problem is by eliminating profit centers....

... And there's another reason why I don't think that profit centers are a good idea here at Thunderbolt. Marketing people are sales oriented, and they perform best if they are measured in terms of sales. If you hold them responsible for profits, and costs, and inventories, and warehousing and this and that, your're just confusing them and taking their attention away from the only thing that really means something to them, namely sales. . . .

Mr. Smith concluded his interviewing with Mr. Ray Alexander, president of Thunderbolt.

SMITH: Mr. Alexander, would you tell me how you judge the performance of a plant manager?

ALEXANDER: Yes. Since we use flexible budgeting, I know what each manager's costs should have been for the period in question, given a particular volume of activity. Then, all I need to do is look at his variances by individual expense classifications to tell how well he has done his job.

SMITH: I gather, then, you don't just look at his profit figure on the P&L report and see how that compares with the budgeted profit?

ALEXANDER: No. I don't. I feel it is more meaningful to look at the variances. Besides, if a manager's costs are in line with his particular volume, then his budgeted profit will result automatically.

In the course of this interview, Mr. Alexander mentioned that he was considering the possibility of discontinuing the profit center approach at Thunderbolt.

SMITH: Mr. Alexander, if you did in fact discontinue the profit center approach, what would you substitute in order to meet the company's needs for management control?

ALEXANDER: I think we would use expense centers. Each plant, for example, would become an expense center, and that would be about the only change here. We would still use a flexible budget, and we would measure performance by variances from the budget. As before, we would expect each plant manager to keep his out-of-stock position down. Also, we'd still judge him on intangibles, such as his labor relations and his community relations.

For the marketing group, we would use sales quotas instead of profit budgets. Sales is a more direct and more meaningful measure for marketing-oriented people. To control their selling expenses, we would use a flexible expense budget and measure their variances from that. Also, we would hold them responsible for keeping finished goods inventories at budgeted levels, similar to the way we do it now. . . .

You see, what we would like to do is to hold each manager responsible only for items he can control. Of course, we probably will never be able to achieve this goal completely; however, I think that this system would be better in this respect than what we have now. . . .

Of course, we'd probably have to pay a price for changing to expense centers. For example, we might lose some profit consciousness at the plant manager level. . . .

However, I feel that there are two offsetting factors here. First, our plant managers would receive corporate financial statements on a monthly basis. Right now, they see these only once a year. For that reason, these corporate statements aren't too meaningful to them; that is, they can't trace the effect of their decisions on the corporate picture. But now, if they become familiar with and use the corporate statements, they will be able to see better the implications of their decisions on the company. And I feel that this will motivate them to act in the best interest of the company.

Second, we are now in the process of installing an advanced computer system, and we expect this to give us at headquarters more and better information for decision making. Without such information available at headquarters, it is probably best to place a good bit of decision making authority in the hands of those managers who are close to the day-to-day operations. However, with the right information available at headquarters, I don't see any good reasons why decisions can't be made there. And if they're made there, they are more likely to be in the best interest of the company, and so we get around the problem of profit consciousness at lower management levels.

Required

1. Would you recommend that Thunderbolt discontinue profit centers?

2. If so, what would you recommend in its place?

3. Precisely how does the acquisition of a computer make centralization of profit responsibility more practicable?

Appendix—Mr. Smith's Notes on the Thunderbolt Manufacturing Company

Nature of the Business. The Thunderbolt Manufacturing Company is in the automotive parts business and is a major supplier of ignition parts for both passenger cars and commercial vehicles. Other major product lines are carburetors and electric motors. Total company sales were about $80 million in 1985. Of this, about 70% was accounted for by ignition parts.

There are nine major classifications of ignition parts: coils, distributors, condensers, spark plugs, points, relays, switches, connectors, and fuses. Within each classification, there may be many different types of items. (For example, spark plugs are made with five different heat ranges, six different reaches, regular and extended tip, three different thread sizes, and four different types of alloys.) As a result of this variety of product lines and types, Thunderbolt manufactures over 3000 different ignition items.

Markets and Customers. The company sells its product both to automobile manufacturers (commonly referred to as original equipment manufacturer or OEM) and to the replacement market (called the aftermarket or AM).

THE OEM MARKET.   This market accounts for about one-third of the total ignition parts volume. Sales are made to two different groups within the automobile companies: OEM production and OEM service. The first group concerns itself with the procurement of materials for the manufacture of automobiles, while the second deals with the parts requirements of the OEM dealers for service and repairs. Even though both groups are integral parts of the same automobile companies, they do their purchasing independently of each other. This means that, although Thunderbolt may supply some ignition parts as original equipment for a certain model of automobile, it does not necessarily furnish replacement parts for the OEM dealers for the same model. Despite these distinctions, however, both groups do their purchasing in the same manner. Thus the Thunderbolt OEM sales engineers, who are responsible for sales to the automobile companies, deal with both groups.

In this business, three major factors determine whether a parts manufactuer will be successful in establishing and continuing a relationship with an OEM. The most important factor is service, and there are two aspects to this: (1) The ability to design ignition parts that meet OEM specifications and to come up with innovations beneficial to the OEM, and (2) the ability to meet OEM delivery requirements, even though these may change drastically from original estimates. (A good example of such drastic change is the Mustang—Thunderbolt was originally scheduled to supply 100,000 distributors, yet actual production for the first year was 250,000 units.)

Close behind service as an important factor is price. Very small differences in unit selling prices of parts can mean the difference between winning or losing a bid.

The third factor is quality. Parts suppliers are expected to meet or exceed OEM quality specifications consistently.

THE AFTERMARKET.   This market accounts for the other two-thirds of Thunderbolt's ignition parts volume. Whereas in OEM sales a relatively small number of sales engineers handle sales to only a few automobile companies, in the aftermarket a national sales force covers a large number of accounts. Also, in the aftermarket a chain of distributors is usually involved in getting the product to the ultimate consumer. A Thunderbolt salesman may sell to a wholesaler, who in turn sells a jobber; from there the product moves to a retailer, who then sells it to the ultimate customer, the car owner.

As in the OEM business, service, price, and quality are essential for success in the aftermarket. Here, however, price is less important than either service or quality.

Competition.   The automobile parts business is keenly competitive. There are other manufacturers who have product lines similar to those of Thunderbolt and strong marketing organizations with established contacts. In addition, there is a further pressure in the OEM market. The automobile companies have value analysis staffs that review a supplier's cost structure and manufacturing methods and, because of their huge purchasing power, often specify what they think the costs—and prices—should be.

Pricing Practices. Thunderbolt's OEM bid prices are calculated by the price esti-mating group, which is located at headquarters. For a particular item, this group obtains the estimated full manufacturing cost from the plant (or plants), making it. The group also gets an estimate from the sales people of what the product can be sold for. If this sales price estimate in view of estimated costs meets certain profit criteria (such as a 10% profit on sales), the estimate then becomes the bid price. If the estimate does not meet the profit criteria, the pricing decision is then usually made by Mr. David Mattson, vice president and general manager of manufacturing.

Because of competitive pressures and the negotiating power of the OEM, the profit criteria usually are not met, and thus top management quite frequently gets into OEM pricing decisions. Also, management may be especially interested in getting an item used in a particular automobile model, in the hope that "a foot in the door" will lead to increased sales later. As a result of these factors, profit margins are generally quite low in this area.

Another factor that complicates OEM pricing decisions is that there is a one to two year lag between the time a bid is submitted and the time the product is delivered. (As an example, in July 1986, Thunderbolt was quoting on parts for the 1988 model.) Even though there is a clause in each purchase contract that permits a renegotiation of the price if there have been increases in material or labor costs, the seller is not always successful in obtaining an increase in bid prices. Thus, it is desirable to take any foreseeable changes in costs into account at the time the bid price is determined.

In the aftermarket, parts suppliers such as Thunderbolt also have limited freedom in setting prices. This is because the OEM service divisions set the retail prices that are charged by automobile dealers for replacement parts that the OEM supplies them, and these prices, in turn, largely determine the retail prices that can be charged for similar parts by the independent dealers. With dealer prices fixed, the prices that a parts manufacturer is able to obtain are also rela-tively fixed, because all distributors involved in handling AM products receive standard mark-ups. About the only area where some pricing flexibility exists is in special designs, such as "hot" coils or special-purpose spark plugs. Even here, however, flexibility is limited by competitive pressures.

With this lack of flexibility in pricing, parts manufacturers' profit margins for a particular product are highly dependent on the level of manufacturing costs. Because of differences in cost structures among companies, some product items can be quite profitable for a particular manufacturer while others are not. Some products may even be loss items, carried only to provide a full line to the aftermarket. However, on the average, the profit margins for AM products are considerably larger than those in the OEM area. This difference in profit margins, however, may be partly due to the method of allocating costs. For example, whenever Thunderbolt manufactures a product for an OEM, the cost of tooling is charged completely to that part of the OEM business. Consequently, if no new tooling is required to produce the same item for the aftermarket, no tooling costs are charged against that part of the AM business.

Organization. In 1978 Thunderbolt had only two plants, one in Ironville, Ohio, the other in Gary, Indiana. The Ironville plant manufactured coils, condensers, and spark plugs, while the Gary plant concentrated on distributors, points, and relays. (Switches, connectors, and fuses were not produced by Thunderbolt at that time.) A single sales force dealt with both the OEM market and the aftermarket and handled the products of both plants.

Each plant was made a profit center in 1978. Under this concept, the plant manager was held responsible for the profits of his operation. The marketing group, however, was not made a profit center at that time. Thus, revenues on the plant P&L statements were shown at the dollar value of sales to the outside, rather than at some (lower) transfer price.

This organization by profit centers was initiated by Mr. Earl Goodwin, who joined Thunderbolt in 1978 as president. He had come from an automobile manufacturing company where profit centers had been used for some time with great success.

According to Mr. Charles Campbell, vice president and treasurer, there were essentially three reasons for introducing profit centers:

1. At the time Earl Goodwin joined Thunderbolt, its competitive position and profits had been dropping and there was considerable pressure for improvement. From his experience, Mr. Goodwin felt that holding operating managers responsible for profits, instead of just for costs, and giving them corresponding authority would improve the situation by inducing in them a strong profit consciousness.

2. There was need for an effective means of developing managers. Under the old approach, plant managers and their immediate subordinates were only supervisors—they just didn't have the opportunity to participate in decisions outside of their own limited areas of responsibility. As a result of this narrow exposure to business problems, they weren't ready to step into top management jobs. Yet Thunderbolt needed good managers. Mr. Goodwin believed that by holding them responsible for profits, and thus forcing them to deal with all phases of the business, they would receive the valuable training they needed to become top managers.

3. Mr. Goodwin had brought with him a number of top-flight managers from his previous employer. Some of these men came to the head office, others went to the plants. They were familiar with profit centers and Mr. Goodwin thought this would be of great help in introducing such centers at Thunderbolt.

CHANGES SINCE 1978. Since profit centers were introduced in 1978, quite a number of changes have taken place at Thunderbolt. The most recent is a change in top management. Late in 1985, Mr. Earl Goodwin became chairman of the board and Mr. Ray Alexander was elected president. Mr. Alexander's background has been in finance.

Second, the company has grown considerably, not only in terms of sales and profits, but also physically and organizationally. Whereas there were only two plants in 1978, there are now four plants: one in Broken Arrow, Oklahoma, and one in Waycross, Georgia, in addition to the two original plants in Ironville, Ohio, and Gary, Indiana.

Third, there has been a trend to specialization by market among the plants. In 1978, the plants were specialized by product line, emphasizing neither the OEM nor the AM business. Now, however, the Ironville plant produces almost 80% of its volume for the OEM market. The other three plants do about 90% of their business in the AM area. As a result of this market specialization, the plants are not limited to the manufacture of certain product lines. Rather, production scheduling by product lines is based mainly on economics with the goal of achieving the lowest total cost (which includes manufacturing, warehousing, and shipping costs) for the company. As a result, each plant now handles a wide mix of items—considerably wider than the original plants did in 1978.

PROFIT CENTERS.   Currently there are six profit centers. All manufacturing under Mr. David Mattson (vice president and general manager of manufacturing) is treated as a profit center (see organization chart, Exhibit 1). The three plants reporting to Mr. Mattson (those at Gary, Broken Arrow, and Waycross) are also profit centers. These plants do not have responsibility for outside sales of their products, as they did in 1978.

The OEM group, under Mr. George Robbins (vice president and general manager of the group) is treated as a profit center. Mr. Robbins also reports to Mr. Mattson. The Ironville plant, which produces mainly the OEM market, is part of this profit center. So also are the OEM sales engineers, who sell only to the automobile manufacturers. The responsibility of this profit center for sales extends to all products purchased by the automobile companies whether manufactured at Ironville or at the other plants. The responsibility of the center for manufacturing, however, includes only production at the Ironville plant.

The sixth profit center is AM marketing, with responsibility for all sales in the aftermarket regardless of which plant manufactured the products or whether they were acquired from outside suppliers. This center is headed by Mr. Larry Kimber, vice president and general manager of AM marketing.

Transfer pricing.   Because all four plants manufacture products for both the OEM and the replacement markets, and because AM marketing is a separate profit center, transfers of finished goods between profit centers are necessary. In addition, there are transfers between profit centers of materials in various stages of completion. For example, partly finished distributors are sometimes transferred from the Ironville plant (mainly OEM production) to the Gary plant (mainly AM production) for special processing and then back to Ironville for sale by the OEM sales engineers. Or, parts manufactured by one plant may be shipped to another for completion and eventual sale by AM marketing.

Transfers of finished and unfinished parts are made at transfer prices. These are based on standard costs as market prices are not readily available. Standard costs are set by headquarters, but are strongly influenced by the level of actual costs at the plants. In setting the prices for transfers of finished goods from the plants to AM marketing, the aim is to allocate the total margin equitably among the involved profit centers on the basis of their costs. (Total margin is the difference between the selling price to wholesalers and the standard cost.)

For ignition parts, transfer prices are determined for the nine product lines rather than for individual items. According to Mr. Campbell, it would be impractical to have a transfer price for each of the 3000 different items. Transfer prices are reviewed at headquarters at least once a year, and a review may take several hours; thus, the total management time involved would be excessive if there was a separate price for each item. Instead, a percentage markup over standard costs is used for each product line. This markup is set by headquarters in such a way that the producing plant and the AM marketing group receive approximately equal profits after all expenses directly associated with the product are included.

Thus, in theory, only nine transfer markups are needed, one for each product line. In practice, however, it has been necessary to make adjustments to these markups for a few items. After agreeing in general with a particular product line markup, the AM marketing group has found instances in which some items could be purchased for less on the outside than from the plants. For these items, a below standard markup is used, so that the outside market price is equaled.

Similarly, for parts transferred between plants, the total margin is allocated between the affected plants. Here, also, a markup over standard costs is used. According to a member of management, this practice has been satisfactory mainly because the volume of parts so transferred is less than 5% of the company's total production.

Transfer prices are not necessary for transfers from OEM manufacturing to OEM marketing inasmuch as both are part of the same profit center.

Budgets. Measurement of performance at Thunderbolt is based on actual profit shown as compared to budgeted profit. Preparation of profit budgets for the coming fiscal year is initiated in July and the "big push" occurs during September, when the budgets are consolidated. Budgets are broken down by months. As a first step, monthly sales forecasts are made by the marketing groups on the basis of expected demand, industry trends, and the state of the economy. Because the forecasts are broken down by items, they take into account such factors as product mix and new products. These forecasts are reviewed by management and revised as necessary.

The approved sales forecasts are then converted into production schedules by the production scheduling group at headquarters. Anticipated changes in inventory levels are taken into account in this step. These schedules are then broken down by plants. Factors such as plant capacity, special manufacturing capabilities, freight costs, and manufacturing costs determine to a large extent which plant will produce what.

These individual plant schedules are used by the plants as a basis for developing their own budgets. For the volume of production scheduled, both revenues (based on transfer prices) and costs are developed. After corporate management has reviewed the completed budgets and agreement has been reached, they become the official budgets for the next year. The budgets for the OEM group and the AM marketing group are prepared in a way very similar to the plant budgets. The differences are that sales volume instead of production volume is the basis of the budget, and, of course, that revenues are derived from actual sales to the outside instead of from transfer prices. A further difference for marketing is that cost of goods sold is based on transfer prices.

In order to control the inventories and fixed assets that are related to a profit center, capital appropriations and monthly inventory budgets are determined at the same time as the profit budgets. These budgets are also developed by the "bottom-up" approach, by which the individual profit centers first arrive at tentative figures, which are then reviewed by top management, revised as necessary, and agreed to.

Responsibilities of Managers. Each manager of a profit center is responsible for achieving his budgeted profit. His performance is not judged on the basis of his profits relative to the investment required to achieve these profits. (However, one member of management stated that the company hopes to measure managers on the basis of return on investment in the future.)

Plant managers, furthermore, are expected to keep their acquisition of fixed assets within the limits set by the capital appropriate budget.[1] Also they are responsible for the out-of-stock position of their plants. Since delivery is one of the critical success factors in the automotive parts business, it is important that out-of-stock position be kept at a minimum. In fact, an out-of-stock position of 2% is the allowed limit for the plant managers. Out-of-stock position of the plants is measured in units and is judged with respect to the forecasts that were used in preparation of the plant production schedules, rather than with respect to sales volume. In this way, the plant managers are not held accountable for incorrect sales forecasts. Instead, if sales exceed scheduled production plus available inventory, such that a back-order position results, AM marketing is held accountable. The reason is that marketing makes the forecasts and is charged with selling the products.

AM marketing is also responsible for the finished goods inventory. This responsibility ranges from maintaining the inventory at the levels set forth in the

---

[1]Only plant managers have capital appropriation budgets, as the plants are the only profit centers with a continuing need for new investments.

monthly inventory budgets, through warehousing, physical security, and paper-work, to obsolescence. The basic reason for holding AM marketing responsible for the inventory is, again, that marketing makes the estimates that determine the inventory levels and is charged with selling the products.

There is a further reason for holding AM marketing responsible for fin-ished goods inventory. Plants are also warehousing points to facilitate national distribution. Because the plants do not all produce the same items, there must be transfers of goods from plants at one location to warehouses at another. If manufacturing were responsible for the inventory, there would be complications. For example, who should be responsible for plant A's inventory at plant B? Should it be the plant that produced the item? Or the one that is warehousing it? Under the present system, this problem does not arise.

As part of its responsibility for the warehousing of the finished goods inven-tory, the marketing group is charged with warehousing expenses. One reason for this is to discourage marketing from exceeding budgeted inventory levels. Be-cause competition is on the basis of delivery (among other factors), marketing has a tendency to stockpile inventory so that products will be available for immediate delivery. Corporate management, of course, does not like to see an already large inventory increase even further; and for that reason, marketing gets charged with these costs. (Finished goods inventories account for almost one-third of total cur-rent assets, and for almost 20% of total assets.)

Degree of Latitude.   Even though managers are held responsible for the profits of their groups, they do not have complete control over all the factors that influence profitability. Plant managers, for example, do not have direct control over their production volume; they are told by the production scheduling group at head-quarters what and how much to produce. They cannot refuse to produce an item, nor may they sell to the outside directly.

Similarly, plant managers have no control over their product mix; this also is fixed by the production schedule determined at headquarters. Yet this factor alone can have a large impact on a plant's profitability as there is a large variation in margins for different products.

Plant managers do have control over their manufacturing costs, and thus partly control their profit margins. Even though standard costs are set at head-quarters for all operations, a plant manager can, for example, reduce his material costs by reducing scrap and rejects. Or he can reduce his labor costs by increasing output per man-hour.

In addition, plant managers have some control over factors such as quality of product and service. As discussed earlier, these factors are important in com-peting in this business, and, thus, plant managers actually do have some indirect control over their volume in the long run.

The AM marketing group also does not have complete control over the important factors that influence its profitability. Although it does have considerably more latitude than the plants in determining sales volume, this element depends to a large degree on external factors, such as competition, number of cars on the road, and the rate at which parts need to be replaced. In addition, another factor that has a direct effect on sales volume is the out-of-stock position at the warehouses.[2] Yet this factor is mainly under the control of the plant managers.

As far as margins are concerned, AM marketing has little control. As pointed out earlier, selling prices for parts are essentially predetermined by the OEM service divisions. Similarly, product costs for AM marketing are relatively fixed. These are determined by transfer prices, which, although reviewed at least once a year, are changed only when conditions change.

On the other hand, AM marketing does have control over its selling and administrative expenses. However, these are relatively small when compared to cost of goods sold.[3]

Another opportunity for the AM marketing group to influence its profits arises from the fact that it is permitted to purchase products outside of the company. This can be done either when the prices charged by the plants are too high or when the plants cannot meet delivery requirements.

Because the OEM manufacturing marketing group is just one profit center, its degree of control over sales volume is slightly greater than that of the three plants supplying AM marketing. Volume, of course, is determined largely by automobile manufacturers and by the vagaries of the automobile market. An OEM will ask Thunderbolt to supply a certain portion of its requirements for an ignition part for a particular model. Then, if demand for that model rises beyond expectations, Thunderbolt will be expected to increase delivery proportionately. If demand is lower than expected, the reverse will be true. However, by being able to develop a particularly good OEM part, the OEM group can gain an advantage over competitors and increase its portion of the OEM requirements.

With respect to margins, the degree of latitude for the OEM group is about the same as for the other three plants. Where negotiated transfer prices determine revenues in their case, negotiated product prices fix revenues for the OEM group; and because of the great purchasing power of the automobile manufctuers, pricing flexibility is limited. Similarly, since manufacturing methods are essentially the same for the Ironville plant as for the other three, flexibility with respect to costs is about the same. However, if the need arises, the OEM group may purchase products from the outside, which is a freedom the other plants do not have.

---

[2]A member of top management estimated that about one-half of the back-ordered AM business is lost. He was unable to provide a similar estimate for the OEM business, as here the buyer/seller relationship is of longer term than in the AM business.

[3]S&A expenses for the AM marketing group amount to about 15% of net sales, while cost of goods sold is over 60%. (The remaining 25% is made up of items such as R&D expense, interest expense, taxes, and profits.)

CASE 13.2 PERKINS ENGINES (A)

In January 1977, James Felker, Finance Director for the Perkins Engines Group, was speaking about the company's management control system:

> In the past two years we have made dramatic improvements in our management control system. The organization of the firm's accounts into cost and profit centers with the associated variance analyses of performance against standards and budgets improved considerably our insight into and control over company operations. A control system, like organization structure, however, never stays static and we are now reassessing it to make sure it still fits our new economic challenges.
>
> When it was installed about a year and a half ago, we were in a depressed order period and its emphasis on the control of production costs helped us to hold down our expenses when revenues were at a minimum. The fact that we had 1,000 redundancies last year gives an idea of the magnitude of the problem then.
>
> Now, however, we are experiencing a totally different phenomenon. With orders coming in faster than we can fill them, the Supply Division, which is our production unit, is willing to alter their production schedule to fit the changing priorities of the Sales Division, providing that alterations be made to their costs so as not to hurt their performance rating. However, because of outside constraints, union pressure, and supplier capacity limitation, there is considerable doubt that even if the brakes were released on manufacturing cost that output could be increased.
>
> On the other hand, the sales people are worried about not getting the important orders produced and delivered at the promised time. They are concerned both with their profit contribution and with their long-term customer contacts. As a result, they are constantly jockeying with each other and complaining about the inability of supply to produce the needed engines. I know that part of the problem is with our suppliers. We are totally out of castings and can't get our orders for these parts filled. But that's not the only problem. I'm also wondering if we might need to make some alterations in the control system. After all, a control system should motivate the employees to work for the good of the whole company, not just their own department.

Company Background

Perkins Engines Group, with headquarters in Peterborough, England, manufactured and sold diesel engines throughout the world (Exhibit 1). In the power range covered by its line of engines, Perkins was the largest producer in the world with 1986 sales of more than $280 million (Exhibit 2). Perkins' line consisted of 3-, 4-, 6-, and 8-cylinder engines for the agricultural, vehicle, industrial, and marine markets. In 1987, Perkins had over 40 basic diesel-engine models as well as two gasoline-engine models.

Founded in 1946 to specialize in diesel engines, Perkins had remained an undiversified diesel-engine manufacturer. In 1948, under Frank A. Perkins, the founder, the company sent sales representatives to Russia, India, and South America.

This case was prepared by Professor F. Warren McFarlan Copyright © by the President and Fellows of Harvard University. Harvard Business School case 9-174-119.

EXHIBIT 1 Perkins Engines (A)

World Distribution of Perkins Engines
Perkins production, 400,000 units p.a. or 14.5% world total
3,000,000 engines are serviced by 11 manufacturing locations, 5 sales companies,
98 national distributors and 1400 authorized dealers

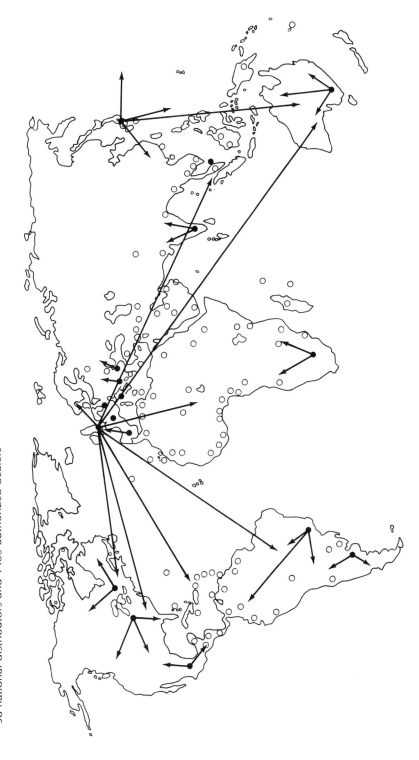

Location of ● Manufacturing Opertations,
Sales Companies and ○ National Distributors

○○ Perkins
○○ Engines

EXHIBIT 2   Perkins Engines (A)

Summary Income Statement and Balance Sheet: Full Year

	1986 ACTUAL	1987 FORECAST AS OF MARCH 16, 1987
SALES		
Third Party	186	239
Massey-Ferguson	100	113
Total Sales	286	352
Standard Variable Cost	212	259
Cost Allowances	2	7
Direct Variable Profit	72	86
DECISION COSTS		
Sales	10	11
Supply	11	11
Engineering	19	20
Services	3	4
Exchange and consolidated adjustments	—	0
Total Decision Costs	43	46
Net Operating Profit	29	40
ASSET REVIEW		
Receivables	37	47
Inventories	38	33
Other Current Assets	(33)	(47)
Current Operating Assets	42	33
Net Fixed and Other Assets	56	62
Decision Costs in Inventory	3	3
Total Assets	103	98

All figures have been disguised and ratios deliberately distorted. Figures are stated in millions of U.S. dollars.

According to Perkins' management, one characteristic of the diesel-engine business was the tendency for large customers to integrate backwards into engine production when their engine purchases became high. Perkins had found its volume thus diminished, particularly by such large vehicle producers as Ford, British Leyland, and Chrysler. In early 1987, management believed that no current customer was in this category.

In 1973, another large customer, Massey-Ferguson Ltd. of Toronto, Canada, had chosen an alternate course of action by making a successful bid to merge with Perkins. In its new relationship, Perkins supplied about 35% of its output by value to Massey-Ferguson but remained independent and autonomous in servicing its other customers, many of whom competed directly with Massey-Ferguson. Perkins' management expressed great pride in their own initiative and operational control of the company.

Organization

Perkins' operations included sales, supply (production), and engineering; a group of service departments supported these three main operations (Exhibit 3). All sales (with the exception of Brazilian sales and those to Massey-Ferguson) were made by regional sales operations. These operations collaborated with the market-development sections to build up Perkins' market share in each area.

In addition to its sales effort, each sales operation was responsible for service and parts for all engines within its territory. Approximately one-half of the U.K. operation's sales went to U.K. original-equipment manufacturers who then exported their equipment; as a result, the remaining sales operations placed much of their service effort (and expense) on engines for which they had received no sales credit. This service effort was relatively profitable. However, spare-parts inventorying and servicing were complicated by the fact that the sales operation was sometimes not aware that certain engines were in its area because of the mobility of the vehicles they powered.

All Perkins' engines were produced by the Supply Division under Richard Perkins, son of the founder Frank Perkins. Richard Perkins was also Deputy Managing Director and General Manager of the autonomous Brazilian subsidiary with its self-sufficient manufacturing operation (Exhibit 4).

The vast majority of Perkins' engines were produced in the five factories in Peterborough. The factories produced the full variety of Perkins' 40-plus engine models. The Fletton factory specialized in V8 engine production; headquarters factory No. 2 specialized in a certain 4-cylinder type; the other three factories produced the remaining varieties of engines.

All Perkins' engines were produced on motorized assembly lines; however, the engines differed substantially, even within one product model. Although basic parts might be similar, there was often great variety in accessory equipment. Such variety might involve the simple substitution of one accessory for another, or it might involve boring entirely different holes into an engine block. On the average, a production order for a group of identical engines averaged about seven; the maximum production order would rarely exceed forty identical engines.

According to Richard Perkins, the company had an adequate labor supply and manufacturing capacity for conceivable future demand. However, many of the company's British suppliers were at full capacity. This tight supply situation

EXHIBIT 3 Perkins Engines (A)

Organization Chart, April 1987

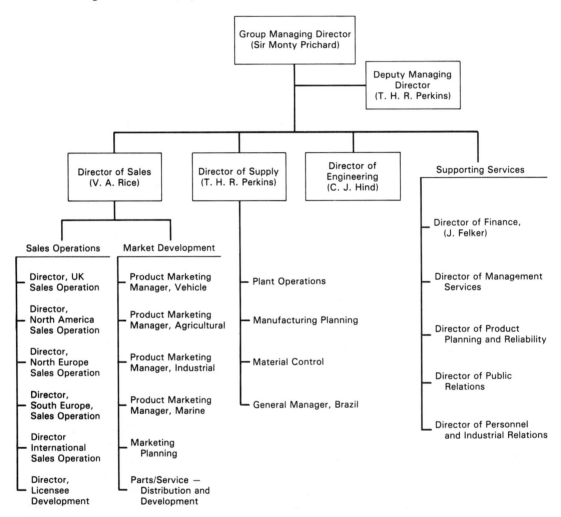

compounded by the high frequency of British strikes had made it attractive to increase imports of parts. For example, some of the company's castings were coming from as far away as Argentina.

Perkins' production was scheduled by three separate departments in the Supply Division. The Planning and Procurement Department prepared the company's monthly production program for 6 months in advance, allocated the engines among customers in times of scarce capacity, and then purchased the parts

EXHIBIT 4 Perkins Engines (A)

Supply Division Organization, January 1987

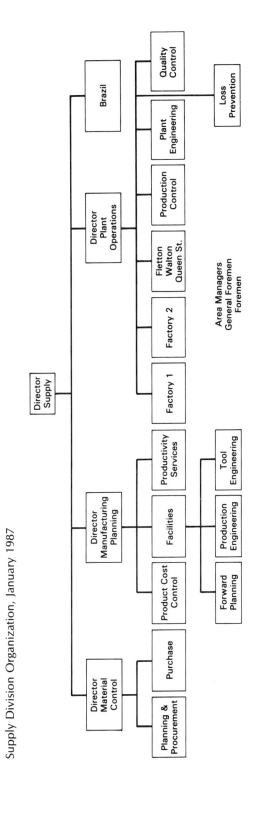

and materials to fill those production needs. This production program was based on Sales Division forecasts and was coordinated with the Purchase Department. The short-term scheduling of the various production lines was done by the Production Control Department.

At one time, Planning and Procurement had been a separate entity, falling under neither the Sales nor the Supply Division. However, in a company consolidation, Planning and Procurement had been placed in the Supply Division because of the close relationship between purchasing and production planning.

The Management Control System

Perkins' planning system was patterned after the Massey-Ferguson system.

The information collected from the books of account was broken down two ways. The first was the legal-entity accounting system which showed the legally reportable results of the individual subsidiaries and the consolidated results of the Perkins Group. The second breakdown formed the management control system. The reports in this system divided the company into profit and cost centers rather than as geographical or legal entities. These reports were used to evaluate managerial performance in each center. Each of the six sales operations was a profit center. The Supply Division, Engineering Division, and support services were cost centers.

The Planning and Reporting Cycle

Senior Massey-Ferguson management began the planning cycle in March. They developed goals for the whole company for the succeeding 3 years. Massey-Ferguson management then informed Sir Monty Prichard, Perkins' Managing Director and a member of Massey-Ferguson's Board of Directors, of the Massey-Ferguson goals and how Perkins supported them.

Upon receipt of this letter, Sir Monty Prichard, in conjunction with Felker, sent out a letter to each operating division (Sales, Supply, and Engineering) setting the general Perkins goals for return on sales and return on assets. At the same time, Felker's department instructed each operating division how the company plans would be formed. Neither of these directives set specific revenue or expense targets for the departments; rather, they provided a framework for planning.

By May, the operating divisions had forwarded their plans to the Finance Department for consolidation into Perkins' tentative 2-year plan with key items projected for 5 years (e.g., sales, capital investment). At the end of May, a presentation involving each operating division was made to the Managing Director; he specified any changes to bring the plan into line with the goals of his March letter. In late June, the plan was presented for approval in Toronto. The final plan was usually approved in November, following a series of discussions.

Perkins' management control involved the comparison of actual results with information generated in the planning process. These results were prepared by the second Friday following the end of each month. Massey-Ferguson headquarters in Toronto received the results by the next Tuesday. A revised forecast for the balance of the year was issued by Perkins on the third Friday after the close of each month. Key sales and expense levels were compared with this revised forecast. Felker felt this constant review and modification of the forecast during the year was a key element in the system's success.

Manufacturing Costs

The heart of Perkins' control system was a manufacturing standard-cost system. Standards for each engine were reviewed annually.

The *direct material costs* of an engine included the vendor's price for the raw materials or finished components incorporated in it, inward freight charges, and import duties, if any. All parts and materials, including packing materials and miscellaneous supplies such as paint and oil, were given standard costs, which were applied to each engine.

The *direct labor costs* for an engine included only those associated with the machining of parts and the assembly and testing of engines. To determine the direct labor cost, the standard time of each production function was multiplied by that function's standard wage rate. Direct labor costs excluded all costs for material handling, maintenance, inspection, and fringe benefits.

The *direct variable overhead costs* included all indirect supervisory labor, direct-labor overtime and night-shift premiums, wage increases, direct-labor fringe benefits, training time, and normal direct-labor idle-time expenses. It also included processing supplies, cutting tools, and labor and material value lost when material was scrapped. Direct variable overhead was charged to an engine at a rate of 117% of direct labor. (The rate was reviewed and redefined every year.)

In addition to the standard costs, the plans provided allowances for increases in costs throughout the fiscal year. These provisions (known as cost allowances) were derived from items like increases in labor contract, price inflation, and labor idle-time.

All costs which were not incorporated in the variable costs for engines were called "decision costs." These were all semi-variable or fixed costs not directly related to increases or decreases in engine production (Exhibit 5). According to Peter Ray, Supply Division Cost Analysis Chief, 80% of these decision costs were personnel-related. Throughout the year, any deviations from the planned standard costs and decision costs were recorded as "variances." These variances were analyzed monthly. In addition a new forecast for the entire year was prepared; this was based on volume, level of inflation, specific supplier increases, etc.

For each production department, a labor-efficiency variance was calculated. This was done weekly by comparing the department's total labor inputs (determined from employee time cards) to the standard labor costs for the depart-

EXHIBIT 5   Perkins Engines (A)

U.K. Supply Division: Decision Cost Variance Analysis
   for 1987 as of March 16, 1987

BY EXPENSE TYPE		*BY SECTION*	
Planned Decision Costs Level as of Jan. 1, 1987	*10,220*	*Planned Decision Costs Level as of Jan. 1, 1987*	*10,220*
PLANT OPERATIONS DEPT.		**PLANT OPERATIONS DEPT.**	
Overtime & Premiums	(119)	Director	2
Salaries & Wages	(144)	Plant No. 1	(43)
Fringes	(23)	Plant No. 2	(12)
Admin. Expenses	(15)	Fletton	(22)
Indirect Materials	(1)	Walton	5
Repairs & Maintenance	(2)	Queen Street	7
Income	—	Production Control	(57)
Other	(21)	Loss Prevention	(4)
Subtotal	(325)	Plant Engineering	(144)
		Quality Control	(57)
		Subtotal	(325)
MANUFACTURING PLANNING DEPT.		**MANUFACTURING PLANNING DEPT.**	
Salaries & Wages	51	Director	9
Outside Services	13	Facilities	33
Other	(8)	Industrial Engineering	18
Subtotal	56	Product Cost	(4)
		Subtotal	56
MATERIAL CONTROL DEPT.		**MATERIAL CONTROL DEPT.**	
Overtime	(18)	Director	2
Other	(1)	Purchase	(13)
Subtotal	(19)	Planning & Procurement	(8)
		Subtotal	(19)
MATERIAL VARIANCES		**MATERIAL VARIANCES**	12
Rebates	12		
Others	—		
Subtotal	12		
POLICY		**POLICY**	(34)
Related Expenses	—		
Holiday Pay under Accrual	(34)		
Other	—		
Subtotal	(34)		
TOTAL SUPPLY DIVISION	(310)		(310)
Forecasted Decision Costs for 1987 as of March 16, 1987	10,530		10,530

All figures have been disguised and are in thousands of U.S. dollars.

ment's output (calculated by multiplying the number of engines processed through each work center by the department's standard labor cost).

All materials purchased by the company were added to the raw-materials inventory at the standard purchase price; the purchase-price variance was identified at that time. Materials were not subtracted from that inventory account until the engine was transferred to finished-goods inventory. Under this system, all raw materials and the materials portion of work-in-process inventories were lumped together. A physical inventory was made once a year.

A finished engine was put into finished-stock inventory for shipment to a customer either in the United Kingdom or overseas. The ex-works price was recorded as an account receivable, against which was charged the standard cost of the engine. Inventory stocks were officially deleted at that time.

For legal-entity reporting purpose, sales to Perkins non-U.K. subsidiaries were made at intercompany prices developed to satisfy tax and customs authorities.

For management control purposes, however, the effect of intercompany transactions was eliminated. To measure management performance, sales revenues were compared with the direct standard manufacturing variable costs (direct materials, direct labor, and direct variable overhead). From this resulting gross-profit figure, the sales-operations decision costs were subtracted (Exhibit 6). This method provided an equivalent basis for evaluation of all sales operations.

All OEM customers (including Massey-Ferguson) were subject to the same pricing policy.

EXHIBIT 6 Perkins Engines (A)

Sales Operation Forecasted Profit Summary as of March 16, 1987
  for South Europe

		YEAR-END FORECAST	
		Forecast for 1987	*Variance from Jan. 1, 1987 Plan*
Sales:	Engines	22,828	777
	Parts	1,037	37
	Total		814
		23,865	
Standard Direct	Engines	4,623	389
Variable Profit:	Parts	336	8
	Total		397
		4,959	
Decision Costs		1,464	29
Profit Contribution		3,495	368

All figures have been disguised and are stated in thousands of U.S. dollars.

Performance Evaluation

Each of the three operating divisions (Sales, Supply, and Engineering) and their subdivisions and each of the support services was evaluated according to its performance versus the 1-year plan. This was accomplished on a month-by-month basis in which year-to-date was compared against plan and the most recent forecast, and the measure of performance varied according to whether the unit was a cost or a profit center.

Each of Perkins' subsidiaries had geographic sales and service responsibilities. With the exception of the independent Brazilian operation, little manufacturing and no engineering was undertaken in these subsidiaries. Each subsidiary reported its results monthly to the Peterborough headquarters where these results were consolidated into Sales Operation Profit Summaries. Each subsidiary and each sales operation was evaluated according to the variation of its profit contribution from the pre-determined plan. This was done on both a monthly and full-year basis (Exhibit 6). A consolidated Sales Division Summary was then calculated from these sales operation reports.

In contrast to the Sales Division, the Supply Division was a cost center. Actual-versus-standard cost comparisons were recorded down to the shop-floor subdepartments. At this level, weekly labor efficiency reports were discussed with the foremen to determine the causes of deviations. Building from this level, the monthly reporting cycle showed the variances in the variable production costs by department and for the whole division (Exhibit 7). It also showed departmental variances in the Supply Division's decision costs; these were broken down by type of expense and by department section (Exhibit 5). In addition to these reports, the Supply Division also generated monthly reports of headcount, productivity, overtime, inventory, engine output, manufacturing arrears, quality, safety, and maintenance downtime.

The Engineering Division and the support services were also cost centers. Since their expenses represented decision costs, each was measured by a decision-cost variance analysis. For the Engineering Division, these cost variances were broken down by work category and by type of expense (Exhibit 8). Each of the support services also broke down the decision-cost variances by type of expense and by cause.

These profit and cost variances were then summarized by operating division in a Sales and Profit Contribution Variance Summary. Also, a Summary Income Statement and Balance Sheet (Exhibit 2) showed the total Perkins performance. The variances in the direct variable profit, decision costs, and assets were then analyzed by cause, and the year-end outcome in each of these areas was projected.

Although Perkins had no formal bonus system, managers were paid and promoted according to their results in comparison with the plan.

EXHIBIT 7   Perkins Engines (A)

U.K. Supply Division: Cost Allowance Forecast
for 1987 as of March 16, 1987

PLANNED COST ALLOWANCES AS OF JAN. 1, 1987	6,052
VARIANCES FROM JAN. 1, 1987, PLAN	
Material Control Dept.	
Volume & Mix	18
Purchase Price Variance	141
Sourcing Variance	157
Sales of Scrap	(21)
Freight Duty & Insurance	3
Other	(7)
Subtotal	291
Manufacturing Planning Dept.	
Volume & Mix	15
Times Revisions	(17)
Consumable Tools	7
Subtotal	7
Plant Operations Dept.	
Volume & Mix	75
Direct Labor Off Standards	(69)
Indirect Labor & O.T. Premiums	(797)
Consumable Materials	(26)
Other	49
Subtotal	(853)
Nondepartmental	
Volume & Mix	(17)
P.P.V. in Inventory	5
Stock Loss Provision	5
Duty Variance	(12)
Other	19
Subtotal	0
Total Supply Division	(555)
Forecasted Cost Allowances as of March 16, 1987	6,607

All figures have been disguised and are stated in thousands
of U.S. dollars.

Company Opinion

In discussing the Supply Division as a cost center, Felker noted that small percentage variations in many items could cause large changes in profits. While materials constituted 80% of the variable standard cost-of-goods sold, there were

EXHIBIT 8 Perkins Engines (A)

Engineering Division Cost Forecast for 1987 as of
March 16, 1987

DECISION COSTS	FORECAST FOR 1987	VARIANCE FROM JAN. 1, 1987, PLAN
WORK CATEGORY		
Cost Saving Work	9,243	154
New Product	775	—
Supply Problems	353	(10)
Product Reliability	928	—
Applications	2,933	85
General	1,183	(103)
Total Direct	15,415	126
Administration	3,889	50
Total	19,304	176
TYPE OF EXPENSE		
Salaries	9,008	—
Wages	3,773	—
Materials	1,568	50
Outside Assistance	1,170	25
Depreciation	1,045	19
Supply Beds	430	188
Consumables	535	29
Other	1,775	(135)
Total	19,304	176

All figures have been disguised and are stated in thousands of U.S.
dollars.

nevertheless 9,000 people working in the Peterborough factories. This large labor expense required careful control.

However, C. Joseph Hind, Director of the Engineering Division, felt that cost-center concept was not particularly helpful. He believed that the monthly reports of costs and variances did not really indicate whether all the money allocated for each particular development project would be spent by the end of the year. Rather than being elated over any positive monthly or year-end variance in a development expense, Hind was often disappointed, since such a surplus probably meant that the project was lagging. Perhaps more importantly, he sensed that a negative expense pressure might discourage the kind of adventurous development so critical in this industry. Furthermore, he felt cost performance was not a good measure of technical productivity.

A marketing manager mentioned his analogous concern that the Supply Division's cost consciousness could inadvertently cause schedule inflexibilities. These in turn might jeopardize long-term customer relationships. In such a case, the company might be sacrificing long-run profits for short-term savings.

According to Victor A. Rice, Sales Division Director, the company was not concerned with trading off the various ways of using a limited production capacity. He acknowledged that there was a significant problem with suppliers; nonetheless, he believed that the company had no foreseeable problems with internal capacity. In his opinion, while his sales subordinates could benefit from additional leverage for influencing the Supply Division's schedule, they also needed firm direction in making more realistic sales forecasts. In his estimation, the current sales forecasts, by which the future production schedules were set, were highly optimistic and reflected two things: salemen were over-selling in 1986–87, effectively stealing sales from 1987–88; and customers were over-ordering in anticipation of an allocation cutback because of under-capacity (as had happened in the past).

Rice believed that the system, which evaluated and pointed up problem areas in the performance reports, tended to look only at the actual-versus-forecast results, with perhaps insufficient attention to the pattern with which forecasts changed.

In looking further at the control system which he had helped design 2 years earlier in his capacity as Finance Director, Rice noted that the responsibility for assets like accounts receivable and inventories was not always assigned on the same basis as the profit-contribution responsibility for inventories; the reason was short transit times and direct contact of customers with planning and procurement. Finance had responsibility for all credit and receivables. The North America Sales Operation Manager, however, was responsible for his receivables assets and inventories.

Questions

1. How appropriate was the management control system to Perkins' needs when it was installed in 1985, assuming that company management at that time forecast a long period of undercapacity utilization of its manufacturing capabilities?

2. How appropriate is this management control system to Perkins in January 1987, when the order books are full and capacity utilization is forecast for the foreseeable future?

chapter 14

TRANSFER PRICING

This chapter is concerned with transactions (principally sales and purchases) among profit centers in the same organization. In general, the magnitude of these transactions is related to the degree of integration. In some industries, large companies produce products from raw material to finished goods. For example, most large paper companies own woodlands from which they produce pulp, which goes through further processing stages until the finished product is finally sold to the ultimate consumer. Where such companies are organized by profit center, several profit centers may be involved in producing and selling a product. At each step there is an intracompany transaction.

There are two decisions that must be made for each product involved in intracompany transactions:

1. Should the company produce (or continue to produce) the product inside the company? This is the *sourcing decision*.
2. At what price should the product be transferred between profit centers? This is the *transfer price decision*.

In order for a company, with any degree of integration, to adopt a profit center form of organization, it must establish a transfer price system. This system can be extremely important because it can affect the ability of a profit center manager to make optimum decisions. Also, the measurement of the financial performance of the profit center manager, as well as the profit center itself, is affected by the transfer price system. Incorrect transfer prices create incorrect measurements which, in turn, result in incorrect decisions.

If two or more profit centers are jointly responsibile for product development, manufacturing and marketing, each share in the revenue that is generated when the product is finally sold. The transfer price system is the mechanism for distributing this revenue. In distributing revenue, the system must do it in such a way as to accomplish three things:

1. It should provide each segment with the relevant information required to determine the optimum trade-off between *company* costs and revenues.
2. Profits should reflect how well the cost-revenue trade-offs have been made. In other words, each segment of the business should be able to maximize company profits by maximizing divisional profits.
3. The profit earned by each segment of the business should respresent the economic contribution of that segment.

Transfer price systems can range from being very simple to being extremely complex, depending on the nature of the business. This chapter starts with the simple situations and describes increasingly complex ones.

SITUATION 1: AVAILABLE MARKETS

The simplest transfer price situation occurs where there are outside markets to which the inside producer can sell its products and outside sources from which the inside user can buy the products it requires. In this instance, the only transfer price policy necessary is to give profit center managers the right to deal with insiders or outsiders at their discretion. The market thus establishes the transfer price. The decision to deal inside or outside is also made by the marketplace. If buyers cannot get a satisfactory price from the inside source, they are free to buy from the outside.

As long as the selling profit center can sell all its products either to insiders or outsiders and as long as the buying profit center can obtain all its requirements from either outsiders or insiders, this method is optimum. The market price represents the opportunity cost to the seller of selling the product inside because if the product were not sold inside, it would be sold outside. From a company point of view, therefore, the relevant cost of the product to the inside buyer is the market price because that is the amount of cash that has been foregone by selling inside.

This is the only situation where a transfer price system fulfills the three requirements stated earlier and yet needs no central administration.

Excess or Shortage of Industry Capacity

Suppose the selling profit center cannot sell all it can produce to the outside market. This situation occurs when there is excess capacity in the market. The company is not optimizing profits to the extent that the buying profit center purchases from the outside while capacity is available on the inside.

On the other hand, suppose the buying profit center cannot obtain all the product that it requires from the outside, whereas the selling profit center is selling to the outside. This situation occurs where there is a shortage of capacity in the market. In this case, the output of the buying profit center is constrained and, again, company profits may not be maximized.

If the amount of intracompany transfers is small or the situation temporary, most companies let the buyers and sellers work out their own relationships without central intervention. Even where the amount of intracompany transfers is significant, some companies still do not intervene on the theory that the benefits of keeping the profit centers independent offsets the loss from suboptimizing company profits.

Some companies allow either the buying or the selling profit center to appeal a sourcing decision to a central person or committee. For example, a selling profit center could appeal a buying profit center's decision to buy a product from outside when capacity was available inside. In the same way, a buying profit center could appeal a selling profit center's decision to sell outside. The person or group (hereafter called an "arbitration" committee) would, then, make the sourcing decision on the basis of the company's best interests. The transfer price would be the competitive price. In other words, the appealing profit center is appealing only the sourcing decision. It must accept the product at the competitive price.

In many companies, given the option, the buying profit centers prefer to deal with outside sources. Some of this is based on service, as outside sources are perceived to provide better service. Some of it may also be based on the internal rivalry often experienced in divisionalized companies. For whatever reason, management should take this situation into account in setting transfer price policy. It is by no means assured that a profit center will voluntarily buy from the inside source when excess capacity exists.

Integrated Costs

There is a second problem that can occur when products are transferred at a competitive price and internal capacity is available. There will always be "upstream" fixed costs and profits that may well *not* be considered by the profit center ultimately selling in the outside market.

To illustrate this problem, assume that Division C manufactures and sells cardboard boxes in an integrated paper company. It buys the paper board from

Division B, who, in turn, buys the pulp to make the paper board from Division A. The prices and costs for a ton of boxes is as follows:

	A	*B*	*C*	*CONSOLIDATED*
Price	$ 75	$150	$350	$350
Cost:				
Inside Material	20	75	150	20
Other Variable Costs	25	25	200	250
Total	$ 45	$100	$350	$270
Contribution	$ 30	$ 50	0	$ 80

Note that the variable cost to Division A was $45 to produce enough pulp to make a ton of boxes. This was sold to Division B for $75 so that Division A earned a contribution of $30. Division B in turn added $25 in variable cost and sold the boxes to Division C for $150. Division C, however, can sell the boxes in the outside market for only $350. As it would earn no contribution on the sale, Division C would have little incentive to pursue such a sale agressively. The company, however, would earn a contribution of $80. Although this example is exaggerated, a somewhat similar situation exists on all sales in an integrated company.

It is always possible for representatives of Division C to meet with representatives of Divisions A and B to decide on an outside selling price and to negotiate a distribution of the contribution that would be earned. If this were done, there would be no problem because the optimum action for the company would be the optimum action for the three divisions. In many cases, however, there may be hundreds of transactions taking place monthly so that there would have to be some formal mechanisms for the three divisions to consult together on bids, or, given a market price, whether or not to sell at that price. Such mechanisms seem to be used rarely in business. In fact, divisions often guard their cost structure jealously so that Division C may not even know the costs of the upstream divisions. This can be a serious problem in transfer pricing because (1) it exists almost universally and will occur to some extent any time there is unused capacity in the upstream profit centers; and (2) rarely is anything done about this problem, except in highly integrated companies (and not always then). Methods for handling this problem are described later in the chapter.

SITUATION 2: LIMITED MARKETS

In many integrated companies, markets for the buying or selling profit centers may be limited. There are several reasons for this. First, the existence of internal capacity might limit the development of external capacity. Where most of the large companies in an industry are highly integrated, as in the pulp and paper industry, there tends to be little independent production capacity for the intermediate products. Thus these producers can handle only a limited amount of demand. When internal capacity becomes tight, the market is quickly flooded with demands for the itnermediate products. Even though outside capacity exists, it may not be available to the integrated company unless this capacity is used on a regular basis. If the integrated company does not purchase a product on a regular basis, it might have trouble obtaining it from the outside when capacity is short.

Second, if a company is the sole producer of a differentiated product, no outside capacity exists. Third, if a company has made significant investment in facilities, it is unlikely to use outside sources even though outside capacity exists, unless the outside selling price approaches the company's variable cost, which is not usual. For practical purposes, the products produced are captive.

Even though outside markets are not used, the transfer price that best satisfies the requirements of a profit center system is still the *competitive* price. Consider the following:

1. Competitive prices will measure the contribution of each profit center to the total company profits. If internal capacity were not available, the company would buy outside at the competitive price. The difference between the competitive price and inside cost is the money saved by making instead of buying.
2. A competitive price measures how well a profit center may be performing against competition.
3. A competitive price is independent of internal conditions.

The problem is, How does a company obtain a competitive price if it does not buy or sell the product in an outside market? Here are some ways:

1. If *published market prices* are available, they can be used to establish transfer prices.
   (a)   However, these should be prices actually paid in the market.
   (b)   Also, the conditions that exist in the outside market should be consistent with those existing within the company. For example, market prices that are applicable to relatively small purchases (a "spot" market) would not be competitive for what is essentially a long-term commitment.
2. Market prices may be set by *bids*. This can generally be done only if the bidder has a reasonable chance of obtaining the business by being the low bidder; for example, one company accomplishes this by buying about one-half of a particular group of products outside the company and one-half inside the company. The company puts *all* the products out to bid but selects one-half to stay inside. The company obtains valid bids because the bidders can expect to get some of the business. Note that a company that requests bids solely to obtain a competitive price will soon find that either no one bids or the bids are of questionable value.
3. If the *manufacturing profit center* sells other products in *outside markets,* it is often possible to replicate a competitive price on the basis of the outside price. For

example, a manufacturing profit center earns 10% over standard cost on the products that it sells to outside markets. It can, then, replicate a competitive price by adding 10% to the standard cost of the proprietary products. Of course, the manufacturing processes for both the competitive and proprietary products must be similar.

4. If the *buying profit center* purchases similar products from the *outside* market, it may be possible to replicate competitive prices for proprietary products. This can be done by calculating the cost of the difference in design and other conditions of sale between the competitive products and the proprietary products.

SITUATION 3: NO VALID COMPETITIVE PRICES AVAILABLE

If there are no ways to approximate valid competitive prices, the remaining option is to develop *cost-based* transfer prices.

Cost-Based Transfer Prices

If competitive prices are not available, transfer prices may be set on the basis of cost plus a profit. Such a transfer price system is usually complex and the results tend to be less satisfactory. There are two basic decisions that have to be made:

1. How to define cost.
2. How to calculate the profit markup.

The Cost Basis.   The usual basis is standard cost. Actual costs should not be used because manufacturing inefficiencies will then be passed on to the buying profit center. If standard costs are used, there is a need to develop an incentive to set tight standards and to improve standards.

The Profit Markup.   It is necessary to decide how to calculate the profit markup. In this case, also, there are two decisions:

1. On what is the profit mark-up to be based?
2. What is the level of profit allowed?

The simplest base is a *percentage of costs*. If this is done, however, no account is taken of capital required. A better base is the amount of *investment*, but there is a major problem in calculating this investment. If the historical cost of the fixed assets is used, new facilities designed to reduce prices could actually increase costs because old assets are undervalued. When the old assets are replaced by new assets, the price could increase.

A second problem with the profit allowance is the amount of the profit. Top management's perception of financial performance of a profit center will be affected by the profit it shows. Consequently, to the extent possible, the profit allowance should be the best approximation of the rate of return that would be earned if the division were an independent company.

The most satisfactory profit allowance appears to be one based on the investment required to meet the volume needed by the buying profit centers. This investment should be calculated at a "standard" volume with fixed assets and inventories at current replacement costs.

Management Considerations

As indicated, there are a number of serious problems with cost-based transfer price. The principal things to be considered are the following:

1. Transfer prices should not encourage the manufacturing profit center to fail to maintain tight standards or fail to improve productivity by making appropriate investments. Manufacturing profit centers should have the same motivation to reduce costs that they would have if their prices were based on outside competition.

2. The performance factors should always be segregated by responsibility. For example, manufacturing inefficiencies should not be passed on to the buying profit center.

3. In general, a fairly elaborate administrative procedure is required if the profit centers are to negotiate their own prices (a wise procedure). When the marketplace is removed as a source of prices, the parties must negotiate on internal conditions, specifically, allowable levels of costs and profits.

If competitive prices are not available or cannot be replicated, the manufacturing operation is usually a captive supplier that manufactures differentiated products entirely within the company. Under these circumstances, serious consideration should be given to making this operation a cost center or at least a "pseudo profit" center, as described in Chapter 13.

UPSTREAM FIXED COSTS AND PROFITS

Most integrated companies face problems because the profit centers that finally sell to the outside customer may not be even aware of the amount of upstream fixed costs and profits included in their internal purchase prices. Even if they were aware of such costs and profits, it might be necessary to reduce their own profits to optimize company profits. Clearly, this is an unsatisfactory situation—yet, it exists in almost all transfer price situations. Some methods that have been used to mitigate this problem are described in this part of the chapter.

Agreement Among Divisions

A company could establish a formal mechanism whereby representatives from the contributing divisions meet periodically to decide on outside selling prices and the distribution of the profit for products having significant amounts of upstream fixed costs and profits in the purchase price to the division that ultimately sells to the outside. To make this mechanism workable, the review process should be limited to decisions that involve a high level of activity. As stated earlier, actions that maximize the profits of the company also maximize the profits of the profit centers affected. This is so because *all* the profits gener- ated are assigned to one profit center involved.

Two-Step Pricing Systems

One way to handle the problem of upstream fixed costs and profits is to establish a transfer price that includes two charges. First, a charge is made for each unit sold that is equal to the standard variable cost of production. Second, a periodic (usually monthly) charge is made that is equal to the fixed costs associ- ated with the facilities reserved for the buying division plus a profit based on a return on the resources reserved for the buying division. For example, assume the following conditions:

Division X (manufacturer)

	PRODUCT A	*PRODUCT B*
Expected sales to Division Y (units)	100,000	100,000
Variable cost per unit	$ 5.00	$ 10.00
Total annual fixed costs assigned to product	480,000	480,000
Investment in working capital and facilities to produce products	1,200,000	1,500,000
Competitive return on investment	10%	10%

The transfer price for product A would be $5 for each unit that Division Y purchases plus $40,000 per month (480,000 ÷ 12) for fixed cost plus $10,000 per month (1,200,000 × 0.10) for profit.

The transfer price for product B would be $10 for each unit that Division Y purchases plus $40,000 per month for fixed costs plus $12,500 (1,500,000 × 0.10) for profit.

The fixed cost calculation is based on the capacity that is reserved for the production of each of the products sold to Division Y. The investment repre- sented by this capacity is then allocated to each of these products. The return on investment that Division Y earns at standard cost on competitive (and, if possible, comparable) products is calculated and multiplied by the investment assigned to the product.

In the example just given, we have calculated the profit allowance as a fixed amount. It would be appropriate under some circumstances to divide the invest- ment into variable (such as receivables and inventory) and fixed (physical assets) components. Then, a profit allowance based on a return on the variable assets would be added to the standard variable cost for each unit sold.

The following points about this method of pricing should be considered.

1. The monthly charge for fixed costs and profits should be negotiated periodically and should depend on the capacity reserved for the buying division.
2. Some questions may be raised as to the accuracy of the cost and investment allocation. Actually, in most situations there is no great difficulty in assigning costs and assets to individual products. In any event, approximate accuracy is all that is needed. Moreover, if capacity is reserved for a group of products sold to the same division, there is no need to allocate fixed costs and investments to individual products in the group. The principal problem is usually not the allocation technique but rather the decision about how much capacity is to be reserved for the various products.
3. Standard variable costs are not always the same as marginal costs. Where there is a real possibility that marginal costs might vary significantly from standard variable costs, some system should be developed for monitoring the costs and communicating to management when such differences develop.
4. Under this pricing system, the manufacturing division's profit performance is not affected by sales volume, which solves the problem that arises when other divisions' marketing efforts affect the profit performance of a purely manufacturing division.
5. There could be some conflict between the interests of the manufacturing division and the interests of the company. If capacity is limited, the manufacturing division can increase its profit by selling outside because the outside selling price will be higher than the standard variable cost. Consequently, if divisional managers have the choice of using their capacity to produce parts for outside sale, it will be to their advantage to do so. (This weakness is mitigated somewhat by stipulating that the selling divisions have first claim on the capacity for which they have contracted.)
6. In some respects this method is similar to the "take or pay" pricing that is sometimes used in public utilities, coal companies, and other long-term contractors.

Profit Sharing

As just described, in those instances where one division markets products produced by another, the transfer price becomes the variable cost to the marketing division in the typical transfer price system. Where the two-step pricing system just described does not appear to be appropriate, a profit sharing system might be used to ensure congruence of divisional interest with company interest. This system operates somewhat as follows:

1. The product is transferred to the marketing division at standard variable cost.
2. After the product is sold, the divisions share the contribution earned, which is the selling price minus the variable manufacturing and marketing costs.

This method of pricing is often appropriate when the demand for the manufactured product is not steady enough to warrant the permanent assignment of facilities as in the two-step method. In general, this method accomplishes the purpose of making the marketing division's interest congruent with the company's. There can be, however, practical problems in calculating the contribution, in finding an equitable method to divide it, and in administering the system.

Two Sets of Prices

A fourth possible solution where a manufacturing division sells only to a marketing division is to have two sets of transfer prices. The manufacturing division's revenue is credited at the outside sales price minus a percentage to cover marketing costs. However, the buying division is charged only the variable standard costs (or, sometimes, the total standard cost). The difference is charged to a headquarters account and eliminated when the divisional statements are consolidated.

This method gives the manufacturing division an incentive to help maximize profits rather than simply minimizing costs. The marketing division is motivated to make correct short-term product and pricing decisions. The method has the disadvantage, however, of making total divisional profits greater than company profits. Consequently, top management must be aware of this situation in evaluating divisional profitability.

Limitations in the Use of Variable Costs

The preceding parts of this section of the chapter have assumed that marketing managers need to make decisions based on an evaluation of the relative contribution and, consequently, they need to know company variable costs. There are many instances where this is not the situation. For example, a company may have a general policy of not pricing below full cost. Or, some companies do not engage in price competition and always price at the competitive level. In some cases, the inability to estimate the elasticity of demand makes contribution analysis of limited value.

Whatever the reason, many companies appear to operate well without using any of the pricing methods described in this part of the chapter. Consequently, it should be understood that these methods should be used only where a significant amount of suboptimizing is taking place and other simpler techniques are not likely to be effective.

SUMMARY

The delegation of significant amounts of authority is dependent upon the ability to delegate responsibility for profits. Profit responsibility cannot be safely delegated unless two conditions exist:

1. The delegatee has all of the relevant information required to make optimum decisions.

2. The delegatee's performance should be measured on how well he or she has made cost-revenue trade-offs.

Where segments of a company share responsibility for product development, manufacturing, and marketing, a transfer price system is required if these segments are to be delegated profit responsibility. This transfer price system must result in the two conditions described above. In complex organizations it can be a difficult problem to devise a transfer price system that assures the necessary knowledge and motivation for optimum decision making.

There are probably few instances in complex organizations where there is a completely satisfactory transfer price system. As with many management control problems, it is necessary to choose the best of perhaps several less than perfect courses of action. The important thing is to be aware of the areas of imperfections and to be sure that administrative procedures are employed to avoid serious suboptimum decisions.

QUESTIONS

14.1 Why is it important for management to know the profit contribution of the different organizational units? What action can it take with this information? Is it necessary to decentralize profit responsibility in order to obtain information of this nature?

14.2 Explain the relationship between a pricing decision and a sourcing decision.

14.3 Develop a proposal for establishing a price arbitration committee. Include in this proposal membership (by title), general duties, procedures for submitting disputes, rights of appeal, and other points that you consider relevant.

14.4 Explain why the marginal cost of an intermediate product is the same as the market price when capacity is limited and there is the alternative of selling it in an outside market. Would this still be true if there were sufficient productive capacity for the intermediate product that an outside sale would not preclude an inside sale? In other words, the internal demand for the intermediate product could be fully satisfied in addition to selling the product in an outside market.

14.5 Explain why there can be a conflict of interest when the transfer price consists of the standard variable cost per unit sold plus a monthly fixed amount to cover fixed costs and profits. What action can be taken to insure that optimum decisions are made in these cases?

14.6 What are the advantages and disadvantages of setting up a Systems and Data Processing Department as a profit center? How would you establish transfer prices?

14.7 How would you go about estimating the opportunity loss from decentralization?

PROBLEMS

14.1 Company X has a pricing formula as follows: standard cost plus 10% of assets assigned to the product. Assets include inventory and fixed assets at book values, receivables at 8% of selling price, and cash at 10% of the selling price. Calculate the transfer price on the following parts:

| | COST AND INVESTMENT PER UNIT AT STANDARD VOLUME | | | |
	Part A	Part B	Part C	Part D
Material	$ 20.00	$ 45.00	$ 6.00	$150.00
Direct labor	10.00	15.00	2.00	20.00
Overhead	20.00	45.00	8.00	70.00
Inventories	10.00	20.00	1.00	20.00
Fixed assets	100.00	100.00	20.00	200.00

14.2 Assume that the X Company, described in Problem 14.1, changes its transfer pricing rules to the following: goods are transferred at a unit price equal to standard variable cost plus 10% of current assets plus a monthly amount equal to the fixed costs plus a profit of 10% of the fixed assets. The fixed overhead is 50% of the total overhead and the annual standard volumes are as follows.

PART	ANNUAL STANDARD VOLUME
A	12,000
B	24,000
C	48,000
D	60,000

Required

Calculate the transfer price of parts A through D.

14.3 Division A of the ABC Company manufactures Product X, which is sold to Division B as a component of Product Y. Product Y is sold to Division C, which uses it as a component in Product Z. Product Z is sold to customers outside of the Company. The intracompany pricing rule is that products are transferred between divisions at standard cost plus a 10% return on inventories and fixed assets. From the information provided below, calculate the transfer price for Products X and Y and the standard cost of Product Z.

STANDARD COST PER UNIT	PRODUCT X	PRODUCT Y	PRODUCT Z
Material purchased outside	$2.00	$3.00	$1.00
Direct labor	1.00	1.00	2.00
Variable overhead	1.00	1.00	2.00
Fixed overhead per unit	3.00	4.00	1.00
Standard volume	10,000	10,000	10,000
Inventories (average)	$70,000	$15,000	$30,000
Fixed assets (net)	30,000	45,000	16,000

14.4 Assume the same facts as stated in Problem 14.3, except that the transfer price rule is as follows: Goods are transferred among divisions at the standard variable cost per unit transferred plus a monthly charge. This charge is equal to the fixed costs assigned to the product plus a 10% return on the average inventories and fixed assets assignable to the product. Calculate the transfer price for Products X and Y and calculate the unit standard cost for Products Y and Z.

14.5 The present selling price of Product Z is $28.00. Listed below is a series of possible price reductions by competition and the probable impact of these reductions on the volume of sales if Division C does not also reduce its price.

Possible competitive price	$27.00	$26.00	$25.00	$23.00	22.00
Sales volume if price of Product Z is maintained at $28.00	9,000	7,000	5,000	2,000	0
Sales volume if price of Product Z is reduced to competitive levels	10,000	10,000	10,000	10,000	10,000

Required

With transfer prices calculated in Problem 14.3, is Division C better advised to maintain its price at $28.00 or to follow competition in each of the instances above? With the transfer prices calculated in Problem 14.4, is Division C better advised to maintain its present price of $28.00 or to follow competition in each of the instances above? Which decisions are to the best economic interests of the company, other things being equal? Using the transfer prices calculated in problem 14.3, is the manager of Division C making a decision contrary to the overall interests of the company? If so, what is the opportunity loss to the company in each of the competitive pricing actions described above?

14.6 Division C of the ABC Company described earlier is interested in increasing the sales of Product Z. A survey is made and sales increases resulting from increases in television advertising are estimated. The results of this survey are provided below. (Note that this particular type of advertising can be purchased only in units of $100,000.)

(IN THOUSANDS)					
Advertising expenditures	$100	$200	$300	$400	$500
Additional volume resulting from additional advertising	10	19	27	34	40

As manager of Division C, how much television advertising would you use if you purchased Product Y at the transfer price calculated in Problem 14.3? How much television advertising would you use if you purchased Product Y for the transfer price calculated in Problem 14.4? Which is correct from the overall company viewpoint? How much would the company lose in suboptimum profits from using the first transfer price? (In all cases, assume that you try to maximize divisional profits.)

14.7 Two of the divisions of the Chambers Corporation are the Intermediate Division and the Final Division. The Intermediate Division produces three products, A, B, and C. Normally these products are sold both to outside customers and to the

Final Division. The Final Division uses Products A, B, and C in manufacturing Products X, Y, and Z, respectively. In recent weeks, the supply of Products A, B, and C has tightened to such an extent that the Final Division has been operating considerably below capacity because of the lack of these products. Consequently, the Intermediate Division has been told to sell all its products to the Final Division. The financial facts about these products are as follows.

Intermediate Division

	PRODUCT A	*PRODUCT B*	*PRODUCT C*
Transfer price	$10.00	$10.00	$15.00
Variable manufacturing cost	3.00	6.00	5.00
Contribution per unit	$ 7.00	$ 4.00	$10.00
Fixed costs (total)	$50,000	$100,000	$75,000

The Intermediate Division has a monthly capacity of 50,000 units. The processing constraints are such that capacity production can be obtained only by producing at least 10,000 units of each product. The remaining capacity can be used to produce 20,000 units of any combination of the three products. The Intermediate Division cannot exceed the capacity of 50,000 units.

Final Division

	PRODUCT X	*PRODUCT Y*	*PRODUCT Z*
Selling price	$28.00	$30.00	$30.00
Variable cost:			
Inside purchases	10.00	10.00	15.00
Other variable costs	5.00	5.00	8.00
Total variable cost	$15.00	$15.00	$23.00
Contribution per unit	$13.00	$15.00	$ 7.00
Fixed costs (total)	$100,000	$100,000	$200,000

The Final Division has sufficient capacity to produce about 40% more than it is now producing because the availability of Products A, B, and C is limiting production. Also, the Final Division can sell all the products that it can produce at the prices indicated above.

Required

1. If you were the manager of the Intermediate Division, what products would you sell to the Final Division? What is the amount of profit that you would earn on these sales?

2. If you were the manager of the Final Division, what products would you order from the Intermediate Division assuming that the Intermediate Division must sell all its production to you? What profits would you earn?

3. What production pattern optimizes total company profit? How does this affect the profits of the Intermediate Division? If you were the executive vice president of Chambers and prescribed this optimum pattern, what, if anything, would you do about the distribution of profits between the two divisions?

14.8   How, if at all, would your answers to Problem 14.7 change if there were no outside markets for Products A, B, or C?

14.9   The Chambers Company has determined that capacity can be increased in excess of 50,000 units, but these increases require an out-of-pocket cost penalty. These penalties are as follows.

VOLUME IN EXCESS OF PRESENT CAPACITY (UNIT)	COST PENALTY		
	Product A	*Product B*	*Product C*
1,000	$10,000	$12,000	$10,000
2,000	25,000	24,000	20,000
3,000	50,000	50,000	35,000
4,000	80,000	80,000	50,000

Each of these increases is independent. That is, increases in the production of Product A do not affect the costs of increasing the production of Product B. Changes can be made only in quantities of 100 units, with a maximum increase of 4000 units for each product. All other conditions are as stated in Problem 14.7.

Required

1. What would be the Intermediate Division's production pattern, assuming that it can charge all penalty costs to the Final Division?
2. The Final Division's optimum production pattern, assuming that it is required to accept the penalty costs?
3. The optimum Company production pattern?

14.10   How would your answer to Problem 14.9 differ if the Intermediate Division had no outside markets for Products A, B, and C?

CASES

CASE 14.1   **BIRCH PAPER COMPANY**

"If I were to price these boxes any lower than $480 a thousand," said James Brunner, manager of Birch Paper Company's Thompson division, "I'd be countermanding my order of last month for our salesmen to stop shaving their bids and to bid full cost quotations. I've been trying for weeks to improve the quality of our business, and if I turn around now and accept this job at $430 or $450 or something less than $480, I'll be tearing down this program I've been working so

This case was prepared by N. E. Harland. Copyright © by the President and Fellows of Harvard University. Harvard Business School case 9-158-001.

hard to build up. The division can't very well show a profit by putting in bids which don't even cover a fair share of overhead costs, let alone give us a profit."

Birch Paper Company was a medium-size, partly integrated paper company, producing white and kraft papers and paperboard. A portion of its paperboard output was converted into corrugated boxes by the Thompson division, which also printed and colored the outside surface of the boxes. Including Thompson, the company had four producing divisions and a timberland division, which supplied part of the company's pulp requirements.

For several years each division had been judged independently on the basis of its profit and return on investment. Top management had been working to gain effective results from a policy of decentralizing responsibility and authority for all decisions but those relating to overall company policy. The company's top officials believed that in the past few years the concept of decentralization had been successfully applied and that the company's profits and competitive position had definitely improved.

Early in 1971 the Northern division designed a special display box for one of its papers in conjunction with the Thompson division, which was equipped to make the box. Thompson's staff for package design and development spent several months perfecting the design, production methods, and materials that were to be used; because of the unusual color and shape, these were far from standard. According to an agreement between the two divisions, the Thompson division was reimbursed by the Northern division for the cost of its design and development work.

When the specifications were all prepared, the Northern division asked for bids on the box from the Thompson division and from two outside companies. Each division manager was normally free to buy from whatever supplier he wished; and even on sales within the company, divisions were expected to meet the going market price if they wanted the business.

In 1971 the profit margins of converters such as the Thompson division were being squeezed. Thompson, as did many other similar converters, bought its paperboard and its function was to print, cut, and shape it into boxes. Though it bought most of its materials from other Birch divisions, most of Thompson's sales were made to outside customers. If Thompson got the order from Northern, it probably would buy its linerboard and corrugating medium from the Southern division of Birch. The walls of a corrugated box consist of outside and inside sheets of linerboard sandwiching the fluted corrugating medium. About 70% of Thompson's out-of-pocket cost of $400 for the order represented the cost of linerboard and corrugating medium. Though Southern had been running below capacity and had excess inventory, it quoted the market price, which had not noticeably weakened as a result of the oversupply. Its out-of-pocket on both liner and corrugating medium were about 60% of the selling price.

The Northern division received bids on the boxes of $480 a thousand from the Thompson division, $430 a thousand from West Paper Company, and $432 a thousand from Eire Papers, Ltd. Eire Papers offered to buy from Birch the outside linerboard with the special printing already on it, but would supply its own inside liner and corrugating medium. The outside liner would be supplied by the Southern division at a price equivalent of $90 a thousand boxes, and would be printed for $30 a thousand by the Thompson division. Of the $30, about $25 would be out-of-pocket costs.

Since this situation appeared to be a little unusual, William Kenton, manager of the Northern division, discussed the wide discrepancy of bids with Birch's commercial vice president. He told the vice president, "We sell in a very competitive market, where higher costs cannot be passed on. How can we be expected to show a decent profit and return on investment if we have to buy our supplies at more than 10% over the going market?"

Knowing that Mr. Brunner had on occasion in the past few months been unable to operate the Thompson division at capacity, it seemed odd to the vice president that Mr. Brunner would add the full 20% overhead and profit charge to his out-of-pocket costs. When asked about this, Mr. Brunner's answer was the statement that appears at the beginning of the case. He went on to say that having done the developmental work on the box, and having received no profit on that, he felt entitled to a good markup on the production of the box itself.

The vice president explored further the cost structures of the various divisions. He remembered a comment that the controller had made at a meeting the week before to the effect that costs that for one division were variable, could be largely fixed for the company as a whole. He knew that in the absence of specific orders from top management, Mr. Kenton would accept the lowest bid, which was that of the West Paper Company for $430. However, it would be possible for top management to order the acceptance of another bid if the situation warranted such action. And though the volume represented by the transactions in question was less than 5% of the volume of any of the divisions involved, other transactions could conceivably raise similar problems later.

Required

1. As commercial vice president, how would you settle this dispute?

2. In what ways, if any, would you change Birch's transfer pricing rules?

CASE 14.2   GENERAL APPLIANCE CORPORATION

Organization

The General Appliance Corporation was an integrated manufacturer of all types of home appliances. As shown in Exhibit 1, the company had a decentralized, divisional organization consisting of four product divisions, four manufac-

This case was prepared by John Dearden. Copyright © by the President and Fellows of Harvard University. Harvard Business School case 9-160-003.

EXHIBIT 1 General Appliance Corporation

Organization Chart

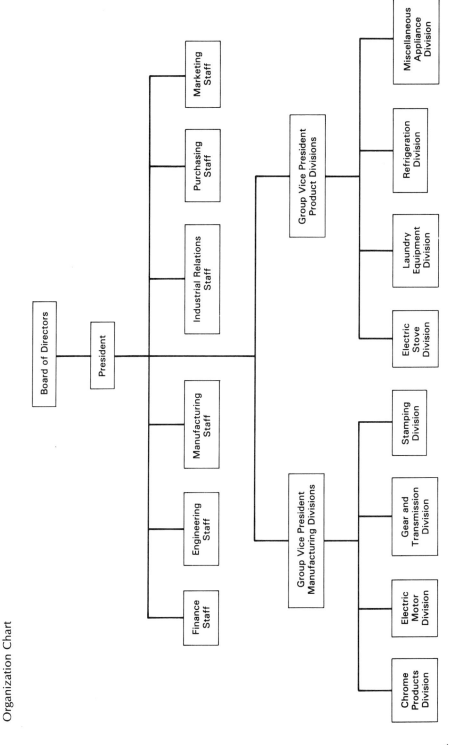

turing divisions, and six staff offices. Each division and staff office was headed by a vice president. The staff offices had functional authority over their counterparts in the divisions, but they had no direct line authority over the divisional general managers. The company organization manual stated: "All divisional personnel are responsible to the division manager. Except in functional areas specifically delegated, staff personnel have no line authority in a division."

The product divisions designed, engineered, assembled and sold various home appliances. They manufactured very few component parts, rather they assembled the applicances from parts purchased either from the manufacturing divisions or from outside vendors.

The manufacturing divisions made most of their sales (approximately 75%) to the product divisions. Parts made by the manufacturing division were generally designed by the product division; the manufacturing divisions merely produced the part to specifications provided to them. Although all of the manufacturing divisions had engineering departments, only about 20% of the total company engineering was done by the manufacturing divisions.

Transfer Prices

The divisions were expected to deal with one another as though they were independent companies. Parts were to be transferred at competitive prices arrived at by negotiations between the divisions. Competitive price levels were generally determined from actual prices paid to outside suppliers for the same or comparable parts. These outside prices were adjusted to reflect differences in the design of the outside part from that of the inside part. Also, if the outside price was based on purchases made at an earlier date, it was adjusted for changes in the general price level since that date.

In general, the divisions established prices by negotiations among themselves. If the divisions could not agree on a price, they could submit the dispute to the finance staff for arbitration.

Source Determination

Although the divisions were instructed to deal with each other as independent companies, in practice this was not always practicable, because the buying divisions did not have the power to decide whether to buy from within the company or whether to buy from an outside supplier. Once a manufacturing division began to produce a part, the only way the buying division could change to an outside supplier was to obtain permission of the manufacturing division, or in case of disagreement, appeal to the purchasing staff. The purchasing staff had the authority to settle disputes between the product and manufacturing divisions with respect to whether a manufacturing division should continue to produce a part or whether it should be manufactured by an outside supplier. In nearly every case of dispute, the purchasing staff had decided that the part would continue to be manufactured within the company. When the manufacturing divisions were instructed to keep producing a part, they had to continue to price the part at the level that the buying divisions could purchase the part from the outside vendor.

In the case of new parts, the buying division had the authority to decide on the source of supply. Even for new parts, however, a manufacturing division could appeal to the purchasing staff to reverse a decision of a product division to purchase a part from an outside vendor.

A. Stove Top Problem

The Chrome Products Division sold to the Electric Stove Division a chrome-plated unit that fitted on the top of the stove; the unit had to be resistant to corrosion and stain from spilled food. It was also essential that the unit remain bright and new-looking. The Chrome Products Division had been producing this unit since January 1, 1985; prior to that time it had been produced by an outside vendor.

The unit in question was produced from a steel stamping. Until June 1986, the stamping was processed as follows:

Operation 1	Machine buffing
Operation 2	Nickel plating
Operation 3	Machine buffing
Operation 4	Chrome plating
Operation 5	Machine buffing

About the middle of 1985, the president of General Appliance Corporation became concerned over customer and dealer complaints about the quality of the company's products. A consumer survey appeared to indicate quite definitely that in the previous year the company's reputation as a producer of quality products had deteriorated. Although this deterioration in reputation was caused principally by the poor performance of a new electric motor which was soon corrected, the president had come to the conclusion that the overall quality of the company's products had been decreasing for the past several years; furthermore, he believed that it was essential for the company to reestablish itself as a leader in the production of quality products. Accordingly, in early 1986, the president called in the vice president for manufacturing[1] and told him that for the next six months, his most important job was to bring the quality of all the products up to a satisfactory level.

In the course of carrying out this assignment, the manufacturing vice president decided that the appearance of the chrome-plated stove-top unit was unsatisfactory. Until now, the bases for rejection or acceptance of this part by the quality

---

[1]The vice president for manufacturing was the director of the manufacturing staff.

control section were a corrosion test and an appearance test; the latter was largely subjective and, in the final analysis, dependent upon the judgment of the quality control person. In order to make the test more objective, three units were selected by the manufacturing vice president and set up as criteria for the minimum acceptable quality. Because the selected items were considerably better than the average units, rejects increased to over 80%. In order to conform to the new quality standards, it was necessary to add copper plating and buffing operations at the beginning of the process and a hand-buffing operation at the end of the manufacturing cycle. These added operations were the result of a study made jointly by the divisional and plant personnel together with representatives from the manufacturing staff. The total cost of these operations was $.40 a unit. As soon as the new operations were put into effect in June 1986, the rejection rate for poor quality declined to less than 1%.

In July 1986, the Chrome Products Division proposed to increase the price of the stove-top unit by $.45; $.40 represented the cost of the added operations necessary for the improved quality and $.05 was the profit markup on the added costs. The current price, before the proposed increase, was $5 a unit. This was developed as follows:

Price charged for the part by the outside producer (12/31/85)	$4.50
Design changes since 12/31/85	.25
Changes in the prices of raw materials and labor since 12/31/85	.25
Price as of June 30, 1985	$5.00

The Electric Stove Division objected to the proposed price increase and, after three weeks of fruitless negotiations, it was decided that the dispute should be submitted to the finance staff for arbitration. The positions of the parties to the dispute are summarized below.

Chrome Products Division. In a letter to the vice president for finance, the general manager of the Chrome Products Division stated that he believed that he was entitled to the increased price because:

1. He had been required by the manufacturing staff to add operations to his manufacturing processing at a cost of $.40 a unit
2. These operations resulted in improved quality that could benefit only the Electric Stove Division
3. The present price of $5 was based on old quality standards. Had the outside supplier been required to meet these new standards, the price would have been $.45 higher.

Electric Stove Division. The general manager of the Electric Stove Division, in appealing the price increase, based his position on the following arguments.

1. There had been no change in engineering specifications. The only change that had taken place was a change in what was purported to be "acceptable appearance." This was a subjective matter which could not be measured with any degree of precision. Further, the manager objected not only to the particular case in point, but to the possible effects of establishing a precedent. He said, "If we were to pay for any change in quality standards, not accompanied by a change in engineering specification, we would be opening up a Pandora's box. Every division would request higher prices based on giving us better quality based on some subjective standard. Every request by this division to a manufacturing division to improve quality would be accompanied by a price increase, even though we were requesting only that the quality be brought up to competitive levels."

2. The Electric Stove Division did not request that quality be improved. In fact, the division was not even consulted on the change. The division should not be responsible, therefore, for paying for a so-called improvement that it neither reviewed nor approved.

3. The general manager doubted if there was any improvement in quality from the customers' viewpoint. He agreed that to the highly trained eye of the quality control personnel, there may have been an improvement. He believed, however, that the customer would not notice a significant difference between the appearance of the part before and after the change in quality standards.

4. Even if there were an improvement in quality that was perceptible to the consumer, the divisional general manager felt strongly that it was not worth 45¢. By adding 45¢ to the cost of the stove, he believed that he could add features that would be far more marketable than the quality improvement.

5. Any improvement in quality only brought the part up to the quality level that the former outside producer had provided. The cost of the improved quality, therefore, was already included in the $5 price.

Finance Staff Review. The finance staff reviewed the dispute. In the course of this review, the manufacturing engineering department of the manufacturing staff was requested to review the added operations and comment on the acceptability of the proposed cost increases. The quality control department of the manufacturing staff was asked to verify whether quality was actually better as a result of the added operations and whether the new units were of higher quality than the units purchased from the outside vendor 18 months ago. The manufacturing engineering department stated that the proposed costs were reasonable and represented efficient processing. The quality control department stated that the quality was improved and that the new parts were of superior quality to the parts previously purchased from outside sources.

B. Thermostatic Control Problem

One of the plants of the Electric Motor Division produced thermostatic control units. The Laundry Equipment Division bought all its requirements for thermostatic control units (about 100,000 per year) from the Electric Motor Division. The Refrigerator Division used a similar unit and until 1982, it had purchased all its requirements (20,000 per year) from the Monson Controls Corporation, an outside supplier. In 1983, at the request of the Electric Motor Division, the Refrigerator Division purchased 25% of its requirements from the Electric Motor Division. In 1984, this percentage was increased to 50%, and in 1985, to 75%. In July 1985 the Refrigeration Division informed the Monson Controls Corporation that beginning January 1, 1986, all the thermostat control units were to be manufactured by the Electric Motor Division. The Refrigerator Division made these source changes as a result of requests from the Electric Motor Division because it was "in the best interests of the company." The outside and inside units were comparable in quality, and the price paid to the Electric Motor Division was the same as the price paid to the Monson Controls Corporation. The Laundry Equipment Division paid this same price to the Electric Motor Division.

In 1982, the demand for this kind of thermostatic control unit was high in relation to the industry's production capacity. Between 1983 and 1986, several appliance companies (including the General Appliance Corporation) built or expanded their own facilities to produce this unit, so that by the middle of 1985 the production capacity of the independent companies considerably exceeded the demand. One of the results of this situation was a declining price level. Prices to the Monson Controls Corporation had been as follows.

1982	1983	1984	1985
$3.00	$2.70	$2.50	$2.40

As a result of these price reductions, the profits of the Electric Motor Division on this product had dropped from a before-tax profit of 15% on its investment in 1982 to nearly zero in 1985.

In August 1985, the Monson Controls Corporation reduced its price to the Refrigeration Division by $.25, retroactive to July 1. The price reduction was not reflected immediately in the intracompany price because the division had agreed to use $2.40 for the entire year.

In October 1985, the Electric Motor Division and the Refrigeration Division were negotiating 1986 prices. The Refrigeration Division proposed a price of $2.15, the price paid to the Monson Controls Corporation for the unit. The Electric Motor Division refused to reduce its prices below $2.40 to either the Refrigeration Division or the Laundry Equipment Division. After several weeks of negotiations, the disagreement was submitted to the finance staff for settlement.

Electric Motor Division. The Electric Motor Division based its refusal to accept the last price reduction of the Monson Controls Corporation on the premise that it was made as a last desperate effort to continue supplying General Appliance Corporation with this part. (Monson Controls Corporation continued to supply General Appliance Corporation with other products, although this control unit had been the major item.) As support for this premise, the Electric Motor Division pointed out the fact that at the lower price it would lose money. Since it was as efficient as the Monson Controls Corporation, the latter must also be losing money. The price was therefore a distress price and not a valid basis for determining an internal price. To support its case further, the Electric Motor Division pointed out the downward trend in the price of this part as evidence of distressed pricing practices growing out of the excess capacity in the industry.

The general manager of Electric Motor Division stated that it was going to take all his ability and ingenuity to make a profit at the $2.40 price. At $2.15, he could never be in a profit position; and if forced to accept a price of $2.15, he would immediately make plans to close the plant and let the outside suppliers produce all the thermostatic control units.

Laundry Equipment Division. The Laundry Equipment Division based its case for a $2.15 price on the intracompany pricing rules that required products to be transferred between divisions at competitive prices. The general manager also pointed out that his annual volume was 100,000 units a year, compared to a total of only 20,000 for the Refrigeration Division. He believed that his higher volume would allow him to obtain an even more favorable price if he were to procure his requirements from outside the corporation.

Refrigeration Division. The Refrigeration Division based its case on the fact that the division not only could, but did, buy the thermostatic control unit from a reliable outside supplier for $2.15. The division was sure that the Monson Controls Corporation had capacity to produce all its requirements and would be happy to do so for $2.15 a unit. Since patronage had been transferred to the Electric Motor Division only as a favor and to benefit the company as a whole, the Refrigeration Division believed it was unjust to make it pay a higher price than it would have paid if the division had never allowed the business to be taken inside the company.

As further evidence to support its case, the Refrigeration Division pointed to an agreement made with the Electric Motor Division at the time that the former agreed to purchase all its requirements of the termostatic control unit from the latter. This agreement read in part:

> In the event of a major pricing disparity, it is agreed that future model requirements will be competitively sourced [i.e., sourced to the lowest bidder].

The Refrigeration Division stated that, in the light of the major pricing disparity, it should be allowed to request quotations from outside suppliers and place the business outside should an outside supplier bid lower than the Electric Stove Division.

Finance Staff Review. In the course of arbitrating this transfer price dispute, the finance staff asked the purchasing staff to review the outside market situation for the thermostatic control unit. The purchasing staff replied that there was excess capacity and that, as a result of this, prices were very soft. Eventually the prices would rise; the rise could occur either when the demand for comparable units increased or when some of the suppliers went out of business. The purchasing staff had no doubt that the Refrigeration Division could purchase all their requirements for the next year or two for $2.15 per unit, or even less. The purchasing staff believed, however, that if all of the corporation's requirements for this unit were placed with outside suppliers, the price would rise to at least $2.40 because this action would dry up the excess capacity.

C. Transmission Problem

Since beginning production of automatic washers shortly after the end of World War II, the Laundry Equipment Division had purchased its transmissions from two sources, The Gear and Transmission Division and the Thorndike Machining Corporation. The transmission was developed and engineered by the Thorndike Machine Corporation. In consideration of an agreement to buy one-half its transmissions from the Thorndike Machining Corporation, the General Appliance Corporation had been licensed to produce the transmission. The agreement ran from 1976 to 1986, and at the expiration of the 10 years General Appliance would have the right to use the design without further restrictions.

In early 1984, nearly two years before the end of the agreement, the mangement of the General Appliance Corporation decided that it would not extend the agreement when it expired, but that it would expand the facilities of the Gear and Transmission Division so that all transmissions could be produced within the company.

Accordingly, in March 1984, the Thorndike Machining Corporation was notified that beginning January 1, 1986, the General Appliance Corporation would manufacture all its own transmissions and, consequently, the current agreement would not be renewed. This notification came as a surprise to the Thorndike Machining Corporation; furthermore, its implications were very unpleasant because the General Appliance Corporation took a major share of the output of an entire plant, and there was little likelihood that the lost business could be replaced. The Thorndike Machining Corporation consequently faced the prospect of an idle plant and a permanent reduction in the level of profits.

In April 1984, the president of the Thorndike Machining Corporation wrote to the president of the General Appliance Corporation, asking that the decision not to extend the current agreement be reconsidered. He submitted a proposed schedule of price reductions to be operative if the current agreement were extended. He stated that these reductions would be possible because (a) it would be better to obtain a lower price than abandon the special purpose machinery used for transmissions and (b) expected increases in productivity. These proposed reductions were as follows.

Present price	$14.00
Price effective 7/1/84	13.50
Price effective 1/1/85	13.00
Price effective 7/1/85	12.50
Price effective 1/1/86	12.00

The letter further stated that the corporation had developed a low-cost transmission that was suitable for economy washers; this transmission was designed to cost $2 less than the present models, and could be made available by January 1, 1986.

On receiving a copy of the letter, the general manager of the Laundry Equipment Division reopened the issue of continuing to buy from the Thorndike Maching Corporation. He had been interested in marketing a low-cost automatic washer, and the possiblity of a $10 transmission appealed to him. The general manager of the Gear and Transmission Division, however, was interested in expanding his production of transmissions and, to satisfy the Laundry Products Division, he offered to develop a unit that would be comparable in price and performance to the proposed Thorndike Machining Corporation's economy unit. The offer was included in a letter signed by the general manager of the Gear and Transmission Division, dated April 22, 1984. The general manager of the Laundry Equipment Division accepted this offer, and no further question was raised about continuing to buy from the Thorndike Machining Corporation.

During the next two months, the engineering departments of the Gear and Trnasmission and the Laundry Equipment Divisions jointly determined the exact performance features that were needed on the economy transmission; some of these features were different from the proposed Thorndike transmissions. In June 1984, the general manager of the Gear and Transmission Division wrote a letter to the general manager of the Laundry Equipment Division, outlining the engineering agreement and including the following price proposal.

Proposed selling price of Thorndike model		$10.00
Probable cost (assuming 10% profit)		9.00
Add:		
Cost of added design features	$.85	
Increased cost of material and labor since date of quotation	.75	1.60
Total cost		$10.60
Profit		1.06
Adjusted price of G. & T. unit		$11.66

The letter went on to say: "Because a price of $11.66 will not give us our objective profit, we propose to sell you this unit for $12. We believe that this is a fair and equitable price and decidedly to your benefit."

This letter was never acknowledged by the Laundry Equipment Division.

In October 1984, the Gear and Transmission Division submitted a project proposal to the Corporation Facilities Committee, requesting money to build facilities to produce the new economy transmission. The project proposal included a profit projection based on a $12 price. The Laundry Equipment Division was quoted in the project proposal as agreeing to the price. There was no objection to this statement from the personnel of the Laundry Equipment Division who were asked to comment on the proposed project. The project was approved, and the Gear and Transmission Division proceeded to buy and install the equipment to produce the new transmission.

In the latter part of 1985, the Gear and Transmission Division opened negotiations with the Laundry Equipment Division on the price of the new transmission, proposing a price of $12 plus some minor adjustments for changes in cost levels since the previous year. The Laundry and Equipment Division refused to accept the proposed price and countered with an offer of $11.21, developed as follows.

Proposed selling price of Thorndike model		$10.00
Adjustments:		
Cost of added design features	$ .85	
Cost of eliminated design features	(.50)	
Increased cost of material and labor since date of quotation	.75	
Net cost change	$1.10	
Profit on added cost	.11	
Total price increase		1.21
Proposed price		$11.21

The Gear and Transmission Division refused to even consider this proposal, and after several days of acrimonious debate, both divisions decided to submit the dispute to the finance staff for arbitration.

Laundry Equipment Division. The Laundry Equipment Division based its case on the following arguments.

1. The division could have purchased a transmission, comparable in performance characteristics to the Gear and Transmission Division's unit, from the Thorndike Machining Corporation for $11.21.
2. The Gear and Transmission Division had agreed to this price in consideration of being allowed to produce all of the transmissions.
3. The intracompany pricing policy was that the supplying divisions should sell at competitive prices.

The general manager of the Laundry Equipment Division stated that it would be unfair to penalize him for sourcing its transmission business inside the corporation as a benefit to the Gear and Transmission Division. In addition, the manager believed that this would be particularly unfair in the light of the promise made by the general manager of the Gear and Transmission Division.

The manager also stated that he did not protest the price proposal included in the May 1984 letter because he believed that it was too early at that time to open negotiations. His cost analysts had not evaluated the proposal, but he assumed that the Gear and Transmission Division was approximately correct in its evaluation of the cost differences from the Thorndike unit. The Laundry Equipment Division's position was that the difference of $.34 between the adjusted Thorndike price and the quoted Gear and Transmission price was not worth negotiating until nearer the production date. The Laundry Equipment Division had naturally assumed that the Gear and Transmission Division would live up to its agreement, and that the rquest for $12 was just a negotiating gimmick.

Gear and Transmission Division. The Gear and Transmission Division based its case on two arguments.

1. The $10 quotation of the Thorndike Machining Corporation was invalid because it represented a final desperate effort to keep a share of the transmission business. A price of this nature, it was contended, could not form a long-term intracompany pricing base. If the Thorndike Machining Corporation had received the business, it would have raised its price eventually.

2. The Laundry Equipment Division did not object to the Gear and Transmission Division's price proposal until after the facilities to build the transmission were already in place. The $12 price was used to authorize the project; if the Laundry Equipment Division wished to object, it should have done so when the project was presented to the facilities committee. Because facilities were purchased on the assumption of a $12 price, the Laundry Equipment Division should not be allowed to object after the money was spent.

Finance Staff Review. A review by the finance staff disclosed the following facts.

1. If the Thorndike Machining quotation of $10 were adjusted for the cost effect of changes in performance characteristics and the increase in general cost levels since the original quotation, the price would be $$11.25 or approximately the same as proposed by the Laundrey Equipment Division. The price of $11.66 developed by the Gear and Transmission Division was in error because it failed to allow for a design elimination that would reduce the cost of the Thorndike unit by $.50.

2. At $12 the Gear and Transmission Division could expect to earn an after-tax profit of 15% on its investment; this was equal to its profit objective. At the $11.25 price, the division would earn about 6% after taxes.

3. The purchasing staff belived that it would be able to buy the transmission from the Thorndike Machining Corporation at the quoted price level for the foreseeable future.

Required

1. As a member of the finance staff, how would you settle these intracompany disputes? How would you explain your decision to the general managers involved?

2. Should the company's intracompany price policy and its procedure for negotiating differences be changed?

CASE 14.3 WARREN CORPORATION

The Warren Corporation is a large conglomerate that is in many types of businesses. A significant portion of its business, however, is in electronics. In this area, the Warren Corporation is quite integrated. There are 15 profit centers in electronics and most of these profit centers deal with each other. More than 50% of the sales in some of these divisions are to internal units. As a consequence, it has been necessary to establish specific procedures to govern intracompany relationships. The Central Finance staff of the Warren Corporation has developed a manual that dictates company policy with respect to intracompany relationships and describes precisely how transfer prices are to be established under a variety of circumstances. This manual changes frequently when decisions of the Price Arbitration Committee make it evident that the manual is incomplete or that policy has been changed. In some respects, the process is like the codification of common law. The decisions of the Price Arbitration Committee are constantly being incorporated into the transfer pricing procedures in the same way that court decisions affect legal procedures.

The *Price Arbitration Committee* (called hereafter the PAC), as the name implies, is a committee that has been set up to arbitrate intracompany pricing disputes. It consists of three staff vice-presidents—finance, manufacturing, and purchasing. The secretary of this committee is the manager of the Price Analysis Department of the Finance staff. This department has the responsibility for providing staff service to the PAC.

This case presents three disputes that were submitted to the PAC by divisional managers of the Warren Corporation. In each instance, the relevant transfer pricing rules are stated. The problem is to decide how each of these disputes should be settled, keeping in mind that any settlement could establish a precedent for future intracompany relationships.

Product Development

The X Division produces a low-volume but high-grade series of electronic products. Its engineering group spent $300,000 developing a new type of unit to be attached to one of the major products. When the development was completed, a marketing survey showed that the number of units that was likely to be sold would not warrant the expenditure required for the tooling and facilities to produce the new unit. The total number of units likely to be sold by the X Division was only 2500 annually. Consequently, the project was shelved.

The Y Division sells an electronic product, with a much higher sales volume, that could use the new unit. Six months after the project was shelved, at a com-

---

This case was prepared by John Dearden. Copyright © by the President and Fellows of Harvard University. Harvard Business School case 9-171-073.

pany-wide meeting of certain research personnel, a research manager of the Y Division learned of this new unit and requested a copy of the blueprints. This was provided to him, since the company policy on research was that all divisions should cooperate and that there should be no secrecy among divisions.

Within the next nine months, Division Y decided to produce the new unit and proceeded to purchase the necessary tools and facilities. About three months later (a year and a half after the X Division had shelved the project) the general manager of the X Division heard that the Y Division was going to produce the unit that had been developed by his division. He immediately called in his controller and told him to send the Y Division a bill for $300,000. He was particularly interested in receiving payment because the X Division's profits were less than budget. Since the costs of development had all been written off in the previous year, the $300,000 would be a direct increase in profitability.

The Y Division refused to pay and the X Division brought the matter to the PAC. The Intracompany Pricing Manual said nothing about the transfer of research.

The X Division based its case on a statement in the manual that said: "In general, divisions will deal with each other in the same way that they deal with outside companies." The X Division's position was that, if it was independent, it could have sold the blueprint for at least $300,000 to an outside company. (Company rules forbade the sale of research findings to outside companies by divisions.)

The position of the Y Division was that the product was marginal. If they had had to pay $300,000 for the blueprints, they would not have gone ahead with the project.

Split Sourcing

The A Division buys a complex electronic component; 50% is purchased from an outside source and 50% is purchased from Division B. The outside source developed the component and licensed the B Division to produce it in consideration of a five-year contract to produce half of Warren's requirements. The contract with the outside source established an initial price, with provision for annual negotiations. These negotiations were to determine the amount that the price should be reduced as the manufacturing efficiency increased. The A Division requested detailed information from the B Division on the manufacturing processes in order to be able to negotiate with the outside source more effectively. If the engineers from the A Division knew precisely in what ways and the extent to which the B Division was increasing its efficiency, it could pinpoint precisely the amount of the price reduction that it should obtain. The B Division refused to provide this information and the A Division submitted the dispute to the PAC.

The Intracompany Pricing Manual stated that split-sourced products should be transferred within the company at the same price as the outside source. Nothing else was said about split-source pricing.

The B Division based its refusal on the statement that "Divisions deal with each other in the same way that they deal with outside companies." Under no conditions, it stated, would we provide our customers with details of our production processes. Furthermore, Division B pointed out that they were "cutting their own throats." The greater the price reduction that Division A negotiated, the lower would be the profits of Division B.

Division A based its case on company welfare. The company profits would be maximized by Division B cooperating with Division A.

Reserved Capacity

Division S is essentially a marketing division. It buys most of its products from Division M. The transfer price agreement is that products are sold at the standard variable cost per unit plus a monthly charge equal to the fixed costs and 10% of the investment assigned to the products produced for Division S. By agreement half the capacity of one plant (Plant M-1) is reserved for Division S. The other half of the capacity of the plant is used by Division M to produce products that it sells to outside customers. The facilities of the Plant M-1 are quite similar. Consequently, the plant can produce either Division S products or Division M products on its facilities.

During 1986, the demand for Division S products declined, while the demand for Division M products increased. As a result, about 75% of the capacity of Plant M-1 was used to produce products for Division M and only 25% was used for products of Division S. Division S objected to paying for 50% of the capacity of Plant M-1. The M Division refused to reduce the price and the case was submitted to the PAC.

The Intracompany Pricing Manual stated that products of the type produced by Division M for Division S should be priced at "the standard variable cost per unit plus a monthly charge equal to the fixed costs and 10% of the book value of the assets assigned to the capacity reserved for the products of the buying division."

The M Division stated that they were reserving 50% of the capacity of Plant M-1 for the S Division. The S Division, however, was not using this capacity this year. Because the demand was sufficiently strong for M Division products, the M Division could utilize this excess capacity. It would be foolish to leave it idle. If, however, the S Division had needed the capacity, the M Division would have been able and willing to provide it.

The S Division felt that it was unfair to pay Division M for capacity that the M Division was using. They were being paid for the capacity and yet utilizing it themselves. The S Division felt that it should pay just for the capacity that it was using, or, at a maximum, for the capacity it used plus any excess capacity up to a total of 50% of Plant M-1's capacity.

Required

How would you settle these disputes? In each case, how would you change the manual?

CASE 14.4   THE CHEETAH DIVISION

The Cheetah Division of the Multi-National Motors Corporation designs and sells Cheetah automobiles and parts to dealers throughout the United States and Europe. The division is responsible for designing, engineering, and marketing its products but the automobiles are manufactured by other divisions of the company and the Cheetah Divison buys its automobiles from the Assembly Division.

Each division of Multi-National Motors is responsible for earning a return on its investment. Investment in Multi-National is calculated as follows:

- Cash   10% of the cost of sales
- Receivables⎤
- Inventories⎦   Average end-of-the-month actual balances
- Fixed assets   Average actual gross book value at end of the month

Profits are the accounted profits, calculated in accordance with the company's accounting system. Because of its rlatively low asset base (few fixed assets) and its high profit potential, the Cheetah Automotive Division had a profit objective of 45% after taxes.

Inventory Control Problem

In addition to marketing autombiles, the Cheetah Division is responsible for supplying repair and replacement parts and accessories to its dealers throughout the country. This requires an extensive warehouse system since parts are supplied for automobiles up to 15 years old. The system handles over 20,000 different parts, with annual sales in excess of $25,000,000.

In 1983, the corporation established an operations research group, with responsibility for reviewing inventory control procedures throughout the company. In carrying out their assignment, members from the group visited the Cheetah Division.

An important inventory control problem was one involving buying current model parts at the end of a model year. At the end of each model year, any parts

This case was prepared by John Dearden. Copyright © by the President and Fellows of Harvard University. Harvard Business School case 9-113-068.

to be discontinued with the new model became past model service parts. A past model service part was usually much more expensive to produce than a current model part because of setup time and the short length of the run of the past model parts. For example, at the end of the 1986 model year, the front fenders were to be changed. During regular production, fenders are run continuously over an automated line. There is no setup cost and production is very efficient. Consequently, the manufacturing cost of a 1986 fender is low during the 1986 model year. Once the part has been discontinued, however, the costs of production can become quite high. It is necessary to pull the dies out of storage, clean them, place them in presses, try them out (usually involving spoiling a certain amount of material), and then run off the required number of parts without any automation. Thus the cost of a past model service part can be several times higher than it was as a current model part.

As a result of this cost differential, it is usual to order, at the end of a model year, a relatively large supply of those parts that are to be discontinued. A formula has been developed that provides the economic order quantity. This formula determines the point where the added cost of carying the inventory is equal to the cost savings from buying at current model prices. The formula is quite complex and need not be considered here. An important feature of the formula, however, is that the cost of carrying inventory includes a return on the capital tied up in the inventory. The operations research group reviewed the formula and agreed that it was a reasonable method for calculating the economic order quantity. The group, however, were surprised to find that the Cheetah Division used 45% as the cost of money tied up in the inventory. Other divisions used between 5% and 10% in their inventory decision formulas and, currently, the corporation had over one hundred million dollars invested in government securities that were earning about 6% before taxes (3% after taxes).

The operations research group raised two questions concerning the economic order quantity formula:

1. They questioned whether 45% was not much too high a percentage for the capital charge of carrying inventories. Their estimate was that it would be no more than 10%.
2. They questioned the fact that the Cheetah Division used their purchase price to calculate the investment in the inventory. The company's out-of-pocket cost of most parts was between 50% and 60% of the purchase price.

The controller of the Cheetah Division met with the operations research group and told them bluntly that he had no intention of changing the formula. This formula, including charging 45% on his purchase price for carrying inventory, was the one that optimized his rate of return. If he followed their suggestions, he would be lowering the rate of return that his division earned. He stated that, if it was really to the benefit of the company for him to use a 10% cost of investment on 60% of his purchase price, he would be glad to comply, if he (the Cheetah Division) were given the benefit of the increased profit that the company would earn. Otherwise, he would continue to do as he was instructed and that was to maximize the division's return on investment.

The Parts Warehouse Problem

In 1985 the Cheetah Division was in the process of building two new parts warehouses on the West Coast. At that time, the Sparrow Division of Multi-National requested that Cheetah provide some space in those warehouses for Sparrow parts. Sparrow was a much smaller division than Cheetah and could not justify economically a new warehouse. The location on the West Coast, however, of two new supply points would improve the effectiveness of Sparrow's distribution system. Sparrow asked for space equal to about 10% of the total.

After the warehouses had been completed and both the Cheetah and Sparrow parts systems were placed in operation, the question of charging for the service came up. Cheetah proposed that Sparrow pay a proportionate share of the cost of running the warehouse plus a return on their proportionate share of the investment. The calculation was made as follows:

10% of cost of operating warehouses	$ 20,000
10% of the investment in warehouses: $200,000[2]	
90% of $200,000	180,000
Total annual charges	$200,000

The Sparrow Division was astounded with the charge. It was several times higher than the highest price for available leased warehouse space. They agreed with the $20,000 but disagreed violently with paying $180,000 for the return on investment. The Cheetah Division pointed out that they had invested $200,000 at the request of Sparrow and that they had to earn $180,000 before taxes on this investment in order to earn 45% after taxes. The Sparrow Division said that they could lease space anywhere on the West Coast for a fraction of Cheetah's charge and that was what they proposed to do. They stated that Cheetah may have a 45% return but Sparrow as lucky to break even *without the exorbitant rental.*

Required

If you were an outside consultant:

1. How would you settle each of these disputes, assuming that the Company would not consider discontinuing its ROI system?

2. What changes in the system would you recommend within an ROI system?

---

[2]Total cost of the warehouse was $2,000,000.

3. What changes would you recommend assuming that the Company was *not* committed to ROI?

CASE 14.5   THE PARTS MANUFACTURING DIVISION

The Parts Manufacturing Division is a division of the General Appliance Corporation. This Division produces metal parts for all types of appliances for both outside manufactuers and other divisions of General Appliance. Its sales are in excess of 125 million annually. The Parts Manufacturing Division is a profit center and the general manager, Mr. Robert Sampson, is responsible for earning a satisfactory return on his investment.

Investment Base

The investment base of the divisions of the General Appliance Corporation are calculated as follows.

- Cash: 8% of sales[1]
- Receivables ⎫   Average end-of-the-month
- Inventories ⎭   actual balances
- Fixed assets: Average end-of-the-month gross book value

The Profit Improvement Conference

Early in 1986, Robert Sampson, the general manager of the Parts Manufacturing Division, was conferring with Daniel Streeter, the controller of the Division. The purpose of the conference was to see what could be done to raise the return on investment. The Division had had several setbacks in 1985. As a result, volume, and consequently profits, were relatively low. One of the possible actions that was discussed was the reduction of the investment base. Following are excerpts from the discussion.

SAMPSON: The equipment in Mill Number 2 is not working at even 50% of capacity. Why don't we scrap it? What is its book value and how would our profits be affected if it were scrapped?

STREETER: Let's see. Our present outlook is to earn about $400,000 on a $10,000,000 investment, or 4% on investment. The equipment in Mill 2 has a gross book value of $750,000 and a net book value of about $350,000. If we

---

This case was prepared by John Dearden. Copyright © by the President and Fellows of Harvard University. Harvard Business School case 9-171-510.

[1]The General Appliance Corporation controls cash centrally. Eight percent of sales is the amount of cash that it is estimated a division would require if it were independent.

closed down Mill 2, our position would look as follows. (Here Streeter handed Sampson a sheet of paper with the figures shown in Exhibit 1.)

SAMPSON: If I read this correctly, we will increase our rate of return from 4% to 5.2% by closing Mill 2 and getting rid of the equipment. What can we sell this equipment for and won't we show a loss if we cannot sell it for its net book value of $350,000?

STREETER: Actually it's mostly special purpose equipment and we will have to sell it for its salvage value. I estimate that the dismantling costs will about equal the salvage value so we will end up with little or nothing from its sale.

Fortunately, we use composite depreciation, so that we do not show a gain or loss when we scrap a fixed asset. The assumption under composite depreciation is that the physical life of any group of assets will be equal to its depreciable life *on the average*. Some equipment will be scrapped sooner than its depreciable life, while other equipment will last longer. As long as the average physical life is equal to the depreciable life, the depreciation will reflect the true reduction in asset values over time. Therefore, under this system, we assume that an asset is always fully depreciated when it is scrapped or sold, so we do not take a gain or loss at the time of disposition.

SAMPSON: But if we keep scrapping equipment, won't our depreciation rates rise?

EXHIBIT 1

Estimated Effect of Closing Mill 2 (figures based on 1986 expectations)

Loss of revenue	$1,000,000
Savings in costs:	
Material, labor, supplies and utilities	800,000
Indirect labor and maintenance	200,000
Depreciation	75,000
Total savings	$1,075,000
Net Increase in profit	$ 75,000
Savings in investment:	
Fixed assets	$ 750,000
Cash (8% of $1,000,000)	80,000
Total savings in investment	$ 830,000

Effect on Expected Rate of Return

	WITH MILL 2	WITHOUT MILL 2
Profits	$ 400,000	$ 475,000
Investment	$10,000,000	$9,170,000
Rate of return	4%	5.2%

STREETER: If most of the divisions in the company continually scrap assets sooner than their average depreciable life, we will eventually have to decrease the estimated average life and this will increase our depreciation rates. Our depreciation rates, however, are company-wide and this is a big company. The effect of scrapping the equipment in Mill Number 2 will have no effect on company-wide rates and, consequently, no effect on our future depreciation costs.

SAMPSON: That's fine, Dan. I'll go ahead and arrange to dispose of the equipment that we have in Mill 2.

Required

1. Is Streeter's analysis correct? Under a composite accounting system, is it true that no loss would be shown when the equipment in Mill Number 2 is scrapped? Does this make sense from an accounting viewpoint?

2. Is Sampson's action in the best interests of the Company? If it is not, why not? How can the system be changed to make the goals of the Division congruent with the goals of the Company?

3. Assume that management would not change the accounting measurement system in any way. What action would you recommend?

CASE 14.6   UNIVERSAL NATIONAL COMPANY

The Universal National Company was a large aircraft and missile manufacturer with a concentration of plants on the West Coast and a number of divisions in other parts of the country as well as overseas. (The basic organization of the company is indicated by the simplified organization chart, included as Exhibit 1.) Its Aircraft Division, the unit from which the company had developed, was located on the West Coast. In 1955, it was awarded a contract for the production and delivery of 100 Sky Haul Troop carriers. The contract was placed on a cost plus incentive fee basis, which means that there was a negotiated target price with an incentive formula under which Universal and the government would share 50/50 any saving below this target. This was the largest award that the Aircraft Division had received in some time, because procurement of military aircraft had been declining with increasing emphasis on missiles. The Aircraft Division in the two previous years had been just breaking even. Management expected that the award of the Sky Haul contract would restore the division to its position as one of the major profit contributors in the company.

In fact, the company's executive vice president, Joseph Sullivan, was deter-

This case was prepared by R. N. Anthony. Copyright © by the President and Fellows of Harvard University. Harvard Business School case 0-113-032.

EXHIBIT 1   Universal National Company

Partial Organization Chart

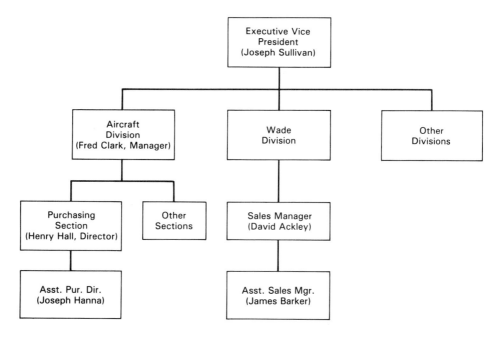

mined that the Aircraft Division would achieve its former profit position, and to this end he called in major mangement personnel from the division and lectured them in rather blunt terms about the need for a dramatic profit improvement. He told them that if they did not do it with the Sky Haul contract, they would never do it.

Fred Clark, the Aircraft Division manager, had recently developed a Profit Improvement Program (PIP). The idea behind it was to get people excited over profits; to get them to concentrate on profit improvement. The initials PIP were written over the walls in the plants and corridors. Each department was given a PIP mandate in terms of cost reduction goals; seminars were held throughout the division; and special PIP announcements were made over the plant loudspeakers.

Henry Hall, divisional director of purchasing, made a comprehensive analysis of the material requirements for the Sky Haul contract. He recognized that, along with several other items, the automatic direction finder was extremely critical to the success of the program. Whereas the Sky Haul contract was let as a straight production contract, the model actually was an advanced one, calling for a number of basic improvements. In particular, the automatic direction finder had to meet requirements that, while within the state of the art, called for considerable improvement over previous production.

Hall determined that there were three logical sources for this radio direction finder: the Bolster Company located in New York; the Acme Radio Electronics Company of Chicago; and the Wade Division of Universal National located in the Midwest. On the basis of previous experience, hall thought that the Bolster Company would probably be the best source. However, he was fairly sure that all three sources would be able to pass the facility survey. He was willing to make the award to whichever company made the best cost proposal, although he did not want the Wade Division to obtain the order.

Hall discussed the problem with Joseph Hanna, his assistant. Hanna felt that the Wade Division looked upon the Aircraft Division as a captive customer. On past jobs it had shown an unwillingness to respond quickly to changes, to keep the Aircraft Division informed of progress, and objectively to evaluate and adopt suggestions. There were times when the Wade Division sales manager, David Ackley, did not even return a critical call for several days. Hall agreed with this opinion. In fact, he wondered if Wade really could be considered a qualified supplier. Two years previously when he was head of quality control, the Aircraft Division had found unsatisfactory a radio transmitter that Wade had produced. Other sources that previously had produced similar radio transmitters had had serious difficulty also, but as Hall said: "The difference was that they did something about it. They didn't sit on their duff or submit long, cumbersome memos blaming everything on the Aircraft Division's specifications and inspection practices."

Hall thought that Wade really did not belong in the electronic business. It had been a small radio manufactuer that branched into electronics in a big way in World War II. Since the middle '40s it had gained an increasingly large part of the market for electronics equipment for commercial aircraft. Hall believed that its chief trouble was that it was trying to cut cost and did not worry enough about quality. Hall said:

> The automatic direction finder should cost somewhere around $150,000, but I am sure Wade, with its five and dime tactics, will bid considerably below that.

Hanna said:

> If you let them bid, we're sunk. They'll come in with a low price and nobody will be able to get them out of here, but their people will never go out of their way to be helpful to us. We'll have to beg for the equipment. Also, it's nothing for them to make a change without even telling us about it. I have to admit some of the changes they have made in past products were pretty ingenious with regard to getting the cost down, but they raised havoc with the rest of the job. No interface at all.

Hall and Hanna spent a few hours reviewing their experience with the only prior order that they had placed with Wade for automatic direction finders. They concluded that there was no doubt about it—Wade's prices were low, but the rejection rate was high and the delivery rate was only fair. They admitted that there had been a number of specification changes on that job and that their own incoming inspection department had been going through a major crisis at that time. Thus, it might be unfair to blame Wade, but both Hall and Hanna still were convinced Wade was wrong for the direction finder job.

Also, they vividly remembered some of the clashes they had had with Mr. Ackley. Ackley refused to respond to urgent calls and refused to incorporate changes immediately. At one point he had refused to take back sets that had to be repaired because of damage during transit. He wanted a memo listing the exact nature of the damage, and a written admission that the Aircraft Division was responsible for filing any necessary claims.

Hall gave much thought to the Wade problem and finally decided that if Wade had not been a division of Universal National he would not consider it for the bid list. He mentioned the problems briefly to Clark, the division manager, who said:

> Henry, if there is any way you can get rid of Wade, get rid of them. It's more difficult to do business inside than it is outside. They are a bunch of prima donnas; but just one thing, Henry, they are always running in to see Sullivan, so make sure you're right.

A month later the Aircraft Division released the request for bids to the two outside vendors. Both had been qualified previously on the basis of investigations including plant survey.

Hall was not surprised that when the bids came in Bolster was low, but he was surprised that the bids ranged from $185,000 each to $220,000. As a result of fairly intensive negotiations with Bolster, Hall was able to negotiate the price down to $180,000 each. A patent problem proved to be more knotty than expected, and all in all it took a month to negotiate the proposed subcontract with Bolster.

Hall had just sent the subcontract to the company's contracting officer for the latter's approval in accordance with the terms of the prime contract, with a request for urgent action because of contract lead time, when he received a call from Clark, the division manager, who said:

> Henry, I just came out of Sullivan's office. Sullivan is hopping mad and I am too. I thought I told you to see that Wade was taken care of on this finder. Ackley and some other clowns were there. They really burned us.

In summary, this is what the Wade people had told Sullivan during a two-hour meeting. They were not even asked to bid on the automatic direction finder, even though in the previous year the division had put something like $1 million of independent research and development money into this product area. They said that troup carriers were going to be one of the biggest markets for the future. They claimed that they had now matched their reputation for low cost with technical proficiency and they were now the leader in the field. They said that they needed this job to start exploiting the independent research and development money the company had spent. They also said they badly needed it to absorb fixed overhead until the radio receiver market recovered—probably the follow-ing year. They claimed also that their reputation in the market place had suffered a staggering blow. Bolster was going all over the industry telling Wade's cus-tomers that Universal National would not even deal with Wade and that on the Sky Haul contract they were not even asked to bid. In fact, Ackley said he did not even know about this procurement until one of his customers asked him if there was any truth to the story that Wade was going out of the finder business. Sullivan was particularly incensed about what he called the waste of independent research and development money and the unabsorbed overhead. "Henry," Clark continued, "I want to talk to you later about how you made this mistake, but right now do one thing first—get a bid quotation from Wade."

Hall tried to remind Clark about their previous conversation. He wanted to give Clark reasons why he felt it was the wrong thing to go to Wade. He also wanted to tell Clark that it was too late. Although the subcontract with Bolster had not yet been executed, it had been written in final form and submitted to the contracting officer.

Hall called Bolster Company and told it that it would have to hold up on the direction finder order. He then put a call through to Sullivan's office for Ackley, whom he thought was there, but was unable to get through to Ackley. He left a message for Ackley to stop by. Not having heard from Ackley in two hours, he called Sullivan's office again and was told that Ackley had just left for Wade. He called Wade and talked to Ackley's assistant, James Barker. He explained the situation and said that the important thing was for Wade to get its estimate in right away. Barker pointed out that he needed the prints before he could make an estimate. He said it might take two or three weeks to evaluate the prints and to price the job. Hall replied, "That's not good enough. You make sure Ackley calls me as soon as his plane gets in." Hall then sent an expediter by plane to Wade with the prints.

Hall called again the next day, but he could not reach Ackley, nor could he reach Barker. However, the secretary to both men said that Ackley had left a message for him as follows:

> Would you please touch base with Wade's regional representative on the West Coast.

This man would receive a commission for the sale and Ackley thought he should earn it. Ackley said they wanted Hall to make sure the company got its money's worth from this sales representative.

About this time, Hall received a call from David Ford, the sales manager of the Bolster Company. Ford wanted to know what to do with the $250,000 in anticipatory costs they had spent in order to meet the short delivery dates on the order. There ensured a long argument between the two men about who was responsible for incurring this expense. Ford said that all he wanted was the $50,000 the company had incurred in trying to help Hall—money that was spent with Hall's full knowledge and agreement.

At this point, Hall had a recurrence of an old ulcer attack and was hospitalized for a week. He had to stay in bed at home for an additional week. When he returned to his office he found that the quote had been received from Wade Division. The price was 250,000, the quoted delivery was four weeks behind that required. And, if this were not enough, Wade had conditioned its bid on a number of waivers being made in the specification.

Hall went into Clark's office with the quotes from Wade. At this point Clark decided that he should take over the problem until it was finally resolved and a subcontractor was selected and a final price determined. He called Ackley and told him that if Wade received the order, he wanted to send a team of Aircraft Division personnel to the Wade plant to help expedite the order in order to meet the prime contractor's delivery requirements. Included in this team would be men from the Aircraft Division's engineering, production, purchasing, quality control, and inspection departments. Their assignment would be to help iron out problems on the spot with Wade personnel.

Ackley's reply to Clark was:

> These panic visits never solve anything. They create more problems than they resolve. There is only one way of doing business and that is in an orderly fashion. As far as I am concerned, I am going to do business the right way. That means that we will perform in accordance with our quotation. If you want to make a change, you should issue a change order in accordance with the changes clause and I will process it like any other change and submit my quotation for an increase in price and delivery time as equitable under the circumstances. The one thing I do not want is a lot of oral communications that no one will remember later on. That's the trouble with doing business inside. People depart from proven business practices and the whole deal gets fouled up.

One week later, Clark got Ackley to agree on a new set of specifications and a compromise delivery date. Ackley also agreed to drop his price $532 to reflect the deletion of a fastener from the equipment.

About this time Clark got a call from the resident Air Force contracting officer wanting to know why his purchasing agent was considering a subcontract with Wade at $250,000, when he could get it from Bolster for $180,000.

Clark believed that he had negotiated as hard as he could to get the Wade Division to reduce its price. He felt that 249,468 was its rock bottom offer, and he believed that this represented an out-of-pocket expense to Wade of about $150,000 per unit for each of the 100 units he was ordering. He wanted to keep peace in the organization. He knew that Sullivan had his eyes on the Aircraft Division's profit figure for this contract. He also knew that he was in trouble for not calling in Wade earlier and that if he did not give it the order, Ackley would take the dispute back to Sullivan. He wondered whether he should present all the facts to Sullivan or let Wade have the contract and absorb part of the difference in his own profit and loss statement or let the Bolster Company go ahead with the order and just wait to see what happened. He wondered, further, what the decision and the consequences for him personally would be if he took the dispute to Sullivan.

Required

1. Is there a problem at Universal? If so, what is it? What caused it?

2. What courses of action could Sullivan take to resolve the general problem (as contrasted to the specific problem described in the case)? What are the advantages and disadvantages of each course of action open to Sullivan?

3. Which of the alternative courses of action would you recommend that Universal adopt?

chapter 15

MEASUREMENT OF PERFORMANCE

This chapter describes methods that are used in measuring the financial performance of profit center managers and profit centers.

MANAGERS VERSUS ORGANIZATIONS

Many companies do not distinguish explicitly between measuring a profit center manager and measuring the organizational unit being managed. This is a questionable practice, as different methods should be used for measuring each. Consider the following:

1. The financial performance of a profit center must be measured in absolute terms, whereas a profit center manager can only be measured against an objective, or in relative terms. Ideally, this objective is the profit potential of the profit center during the period being measured.
2. The extent to which an item of revenue or expense is controllable is irrelevant in measuring the financial performance of a profit center. Controllability, however, is very relevant to judging a manager's performance. For example, the impact of foreign currency fluctuations on profits may be important in judging the profitability of a foreign subsidiary. It is usually entirely irrelevant in judging the performance of the manager of that subsidiary.

3. The methods used to measure managers will affect their future actions. Managers try to optimize the criteria against which they are measured. Whereas the criteria used to measure the financial performance of a profit center will not influence managers as long as they are not used to measure them. For example, if managers are measured on return on investment, they will act to optimize this ratio. This could result in the dysfunctional consequences described in the next part of this chapter. If return on investment is used to measure the profit center but not the manager, there would be no reason to optimize this measure.

4. In general, profit center performance needs to be measured no more frequently than once a year. Managerial performance is measured monthly or at least quarterly.

Because of the differences between these two measurement systems, each is discussed separately in this chapter.

MEASURING MANAGERS

Types of Profit Measurement

In this part of the chapter, the three types of profit measures most commonly used are considered: *return on investment* (ROI), *residual income* (RI), and *actual profits compared to budget.* Many companies use both ROI and profits compared to budget. Some companies use all three measures. Where more than one measure is used, one is considered more important than the other, and this is the one that tends to be optimized by managers. Where incentive compensation is based on a particular measure, this almost invariably is the one optimized. One measure will almost always predominate where there is a conflict between different measures.[1] Companies that say that they use more than one measure of profitability probably do not. Thus two companies having indentical accounting measurement systems could have different effective measurement systems.

(ROI).   ROI is a ratio; the numerator is profits and the denominator is investment. The calculation of profits differs among companies. Three common variations are as follows: Profits may be before taxes and headquarters allocation, before taxes but after headquarters allocation, or after taxes and headquarters allocation. The investment may be total assets, with the fixed assets included at gross book value, total assets with fixed assets at net book value, or total assets minus the current liabilities, again to name three common variations. There are also a number of less commonly used variations. Thus return on investment for one business segment can be compared to another only when the profits and investments are calculated consistently and, as described next, not always then.

---

[1]An exception to this generalization occurs when multiple measures are so complex that the manager is unable to decide which measure is the most important.

ADVANTAGES OF ROI.   Return on investment has two principal advantages. First, it is the only measure that provides a direct comparison of the financial performance of dissimilar businesses or types of investment. It is a universal measure of financial effectiveness. Second, it is a measure so comprehensive that it is affected by changes in any item on either the balance sheet or the income statement. ROI includes both operating performance and investment performance in a single measure.

These are clearly powerful advantages, which undoubtedly account for its widespread use in the United Sates. The use of ROI as a measure of managerial performance can, however, have serious undesirable side effects. These occur because there are situations in which the optimization of divisional ROI may require managers to take actions that are contrary to the overall interests of the company. Some of these situations are described in the next part of this chapter.

DISADVANTAGES OF ROI.   The first, and perhaps the most serious undesirable, side effect of using ROI is that it can discourage managers of divisions with high rates of return from making new investments. If a company's hurdle rate is 15%, for example, and the current divisional ROI objective is 30%, investments above the hurdle rate but below 30% would reduce the divisional ROI. For the same reason, divisions with low rates of return can improve their ROI by investing at a rate that is less than the company's hurdle rate.

Second, under most ROI measures, new investments that will eventually yield satisfactory returns earn a low return at the outset. This occurs because new assets are initially included in the investment base at cost (gross book value). Thus an investment that may have an average return of 20%, for example, would have a much lower return in the early years. This might discourage investment by divisional managers who expect to be transferred in a relatively short period of time.[2] Another manifestation of this situation is that ROI will increase simply by the passage of time as the fixed assets become older and, consequently, more depreciated.

Third, although the concept of return on investment is widely understood, the return on investment as calculated by the divisional measurement system is not. Few managers understand the extent to which the return as calculated for divisional measurement can differ from the true return that, for example, is calculated for bonds or stock yields. Much of the investment in marketing divisions is not capitalized; therefore, the accounting investment as reflected on the balance sheet may be minimum and the indicated rate of return very high. In fact, an investment in product development, new markets, or an expanded dealer organization is just as much an investment as one in brick and mortar. Only the latter is capitalized, however, This situation leads to erroneous conclusions on

---

[2] This problem also exists in other contexts, for example, investment in research and development. The use of ROI can exacerbate this problem.

the part of management with respect to divisional profitability. Even within the same company, where divisions have the same accounting system and the same ROI measurement system, results may be inconsistent because of capitalization policies. For example, a marketing division may have a different ROI from a manufacturing division, even when the true return is identical.

There are other problems with some ROI systems. For example, in some cases, perfectly good assets can be scrapped without penalty and thus reduce divisional investment.

The bottom line is that maximizing divisional ROI will not insure maximization of company financial performance. Company financial performance is maximized when divisional managers maximize the long-run cash flow from the resources at their disposal and invest in new resources when, and only when, the additional investment will earn a true financial rate of return higher than the company's cost of capital.

The problems just described can to some degree be avoided (or at least mitigated) by administrative actions. This, of course, is the reason that companies are able to use ROI with some degree of effectiveness. However, why set up a measurement system that requires administrative action to prevent undesirable side effects? Why not measure managers on their effectiveness in accomplishing the things that maximize the company's financial performance?

Two surveys indicated that a large proportion of decentralized companies in the United States used ROI to measure divisional managers.[3] However, in many companies that measure divisional ROI, some other measure, principally profit compared to budget, is the measure used by senior management to evaluate managerial performance. Consequently, surveys similar to the two cited tend to exaggerate the use of ROI. There is no question, however, that a number of large companies do use ROI as the principal measure of divisional performance.

RI.   RI uses the same profit and investment as ROI except that, instead of dividing the profits by the investment, the profits are reduced by a quotient calculated by multiplying the investment by an interest-type charge. For example, suppose a division had a budgeted ROI of 20% calculated by dividing a budgeted profit of $2 million by a budgeted investment of $10 million. Assume also that the company's hurdle rate is 10%. Instead of measuring divisional managers against a 20% ROI, they are measured against a residual income calculated as follows. The general equation is:

Residual income = budgeted profits − [(investment)(interest charge)]

---

[3]Richard F. Vancil, *Decentralization: Management Ambiguity by Design,* Dow Jones-Irwin, 1979. James S. Reece and William R. Cool, "Measuring Investment Center Performance," *Harvard Business Review,* May–June 1978.

In the specific situation just described, the equation is:

$$\text{Budgeted RI} = 2 - (10 \times 0.1) = \$1 \text{ million}$$

Suppose that actual profits turned out to be $1.9 million and actual investment was $11 million. On a rate of return basis, the divisional ROI would be 17%, or 3 percentage points less than the objective. The RI evaluation would be:

$$\text{Actual RI} = 1.9 - (11 \times 0.10) = 1.9 - 1.1 = 0.8$$

Actual profit performance, therefore, was $200,000 less than budget.

RI corrects the most serious problem of ROI because the RI charge can be made equal to the company's hurdle rate. Thus divisional investment objectives can be made consistent with the company's cost of capital. No matter how high the rate of return a division is curently earning, the residual income can be improved by investing in any project that earns more than the company's cost of capital. All managers, therefore, are motivated to take advantage of any investment that exceeds this rate.

There are, however, at least two problems with RI. First, the problem of new investment in fixed assets still exists. Although the return on an investment may exceed the hurdle rate over its life, it may not do so in the first few years. Thus a desirable investment may reduce RI initially. Also, RI will increase over time as the fixed assets are simply allowed to get older. The basic problem is that there is no satisfactory way to include fixed assets in the investment base. In the typical division, fixed assets have been acquired over a period of time by a number of managers. Their book value is a meaningless figure for judging future performance. Regardless of book value, the manager should use them in such a way as to obtain the maximum cash flow.

Second, the residual income calculation requires a profit and investment calculation. There is an almost universal tendency also to calculate ROI. All that is required is a transposition of the figures. Since ROI appears to be a much easier concept to understand, managers then tend to make judgments based on the ROI and more or less ignore the RI.

Actual Profits Compared to Budget. Just about all decentralized companies throughout the world have profit budget systems for planning and control. As described in earlier chapters, profit budgets are required for resource allocation, coordination, and control. Results are monitored through a system of reporting that provides managers at all levels with analyses of variances, explanation of causes of variances, and descriptions of actions being taken to correct problems when the analyses show such problems exist.

Clearly, a system of profit budgeting with subsequent reports is a much more effective method of planning and control than simply comparing the actual ROI or RI result with some objective. Since all United States decentralized companies use profit budgets and a large proportion of them use ROI,[4] how do these two measures interrelate? The next part of this chapter describes the common interrelationships of the two measures of performance.

RELATION OF PROFIT BUDGETS AND ROI. At one extreme, return on invest-ment is calculated as part of the budget review process, but subsequent reporting is based on actual profits against budgeted profits. In this instance, the return on investment might be a factor in budget approval but its effect on the perform-ance measurement system is minimal. Many companies that reported using ROI in the surveys previously cited seem to be in this category. (No systematic empiri-cal evidence has been collected to support this opinion.)

In some companies, the return on investment is used to evaluate divisional strategic plans. That is, profit improvements are expressed as a return on invest-ment. In this case, divisional managers will base their plans on improving the rate of return, and actions described earlier in this note may be likely. For example, divisional managers will be reluctant to plan investments that do not raise their rates of return; consequently, this could encourage low growth rates in the most profitable divisions.

In addition to using rate of return as a criterion for profit improvement in strategic plans, some companies also measure current performance on the basis of ROI. For example, budgeted profits are expressed as a rate of return instead of a dollar amount of profits. Subsequently, performance reports are analyzed in terms of ROI. Thus managers could meet their ROI objectives by a combination of profit and investment performance. For example, if profits fall below bud-geted levels, ROI may be increased by reducing the investment base, and some of these actions may be undesirable. If profits are less than budget, a manager might be able to postpone planned investments in fixed assets. If the investments were desirable before the actual profits dropped below plan, it is usually unlikely that the situation would change. Short-term fluctuations in profits are not likely to affect long-run investment decisions.

Actual profits should be measured against budget, without any reference to ROI or RI. In addition, there should be an interest charge (similar to an RI charge) for controllable working capital. Receivables, inventories, and payables are often controlled by the divisional manager. There are trade-offs between the amount of working capital and profits, and these trade-offs are only known to divisional managers and, in fact, will change during any period of time. Invento-ries may be increased to increase profits through additional sales; or, credit terms may be liberalized to increase sales. These are current operating decisions and usually only the divisional manager has the information to make them. Con-sequently, these decisions should be delegated to divisional managers, and it is only by making them responsible for the level of working capital that the effec-

---

[4]Since relatively few companies use RI, discussion is confined to the use of ROI with profit budget systems.

tiveness in making these decisions can be measured. The interest charge should be based on the interest that the company would save if working capital items, such as inventory, were reduced.

Profitability Measures

When the financial performance of a divisional manager is measured against budgeted profits, the problem arises as to which income statement items should be included in measuring performance. This part of the chapter describes some of the possible options.

The profitability of a profit center manager can be measured in essentially five different ways; (1) as the contribution margin, (2) as direct divisional profit, (3) as controllable divisional profit, (4) as income before income taxes, or (5) as net income. The nature of these measures is indicated by Exhibit 1, and each is discussed next.

1. *Contribution margin.* The principal argument for measuring profit center performance on the basis of contribution margin is that the fixed expenses are noncontrollable by the profit center manager, and that the managers should therefore focus their attention on maximizing the spread between revenue and variable expenses. The problem with this method is that some fixed expenses are entirely controllable and almost all fixed expenses are partially controllable. Many items of expenses, although not varying with the level of activity, can be changed at the discretion of the profit center manager. Presumably, senior management wants the profit center to be concerned with these discretionary expenses and to keep them in line with amounts agreed on in the budget formulation process. A focus on the contribution margin tends to direct attention away from this responsibility.

EXHIBIT 1

Income Statement

			MEASURE
Revenue		$1,000	
Cost of sales		600	
Gross margin		$ 400	
Variable period expenses		180	
Contribution margin		$ 220	◄——— (1)
Other divisional expenses	$60		
Charges from other divisions	30	90	
Direct divisional profit		$ 130	◄——— (2)
Controllable corporate allocations		10	
Controllable divisional profit		$ 120	◄——— (3)
Other corporate allocations		20	
Income before taxes		$ 100	◄——— (4)
Taxes		50	
Net Income		50	◄——— (5)

This problem could be corrected by defining contribution margin as revenues minus all controllable divisional expenses. There can, however, be differences of opinion with respect to the controllability of expenses. In fact, there are probably very few divisional expenses that cannot in some way be influenced by the divisional manager. Insurance and property taxes, for example, are in some cases noncontrollable by the profit center manager because the insurance coverage is set by corporate policy and property taxes by the municipality; however, the profit center manager may be able to reduce insurance expenses by reducing the amount of insured property (such as inventory and fixed assets), or by reducing fire or safety hazards. Consequently, many companies measure the performance of the divisional manager as profits after deducting all expenses for which the divisional manager is directly responsible.

2. *Direct divisional profit.* This measure shows the amount that the division contributes to the general overhead and profit of the corporation. It incorporates all expenses incurred in or directly traced to the division, regardless of whether or not these items are entirely controllable by the divisional manager. With the use of this measure, it is not necesary to allocate corporate expenses to divisions.

   The principal weakness of this measure is that it cannot be used as a realiable economic measure of performance because it excludes some headquarters expenses that may have been incurred specifically on behalf of the division.

3. *Controllable divisional profit.* Headquarters expenses should be divided into two categories: controllable and noncontrollable. The former includes headquarters expenses that are controllable, at least to a degree, by the divisional manager. Consequently, if these costs are included in the measurement system, the profit will be after the deduction of all expenses that may be influenced by the divisional manager. Controllable divisional profits, however, cannot be compared directly with published data or trade association data that report the profits of other companies in the industry because it excludes general headquarters expenses. Consequently, the next measurement would be divisional profits after subtracting the division's share of *all* headquarters expenses. This is income before taxes.

4. *Income before taxes.* In this measure, all pretax expenses are allocated to some division. The basis of allocation reflects the relative amount of expense that is incurred for each division or, alternatively, the amount of benefit received by each division.

   The sum of the profits of all the divisions equals the pretax profit of the company. Division managers are given the message that the division has not earned a profit unless all expenses are covered, and they may be motivated to raise questions about the amount of corporate overhead, which can lead to desirable actions. (One company sold its corporate airplane because of complaints about its costs from profit center managers.) This measure can be used as a basis for comparison with published data and for other economic analyses of the inherent profit potential of the division.

5. *Net income.* Not many companies measure performance of domestic divisions at the "bottom line," the amount of net income after income tax and interest. There are two principal reasons for this: (a) In many situations, the income after tax is a constant percentage of the pretax income, so there is no advantage in incorporating income taxes; and (b) decisions that have an impact on income taxes are made at headquarters, and it is believed that divisional profitability should not affect or be affected by these decisions.

   In some companies, however, the effective income tax rate *does* vary among divisions. Particularly, foreign subsidiaries or divisions with foreign operations may have different effective income tax rates. In these situations, it may assign income tax expenses, not only to measure the economic profitability of the division but also to motivate the divisional manager to minimize taxes.

Conclusion

All the measurements described in this part of the chapter are used by some companies. Most companies in the United States include some, if not all, of the costs just described, whether or not they can be influenced by the divisional manager. For example, a large proportion of United States multinational corporations measure the performance of managers of foreign subsidiaries in dollars. Performance is thus affected by fluctuations in the value of the dollar relative to the home currency. There are few if any instances where individual managers can exercise any influence over the value of the dollar.

It is my opinion that most of the confusion in measuring profit center managers is the result of *not* separating the measurement of the manager from the measurement of the division. If we consider the measurement of the manager alone, the solution becomes evident. That is, managers should be measured against those items that they can influence. In the typical company, this would probably be all expenses directly incurred by the division plus any corporate expenses incurred directly for the division. The managers would be measured on an after-tax basis only if they can influence the amount of tax that they pay. Items that they clearly cannot influence, such as currency fluctuation and general administrative expenses, should be eliminated.

Following the guide of including only those items that the manager can influence does not solve all the problems. There are many degrees of influence. There will always be items over which a manager may exercise some influence but little real control. This is why variance analysis is always important in judging management performance. Even with the best variance analysis system, however, judgment will always be necessary in evaluating managerial performance. If all items over which the manager has no influence are eliminated, however, it will make the exercise of this judgment more reliable.

MEASURING DIVISIONAL PROFITABILITY

Chapter 7 described techniques for measuring the profitability of manufactured products. A product is the smallest segment of a business for which meaningful profitability can be calculated. The division or subsidiary is usually the largest segment of a business for which profitability is calculated. Nevertheless, the principles are exactly the same. Senior managers need to know on a systematic basis how many resources are being generated by each division. Any item of revenue or expense that can be directly associated with the operation of the division should be assigned. This would include all revenues earned and costs incurred at the divisional level plus all costs incurred at headquarters or in other divisions on behalf of the division.

One important question with respect to costs is the joint headquarters cost—that is, those costs incurred at headquarters that would not be affected if the division were to be disposed of. One school of thought is that divisions benefit from headquarters activity, even though expenses were not incurred for specific divisions. For example, the development by headquarters of an effective standard cost system benefits the division even though it was not designed specifically for that division. A second reason for including all headquarters cost is to make the profitability of a division and outside companies more comparable. Whether all headquarters are included or not is a matter of judgment. However, if joint headquarters costs are allocated to divisions, they should be clearly identified so that resources generated with and without these joint costs can be readily calculated.

The evaluation of the resources that a division generates can be made only when related to the resources invested in that division. There are two issues to be resolved:

1. How is the amount of investment to be calculated?
2. Should ROI or RI be used?

With respect to the amount of the investment, it should include the average working capital used during the period plus the noncurrent assets. The question is whether the fixed assets should be at cost, net book value, or replacement cost. Replacement cost is often best, but other values might be satisfactory.

With respect to the use of ROI or RI, both should be calculated. Although the use of RI is preferable for reasons given in Chapter 7, it is inevitable that if RI is calculated, so will ROI be determined. Note that the use of ROI or RI will not have the dysfunctional consequences described earlier in this chapter because the division is being measured on this basis, *not* the manager.

As with product profitability analysis, the purpose of measuring the past profitability of the division is to diagnose areas requiring management attention. Once the diagnosis is made, any action taken will be aimed at improving future cash flows from facilities already in place and adding resources only where they are expected to earn at least the company's cost of capital. Profitability analysis is, of course, necessary for effective strategic planning.

SUMMARY

The measurement of divisional financial performance should be separated from the measurement of the performance of the divisional manager for reasons given in this chapter. Divisional managers should be measured only against the things that they can influence, and they should be measured against budgeted profit objectives rather than return on investment or residual income. On the other hand, financial performance of the division should include everything that affects the flow of resources and performance measurement should include either return on investment, residual income, or both.

QUESTIONS

15.1 Give some examples of managerial actions that are *not* reflected in the ROI in the year that these actions are taken.

15.2 Explain why divisional ROI is usually not consistent with the return on investment in government or corporate bonds. For example, a 6% rate of return calculated on a divisional investment is not the same as a 6% return on a government bond.

15.3 Assume that you were told by your superior to develop a system for estimating the economic value of the divisional investments. Outline the best procedure that you can, consistent with a realistic appraisal of available data.

15.4 Explain how residual income differs from ROI. If it has the advantages stated in the text, why do you think it is used so little?

15.5 Name some performance variables that are not controllable by the divisional manager. Name some performance variables that are only partially controllable by the divisional manager.

15.6 It has been stated that a serious problem in communication is that a system that works very well for transmitting favorable news can be ineffective in transmitting unfavorable news. Is this true? If so, can you think of examples in which this has happened? How do you guard against this situation in a management control system?

CASES

CASE 15.1   **WESTPORT ELECTRIC CORPORATION (B)**

James Snell, the general manager of the Laundry Division of the Home Appliance Group of Westport Electric Corporation, was discussing a reduction in the profits earned by the division with his controller, Frederick Beck. (Exhibit 1 is an organization chart of the Westport Electric Company.) The problem arose because the Laundry Division's rate of return on investment, for the first half of 1985, was less than objective and, also, less than the rate of return earned in 1984. Furthermore, the situation was not expected to improve during the remainder of the year. Beck was explaining to Snell that the lower rate of return was caused principally by a new plant that had started in operation in early 1985. The new

This case was prepared by John Dearden. Copyright © by the President and Fellows of Harvard University. Harvard Business School case 9-113-073.

EXHIBIT 1 Westport Electric Corporation

Organization Chart—January 1, 1982

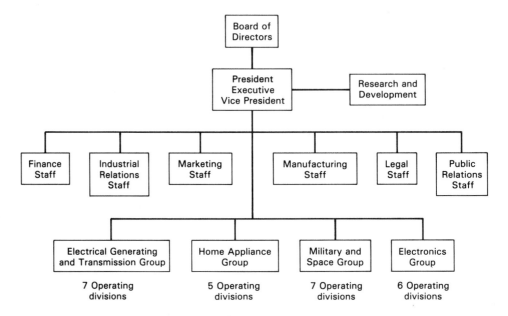

plant was performing well and the analysis submited at the time that the investment was approved indicated that the new plant would increase the divisional
rate of return. Snell was therefore both perplexed and annoyed. The lower rate
of return would result in a lower bonus for him at the end of the year.

Organization of Westport

Westport Electric is one of the giant United States corporations that manufactures and sells electric and electronic products. Sales in 1983 were in excess
of $30 billion and profits after taxes were over $1.25 billion. The operating activities of the corporation are divided into four groups, each headed by a group vice
president. These groups are: the Electrical Generating and Transmission Group;
the Home Appliance Group; the Military and Space Group; and the Electronics
Group. Each of these groups is comprised of a number of relatively independent
divisions, each headed by a divisional manager. The division is the basic operating unit of the corporation and each is a profit center. The divisional manager
is responsible for earning a specific return on his investment. There are 25 divisions in the corporation.

Profit Evaluation

Each profit center is evaluated on the basis of its return on investment (ROI). The return on investment is calculated by dividing the profits earned during a period by the average assets employed during that period. The profits are calculated in accordance with generally accepted accounting principles and conventions and come off the regular income statement. The investment, however, is reported on a separate schedule (not the balance sheet) and is calculated as follows.

Cash	7% of annualized net sales
Receivables	Actual end of the month balances
Inventories	Actual end of the month balance, calculated on a LIFO basis
Fixed Assets	Average monthly net book value of completed assets. (Fixed assets in the process of being constructed are not included.) Westport uses a composite, declining-balance system of depreciation.

Capital Investment Analysis. In 1980, Westport Electric adopted a time-adjusted rate of return method for evaluating proposed capital expenditures. This method involves discounting the estimated cash flows at various rates until one is found that makes the algebraic sum of all the cash flows equal to zero. For example, suppose that a proposed investment of $3000 was expected to result in an out-of-pocket saving of $1000 a year for 5 years. By discounting the cash flows at 3 discount rates, 10%, 20%, and 30%, the results are as follows.

ITEM	*AMOUNT*	*10%*	*20%*	*30%*
Investment	*$ – 3000*	*$ – 3000*	*$ – 3000*	*$ – 3000*
SAVINGS:				
Year 1	+ 1000	+ 909	+ 833	+ 769
Year 2	+ 1000	+ 826	+ 694	+ 592
Year 3	+ 1000	+ 751	+ 579	+ 455
Year 4	+ 1000	+ 683	+ 482	+ 350
Year 5	+ 1000	+ 621	+ 402	+ 269
		+ 790	– 10	– 565

As you can see, the rate of return is approximately 20%. This means that $1000 a year for 5 years yields a 20% return on an investment of $3000.

Although Westport has no hard-and-fast rule on the return a proposed investment must earn, the rule of thumb is that an investment should yield 10% after taxes in order to be acceptable.

Investment proposals are prepared by the operating divisions and submitted to the Executive Committee, where they are either approved, modified, or rejected.

Prior to 1984, Westport used the so-called "accounting" method for evaluating capital investment proposals. This method involved subtracting the average annual depreciation from the average annual gross cash inflow. (This gave the estimated accounted profit.) The profit was divided by one-half the gross investment. In the examples cited above the rate of return would be calculated as follows.

$$\text{Return on investment} = \frac{\text{Gross cash inflows} - \text{depreciation}}{\frac{1}{2}\ (\text{investment})}$$

$$= \frac{1000 - (3000/5)}{1500}$$

$$= \frac{400}{1500} = 26.7\%.$$

One-half the total investment was used in the denominator of the fraction on the assumption that the investment would be gradually returned over its life and, therefore, the *average* outstanding investment was one-half the gross amount.

The accounting method was discontinued because it did not take into account the time value of money and was, therefore, not an accurate method for determining the expected rate of return on a proposed investment.

The Problem.   As indicated in the opening paragraph of the case, the problem Snell was facing resulted from the fact that, although an investment analysis indicated that the new plant would increase his return on investment, it actually reduced his rate of return in 1985.

At the time that the original capital investment procedure went into effect in 1980, the company used straight-line depreciation in their accounting system. Also, the divisional assets employed for determining the divisions's return on investment were calculated using one-half the gross book value of the fixed assets. In 1985, however, Westport changed to double declining balance depreciation. Also, as indicated earlier in the case, the fixed assets are now included in the investment base at net book value. This change was made when it was discovered that using one-half the gross book value encouraged too early disposition of equipment. These two changes, together with using the time-adjusted rate of return for evaluating capital investment proposals, have made the rate of profit calculated for management control different from that used in making the capital investment decision. This can be indicated from the following analysis of the new plant investment made in the Laundry Division.[1]

---

[1] The figures have been simplified from those actually used.

Expected investment in plant $166,000
After tax cash flow resulting from investment:

YEAR	AMOUNT	DISCOUNTED AT 15%	DISCOUNTED CASH FLOW
1 (1968)	40,000	.87	34,800
2	38,000	.76	28,880
3	36,000	.66	22,760
4	35,000	.57	19,950
5	33,000	.50	16,550
6	31,000	.43	13,330
7	27,000	.38	10,260
8	25,000	.33	8,250
9	22,000	.28	6,160
10	20,000	.25	5,000
	307,000		165,890

As you can see, the investment of $166,000 was expected to earn 15% over the next ten years.

The net cash flow for year 1 was calculated as follows.

Cash flow before taxes	$46,800
Depreciation (double declining balance)	33,200
Taxable income	13,600
Tax	6,800
After tax cash flow	$40,000

The accounting return on this investment in 1985, however, would be as follows.

Gross earnings		$ 46,800
Less:		
Depreciation	33,200	
Taxes	6,800	40,000
After tax profit		$ 6,800
Average investment during year:		
166,000 − (33,200/2)		149,400
Rate of return		4.6%

As Frederick Beck explained to Snell, the return for 1985 would be only 4.5%. In future years, however, Beck pointed out that Snell's return on investment would more than offset the poor showing in 1985. He prepared the following table to show the rate of return that would be earned over the entire 10 years if the plant operated according to plan.

Year	(1) Earnings after taxes but before depreciation	(2) Depreciation[a]	(3) Accounted profits (1) − (2)	(4) Investment[b]	(5) Rate of return (3) ÷ (4)
1	$ 40,000	$ 33,200	$ 6,800	$149,400	4.6%
2	38,000	26,560	11,440	119,520	9.6
3	36,000	21,248	14,752	95,616	15.4
4	35,000	16,998	18,002	76,493	23.5
5	33,000	13,599	19,401	61,194	31.7
6	31,000	10,879	20,124	48,954	41.1
7	27,000	10,879	16,121	38,075	42.3
8	25,000	10,879	14,121	27,196	51.9
9	22,000	10,879	11,121	16,317	68.2
10	20,000	10,879	9,121	5,438	167.7
Total	$307,000	$166,000	$141,000	$638,203	
Average	30,700	16,600	14,100	63,820	22.1%

[a]For the first six years, depreciation is calculated by multiplying double the straight-line rate (20%) by the net book value at the beginning of the year. For years 7 through 10, the company would change back to straight-line depreciation for the undepreciated balance at the beginning of year 7.

[b]This is the average of the net book value at the beginning of the year and at the end of the year.

Snell was surprised to see the results. He told Beck that the system made no sense at all to him. The investment was approved because it earned 15%, supposedly calculated in a correct mathematical manner. "Yet," he stated, "the division *never* earned 15%. It will earn from 4.6% to 167.7% and *average* 22.1%." He observed that no matter what he did by 1983 and 1984, he would look bad. Thereafter, he felt, he would look good even if he failed to make all the profits that he forecast. He was concerned that he might leave the division and the new man would be given credit for improving the rate of return, even though it was the result of the declining investment base.

Questions

1. Will the system act in the way that Beck indicates? If not, how will it act? If so, what causes it to act in this way?

2. How will this system motivate management to act? Is this desirable? If not, how should the system motivate management to act?

3. Assuming that management still wants to use ROI, what changes if any, would you recommend?

4. Assuming that management wants to use ROI based on the accounting treatment for fixed assets (i.e., use the fixed assets and depreciation from the accounting records in the investment base), what changes, if any, would you recommend?

CASE 15.2   MULTI-NATIONAL MOTORS

Multi-National Motors is a large corporation producing automobiles, trucks, and many other related products on a world-wide basis. Its sales are several billion dollars per year. The Company is organized on a profit center basis. It has 25 domestic divisions. Each division is managed by a relatively autonomous divisional manager who is assigned the responsibility for earning a satisfactory profit.

This case is concerned with the method used to compensate the executives of the domestic corporation. (Executives of foreign subsidiaries are compensated on a different basis.) In particular, it is concerned with the profit-sharing system that provides executives with a bonus over and above their salary if profits are above a certain level.

The Present Bonus System

Each executive eligible for a bonus has a number of bonus points. Although there is some flexibility in giving an executive bonus points, for practical purposes it is a function of his salary. It is not a linear function, however (i.e., his bonus points are not proportionate to his salary). Up to a certain salary level, the higher the salary, the greater the number of bonus points per thousand dollars of salary. Above this level, the bonus points per thousand dollars of salary remains constant.

Each year, 10% of the profits after taxes in excess of 10% of capital (net worth) is set aside for executive bonuses. This amount is divided by the total number of bonus points in the company and a "standard award per bonus point" is calculated. From this standard award per point, the standard bonus for each executive is calculated. No bonuses are paid in excess of 100% of salary. When the standard bonus of an executive is over 100%, the excess is returned to the general funds of the company. Also, the bonus is paid each year out of the current year's profits. Bonuses are not carried forward to future years.

In summary, each executive is given an annual bonus. This bonus is equal to the total annual bonus award divided by the total number of bonus points awarded by the company multiplied by the bonus points he holds; however, no one can receive a bonus of more than 100% of his base salary. The bonus is awarded automatically. The funds are returned to the company to the extent that the standard bonus of an executive exceeds 100% of his salary. There is no carry-over of bonus from year to year.

This case was prepared by John Dearden. Copyright © by the President and Fellows of Harvard University. Harvard Business School case 9-171-511.

Proposed Bonus System

One of the major objections to the present bonus system is that it provides no rewards to the divisional managers who have made the greatest contributions in a given year. To correct the situation, the Central Finance Staff proposed that the divisional bonuses be based on divisional profitability. (Central staff executives would continue to be paid their bonus on the basis of total company profits.) The proposed divisional bonus plan had the following principal provisions.

1. An Incentive Compensation Committee would be organized, consisting of the President, the Executive Vice President and the Vice President in charge of Finance. This committee would be responsible for setting "profit potential" targets for each division. These targets would be set at the beginning of each year, and would be in total dollars.

2. Each division would be given a profit objective as follows: Potential profit minus budgeted assets multiplied by 10%. For example, assume that a division had a profit potential of $100,000 and a budgeted investment of $500,000. The profit objective would be 100,000 − 50,000 or $50,000.

3. The actual investment base is as follows:

Cash	10% of cost of sales
Receivables Inventories	average actual month-end balances
Fixed assets	average actual end-of-the-month gross book value

The budgeted investment base is the beginning-of-the-year estimate of what the actual investment base will be.

4. At the end of the year, the actual profits are to be compared to objective. In the example given above, assume that actual profits were $105,000 and actual investment was $600,000. The calculated actual profit performance would be 105,000–60,000 or $45,000. Therefore the division earned $5000 less than objective.

5. If the profit performance were exactly equal to objective, the standard bonus for all executives in the division would be 30% of salary.[1] This would increase by five percentage points for each $100,000 above the objective and be reduced by five percentage points for each $100,000 below the objective. The maximum bonus would be 100% of salary; the minimum bonus would be zero.

Required

1. Determine the percentage bonus allowance in each of the following cases.

    (a) Division A's profit potential is $500,000; the budgeted investment is $4,000,000; actual profits are $700,000; actual investment is $3,500,000.

---

[1]Divisional executives had averaged bonuses of 30% of salary for the past three years.

(b) Division B's profit potential is a $50,000 loss; budgeted invest-ment is $2,000,000; actual loss is $40,000; actual investment is $2,100.000.

(c) Division C's profit potential is $1,000,000; the budgeted invest-ment is $5,000,000; actual profits are $800,000; actual investment is $6,000,000.

2. Evaluate the present bonus system.

3. Evaluate the proposed bonus system.

4. If you could make the decisions, what kind of an executive bonus system would you design for Multi-National Motors?

CASE 15.3   PURITY STEEL CORPORATION

"I'm no expert in high finance," said Mr. Hoffman, manager of the Denver branch for the Warehouse Sales Division of Purity Steel Corporation, "so it didn't occur to me that I might be better off by leasing my new warehouse instead of owning it. But I was talking to Jack Dorenbush over in Omaha the other day and he said that he's getting a lot better return on the investment in his district be-cause he's in a leased building. I'm sure that the incentive compensation plan you put in last year is fair, but I didn't know whether it adjusted automatically for the difference between owning and leasing and I just thought I'd raise the question. There's still time to try to find someone to take over my construction contract and then lease the building to me when it's finished, if you think that's what I ought to do."

Purity Steel Corporation was an integrated steel producer with annual sales of about $900 million in 1984. The Warehouse Sales Division was an autonomous unit that operated 21 field warehouses throughout the United States. Total sales of the division were approximately $45 million in 1984, of which roughly half represented steel products (rod, bar, wire, tube, sheet, and plate) purchased from Purity's Mill Products Division. The balance of the volume in the Warehouse Sales Division was for copper, brass, and aluminum products purchased from large producers of those metals. The Warehouse Sales Division competed with other producer-affiliated and independent steel warehousing companies, and purchased its steel requirements from the Mill Products Division at the same prices paid by outside purchasers.

Mr. Harold Higgins had been appointed general manager of the Warehouse Sales Division in mid-1984 after spending 12 years in the sales function with the Mill Products Division. Subject only to the approval of his annual profit plan and proposed capital expenditures by corporate headquarters, Mr. Higgins was

This case was prepared by R. F. Vancil. Copyright © by the President and Fellows of Harvard Univerity. Harvard Busines School case 9-110-065.

given full authority for the operations of his division and charged with the responsibility to "make the division grow, both in sales volume and in the rate of return on its investment." Prior to his arrival at division headquarters in St. Louis, the Warehouse Sales Division had been operated in a centralized manner; all purchase orders had been issued by division headquarters and most other operating decisions at any particular warehouse had required prior divisional approval. Mr. Higgings decided to decentralize the management of his division by making each branch (warehouse) manager responsible for the division's activities in his geographic area.

In Mr. Higgins' opinion, one of the key features of his decentralization policy was an incentive compensation plan which was announced in late 1984 to become effective on January 1, 1985. The description of the plan, as presented to the branch managers, is reproduced in Exhibits 1, 2, and 3. Monthly operating

EXHIBIT 1   Purity Steel Corporation

Branch Managers' Compensation Plan—Warehouse Sales Division

I. OBJECTIVES

The Warehouse Sales Division has three major objectives.

A. To operate the division and its branches at a profit.
B. To utilize efficiently the assets of the division.
C. To grow.

This compensation plan is a combination of base salary and incentive earnings. Incentive earnings will be paid to those managers who contribute to the achievement of these objectives and in proportion to their individual performance.

II. COMPENSATION PLAN COMPONENTS

There are three components to this plan.

A. Base Salary
Base salary ranges are determined for the most part on dollar sales volume of the district(s) in the prior year. The higher the sales volume, the higher the range to which the manager becomes eligible. The profitability of dollar sales or increases in dollar sales is an important consideration. Actual salaries will be established by the General Manager, Warehouse Sales Division, and the salary ranges will be reviewed periodically in order to keep this division competitive with companies similar to ours.

B. Growth Incentive
If the district earns a net profit before federal income tax for the calendar year, the manager will earn $350 for every $100,000 of increased sales over the prior year. Proportionate amounts will be paid for greater or lesser growth.

C. Return on Investment Incentive
In this feature of the plan, incentive will be paid in relation to the size of investment and the return on investment. The manager will be paid in direct proportion to his effective use of assets placed at his disposal.

The main emphasis of this portion of the plan is on increasing the return at any level of investment, high or low.

III. *LIMITATIONS ON RETURN ON INVESTMENT INCENTIVE*

A. No incentive will be paid to a manager whose branch earns less than 3% return on investment before federal taxes.

B. No increase in incentive payment will be made for performance in excess of 20% return on investment before federal taxes.

C. No payment will be made in excess of $10,000 regardless of performance.

IV. *CALCULATIONS ON RETURN ON INVESTMENT INCENTIVE*

Exhibit 2 is a graphic presentation of this portion of the incentive. Since all possible levels of investment and return on investment cannot be detailed on the chart, exact incentive figures cannot be determined. However, a rough estimate can be made by:

A. Finding the approximate level of investment on the vertical scale.

B. Drawing a line horizontally from that point to the approximate return on investment percent.

C. Dropping a line vertically from that point to the bottom scale which indicates the approximate incentive.

The exact amount of incentive can be determined from Exhibit 3 by the following procedure and example.

EXAMPLE

- Investment $1,652,750
- ROI   7.3%
- Step 1   Divide the last five digits of investment figures by 100,000. The result is a percentage.

    Example

    $$\frac{52,750}{100,000} = .5272$$

- Step 2   In the 1% Column in Exhibit 3, take the difference between the next highest investment and next lowest investment.

    Example

Investment	1%	Difference
$1,600,000	$420	
		$10
$1,700,000	$430	

- Step 3   Multiply the result of Step 2 by the result of Step 1 and add to the 1% Column figure for the next lowest investment.

    Example

    $10 × .5275 = $5.275 + $420 = $425.275

- Step 4   Multiply the result of Step 3 by the actual ROI %.

    Example

    $425.275 × 7.3 = $3,104.51 *Incentive Payment.*

EXHIBIT 2 Purity Steel Corporation

Incentive Payments @ Various ROI's

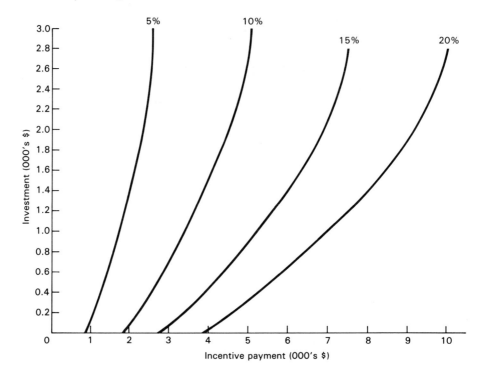

statements had been prepared for each warehouse for many years; implementing the new plan required only the preparation of balance sheets for each warehouse. Two major asset categories, inventories and fixed assets (buildings and equipment), were easy to attribute to specific locations. Accounts receivable were collected directly at Purity's central accounting department, but an investment in receivables equal to 35 days' sales (the average for the Warehouse Sales Division) was charged to each warehouse. Finally, a small cash fund deposited in a local bank was recorded as an asset of each branch. No current or long-term liabilities were recognized in the balance sheets at the divisional or branch level.

At the meeting in December 1984, when the new incentive compensation plan was presented to the branch managers, Mr. Higgins had said,

> "Howard Percy (division sales manager) and I have spent a lot of time during the last few months working out the details of this plan. Our objective was to devise a fair way to compensate those branch managers who do a superior job of improving the performance in their areas. First, we reviewed our salary structure and made a few adjustments so that no branch manger has to apologize to his wife for the regu-

EXHIBIT 3 Purity Steel Corporation

Incentive Payments @ Various Investments and ROI %'s

	ROI %					
Investment	*1%*[a]	*3%*	*5%*	*10%*	*15%*	*20%*
$ 100,000	$209	$ 627	$1,045	$2,090	$3,135	$ 4,180
200,000	225	675	1,125	2,250	3,375	4,500
300,000	241	726	1,205	2,410	3,615	4,820
400,000	257	771	1,285	2,570	3,855	5,140
500,000	273	819	1,365	2,730	4,095	5,460
600,000	289	867	1,445	2,890	4,335	5,780
700,000	305	915	1,525	3,050	4,575	6,100
800,000	321	963	1,605	3,210	4,815	6,420
900,000	337	1,011	1,685	3,370	5,055	6,740
1,000,000	350	1,050	1,750	3,500	5,250	7,000
1,100,000	362	1,086	1,810	3,620	5,430	7,240
1,200,000	375	1,125	1,875	3,750	5,625	7,500
1,300,000	387	1,161	1,935	3,870	5,805	7,740
1,400,000	400	1,200	2,000	4,000	6,000	8,000
1,500,000	410	1,230	2,050	4,100	6,150	8,200
1,600,000	420	1,260	2,100	4,200	6,300	8,400
1,700,000	430	1,290	2,150	4,300	6,450	8,600
1,800,000	440	1,320	2,200	4,400	6,600	8,800
1,900,000	450	1,350	2,250	4,500	6,750	9,000
2,000,000	460	1,380	2,300	4,600	6,900	9,200
2,100,000	465	1,395	2,325	4,650	6,975	9,300
2,200,000	470	1,410	2,350	4,700	7,050	9,400
2,300,000	475	1,425	2,375	4,750	7,125	9,500
2,400,000	480	1,440	2,400	4,800	7,200	9,600
2,500,000	485	1,455	2,425	4,850	7,275	9,700
2,600,000	490	1,470	2,450	4,900	7,350	9,800
2,700,000	495	1,485	2,475	4,950	7,425	9,900
2,800,000	500	1,500	2,500	5,000	7,500	10,000
2,900,000	500	1,500	2,500	5,000	7,500	10,000
3,000,000	500	1,500	2,500	5,000	7,500	10,000

[a]This column for calculation purposes only. No incentive will be paid for less than 3% ROI.

lar pay check he brings home. Next, we worked out a simple growth incentive to recognize that one part of our job is simply to sell steel, although we didn't restrict it to steel alone. But more importantly, we've got to improve the profit performance of this division. We established 3% as the return-on-investment floor representing average performance. As you know, we won't even do that well for 1984, but our budget for next year shows that we'll earn about 3% before taxes. Thus, in 1985 we expect about half the branches to be below 3%—and earn no ROI bonus—while the other half will be the ones who really carry the weight. This plan will pay a bonus to all managers who help the division increase its average rate of return. We also decided on a sliding scale arrangement for those above 3%, trying to recognize that the manager who makes a 5% return on a $2 million investment is doing as good a job as one who makes a 10% return on only half a million dollars. Finally, we put a $10,000 limit on the ROI bonus because we felt that the bonus shouldn't exceed 50% of salary, but we can always make salary adjustments in those cases where the bonus plan doesn't seem to adequately compensate a man for his performance."

After the telephone call in May 1986 from Mr. Hoffman, quoted in the opening paragraph, Mr. Higgins called Mr. Percy into his office and told him of the question that Hoffman had raised. "We knew that we probably had some bugs to iron out of this system," Percy responded. "Let me review the Denver situation and we'll discuss it this afternoon."

At a meeting later that day, Mr. Percy summarized the problem for Mr. Higgins in the following way.

"As you know, Larry Hoffman is planning a big expansion at Denver. He's been limping along in an old multistory building with an inadequate variety of inventory, and his sales actually declined last year. About a year ago he worked up an RFE (Request for Expenditure) for a new warehouse which we approved here and sent forward. It was approved at corporate headquarters last fall, the contract was let, and it's to be completed by the end of his year. I pulled out one page of the RFE which summarizes the financial story (Exhibit 4). Larry forecasts nearly a triple in his sales volume over the next eight years, and the project will pay out in about $7\frac{1}{2}$ years.

"Here (Exhibit 5) is a summary of the incentive compensation calculations for Denver that I worked up after I talked to you this morning. Larry had a very high ROI last year, and received one of the biggest bonuses we paid. Against that background, I next worked up a projection of what his bonus will be in 1987, assuming that he moves into his new facility at the end of this year. As you can see, his ROI will drop from 17.3% to only 7.2%, and even on the bigger investment his bonus in 1987 will go down substantially.

"Finally, I dug out the file on New Orleans where we're leasing the new warehouse that was completed a few months ago. Our lease there is a so-called net lease, which means that we pay the insurance, taxes, and maintenance just as if we owned it. The lease runs for 20 years with renewal options at reduce rates for two additional ten-year periods. Assuming that we could get a similar deal for Denver, and adjusting for the difference in the cost of the land and building at the two locations, our lease payments at Denver during the first 20 years would be just under $50,000 per year. Pushing that through the bonus formula for Denver's projected 1987 operations shows an ROI of 7.3%, but Larry's bonus would be about 10% less than if he was in an owned building."

"On balance, therefore," Mr. Percy concluded, "there's not a very big difference in the bonus payment as between owning and leasing, but in either event Larry will be taking a substantial cut in his incentive compensation."

Required

1. Evaluate the Branch Manager's Compensation Plan. In what ways, if any, would you change it?

2. Evaluate the financial relationship between the Warehouse Sales Division and the Mill Products Division. Will the Mill Products Division optimize Purity's profits by optimizing the Divisional profits?

EXHIBIT 4 Purity Steel Corporation

Warehouse Sales Division—Denver Branch

Forecast sales, expenses, and after-tax profits due to new facility (000's)

	ESTIMATED TO 12/31/85	1ST YEAR	2ND YEAR	3RD YEAR	4TH YEAR	5TH YEAR	6TH YEAR	7TH YEAR	8TH YEAR
Sales dollars	$2,460.0	$313.0	$603.0	$1,216.0	$1,899.0	$2,513.0	$3,326.0	$3,927.0	$4,534.0
Gross profit dollars	447.0	49.0	94.0	194.0	310.0	403.0	522.0	613.0	712.0
Service income	51.0	(25.0)	(24.0)	(22.0)	(20.0)	(18.0)	(16.0)	(16.0)	(16.0)
Total income	528.0	24.0	70.0	172.0	290.0	385.0	506.0	597.0	696.0
Less: expenses excluding depreciation	329.0	61.0	117.0	157.0	200.0	235.0	291.0	322.0	331.0
Pre-tax net profit excluding depreciation	199.0	(37.0)	(47.0)	15.0	90.0	150.0	215.0	275.0	365.0
Additional mill profit		13.0	24.0	58.0	99.0	125.0	157.0	184.0	233.0
		(24.0)	(23.0)	73.0	189.0	275.0	372.0	459.0	598.0
Less: relocation		(20.0)	—	—	—	—	—	—	—
		(44.0)	(23.0)	73.0	189.0	275.0	372.0	459.0	598.0
Less: depreciation		10.6	10.6	10.6	10.6	10.6	10.6	10.6	10.6
		(54.6)	(33.6)	62.4	178.4	264.4	361.4	448.4	587.4
Less: 50% tax		27.3	16.8	31.2	89.2	132.2	180.7	224.2	293.7
Net income		(27.3)	(16.8)	31.2	89.2	132.2	180.7	224.2	293.7
Add: back depreciation and relocation		36.6	10.6	10.6	10.6	10.6	10.6	10.6	10.6
Annual return of funds		3.3	6.2	41.8	99.8	142.8	191.3	234.8	304.3

Total return over 8 years $1,011,710

Capital expenditures required:
Land	$ 60,000
Building	522,500
Equipment	211,930
Relocation expense	20,000
Total	814,430
Pay-back period	7.4 years

EXHIBIT 5 Purity Steel Corporation

Return on Investment and Incentive Compensation

	TOTAL WAREHOUSE SALES DIVISION 1985 ACTUAL	DENVER BRANCH		
			1987 PROJECTED	
		1985 Actual	Owned Building	Leased Building
INVESTMENT AT YEAR-END				
Land	$ 1,028,900	$ 24,900	$ 60,000	—
Buildings (net of depreciation)	2,790,100	64,900	513,792	—
Equipment (net of depreciation)	544,400	6,400	202,085	$ 202,085
Subtotal	$ 4,363,400	$ 96,200	$ 775,877	$ 202,085
Cash fund	276,500	10,000	10,000	10,000
Accounts receivable	4,503,500	248,300	277,300	277,300
Inventories	11,059,100	626,400	693,250	693,250
Total year-end investment	$20,202,500	$ 980,900	$1,756,427	$1,182,635
Investment at start of year	$19,959,100	$1,052,700	$1,679,130	$1,096,630
Average investment during year	20,080,800	1,016,800	1,717,779	1,139,630
Profit before depreciation and taxes	$ 829,462	$ 183,574	$ 142,000	$ 142,000
Less: Depreciation	(129,741)	(8,000)	(18,553)	(9,845)
Lease payments	(84,113)	—	—	(48,640)
Net pre-tax profit	$ 615,608	$ 175,574	$ 123,447	$ 83,515
Return on investment	3.1%	17.3%	7.2%	7.3%
INCENTIVE COMPENSATION				
Sales volume increase (decrease)		$ (174,000)	$ 313,000	$ 313,000
Bonus @ $350 per $100,000		—	$ 1,096	1,096
ROI bonus:				
Base investment		$1,000,000	$1,700,000	$1,100,000
Value from 1% column, Exhibit 3		$350.00	$430.00	$362.00
Difference to next base		12.00	10.00	13.00
Interpolated portion		2.02	1.78	5.15
Total value per percentage point		$352.02	$431.78	$367.15
ROI bonus		$6,090	$3,109	$2,680
Total incentive compensation		$6,090	$4,205	$3,776

Assumptions used for 1987 projections at Denver:

1. Old facility and equipment sold at end of 1987, proceeds remitted to corp. hq.

2. Depreciation on new facilities in 1987 is $8,708 on building (60 years, straight line) and $9,845 on equipment (various lives, straight line).

3. Year-end investment in receivables and inventory will approximate 1985 relationship: receivables at 10% of annual sales, inventories at 25% of annual sales.

4. Average total investment assumes that new fixed assets are acquired on December 31, 1986, and that other assets at that date are the same as at the end of 1985.

5. Profit taken from RFE (Exhibit 4) as $199,000 less $37,000 first year decline, less $20,000 relocation expense. Additional mill profit of $13,000 does not reflect on divisional books and was used only at corporate headquarters for capital expenditures evaluation purposes.

CASE 15.4 GENERAL ELECTRIC COMPANY (A)[1]

The General Electric Company is a large, multi-location corporation engaged in the manufacture and marketing of a wide variety of electrical and allied products. In 1961 there were almost 400 separate product lines and over three million catalog items. Sales volume in that year totaled $4457 million, and net income was $242 million. Total employment was about 250,000.

Early in the 1950's, General Electric initiated an extensive decentralization of authority and responsibility for the operations of the company. The basic unit of organization became the product department. As of 1961, there were over 100 of these departments.

The company recognized that, if this decentralization was to be fully effective, it would need an improved system of management control. It also recognized that any improved system of control would require better measures of performance. To meet this need, the company established a Measurements Project and created a special organizational unit to carry out this project. This case summarizes the main features of this project, with particular emphasis on the measuring of performance of the operating (i.e., product) departments.

The Measurements Project

The Measurements Project was established in 1952. Reponsibility for the project was assigned the Accounting Services, one of the corporate functional services divisions. A permanent organization unit, initially called Measurements Service, was set up to carry out this project.

An early step in the Measurements Project was the development of a set of principles by which the project was to be governed. Five such principles were formulated.

1. Measurements were to be designed to measure the performance of *organizational components,* rather than that of *managers.*
2. Measurements were to involve common *indexes* of performance, but not common *standards* of performance. (For example, rate of return on investment might be the index of performance common to all product departments, but the standards in terms of this index might be 12% for one department and 25% for another.)

---

[1]With the exception of the statistical information and publicly known facts presented in the introduction of this case, the sources for the facts making up the body of this case are *Executive Control—The Catalyst,* by William T. Jerome III (New York, Wiley, 1961) pages 217–237, and Robert W. Lewis, "Measuring, Reporting and Appraising Results of Operations with Reference to Goals. Plans and Budgets," in *Planning, Managing and Measuring the Business,* A Case Study of Management Planning and Control at General Electric Company (New York, Controllership Foundation Inc., 1955).

This case was prepared by R. H. Caplan and Robert Anthony. Copyright © by the President and Fellows of Harvard University. Harvard Business School case 9-113-121.

3. Measurements were to be designed as aids to judgment in appraisal of perform-ance, and not to supplant judgment.

4. Measurements were to give proper weight to future performance as well as cur-rent performance, in order to facilitate the maintenance of a balance between the long run and the near term.

5. Measurements were to be selected so as to facilitate constructive action, not to restrict such action.

The overall Measurements Project was divided into three major subprojects.

1. Operational measurements of the results of a product department.

2. Functional measurements of the work of engineering, manufacturing, market-ing finance, employee and plant community relations, and legal components of the organization.

3. Measurements of the work of managing as such—planning, organizing, integrat-ing, and measuring itself.

    The first step in the subproject on operational measurements was to de-velop an answer to the following question.

    What are the specific areas for which measurements should be designed, bearing in mind that sound measurements of overall performance require a proper balance among the various functions and among the aspects (planning, organizing, for example) or managing?[2]

In seeking an answer to this question, the organization made a careful anal-ysis of the nature and purposes of the basic kinds of work performed by each functional unit with the purpose of singling out those functional objectives that were of sufficient importance to the welfare of the business[3] as a whole, to be termed "key result areas."

The Key Result Areas

In order to determine whether an area tentatively identified according to the preceding analytical framework was sufficiently basic to qualify as a key result area, the organization established a criterion in the form of the following test question.

Will continued failure in this area prevent the attainment of management's respon-sibility for advancing General Electric as a leader in a strong, competitive economy, even though results in all other key areas are good?[4]

As an outcome of analysis and application of this test, eight key result areas were decided on. These were as follows:

---

[2]Lewis, "Measuring, Reporting, and Appraising Results," 30.
[3]The word "business" is used here to refer to a product department, not to the whole company.
[4]*Ibid.*

1. Profitability
2. Market position
3. Productivity
4. Product leadership
5. Personnel development
6. Employee attitudes
7. Public responsibility
8. Balance between short-range and long-range goals

Each of these key result areas is described below.

1. Profitability

The key index used by General Electric to measure profitability was "dollars of residual income." Residual income was defined as net profit after taxes, less a capital charge. The capital charge was a certain percentage (say, 6%) of the net assets assigned to the department; it corresponded to an imputed interest charge. The criteria formulated to guide the development of a satisfactory measure of profitability were expressed as follows:

(a) An index that recognized the contribution of capital investment to profits.
(b) An index that recognized what human work and effort contribute to profits.
(c) An index that recognized the "corporate facts of life" (e.g., one consistent with General Electric's needs and organizational objectives).
(d) An index that served to make the operating decisions of individual managers in the company's best interests.

In the process of selecting and developing a measure of profitability, the measurements organization considered several more conventional indices, including rate of return on investment, ratio of profit to sales, and ratio of profit to value added. A weakness of these ratios or indices was stated in this way.

> " . . . the acid test of an index should be its effectiveness in guiding decentralized management to make decisions in the best interests of the company overall, since operating managers' efforts naturally will be to improve the performance of their businesses in terms of the index used for evaluation. This test points up the particular weakness of rate of return and of other ratio indexes, such as per cent profit to sales. This weakness is the tendency to encourage concentration on improvement of the *ratios* rather than on improvement in *dollar* profits. Specifically, the business with the better results in terms of the ratios will tend to make decisions based on the effect the decisions will have on the particular business's current ratios without consideration of the dollar profits involved. This tends to retard incentive to growth and expansion because it dampens the incentive of the more profitable businesses to grow."[5]

---

[5]*Ibid*, 32.

2. Market Position

Performance in this key result area was measured in terms of the share of the market obtained during a given measurement period. The measurement was expressed as a percentage of available business in the market. "Market," as used in this sense, was expressed in dollars or units, kilowatt-amperes, or other meaningful terms.

"The first major consideration in designing market position measurements is a determination of what constitutes a product line and what constitutes the market for each product line of a business. A product line may be defined as a grouping of products in accordance with the purposes they serve or the essential wants they satisfy. The definition is somewhat misleading in that a product line may be a broad classification, such as clocks, or it may be a narrow classification, such as alarm clocks, kitchen clocks, or mantel clocks. In addition, product lines may overlap so that a particular product could be included in several product lines. Hence, the actual grouping of products by product lines must be accruately identified.

"There may be wide variations in the interpretation of what constitutes the market for a given product line. Therefore, it is important that for each of their lines, our product departments identify such things as:

1. Whether the market includes not only directly competing products but also indirectly competing products (electric ranges vs. electric ranges; electric ranges vs. all types of ranges—electric, gas, oil, and others).
2. Whether the market includes sales by all domestic competitors or only those reporting to trade associations.
3. Whether the market includes imports, if foreign sellers are competing in the domestic market.
4. Whether the market includes export sales.
5. Whether the market includes captive sales.
6. Whether the market is considered to be represented by sales to distributors, or to retailers, or to ultimate users.

"In other words, in establishing measurements of market position there should be a clear understanding of precisely what comprises the product line and what comprises the market. The purpose of having sharp definitions of these two items is, of course, to avoid being misled into thinking we are doing better than we actually are simply because of failure to identify the nature and extent of our competition."[6]

3. Productivity

Although the concept of productivity is a relatively simple one—a relationship of output of goods and services to the resources consumed in their production—this concept proved a difficult one to make operational as a measure of performance. For the national economy as a whole, it has been the practice to

---

[6]*Ibid,* 33.

look at productivity simply in terms of the amount of output per unit of labor input. In any given firm, however, labor is only one of the factors contributing to output. Therefore, the company sought to develop an index that would accomplish two things: (1) broaden the input base so as to recognize that capital as well as labor contributed to improvements in productivity, and (2) eliminate from the measure those improvements contributed by suppliers of materials.

On the output side of the productivity ratio, the company considered several refinements of "sales billed." One such refinement was the use of "value added" (e.g., sales billed less the cost of goods or services acquired outside the company). On the input side, the company considered payroll dollars plus depreciation dollars. Payroll dollars were employed as the variable, rather than labor hours, so as to give effect to differences in the labor skills employed. The inclusion of depreciation charges constituted an attempt to include the consumption of capital resources. All factors were to be adjusted for changes in the price level, so that changes in the resulting ratio would more nearly reflect real changes in productivity.

4. Product Leadership

Product leadership was defined as "the ability of a business to lead its industry in originating or applying the most advanced scientific and technical knowledge in the engineering, manufacturing and marketing fields to the development of new products and to improvements in the quality or values of existing products."[7] To make this definition operational, procedures were established for appraising periodically the products of each department. These appraisals were directed at providing answers to the following questions:

(a) How did each product compare with competition and with company standards?

(b) Where within the company was the research conducted upon which the product was based?

(c) Who first introduced the basic product and subsequent improvements, General Electric or a competitor?

The appraisal procedures were based largely on qualitative rather than quantitative considerations. Appraisals were made by appropriate experts from the areas of engineering, marketing, accounting, and manufacturing. In general, these experts were located within the product department for which the appraisal was to be made. Standard forms were employed so as to facilitate as high a degree of consistency as possible.

The trends revealed by these appraisals over a period of time were considered to be as significant as the specific information revealed by an appraisal for a particular period.

---

[7]*Ibid*, 35–36.

5. Personnel Development

For the purposes of measurement, personnel development was defined as "the systematic training of managers and specialists to fill present and future needs of the company, to provide for further individual growth and retirements and to facilitate corporate growth and expansion.[8] Management of General Electric defined personnel development as including "programs in each field of functional endeavor, such as engineering, manufacturing, marketing and finance, and broad programs aimed at developing an understanding of the principles of managing. Such programs must be designed to provide a continuous flow of potentially promotable employees in sufficient numbers to permit proper selection and development of individuals for each position. And, at the same time, these programs must encourage competition and initiative for further individual growth."[9]

Three steps were involved in the Measurement of performance in this Key Result Area. (1) The basic soundness of the various programs or techniques being sponsored by a product department for the development of its employees was appraised. (2) An inventory was taken of the available supply of trained men, as well as their qualifications, for the key positions that must eventually be filled within the department. (3) The effectiveness with which the department executed its personnel development programs was evaluated.

The first step consisted of judgments regarding the adequacy of the following elements in the development process.

- *Recruitment.* How good a job was being done in the selection of candidates for the development process?
- *On-the-job training.* What programs were available for training candidates, for providing information and knowledge about both general company matters and job particulars, and for advanced training for those who had been on the job for a while?
- *Review and counsel.* Was there any provision for periodically reviewing the performance of the men, for discussing with an individual the caliber of his work, for providing help and consultation, and for identifying especially promising talent?
- *Placement.* What was being done to see that recruits were placed in jobs commensurate with their interests and abilities, that the more promising were rotated, and, that promotions came to those who merited them?

The second step was accomplished with the aid of manning tables and related inventorying procedures. These procedures were directed primarily at determining the training background of each man in the inventory; i.e. graduates of company-sponsored programs, those hired from outside the company, and

---

[8]*Ibid*, 37.
[9]*Ibid.*

those who attained their positions without the benefit of a company-sponsored program.

The investigating group used two statistical measures in carrying out the third step. The first of these was the ratio of the number of men promoted (both within department and through transfer to another department) in a given period (usually a year) to the total number of men regarded as "promotable" during the same period. The second measure was tied in with the personnel rating procedure that was employed throughout the company. At the conclusion of each performance review cycle, the rating forms for a particular department were analyzed to determine the proportions of employees whose performance was considered to be (a) improving, (b) unchanged, and (c) deteriorating.

6. Employee Attitudes

For purposes of developing measures of performance in this key area, the group defined an attitude as "a generalized point of view toward objects, events or persons which might serve to influence future behavior." It used two basic approaches to the measument of attitudes. The first involved the use of statistical indicators, such as turnover rate, absenteeism, number of grievances, lateness, accident experience, etc. The second approach involved a periodic survey of employees through questionnaires.

Several shortcomings were recognized in the first approach. (1) The statistical indicators provided little or no information about underlying causes. (2) In general, the indicators told of trouble only after the harm had been done. (3) Because these indicators were traditionally associated with the pesonnel functions, managers tended to minimize their importance or else place responsibility for improvement on the personnel function. (4) Unfavorable trends in certain of these indicators might be due to external factors (e.g., short labor supply) rather than to some shortcoming of management.

The attitude survey made use of a standardized questionnaire designed to reveal the attitudes of employees in a number of broad areas. The survey was administered at intervals of about eighteen months. Results for each attitude area were tabulated in terms of proportion of responses that were favorable. Tabulations were made by work groups and not by individual employees; this practice helped protect the anonymity of responses, and thus the validity of the surveys.

7. Public Responsibility

This Key Result Area evolved from General Electric's recognition of its obligation to conduct itself as a good citizen within society, complying faithfully with the laws and ethics governing business conduct. The company believed its progress required not only an active recognition of the broad public interest, but also a responsiveness to certain special "publics" who had a stake in the success of the business: namely, shareowners, customers, employees, vendors, dealers and distributors, the plant community, educational institutions, and government.

While the resonsibility to certain "publics," such as shareowners, educational institutions, and the Federal government could best be measured from an overall company viewpoint rather than departmentally, nevertheless, the actions taken by a product department (including the individual acts of employees of that department) could have an important impact on the whole company's reputation as a good corporate citizen. Accordingly, the company attempted to assure wholehearted observance of the legal and ethical standards of business by insisting that all managerial and professional employees conduct periodical surveys at least once a year of the activities of those who reported to them with respect to antitrust compliance, conflict of interest, and other areas of business practice. These matters were discussed with each individual, who then signed a statement affirming his understanding and compliance.

Other measurements related to the effectiveness of department action in strengthening the company's reputation and business relationships. With respect to fulfilling obligations to customers, it was determined that the previously mentioned product leadership and market position areas were the best indicators. For the remaining "publics" the following measures were recommended.

Shareowners. The total shares of General Electric Company stock were to be "allocated" to the various operating components that were assigned responsibility for preserving and enhancing "their portion" of the shareowner's investment in the company.

Vendors, Dealers, and Distributors. Suppliers of raw materials and parts were to be surveyed periodically to determine their appraisal of the department's practices in conducting its business as compared with the practices of others who bought from them. Dealers and distributors were likewise to be interviewed from time to time, to measure whether these important relationships were being responsibly maintained.

Plant Community. Again, comprehensive reaction surveys were to be used, aimed at identifying the impact of the actions of a product department on the individuals who made up the community. These reactions disclosed by the opinion surveys were to be supplemented by use of trends developed from various types of data such as community wage rates, number of employment applications received, volume of purchases made locally, contributions to local charities, and participation in civic, church, and business organizations.

8. Balance Between Short-Range and Long-Range Goals

This factor was set out separately as a Key Result Area in order to emphasize the importance of the long-term survival and growth of the company. Short-range goals and performance had to be balanced against the need for satisfactory performance five, ten, fifteen years in the future, since undue pressure for current profits could, in effect, borrow from the future.

Various means were employed to experiment with suggested measures in their Key Result Area. However, it is important to note that when the eight Key Result Areas were established, each of the first seven had both short-range and long-range dimensions. The eighth area, balance between short-range, and long-range goals, had been specifically identified to make sure that the long-range health of the company would not be sacrificed for short-term gains. The plans, goals, and actions in each of the other areas were, therefore, to be appraised in terms of both their short-term and long-term implications.

During the period after the Measurements Project was established in 1952, deep research work was carried on to establish the specific measurements in each of the eight Key Result Areas. Before communicating these measures to the product departments, the investigators reviewed the recommendations in each area with operating personnel and with officers, for their comments, suggestions, and final approval.

The company's business planning, budgeting, and forecasting program incorporated the use of selected Key Result Areas in (1) reviewing the recent history and current status, (2) setting standards for each department, (3) planning to achieve the standards, and (4) periodic reporting and measurement of accomplishment. Since the first four Key Result Areas lent themselves readily to numerical evaluations, they were a part of the planning, budgeting, forecasting, reporting, and measuring system. Building on this experience in using the Key Result Areas to plan and measure performance, management at the General Electric Company made the search for effective business measurements a continuing, evolutionary process.

Required

Evaluate the success of General Electric's Measurements Project in accomplishing its stated objectives.

CASE 15.5   GENERAL ELECTRIC COMPANY (B)

In early May 1974, Mr. Standley Hall,[1] Manager of the Business Analysis and Cost Accounting Operation in the Comptroller's Department of General Electric Company, was trying to identify and evaluate alternative procedures for assigning interest expense to the operating components of the company. His investigation had been instigated by Mr. R. H. Smith, Chairman and Chief Executive Officer, when, at the end of 1973, Mr. Smith had discovered that the total amount of

---

This case was prepared by Richard Vancil. Copyright © by the President and Fellows of Harvard University. Harvard Business School case 9-175-053.

[1]The names of individual executives in this case have been disguised.

corporate interest expense was substantially underliquidated in terms of assignment to operating units. The problem had wound up on Mr. Hall's desk for analysis and recommendation because he was the staff executive responsible for the design of all internal financial measurements used within the company.

Background

In 1974, GE was the largest diversified industrial organization in the world. In the early 1950s, as sales volume passed the three billion dollar level and the prospects for continued growth were good, management had adopted a decentralization philosophy. The corporation was reorganized into product departments, each one small enough and cohesive enough to be analogous to a separate business and headed by a general manager who was responsible for running it in a manner consistent with overall corporate objectives.

By 1974, there were approximately 160 product departments in GE. Department general managers reported to division general managers, numbering about 40, who were also vice presidents of the company. Division managers reported to one of ten vice presidents and group executives who, in turn, reported to one of three vice chairmen and executive officers. The vice chairmen and Mr. Smith, collectively referred to as the Corporate Executive Office, were assisted by six senior vice presidents who comprised the Corporate Executive Staff. In addition, the Corporate Administrative Staff consisted of about two dozen vice presidents with functional or technical responsibilities.

At the time of the reorganization, corporate management realized that effective decentralization would require appropriate and comprehensive measures of the performance of the operating units down to the product department level. A measurements project was established to design and install a new set of internal operating reports [see the General Electric (A) case]. "Profitability" was identified as one of eight "key result areas" for which the performance of a product department should be measured. Profitability was to be measured in terms of "dollars of residual income," where residual income was defined as net income (after taxes) less a capital charge equal to 5% (after taxes) of the net assets assigned to the department. At about this time, the shareholders of GE approved a new incentive compensation plan: the total bonus pool each year would be 10% of corporate net income after deducting 5% of total invested capital. The distribution of this pool among GE executives was not specified by formula.

As the new reporting system evolved in its early years, corporate management found it desirable to use two measures of the profitability of operating components, residual income as defined above and net income before deducting the capital charge. In Mr. Hall's opinion, "Top management needs to look at net income on a monthly basis because it measures what they are responsible for and is reported to the stockholders quarterly and at the end of the year. If corporate net income doesn't meet budgeted goals, top management needs to be able to identify the components that are responsible for the variance."

Imputed Interest Expense

"The new reporting system worked pretty well for the first ten years or so," Mr. Hall continued, "but in the middle sixties the net amount of corporate-level adjustments turned red. Up until then, other income, like dividends from investments, had about equaled net interest expense. But our rate of growth was accelerating and, increasingly, we had to use debt as a source of funds for expansion. Total borrowings have increased by more than a billion dollars in the last ten years. Realizing that interest expense would become a significant cost of doing business, we had to find a way to assign it to the operating components so that their net income would continue to approximate the corporate net income.

"The approach we finally adopted in late 1967 was intended to reflect the situation we were coping with. Our businesses were growing faster than we could generate funds internally to finance the growth. So we established January 1, 1966, as a retroactive starting point and told the department managers that, from that point on, there would be no more free money from the Treasurer's office. We referred to it as a cash flow approach to financial management."

The imputed interest calculation was performed at the end of each month. Using the balance sheet maintained for each component, the change in the corporation's investment in the component was readily determinable. All cash was managed centrally in GE, so the component balance sheets contained only working capital items (receivables and inventories less payables and accruals) plus the net book value of plant and equipment. Component's monthly cash flow analysis typically showed two sources of cash: component net income and depreciation. The typical uses of cash were an increase in working capital and the cost of new investments in plant and equipment. The net difference of these four items represented cash that the component had provided to or drawn from the corporate treasury.

"In order to make the whole thing work," Mr. Hall went on, "we also had to assess dividends paid to stockholders as a use of funds at the component level. Not all our net income can be invested in financing expansion, only the retained earnings. The net effect was that a department manager would not be charged any imputed interest as long as he was able to finance his own growth out of his retained earnings plus the cash flow from depreciation. If he needed more funds, we'd provide them, but he'd have to pay interest on the excess. If he was throwing off more cash than he needed then he was really helping to finance other units, and we'd credit him with imputed interest income. The interest rate, either way, was a four-year rolling average of the actual cost of all money borrowed by the corporation.

"The calculation of imputed interest was a little complex, so it took a while for all the general managers to understand it, and some of them complained that the starting rate was arbitrary. But there's no question that it worked. First, over the next several years, this routine did succeed in assigning the increase in the corporate interest expense to the components. That made top management happy. Second, and probably more important, the general managers had to learn a lot about financial management. During the first five years after the routine was installed, working capital at the component level increased less than 10%, even though sales volume rose over 30%. That made top management even happier."

The Problem in 1973

"The magnitude of the underliquidation in 1973," Mr. Hall said, "came as something of a surprise. The amount of net interest expense that we actually charged to the components was only about 55% of the amount that should have been liquidated. If we define the problem narrowly, then a simple variance analysis can explain the shortfall. There are two causes: the interest rate we use and the investment base to which it's applied. In 1973, the formula rate was 6% and that was also the prime rate at the start of the year. But the prime skyrocketed to 10% before the year was out and we've got a few hundred million dollars of bank debt and commercial paper that moves with the prime. Our actual average interest rate on short- and long-term debt in $973 was about $7\frac{1}{2}$%.

"The bigger cause of the variance, though, was in the deterioration of our investment base during recent years. The total increase in the company's investment in the operating components since the beginning of 1966 is about a billion dollars. During those years, however, we've launched a lot of new products and ventures, some of which have failed, and we've also discontinued some of our old product lines. The Comptroller adopted a policy a few years ago of 'forgiving' the cumulative investment in product lines that were abandoned; it didn't seem fair to continue to impute an interest expense to a defunct line of business. By 1973, such abandonments had wiped out about 30% of our base.

"Well," Mr. Hall continued, "the large, sudden underliquidation sure got Smith's attention. In discussions with my boss, Maurice Mott, the Comptroller, and his boss, Al Woods, the Vice President–Finance, we've decided that maybe we shouldn't define the problem narrowly as: How do we fix the formula to eliminate the variance? Given the magnitude of the problem, fixing the formula might involve bending it out of shape in any event. Instead, we've decided to use this problem as an opportunity to review the fundamental philosophy behind our imputed interest procedure and, perhaps, adopt a whole new approach. A problem like this can make people more receptive to a major change than would be feasible in the normal course of events, and there are some aspects of the current procedure that are troublesome, quite apart from the underliquidation.

"First, several of us think that charging interest as we do may make it harder to implement GE's broad strategy for continued growth. Mr. Smith has made the strategy quite explicit: The allocation of corporate resources must be biased in favor of our high-growth, high-potential, newer businesses even if that means a reduction in the resources available for our mature businesses that are growing more slowly. Making such allocation decisions is always tough, and one important criterion is the trend in the bottom line for each business; they look at the net income over the last three years and the forecast for the next three. One effect of the way that we imput interest expense is that it makes the net income of the mature businesses appear to be growing faster than it really is, and it dampens the apparent growth rate of our high-growth businesses.

"Another aspect of this same effect," Mr. Hall went on, 'is the protection that imputed interest income provides for the net income of mature businesses. We're fortunate in having several highly profitable businesses that aren't growing very fast anymore so they have a substantial cash throwoff. Last year, the largest of these earned more than a million dollars of interest income, and that figure grows each year. Theoretically, the day might come when the imputed interest income of such a business will exceed its operating income. To the extent that there's a problem in that, it's compounded by the fact that our general managers tend to get new assignments every three or four years and a new man coming into such a business has two things going for him—a fine business and an annuity from prior cash flow—not just one.'

Alternative Solutions

"So," Mr. Hall said, "we're in the midst of a review of the whole procedure. Without being too academic about it, Al Woods, Maurie Mott, and I have tried to identify the criteria that our recommendation to Smith should fulfill. First, the procedure should be as simple as possible, not just to facilitate computation but to make it easy for the general managers to understand. Second, the procedure should be effective in liquidating corporate interest expense into the components, although a modest over- or underliquidation would be tolerable. Finally, the procedure should help to increase the awareness of our general maangers about the major increase in the cost of borrowing money. Prime interest rates (inserted by the casewriter at the bottom of Exhibit 1) have really climbed and stand at 11% today. That may come down a little, but we think high rates are going to be with us for several years.

"At the moment, we're trying to conceptualize alternative procedures that might meet these criteria, focusing really on what investment base to use. We also had to decide on what rate to use and there's a nest of issues there—whether to use one rate or several different ones; whether the rate should be a 'policy' rate, a cost-based rate, or a current market rate; and how often the rate should be changed—but we've decided to defer dealing with that until we get some resolution on the conceptual issue. So far, we've identified four main alternatives, although a couple of them are rather theoretical.

No Capital Charge. "Any exhaustive list of alternative ways to assign interest expense," Mr. Hall said, "would have to start with the question of why do it at all? The basic reason, I think, is that a capital charge of some sort is required by criterion number three. Also, our general managers have gotten used to the idea of having their net income be a "realistic" number. They know that interest is a cost of doing business and believe that it should appear on their operating statement. The primary argument against liquidation of the actual corporate interest expense is that it is a function of GE's capital structure and dividend policy, and the component general managers really don't control that."

Complete Capital Charge. "That brings us to the second alternative," Mr. Hall continued. "Why not charge for the total corporate investment in each component, rather than just for its cumulative cash flow requirements since 1966? That brings us right back to residual income, of course, so it would be the simplest of all procedures. The rationale for residual income is that it's the total investment in a component—not just the portion of it that the corporation finances with borrowed money—that is important, and the general manager is the person who is responsible for the total investment.

"The major problem with this approach is that the components' new income would not be realistic—there'd be a major overliquidation at the corporate level. Nevertheless, I've given this approach some thought. If we could agree to just change the name—to call residual income at the component level 'net income'—and to adjust our thinking to accept a positive variance between corporate net income and component net income—it would be a big step forward. As a practical matter, however, I'm sure this is too revolutionary a change. It just won't happen."

Modified Cash Flow Approach. "Some modification of our existing procedure is clearly the most feasible alternative," Mr. Hall went on. "It's now widely accepted because it's been applied for several years and everyone is used to it and understands it more or less. This is a huge company with a great diversity of businesses and when you finally get something that works you don't change it lightly—and sometimes you can't change it even if you want to.

"If we do keep it, then criterion number two dictates that we'll have to modify it immediately, and I'm not sure how to do that in any way that isn't totally arbitrary. Also, when we make a modification this time, we ought to build some flexibility into the formula so that it will continue to be effective. For example, in explaining the need for a change, we'll have to disclose that, in part, it was caused by the Comptroller's forgiveness of the investment in abandoned product lines. Now, most general managers didn't realize that such forgiveness was possible, but when they find out I think that Maurie will get a lot more requests. Any change in the procedure ought to anticipate the need to deal with that issue on a continuing basis."

Net Working Capital Approach. "Finally," Mr. Hall said, "I can only think of one other way to deal with the problem. The idea is simple, and my calculations indicate that it would achieve a reasonable liquidation of corporate interest expense.

The big problem is that it's a totally different approach, and, as I'll describe in a moment, some managers will be upset.

"You know, once you get a new idea, it's hard not to get enamored with it. At first blush, this idea looked flawless. The proposal is simply to charge each component for the investment in net working capital shown on its balance sheet. I see two big advantages to this approach. First, it focuses on that part of the component investment that the general manager really can control on a current basis. Through our capital budgeting procedures, we already have explicit controls on new investments in plant and equipment, and this approach would provide a decentralized control over working capital. Second, this new approach would treat all components in exactly the same way on a current basis, no matter whether it's a new business or an old one. That would mean that no component would earn imputed interest income, but that any unit could lower its interest expense by reducing working capital. Product abandonments under this proposal would be adjusted for automatically; if you closed out a product line, the working capital supporting it would be eliminated and so would the interest expense.

"So," Mr. Hall continued, "I took the idea to Maurie and then to Al. They thought it was interesting enough to be explored further, but both were concerned about how it might be accepted in the components. I agreed that I ought to try the idea on the Managers of Finance in the operating units—and did I get an earful.

"I've only talked to a handful so far, but I haven't yet found anyone who likes it. A variety of concerns have been expressed, but some patterns are emerging. First, everyone I've talked to is worried about what it would do to the pattern of their net income. Even if we recast the imputed interest calculation for the last five years—and that could be done—they can't predict how the recast— and their forecast—using the new method would be affected. The components with interest income know that they'd be hurt, but it's not the drop in net income that bothers them as much as the caprious ways that the new approach might change the earnings trend.

"Another worry is with the general fairness of the new approach. As one finance manager in a profitable, mature business put it, 'It doesn't seem right that, with all the cash we throw off that we should also have to pay interest expense. In effect, we get no credit for our cashflow, and it is used to pay for plant and equipment that is built—interest-free—for a growing business.' A similar criticism but expressed a little more broadly is that this approach is just another type of corporate assessment, like corporate overhead but assessed on a different basis, and that it will fail to get and keep the general manager focused on financial management the way that our cash flow method does.

"So, I went back to the drawing board to search for a way to modify the cash flow approach. One idea, that one of my assistants suggested, would be to adopt a banker's method of doing business. A savings bank, for example, accepts deposits and pays, say, 6% interest on them and then turns around and loans the money to borrowers at, say, 8%. We might try something like that, paying a lower rate of interest to components that provide cash than we charge to components that use it.

"An alternative set of modifications would be to charge components interest on their beginning-of-the-year "long-term debt" and charge (or credit) them for their cumulative use or generation of cash during the year at the current monthly prime rate of interest. This proposl would retain the case flow approach although it would eliminate January 1, 1966, as the starting date. In addition, the use of one rate to apply to past as well as current uses of cash would be replaced by a long and short term rate concept.

"The beginning-of-the-year debt for each component would be established by multiplying the corporation's investment in that component by the parent Company's ratio of debt to debt plus equity. In recent years, this ratio has been roughly 30%. By resetting the debt each year, the need to adjust for abandonments will no longer be necessary. A conventional cash flow analysis, as we do it now, would calculate the net cash provided or used during the current year, to which the monthly prime rate would be applied."

"I don't know," Mr. Hall concluded, "what the reactions will be to either of these modifications, but I'm not very optimistic. Some part of the negative reactions to the working capital approach could be labeled simply as resistance to change, but the resistance is real nonetheless. Beneath that there may also be substantive concern that any new proposal won't have the effect on managers that we expect or want. I admit that a change in the measurement system can affect behavior, and that it might affect one manager differently than another because the people as well as the businesses are different. But we've got over 200 component general managers and the same measurement procedure has to be applied to all of them. How could we tailor it to the personalities of each one—particularly when they keep changing jobs? About all I can hope to do is to find the right answer—whatever that is."

Required

1. How does General Electric's cash flow system operate? What are its purposes? Which of these purposes do you believe the most important? How well has it accomplished those purposes in the past? Do you believe that it motivates department managers to act consistently with General Electric's goals? Does it provide a fair measurement of performance?

2. What is the purpose of allocating interest expense to the departments? Why assign just interest expense? Why not equity capital? Does this allocation affect managerial behavior? Should it?

3. What alternative methods is General Electric considering? Of the three objections to the working capital charge method, which of these objections, if any, are valid? Which of the alternative methods would you recommend?

CASE 15.6 THE GALVOR COMPANY[1]

M. Boudry, Universal Electric's Regional Controller for Europe, was optimistic about Galvor's future.

"Galvor is small," he said, "and we don't give it much time or help unless its variances appear to be off. This happened in the second half of 1986 when we became increasingly concerned about the level of Galvor's inventories. This brought M. Poulet into the picture. M. Poulet is Director of Manufacturing on the regional headquarters staff here in Geneva. If you want to see how our system works, you might take a look at this series of telex messages (Exhibits 2 through 5) between him and Galvor's Managing Director.

"We feel that the situation is under control now, and that the outlook for Galvor is okay despite the flat performance between 1983 and 1985 and the downturn in 1986. The company has been turned around and 1987 looks promising."

The variances referred to by M. Boudry were shown on Galvor's regular monthly operating reports, a key feature in the financial planning and reporting system used by Universal to control its far-flung subsidiaries. This case describes the Universal system and its implementation at Galvor. The description is divided into six major sections.

    A. Development of the business plan
    B. Headquarters reporting
    C. Providing information for Galvor's management
    D. Organization of the controller's department at Galvor
    E. Cost of the system
    F. Management's evaluation of the system

A. Developing the Business Plan

The heart of Universal's reporting and control system was an extremely comprehensive document called the Business Plan. Prepared annually by each operating unit, the Business Plan was the primary standard for evaluating the unit manager's performance.

Development of the plan was a four-phase process, spread over a ten-month period:

This case was prepared by Professor L. E. Morrissey as a basis for class discussion rather than to illustrate either effective or ineffective handling of an administrative situation. Copyright by IMEDE (International Management Development Institute), Luasanne, Switzerland. Reproduced by permission.

[1]The Galvor Company, supplying electric and electronic measuring instruments primarily to the French market, became a Universal subsidiary in April, 1984.

- *Phase 1*: Establishment of Broad Objectives
- *Phase 2*: Preparation of a tentative plan
- *Phase 3*: Headquarters review and approval
- *Phase 4*: Preparation of detailed budget schedules

1. Establishment of Broad Objectives. Each January, Universal's regional headquarters staff in Geneva set tentative objectives for the following two years for each of the company's European operating units. Objectives were established for five key measures:

- **(a)** Sales
- **(b)** Net income
- **(c)** Total assets
- **(d)** Total employees
- **(e)** Capital expenditures

For operating units which produced more than a single product line, objectives were established both for the unit as a whole and for each product line. Primary responsibility for establishing these tentative objectives rested with eight product-line managers located in Geneva, each of whom was responsible for several of the 300-odd lines that were marketed in Europe by Universal. The product-line manager set these tentative objectives on the basis of his knowledge of the product lines and his best judgment of their market potential.

For planning and reporting purposes, Universal considered that Galvor represented a single product line, even though Galvor's own executives viewed their products as falling into three distinct lines—multimeters, panel meters, and electronic instruments.

From January to April, these tentative objectives were "negotiated" between Geneva headquarters and the operating managements. Formal meetings were held in Geneva to resolve differences between the operating unit managers and product-line managers or other headquarters personnel.

Negotiations also took place at the same time on products to be discontinued. Mr. Hennessy, Galvor's Managing Director, described this process as a "sophisticated exercise which includes a careful analysis of the effect on overhead costs of discontinuing a product and also recognizes the cost of holding an item in stock. It is a good analysis and one method Universal uses to keep the squeeze on us."

During May, the negotiated objectives were reviewed and approved by Universal's European headquarters in Geneva and by corporate headquarters in the United States. The approved objectives provided the foundation on which the unit managers could build their Business Plans.

2. Preparation of a Tentative Plan. In June and July of each year, each operating unit prepared a tentative Business Plan for the two years beginning in the following January. This plan showed how the unit intended to achieve its objectives.

The Business Plan was a lengthy document, containing as many as 100 pages. It consisted of five parts:

(a) A one-page financial and operating summary

(b) A summary analysis of the causes of anticipated changes in net income

(c) A set of projected financial statements, with detailed commentary

(d) A description of the major management actions planned for the next two years

(e) Simulated financial results for sales of 60%, 80%, and 120% of forecast levels

2A ONE-PAGE SUMMARY. The one-page summary contained actual data for the preceding year and planned or forecasted data for the current year, each of the next two years, and the fifth year ahead. A line was provided for each of the following measures.

- Net income
- Sales
- Total assets
- Total capital employed (sum of long-term debt and net worth)
- Receivables
- Inventories
- Plant, property, and equipment
- Capital expenditures
- Provision for depreciation
- % return on sale
- % return on total assets
- % return on total capital employed
- % total assets to sales
- % receivables to sales
- % inventories to sales
- Orders received
- Orders on hand
- Average number of full-time employees
- Total cost of employee compensation
- Sales per employee
- Net income per employee
- Sales per $1000 of employee compensation
- Net income per $1000 of employee compensation
- Sales per thousand square feet of floor space
- Net income per thousand square feet of floor space

2B ANTICIPATED CHANGES. Anticipated changes in net income for the current year and for each of the next two years were summarized according to their cause, as follows:

- Volume of sales
- Product mix
- Sales prices
- Raw material purchase prices
- Cost reduction programmes
- Accounting changes and all other causes

This analysis of the causes of changes in net income was intended to force operating managements to appraise carefully the profit implications of all management actions affecting prices, costs, volume or product mix.

2c PROJECTED FINANCIAL STATEMENTS. This analysis was followed by a complete set of projected financial statements—income statement, balance sheet, and statement of cash flows—for the current year and for each of the next two years. Each major item on these statements was then analyzed in detail, covering such matters as transactions with headquarters, proposed outside financing, investment in receivables and inventory, number of employees and employee compensation, capital expenditures, and nonrecurring write-offs of assets.

2d DESCRIPTION OF MAJOR MANAGEMENT ACTIONS. The fourth section of the Business Plan consisted of a description of the major management actions planned for the next two years, with an estimate of the effect each action would have on total sales, net income, and total assets. For example, the following actions were among those described in Galvor's 1986 Business Plan (prepared in mid-1985).

- Implement standard cost system
- Revise prices
- Cut oldest low margin items from line
- Standardize and simplify product design
- Create forward research and development plan
- Implement product planning

Detailed plans were also presented for each functional area: marketing, manufacturing, research and development, financial control, and personnel and employee relations. These functional plans began with a statement of the function's mission, an analysis of its present problems and opportunities, and a statement of the specific actions it intended to take in the next two years. For example, M. Barsac, Galvor's new controller, included the following objectives for his department in the 1986 Business Plan.

- Distribute tasks more efficiently
- Make more intensive use of IBM equipment
- Replace nonqualified employees with better trained and more dynamic people

2E SIMULATED FINANCIAL STATEMENTS. The final section of the Business Plan consisted of a series of comparative financial statements which depicted the estimated item-by-item effect if sales fell to 60% or to 80% of forecast or increased to 120% of forecast. For each of these levels of possible sales, costs were divided into three categories: fixed costs, unavoidable variable costs, and management discretionary costs. Management described the specific actions it would take to control employment, total assets and capital expenditures in case of a reduction in sales and when these actions would be put into effect. In its 1986 Business Plan, for example, Galvor indicated that its program for contraction would be put into effect if incoming orders dropped below 60% of budget for two weeks, 75% for four weeks or 85% for eight weeks. It noted that assets would be cut only to 80% in a 60% year and to 90% in an 80% year "because remodernization of our business is too essential for survival to slow down much more."

3. Review and Approval of Plan.

The completed Business Plan was submitted to Unviersal's headquarters about the end of July. The plans of the individual companies were then reviewed and defended at a series of meetings held in Geneva early in autumn. These meetings were attended by senior executives from both Universal's European and American headquarters and by the general managers and funcional mangers of many of the operating units. Universal viewed these meetings as an important element in its contsant effort to encourage operating managements to share their experiences in resolving common problems.

Before final approval of a company's Business Plan at the Geneva review meeting, changes were often proposed by Universal's top management. For example, in September 1986, the 1987 forecast of sales and net income in Galvor's Business Plan were accepted, but the year-end forecasts of total employees and total assets were reduced about 9% and 1%. Galvor's proposed capital expenditures for the year were cut 34%, a reduction primarily attributable to limitations imposed by Universal on all operating units throughout the corporation.

4. Preparation of Detailed Budget Schedules.

The approved Business Plan became the foundation of the budget for the following year, which was due in Geneva by mid-November. The general design of the budget resembled that of the Business Plan except that the various dollar amounts, which were presented in the Business Plan on an annual basis, were broken down by months.

The annual totals in the budget had to agree with the figures shown in the approved Business Plan unless advance approval for a change in the plan had been obtained from Geneva. Requests for approval of such changes had to be submitted to Geneva no later than mid-October. To conserve management's time, only major changes could be submitted; adjustment for minor changes in conditions or forecasts were not allowed.

B. Headquarters Reporting

The second pillar in Universal's financial control structure was the periodic financial and statistical reporting system. Each operating unit submitted 13 reports to regional and world-wide headquarters each month, covering the unit's activities for the previous month and in some cases for the year to date as well:

- Preliminary income statement (due during the first week of the month)
- Income statement
- Balance sheet
- Statement of changes in retained earnings
- Statement of cash flows
- Employment statistics
- Status of orders received, canceled and outstanding
- Statement of intercompany transactions
- Statement of transactions with headquarters
- Analysis of inventories
- Analysis of receivables
- Status of capital projects
- Controller's monthly operating and financial review

In addition to the monthly reports, each operating unit was required to submit about a dozen other reports, some quarterly, some semiannually, and some once a year.

1. Focus on Variances. The main focus in most of the reports submitted to Universal was on the variance between actual results and the budgeted plan. For this reason, the controller's monthly operating and financial review (the last report on the list above) often ran to 20 pages or more. It contained an explanation of the significant variances from budget as well as a general commentary on the financial affairs of the unit. Differences between the current year and the prior year were also reported because these were the figures submitted quarterly to Universal's shareholders and to newspapers and other financial reporting services.

To assist M. Barsac in preparing this report, Galvor's department heads had been required since the beginning of 1986 to explain the variances from their budget for the month. M. Barsac hoped that the need to make these explanations would make the operating executives more familiar with the financial side of their operations, thus permitting them to play a greater role in the annual planning process.

2. Uniformity Within the Universal Electric Group. All units in Universal, whether based in the United States or elsewhere, adhered to essentially the same reporting system. Identical forms and account numbers were used throughout the Universal organization. Since the reporting system made no distinction between units of different size, Galvor submitted the same reports as a unit with many times its sales. Computer processing of these reports facilitated combining the results of Unviersal's European operations for prompt review in Geneva and transmission to corporate headquarters in the United States.

3. Headquarters Performance Review. Galvor's periodic financial reports were forwarded to M. Boudry in Geneva. The reports were first reviewed by an assistant to M. Boudry, one of four financial analysts who together reviewed all reports received from Universal's operating units in Europe.

In early 1987, M. Boudry described the purpose of these reviews.

> "The reviews focus on a comparison of performance against budget for the key measures—sales, net income, total assets, total employees, and capital expenditures. These are stated as unambiguous numbers. We try to detect any trouble spots or trends which seem to be developing. Of course, the written portions of the reports are also carefully reviewed, particularly the explanations of variances from budget. If everything is moving as planned, we do nothing.
>
> "The reports may contain a month-by-month revision of forecasts to year-end, but if the planned objectives for the year are not to be met we consider the situation as serious.
>
> "If a unit manager has a problem and calls for help, then it becomes a matter of common concern. He can probably expect a bad day in explaining how it happened, but he can expect help too. Depending on the nature of the problem, either Mr. Forrester, Galvor's product line manager, or one of our staff specialists would go down to Bordeaux. In addition to the financial analysts, one of whom closely follows Galvor's reports, we have specialists on cost systems and analysis, inventory control, credit and industrial engineering.
>
> "We have not given Galvor the help it needs and deserves in data processing, but we have a limited staff here in Geneva and we cannot meet all needs. We hope to increase this staff during 1987.

Deviations from budget, as well as problems identified by unit management, were discussed at regular, periodic meetings with regional and headquarters personnel. Separate meetings were held for each of Universal's world-wide product groups. Unit managers were expected to identify their problems and to propose solutions in writing prior to each such meeting. The meetings were meant to assure that relevant experiences would be shared, that specific individuals would be assigned to solve pressing problems, and that all such problems would be identified and placed under study.

C. Providing Information for Galvor's Management

Although most of M. Barsac's efforts during his first two and a half years with Galvor had gone into meeting Universal's planning and reporting requirements, a good deal of progress was also made in providing information for use by Galvor's management.

For example, Mr. Hennessy and M. Barsac prepared the 1985 Business Plan themselves. In 1985, however, each department head prepared his own part of the 1986 plan and submitted it to Mr. Hennessy. M. Gevrey, Manager of Materials Control, had the following reaction at the time.

> "This is, of course, the first time we have prepared our own budget. I was asked to project my personnel expenses and purchasing expenses. Mr. Hennessy called me in with Barsac to review my figures, and he asked me how I had obtained certain of them which he thought were too high. He will reduce these, although he hasn't yet told me by how much. This budget review session is a little like a father controlling the expenses of his child. The father has a lot of experience and more judgment than the child. This new tool is not perfect, but it has the advantage of being established."

Mr. Hennessy commented:

> "Most of the people at Galvor are not fully committed to the objective of cost cutting and they don't put figures down for savings. When they do see figures or financial results they shake their heads, a little unconvinced. They accept the idea of preparing a budget, but they are not yet fully committed to the results."

Nevertheless, Mr. Hennessy cited a 7% reduction in manufacturing costs as evidence that some progress was being made, even at that early date.

A key element in the new financial control system was a standard costing system, adapted from the system used by Universal in its other manufacturing companies, and covering development, tooling, machining, and assembly costs. A tight time table for this project was established immediatley after the merger, and Galvor embarked on a crash program of standardizing and codifying all the piece parts used in its products. This required the establishment of 8000 machining and 300 assembly standard times and the codification of 15,000 piece parts, all in a very short space of time.

Galvor had great difficulty in meeting the time table for this project, due largely to the lack of reliable historical data and a shortage of qualified personnel. For example, Universal's United States headquarters called for complete standard price lists from all of its subsidiaries by January, 1986. By July, 1985 only 30% of these prices had been prepared.

> "Universal's European headquarters has asked us to do this and we have had to do it too quickly," M. Gevrey, Manager of Materials Control, said at the time. "Therefore, we have taken present prices and made these standard. . . . I have talked to Mr. Hennessy about it but he is being pressured by Universal's headquarters. They are always pushing us, and telling us, 'you must, you must, you must.' Everything is dominated by numbers and the financial control system. You know, we have asked for a great effort on the part of all the people in my department and although things are beginning to take shape, it is a little discouraging to have no results yet."

Progress on the development of standard prices was slowed by the delays encountered in installing Universal's standard production and inventory control system. As of July 1985, however, 30% of Galvor parts were still not codified, and the IBM expert explained that most of his results were still not exploitable and that no one paid any attention to them. Further mechanization had not solved any of Galvor's problems and the old systems were still running in parallel. If the mechanization plan were to be thrown out tomorrow, he commented, no one would notice the difference.

Despite these difficulties, Galvor managed to put its standard cost system into operation in March, 1986, only two months behind schedule, and a formal inventory control system went into effect ten months later, in January 1987.

One feature of the new standard costing system was an improved method of applying factory overhead costs to individual products. Before Universal acquired Galvor, a single factory-wide rate was used for this purpose. For many years the rate was 310% of direct labor cost. In 1986, as part of the new standard costing system, Galvor replaced this with departmental burden rates. Fifteen different cost centers were established in the factory, each with a separate burden rate. These rates, which combined direct labor cost and overhead, ranged from 13.19 francs to 38.62 francs per direct labor hour.

Impressive as these changes were, however, it remained true that the bulk of the work of the Controller's department was devoted to routine clerical work or to meeting Universal's reporting requirements.

D. Organization of the Controller's Department at Galvor

Technical responsibility for compliance with the requirements of Universal's planning and reporting system was lodged in the controller's department at Galvor. Despite many difficulties, Galvor managed to meet Universal's reporting deadlines from the early part of 1985 onward.

Headquarters reporting was only one part of M. Barsac's responsibility, however. His second task was to supervise Galvor's internal accounting operations, including the preparation of reports for the use of Galvor's own management and the installation of a new IBM data processing system.

Mr. Hennessy regarded M. Barsac as one of the key men in the Galvor management team. Commenting early in 1985 on M. Barsac's role and qualifications, Mr. Hennessy said:

> "He is very well trained and has had 10 years of experience in the second largest Universal subsidiary in France. He has trained himself by moving around the various control areas of the subsidiary. He knows the requirements of the Universal policies and he has a broad feeling for management. He will be part of my management triumvirate. I will use him more than I will train him."

When M. Barsac first came to Galvor, he found that no one on the staff was qualified to prepare accounting statements. His predecessor, M. Chambertin, had always prepared Galvor's financial statements himself. Consequently, M. Barsac faced a serious shortage of trained personnel when he took over in 1984. "Most of my accountants can only prepare statements if you explain every step of the procedure," he complained in 1985. "They have no initiative and I have to check everything because they always make mistakes."

To relieve himself of much of this detailed work, M. Barsac hired M. Dussex in the fall of 1985 to fill the newly created position of chief accountant. M. Dussex's place in the organization structure is shown in Exhibit 1. As the exhibit shows, most of M. Barsac's people were under M. Dussex, doing routine book-keeping and accounting work.

EXHIBIT 1 The Galvor Company

Organization of Controller's Department (January 1987)

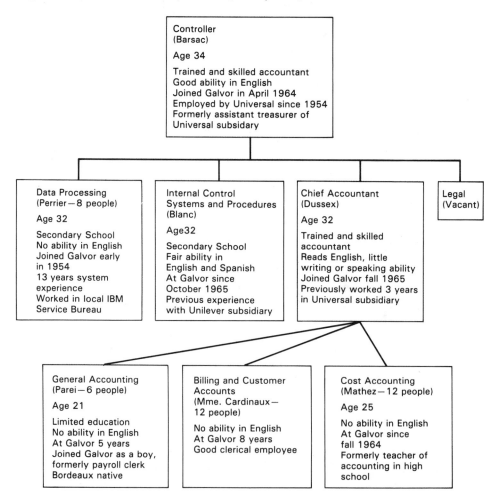

Controller
(Barsac)

Age 34

Trained and skilled accountant
Good ability in English
Joined Galvor in April 1964
Employed by Universal since 1954
Formerly assistant treasurer of
Universal subsidary

Data Processing
(Perrier—8 people)

Age 32

Secondary School
No ability in English
Joined Galvor early
in 1954
13 years system
experience
Worked in local IBM
Service Bureau

Internal Control
Systems and Procedures
(Blanc)

Age32

Secondary School
Fair ability in
English and Spanish
At Galvor since
October 1965
Previous experience
with Unilever subsidiary

Chief Accountant
(Dussex)

Age 32

Trained and skilled
accountant
Reads English, little
writing or speaking ability
Joined Galvor fall 1965
Previously worked 3 years
in Universal subsidiary

Legal
(Vacant)

General Accounting
(Parei—6 people)

Age 21

Limited education
No ability in English
At Galvor 5 years
Joined Galvor as a boy,
formerly payroll clerk
Bordeaux native

Billing and Customer
Accounts
(Mme. Cardinaux—
12 people)

No ability in English
At Galvor 8 years
Good clerical employee

Cost Accounting
(Mathez—12 people)

Age 25

No ability in English
At Galvor since
fall 1964
Formerly teacher of
accounting in high
school

E. Cost of the System

Universal's financial planning and reporting system imposed a heavy burden in both time and money on the management of an operating unit. The load on Galvor was particularly heavy during the first few years after the company's acquisition by Universal. M. Barsac recalled vividly his early days as Galvor's controller:

> "I arrived at Galvor in early April, 1984, a few days after M. Chambertin had left. I was the first Universal man here in Bordeaux and I became quickly immersed in all the problems surrounding the change of ownership. For example, there were no really workable financial statements for the previous two years. This made preparation of the Business Plan, which Mr. Hennessy and I began in June, extremely difficult. This plan covers every aspect of the business, but the great secrecy which had always been maintained at Galvor about the company's financial affairs made it almost impossible for anyone to help us."

The burden on M. Barsac's staff was no lighter a year later. Commenting on his role in the preparation of Galvor's 1986 Business Plan, M. Barsac said:

> "Galvor's previous Administrative Manager (Controller), who was a tax specialist above all, had to prepare a balance sheet and statement of income once a year. Cost accounting, perpetual inventory valuation, inventory control, production control,

EXHIBIT 2 The Galvor Company

Telex from Poulet to Hennessy Concerning Level of Inventory

TO:	HENNESSY – GALVOR
FROM:	POULET – UE
DATE:	SEPT. 26, 1986

FOLLOWING ARE THE JULY AND AUGUST INVENTORY AND SALES FIGURES WITH THEIR RESPECTIVE VARIANCES FROM BUDGET.

THOUSANDS OF DOLLARS

	ACTUAL	*JULY* *BUDGET*	*VARIANCE*	*ACTUAL*	*AUGUST* *BUDGET*	*VARIANCE*
INVENTORY	2010	1580	(430)	2060	1600	(460)
SALES TO DATE	3850	3900	(50)	4090	4150	(60)

LATEST AUGUST SALES FORECAST REFLECTS DECREASE IN YEAR-END SALES OF 227 VS INCREASE OF 168 IN YEAR-END INVENTORIES OVER BUDGET.

REQUEST TELEX LATEST MONTH-BY-MONTH INVENTORY AND SALES FORECAST FROM SEPTEMBER TO DECEMBER, EXPLANATION OF VARIANCE IN INVENTORY FROM BUDGET AND CORRECTIVE ACTION YOU PLAN IN ORDER TO ACHIEVE YEAR-END GOAL. INCLUDE PERSONNEL REDUCTIONS, PURCHASE MATERIAL CANCELLATIONS, ETC.

POULET

EXHIBIT 3   The Galvor Company

Telex from Hennessy to Poulet Concerning Level of Inventory

TO: POULET – UE
FROM: HENNESSY – GALVOR
DATE: SEPT. 27, 1986

YOUR 26.9.86
MONTHLY INVENTORY FORECAST SEPTEMBER TO DECEMBER BY CATEGORY FOLLOWS:

THOUSANDS OF DOLLARS

	SEPT. 30	*OCT. 31*	*NOV. 30*	*DEC. 31*
RAW MATERIALS	53	51	50	50
PURCHASED PARTS	180	185	190	195
MANUFACTURED PARTS	95	93	93	91
WORK IN PROCESS	838	725	709	599
FINISHED GOODS	632	694	683	705
OTHER INVENTORIES	84	84	82	80
ENGINEERING IN PROCESS	55	58	48	44
RESERVE	(14)	(14)	(14)	(20)
INDICA	50	52	55	55
TOTAL	1973	1928	1896	1799

THE MAIN EXPLANATIONS OF PRESENT VARIANCE ARE THREE POLICIES ADOPTED END 1985 AND DISCUSSED IN MONTHLY LETTERS BUT WHICH LEFT DECEMBER 1986 BUDGET OPTIMISTICALLY LOW. FIRST WAS TO HAVE REASONABLE AMOUNTS OF SELLING MODELS IN STOCK WITHOUT WHICH WE COULD NOT HAVE ACHIEVED 19% INCREASE IN SALES WE ARE MAKING WITH OUTMODED PRODUCT.

SECOND POLICY WAS TO MANUFACTURE LONGER SERIES OF EACH MODEL BY DOUBLE WHEREVER SALES WOULD ABSORB IT, OTHERWISE MANY OF OUR COST REDUCTIONS WERE NEARLY ZERO. THIS MEANS OUR MANUFACTURING PROGRAM ANY MONTH MAY CONTAIN FIVE MONTHS WORTH OF 15 MODELS INSTEAD OF 10 WEEKS WORTH OF 30 MODELS (OUT OF SEVENTY).

THIRD WAS NEW POLICY OF REDUCING NUMBER OF PURCHASE ORDERS BY MAINTAINING A MINIMUM STOCK OF MANY THOUSANDS OF LOW VALUE ITEMS WHICH YOU AGREED WOULD AND DID INCREASE STOCK UPON FIRST PROCUREMENT BUT WE ARE ALREADY GETTING SLIGHT REDUCTION.

CORRECTIVE ACTIONS NUMEROUS INCLUDING RUNNING 55 PEOPLE UNDER BUDGET AND ABOUT 63 BY YEAR END PLUS REVIEWING ALL PURCHASE ORDERS MYSELF PLUS SLIDING A FEW SERIES OF MODELS WHICH WOULD HAVE GIVEN SMALL BILLING IN 1986 INTO 1987 PLUS THOSE POSTPONED BY CUSTOMERS. THIS WILL NOT HAVE DRAMATIC EFFECT AS NEARLY ALL THESE SERIES ARE PROCURED AND HAVE TO BE MADE FOR RELATIVELY SURE MARKETS BUT SOME CAN BE HELD IN PIECEPARTS UNTIL JANUARY. WE ARE WATCHING CAREFULLY STOCKS OF SLOW MOVING MODELS AND HAVE MUCH CLEANER FINISHED STOCK THAN END 1985.

FINAL AND GRAVE CONCERN IS ACCURACY OF PARTS, WORK IN PROCESS, AND FINISHED GOODS VALUATION SINCE WE BEGAN STANDARD COST SYSTEM. INTERIM INVENTORY COUNT PLUS VARIANCES VALUED ON PUNCH CARDS STILL DOESN'T CHECK WITH MONTHLY BALANCE USING CONSERVATIVE GROSS MARGINS BUT NEARLY ALL GAPS OCCURRED FIRST FOUR MONTHS OF SYSTEM WHEN ERRORS NUMEROUS AND LAST 4 MONTHS NEARLY CHECK AS WE CONTINUE REFINING. EXTENSIVE RECHECKS UNDERWAY IN PARTS, WORK IN PROCESS, AND FINISHED GOODS AND CORRECTIONS BEING FOUND DAILY.

YOUR INVENTORY STAFF SPECIALISTS ARE AWARE OF PROBLEM AND PROMISED HELP WHEN OTHER PRIORITIES PERMIT. WILL KEEP THEM INFORMED OF EXPOSURE WHICH STARTED WITH RECORDING ALL PARTS AND BEGINNING NEW BALANCES WITH NEW STANDARDS AND APPEARS CLOSELY RELATED TO ERRORS IN THESE OPERATIONS. WE CAN ONLY PURGE PROGRESSIVELY WITHOUT HIRING SUBSTANTIAL INDIRECT WORKERS.

HENNESSY

customer accounts receivable control, budgeting, etc. did not exist. No information was given to other department heads concerning sales results, costs and expenses. The change to a formal monthly reporting system has been very difficult to realize. Due to the low level of employee training, many tasks such as consolidation, monthly and quarterly reports, budgets, the Business Plan, implementation of the new cost system, various analyses, restatement of prior year's accounts, etc. must be fully performed by the Controller and Chief Accountant, thus spending 80% of their full time in spite of working 55–60 hours per week. The number of employees in the Controller's Department in subsequent years will not depend on Galvor's volume of activity, but rather on Universal's requirements."

EXHIBIT 4 The Galvor Company

Telex from Poulet to Hennessy Concerning Level of Inventory

TO: HENNESSY – GALVOR
FROM: POULET – UE
DATE: NOV. 10, 1986

SEPTEMBER INVENTORY INCREASED AGAIN BY 64,000 COMPARED TO AUGUST WHILE SEPTEMBER SALES WERE 145,000 UNDER BUDGET REFERRING TO YOUR LATEST TELEX OF SEPTEMBER 27 IN WHICH YOU GAVE A BREAK-DOWN OF THE SEPTEMBER FORECAST. REQUEST DETAILED EXPLANATION FOR NOT MEETING THIS FORECAST IN SPITE OF YOUR CURRENT CORRECTIVE ACTIONS.

SEPTEMBER	*YOUR FORECAST*	*ACTUAL*	*VARIANCE*
RAW MATERIALS	53	96	(43)
PURCHASED PARTS	180	155	25
MANUFACTURED PARTS	95	108	(13)
WORK IN PROCESS	838	917	(79)
FINISHED GOODS	632	723	(91)
OTHER INVENTORIES	84	87	(3)
ENGINEERING IN PROCESS	55	52	3
RESERVE	(14)	(14)	—
INDICA	50	51	(1)
TOTAL NET	1973	2175	(202)

IN ORDER TO MEET YOUR DECEMBER FORECAST OF 1799 YOUR WORK IN PROCESS HAS TO BE REDUCED BY 318. THIS MEANS A REDUCTION OF ABOUT 100 PER MONTH FROM SEPTEMBER 30 TO DECEMBER 31. THEREFORE, I ALSO WOULD LIKE ACTUAL ACHIEVEMENTS AND FURTHER REDUCTION PLANS DURING OCTOBER, NOVEMBER, AND DE-CEMBER CONCERNING THE POINTS MENTIONED IN YOUR SAME TELEX OF SEPTEMBER 27. CONSIDER AGGRESSIVE ACTIONS IN THE FOLLOWING SPECIFIC AREAS:

1. REALISTIC MASTER PRODUCTION SCHEDULES.
2. SHORT TERM PHYSICAL SHORTAGE CONTROL TO INSURE SHIPMENTS.
3. WORK-IN-PROCESS ANALYSIS OF ALL ORDERS TO ACHIEVE MAXIMUM SALEABLE OUTPUT.
4. MANPOWER REDUCTION.
5. ELIMINATION OF ALL UNSCHEDULED VENDOR RECEIPTS. HAVE YOU ADVISED OTHER UNIVERSAL HOUSES NOT TO SHIP IN ADVANCE OF YOUR SCHEDULE UNLESS AUTHORIZED?
6. ADVISE FULL DETAILS ON ALL CURRENT SHORTAGES FROM OTHER UNIVERSAL HOUSES WHICH ARE RESPON-SIBLE FOR INVENTORY BUILD-UP.

POULET

The events of the next year and a half did nothing to lighten M. Barsac's load. When interviewed early in 1987, he commented:

> "Getting the data to Universal on time continues to be a problem. We simply don't have the necessary people who understand the reporting system and its purpose. The reports are all in English and few of my people are conversant in English. Also, American accounting methods are different from procedures used in France. Another less serious problem concerns the need to convert all of our internal records, which are kept in francs, to dollars when reporting to Universal."

Mr. Hennessy also commented on meeting the demands imposed by Universal's reporting system:

> "Without the need to report to Universal, we would do some things in a less formal way or at different times. Universal decides that the entire organization must move to a certain basis by a specified date. There are extra costs involved in meeting these deadlines. An example was applying the punch card cost system to our piece parts manufacturing operation before we were really ready to tackle the job. It should be noted, also, that demands made on the Controller's Department are passed on to other areas such as marketing, engineering and production."

EXHIBIT 5 The Galvor Company

Telex from Hennessy to Poulet Concerning Level of Inventory

TO: POULET – UE
FROM: HENNESSY – GALVOR
DATE: NOV. 15, 1986

YOUR 10.11.86

WE NOW HAVE OCTOBER 31 FIGURES. OUR ACTUAL ACHIEVEMENTS FOLLOW:
RAW MATERIALS 54 VARIANCE PLUS 3, PURCHASED PARTS 173 VARIANCE MINUS 12, MANUFACTURED PARTS 110 VARIANCE PLUS 17, WORK IN PROCESS 949 VARIANCE PLUS 224, FINISHED GOODS 712 VARIANCE PLUS 18, OTHER 82 VARIANCE MINUS 2, ENGINEERING 54 VARIANCE MINUS 4, RESERVE MINUS 14 VARIANCE NIL, INDICA 55 VARIANCE PLUS 3, TOTAL 2175 VARIANCE PLUS 247. EACH ITEM BEING CONTROLLED AND THE ONLY SIGNIFICANT VARIANCES 224 WORK IN PROCESS AND 18 FINISHED GOODS ARE MY DECISION UPON SALES DECLINE OF SEPTEMBER AND OCTOBER OF 311 TO DELAY COMPLETION OF SEVERAL SERIES IN MANUFACTURE IN FAVOR OF ANOTHER GROUP OF SERIES, MOSTLY GOVERNMENT, WHICH ARE LARGELY BILLABLE IN 1986 IN ORDER TO PARTLY REGAIN SALES. LAST EIGHT DAYS ORDERS AND THEREFORE SALES ARE SHARPLY UP AND NONE OF THIS WORK IN PROCESS WILL BE ON HAND MORE THAN 3 TO 6 WEEKS LONGER THAN WE PLANNED.

NEVERTHELESS YOU SHOULD BE AWARE WE MANUFACTURE 4 TO 8 MONTHS WORTH OF MANY LOW VOLUME MODELS AND EXAMPLE OF HOW WE DETERMINE ECONOMIC SERIES WAS FURNISHED YOUR STAFF SPECIALIST THIS WEEK. WE CANNOT OTHERWISE MAKE SIGNIFICANT COST REDUCTIONS IN A BUSINESS WHERE AT LEAST 70 OF 200 MODELS HAVE TO BE ON SHELF TO SELL AND TYPICAL MODEL SELLS 15 UNITS MONTHLY. REGARDING YOUR 5 SUGGESTIONS AND TWO QUESTIONS WE ARE CARRYING OUT ALL 5 POINTS AGGRESSIVELY AND HAVE NO INTERHOUSE SHORTAGES OR OVERSHIPMENTS.

                                                              HENNESSY

M. Boudry, Universal's Regional Controller in Geneva, acknowledged that the cost of the planning and reporting system was high, especially for smaller units:

"The system is designed for a large business. We think that the absolute minimum annual sales volume for an individual unit to support the system is about $5 million; however, we would prefer at least $10 million. By this standard, Galvor is barely acceptable. We really don't know if the cost of the system is unnecessarily burdensome in the sense that it requires information which is not worth its cost. A reasonable estimate might be that about 50% of the information would be required in any smartly managed independent business of comparable size, another 25% is required for Univesal's particular needs, and 25% is probably 'dead underbrush' which should be cleaned out. Ideally, every five years we should throw the system out the window and start again with the essentials."

F. Management's Evaluation of the System

Univeral attributed much of its recent success to the operation of this system, and placed a good deal of emphasis on it. M. Boudry was particularly enthusiastic:

In addition to measuring our progress in the conventional sense of sales, earnings and return on investment, we believe the reporting system causes our operating people to focus their attention on critical areas which might not othewise receive their major attention. An example would be the level of investment in inventory. The system also forces people to think about the future and to commit themselves to specific future goals. Most operating people are understandably involved in today's problems. We believe some device is required to force them to look beyond the problems at hand and to consider longer range objectives and strategy. You could say we view the reporting system as an effective training and educational device."

Commenting on the new inventory control system. Mr. Hennessy said:

"This, together with the standard cost system, allows us for the first time to really determine the relative profitability of various products, and to place a proper valuation on our inventory.
"All standards were reviewed last December on the basis of our experience in 1986 and were revised if necessary. We now have a history of development and tooling experience which we have been accumulating since 1985. This has proved extremely useful in setting cost standards. Simultaneously, we have integrated market and sales forecasts more effectively into our pricing decisions."

M. Barsac argreed fully with the objectives of the system, but felt that most of the benefits to Galvor's management were yet to come:

"I am especially concerned that few of the reports we prepare for Universal are useful to our operating people here in Bordeaux. Mr. Hennessy, of course, uses the reports as do one or two others. I am doing all that I can to encourage greater use of these reports. My job is not only to provide facts, but to help the managers understand and utilize the figures available. We have recently started issuing monthly cost and expense reports for each department showing the variances from budget. These have been well received."

Required

1. What are the purposes of Universal Electric's accounting and financial control system? That is, what is this system supposed to accomplish for either Universal National or Galvor? The following three criticisms have been made of Universal National's financial control system as it applies to Galvor:

(a) There is too much detail. The system requires too much management time. It is also too expensive for such a small company.

(b) The system does not leave enough initiative to management. There is too much staff interference and too much control by headquarters.

(c) The system encourages short-term action that may not be in the best long-run interests of the company.

2. Review the reports that Galvor is required to prepare. In what ways would you modify Galvor's reporting requirements?

3. What is Universal National trying to accomplish with their "tight" control system? What are the alternatives? What would you do?

CASE 15.7   TEXAS INSTRUMENTS INCORPORATED (B)

In May 1985 Tom Pringle, the manager of the Industrial Metals product department at Texas Instruments' Metals & Controls Division, was considering several courses of action in the face of his department's failure to meet forecasted sales and profits during the first four months of 1985. The rebuilding of inventories by M & C's customers, which had been expected as an aftermath of the settlement of the 1984 steel strike, had not materialized and shipments from Pringle's product department were running about 12% below forecast. Furthermore, incoming sales commitments during these four months were 15% below expectations. The product department's direct profit, according to preliminary statements, was 19% below plan.

In light of these adverse developments, Pringle was studying the advisability of three specific moves which would improve his profit performance: (1) eliminating his $30,000 advertising budget for the latter half of 1985, (2) postponing the addition of two engineers to his engineering group until 1986, and (3) reducing further purchases of raw materials in order to improve his department's return on assets ratio. Until now, Pringle had been reluctant to make any conces-

This case was prepared by H. E. Wrapp. Copyright © by the President and Fellows of Harvard University. Harvard Business School case 9-306-066.

sions in his department's scale of operations since there was a very strong accent on rapid growth throughout the Texas Instruments organization. This attitude towards expansion also appeared to prevail in the new top management group in the Metals & Controls Division. The enthusiasm of the Texas Instruments' management had caught on at Metals & Controls with the formation of the product-centered decentralized organization.

The 1984 Reorganization

In June 1984, just three months after Metals & Controls Corporation had become a division of Texas Instruments Incorporated, Mr. Edward O. Vetter, the division vice president, instituted a product-centered organization. This decentralization was carried out in accordance with Texas Instruments' policy of placing ultimate responsibility for profitable operation at the product level. The framework that emerged was similar to that which existed elsewhere in the company.

Mr. Vetter organized four major product groups at Metals & Controls: General Plate, Spencer Controls, Nuclear Products, and International Operations. To augment these groups, six centralized staff units were organized at the division level: Research and Development, Legal, Industrial Engineering, Control, Marketing, and Personal (Exhibit 1). The four managers of the product groups and the six managers of these staff departments, along with Mr. Vetter, comprised the management committee for the Metals & Controls Division. This committee was a sounding board for helping each responsible manager make the proper decision as required by his job responsibility. In the case of profit performance, the ultimate responsibility for the division was Vetter's.

Within each product group, several product departments were established. The General Plate products group, for example, included the Industrial Metals, Electrical Contacts, Industrial Wire, and Precious Metals departments (Exhibit 2). The manager of each of these departments was responsible for its "profit performance." He was supported by staff units such as Industrial Engineering and Administration which reported directly to the group manager (Burt Turnbull for General Plate products). The expense of these staff units was charged to the individual product departments proportionally to the volume of activity in the various departments as measured by direct labor hours or by sales dollars less raw materials cost. The product departments were also charged with those expenses over which the manager and his supervisory group were able to exercise direct control, such as labor and materials.

The field sales force of 50 men was centralized under the manager for marketing, Al Scofield (Exhibit 1). These men were divided about evenly into two major selling groups: one for General Plate products, and the other for Spencer products. The 25 salesmen assigned to General Plate and the 25 salesmen assigned to Spencer were shared by the four General Plate and four Spencer product departments. Each individual product department also maintained "inside"

EXHIBIT 1

Organization Chart, Metals and Controls Division

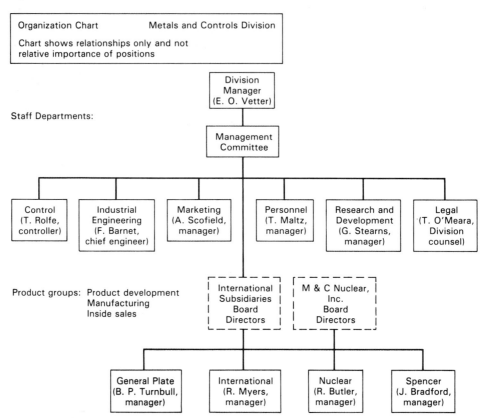

marketing personnel who performed such functions as pricing, developing marketing strategy, order follow-up and providing the field sales engineers with information on new applications, designs, and product specifications for its particular line.

The Industrial Metals Department. Tom Pringle was manager of the Industrial Metals department of the General Plate products group. Sales of this department in 1984 were approximately $4 million.[1] Pringle was responsible for the profitability of two product lines: (1) industrial metals and (2) thermostat metals. His department's sales were split about evenly between these lines, although industrial metals had the greater growth potential due to the almost infinite number of possible clad metals for which an ever increasing number of applications was being found. He was in charge of the marketing, engineering, and manufacturing activities for both these lines and had six key subordinates:

---

[1]All figures have been disguised.

Industrial Metals Department
Years of service with the Metals and Controls organization.

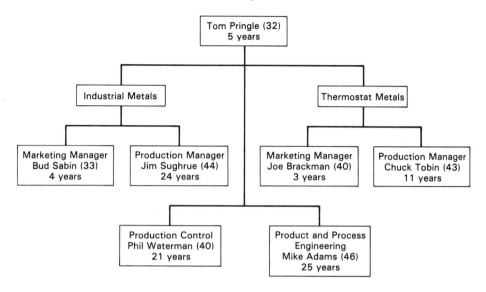

EXHIBIT 2

Organization Chart, General Plate Products Group

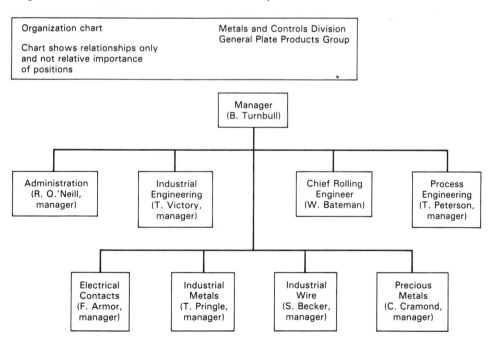

The function of the marketing managers in the Industrial Metals department (Bud Sabin and Joe Brackman) was to supervise the "inside selling units." These units were responsible for developing marketing strategy, pricing, contacting customers on special requests and factory problems, for promotional activiites, and for coordinating product development and sales. In May 1985, in addition to its regular work, the Industrial Metals inside selling unit was developing a manual of special applications for its products which it hoped would improve the ability of the field sales force to envision new uses. The production managers had line responsibility for the efficient use of manufacturing facilities, for meeting delivery promises to customers, and for expenses incurred in producing the department's products. The product and process engineering group had responsibility for designing new products and devising new production processes. The production control manager formulated guidelines to aid the foremen in scheduling work through the plant, supervised the expediters and clerks who served as a clearing house for information on delivery dates, and was responsible for ordering raw material and maintaining a balanced inventory.

In accordance with Texas Instruments' policy of placing ultimate responsibility for profitable operation at the product level, Tom Pringle's performance was measured, to a large extent, by the actual profits earned by the Industrial Metals department. The old M & C system of evaluating performance according to fixed and variable departmental budgets had been supplemented by the establishment of these "profit centers." Athough the system passed actual profit responsibility to the product department manager level, the Texas Instruments' top management had always retained some control over the profit centers by requiring each manager to formulate a one-year plan which was subject to review by higher management. As a result, profit planning was instituted whereby each manager set forth a detailed plan for the year's operations under the direction of the management committee. His actual performance was continually being evaluated against the plan.

FORMULATION OF THE PROFIT PLAN.   In October 1984 Tom Pringle began to prepare his department's profit plan for 1985. This was part of a companywide effort in which all department managers participated. The first step in the process was to prepare a detailed estimate of expected sales for the year. These estimates were gathered from two sources: the inside selling units and the field sales force. Management felt that one would serve as a good check on the other, and, furthermore, believed that widespread participation in preparing the plan was one way to insure its effectiveness. Bud Sabin and Joe Brackman then began to prepare estimates of 1985 sales by product lines with the help of the individual product specialists within the inside marketing group. Sabin and Brackman were also aided by the Texas Instruments central marketing group which prepared a report which estimated normal growth for their product lines. Pringle suggested that they prepare their estimates by subdividing the market into three parts: sales resulting from normal industry growth at current levels of market penetration;

increased sales resulting from further penetration of the market with existing products; and increased sales from new products detailed by specific customers. At the same time, Herb Skinner, the manager of the General Plate field sales force, asked the field engineers to predict the volume of orders that each Industrial Metals customer would place in 1985, without referring to the reports being readied by the product marketing groups. In this way, the marketing managers made forecasts by product line and the field force made forecasts by customer.

The field selling force came up with estimated thermostat metal sales of $2,350,000 for 1985, and the inside group estimated sales of $2,420,000. Pringle felt that these two estimates were in reasonably good agreement. On the other hand, Bud Sabin, the Industrial metals marketing manager, estimated sales of $3,050,000, while Skinner's group predicted only $2,500,000. Sabin predicted that 20% of the increase would come from normal growth, 50% from increased market penetration with existing products, and 30% from new products. Sales for Sabin's group had been $1,400,000 in 1983 and $2,100,000 in 1984. Pringle felt that the disparity between the two estimates was significant and he discussed the matter with both men. All three men finally decided that the sales force had submitted a conservative estimate and agreed that Sabin's figure was the more realistic goal.

Once the sales estimate of $5,470,000 was agreed on by Pringle and his marketing managers, the process of estimating manufacturing costs began. The manufacturing superintendents, Huck Tobin and Jim Sughrue, were furnished the thermostat and industrial metals sales expenses. These forecasts were to be made for each manufacturing area, or cost center, under their supervision. Sughrue was responsible for five cost centers and Tobin for four, each of which was directly supervised by a foreman. These expenses were to be forecast monthly and were to be used as a yardstick by which the actual expense performance of the manufacturing personnel could later be measured.

Jim Sughrue had previously calculated the hourly labor cost and the output per hour for each of his cost centers for 1984. To estimate 1985 salaries and wages, he then increased 1984 expenses proportionately to the expected sales increase. He followed the same procedure in supplies, and general supplies. Chuck Tobin's task was somewhat simpler since the sales projection for his cost centers required a level of output that exactly matched the current production level. For salaries and wages, he merely used as his 1985 estimate the actual cost experience that had been reported on the most recent monthly income statement he received. For overhead, he applied a historical percent of sales ratio and then reduced his estimate by 3% to account for increased efficiency. In discussing the overhead estimate with his foremen, Tobin informed them that he had allowed for an 8% efficiency increase.

Since this was the first time any attempt at such detailed planning had been made at M & C, and since the M & C accounting system had recently been changed to match Texas Instruments', very little historical information was available. For this reason, Pringle did not completely delegate the responsibility for the various marketing and manufacturing estimates to his subordinates. Instead he worked in conjunction with them to develop the forecasts. He hoped that his participation in this process would insure a more accurate forecast for the year, Furthermore, he hoped to develop the ability of his supervisors to plan ahead.

Pringle estimated direct materials cost and consumption factors himself. Since it was impossible to predict what all the various strip metal prices would be, he calculated the ratio of materials expense to sales for 1984 and applied it to the 1985 sales projections for each of the product lines in his department.

The marketing, administration, and engineering groups that serviced Pringle's Industrial Metals group forecast their expenses by detailing their personnel requirements and then applying historical ratios of expenses to personnel to estimate their other expenses. From these dollar figures, Pringle was able to estimate what proportion of these amounts would be charged to his department.

With the various forecasts in hand, Pringle estimated a direct profit of $1,392,000 on a sales volume of $5,470,000. Once this plan had been drawn up, it was reviewed by the division management committee in relationship to the specific profit and sales goals which it had established for the division. In reviewing the plans of each product department in terms of the specific group goals, it became obvious that the combined plans of the General Plate product departments were not sufficient to meet the overall goal, and that based on market penetration, new product developments, and other factors, the planned sales volume for Industrial Metals should be revised upward to $6,050,000 and direct profit to $1,587,000 (Exhibit 3). This was discussed among Vetter, Turnbull, Scofield, and Pringle and they agreed that it was a difficult but achievable plan.

ACTUAL PERFORMANCE, 1985. On May 10 Tom Pringle received a detailed statement comparing the actual performance of his department for January through April with his budget (Exhibit 4). Sales were 12% below plan, and direct profit was 19% below plan.

EXHIBIT 3

Industrial Metals Department
Initial and revised profit statements for 1985

	INITIAL	*REVISED*
Sales	$5,470,000	$6,050,000
Direct labor	435,000	480,000
Direct material	1,920,000	2,115,000
Overhead	875,000	968,000
Marketing	305,000	346,000
Administration	161,000	161,000
Engineering	382,000	393,000
Direct profit	1,392,000	1,587,000

All figures have been disguised.

EXHIBIT 4

Comparison of Actual and Budgeted
Performance January–April 1985

	BUDGETED	ACTUAL
Sales	$2,020,000	$1,780,000
Direct labor	160,000	142,400
Direct material	704,000	593,000
Overhead	322,000	287,000
Marketing	100,000	116,400
Administration	54,000	55,800
Engineering	126,000	136,600
Direct profit	554,000	448,800

All figures have been disguised.

In addition to these figures, manufacturing expenses by cost centers were accumulated for Pringle. He passed these along to the production superintendents after he had made adjustments in the budgeted expense figures to allow for the sales decline. Pringle had devised a variable budget system whereby he applied factors to the forecast expenses to indicate what an acceptable expense performance was at sales levels other than the planned volume. Chuck Tobin and Jim Sughrue then analyzed the actual expenses and, one week later, held meetings with their foremen to discuss the causes of both favorable and unfavorable variances. The most common explanation of favorable manufacturing variances was either extremely efficient utilization of labor or close control over overhead. Unfavorable variances most frequently resulted for machine delays which necessitated overtime labor payments.

SPECIFIC PROBLEMS.   Pringle was currently faced with three specific problems. In light of his department's poor performance these past months, he was considering the effects of eliminating his $30,000 advertising budget for the remainder of 1985, postponing the addition of two new engineers to his staff for six months, and reducing raw materials purchases in order to decrease inventory and thus improve his department's return on assets performance.

He had discussed the possibility of eliminating the advertising budget with Bud Sabin and Joe Brackman but had not yet reached a conclusion. Advertising expenditures had been budgeted at $30,000 for the final six months of 1985. The Industrial Metals department advertisements were generally placed in trade journals read by design engineers in the electrical, automobile, and appliance industries. Pringle did not know for certain how important an aid these advertisements were to his sales force. He did know that all of his major competitors allocated about the same proportion of sales revenue for advertising expenditures and that Industrial Metals advertisements were occasionally mentioned by customers.

In late 1984 Pringle had made plans to increase his engineering staff from eight men to ten men in mid-1985. He felt that the two new men could begin functioning productively by early 1986 and could help to revise certain processes which were yielding excessive scrap, to develop new products, and to assist the field engineers in discovering new applications for existing products. Pringle estimated that postponing the hiring of these men for six months would save $20,000 in engineering salaries and supporting expenses.

Pringle also knew that one of the important indicators of his performance was the department's ratio of direct profit to assets used. This figure had been budgeted at 40% for 1985, but actual results to date were 31%. Pringle was considering reductions in raw material purchases in order to decrease inventories and thus improve performance. He had discussed this possibility with Phil Waterman, the production control manager for Industrial Metals. Pringle knew that significant improvements in the overall ratio could be made in this way since raw materials inventories accounted for almost 20% of total assets and were at a level of ten months' usage at present consumption ratios. He recognized, however, that this course of action required accepting a greater risk of running out. This risk was important to assess since most customers required rapid delivery and Pringle's suppliers usually required four months' lead to manufacture the nonstandard size metals in relatively small lots required for the Industrial Metals' cladding operation.

THE PURPOSE OF THE PROFIT PLAN. The degree to which the plan was used as a method for evaluating performance and fixing compensation was not completely clear to Pringle. Everyone seemed to recognize that this first effort was imperfect and had errors built in because of inadequate historical data. He had never been explicitly informed of the extent to which top management desired product department decision making to be motivated by short-run effects on planned performance. Pringle stated that during the months immediately following the initiation of the plan he had concluded that short-term performance was much less significant than long-run growth and that he had preferred to concentrate on the longer-run development of new products and markets.

Pringle knew that the Metals & Controls operating committee met every Monday to review the performance of each product department from preliminary reports. Customarily Burt Turnbull, the manger of the General Plate group, discussed both Pringle's incoming sales commitments and actual manufacturing expenses with him before each meeting. Pringle also knew that each manager was given a formal appraisal review every six months by his superior. It was common knowledge that the department's performance in relation to its plan was evaluated at both these sessions. Furthermore, Pringle was aware of the fact that Turnbull's performance as product group manager would be affected by his own performance with Industrial Metals. Over a period of months, Pringle had learned that the management committee utilized the comparison of actual and planned performance to pintpoint trouble spots. On occasion Vetter had called him in to explain any significant deviations from plan but normally he was represented at these meetings by Burt Turnbull. It was Pringle's impression that Vetter had been satisfied with the explanation he had given.

In their day-to-day decisions, Pringle's subordinates seemed to be influenced only in a very general way by the profit plan. They reviewed their monthly performance against plan with interest, but generally tended to bias their decisions in favor of long-run development at the expense of short-run deviations from the plan. More recently, however, Pringle realized that top management was not satisfied with his explanations of failure to meet plans. The message, though not stated explicitly, seemed to be that he was expected to take whatever remedial and alternate courses of action were needed in order to meet the one-year goals. He was certain that real pressure was building up for each department manager to meet his one-year plan.

In commenting on the use of planning at M & C, Mr. Vetter, the division vice president, stated four major purposes of the program:

To set a par for the course. Vetter believed that performance was always improved if the manager proposed a realistic objective for his performance and was informed in advance of what was expected of him.

To grow management ability. Vetter believed that the job of management was to coordinate all the areas for which he was given responsibility. He saw the planning process as a tool for improving these managerial skills.

To anticipate problems and look ahead. Vetter felt that the planning process gave the department a convenient tool for planning personnel requirements and sales strategy. It also set guideposts so that shifts in business conditions could be detected quickly and plans could be altered.

To weld Texas Instruments into one unit. The basic goals for each division were formulated by Vetter in recognition of overall company goals as disseminated by Haggerty, the company president. These were passed down to the product department level by the product group manager at each Texas Instruments division. Profit planning was thus being carried out by the same process by every department manager in the corporation.

Vetter recognized, however, that many reasons could exist for performance being either better or worse than planned. He stated that in his experience extremely rigid profit plans often motivated managers to budget low in order to provide themselves with a safety cushion. In his view, this made the entire profit planning process worthless.

Required

1. Evaluate Texas Instruments' management control system, assuming that the organizational structure remains unchanged.

2. Should the organization structure of the Industrial Metals Department be changed? If so, why?

chapter 16

COST ACCOUNTING AND CONTROL IN SERVICE INDUSTRIES

Service industries are responsible for an increasing percentage of both total employment and gross national product. The problem in cost accounting is that whereas manufacturing operations have a reasonable degree of homogeneity, service industries are extremely diverse. Most manufacturing operations are conducted in physical plants, which use direct labor to convert raw materials into finished products. Although the number and type of products are extremely large, the processes are similar enough so that a limited number of basic cost accounting systems can be used to account for a large percentage of manufacturing processes. This is not true of service industries. The type of different processes that exist in service industries is extremely diversified. The types of financial control that are employed and the degree of control that can be exercised differs widely among different service industries.

Service industries can be generally divided into those that sell physical goods and those that do not. In the former category are: retailers, wholesalers, distributors of various types, repair shops of all kinds, retaurants and eating establishments, and so forth. Industries that have small or no finished goods inventories are public utilities (electricity, gas, transportation, and so forth), newspapers and other publishers, and all financial and professional services as well as many not-for-profit organizations.

INDUSTRIES SELLING FINISHED GOODS INVENTORIES

The difference between a service and a manufacturing industry is the "production" function. Any accounting differences, therefore, will be a result of differences between the production function in the particular service industry and its counterpart in a manufacturing industry. Service industries that sell finished goods inventory have no production function. They buy the goods that they sell and these industries have only a delivery function. (This contrasts to manufacturing, which has both a production and a delivery function.) These industries are in the same position as a manufacturing industry *after* the production of goods has been completed.

As stated in earlier chapters, the three uses of a cost accounting system are providing information for inventory valuation, cost control, and product profitability analysis. This information is all available through the procurement process and, consequently, service industries that sell finished products have no new problems in accounting or control. For the most part, therefore, these types of services have well-established systems for accounting and control and are not considered further in this chapter. Service industries that sell intangible services are considered in the remainder of this chapter and are called simply *service industries.*

INDUSTRIES THAT SELL INTANGIBLE SERVICES

Industries that produce and sell intangible services *do* have a production function. Not only can this function differ widely from a typical manufacturing industry, but these production functions can differ even more widely among different service industries. For the most part, many of these institutions do *not* have as effective cost accounting and control systems as are available in manufacturing industries. One reason is that the problems of measurement and control are more difficult in most of these industries. Also, it has only been in the past few years that many of these institutions have attempted to install sophisticated control systems.

This part of the chapter describes the problems with cost accounting and control systems in these industries. Since they have no finished goods inventories, inventory valuation is not a problem. Cost control and product profitability analysis are, however.

This part of the chapter is divided into three parts: unique characteristics of service industries, cost control, and product profitability analysis.

Unique Characteristics of Service Industries

Service industries have certain characteristics that make the problems of accounting and control different from manufacturing industries. These characteristics are as follows:

1. *No finished goods inventories.* The absence of finished goods inventories means that there is no buffer between production and sales. This means that the production and delivery function must generally be done simultaneously and are often inseparable.

2. *No product costs.* Almost all costs in service industries are period costs. There may be only minor amounts of direct material costs and often limited direct labor and variable overhead. As a result, it is very difficult to set standards and measure performance against those standards. Often, meaningful standards can be set only for a minor number of service activities.

3. *Measurement of output.* In many service industries it is difficult even to measure output. (This is the same problem experienced with service departments within a manufacturing industry, as described earlier.) For example, how do you measure the output from an accounting firm or an investment banking firm? The only measure of output is the fee received. Yet this may be an unreliable measure of output. For example, deterioration of service could go on for a considerable amount of time before it was reflected in income. This means that financial measures often have limited effectiveness in service industries. As a consequence, professional firms must put great emphasis on trying to measure the quality of service. These measures, however, are often not quantitative and are rarely financial.

4. *Few variable costs.* Service industries are labor intense, with most of this labor fixed, at least in the short term. For the most part, nonlabor costs are also fixed. Where sales vary, therefore, the change in the contribution is nearly equal to the change in revenue. This can cause profits to be very volatile, particularly in the short run. This, in turn, makes interim evaluation of financial results more difficult.

5. *No foreign competition.* With some exceptions (such as, airlines), service industries are generally free from foreign competition, and many are affected only by local competition.[1] In some respects, this makes planning easier. In other respects, however, the more restricted customer base could cause wider cyclical swings—for example, the volume of services could be seriously affected in areas dependent upon employment in a single industry, such as steel.

Cost Control

Because of the unique characteristics just described, the application of traditional cost control technique is greatly limited in many service industries.

In very few service industries can the concept of standard cost be employed. It is difficult to develop standard products. It is difficult to measure quality. It is difficult to measure quantity. Almost all costs are fixed in the short run. As a result, it is difficult to measure either efficiency or effectiveness through the accounting system. Measurement in most service industries has somewhat the same limitations that were described in Chapter 11 for discretionary cost centers. Consequently, the technique generally used to control costs at the production level is through a fixed annual budget with monthly variance reports. (Case 16.3, Pied-

---

[1]Foreign competition is already entering domestic markets through the acquisition of domestic service institutions. This type of competition has not been extensive until recently.

mont Power Company, describes such a system in a public utility.) Note that heavy reliance on nonquantitative factors is necessary in evaluating performance.

It should be noted, however, that in a limited number of service industries it is possile to exercise reasonable cost control, as in service industries where the production involves repetitive and specified services. Wellesley Press (Case 16.1) and Wilkinson Transport (Case 16.2) are examples of these types of control systems.

Product Profitability Analysis

The principal application of traditional cost accounting techniques in service industries is generally limited to product profitability analysis.

Individual services are the *products* of service industries. The term *product* is used to mean any identifiable service, such as a NOW checking account in a bank or a type of policy in an insurance company. The term *product group* means a group of related services, and the term *product line* is used to mean a number of related product groups. Profitability analysis is used in the following ways, all of which direct management's attention to situations for possible action:

1. *Product diagnosis.* To identify those products that are earning a less than satisfactory profit, products are ranked in the order of their profitability. Unprofitable or low-profit products are then analyzed further to see why the profits are low and what can be done to remedy the situation. Where no improvement appears feasible, an analysis is made to see whether the product should be discontinued.
2. *Planning guide.* Products with better than average profits become the basis for studies of possible expansion programs.
3. *Trend analysis.* Analysis of changes in profitability, particularly if they are downward, is a tool for diagnosing certain types of potential problems before they become acute.
4. *Price guide.* Profitability analysis can be used as a guide in setting selling prices. Even where—for competitive or policy reasons—a price cannot be changed, the analysis informs management of the extent to which a particular service is being subsidized.

Determination of Cost. Information describing the profitability of a product should have real economic meaning if it is to be useful. That is to say, it should quantify a real financial change in the net worth of an organization. Product profitability is the decrease in earnings that would have resulted had the product in question not been produced and sold. Conversely, a loss is the increase in total earnings that would have resulted had the product not been produced and sold. The problem with the typical service industries is that there are few direct costs and almost no variable costs. In order to calculate product profitability, therefore, it is necessary to find a relevant basis for allocating costs to product. The only relevant costs for product profitability analysis are those that can be uniquely attributed to the production and the sale of that particular product.

As explained in Chapter 7, the concept of uniquely attributable costs differs from the traditional cost accounting differentiation between variable and fixed cost. The unique cost concept assumes that no amount of the product would have been produced. At zero volume, many costs can be eliminated that would have to be incurred at higher levels. Revenues minus uniquely attributable costs constitute the total profit contribution of a product for the period.

Many, if not most, service industries have a great deal of difficulty in identifying unique costs for individual services. This occurs because there are relatively large amounts of joint costs and interrelated products in the typical service industry. This may mean that the products are "joint products" for practical purposes and must be treated as such in making decisions about them. Some companies allocate these joint costs to products. This really accomplishes nothing because the allocation of joint costs does not represent the economic realities. With the present state of the art, the only available solution in many instances is to calculate product profitability for a group of services.

MANAGEMENT CONTROL SYSTEMS

In general, management control techniques do not differ materially in service industries from other industries except at the cost control level, as previously described. (A great many service companies are so small that they require no formal management control system.) Almost all decentralized companies have service subsidiaries that are subject to control techniques similar to those used to control the manufacturing units. That is, profit budgets are prepared and approved and actual results are compared to budget and variances explained. Often, the variance analysis report is modified to take into account some of the unique features of the service subsidiary. Service companies often treat units within the company as profit centers where the appropriate revenues and costs can be segregated. Case 16.4, Chemical Bank, illustrates some of the unique problems that may be encountered in delegating profit responsibility in a large bank.

SUMMARY

While management control principles are generally applicable to manufacturing and service industries alike, cost accounting principles are not. Manufacturing cost control and product profitability techniques have very limited applications in many service industries. No set of techniques applicable to service industries has been developed. There are probably two reasons why this is so. First, service industries differ so widely in their production processes that no universally applicable set of techniques is possible; any developments, therefore, are applicable only to specific industries. Second, the problems of developing techniques to control costs and calculate product profitability are much more intractable in service industries than in manufacturing industries. The cases at the end of this chapter have been selected to illustrate cost accounting and control problems in a variety of service industries.

QUESTIONS

16.1   What are the characteristics of a bakery that makes it a service industry rather than a manufacturing industry? Does its designation as a service industry affect its operations in any way?

16.2   Give additional examples of service industries "selling finished goods."

16.3   Give additional examples of industries that sell intangible services.

16.4   Give examples of service industries that are affected by foreign competition.

16.5   Give additional examples of service industries that can utilize formal cost control systems effectively.

16.6   How, if at all, does the concept of "unique cost" in service industries differ from this concept when applied to manufacturing industries?

16.7   Explain why the problems of management control in service industries are similar to those in manufacturing industries.

CASES

CASES 16.1   WELLESLEY PRESS, INC.

Introduction

The Wellesley Press did about a million dollars worth of business in 1970, printing several thousand different orders (Exhibits 1 and 2). The orders customarily processed varied from single sheet forms and cards to multipaged weekly newspapers and magazines.

The cost accounting system was based upon the conventional usage of various standard machine rates in the printing industry to cover labor, overhead and profit for different machine centers. The industry had always been faced with either difficulties of accounting for the costs of many different orders and had consequently developed standard hourly rates to simplify job order costing. Most plants divided their facilities, for accounting purposes, into several production centers which performed distinct functions. Total operating costs were then allocated to each center and reduced to hourly rates by dividing the allocation by the hours the center was normally used during the accounting period.

These rates provided a "standard" for estimating costs, and for costing

---

This case was prepared by E. Bennett. Copyright © by the President and Fellows of Harvard University. Harvard Business School case 9-103-009.

EXHIBIT 1 Wellesley Press, Inc.

Balance Sheet as of September 30, 1970

ASSETS

CURRENT ASSETS

Accounts receivable	$ 35,309.30
Cash	48,534.81
Stamps meter	1,713.16
Ink inventory	250.00
Paper inventory	19,932.70
Prepaid insurance	3,359.35
Work in process	14,565.22
Total current assets	$123,664.54

FIXED ASSETS

Machinery and equipment (net)	$153,454.61
Total assets	$277,119.15

LIABILITIES

CURRENT LIABILITIES

Accounts payable	$ 12,312.96
Accrued payroll	2,488.00
Accrued taxes	5,527.44
Accrued expenses	89.62
Reserve—holiday pay	1,877.04
Reserve—old age	446.47
Reserve—taxes	4,539.65
Provision for vacations	498.00
Total current liabilities	$ 27,779.18
Notes payable	$ 6,300.00

CAPITAL

Capital stock	$ 56,000.00	
Surplus	187,039.97	
Total capital		$243,039.97
Total liabilities and capital		$277,119.15

every job. However, most firms relied upon conventional profit and loss statements to indicate their operating efficiency, and the extension of standards as a control device was very limited.

Production Process

Production at the Wellesley Press commenced with the receipt of "copy," which was marked with all specifications in the office, indicating such information as size of type, colors, and margin dimensions. A stock card was made out

EXHIBIT 2   Wellesley Press, Inc.

Profit and Loss Statements

	MONTH OF SEPT. 1970		JAN. 1, 1970 TO SEPT. 30, 1970	
GROSS INCOME		$74,417.09		$664,326.52
Deductions:				
Sales discounts	$ 99.49		$ 533.13	
Sales returns	103.53		1,100.36	
Stamped goods	9,323.70		96,718.96	
Spoilage	28.50		2,157.11	
Miscellaneous	3,272.93	12,828.15	27,847.19	128,356.75
NET SALES		$61,588.94		$535,969.77
Direct purchases:				
Addressing, binding, etc.	$ 1,594.29		$ 20,985.55	
Cuts and electros	808.72		7,066.38	
Ink	1,862.08		10,876.35	
Paper	6,137.83		56,145.69	
Stencils	—		1,217.98	
Adjustment	(3,168.70)	7,234.22	—	96,291.95
GROSS PROFIT		$54,354.72		$439,677.02
Operating expense:				
Auto expense	$ 228.37		$ 2,105.62	
Depreciation	2,060.12		15,236.30	
Light, power, etc.	586.25		5,737.50	
Manufacturing expense	795.05		7,691.74	
Rags	167.71		2,680.83	
Repairs	2,004.27		17,240.30	
Rollers	406.38		2,930.88	
Express expenses	851.04		7,550.57	
Wages	27,602.55		228,196.82	
Holiday pay	475.00	35,176.74	1,877.04	291,247.68
OPERATING PROFIT		$19,177.98		$148,430.14
General and administrative expense:				
Advertising	$ 66.40		$ 1,068.28	
Insurance	544.64		3,557.29	
Salaries	5,652.00		51,502.44	
Selling expenses	898.29		10,131.03	
Rent	1,035.72	8,197.05	8,215.76	74,474.80
NET PROFIT BEFORE TAXES		$10,980.93		$ 73,955.34

at this time, and the copy and specifications were sent to the Composition Department where type was set in galley form. This operation was done either by hand or by linotype machinery and did not include any arranging or spacing of type. Galleys were taken to the proof room by the "bank boy," and returned to Composition for correction, or when no corrections were necessary, for make up into spaced pages. Then a proof was sent to the customer. When the customer's approval was received, or when his alterations were effected, the pages were "locked" into steel chases or frames. Usually several pages were locked together in such a way that they could print a large sheet of paper which could subsequently be folded into several successive pages. When a page was locked and ready for printing, the stock was issued and the presses were set up. Then copies were run off, trimmed, bound, and shipped (Exhibit 3).

The plant had been operating at about 90% of capacity since a major expansion in 1980. Capacity was defined as a 24-hour day, six days a week. The company employed two eight-hour shifts which worked enough overtime to meet production requirements. The superintendent pointed out that this procedure, as compared to three-shift operations, passed on to employees those company savings due to decreased vacation pay and shift change-over time.

Accounting at the Wellesley Press

When the copy, "specs," and stock card for an order were forwarded to Composition from the office, a Job Cost Sheet (Exhibit 4) was filled out with the job order number, customer's name, and the materials needed. The materials were entered at current purchase costs and marked up 32% to cover various inventory expenses and a profit. This markup usually amounted to slightly less than the company's cash and quantity purchase discounts.

EXHIBIT 3 Wellesley Press, Inc.

Production Flow

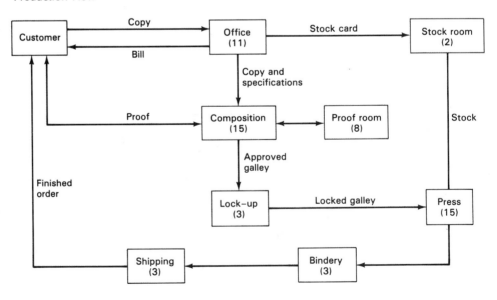

EXHIBIT 4 Wellesley Press, Inc.

Job Cost Sheet

CUSTOMER: JONES COMPANY *JOB: 10M RESERVATION FORMS*			*DATE DUE: SEPTEMBER 10, 1970* *NUMBER: 7465*	
Operation	*Hours worked, date, operator*		*Total hours*	*Charge*
MACHINE:				
Composition	1.3–8/10–R.P.	0.2–8/11–D.R.	1.5	$ 12.00
Proof	0.1–8/11–R.P.		0.1	.30
Customer's changes	1.2–8/12–R.P.	0.3–8/13–D.R.	1.5	12.00
HAND:				
Composition and lockup	0.8–8/10–J.M.	0.6–8/11–D.M.	1.4	9.80
Makeup	1.0–8/14–D.H.		1.0	7.00
Customer's changes	0.2–8/13–J.M.		0.2	1.40
PRESS:				
#4	2.8–8/16–F.H.	2.8–8/17–L.L.	5.6	50.40
#				
#				
BIND:				
Tip-on	None			
Other	0.4–8/18–E.F.	0.6–8/18–U.S.	3.7	20.35
	2.3–8/19–G.M.	0.4–8/20–G.M.		
MAILING:	0.9–8/20–D.M.	0.3–8/20–R.M.	1.2	3.00
Total std. charges				$116.25
Stock				57.00
Markup				18.24
Total charges				$191.49

All other costs for each order were determined by accumulating from time cards the number of hours that the job was processed in each function and applying standard hourly charges (Exhibit 5) which were intended to cover direct costs, overhead, and profit margin. For example, in Exhibit 4, it can be seen that there was a total of 1.5 hours of machine composition on this job, and with a standard rate of $8 per hour for the machine composition function, a $12 charge was obtained. The total of such charges for all functions, plus the material charges, was the indicated selling price of a job.

However, the indicated selling price of a job, shown as the final total on the Job Cost Sheet, was not always used for billing purposes. About one-half of the company's jobs were usually obtained from bidding and their prices were determined as described below. On nonbid jobs, the final price was usually arrived at arbitrarily. The superintendent pointed out that on most jobs the final price

EXHIBIT 5 Wellesley Press, Inc.

Standard Hourly Rates

	WELLESLEY PRESS	INDUSTRY
Linotype composition	$ 8.00	$7.70
Customer's alterations—machine	8.00	8.00
Proof	3.00	N.A.
Hand composition and lockup	7.00	7.70
Customer's alterations—hand	7.00	7.70
Makeup	7.00	7.70
PRESSES:		
#1,2 two-color miller	14.50	N.A.
3,4,5 one-color miller	9.00	8.60
6 horizontal	7.00	7.75
7 poly	6.00	6.05
8 vertical	6.00	6.05
9–11 jobbers	4.50	4.80
12 multilith	2.50	N.A.
BINDERY:		
Cut, fold, operate, stitch, trim, and punch	5.50	5.60
Tip-on	4.00	4.10
Mailing	2.50	2.95

indicated by the Job Cost Sheet was adjusted to meet special competitive situations, to counteract any unusual variations in production expense, and to approximate the price of any similar jobs recently done for the same customers. Either the superintendent or the chief accountant would make these adjustments in accordance with their knowledge of competitors' prices and experience with costs at the Wellesley Press.

When a final billing price had been determined, that figure and the total hours and charges on the Job Cost Sheet were posted to the Order Journal and Sales Analysis (Exhibit 6). It was expected that the "selling price" column would total approximately the same as the "total charges" column; any difference would raise or lower the profit included in the standard charges.

At the end of each month all finished jobs had been posted to the Order Journal and Sales Analysis, and all remaining Job Cost Sheets, representing work in process, were posted to a Work-in-Process Summary (Exhibit 7, Part I).

The hours of work recorded on these unfinished jobs were charged at the standard rates to determine their values which were debited in totals to Work-in-Process Inventory and credited to sales.

In the following month, operations to complete the unfinished jobs were recorded on their original Job Cost Sheets at standard rates. Then the total

EXHIBIT 6 Wellesley Press, Inc.

Order Journal and Sales Analysis as of September 30, 1970

DATE FINISHED	*CUSTOMER*	*JOB DESCRIPTION*	*HOURS (LABOR)*	*TOTAL CHARGES*	*SELLING PRICE*
Balance forward:				$35,104.71	$35,437.78
Sept. 26 (cent.)	Co. A	Address env.	15.3	35.22	37.00
26	X	Fold 3 p. letter	3.7	12.07	13.00
27	C	Notices	1.7	3.75	4.00
27	Mr. A.	20 M folders	30.4	197.55	229.00
28	Co. H.	500 M flyers	1.8	26.51	25.47
28	D.	Calendars	4.2	75.00	75.00
28	Mr. F.	500 menus	9.1	46.45	46.50
30	Church	Fund envelope	1.5	12.70	13.75
30	N.E. Assoc.	Jan. issue of magazine	77.4	705.81	610.91
Totals				$36,219.77	$36,492.41

Reconciliation of total sales figures:

Total September sales (as above)	$36,492.41
Work-in-process—September 30 (Exhibit 7, Part 1)	14,565.22
Value added to beginning inventory (Exhibit 7, Part 2, $36,438.83 minus $13,079.37)	23,359.46
Total sales (See Exhibit 2.)	$74,417.09

EXHIBIT 7

Work-in-process Summaries—Part 1 Summary as of September 30, 1970

			WORK IN PROCESS			
DATE FINISHED	*CUSTOMER*	*JOB DESCRIPTION*	*Hours (labor)*	*Total charge to date*	*TOTAL CHARGES AT COMPLETION*	*SELLING PRICE*
Balance forward:				$14,323.23		
	Co. A	1 m flyers	4.2	28.42		
	Mr. X	1 × 4 cards	1.4	8.36		
	Co. E	2 m envelopes	0.1	33.87		
	Town X	10 m reports	20.4	160.93		
	Church X	500 3 × 6 forms	3.7	10.41		
				$14,565.22		

Part 2 Summary as of August 31, 1985

Balance forward:				$12,541.97	$33,626.39	$35,602.39
September 28	Co. E	newspaper	64.1	354.10	510.90	500.00
28	Mr. B	500 stationery	1.2	3.51	5.62	6.00
29	Church H	1 m envelopes	2.4	8.50	10.11	10.00
30	Co. M	10 m flyers	10.4	62.85	120.44	120.44
30	Co. C	1 m booklets	21.2	108.44	221.96	200.00
				$13,079.37	$34,495.42	$36,438.83

charges and final billing prices were posted from the Job Cost Sheet to the Work-in-Process Summary (Exhibit 7, Part II). The difference between the total Work-in-Process column and the selling price column on this summary was considered value added, and included in the current month's sales figure.

In summary, monthly sales figures came from three sources:

1. The total of the "selling price" column on the Order Journal and Sales Analysis.
2. The total Work in Process from the current Work-in-Process Summary and
3. The difference between the "selling price" and Work-in-Process columns on the Work-in-Process Summary of the preceding period.

Raw materials (paper and ink) were valued at the lower of average cost or market and accounted for by a perpetual account of goods received and requisitions from the plant. A quarterly physical inventory was used to maintain the accuracy of these accounts. Finished goods, which were sometimes held temporarily for a customer, were valued at their selling prices.

Profit and loss statements did not utilize costs developed on Job Cost Sheets or Order Journal and Sales Analyses. Actual costs were accumulated by natural expense classifications for the preparation of monthly income statements (Exhibit 2). If the net profit was 7% or more of sales, the standard rates were generally not revised. However, sustained deviations from this profit goal usually led to an upward or downward revision of the rates. Another way of determining whether the standard rates were in line was to review the proportion of bids won. The superintendent said that, as a rule of thumb, they should receive about one-half of the jobs which they bid on; if they received less, rates were too high and if they were awarded more than one-half, rates were too low.

The standard rates had been established in 1959 by a consulting firm, and included charges for all expenses and a 7% profit margin. The rates had been raised several times since then to cover increased costs. In June 1982, for example, an unfavorable change in the monthly profit and loss figures indicated the need to raise standard rates. The superintendent, in reviewing operations to see what rates should be raised, remembered that 20 new pieces of equipment had been recently installed in the press room without an accompanying rate increase. Consequently, he raised several rates on the presses which were most "underpriced," relative to the trade association data (Exhibit 5). The next month the profit margin was back to approximately 7%.

The standard machine rates had been originally established by allocating all costs to various production centers. Labor and depreciation were readily assignable to different machines, and almost every other expense was allocated on a square foot basis. This procedure had not been applied to rate changes since then, and the superintendent stated that he was not sure whether the current rates resulted in uniform profitability in each function. When new machinery was purchased, a rate was established by weighing industry prices, the rate of the machinery replaced, and incremental power and depreciation costs.

On about one-half of the jobs, cost estimates had been prepared in order to bid on them. In these cases, cost accounting was the same as for nonbid jobs. The estimates made by the chief accountant or superintendent were developed by listing the operations required to print the copy and then by estimating the time needed for each operation. The estimated time per operation was then multiplied by the standard rates and added to material costs to obtain a total cost which, like all Wellesley Press's costs, included a profit margin and could be adjusted at the discretion of the estimator.

Both of the men who did this work emphasized the need for experience in making estimates of the time needed to process a job through different operations. They usually compared the actual cost figures on bid jobs with the detailed estimates to determine how well they were estimating costs and to find out if the plant was maintaining normal efficiency.

Wellesley Press's chief accountant stated that their auditors considered their accounting system very primitive. He pointed out that they had to revalue work in process for the annual balance sheets by multiplying the total labor hours on the Work in Process Summary by the average hourly wage and adding total material costs from unfinished Job Cost Sheets. However, both the chief accountant and the superintendent were of the opinion that their system was doing an adequate job, and because the funds available for accounting were limited they contemplated no immediate changes. The superintendent pointed out that all estimating, pricing, payroll and accounting work was done very simply under the present system and required two clerical workers in addition to the chief accountant and himself. He indicated that the various standard charges were not necessarily indicative of actual function costs, but pointed out that as long as their rates maintained a 7% profit margin and reflected competitive conditions, they were fulfilling their purpose.

Required

1. Evaluate Wellesley's cost accounting system with respect to its adequacy in inventory valuation, cost control, and marketing decisions.

2. What changes would you make? Be sure to explain how these changes would overcome the limitations described in Question 1.

CASE 16.2   **WILKINSON TRANSPORT**

In December 1979, the managing director of Wilkinson Transport was considering a change in the organization. Wilkinson Transport was a wholly owned subsidiary of the Lex Service Group Limited. Lex was a diversified service company

---

This case was prepared by John Dearden. Copyright © by the President and Fellows of Harvard University. Harvard Business School case 9-181-056.

with 1979 sales of £500 million and profits of £22.8 million before taxes and £19.7 million after taxes. It was organized into seven business groups. Wilkinson Transport was one of the five subsidiaries included in the Transportation Business Group.

In general, Lex Service was highly decentralized. The top management of the business group participated in strategic planning; it reviewed and approved the annual budget. It reviewed accounting and budget performance reports each month. As long as Wilkinson was performing within expectations, top management did not involve itself in the day-to-day operations.

Operations

Collection and Delivery Operations.   Wilkinson Transport was an express parcel company that collected and delivered parcels weighing between ten kilograms and one metric ton. It operated throughout the United Kingdom and in Ireland through an arrangement with an associated company located there. Wilkinson typically collected 58,000 parcels a day from 2,300 customers and delivered these parcels to 10,000 addresses, ranging from retail outlets to industrial users. The average consignment was 5.3 parcels weighing 80 kilograms.

Wilkinson operated 16 depots throughout the United Kingdom. Each depot was responsible for a georgraphic area. Daily, it collected parcels from the customers in its area and delivered parcels for the entire network to the consignees within its area.

Each morning vans from each depot delivered parcels to the consignees within its area, and then collected the consignments from its customers. The vans returned to the depot, were off-loaded, and the parcels consolidated for the depot located in the area to which the parcels were to be deliverd. Thus, each day a depot would have 15 different consolidations for delivery to other depots, plus the retention of its own delivery traffic.

Trunking.   Each consolidation was loaded into vans and, during the night, the vans delivered the parcels to the appropriate depot and collected the parcels for consignees within its area. This operation was known as "trunking." There were a variety of trunking configurations. For example, Depot A and Depot B vans would meet at an intermediate point and exchange loads. Or Depot A would do the entire trunking for Depot B by delivering to Depot B and picking up its own parcels. In some instances, a depot would not have enough activity to warrant direct shipments from all depots. In this case, Depot A might deliver to Depot B parcels for delivery by Depot C. The next day Depot B delivered the parcels to Depot C. This was called transshipment. About 80 percent of the trunking was made directly to the depot that was to deliver the parcels and about 20 percent were transshipped. The trunking configurations were determined periodically by a computer model that simulated the optimum trunking configuration based on the past six months' collections and delivery patterns.

The delivery schedule for a typical parcel was as follows:

- *Monday*: The parcel was collected from the customer.
- *Monday Night*: The parcel was trunked to the depot that was to deliver it.
- *Tuesday*: The parcel was unloaded and assigned to the appropriate route.
- *Tuesday Night*: The parcel was loaded onto a delivery van.
- *Wednesday*: The parcel was delivered.

About 10 percent of deliveries were overnight shipments. In this case, parcels were placed onto the back of the appropriate van that evening and removed immediately upon arrival at the delivery depot and loaded onto delivery vehicles.

Marketing

The volume and quality of sales depended on three factors: service, price, and personal sales effort. Each is discussed below.

Service. The most important factor in retaining present customers was the reliability of the service provided. Also, to a considerable extent, the ability to obtain new customers was affected by the company's reputation for service. Service is measured by the speed and reliability of delivery, although other factors, for example, the ability to inform the customer quickly as to the status of a consignment or the prompt settlement of claims for lost or damaged goods, were also important.

Speed and reliability depended on:

1. The proper marking of the parcel and the correct information on the waybill;
2. The correct classification of the destination at the collection depot;
3. The correct classification of the route at the delivery depot;
4. The handling of parcels to minimize damage; and
5. The control of theft.

Price. The transport business was extremely competitive and price was an important factor in obtaining new customers and retaining present customers. Wilkinson published a price card that provided the prices for all of the usual types of deliveries. Prices were based on the weight of the consignment and the distance traveled. Discounts from the price card were made for special circumstances. For example, large customers were sometimes quoted a fixed price per kilogram delivered. Or, salespersons discounted the list price to take account of competition.

Salespersons. A third factor in selling the service was the personal contacts made by individual salespersons. Salespersons also handled complaints or contacted present customers to ascertain that the service was satisfactory.

Recent Developments

By July of 1980 Wilkinson Transport had largely completed a program of computerization and mechanization started two years previously. This part of the case describes these programs.

WILKONTROL

WILKONTROL was the name of the computer system that had been designed to:

1. Keep track of consignments during the collection and delivery process; and
2. Provide current operating data to management.

The WILKONTROL system was installed in 1979.

The Consignment Note. The consignment note was the main source of information in the WILKONTROL system. The consignment note was initially prepared at the collection point and contained all of the relevant information about the consignment: for example, the shipper's name and address, the consignee's name and address, and the number and weight of the packages in the consignment. The consignment note was prepared in duplicate and was numbered for identification. One copy of the consignment note remained with the consignment; the other copy was retained by the depot.

Keeping Track of Consignments. The information from the consignment notes was recorded in the memory of a central computer by clerks in the depot. From this information, the computer calculated additional data such as the revenue from the consignment.

When the consignment moved from the collecting depot to the delivery depot, this information was recorded into the computer memory. The information was continually updated as the consignment was moved through the system. Finally, after the consignment was delivered, the driver returned the receipted copy of the delivery manifest to the depot and the final delivery was recorded.

Throughout the system there were computer terminals with visual display devices that gave access to the information stored in the central computer memory. Thus, the status of any consignment could be ascertained within four seconds from any pont within the system. The WILKONTROL system allowed management to identify quickly shipments that deviated from the standard pattern and to take appropriate corrective action.

Wilkinson was the only transport company in the United Kingdom that employed such a computer control system in 1980.

Operating Statistics. The WILKONTROL system made it possible to provide detailed operating statistics on a daily and weekly basis. For example, at 10 A.M.

every morning, the following information about the previous day's operation was available by depot and, if desired by route:

- Number of consignments
- Number of waybills
- Total weight
- Number of packages
- Total revenue.

In short, it was possible on a daily basis to observe the "profile" of the business being done on the preceding day down to the smallest organization unit. This information was then summarized by week and month.

In addition to the profile information, the depot managers were provided daily or weekly with all information relevant to the effective operation of the system. Statistics on any deviations from standard were available. This information was also required by regional and headquarter executives.

Depot Mechanization

It was Wilkinson's plan to mechanize most depots by 1983. It was expected that mechanization would increase both the efficiency and the capacity of the depots. Also, since much of the labor would be machine-paced, better standards and performance measures against these standards would be possible.

The Hub

The Hub, a highly mechanized central depot, was built in Nuneaton, a town near Birmingham. It was designed to be fully operational in the latter part of 1980. The Hub would completely transform the trunking patterns. When operational, *all* depots would send their collection to the Hub. There, the parcels would be sorted mechanically and trunked to the delivery depots. This had several important advantages.

First, the collecting depots would not be required to sort and consolidate the collected parcels except those that were to be delivered within their area. This increased the effective capacity of the depots.

Second, vans from both the depots and the Hub would move fully loaded because all collections and deliveries were made to the same location. Under the present system, each depot sent vans to 15 other locations, many of them with less than a full load.

Third, it would be possible for all drivers to reach the Hub in eight hours. EEC regulations by 1981 would require that a driver work a maximum of eight hours. Under the present system, some locations required more than eight hours driving time to reach their destination.

Fourth, the Hub was designed to provide a highly mechanized, efficient method for handling parcels. It would be possible to exercise greater control over all of the aspects of parcel handling.

The Organization

Exhibit 1 is an organization chart of Wilkinson Transport as of July 1, 1980. There were five staff officers and three regional managers reporting to the managing director. The commercial manager was responsible for the rate structure, the settlement of claims, public relations and advertising. Other staff offices are self-explanatory.

The Region. Each region was a profit center. Four staff officers and the general managers of the depots reported to the regional manager.

The Depot. Each depot was also a profit center. The depot manager was responsible for operations, sales, accounting, and the repair shop. Although depot managers came from a variety of backgrounds, many had worked their way up from hourly employment. Each depot had its own accounting system, which collected from customers and paid supplier. Throughout the system costs were recorded in the area where they were incurred and revenues were recorded in the area where they were received. Each month, the depot accounts were consolidated by

EXHIBIT 1 Wilkinson Transport (B)

Current Organization

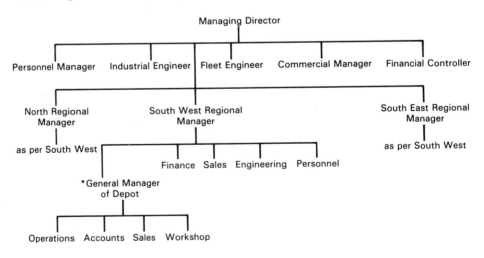

*N.B. Typical profit center consolidation at region.

the regional accounting staff and the regions were consolidated by the headquarters staff.

Purchasing was also done locally, although some items were controlled through company-wide contracts.

The Financial Control System. The Lex organization exercised short-term control through an annual profit budget. Each year a budget was presented by Wilkinson's management to the management of the Transportation Business Group. The proposed budget was reviewed and either accepted or adjusted. The final version became the basis for the monthly reports that provided a comparison of the actual results with the budget on both a monthly and year-to-date basis. The report included the analyses of variances and explanations of the causes of the variances and the action being taken.

Within Wilkinson a similar type of control was used for each region and for each depot within the region. Each depot prepared a profit plan which was approved by the regional manager and each region prepared a regional profit plan that was approved by the managing director. Comparisons of actual performance to plan were made monthly by depot and consolidated by region. These reports included a great deal of operating statistics in addition to the financial comparisons.

In addition, there was a weekly information system that provided network profit contribution and efficiency indicators.

TRANSFER PRICING.   Each depot typically performed two services for other depots and used similar services from other depots. The most important was to deliver parcels collected by other depots. Since the entire revenue was paid to the collecting depot, under a profit center system, part of this revenue had to be reassigned to the delivering depot. Several methods of transfer pricing had been used. Currently, the intracompany charge made by the delivering depot to the collecting depot was a flat charge of £2.50 for each delivered consignment plus a variable charge of £10 per metric ton. This charge, on average, would compensate the delivery depot for its costs plus providing an allowance for profits.

The second service performed by one depot for the other was trunking, or delivering consignments between depots. This charge was £.40 a mile, which also was sufficient to cover costs plus providing a profit.

OPERATING CONTROL.   Although the profit plan was an important tool for measuring managerial performance, management at all levels had access to detailed operating statistics daily and weekly. (These operating statistics were developed through the WILKONTROL system previously described.) For example, each week four pages of operating statistics were developed for each depot. One of the unique features of Wilkinson's measurement system was the amount of operating statistics that was available to management on a current basis.

Consideration of Change

In 1980, the managing director began to consider seriously whether the organization of Wilkinson Transport should be changed. In particular, he wondered whether the profit center system should be abandoned in favor of some other form of organization. Although he had always had some reservations about the profit center system, recent events had made it desirable to consider a change at this time. It seemed logical to him that if the organization were to be changed, it should be done in 1980.

The Strategic Plan.   In 1979, Wilkinson Transport, together with the management of Lex, developed a new strategic plan. Among other things, the plan called for sales volume to be increased by 1985 to $2\frac{1}{2}$ times the 1979 volume *at 1979 prices.* The managing director wondered whether volume increases of this magnitude could be accomplished with the present organization. Of principal concern was whether such a large increase in sales could be realized with a sales force that was decentralized into 16 separate depot organizations.

The Hub and Depot Mechanization.   It was expected that the Hub would change significantly network operations and would result in a greater central control. In the same way, the mechanization of the depots would change the way that parcels were handled and, to some extent, would make central control easier. Although neither the Hub nor the depot mechanization would have an important direct impact on the profit center system, the managing director believed that these developments would have an impact on the timing of any organizational change. The operations of the depots would be changed considerably by these developments. It seemed to him that a change in organization, if one was to be made, would be more acceptable to those executives affected, if it were done coincidentally with the operating changes.

Concerns About the Profit Center System.   Although the adoption of the 1979 strategic plan was the immediate cause for reconsidering the profit center from of organization, the top management of Wilkinson had experienced some concerns about the profit center system for some time. These concerns are described in this part of the case.

First, there was a question as to whether the depot manager controlled the critical elements of profit generation. For example, most of the delivery business was generated by other depots and most of the business generated by a depot was completed by other depots.

Second, there were questions as to whether excessive demands were being made on the depot manager. Was it not enough for the depot managers to be responsible only for operating the depot? Should not responsibility for sales, finance, and purchasing be assigned to functional experts? In fact, did the depot manager even have enough expertise in these areas?

Third, the profit center system tended to encourage depot managers to optimize depot profits at the expense of company profits. There was simply no incentive to sacrifice depot profits for the benefit of the company. For example, a depot manager could turn down (or, at least, not pursue aggressively) business that might benefit the company. If a depot was very busy, additional business might not be profitable to the collecting depot even though it might benefit the company. On the other hand, business that might be profitable to collect but marginal to deliver might be pursued aggressively. The problem was that the depot manager evaluated the desirability of business from the collection point of view only.

Finally, there was a question as to whether the transfer price system divided the revenue among contributing depots fairly. A related concern was whether the paper work required to implement the transfer price system was not only a waste of money but might even be producing misleading information.

Advantages of Profit Centers. In deciding upon any organizational changes, the managing director was well aware of the benefits that had accrued to the company because the profit center system *had* worked very well in the past. The depot general managers viewed themselves as managing their own business. Parcel collection and delivery was a geographic function and the depot general manager controlled all aspects within his area.

Three considerations were of particular importance in any change from the profit center system.

First, what would be the effect if responsibility for sales was taken from the depot manager? How would the trade-off between simply increasing the level of sales volume and increasing the quality of the sales be resolved? For example, additional business obtained from customers on established routes required almost no additional cost to collect; however, business in other locations might require considerable additional cost. If salespersons did not report to the depot manager, would they not be motivated to increase the level of sales regardless of location?

Second, the level of costs were to some extent a function of volume. The volume of activity, particularly of deliveries, was largely outside the control of the depot manager. Without the profit center system, how could the performance of a depot manager be measured?

Finally, the depot manager controlled the most important element of sales volume—service. Without profit centers, how would this be taken into consideration in the measurement system?

Required

1. Should Wilkinson Transport change its organization? If so, how? If not, explain why the present system should not be changed.

2. How would you change the performance measurement system to accompany your revised organization? In particular, how would you measure depot managers to insure goal congruence?

3. In order of potential severity, list the problems that you anticipate would occur in implementing your revised organization and measurement system. How would you handle these problems?

CASE 16.3 PIEDMONT POWER COMPANY

The Piedmont Power Company is a large privately owned utility company whose main business is the generation and distribution of power over a wide area in the eastern United States. While the U.S. electric utility industry as a whole has been growing at a compounded annual rate of 7.2% since 1920, Piedmont Power's growth was 7.9% per year. An exponent of low rates and high sales volume, Piedmont has kept its average 25% to 38% below the national figure, emphasizing technological advance on every front in the generation and distribution of electricity. In the last ten years, the company has doubled its sales revenue while cutting the employee work force from around 10,000 to around 8500 people.

However, despite this outstanding record, the president of Piedmont, Mr. James Wade, was not satisfied. He said, "We are doing a good job, but I am convinced that we can do a better job."

The electric power industry is characterized by stable growth. The consumption of electric power tends to grow at about the same rate, year after year, without large business-cycle swings that affect other industries. For a given area, projected movements of population, changes in population, movement in industry, and other such factors can be weighed and used to extrapolate the demand for electric power.

Sales can be accurately predicted for an electric utility because typically it is the only supplier of electric power in its service area. While electricity has to compete with other forms of energy in many instances, and these other forms of energy (gas, oil, etc.) are usually sold by other companies, the utility normally has a local monopoly on the sale of electric power.

This gives rise to government regulation of electric utilities. The Federal Power Commission exercises a limited supervision over the utilities generally, regarding their accounting, interstate sales, and operation of hydroelectric plants on navigable rivers. Most regulation, particularly concerning rates and profits, is carried out by state commissions. These commissions set rates so that the company will receive a "fair" return on its investment but no more than a fair return. The rate of return is defined by the commission. Although the public utility has the right to submit evidence to the commission and in some cases to appeal its decisions to the courts, it generally does not have any control over the commission's decisions and has to make the best of whatever rates the commission

This case was prepared by E. R. Helfert and J. Yeager. Copyright © by the President and Fellows of Harvard University. Harvard Business School case 9-165-010.

EXHIBIT 1 Piedmont Power Company

Summarized Industry-Wide Balance Sheets, 1979–1982 ($ millions)

	1978	1979	1980	1981	1982
Utility plant	43,485	46,853	50,308	53,241	56,158
Depreciation	8,192	8,963	9,851	10,692	11,672
Net utility plant	35,293	37,889	40,456	42,549	44,486
Current assets	2,773	2,943	3,066	3,151	3,320
Other debts	1,212	1,273	1,220	1,309	1,386
Total	39,278	42,106	44,742	47,010	49,191
Common stock	8,051	8,520	9,041	9,452	9,827
Preferred stock	4,023	4,115	4,280	4,349	4,498
Other paid-in capital	1,483	1,729	1,747	1,903	1,990
Earned surplus	3,042	3,356	3,736	4,011	4,481
Long-term debt	18,558	19,818	21,035	22,028	22,912
Current liabilities	2,781	2,966	3,112	3,286	3,285
Other liabilities	1,339	1,601	1,790	1,979	2,199
Total	39,278	42,106	44,742	47,009	49,192

NOTE: Figures may not sum owing to rounding.

awards. Both privately owned and publicly owned utilities operate within this framework.

Comparative income accounts for the calendar years 1978–1983 for the Piedmont Power Company are given in Exhibit 2, while the related balance sheets are set forth in Exhibit 3.

The operations of a typical electric utility company can be divided into five broad functions—generation, transmission, distribution, commercial, and administrative. In Piedmont Power, the generation of power is regarded as a separate function from the others. Engineering and economic considerations dictate the location of power plants and the power from these plants is then fed into the transmission system to be carried to its destination. The division managers are not held responsible for the generating plants, which are under separate jurisdiction.

The transmission system consists of the high-voltage lines suspended from towers, which carry power over long distances. The division managers are charged with certain portions of the operation and maintenance of those lines which lie within their area, whether they draw power from them or not. Other portions of transmission maintenance is performed by crews working out of company headquarters. The cost of such work is not usually a high proportion of the total cost of running the division.

The distribution of power to the ultimate customers is the purpose of the distribution function. The power from the transmission lines is tapped, transformed down to household or industrial voltage, and fed into the system of distribution lines. These may be on small towers, but are more commonly carried on

EXHIBIT 2 Piedmont Power Company

Comparative Income Statements, Years Ended December 31, 1978 Through 1983 ($ thousands)

	1983		1982	1981	1980	1979	1978
Operating revenues	$295,568	100.0%	$282,052	$264,332	$253,559	$242,705	$222,410
Operating expenses	95,555	32.2	89,954	84,454	85,624	82,509	76,955
Maintenance	22,844	7.2	21,485	20,891	18,567	17,990	16,288
Depreciation	40,841	13.3	38,688	37,215	33,662	31,755	28,667
Federal income tax	27,751	9.2	24,041	20,357	21,199	18,545	15,872
Provision for deferred tax	13,444	4.2	16,622	17,399	15,127	13,776	13,165
Prior deferrals (cr)	3,146	1.0	2,215	1,917	1,826	—	—
Other taxes	24,796	8.1	24,207	22,802	22,040	21,593	18,922
Other net income (cr)	955	(0.4)	1,053	340	499	607	469
Gross income	74,438	25.2	70,323	63,471	59,665	57,144	53,415
Interest on debt (long-term)	23,056	7.8	21,787	19,781	19,039	20,027	18,097
Amortization, debt discount (cr)	99	0	101	97	100	98	87
Interest, short-term debt	426	.2	417	696	1,072	886	1,031
Interest charged to capital (cr)	4,295	(1.5)	2,936	1,468	4,076	3,872	4,032
Net income	55,350	18.7	51,156	44,559	43,730	40,201	38,001
Preferred dividend required	3,233	1.1	3,240	3,249	3,252	3,256	3,263
Balance for parent company common stock	52,117	17.6	47,916	41,310	40,478	36,945	34,738

EXHIBIT 3 Piedmont Power Company

Comparative Balance Sheets as of December 31 (In Thousands)

	1983	1982	1981	1980	1979	1978
Net utility plant and fixed assets	$1,183,593	$1,137,141	$1,076,804	$1,044,152	$1,007,501	$ 955,149
Current assets	106,165	100,510	90,431	81,405	80,696	82,124
Other assets and debits	3,580	3,424	3,598	4,835	5,161	5,900
	$1,293,338	$1,241,075	$1,170,833	$1,130,392	$1,093,358	$1,043,173
Stockholders' equity	$ 369,444	$ 353,586	$ 339,015	$ 328,628	$ 315,475	$ 263,084
Long-term debt	638,685	609,746	563,157	538,723	542,362	536,243
Preferred stock of subsidiaries	75,853	75,886	76,180	76,296	76,332	76,363
Current liabilities	82,345	85,165	90,325	100,106	85,761	107,830
Deferred income tax	120,836	110,539	96,131	80,649	67,349	53,572
Other credits	6,175	6,153	6,025	5,990	6,079	6,081
	$1,293,338	$1,241,075	$1,170,833	$1,130,392	$1,093,358	$1,043,173

poles. The division managers are held responsible for the distribution of power in their region. The cost of this operation is a direct function of its nature. The area to be covered by the system, the number of customers that can be served from one connection, and the nature of the terrain all affect costs. A large, moun-tainous, rural area will be more costly to serve (per kilowatt hour) than a small, level, urban area.

The cost of maintenance of the distribution system is a function of area, terrain, climate, and number, type and dispersion of customers. It is more expen-sive to maintain a system when the maintenance crews have to travel greater distances, over inhospitable territory. Also if the climate is damp, the vegetation may grow faster and interfere with the power lines more frequently.

The commercial section of the operation is that associated with sales and customer relations. Selling electricity, of course, is a matter of selling ways of using it. Therefore the sales personnel work with the manufacturers of electrical appliances and heating equipment. They also attempt to get industry to locate in the area and to convert to electric energy. The cost of their work will depend on the sales program adopted, which is subject to the approval of the division managers.

The cost of customer accounting depends on the nature of the division. While the bookkeeping is virtually a fixed cost per account, the cost of reading the meters will vary by division. Mr. John Porter, assistant general manager of the company, stated: "In one area, the meters will be clustered, and a great many people will be in the same geographical area. In another divison there will be substantial distances to be traveled by meter readers and hence the meter reading costs will be much less attractive than in the former location, yet perfectly justi-fied because of the physical conditions of the terrain."

For many years both the top management of Piedmont Power Company and the controller's group at headquarters had felt that there was a need for a system of control reports which would be of value both to headquarters in evalu-ating the divisions and also to the divisions themselves in the running of their operations. Until 1977, no attempt had been made to collect accounting data other than in the form specified by the Federal Power Commission, which de-signed its requirements to satisfy the needs of ratesetting commissions, rather than to provide management information.

These persons thought that there was need for a measure of performance, so that some systematic evaluation of the operations of the company could be made. They also felt that the use of expected levels of performance would help by telling the division manager, in time, where he was in danger of losing control, if at all. Accordingly, the idea of budgeting was introduced to the company. It was reasoned that if the manager were asked to write down what he expected to do in the coming period, giving details of what he thought he would have to spend, then top management would be able to evaluate the division (and the manager) twice. A review could be made when the budget was submitted at the beginning of the period, and again when the actual results became available for comparison with budget. From the manager's viewpoint, it was considered that the discipline of having to sit down and figure out what his expenditures were going to be would be valuable, in that it would keep him on top of his work, and enable him to foresee problems he might otherwise have missed.

In 1981, therefore, a system of "managerial accounting" reports prepared by means of an electronic computer, was put into use. Exhibit 4 of the case presents a typical report produced under this system. In explaining the need for such a report, Mr. James Wade, president of Piedmont said: "I am interested in getting better control of our operation. When I receive one of these managerial reports on one of our operating companies I can tell in a hurry how that overall company is performing. I know where to look in the figures to tell what is going on. I know all the keys on the piano; but these are just over-all reports. We need more detail on how each of the smaller units is performing.

"I am very suspicious of general reports that homogenize a lot of information. These general reports tend to cover up organizational shortcomings. I start with the premise that some organizational units perform better than others. I want some reports that will show this up right down to the smallest unit such as a division. This should highlight where the weaker units are, and we can go to work to bring these up to the level of the best units. I think competition of that kind is a healthy thing. It gets the necessary tension into the organization.

"We want to set up what you might call some controllership groups to help us strengthen our organization. These groups will act as 'gadflies on the flank of line management.' We might want to set up the units at different levels of the management hierarchy. I think we need a substantial number of these units in our field organizations and smaller but significant groups here at headquarters."

In an address to a management seminar at which many of the mangement teams of the operating companies were present, Mr. Sydney Harcourt, assistant controller of the corporation, gave an address on the subject: "Using the Managerial Accounting Reports," from which the following are abstracts.

"Why managerial accounting—why more accounting reports? The answer to this question is that the Federal Power Commission uniform system of accounts for the electric utility industry which has been the basis of our accounting systems since 1937 was designed primarily for regulatory commissions and is of limited value to us from a management standpoint. On the other hand, the managerial accounting reports are *designed for managers*. Such reports give each manager the cost which he incurred and for which he is responsible.

"The reports for line managers are prepared monthly and show current month as well as year-to-date figures. They show budget figures for each detail account so there is a bench mark from which to appraise performance.

"What we have with mangerial accounting is a reporting system which we can use in running our business and with IBM equipment we can reassemble the data from the managerial accounting reorts in the form necessary to comply with Federal Power Commissions regulations. In Piedmont Power, our belief in excellence as a working philosophy means that a great deal is expected from mana-

EXHIBIT 4 Piedmont Power Company

Southern Division—Year-to-Date Report, September 1984 (–Indicates Favorable Variance)

(In thousands of dollars)

DESCRIPTION	VARIANCE	TOTAL	MANAGERIAL	ACCOUNTING	PERSONNEL	COMMERCIAL	TRANSMISSION AND DISTRIBUTION
Transmission operation	44	4,469	—	—	—	—	4,469
Transmission maintenance	4,252	21,284	—	12	—	—	21,272
Total	4,296	25,753	—	12	—	—	25,741
Distribution operation	6,453	140,998	346	4,886	—	2,332	133,434
Distribution maintenance	7,951–	221,620	355	329	—	—	220,936
Total	1,498–	362,618	701	5,125	—	2,332	354,370
Customer accounting	5,799	148,098	100	135,285	—	—	12,713
Residential and rural	8,121	123,120	208	2,417	—	120,406	89
Commercial and industrial	6,421	37,521	8	—	—	37,513	—
Total	14,542	160,641	216	2,417	—	157,919	89
Area development	6	96	28	—	—	68	—
Public relations	123–	1,347	1,233	89	—	25	—
Pension/insurance and credit	217–	1,324–	246	—	1,078–	—	—
Other personnel	2,711–	12,157	2,851	—	9,053	—	253
Total	2,928–	10,833	2,605	—	7,975	—	253
Other A. & G. operating expenses	7,013	50,299	27,741	18,261	247–	2,191	2,353
Other A. & G. maintenance	2,350–	3,098	172	415	3	397	2,111
Total	4,663	53,397	27,913	18,676	244–	2,588	4,464
Operation and Maintenance	24,757	762,783	32,796	161,694	7,731	162,932	397,630
Variance	—	24,757	954	12,312	303	14,017	2,829–

gerial accounting. We don't want to turn out reams and reams of beautiful look-ing reports that in the final analysis do nothing for us. Management expects the report to be used deliberately and methodically as a device to reduce costs. This is our goal. An information system should not simply report what happens, it should help make things happen. I submit that detailed insight into the costs of various jobs can trigger improved ways of doing things—in the final analysis the only way in which costs can be significantly reduced. This is what we want from managerial accounting."

Some members of the controllership group at headquarters were of the opinion that the operating personnel at the division level had been opposed to the introduction of the managerial accounting reports at first. However, this opposition had, they thought, disappeared as the division managers became ac-customed to the reports.

The Preparation of Budgets and the Managerial Accounting Report

The data given in Exhibit 4 of the case is a complete report of the activities of the Southern division. It is compiled from series of reports on smaller units summarized into it. Likewise, the divisional reports for Southern are consoli-dated with those for other divisions to give the over-all company report.

In the last column of Exhibit 4 of this case are shown the figures for "T&D" which means "transmission and distribution" department. This column is the result of the collection of costs described in Exhibit 5, which is the detail report of the transmission and distributon section of the Southern division. In the inter-est of brevity some of the more detailed subdivisions of accounts in Exhibit 5 have been omitted, the principal account only being shown. A full breakdown, however, is given of the "distribution maintenance" group of accounts, #59,000–#59,890, many of which can be varied at the discretion of the manager of the responsibility unit. Two asterisks in the "Resp Unit" column mean that the ac-count is a total, just as "Distribution Maint" is a total of the ones inset above it. Three asterisks indicate a summary account of all preceding totals. The column of the exhibit labeled "% Discret," suggests the proportion of the dollar amount in each expense group which can be varied at the discretion of the departmental head.

The division managers are responsible for setting their budget for the pe-riod, in this case one calendar year. The expected level of power consumption is extrapolated, on the basis of estimated changes in significant factors such as the number of customers, movements in industry and so on. Hence the expected levels of the various expenses are estimated by all levels of operating manage-ment, and from these projections budget estimates for each of the numerous cost categories are prepared by consolidating the projections into a divisional total. These budget estimates are allocated over the months of the year according to a pattern established by experience so that at the end of any given month expected totals for the year to date for each of the expense categories can be found. Those

EXHIBIT 5

Transmission and Distribution Department Year-to-Date and Current Month Report, September 1984 (–Indicates Favorable Variance)

| YEAR TO DATE | | | | | | | | | CURRENT MONTH | | | | | | | | |
| Payroll labor | | | | | | | | | | | Payroll labor | | | | | | |
Hours	Amount	Total	Budget	Variance	Account	Description	Resp Unit	% Discret	Variance	Total	Hours	Amount	Outside services	Materials	Automotive	Employee expenses	All other
788	2,860	4,469	4,425	44	**	Transmission oper	**	0	99–	370	71	249	7	—	22	—	99
2,921	11,792	21,272	17,032	4,240	**	Transmission maint	**	50	1,037–	2,082	437	1,761	—	146	168	—	—
29,228	106,959	133,434	127,293	6,141	**	Distribution oper	**	0	1,206–	15,377	3,215	11,715	546	670	1,464	55	957
2,180	11,324	12,004	10,143	1,861	59.000	Maint supv and eng			241	1,368	256	1,421	—	—	115	9	177
206	814	1,304	252	1,052	59.100	Maint structures			134	162	—	—	105	57	—	—	—
297	1,148	1,485	900	585	59.210	Mt station ckt breaker			18	118	28	108	—	—	10	—	—
288	1,118	1,752	1,665	87	59.220	Mt sta transf/regltr			80–	105	—	—	105	—	—	—	—
135	525	948	657	291	59.230	Mt station buses/disc			52	105	—	—	105	—	—	—	—
—	—	—	100	100–	59.240	Doble test station eqp			0	—	—	—	—	—	—	—	—
830	3,173	4,846	1,863	2,983	59.290	Maint station eqp-ad			143	64	14	54	—	5	5	—	15
38	138	17,990	23,947	5,597–	59.311	Tree trimming			2,024–	4,624	38	138	4,402	41	28	—	—
59	213	4,155	5,352	1,197–	59.312	Tree removal			573–	599	10	34	558	—	7	—	—
98	356	58,828	70,349	11,521–	59.313	Reclearing			1,184–	9,762	98	356	9,333	—	73	—	—
—	—	—	586	586–	59.314	Spraying			—	—	—	—	—	—	—	—	—
1,792	6,807	13,798	12,873	925	59.321	Mt poles/tower/fixt			468–	1,129	114	413	504	136	82	—	6
5	18	21	40	19–	59.322	Mt ptf-ovhd lg instal			0	—	—	—	—	—	—	—	—
6,808	25,856	51,102	51,893	791–	59.331	Maint ovhd cors/devc			244	6,346	654	2,387	3,098	342	514	5	—
5	16	18	—	18	59.332	Mt ocd-ovdr lgt instal			0	67	16	62	—	—	—	—	—
720	2,755	3,673	1,314	2,359	59.340	Maint line recls/sctlz			79–						5		
3,753	14,309	20,351	19,971	380	59.350	Maint ovhd services			81	2,300	388	1,420	368	179	329	4	—
—	—	20	207	187–	59.390	Maint ovhd lines-ad			23–								
2,177	8,290	14,332	15,345	1,013–	59.510	Maint line transf/devc			175	1,880	234	857	543	298	182	—	—
497	1,931	2,280	3,060	780–	59.520	Maint line regulators			340–								
135	508	576	45	531	59.590	Maint line trans-ad			5–								
581	2,143	3,967	4,623	656–	59.601	Mt ovhd st lgt/sig sys			906–	159–	12	46	37	251–	9	—	—
2	8	9	225	216–	59.602	Mt undg st lgt/sig sys			25–								
860	3,321	4,080	2,394	1,686	59.790	Maint meters-ad			80	346	79	294	—	1–	53	—	—
160	607	2,012	1,242	770	59.810	Mt cust ovdr lgt units			127	265	13	47	—	207	11	—	—
32	102	799	594	205	59.890	Mt misc distrbn plt-ad			39–	27	6	18	9	—	—	—	—
21,658	85,480	220,936	229,054	8,118–	**	Distribution maint	**	80	659	29,108	1,960	7,655	19,167	1,013	1,423	18	168–
2,856	10,664	12,713	13,473	760–	**	Customer accounting	**	0	398–	1,099	251	891	—	—	208	—	—
21	78	89	50	39	**	Residential and rural	**	0	27–	23	5	19	—	—	4	—	—
—	—	—	135	135–	**	Public relations	**	0	45–	—	—	—	—	—	—	—	—
104	253	253	3,120	2,867–	**	Other personnel	**	0	0	—	—	—	—	—	—	—	—
213	628	2,353	1,377	976	**	Other A. & G. oper	**	50	8	161	24	72	—	89	—	—	—
314	1,190	2,111	4,500	2,389–	**	Other A. & G. maint	**	50	308–	192	42	158	—	15	19	—	—
58,103	219,904	397,630	400,459	2,829–	***	Oper and maint	***		41–	48,412	6,005	22,520	19,720	1,933	3,308	73	858

items of expense in the transmission-distribution departments not stated to be variable at the discretion of the manager responsible are predetermined either by company policy, by technical constraint or by the historically established relationship of the expense with the level of production anticipated. Distribution operation, for example, although a highly significant quantity, is largely a function of the demands of the customers over which the manager of the responsibility unit has little control. Similarly, customer accounting, residential and rural sales, and public relations, are for the most part outside the control of the sectional head.

On the other hand, some of the expenses under distribution maintenance can be controlled by the division manager. While the cost of doing any given piece of work is largely predetermined, the division manager has it within his power to defer the work to a later period; as long as he does not defer work too long, so that the distribution system is in danger of failing altogether, he can exert a substantial degree of independent judgment as to when to carry out maintenance work.

Some of the most important items in this group are accounts 59,311–59,314 those dealing with the prevention of interference by trees and other growth with the power lines. These four accounts amount to $81,559 for the nine months to date, which is more than a third of the distribution maintenance total. Other accounts in the distribution maintenance section are also within the control of the division manager.

Not all of the accounts are equally easy to estimate for budgetary purposes. While some expenses are technically predetermined, and others are a direct function of the power generated, some can vary almost without limit. One example of the last kind is 59,210, maintenance station circuit breaker expense. Although not a very large account in the distribution maintenance department, this account is substantial for transmission maintenance. Another difficult account is 59,510, maintenance line transformers and devices. These and other accounts are particularly prone to unexpected events, which throw out the predictions of the managers. Frequently nothing can be done to improve the predictions, although sometimes by a careful and conscientious examination of the probable future situation improved estimates can be made.

As it is impossible to define the degree of difficulty that makes an account "hard" to estimate, no dollar figure can be attached to the problem account total. Certain of the managers have estimated that nearly 25% of the total distribution and transmission cost is of this type.

Once estimates of expenditures and revenues from the several divisions have been made by the operational personnel, an estimate of the profit for the entire company is derived for the period. This is done simply by taking the estimated revenue of the divisions and deducting the budgeted expenses. The revenues are also broken down into categories though they are not usually regarded as controllable. In this manner, a divisional income statement estimate is prepared. The income statement developed from the budget figures is examined with great care by the controller and by the president. The latter expresses an opinion on whether or not the performance budgeted is satisfactory. If satisfactory, no further action is taken. If the president is dissatisfied with the budgeted profit, however, the budget will be returned to the division with some injunction such as "increase budgeted profits."

When an unsatisfactory budget has been returned to him, an operating manager will adjust some of the accounts which can be varied at his discretion. He may, for example, reduce expenditure on tree removal for distribution maintenance, being aware that he can meet such a reduced budget simply by removing fewer trees during the period under review. Alternatively, he may cut back on promotion or some other nonoperating item. Once adjusted, the budget is resubmitted to headquarters, usually in acceptable form. In due course, a complete budget for the entire company is compiled and the budgeted profits for each subdivision of the corporation are available for consolidation into an overall company income statement. Deviation from this target will have to be explained by the creator of such a difference.

The Managerial Accounting System—1984 Review

Over the three-year period in which the managerial accounting system has been in operation, certain facts have come to light concerning its use. It has been found that while the operating personnel regard the receipt of a managerial report as being a reliable indication of personal prestige, they are less inclined to regard the report as a reason for action. Mr. Sydney Harcourt, assistant controller of Piedmont, said; "We have some trouble getting them (the operating people) to take the report seriously."

While other factors may be involved, he felt the stability of the industry as a whole probably contributes greatly towards this attitude. For example, the dismissal of personnel is a rare event, and natural attrition is relied upon to bring down the payroll to a desired level. The industry as a whole, whether privately or publicly owned, has an unwritten proscription on the wholesale dismissal of personnel which characterizes other industries. Considerable security of employment extends to managers, salaried employees and nonsalaried employees. In the light of this, an unfavorable labor variance will not usually be regarded as a basis for action.

The Multiple Correlation Analysis Procedure

Mr. Harcourt explained that as one step in the direction of closer and more effective control, experimental use is being made of a new multiple correlation procedure for the analysis of performance of divisions. The effect of certain of the variables involved in the profitability of a division is being investigated. This is described in detail in the appendix to this case. Once the most important group of variables has been established, applicable data for the year are fed into the computer for analysis and on this basis an *expected total distribution cost* for that division is prepared. The objective of the experiments is to try to pick out divisions that are doing outstandingly well or badly, in order to analyze the reasons for good performance and to try to correct serious problems.

Once the significance of the relationship between the independent variables listed in the appendix and the total distribution costs has been established by means of the correlation analysis, the most significant group of these variables is used as a basis from which to compute the expected total distribution cost for each division. The latter figure is then compared with the actual distribution costs. Exhibit 6 shows a listing of the divisions. In the "Deviation" column a large

EXHIBIT 6 Piedmont Power Company

Printout from Correlation Analysis

	PREDICTED VERSUS ACTUAL RESULTS		
Division no.	*Actual*	*Predicted*	*Deviation*
1	994.88900	873.97665	120.91235
2	846.67300	819.11222	27.56078
3	605.51900	630.63419	− 25.11520
4	463.54600	548.38319	− 84.83719
5	722.19700	708.82148	13.37552
6	489.76800	521.70649	− 31.93849
7	572.88599	539.74282	33.14317
8	387.79000	410.70629	− 22.91629
9	700.05399	648.44309	51.61090
10	364.52000	377.06149	− 12.54149
11	791.57500	694.88955	96.68545
12	1326.58699	1321.88506	4.70193
13	778.42300	730.11306	48.30994
14	362.61800	520.83471	−158.21671
15	336.22000	443.87338	−107.65339
16	889.40800	972.38593	− 82.97793
17	328.15000	396.94847	− 68.79848
18	988.02499	1034.93004	− 46.90504
19	929.06699	871.24320	57.82379
20	774.77000	609.17689	165.59311
21	511.27400	564.04809	− 52.77409
22	648.84900	704.69079	− 55.84179

Independent variables

3. Number of meters

8. Residential MWH, January 1964 (surrogate for system capacity)

4. (negative coefficient) Number of residential customers

Division #14   Southern

Division #16   Northern

Division #11   Eastern

positive number as in divisions 1, 11, and 20, indicates that the division's actual cost substantially exceeded the quantity predicted by the correlation analysis procedure. A large negative number, on the other hand, as in divisions 4, 14, 15, and 16, indicates that actual costs were substantially less than had been anticipated.

Mr. Sydney Harcourt, the assistant controller of the corporation, explained that he did not think there was any significance in the numerical value of the deviation, but did think that some indication could be derived of the performance of a division from the new procedure. He thought that further investigation was merited in those cases where the deviation was substantial in either direction.

Required

1. What are the major variables the management of this company has to consider in setting up operational plans?

2. What are some of the major problems this company faces in budgeting for and controlling its operations, which are

    (a)   unique to this industry?

    (b)   generally applicable?

3. How do you appraise the approach Piedmont has taken to establish budgetary controls? What values do you see in the procedures from

    (a)   the point of view of top management?

    (b)   the point of view of divisional management?

Appendix

The company is divided into twenty-two divisions. For each of these, the current values of the eleven independent variables listed below was obtained. Also, the total cost of distribution for each division for a typical period was selected. These data are fed into the company's IBM 1401 computer, together with the divisions' actual costs and a standard program for multiple correlation analysis.[1]

Independent Variables.

1. Area (square miles)
2. Number of customers
3. Number of meters
4. Number of residential customers
5. Number of nonresidential customers
6. Number of large power customers
7. Pole Miles of distribution lines

---

[1]For a more detailed discussion of multiple correlation analysis, see Wallis and Roberts, *Statistics: A New Approach*, pp. 526–528.

8. Residential MWH[2,3]
9. MWH to ultimate customers[2]
10. Nonresidential MWH[3]
11. Population of largest city

The output from this program gives the sets of the independent variables which relate most closely to the total distribution cost figures. The most closely related single variable (which proved to be number of meters), the most closely related pair (number of meters and residential megawatt hours), the most closely related triplet (meters, MWH, and the number of residential customers)[4] and so on are all detailed.

Given this information, it is possible to use this historically established relationship as an analytical tool, using the known values of the independent variables as a basis. To avoid the risks involved in using one variable and the undue complexity of using too many, it was decided to use the triplet of number of meters, residential megawatt hours, and the number of residential customers as the basis for the analytical portion of the study.

The computer program then derived expected values for total distribution costs for each of the divisions by manipulating the independent variable values and their coefficients until (1) the total expected distribution cost for all divisions equaled the actual total and, (2) the sum of the squared differences between the derived and actual costs was minimized. The results of this computation, the expected total distribution costs by divisions, are printed in the third column of Exhibit 6.

CASE 16.4   CHEMICAL BANK

Chemical Bank, with deposits averaging well over a billion dollars, was one of the largest banks in the United States. Its banking operations were conducted in a main office and several dozen branch offices located throughout the metropolitan area that it served. A condensed organization chart is shown in Exhibit 1.

Branch offices operated as if they were independent banks. They served individual, commercial, and industrial customers by accepting demand, savings,

---

[2]MWH = megawatt hours, thousands of KWH.

[3]The values of these three variables for the peak load month of January were used, as being the best measures available of system capacity. One of them was found to be significantly related to total distribution cost.

[4]The number of residential customers had a negative coefficient. In conjunction with the number of meters, this means that it should cost more to serve a nonresidential (commercial, industrial, etc.) consumer than a residential customer.

This case was prepared by Mr. Chei-Min Paik, Research Assistant, under the direction of Professor Robert N. Anthony. Copyright © by the President and Fellows of Harvard College. Harvard Business School case 9-172-228.

EXHIBIT 1 Chemical Bank

Partial Organization Chart

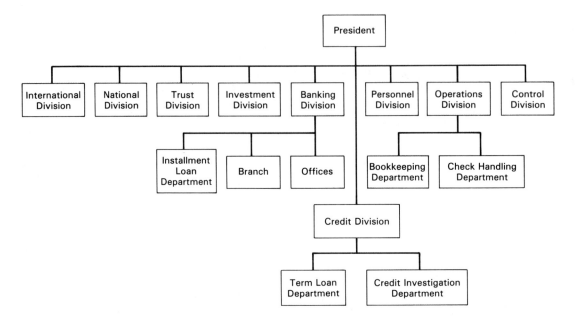

and time deposits, by extending various types of loans, and by performing other services normally expected of a bank. The sizes and operating characteristics of the branches varied over a wide range. Average deposits outstanding ranged from $1 million to over $100 million; average loans outstanding, from no loans to over $100 million. Moreover, the ratio of deposits to loans varied considerably from one branch to another; most branches had more deposits than loans, but a few had more loans than deposits. In brief, both the magnitude and composition of assets and liabilities were significantly different among the different branches. Inasmuch as these differences were related to the geographical location of the branches, the difficulty of evaluating and comparing the performances of branches for the purpose of over-all planning and control was inherent in the situation. The design and operation of a planning and control system for this purpose was the responsibility of the control division.

Among various reports reaching top management, the quarterly comparative earnings statement (see Exhibits 2 and 3) played a central role in the evaluation of branch performance. The report was designed to show the extent to which branches attained three important goals: (1) branches should operate within their budgets; (2) branches should grow in deposits and loans; and (3) for each office the budgeted and actual amounts of deposits and loans outstanding, and income, expenses and earnings for the current quarter, the year to date, and the year to date for the preceding year.

EXHIBIT 2

Comparative Statement of Earnings: Branch A

3RD QUARTER			JANUARY 1 THRU SEPTEMBER 30		
1960	*1960*		*1960*	*1960*	
Actual	*Budget*	**INCOME**	*Actual*	*Budget*	*Actual*
13,177	12,600	Interest on Loans	33,748	35,200	
6,373	4,800	Service chgs.—Regular A/C's.	14,572	14,100	
3,816	3,600	Service chgs.—Special Ck.	11,114	10,700	
1,168	1,300	Safe deposit rentals	4,317	4,500	
2,237	2,154	Installment loans (net)	5,126	5,406	
—	—	Special loans (net)	—	—	
1,010	1,200	Fees, comm., other income	3,321	3,300	
27,781	25,654	Total Direct Income	72,198	73,206	
104,260	102,148	Int. on excess (borr.) funds	324,434	306,166	
132,041	127,802	**GROSS INCOME**	396,632	379,372	
		EXPENSES			
32,363	32,617	Salaries	96,151	97,164	
2,955	2,955	Deferred compensation	8,865	8,865	
5,232	4,689	Employee benefits	14,925	14,067	
11,485	11,489	Rent and occupancy	34,398	33,947	
6,824	7,560	Interest on deposits	20,455	21,780	
9,458	8,090	Other direct	25,688	23,930	
3,128	3,097	Office administration	9,676	9,725	
19,183	17,642	Service departments	57,059	52,399	
6,415	5,061	Indirect & overhead	14,964	14,273	
97,043	93,200	**GROSS EXPENSES**	282,181	276,150	
34,998	34,602	**NET EARN. BEFORE TAXES**	114,451	103,222	
18,955	18,741	Income Tax Prov. (credit)	61,987	55,906	
16,043	15,861	**NET EARN. AFTER TAXES**	52,464	47,316	
12,655,000	12,550,000	Average Deposits—Demand	13,134,000	12,650,000	
979,000	1,100,000	Savings	986,000	1,057,000	
55,000	55,000	Time	40,000	43,000	
233,000	190,000	U.S.	213,000	183,000	
13,922,000	13,895,000	Total	14,373,000	13,933,000	
900,000	870,000	Average Loans	775,000	827,000	
5.82	5.76	Average Loan Rate	5.82	5.69	
		Earn. Rate on:			
4.08	3.95	Excess (borr.) funds	4.05	3.95	
6.50	6.40	Savings deposits	6.46	6.40	
26.5%	27.1%	Net Earn. Ratio (before taxes)	28.9%	27.2%	
		MEMO			
—	—	Losses · Before taxes	—	—	
—	—	Recoveries · Before taxes	—	—	

EXHIBIT 3

Comparative Statement of Earnings: Branch B

3RD QUARTER		INCOME	JANUARY 1 THRU SEPTEMBER 30		
1960	*1960*		*1960*	*1960*	
Actual	*Budget*		*Actual*	*Budget*	*Actual*
951,617	833,300	Interest on Loans	2,646,813	2,202,750	
7,015	7,400	Service chgs.—Regular A/C's.	24,020	21,900	
8,211	7,600	Service chgs.—Special Ck.	23,384	22,600	
2,049	2,100	Safe deposit rentals	6,712	7,100	
9,202	9,478	Installment loans (net)	21,402	23,790	
—	212	Special loans (net)	85	556	
8,081	3,100	Fees, comm., other income	22,517	12,800	
986,175	863,190	Total Direct Income	2,744,933	2,291,496	
(191,650)	(121,960)	Int. on excess (borr.) funds	(430,444)	(121,493)	
794,525	741,230	**GROSS INCOME**	2,314,489	2,170,003	
		EXPENSES			
69,308	62,633	Salaries	197,572	185,634	
5,646	5,646	Deferred compensation	16,938	16,938	
9,180	7,989	Employee benefits	25,833	23,967	
27,674	27,775	Rent and occupancy	82,726	83,375	
15,878	18,230	Interest on deposits	47,589	52,650	
25,637	23,660	Other direct	86,112	71,400	
17,232	17,072	Office administration	53,321	53,606	
89,724	95,719	Service departments	290,082	283,531	
22,406	18,001	Indirect & overhead	53,643	51,166	
282,685	276,725	**GROSS EXPENSES**	853,816	822,267	
511,840	464,505	**NET EARN. BEFORE TAXES**	1,460,673	1,347,736	
277,212	251,576	Income Tax Prov. (credit)	791,100	729,934	
234,628	212,929	**NET EARN. AFTER TAXES**	669,573	617,802	
67,901,000	70,000,000	Average Deposits—Demand	69,425,000	72,667,000	
2,354,000	2,700,000	Savings	2,328,000	2,600,000	
74,000	90,000	Time	52,000	66,000	
5,194,000	1,900,000	U.S.	4,086,000	1,733,000	
75,523,000	74,690,000	Total	75,891,000	77,066,000	
72,129,000	65,000,000	Average Loans	67,446,000	57,666,000	
5.25	5.10	Average Loan Rate	5.24	5.10	
		Earn. Rate on:			
4.08	3.95	Excess (borr.) funds	4.05	3.95	
6.50	6.40	Savings deposits	6.46	6.40	
64.4%	62.7%	Net Earn. Ratio (before taxes)	63.1%	62.1%	
		MEMO			
—	—	Losses · Before taxes	5,559	—	
66	—	Recoveries · Before taxes	798	—	

Budget. In early November, each branch prepared a budget for the following year for submission to headquarters of the banking division and to top management. The branches were furnished a booklet containing sample forms, 24 pages of detailed instructions, and a brief set of policy guides from top management to facilitate the preparation of their budgets. The policy guide for 1961 is given in its entirety in Exhibit 4. The instructions gave the procedures to be followed in arriving at the budget amounts for specific items. It was, for instance, specified that the starting point for forecasting was to be the prior year's figures on the quarterly basis, that the income item interest on loans, was to be derived from the projected volume of loans and loan rates, that painting costs should not be included in the item for building maintenance expense, and so on.

Since salaries were the biggest single expense item, and the hiring and releasing of employees involved considerable cost, utmost care was required in budgeting this item. Branches were instructed to arrive at staffing requirements

EXHIBIT 4 Chemical Bank

Covering Memorandum for 1961 Budget Instructions

It is customary for the committee to summarize for your general guidance current thinking regarding deposits, loans, and loan rates. The expectations outlined below are for the overall bank. Therefore, it is important that the head of each earning unit analyze the impact of expected general economic trends on the conditions peculiar to his own area of activity in order to project specific goals which he may reasonably expect to attain.

Deposits

There is every indication that money market conditions will be such that demand deposit levels in our area will expand. In our judgment, we anticipate at least a 5% growth in demand deposits for all banks. Our overall goal, however, should be set somewhat higher to reflect an improvement in our relative position. Savings deposits will continue to climb moderately. Current rates for time and savings deposits should be used to project interest costs.

Loans and Loan Rates

In all probability loan demand will slacken seasonally in the early months of 1961; in fact, many economists believe that the decline may continue through the second quarter of the year. We firmly believe that sometime between the March tax date and early in the third quarter, loan demand should strengthen.

For the most part, the recent decline in the prime rate is reflected in the loan rate structure at this time. Accordingly, excepting where necessary rate adjustments are still anticipated, the existing rate structure should prevail.

(continued)

EXHIBIT 4 (continued)

Expenses

Before preparing the budget, it is imperative that each supervisor closely evaluate every controllable expense in his area and consider all means of economizing and reducing costs, particulary in such areas as personnel staffing, overtime, entertainment, stationery, etc. The salary administration policies explained on pages 19 and 20 in the Budget Instructions* should be strictly followed.

In order to complete the budget for the entire bank by year-end, your full cooperation is necessary in meeting the deadlines which appear in the attached General Instructions.

BUDGET COMMITTEE

October 7, 1960

*These policies referred to are as follows: Your current appraisal of each employee's performance as E (excellent), AA (above average), A (average), or P (poor) is to be shown immediately following the individual's name on Schedule 4A, as a guide for your own budgeting and for the subsequent review by the Budget Committee.

Salary administration policies, as expressed in Bulletin III of the Personnel Policies Manual, are not expected to change during 1961. Our salary rates are competitive, and as in recent years, any projected increases should be based solely on merit or, where plans are sufficiently advanced, on anticipated bona fide promotions.

In general, the budget committee anticipates that we will be able to maintain our competitive position with total bankwide increases to deserving employees, averaging no more than 5% of their salaries. In order to achieve this purpose, all departments must cooperate in observing the following guides:

(a) In all cases, *merit* and not length of service, is to be the basis for the forecasting of increases.

(b) Individual merit increases should be roughly 5% to $5\frac{1}{2}$% of the range midpoint, with no increase less than $156 nor more than 10% of the range midpoint, ($500 maximum), and in multiples of $1.00 weekly.

(c) Individual increases exceeding the guide lines in (b) above should be thoroughly documented both in budget submittal and in subsequent actual review for salary purposes.

(d) An employee rated average should not receive appreciably more than the midpoint of his salary range. The top half of the range is reserved for those employees who demonstrate above-average performance.

(e) In case of promotion, the increase or increases to be scheduled should normally bring the salary within a reasonable period to the minimum for the new job.

for the next year after a thorough examination of anticipated increases in productivity arising from mechanization or otherwise improved operating procedures, of anticipated changes in the volume of activity, and of advantages and disadvantages of using overtime and temporary or part-time help. If the number of the required staff of a branch thus determined exceeded the number previously authorized by top management, the reason for the difference had to be thoroughly documented for and substantiated to banking division headquarters and the budget committee. Top management was extremely critical of subsequent requests by the branches for staff increases which had not been reflected in the budgets.

In general, there were two types of income and expense items—those directly identifiable with a particular branch, and those not directly identifiable with a particular branch. Branches were instructed to budget only those direct expenses under their control. Indirect expenses were allocated to branches by the control division. In addition, the budgeting of certain direct expenses, such as depreciation of fixtures, employee benefits, and deferred compensation, was done by the control division because the branches had only secondary control over these expenses.

Deposits and Loans. In the lower part of the comparative statement were shown the budgeted and actual loans and deposits outstanding. Both top management and branch managers exercised a close watch over these primary indicators of the level of the branch's operation. The controller, however, expressed the opinion that the ultimate test of the office performance should not rest with these items, but, rather, with earnings. He maintained that the effect of changes in deposits and loans should and would, be reflected in the earnings statement.

Earnings Statement. The control division had encountered a number of serious problems in trying to produce an earnings statement that would be most useful for the branches and for the management of the banking division. Some problems were basic to all types of business; some were peculiar to banking. The fundamental cause of the problems, however, lay in the fact that not all income and expense items could be measured precisely or directly identified with particular offices. Specifically, some of the questions asked were: What should be the basis for determining the credit for a branch which generated deposits in excess of its own requirements for funds? What share of general administrative expenses, including the salaries of top management, should be charged to each branch? How should the expenses of the personnel division, the bookkeeping department, the check clearance department, the credit department, etc. be allocated to branches?

The control division resolved some of these problems in the following ways.

Installment Loans. Record-keeping, issuance of coupon books, and part of collection work for installment loans generated by all branches were handled centrally by the installment loan department, and income earned from installment loans was, therefore, credited initially to this department. This income was, in large part, attributable to the branches that generated the loans, and was, therefore, redistributed to them. The current procedure was to distribute gross operating income less the cost of "borrowed" funds and operating expenses of the department on the basis of the total direct installment loans generated by the branch during a revolving annual cycle.

An alternative basis that had been considered was to apportion the net income of the installment department according to the number of payments received by branches, since this measure of activity reflected the clerical time spent for coupon handling. This alternative was not adopted, on the grounds that it did not give branches enough motivation to seek more new installment loans, particularly since customers could make their installment payments at any branch they chose. An alternative basis considered was the amount of average loans outstanding. The controller thought this might be more equitable than the currently used basis, but he was of the opinion that the gain to be obtained from the adoption of the new basis was not large enough to offset the additional necessary record-keeping.

Interest on Excess (or Borrowed) Funds. Branches and other operating units with funds available for investment in excess of their own requirements for loans, cash, and other assets shared in the net earnings of the investment division; branches and other operating units whose asset requirements exceeded their available funds were charged for funds "borrowed." There was a wide variation in the ratio of deposits to loans among branches, and some branches were credited with the interest on excess funds in an amount higher than their direct income. An example of the calculation of this important income or charge item is shown in Exhibit 5.

EXHIBIT 5   Chemical Bank (A)

Calculation of Interest Income on Excess Funds, Branch A First Three Quarters of 1960

CALCULATION OF EXCESS FUNDS:

	(In thousands)	
Total demand deposits	$13,134	
Less: Reciprocal bank balances; float	(727)	
Plus: Treasury tax and loan a/c	221	
Adjusted demand deposits	$12,628	
Less: Reserve at 18%	(2,273)	
Net demand deposits		$10,355
Savings Deposits	$ 1,026	
Less: Reserve at 5%	(51)	
Net savings deposits		975
Net deposits available for investment		$11,330
Less: Loans, cash, other assets		(1,229)
Net excess funds		$10,101

CALCULATION OF INTEREST INCOME ON EXCESS FUNDS

	Principal		*Annual Rate*		*Three Quarters*		*Interest*
In special investment pool (63%)	$614,000	×	7.88%	×	$\frac{3}{4}$	=	$36,267
In regular investment pool (37%)	361,000	×	4.05%	×	$\frac{3}{4}$	=	10,965
Savings deposits (100%)	$975,000	×	6.46%	×	$\frac{3}{4}$	=	$47,232
In regular investment pool—demand deposits	9,126,000	×	4.05%	×	$\frac{3}{4}$	=	277,202
Net excess funds	$10,101,000						
Interest on excess funds							$324,434

As shown in the top section of Exhibit 5, the first step was to compute the amount of excess (or borrowed) funds for the branch. Funds were divided into two pools: (1) special pool—earnings from special long-term, high-yield municipal securities which were considered as an investment of part of the savings and time deposits; and (2) regular pool—earnings from other portfolio securities investments, interest on certain loans, and sundry earnings. As a rule, the special-pool investment yielded a higher rate of return than the regular-pool investments.

Third, branches with savings deposits were credited at the interest rate of the special pool on the basis of their pro rata share of savings deposits. Net savings deposits in excess of the principal of investment in the special pool, together with excess funds other than savings deposits, received pro rata credit from the earnings of the regular investment pool. Branches that borrowed funds were charged at the regular pool rate. In summary, the two rates from the two pools were as follows:

- Special pool rate: Net earnings of special pool/special pool securities principal (part of total savings deposits)
- Regular pool rate: Net earnings from regular pool/excess funds less borrowed funds less special securities principal

For the first three quarters of 1960, the budgeted regular pool rate and special pool rate were 3.95% and 7.81%; the actual rates, 4.05% and 7.88%, respectively. Thus for Branch A the interest on excess funds for the first three quarters was calculated as shown in the lower section of Exhibit 5.

Rent and Occupancy Cost.   Some branches operated in leased space while others operated in bank-owned buildings. The first group was charged with the actual rent paid, but the second was charged with the "fair rental value," which was determined by outside real estate appraisers. The practice was thought to put the two groups in the same footing. The fair rental value charges were internal bookkeeping entries offset by credits to real estate accounts which were maintained for each bank-owned building. These accounts, therefore, indicated the profitability of each building. The determination of the fair rental value was not difficult, and there had been no significant controversies involving its calculation.

Advertising.   General or institutional advertising was charged to other indirect expenses. (See below for the allocation of other indirect expenses.) Advertising related to a specific branch was charged directly to that branch, except that when advertising was placed through mass media such as radio, television, and newspapers with general circulation, 33% of the expense was allocated to other indirect expenses and 67% was allocated to the specific branches involved. The theory of the exception was that when mass media were used, the whole bank benefited to a certain extent.

Banking Division Headquarters and General Administration. All expenses of the banking division headquarters, including the salaries of officers in the divison headquarters, were allocated to branches on the basis of their prior year's average gross deposits. The figure for average gross deposits was considered as the best single measure of branch activity.

The salaries of general administrative officers of the bank were first allocated among divisions on the basis of the time spent on problems of each division as estimated by each officer. The amount of general administrative salaries thus allocated to the banking division was, in turn, allocated among branches on the basis of gross deposits in the prior year. All other general administration expenses were charged on the same basis.

Bookkeeping Department. Much of the bookkeeping work was centralized for the whole bank. However, since the central department was established only in 1959, several offices continued to do their own bookkeeping in 1960. The expenses of the central bookkeeping department were, therefore, allocated only to branches which it serviced. There were eight functional cost centers in the bookkeeping department, and each cost center had its own basis of allocation. The bases of four of the cost centers are given below.

1. *Regular bookkeeping cost center.* In the bookkeeping department a permanent clerical staff was assigned to process the accounts of each branch. Allocations to branches were based on the salaries of this assigned staff, plus fringe benefits and related overhead costs.
2. *Bank ledgers cost center.* Allocation was on the basis of debit and credit activity as determined by an analysis made from time to time. Inasmuch as the main activity of this cost center was the posting of transactions to ledger sheets, the number of debit and credit entries was preferred to any other basis, e.g., number of accounts. A new survey of debit and credit statistics was made by the analysis department whenever it was believed that there had been a material change from the prior survey period and, in any event, at least once a year.
3. *Special checking cost center.* Same as 2.
4. *Special statement section.* Allocation on the basis of number of accounts handled. The activity of the section was to send out special statements on customers' special requests.

Before adoption of the current method based on the cost-center concept, weight of statements mailed out had been the basis of allocation for the expenses of the entire department. The current practice was regarded as more accurate, because there were very few temporary movements of staff and machine services from one cost center to another and because there was a significant variation in the activity measures of the cost centers.

According to the controller, the main controversy involving the expenses of the bookkeeping department was not with respect to the basis of allocation but, rather, with respect to the absolute level of expenses of the department. Complaints were heard from those branches serviced by the department to the effect that they were handicapped relative to branches that did their own bookkeeping, because the cost charged by the central bookkeeping department was considerably higher than the cost that would be incurred if the branch did its own bookkeeping. The controller thought branches that had this opinion failed to recognize that the bookkeeping expenses shown in the earnings statements of the branches with their own bookkeeping were only part of the true bookkeeping cost, because an appropriate portion of supervisory salaries, keeping was centralized for a branch, the benefit gained from relieving the supervisors of supervising bookkeeping activity usually appeared as increased loans and deposits and better management generally.

Check Clearance Department. The total cost of this department was divided among 12 functional cost centers, based on the number of employees assigned to each and the volume of its work. The cost of each cost center was, in turn, charged to branches. Examples of the basis of allocation are given below.

1. *IBM proof machine operation—exchanges*: allocated on the basis of number of checks handled.
2. *IBM proof machine operation—deposits*: allocated on the basis of the number of deposit items.
3. *Check desk*: allocated on the basis of number of checks handled.
4. *Transit clerical*: allocated on the basis of number of deposit items.
5. *Supervision*: allocated to the various check clearance department cost centers in ratio to labor costs.

As was the case with the bookkeeping cost centers, the measures of activity (checks handled and number of deposit items) were based on periodic surveys and remained unchanged until significant changes in the relative activity of branches indicated the need for a new survey. Every cost center's activty was reviewed at least once a year for this purpose.

There were two important sources of trouble in allocation of the expenses of the check clearance department. One was that branches cashed checks issued by other branches; the other was that branches received deposits for customers whose accounts were in other branches. In the periodic activity analyses made to determine the basis of allocating cost, the "number of checks cashed" was the number of checks actually cashed in the branch, whether or not the account was located in the branch. Similarly, the "number of deposit items" was the number of deposits made in the branch. Although it had been believed that the effect of these interbranch services largely offset one another, a recent study by the control division indicated that they, in fact, resulted in distortions with respect to certain branches. The control division was currently working on a method of allocation by which the charge would be made to the branch that benefited most; that is, the branch in which the account was located.

Credit Investigation Department.   Although most branches had their own credit analysis staffs, they often requested the central credit department to make investigations. The expenses of the central credit investigation department, therefore, were allocated to the branches that requested its service. The basis of allocation was the number of requests for credit investigation weighted by the typical time required for the analysis performed. The weight for the various types of investigation was determined by the analysis department on the basis of an actual time study.

Term Loan Department.   Income from term loans was credited to the branches which generated the loans. Officers of the term loan department actively counseled the branches in negotiating terms with customers, in drawing up loan contracts, and in reveiwing existing loans. It was therefore necessary that the expenses of the term loan department be allocated to the branches that used its services. The basis of allocation was the number of loans considered, the number of loans outstanding, and the number of amendments to existing loans, weighted by the unit-handling time of each of three classes. In order to determine the weight, the analysis department asked the staff of the term loan department to estimate the time spent on each class.

Personnel Division.   The expenses of this division were allocated to all operating units in the ratio of the number of employees in each operating unit to the total.

Other Indirect Expenses.   Items of a general overhead nature, such as expenses of the accounting division, (except the direct cost of examining a branch, which was charged directly) cost of the senior training program, general institutional advertising, contributions, etc., were included under this heading. The basis of allocation of these expenses among branches was the ratio of annual operating expenses (excluding other indirect and interest on deposits) of each branch to the total operating expenses of all branches.

Controller's Views on Allocations

The controller believed that some arbitrariness was inevitable in the allocation of the income and expense items described above. With dozens of branches, each with its own operating characteristics, it was impossible to have a "perfect" or "right" system for all of them. What was more important, according to the controller, was agreement on the part of the branch managers that the system was generally equitable. If managers agreed on the fairness of the system, he believed, it was likely to be a success. They, therefore, let it be known to branch managers that the system was always open for revision, and he encouraged them to make known any criticisms they had. After the control division had done its best to find a workable system, the initiative for suggesting changes was with the branch managers. The controller said that several changes had been made as a result of branch managers' suggestions.

He warned them, however, against a blind and apathetic acceptance; the acceptance should be positive and constructive. On acceptance of the system, branch managers should be concerned with the reported result and make necessary efforts to improve it. Thus, he said, branch mangers were told clearly that the earnings statement was used to evelute their performance. This, he thought, attached sufficient importance to the matter to prevent any possible indifference.

Attitudes of Branch Managers

The managers of two offices, A and B, held different opinions about the system. The operating characteristics of these branches were different, as indicated by their comparative statements of earnings for the third quarter of 1960, reproduced in Exhibits 2 and 3. Branch A was relatively small and deposit-heavy, did its own bookkeeping, and operated in a leased space, whereas Branch B was larger, loan-heavy, used the centralized bookkeeping department, and operated in a bank-owned building. Their annual earnings statements of recent years are shown in Exhibits 6 and 7.

Comment by Manager of Branch A.   The statement is useful because I like to see, at least quickly, whether I am within the budget and what caused the deviations from it, if any.

The earnings of our branch are relatively low, because the volume of business is limited by the location. We have more deposits than our loan requirements; consequently, we get credit for the excess funds. In fact, as you see, for the first three quarters of 1960, interest on excess funds was more than four times the total direct income. The 4.05% rate on the excess funds seems fair enough, but we try always to increase our own loans in order to increase our earnings. However, the location of our office is a limiting factor.

Since rent and occupancy is the actual rent paid to the owner of the building, we can't have any quarrel about that, but the service department charges are certainly too high. We don't have any control over these costs; yet we are charged for them. I am not complaining that this is unfair; on the contrary, I believe branches should share the burden. My only misgiving is whether those service departments are doing enough to cut down their costs.

About one-half of the service department expenses charged to our branch is for check clearing service. Although I don't know the basis of allocation, I don't doubt that it is fair. Besides, even if I should have some questions about the basis, probably it wouldn't reach up there; the communication channel from here to the top is long and tedious.

At present, we do our own bookkeeping, but soon this will be centralized. I have heard some managers complain that the cost charged to them for the centralized bookkeeping is higher than the cost when they did their own bookkeeping. However, such intangible gains as prestige and customer relations may justify a little higher cost. At any rate, we wouldn't have any choice if top management decides to centralize our bookkeeping. It may be better in the long run.

EXHIBIT 6 Chemical Bank (A)

Condensed Annual Earnings Statements, Branch A (thousands of dollars)

	1960 BUDGET	1959 BUDGET	1959 ACTUAL	1958 BUDGET	1958 ACTUAL	1957 BUDGET	1957 ACTUAL	1956 ACTUAL	1955 ACTUAL
Total direct income	$ 98	$ 93	$ 90	$ 87	$ 89	$ 99	$ 90	$ 99	$ 82
Interest on excess funds	409	364	381	327	316	299	287	263	355
Gross income	507	457	471	414	405	398	377	362	437
Expenses									
Salaries	130	129	125	125	125	140	147	132	114
Deferred compensation	12	10	10	8	9				
Employee benefits	19	19	18	17	17				
Rent and occupancy	45	46	45	45	47	47	49	43	43
Interest on deposits	30	30	27	19	19	9	11	6	4
Other direct	32	29	31	30	30	[a]	[a]	[a]	[a]
Office administration	13	15	13	17	16	[a]	[a]	[a]	[a]
Service departments	70	58	61	57	57	67	69	62	44
Indirect overhead	18	18	21	19	16	[a]	[a]	[a]	[a]
Gross expenses	369	354	351	337	336	315	329	296	256
Net earnings before taxes	138	103	120	77	69	83	48	66	181
Average gross deposits	13,975	13,550	13,707	13,573	12,948	14,540	13,442	15,057	21,504
Average loans	820	820	810	746	737	990	927	1,139	1,093

[a] Changes in accounting procedure make these items noncomparable with later years.

EXHIBIT 7 Chemical Bank (A)

Condensed Annual Earnings Statements, Branch B (thousands of dollars)

	1960 BUDGET	1959 BUDGET	1959 ACTUAL	1958 BUDGET	1958 ACTUAL	1957 BUDGET	1957 ACTUAL	1956 ACTUAL	1955 ACTUAL
Total direct income	$ 3,077	$ 2,725	$ 2,532	$ 2,214	$ 2,201	$ 2,338	$ 2,395	$ 1,959	$ 1,172
Interest on excess (borr.) funds	(177)	157	222	154	263	73	(32)	209	556
Gross income	2,900	2,882	2,754	2,368	2,464	2,411	2,363	2,168	1,728
Expenses									
Salaries	249	255	256	245	247	250	264	236	232
Deferred compensation	22	19	21	17	18				
Employee benefits	32	34	33	30	31				
Rent and occupancy	111	105	104	104	105	106	108	65	85
Interest on deposits	71	75	66	51	52	19	25	12	10
Other direct	95	93	108	84	86	[a]	[a]	[a]	[a]
Office administration	71	85	76	86	83				
Service departments	379	383	360	356	345	361	380	315	224
Indirect and overhead	65	64	72	60	51	[a]	[a]	[a]	[a]
Gross expenses	1,095	1,113	1,096	1,033	1,018	878	928	829	814
Net earnings before taxes	1,805	1,769	1,658	1,335	1,446	1,533	1,435	1,339	914
Average gross deposits	77,410	79,885	75,853	72,063	73,899	73,415	69,683	70,740	73,433
Average loans	58,000	56,000	49,702	48,971	47,095	50,000	49,945	44,460	28,378

[a]Changes in accounting procedure makes these items noncomparable with later years.

Although I don't know exactly what items are included in other direct and indirect and overhead expenses, I don't think they are excessive. The control division is trying to be fair.

In summary, I think the statement is useful, but there are many factors you should consider in interpreting it.

Comment by Manager of Branch B.   The statement is a fair measure of how branches are doing. It is true that the location of a branch has a lot to do with its operation; in evaluating a particular branch, the location is an important element to be taken into account. To take the extreme case, you don't need a branch in a desert. If a branch can't show earnings after being charged with its fair share of all costs, perhaps the purpose of its existence is lost.

High volume and efficient operation have contributed to our high level of earnings. Our branch has more loans than can be sustained by our own deposits; thus, we are charged with interest on borrowed funds on the theory that we would have to pay the interest if we borrowed from outside. Of course, by increasing deposits we could meet the loan requirements and add to our earnings a good part of the interest on borrowed funds; indeed, we have been trying to lure more deposits to our branch. Quite apart from this special effort, however, we do not neglect to seek more loan opportunities, for loans increase earnings even after the interest charge.

Our office is in a bank-owned building, but, instead of controversial depreciation and maintenance charges, we are charged with the fair rental value. We are satisfied with this practice.

The bookkeeping of our branch is centralized. I believe we could do it for less money if we did our own bookeeping; but competing banks have centralized bookkeeping departments, and we have to go along. I suspect there are some intangible benefits being gained, too.

If I really sat down and thoroughly examined all the allocation bases, I might find some things that could be improved. But the fact of life is that we must draw a line somewhere; some arbitrariness will always be there. Furthermore, why should our branch raise questions? We are content with the way things are.

Comments by Banking Division Headquarters.   We call this report (Exhibits 2 and 3) our Bible, and like the actual Bible, it must be interpreted carefully. Many factors affect the performance of a branch that do not show up on the report. For example, in an area that is going downhill, the manager of a branch has to work terribly hard just to keep his deposits from declining, whereas in a growing area, the manger can read the *New York Times* all day and still show an impressive increase in deposits. The location of the branch in the neighborhood, its outward appearance, its decor, the layout of its facilities—all can affect its volume of business. Changes in the level of interest rates, which are noncontrollable, also have a significant effect on income. At headquarters we are aware of these factors and take them into account when we read the reports. The unfortunate fact is that some managers—for example, those in declining areas—may not believe that we take them into account. Such a manager may worry about his apparently poor performance as shown on the report, and this has a bad psychological effect on him.

One other difficulty with the report is that it may encourage the manager to be interested too much in his own branch at the expense of the bank as a whole. When a customer moves to another part of town, the manager may try to persuade him to leave his account in the same branch, even though the customer can be served better by a branch near his new location. We even hear of two branches competing for the same customer, which certainly doesn't add to the reputation of the bank. Or, to take another kind of problem, a manager may be reluctant to add another teller because of the increased expense even though he actually needs one to give proper service to his customers.

Of course, the earnings report is just one factor in judging the performance of a branch manager. Among the others are the growth of deposits compared with the potential for the area; the number of calls he makes soliciting new business (we get a monthly report on this); the loans that get into difficulty; complaint letters from customers; the annual audit of his operations made by the control division; and, most important, personnel turnover, or any other indications of how well he is developing his personnel. Some of these factors are indicated in these statistics (see Exhibits 8 and 9 on pages 602–5) which are prepared at banking division headquarters.

Required

1. The general question is: What are the strong and weak points of the budget-reporting-performance evaluation system of the bank in reference to its branch operations? What improvement would you suggest?

    a. What characteristics of banking make its management control system different from that of a manufacturing operation?

    b. What is the relationship between the earnings statement and the branch office reports?

    c. Would you recommend calculating a return on investment for each branch? If so, how would you determine the investment base?

    d. Should noncontrollable costs be omitted from the earnings statement? If so, what items would be affected?

    e. In comparing actual with budgeted interest on loans, should a noncontrollable variance be developed which represents the effect of changes in the general level of interest rates?

2. Bank of America, charged its profit centers for the use of money at current interest rates for obtaining funds of like maturities and risk. For example, if a branch makes a 90-day loan, it would be charged at the current rate that the bank pays on 90-day certificates of deposits. Should Chemical Bank adopt this practice?

EXHIBIT 8 Branch Office Report

Location and Office No. A

1960

All Dollar Amounts in Thousands Unless Otherwise Stated

		$	JAN.	FEB.	MAR.	APRIL	MAY	JUNE	JULY	AUG.	SEPT.	OCT.	NOV.	DEC.	YEAR AVERAGE	
DEPOSITS — AVERAGE																
1	DEMAND — (Ind., Part., Corp.)	$	14,038	13,473	12,330	12,919	13,108	12,911	12,596	11,907	12,746	12,202				1
2	DEMAND — BANKS	$	50	50	–	–	–	–	–	–	–	–				2
3	SPECIAL CHECKING		221	218	220	251	235	216	237	244	236	219				3
4	TREAS. TAX & LOAN ACCOUNT		118	149	238	124	270	321	232	202	265	196				4
5	SAVINGS		987	974	1,001	990	976	1,012	972	978	986	1,013				5
6	CHRISTMAS CLUB		15	23	30	35	41	46	51	55	60	63				6
7	TIME		–	–	–	–	–	–	–	–	–	–				7
8	TOTAL	$	15,429	14,887	13,819	14,319	14,630	14,506	14,088	13,386	14,293	13,693				8
NUMBER OF ACCOUNTS																
9	DEMAND (Ind., Part., Corp.)		1,515	1,513	1,507	1,503	1,516	1,511	1,514	1,497	1,478	1,473				
10	DEMAND — BANKS		1	1												
11	SPECIAL CHECKING		868	865	884	892	894	900	903	911	939	948				
12	SAVINGS		585	587	593	589	587	591	593	587	621	645				
13	CHRISTMAS CLUB		540	536	534	538	533	530	526	519	516	511				
14	TIME		–	–	–	–	–	–	–	–	–	–				
15	TOTAL		3,509	3,501	3,518	3,522	3,530	3,532	3,536	3,514	3,554	3,577				
LOANS																
16	TOTAL LOANS — AVERAGE	$	723	755	720	627	672	773	841	889	971	961				16
17	INSTALMENT LOAN VOLUME	$	20	24	36	31	35	22	25	34	27	39				17
18	SPEC. LOAN DEPT — Month End	$	–	–	–	–	–	–	–	–	–	–				18
NUMBER OF BORROWERS																
19	TOTAL LOANS		48	58	50	49	51	54	55	60	62	63				
20	INSTALMENT LOANS MADE		24	37	46	50	32	30	28	45	44	39				
21	SPECIAL LOAN DEPT		–	–	–	–	–	–	–	–	–	–				
22	STAFF — Number of Officers		4	4	4	4	4	4	4	4	3	3				
23	No. of Employees — Auth. Budget		25	25	25	25	25	25	25	25	25	25				
24	TOTAL		29	29	29	29	29	29	29	29	28	28				
25	OVERTIME & SUPPER MONEY PAYMENTS (To nearest dollar)	$	276	135	273	93	496	123	536	370	350	220				25
SERVICE CHARGES (To nearest dollar)																
26	REGULAR CHECKING ACCOUNTS	$	1,543	1,578	1,445	225	2,550	858	2,378	1,998	1,997	1,833				26
27	SPECIAL CHECKING ACCOUNTS	$	1,017	1,119	1,220	1,397	1,223	1,322	1,313	1,237	1,266	1,340				27
28	TOTAL	$	2,560	2,697	2,665	1,622	3,773	2,180	3,691	3,235	3,263	3,173				28

YEAR — AVG.   YEAR — TOTALS

INCOME AND EXPENSE BY QUARTERS AND CUMULATIVE

To Nearest Dollar		1st Quarter	2nd Quarter	Jan. thru June	3rd Quarter	Jan. thru Sept	4th Quarter	Jan. thru Dec.
GROSS INCOME	$	133,060	131,531	264,591	132,041	396,632		
GROSS EXPENSES	$	92,050	93,088	185,138	97,043	282,181		
NET BEFORE TAXES	$	41,010	38,443	79,453	34,998	114,451		
NET AFTER TAXES	$	18,799	17,622	36,421	16,043	52,464		
Average Loan Rate		5.80	5.83	5.81	5.82	5.82		
Earn. Rate Excess Funds		4.02	4.06	4.04	4.08	4.05		
Earn. Rate Savings Deposits		6.52	6.55	6.54	6.59	6.55		

EXHIBIT 8 (continued)   Branch Office Report – Supplement

1960

Location and Office No. A

All Dollar Amounts in Thousands	JAN.	FEB.	MAR.	APR.	MAY	JUNE	JULY	AUG.	SEPT.	OCT.	NOV.	DEC.	YEAR TOTALS	
Regular Checking Accounts-Number														
1 OPENED – NEW	26	17	7	15	16	17	10	9	14	11				1
2 OPENED – A/C Trans. within Office	–	1	1	–	4	–	–	–	1	–				2
3 OPENED – A/C Trans. from other Off.	–	1	1	–	3	–	2	–	1	–				3
4 Total Number Opened	26	19	9	16	23	17	13	9	15	11				4
5 CLOSED	24	17	12	17	6	19	9	17	24	14				5
6 CLOSED – A/C Trans. within Office	–	2	1	2	2	–	–	8	6	1				6
7 CLOSED – A/C Trans. to other Offices	4	3	2	1	2	3	1	1	4	1				7
8 Total Number Closed	28	22	15	20	10	22	10	26	34	16				8
9 NET OPENED OR CLOSED	– 2	– 3	– 6	+ 4	+ 13	– 5	+ 3	– 17	– 19	– 5				9
Regular Checking Accounts Average Deposits Closed – Monthly														
10 CLOSED $	16	7	3	15	7	14	4	11	18	7				10
11 CLOSED – Trans. within Office $	–	19	2	4	2	–	–	6	4	1				11
12 CLOSED – Trans. to other Offices $	5	6	2	1	1	3	1	1	2	2				12
13 Total Average–Closed Accts. $	21	32	7	19	10	17	5	18	24	10				13
Accounts Since Jan. 1st–Cumulated*														
14 *No. opened (Line 1)	26	43	50	65	81	98	108	117	131	142				14
15 No. closed (Line 5)	24	41	53	70	76	95	104	121	145	159				15
16 *Opened–Current Month Aver. (Line 14) $	83	191	162	143	120	102	120	109	114	127				16
17 Closed–Total Avg. Bal. (Line 10) $	16	23	26	41	48	62	66	77	95	102				17
Business Development														
18 No. of calls – Customers	3	8	7	4	10	8	*6	9	5	5				18
19 No. of calls – Prospects	3	4	4	4	1	4	2	6	5	5				19
20 Total	6	12	11	8	11	12	8	15	10	10				20
21 Spec. Checking Accts. – Opened	26	21	31	21	19	22	15	33	37	29				21
22 Spec. Checking Accts. – Closed	13	24	12	13	17	16	12	25	9	20				22
23 Spec. Checking Accts. – Net	+ 13	– 3	+ 19	+ 8	+ 2	+ 6	+ 3	+ 8	+ 28	+ 9				23
24 Savings Accounts – Opened	17	9	22	9	15	24	15	9	52	39				24
25 Savings Accounts – Closed	21	7	16	13	17	20	13	15	18	15				25
26 Savings Accounts – Net	– 4	+ 2	+ 6	– 4	– 2	+ 4	+ 2	– 6	+ 34	+ 24				26
27 S. D. Boxes – New Rentals	9	6	3	9	3	6	5	6	4	4				27
28 S. D. Boxes – Surrendered	9	4	9	11	12	10	6	7	7	3				28
29 S. D. Boxes – Net	–	+ 2	– 6	– 2	– 9	– 4	– 1	– 1	– 3	– 3				29
30 No. of Personal Money Orders Sold	523	543	583	643	421	467	447	419	452	367				30

EXHIBIT 9 Branch Office Report

1960

Location and Office No. __B__

DEPOSITS — AVERAGE
(All Dollar Amounts in Thousands Unless Otherwise Stated)

		JAN.	FEB.	MAR.	APRIL	MAY	JUNE	JULY	AUG.	SEPT.	OCT.	NOV.	DEC.	YEAR AVERAGE	
1	DEMAND – (Ind., Part., Corp.) $	76 738	68 526	68 509	68 654	65 716	67 602	66 723	64 335	70 017	70 912				1
2	DEMAND – BANKS $	475	475	350	150	275	520	524	350	258	125				2
3	SPECIAL CHECKING	506	506	509	562	534	516	512	508	475	465				3
4	TREAS. TAX & LOAN ACCOUNT $	1 689	3 065	4 776	1 824	5 078	4 761	4 757	4 786	6 038	6 026				4
5	SAVINGS	2 359	2 301	2 340	2 320	2 359	2 210	2 349	2 328	2 385	2 493				5
6	CHRISTMAS CLUB $	19	28	35	45	54	61	67	75	81	89				6
7	TIME $	—									—				7
8	TOTAL $	81 786	74 901	76 519	73 555	74 016	75 670	74 932	72 382	79 254	80 110				8

NUMBER OF ACCOUNTS

		JAN.	FEB.	MAR.	APRIL	MAY	JUNE	JULY	AUG.	SEPT.	OCT.	NOV.	DEC.	YEAR AVERAGE
9	DEMAND (Ind., Part., Corp.)	3 561	3 585	3 631	3 622	3 565	3 556	3 569	3 617	3 619	3 591			
10	DEMAND – BANKS	1	1	1	1	1	1	1	1	1	1			
11	SPECIAL CHECKING	1 840	1 862	1 853	1 850	1 893	1 891	1 871	1 894	1 885	1 909			
12	SAVINGS	1 509	1 510	1 511	1 518	1 507	1 531	1 523	1 526	1 642	1 707			
13	CHRISTMAS CLUB	600	602	734	731	728	723	721	720	715	708			
14	TIME	—									—			
15	TOTAL	7 511	7 560	7 730	7 722	7 694	7 702	7 685	7 758	7 862	7 916			

LOANS

		JAN.	FEB.	MAR.	APRIL	MAY	JUNE	JULY	AUG.	SEPT.	OCT.	NOV.	DEC.	YEAR – AVG.	
16	TOTAL LOANS – AVERAGE $	64 277	67 796	66 835	62 033	61 763	67 926	72 386	71 644	72 356	65 851				16
17	INSTALMENT LOAN VOLUME $	80	86	134	124	103	110	98	115	90	123				17
18	SPEC. LOAN DEPT. Month End $	3	—	—	—	—	—	—	—	—	—				18

NUMBER OF BORROWERS

		JAN.	FEB.	MAR.	APRIL	MAY	JUNE	JULY	AUG.	SEPT.	OCT.	NOV.	DEC.	YEAR AVERAGE
19	TOTAL LOANS	378	381	372	390	398	403	408	430	434	409			
20	INSTALMENT LOANS MADE	86	83	118	121	97	107	106	120	112	110			
21	SPECIAL LOAN DEPT.	1												
22	STAFF – Number of Officers	8	9	9	9	9	9	9	9	9	9			
23	No. of Employees – Auth. Budget	42	42	43	43	43	43	43	43	43	43			
24	TOTAL	50	51	52	52	52	52	52	52	52	52			
25	OVERTIME & SUPPPER MONEY PAYMENTS (To nearest dollar) $	756	238	139	127	139	21	195	78	16	80			25

SERVICE CHARGES
(To nearest dollar)

		JAN.	FEB.	MAR.	APRIL	MAY	JUNE	JULY	AUG.	SEPT.	OCT.	NOV.	DEC.	YEAR – TOTALS	
26	REGULAR CHECKING ACCOUNTS $	3 081	2 786	2 263	3 048	2 430	3 399	2 620	2 067	2 328	2 876				26
27	SPECIAL CHECKING ACCOUNTS $	1 963	2 251	2 504	2 834	2 755	2 867	2 865	2 645	2 701	2 674				27
28	TOTAL $	5 044	5 037	4 767	5 882	5 185	6 266	5 485	4 712	5 029	5 550				28

INCOME AND EXPENSE BY QUARTERS AND CUMULATIVE

To Nearest Dollar	1st Quarter	2nd Quarter	Jan. thru June	3rd Quarter	Jan. thru Sept	4th Quarter	Jan. thru Dec.
GROSS INCOME $	766 538	753 426	1 519 964	794 525	2 314 489		
GROSS EXPENSES $	290 733	280 398	571 131	282 685	853 816		
NET BEFORE TAXES $	475 805	473 028	948 833	511 840	1 460 673		
NET AFTER TAXES $	218 109	216 836	434 945	234 628	669 573		
Average Loan Rate	3.18	5.29	5.24	5.24	5.24		
Earn. Rate–Excess Funds	4.02	4.06	4.04	4.04	4.05		
Earn. Rate–Savings Deposits	6.52	6.55	6.54	6.59	6.55		

EXHIBIT 9 (continued) Branch Office Report – Supplement

1960

Location and Office No. B

All Dollar Amounts in Thousands	JAN.	FEB.	MAR.	APR.	MAY	JUNE	JULY	AUG.	SEPT.	OCT.	NOV.	DEC.	YEAR TOTALS	
Regular Checking Accounts-Number														
1 OPENED – NEW	54	54	38	32	21	32	33	49	43	46				1
2 OPENED – A/C Trans. within Office	10	9	50	5	6	10	5	46	8	4				2
3 OPENED – A/C Trans. from other Off.	4	4	7	5	1	5	11	9	3	6				3
4 Total Number Opened	68	67	95	42	28	47	49	104	54	56				4
5 CLOSED	32	17	40	31	47	30	21	39	32	28				5
6 CLOSED – A/C Trans. within Office	14	19	2	16	35	20	12	7	10	53				6
7 CLOSED – A/C Trans. to other Offices	5	7	7	4	3	6	3	10	10	3				7
8 Total Number Closed	51	43	49	51	85	56	36	56	52	84				8
9 NET OPENED OR CLOSED	+ 17	+ 24	+ 46	– 9	– 57	– 9	+ 13	+ 48	+ 2	– 28				9
Regular Checking Accounts Average Deposits Closed — Monthly														
10 CLOSED $	129	37	181	153	160	32	72	42	40	91				10
11 CLOSED – Trans. within Office $	226	48	31	42	34	694	39	107	346	157				11
12 CLOSED – Trans. to other Offices $	204	107	15	20	5	247	36	44	70	67				12
13 Total Average - Closed Accts. $	649	192	227	220	199	973	147	193	456	315				13
Accounts Since Jan. 1st - Cumulated*														
14 *No. opened (Line 1)	54	108	148	178	199	231	264	313	356	402				14
15 No. closed (Line 5)	32	49	89	120	167	197	218	257	289	317				15
16 *Opened - Current Month Aver. (Line 14)$	603	907	1 378	1 584	1 544	1 709	2 419	2 634	2 484	3 066				16
17 Closed - Total Avg. Bal. (Line 10) $	129	166	347	505	665	697	769	81	851	942				17
Business Development													YEAR TOTALS	
18 No. of calls – Customers	129	148	153	115	140	215	117	103	160	136				18
19 No. of calls – Prospects	89	46	39	48	51	44	29	50	33	34				19
20 Total	218	194	192	163	191	259	146	153	193	170				20
21 Spec. Checking Accts. – Opened	70	62	28	66	64	55	67	60	91	87				21
22 Spec. Checking Accts. – Closed	33	40	37	69	21	57	87	37	100	63				22
23 Spec. Checking Accts. – Net	+ 37	+ 22	– 9	– 3	+ 43	– 2	– 20	+ 23	– 9	+ 24				23
24 Savings Accounts – Opened	63	54	54	63	47	65	56	53	173	122				24
25 Savings Accounts – Closed	93	53	53	56	58	64	64	50	57	57				25
26 Savings Accounts – Net	– 30	+ 1	+ 1	+ 7	– 11	+ 24	– 8	+ 3	+ 116	+ 65				26
27 S. D. Boxes – New Rentals	8	11	7	14	15	10	14	6	15	7				27
28 S. D. Boxes – Surrendered	8	9	8	8	9	13	14	6	14	13				28
29 S. D. Boxes – Net	–	+ 2	– 1	+ 6	+ 6	– 3	–	–	+ 1	– 6				29
30 No. of Personal Money Orders Sold	1 410	1 636	1 578	1 648	1 165	1 140	1 244	1 157	1 134	1 084				30

chapter 17

COMPREHENSIVE CASES

This chapter contains three comprehensive management accounting cases involving the control of foreign subsidiaries. The control of foreign subsidiaries involves complexities that are not normally experienced in the control of domestic divisions. Consequently, these cases provide an additional dimension to most of the other cases included in this book.

CASES

CASE 17.1   BULOVA WATCH COMPANY

Bulova's controller described the highlights of the company's control system and some of the features of the company's operations that complicated the control process. His comments are summarized in the next few pages.

Manufacturing

Above all else, Bulova's control system had to take into account the rather unusual features of the company's manufacturing operations. In 1973, the company made its products in 21 plants, 12 located in the United States, 9 overseas.

This case was prepared by F. T. Knickerbocker. Copyright © by the President and Fellows of Harvard University. Harvard Business School case 9-374-052.

(See organization chart in Exhibit 1.) Though the number and size of the plants, compared to what was common in other industries, was not large, the degree to which output moved around the world and from one plant to the next was out of the ordinary. Exhibit 2 gives a rough picture of the product flows within the Bulova manufacturing system. In addition, Exhibit 3 gives an example of the build-up from cost to selling price of a typical quality jeweled-lever watch.

The description of manufacturing flows pinpointed one fact. Within Bulova, intercompany sales and/or purchases were frequent and important. The best example of this was the domestic company's reliance on overseas production. In the early 1970s, of all the watches sold by Bulova in the United States, about 85% contained movements imported from abroad. In some instances, from the time components were manufactured at a foreign site to the time finished watches were ready for sale in the United States, as many as five intercompany transactions took place.

Bulova's policy was to have all intercompany transfers billed at standard cost plus 10%. Exceptions to this policy were rare. Bulova operated on the basis of a standardized, worldwide cost accounting system. The standard costs for manufacturing subsidiaries were based on a full costing system with the standards set by the Production Engineering Department with the assistance of the Cost Accounting Department. Management did not regard intercompany pricing as an issue that was negotiable among sub-units.

A second implication of Bulova's manufacturing flows was that the company was almost always moving products across national boundaries and, hence, across currencies.[1] With watches, for example, in nearly eight cases out of ten, all or a major part of the costs associated with their production were accumulated in one currency, while the revenues associated with their sales were generated in a second currency. Only four operations within Bulova did not involve a currency shift between costs and revenues, but three of the four were not, as of the early 1970s, of great importance to the firm:

1. Bulova made and sold a few watches within Switzerland,
2. It made watches in Switzerland for export, billed in Swiss francs, to third party distributors, and
3. Its joint venture made and sold watches in Japan.

Of course, these three operations eventually involved a second type of cross-currency transaction when profits, upon remittance to the parent company, were converted into U.S. dollars. The one important watch activity within Bulova that did not involve cross-currency transactions was the manufacture and sale of watches in the United States. This activity generated about 25% of Bulova's total *domestic* consumer business by fiscal 1973.

---

[1] A third implication, not discussed here, was that Bulova was almost always moving products across tariff barriers.

EXHIBIT 1   Bulova Watch Company, Inc.

Organization Chart as of September 1975

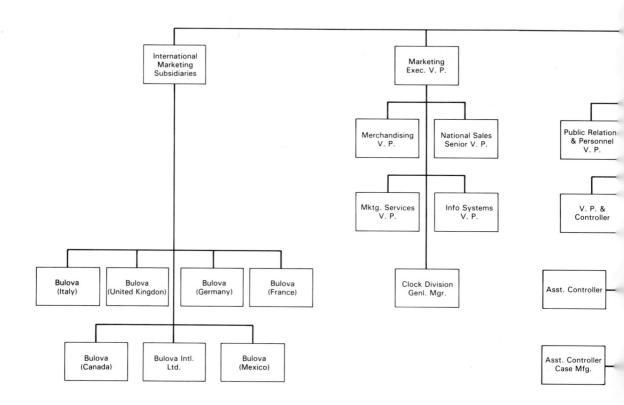

Bulova's controller summed up the matter this way:

> Many of the large multinational firms don't face the cross-currency complexities
> we do. They have numerous subsidiaries that make and sell products within single
> countries. Thus, they are largely operating within single currencies. Only when
> profit remittance comes up do they face, as of course we do, the problem of convert-
> ing currencies.

He added:

> Looking at the company as a whole, you might say that our income statement is
> made up of sales denominated in one bundle of currencies while cost of goods sold
> and expenses enter the statement denominated in a second bundle of currencies.

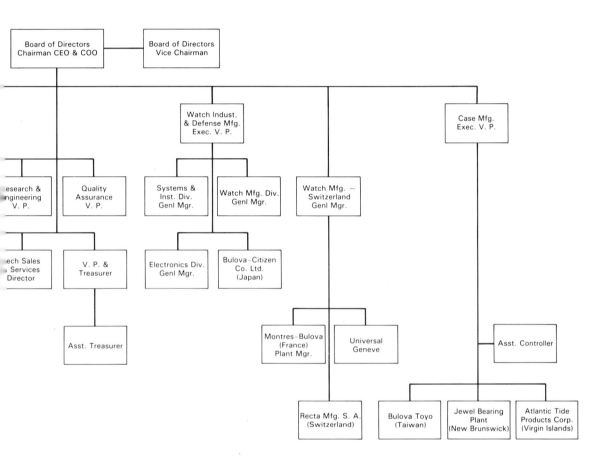

Thus, exchange rate considerations play a part in practically every control matter we handle.

Operations in the US Virgin Islands and American Samoa

Within Bulova's manufacturing system, its movement assembly operations in the Virgin Islands and American Samoa raised special problems. Since, in unit terms, the number of movements flowing through the Virgin Islands and Samoan plants was approaching 30% of Bulova's annual domestic requirements, close control to these activities was obviously critical. But there were complications.

First, in order to gain the tariff advantages associated with production at the island sites, Bulova had to insure that local value added exceeded 50% of the

EXHIBIT 2 Bulova Watch Company, Inc.

Manufacturing Flows Within Bulova for Consumer Products

SOURCE	PRODUCT	DESTINATION
Swiss plants (including that of Bulova's subsidiary, Universal Geneve).	Movements and finished watches.	Bulova's 8 and Universal Geneve's 7 foreign marketing subsidiaries.
	Finished watches.	Bulova's and Universal Geneve's third-party distributors.
	Finished watches.	Bulova's Hong Kong and Tokyo distribution centers.
	Components.	Bulova's Virgin Islands and American Samoa assembly plants.
Bulova's Virgin Island plant.	Assembled movements.	Bulova's Flushing, N.Y., plant.
Bulova's American Samoa plant.	Assembled movements.	Bulova's Flushing, N.Y., plant.
Bulova's joint venture Taiwan plant.	Watch cases.	Bulova's Flushing, N.Y., plant, Toyo Corp., Japan, and third-party customers.
Bulova's joint venture Japan plant.	Finished tuning-fork watches.	Bulova brand products; all world markets except the U.S.;
		Citizen brand products: Japan and other selected markets, especially the Middle East.
Citizen Watch Co., Japan (independent supplier to Bulova for 13 years).	Components, movements.	Bulova's Virgin Islands, Flushing, N.Y., and Toronto, Canada, plants.
Bulova's Flushing, N.Y., plant.	Finished tuning-fork, quartz, and conventional jeweled-lever watches.	Bulova's U.S. marketing subsidiaries;
		Bulova's overseas marketing subsidiaries: Accuquartz watches only.
Bulova's Flushing, N.Y., plant.	Tuning-fork movement subassemblies.	Bulova's Swiss plants during start-up phases of production.
Bulova's 2 U.S. watch case plants.	Cases.	Bulova's Flushing, N.Y., and Swiss plants and its marketing subsidiary in Canada.

This list ignores manufacturing flows within Bulova for industrial defense products. With very minor exceptions, all such products were made and sold in the United States. As of 1973, industrial defense production took place in 8 plants. In 5 of the 8, Bulova also manufactured consumer products: watch movements, cases, clocks, etc.

EXHIBIT 3 Bulova Watch Company, Inc.

Estimated Manufacturing and Distribution Costs
  For a Quality Jeweled-Lever Watch

U.S. jeweler's selling price		$100.00
U.S. jeweler's mark-up		50.00
Manufacturer's selling price		$ 50.00
Manufacturer's mark-up		18.75
Manufacturer's assembled cost		$ 31.25
Materials and labor cost for adding, in the U.S., the case, dial, bracelet, and packaging		15.00
Manufacturer's landed cost of movement:		$ 16.25
Duty	$ 2.70	
Transportation and Insurance	.10	2.80
Manufacturer's movement cost F.O.B. Switzerland		$ 13.45
Manufacturing mark-up		2.50
Total movement cost, of which:		$ 10.95
Direct labor	$ 4.10	
Indirect labor and overhead	5.75	
Materials	1.10	
	$10.95	

    The assumed watch is a 17-jewel watch, containing a Swiss-made automatic movement, with a day and date display and a stainless steel case and bracelet.
    The figures are not actual data taken from any one firm. Rather, they indicate what might be regarded as industry-typical numbers starting from an assumed jeweler's U.S. selling price of $100.

selling price of the assembled movements.[2] Four different sets of prices or cost were involved:

1. Transfer prices for incoming components from Bulova's Swiss plants,
2. Purchase prices for incoming components from Bulova's Japanese supplier,
3. Locally generated costs, and
4. Transfer prices for sales between the two island plants and Bulova's domestic operations.

    Second, in the case of the Samoan operation, though not the Virgin Islands one, Bulova had a ten-year exemption from taxation. Naturally, the company wanted to take advantage of the exemption to the greatest extent possible.
    The two island operations were profit centers, but whether it made sense at all to treat them as such represented one side of the control problem. Yet,

---

    [2]The U.S. tariff law stipulates that goods can be imported duty free into the United States from its insular possessions (the U.S. Virgin Islands, American Samoa, and Guam) provided that local value added exceeds 50% of the selling price in the islands. In 1965 Bulova established a subsidiary in the Virgin Islands; in 1971, it established one on American Samoa. In the case of Samoa, Bulova received the ten-year tax exemption as an investment inducement.

given their importance to the whole manufacturing system, how to exert pressure on their local managers for better performance constituted the other side of the control problem.

Swiss Manufacturing and the Foreign Marketing Subsidiaries

Other factors complicating the control process arose out of the relationships between the Swiss manufacturing plants and the foreign marketing subsidiaries. As of the early 1970s, about 40% of the output from Bulova's Swiss plants was shipped to its overseas marketing subsidiaries or to third-party customers in foreign countries. The remainder was shipped, directly or indirectly, to Bulova-U.S.

The usual arrangements between Swiss manufacturing and the foreign marketing subsidiaries were as follows: The Swiss plants sold the subsidiaries on open account. That is, the intercompany billings had no stipulated repayment time. Management had adopted this practice as a means to finance, in an indirect way, the growth of the fledgling marketing subsidiaries. The billings were denominated, of course, in Swiss francs, and as per company policy, the Swiss plants billed the subsidiaries at standard cost plus 10%.

Management had also decided that the foreign marketing subsidiaries should have a high degree of purchasing autonomy. The subsidiaries were required to purchase movements, either jeweled-lever or tuning-fork, from Bulova's Swiss plants, but they were not obliged to accept what the plants offered in the way of finished watches. The subsidiaries could buy all the exterior components of watches from outside suppliers and finish the watches in their own local assembly facilities. Moreover, if the subsidiaries bought finished watches from the Swiss plants, they had the option of returning them to Switzerland if they did not sell in local markets. According to management, this policy was designed to insure that market pressures worked their way back to Swiss manufacturing. As Bulova's president put it, the system guaranteed that Bulova manufactured what could be sold rather than sold what could be manufactured. From the control standpoint, though, the policy made it a good bit more difficult to measure how well the Swiss plants planned their production and managed their inventories.

Control System

During the 1960s, Bulova developed a formal annual budgeting program, and this became the key to its control system.[3] Since little about the mechanics of the system was unusual, only a few of its main characteristics will be mentioned here.

---

[3]Most, though not all, of the budgeting and reporting system was formalized. Management did not disseminate performance goals in a formal way. Generally, line management learned about management's performance expectations in meetings conducted by Bulova's president or in conversations between individual managers and the president.

Foremost of these characteristics was management's attempt to use the profit center concept to the maximum extent possible.

As of 1973, Bulova was composed of 32 operating sub-units, each with its own profit responsibility. Of the total number of profit centers, 22 were located outside the United States. They were:

- 15 marketing subsidiary profit centers;
- 3 manufacturing profit centers in Switzerland;
- 2 profit centers, one each in the Virgin Islands and American Samoa;
- 2 joint venture profit centers, one each in Japan and Taiwan.

Each of these was a separate planning and reporting unit responsible for performance down to the profit-after-tax level.

When asked about what led management to focus heavily upon the profit center concept in Bulova's foreign sub-units, the corporate controller responded that the manufacturing and foreign marketing subsidiaries were separate corporations or taxable entities. He further noted that these sub-units operated under the laws of countries which require that they be legally constituted and taxable therein. There was no way, he said, that they could exist except as separate profit centers.

At home, 11 of Bulova's 12 manufacturing plants were organized into 4 profit centers, each responsible for performance down to the profit-before-tax level.[4] On the marketing side, the company was organized into 6 product divisions, each held for performance down to the operating profit level. General administrative expenses were allocated to both the manufacturing operations and the product divisions. Only general corporate expenses, e.g., interest expense, were not charged to the domestic profit centers.

The budgeting and reporting procedures followed by the domestic operations were fairly routine, and, because the profit centers were near at hand, headquarters management could easily get supplementary facts or explanations whenever needed. The flow of information from overseas was somewhat less detailed and frequent. The foreign marketing subsidiaries prepared and forwarded to New York these reports:

ANNUALLY	*QUARTERLY*	*MONTHLY*
Income Statements; Balance Sheets; Cash flow statements: For the forthcoming year.	Income Statements; Balance Sheets; Cash flow statements: Actual for last quarter and Revised for the remaining quarters of the year.	Trial Balances; Sales reports by product and territory; Statements of inter-company cash remittances.

---

[4]In those domestic plants where joint production of consumer products and industrial defense products took place, overhead, general expenses, etc., were allocated to the various product lines on the basis of direct labor costs. One Bulova plant was run on a fee basis for the U.S. Government.

On an annual and quarterly basis, the 3 Swiss-based manufacturing profit centers submitted to New York the same reports as those sent in by the marketing subsidiaries.[5] On a monthly basis, they submitted reports, beyond those listed above, on shipments, sales by product and destination, and intercompany payables and receivables. Among other things, this reporting system made it possible to centralize cash flow management in New York.

As regards data on the manufacturing costs of the Swiss plants, headquarters received a complete report only once a year. Bulova's controller stated that headquarters did not get into the detail of manufacturing costs, but rather left that up to the managers of the three profit centers in Switzerland. He explained that the real mechanism by which headquarters controlled manufacturing costs in Switzerland was through exerting competitive pressures on the Swiss plants. That is, headquarters kept the Swiss plants well informed of the intercompany prices the domestic company could afford to pay for movements. These prices were derived from predicted competitors' retail prices in the United States. A Bulova's controller put it:

> Our Swiss plants know a year or so in advance what sort of manufacturing costs they will have to meet for movements if we are to stay competitive in the U.S. marketplace. They are expected to meet these targets. How they do it is the job of the managers in Switzerland.

By and large the various other overseas manufacturing operations within Bulova, the plants in the Virgin Islands and Samoa, the Japanese and Taiwanese joint ventures, followed the same budgeting and reporting procedures, though the joint ventures did submit monthly income statements, balance sheets, etc.

Since all information and documentation flowed to New York, the overall picture was one of a highly centralized control system. In effect, no layers of management intervened between the field profit centers and headquarters.

Bulova did not have a long-range budgeting system. Domestic and foreign profit centers budgeted only for the forthcoming fiscal year, and as the budget year progressed, they revised their plans only to the end of the current fiscal year. Yet, separate from the control system, Bulova carried out a type of long-range planning.

Business Plans

Each year, the managers of all profit centers submitted directly to Bulova's president a business plan that extended beyond the next fiscal year. Usually, these,

---

[5]On an annual basis, all manufacturing profit centers, domestic and foreign, also submitted capital expenditure budgets, which went to the Board of Directors for approval. How changes from budget were handled differed depending on whether the changes arose in foreign or domestic profit centers. Overseas units were permitted to modify the composition of their capital budgets so long as they stayed within their total approved limits. All changes taking them beyond their approval limits had to be forwarded to New York for review. In the case of domestic units, any change from budget had to be forwarded to headquarters for review.

covered two years though some, upon the request of the president, carried planning five years forward. Year one of the business plans matched each sub-unit's budget for the next fiscal year. Years two and on of the business plans presented, largely in narrative form, the goals and programs of the profit centers. More often than not, the plans concentrated on marketing objectives such as growth goals, market share goals, etc. Executives in Bulova described these reports as personal plans of the profit center managers, and they were viewed as private interchanges between these managers and Bulova's president.

Measurement and Rewards

Though Bulova was organized, for control purposes, around profit centers, the performance criteria that operating managers seemed to follow most closely were gross margins and the levels of inventories and receivables. Still, top management kept a careful eye on the bottom line.[6] When asked if the profit center system had any teeth in it, the controller observed:

> Those managers who haven't been able to meet their profit goals haven't stayed around in the company very long. I can think of three or four instances of this in the last few years.

Complicating this picture, however, was the nature of the company's reward system for its managers. In the mid-1960s, Bulova's management had instituted a version of management by objectives. Individual managers, in consultation with Bulova's president, set specific goals for the forthcoming year or two, e.g., share of market for a new watch line. Attainment of these goals was factored into the performance review of each manager. However, there was more to the reward system than this. As a general policy, therefore, all the more important line and staff managers of the company, domestic and foreign, were rewarded on the basis of the company's overall performance. According to Bulova's president, the nature of the company's operations precluded any other sort of reward system.

The Issue

Bulova's controller summed up his comments:

> We think our control system, and our commitment to profit centers, make good sense. Yet, for a number of reasons, I think our control problems are tougher than a lot of firms face. For one thing, we are not only a highly integrated company but also we are a highly international company.

---

[6]Top management, naturally, also measured progress against return on investment, but, given the nature of the company's operations, managers under the top echelon seemed to give little attention to the ROI criterion. Rather, they focused more on managing current assets largely by applying certain rules of thumb to determine acceptable levels of receivables and inventories.

Sure, so are all the oil companies, some of the other mineral companies, some of the metal companies, so why should our control problems be special? I'll tell you. First, we're in the fashion business, so we are constantly facing market instability. Second, our entire industry is a drop in the bucket compared to these other industries. We simply don't have the resources for elaborate administrative systems.

I suppose what bothers me is that we have pushed the profit center concept pretty far in our company. Maybe too far? I'd love to have somebody take a good look at us and suggest alternative ways of controlling the company.

Got any ideas?

Required

1. Evaluate Bulova's transfer price system in terms of its advantages and disadvantages. Assuming that Bulova wishes to retain its profit center system, what changes would you recommend?

2. Evaluate Bulova's measurement and control system with respect to its foreign manufacturing subsidiaries. In what ways, if any, would you change their system?

3. Evaluate Bulova's measurement and control system with respect to its foreign marketing subsidiaries. In what ways, if any, would you change the system?

In answering each question, discuss the major alternatives you have identified to the changes you recommend and indicate the reasons why you have decided against them. In answering Questions 2 and 3, be sure to evaluate the subsidiary manager's influence over the determinants of profitability.

CASE 17.2   SKA, LTD.

In July 1980 the management of SKA, Ltd. were considering how to reply to a proposal, received from their parent company, to implement a system of measuring the amount of resources either contributed or used by each business area and product throughout the world.

SKA, Ltd. was a wholly owned Australian subsidiary of Svenska Kemisk Akiebolag (hereafter called SKA, Sweden). SKA, Sweden, was a large, multinational manufacturer of chemicals and related products with headquarters based in Uppsala, a city in the southeast part of Sweden. SKA, Ltd., located in Newtown, Australia, manufactured fertilizers and related chemical products which were sold in Australia, New Zealand, and other countries in the Far East.

This case was prepared by John Dearden. Copyright © by the President and Fellows of Harvard University. Harvard Business School case 9-181-063.

Products and Organization

SKA, Ltd. was divided into three business areas as follows:

1. Agricultural products
2. Industrial products
3. Services (e.g., power, water, and steam).

Each of the business areas had its own plants and its own marketing organization. Most of SKA, Ltd.'s production facilities were located in a large industrial complex in Newtown, although three other smaller plant were located in South-eastern Australia. The corporate staffs and the central research department were also located in Newtown.

Each business area was a profit center. Except for marketing, almost all managers had a dual reporting responsibility. For example, all plant mangers reported to the production management at the staff level on a functional basis and to the business area manager on a line basis. A similar dual relationship existed for accounting, personnel, research, industrial engineering, and so forth. A unique features of the organization was that many managers held two positions. For example, the production manger was also the general manager of the fertilizer business area.

Cost Accounting

SKA, Ltd. used a process cost accounting system. Costs were accumulated by each production department and transferred to subsequent departments as the product was transferred. Thus, at all points in the production process, all costs incurred in the manufacture of a product to that point had been charged to it.

Dual Systems. SKA, Ltd. maintained two parallel systems. One system collected the actual costs incurred by each department and transferred these costs to subsequent departments. This was called the *roll-through* system. A second system transferred certain intermediate products at a transfer price. This was called the *transfer-price* system. The products transferred at a price were independent products (e.g., ammonia and nitric acid) that were normally traded in the market. The market price determined the transfer price.

A dual system was maintained because the management of SKA, Ltd. exercised two types of control. First, control over products was exercised through a system of product profitability analysis. The roll-through was used for product control. Second, operating control was exercised through a profit budget. The transfer price system was used for operating control.

Standards. Standard costs were set for all products. As explained above, however, products were transferred through the system at actual costs, contrary to many standard costs systems. Standard costs were calculated for the products produced and then the total standard costs were compared to the actual costs incurred *outside* of the books of account. Inventories, however, were maintained at standard costs.

Product Profitability Analysis

Annually and sometimes twice a year, the profitability of all product groups were analyzed. A unique feature of this analysis was that it was made on the basis of both historical and inflation adjusted costs (called current costs hereafter). Management relied principally on current costs in making product decisions.

Calculating Current Costs. Current costs were calculated by adjusting fixed assets and inventories for the effect of inflation. These adjustments are explained in this part of the case.

FIXED ASSETS. The construction index for the chemical industry was the basic means for adjusting fixed assets for the effect of inflation. However, this was modified for the following circumstances:

1. An independent estimate of replacement cost of each facility was made by the plant engineering department. Where this estimate differed by more than 15% from the index adjusted amount, further study was made and the discrepancy resolved.
2. Specific information was used where available. For example, where major new plants have been recently completed, the existing plants were valued on this basis, adjusted for differences in capacity, if appropriate.
3. Where excess capacity existed, only the replacement cost of the capacity being used was included.
4. Anti-pollution and environmental improvements were excluded in the replacement cost estimate where these were not part of the existing facilities. (This was a rule laid down by Uppsala.)

Two other points on the fixed asset replacement cost calculations were of importance:

1. In the interests of simplicity, it was decided to do the following:
   (a) Replacment costs were calculated on a "site" basis only. For example, calculations would not assume a different plant in a different place or a leased plant instead of a purchased plant. In short, replacement costs assumed the same facilities in the same location.
   (b) Adjustments were not made for greater efficiency, more advantageous location, or any other technological change except for capacity.
2. Current costs reflected the best estimates of the expected lives of the assets. This was important because, in some instances, the historical accounting lives of fixed assets were shorter than the expected lives partly to offset the effects of inflation.

IVENTORIES. Inventories were valued at standard costs which approximated the current (replacement) cost of the inventories. Standard costs were changed *each quarter* to reflect expected changes in price levels. (The technique for setting quarterly standard costs is explained later in the case.)

Return on Capital (ROC). The final result of the profit profitability analysis was a rate of return on capital. This was calculated by business area, product-line and, individual products. All analyses were on a company-wide consolidated basis and were calculated for both historical costs and current costs.

EXHIBIT 1 SKA, Ltd(A)

Work-In Process Inventory

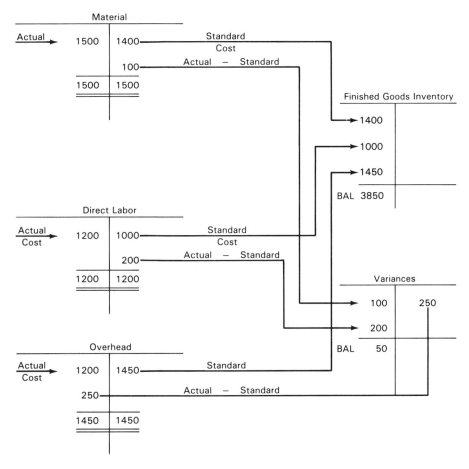

REVENUES.   The revenues were those actually realized from the sale of the product to outside customers. (Also included were some sales to other subsidiaries of SKA, Sweden.)

COSTS.   All costs incurred by the SKA, Ltd., including a corporate assessment from Uppsala, were assigned to business segments except income taxes.

CAPITAL.   Investment was equal to the working capital plus fixed assets at gross book value. Inventories and fixed assets were included at both historical costs and replacement value.

Use of Product Profitability Analysis.   The profitability of business areas and product lines was reviewed periodically by the top management of SKA, Sweden and SKA, Ltd., as well as by all of the managers responsible for individual segment profitability. These analyses had four principal uses:

- First, they were used as a guide in setting selling prices. (The prices of all basic products were reviewed and approved by the top management of SKA, Ltd.)
- Second, they acted as a discipline to the marketing organization to keep prices in line with inflation.
- Third, they were used to identify products that were not earning a sufficient profit.
- Fourth, they were used in the analysis of budget proposals. For example, if the ROC was declining, an analysis was made to determine which business areas and products were contributing to this decline and why.

Budgeting

SKA, Ltd. presented an annual profit budget to top management in Uppsala, Sweden, for review and approval. Monthly reports showing actual results compared to budget, analysis of variances and explanations of significant deviations from budget were submitted monthly to Uppsala.

Within SKA, Ltd. budgets were also used for the day-to-day control of operations. (The transfer price system was used for budgeting.) Each of the business areas prepared a profit budget which was reviewed and approved by the company management. Staff offices and the research department prepared expense budgets which were similarly reviewed and approved. Monthly, actual results were compared to budget and deviations analyzed and explained.

Current Costs.   A unique feature of SKA, Ltd.'s budgeting system was that it took into account the amount of inflation expected during the year. Revenues and nonmanufacturing costs were calendarized by month. Standard costs were projected for each quarter. Thus, four sets of standard costs were incorporated in the budget and new standard costs were introduced at the beginning of each quarter.

In setting these quarterly standards, the following techniques were used:

1. An estimated average price was used for commodities in which prices fluctuated randomly through the year.
2. Where materials were purchasd by contract, an estimate of the new price was phased in at the appropriate time.
3. Other material prices were forecast as follows:
   (a) The prices of all major materials were estimated individually.
   (b) The prices of non major materials were adjusted for the forecast of the wholesale price index.
4. Direct labor was based on the expected changes in the labor contracts.
5. Important overhead costs such as maintenance, supplies, and power, were forecast individually.

The Proposal From Uppsala

The top management of SKA, Sweden, as concerned with identifying business and products worldwide that were not contributing sufficient cash to enable the company to realize its strategic plans. A study was undertaken by the corporate director of finance to develop a method for systematically identifying such business segments.

A task force, assigned to this project, developed an objective rate of return on capital. Any subsidiary, business area, or product earning less than this return was considered not to be generating its share of the cash required for SKA, worldwide to accomplish its strategic plans. This part of the case describes how this objective rate of return was developed.

- *Step 1,* the task force prepared a forecast of the amount of cash that must be generated from operations on a worldwide basis if SKA was to have enough financial resources to accomplish its strategic plan.
- *Step 2,* the total noncash expenses (principally depreciation) that would be generated worldwide from all operations were estimated. (These noncash expenses were based on the *current cost* estimates.) This amount was subtracted from the amount calculated in Step 1 above.
- *Step 3,* the amount of income taxes expected to be paid worldwide was calculated and *added* to the amount calculated in Step 2. Steps 2 and 3, therefore, translated the required cash flow into operating profits before taxes. In other words if all operations earned a total profit before taxes equal to the amount calculated in Step 3, the net cash flow would equal the amount estimated in Step 1.
- *Step 4,* the total capital (working capital and gross fixed assets on a current cost basis) that would be employed by all operating units worldwide was calculated.
- *Step 5,* the amount calculated in Step 3 was divided by the amount calculated in Step 4. This was the objective rate of return that all business segments must earn if they were to contribute their shares to the cash requirements of the company.

It was reasoned, therefore, that any business or product not earning this return was a cash drain and the amount of this drain was equal to the capital employed multiplied by the difference between the actual or projected rate of return and the objective. A hypothetical calculation is as follows assuming an objective of 10%:

Product A—Thousands of Australian Dollars

		ACTUAL			*PROJECTED*	
	1977	*1978*	*1979*	*1980*	*1981*	*1982*
Profit before Taxes	100	90	80	90	100	110
Capital	1,500	1,600	1,800	1,700	1,600	1,500
Rate of Return	6.7%	5.6%	4.7%	5.3%	6.3%	7.3%
Excess/(Deficiency):						
%	(3.3%)	(4.4%)	(5.3%)	(4.7%)	(3.7%)	(2.7%)
Amount	(49.5)	(70.4)	(95.4)	(79.9)	(59.2)	(40.5)

Uppsala proposed that worldwide all business segments be evaluated in terms of this objective rate of return, and that excesses or deficiancies represent cash contribution or drain. Segments that were creating a cash drain were to be carefully evaluated to see if the situation could be corrected. If not, there should be valid reasons why the business segment should not be dropped or, at least, curtailed.

SKA, Ltd., Analysis

The finance director of SKA, Ltd. was puzzled by the proposal from the Uppsala task force. SKA, Ltd. had been remitting significant amounts of cash to the parent company consistently over the past several years. Yet, on the basis of the standard criteria, most products of SKA, Ltd. were cash drains and the subsidiary as a whole was a significant net cash user. On further reflection and analysis, the finance director determined that four conditions caused this inconsistency.

First, the formula did not take into account capital grants or rapid depreciation. In the part of Australia where SKA, Ltd. was located, it was possible to obtain a 25% grant on most investments and to write off the entire investment for tax purpose in the first year. Thus, an investment of A$1,000,000 would include a cash outlay of only A$250,000 (1,000,000 − 500,000 tax savings − 250,000 capital grant).

Second, effective income tax rates differed widely among countries. This was not so much because statutory rates were different but because some countries were more liberal in allowable deduction than others. The finance director believed that Australia had one of the lowest effective tax rates.

Third, the rate of growth differed widely among business segments. The higher the growth rate of a subsidiary or product, the more cash would be required. The Australian company with its lower growth rate was subsidizing higher growth segments of the Company.

Finally, the proportion of working capital to total capital varied widely among subsidiaries, business areas and products within business area. Working capital required a constant investment, whereas the actual investment in fixed assets declined over time because depreciation represented a partial return of the original investment.

SKA, Ltd., being heavily capital intensive, would have a lower real investment than a subsidiary with the same total amount of capital that included a larger percentage of working capital.

Required

1. Evaluate the product profitability and budgetary control systems of SKA, Ltd. In particular, how do you evaluate their current cost procedures, both in principle and execution? How would you change them if at all?

2. Evaluate the proposal of the Uppsala task force:

(a) Do you agree with their general method for identifying cash contributors and users?

(b) If you disagree how would you identify cash contributors and user?

(c) To what extent would you take into account the points raised by the finance director of SKA, Ltd.?

(Remember, the objective is to develop standard criteria that can be applied worldwide to any subsidiary, business area or product.)

CASE 17.3 **VEREINIGTE DEUTSCHE WAGEN, A.G.**

In October 1980, Rolf Ernst, financial director of Vereinigte Deutsche Wagen, A.G. (VDW), was considering what, if any, changes should be made to that part of the accounting system used to measure the financial performance of the company's sales subsidiaries. The system had operated without significant change for many years; however, the events of 1980 brought out in a rather dramatic fashion some of the problems with measuring the profitability of the sales subsidiaries. The immediate impetus for considering a change was a letter describing the 1980 situation of VDW, Suisse, from Hans Weber, the financial director of that sales subsidiary (Appendix A). Consequently, Mr. Ernst believed that this would be an appropriate time to review the entire accounting and control system for the sales subsidiaries.

The Organization

VDW was a multinational manufacturer of passenger automobiles with 1980 revenues in excess of DM 15 billion. Headquarters were located in Munich,

---

This case was prepared by John Dearden. Copyright © by the President and Fellows of Harvard University. Harvard Business School case 9-181-125.

Germany, and manufacturing and sales were conducted throughout Europe and parts of Africa.

Staffs. Exhibit 1 is an organization chart of VDW as of January 1, 1981. The headquarters staff, although reporting to the managing director, was also responsible for providing the operating director with the appropriate staff services.

Most of the functions of headquarters personnel were duplicated at all operating levels down to the manufacturing plants and the sales subsidiaries. For example, there was a finance function in product development, manufacturing, and marketing. There was a finance director for stampings, engine and power train, and assembly. Each of the manufacturing plants had financial directors. Each of the sales subsidiaries had finance directors. With the exception of prod-

EXHIBIT 1   Vereinigte Deutsche Wagen, A. G.

Organization as of January 1, 1981

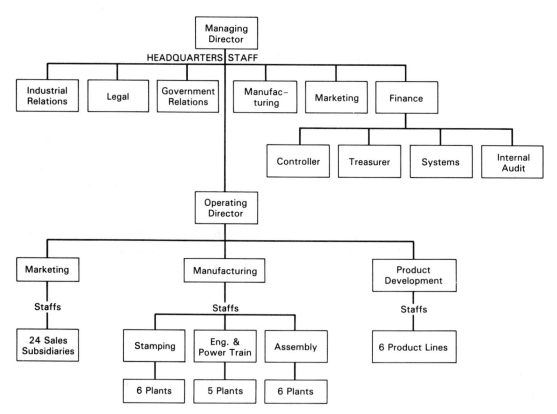

SOURCE: Company Organization Manual.

uct development, staff members reported directly to the operating manager and functionally to a headquarters staff counterpart. All product-planning personnel were responsible directly to the director of product development, regardless of their geographical location.

Operations.   Operations were divided into three functional areas: product development, manufacturing, and marketing.

Product development was responsible for the styling and engineering of all new products lines and the improvement of all existing product lines. Both the marketing and manufacturing operations had product planning personnel assigned to them. These people reported directly to the director of product development.

Manufacturing operations were divided into three groups: stampings, engine and power train, and assembly. There were several plants in each group.

Manufacturing operations were located in three countries: Germany, France, and Italy. All three countries had stamping plants, engine and power train plants, and assembly plants. For the most part, the stamping plants located in each country provided stamped parts for the assembly plants within the same country; however, all stamping plant provided some parts for assembly plants in the other two countries. For the most part, the engine and power train plants were rationalized to obtain the maximum economies of scale. Consequently, all engine and power train plants produced parts for all assembly planst. Some assembly plants assembled only one product line, some assembled several. Some product lines were assembled exclusively in one assembly plant. Other product lines were assembled at two assembly plants.

The total manufacturing capacity by country was Germany 50%, France 30%, and Italy 20%.

Marketing operations were composed of 24 sales subsidiaries, one for each country within which the company sold vehicles. Most of these subsidiaries were in Europe although some were located in Africa. All sales subsidiaries sold the full range of product lines.

Accounting and Control

VDW employed a dual accounting system. First, there was an accounting system for fiscal and tax purposes. Second, there was a system for management control.

The Fiscal Accounting System.   An accounting system was maintained in each country for fiscal and tax purposes. Under this system, each country was a profit center, and products were bought and sold among units of the company at transfer prices. Transfer prices were negotiated by the financial directors of the units involved. The objective of these negotiations was to develop prices that distributed the profits or losses among the participating units as fairly as possible, so as to avoid conflict with fiscal authorities. The fiscal accounting system was *not* used to measure the financial performance of either the operations within a country or the financial performance of the managers of those operations.

The Management Control System. For control purposes, the top management of VDW looked only at companywide revenues, costs, and profits. Each quarter, total company profits were assigned first to product line, and then reassigned to market area. *All* costs and revenues were assigned to some product and to some market area. Thus, the sum of the profits before taxes of all product lines equalled the sum of the profits of all market areas, which in turn equalled the total company profit shown on the external financial statement. The perform-ance of managers in manufacturing and product development was measured on the basis of cost targets and a number of nonfinancial objectives, for example, quality, meeting time commitments, and so forth. Since the issue in this case concerns the measurement of market area financial performance, the specific methods for measuring product development or manufacturing performance are not described.

Measuring Market Performance

Market area profitability analysis was based on two underlying principles:

1. Only companywide revenues, costs and returns were considered. All accounting transactions involving transfer prices for the sales and purchases of vehicles and components were eliminated.
2. *All* companywide costs, revenues and assets were assigned to some market area.

Revenues. Revenues were the actual revenues received in each market area con-verted to Deutsche marks.

Variable Costs. Variable manufacturing costs included direct material, direct la-bor, and variable overhead. The latter included the variable portion of indirect labor, utilities, supplies, maintenance, and fringe benefits. The variable costs of the components produced by the engine and power train plants, the stamping plants, and the assembly plant were calculated each quarter for each product line and each model within the product line. Each marketing area was charged with the specific variable cost for each product and model sold. Where two products were produced at different assembly plants, the variable costs incurred by the assembly plant that produced the specific vehicle were charged to the marketing area receiving the vehicle. Then companywide manufacturing costs were calcu-lated for each type of vehicle.

Fixed Costs

MANUFACTURING. An average unit-fixed manufacturing cost was calculated for each component based on the relative standard direct labor content. Then a total unit-fixed manufacturing cost was assigned to each product line and model, representing the sum of the unit-fixed manufacturing costs for all manufactured components included in the vehicle, plus the unit-fixed cost of assembly.

Special Tools, Launching Costs and Product Development. The amortization of special tools, launching costs, and product development was assigned directly to product line and model where possible. Common costs were assigned to applicable product lines on the basis of relative unit sales volume. Unit costs were calculated by dividing the total costs by the unit sales volume for each product line and for each model within product line.

Marketing. Marketing costs were assigned directly to sales subsidiaries where this was possible. Common marketing costs were allocated to market area on the basis of the relative volume of sales revenues.

Administration. Administration costs were assigned directly to market area where possible. Common administrative costs were allocated to market area on the basis of relative volume of sales revenues.

Summary. A unit-fixed manufacturing cost, special tool cost, launching cost, and product development cost were calculated for each model. These unit costs were multiplied by the number of the appropriate models sold by each sales subsidiary. In addition to the above, each sales district was assigned unique marketing and administrative costs plus a share of the common costs based on the relative sales revenue in each market area.

Assets were also assigned to product and marketing area so that a "return on assets" could be calculated.

An Example of Profitability Analysis. The following example provides a hypothetical and somewhat simplified picture of how the profitability of the sales subsidiaries was calculated. This example assumes that there are two product lines and two models within each product line. Product line 1 has model A and model B. Product line 2 has model C and model D. There are four sales subsidiaries; W, X, Y, and Z.

Product Line Statistics—First Quarter, 1981

	PRODUCT LINE 1		**PRODUCT LINE 2**	
	Model A	*Model B*	*Model C*	*Model D*
Unit Volume	1,000	2,000	3,000	4,000
Price per Unit	DM 10,000	DM 12,000	DM 20,000	DM 25,000
Cost per Unit				
Variable Cost:				
Italy		6,000[a]	9,000	13,000[b]
Germany	4,000	5,000[c]		11,000[d]
Fixed Mfg Costs	2,000	3,000	4,000	5,000
Other Fixed Costs[e]	1,000	1,000	1,500	2,000

[a]Vehicles delivered to subsidiaries W and X

[b]Vehicles delivered to subsidiaries W and Y

[c]Vehicles delivered to subsidiaries Y and Z

[d]Vehicles delivered to subsidiaries X and Z

[e]Other fixed costs include special tools, launching and product development.

Subsidiary Statistics—First Quarter, 1981

		UNIT SALES VOLUMES			
MODEL	Subsidiary W	Subsidiary X	Subsidiary Y	Subsidiary Z	Total
A	250	200	300	250	1,000
B	1,000	500	300	200	2,000
C	1,000	500	500	1,000	3,000
D	1,000	1,000	1,500	500	4,000
Total	3,250	2,200	2,600	1,950	10,000

Marketing and Administrative Costs

		(DM 000)			
	Subsidiary W	Subsidiary X	Subsidiary Y	Subsidiary Z	Total
MARKETING					
Unique	3,000	5,500	5,000	4,000	17,500
Common					15,000
ADMINISTRATION					
Unique	100	300	600	500	1,500
Common					16,000

Market Area Profitability: First Quarter 1981

		(DM 000)			
	Subsidiary W	Subsidiary X	Subsidiary Y	Subsidiary Z	Total
REVENUE					
Model A	2,500	2,000	3,000	2,500	10,000
Model B	12,000	6,000	3,600	2,400	24,000
Model C	20,000	10,000	10,000	20,000	60,000
Model D	25,000	25,000	37,500	12,500	100,000
Total	59,500	43,000	54,100	37,400	194,000
VARIABLE COST					
Model A	1,000	800	1,200	1,000	4,000
Model B[a]	6,000	3,000	1,500	1,000	11,500
Model C	4,000	2,000	2,000	4,000	12,000
Model D[a]	13,000	11,000	19,500	5,500	49,000
Total	24,000	16,800	24,200	11,500	76,500
CONTRIBUTION	35,500	26,200	29,900	25,900	117,500

[a]Calculation of variable costs for models B and D.

Market Area Profitability: First Quarter 1981 (continued)

	Subsidiary W	Subsidiary X	Subsidiary Y	Subsidiary Z	Total
	(DM 000)				
FIXED COSTS*					
Model A	750	600	900	750	3,000
Model B	4,000	2,000	1,200	800	8,000
Model C	5,500	2,750	2,750	5,500	16,500
Model D	7,000	7,000	10,500	3,500	28,000
Total	17,250	12,350	15,350	10,550	55,500
	18,250	13,850	14,550	15,350	62,000
Mkt. 2 adm.**	12,586	12,682	14,249	10,483	50,000
Net profit	5,664	1,168	301	4,867	12,000
MODEL B					
Volume	1,000	500	300	200	
Unit Var. Cost	6,000	6,000	5,000	5,000	
Total Var. Cost (DM 000)	6,000	3,000	1,500	1,000	DM 11,500
MODEL D					
Volume	1,000	1,000	1,500	500	
Unit Var. Cost	13,000	11,000	13,000	11,000	
Total Var. Cost (DM 000)	13,000	11,000	19,500	5,500	DM 49,000
Percent of sales revenue	30.6	22.2	27.9	19.3	100.0%
Unique costs	3,100	5,800	5,600	4,500	19,000
Common costs	9,486	6,882	8,649	5,983	31,000
Total	12,586	12,682	14,249	10,483	50,000

*Includes manufacturing fixed costs, special tool amortization, launching costs, and product development costs.

**Allocation of Marketing and Administrative Costs*

Measuring the Performance of Sales Subsidiary Managers

Responsibilities of Sales Subsidiary Managers

PRICING. Vehicle price recommendations were submitted to the headquarter's marketing staff for review. Differences of opinion between the subsidiary manager and the staff were negotiated; disputes that could not be resolved readily were reviewed with the top operating management for decision.

SALES VOLUME AND MIX. The subsidiary manager was entirely responsible for all of the sales within the country, although headquarters staff units often provided guidance. The subsidiary manager was responsible for dealer recruitment, development, and control. He or she was also responsible for all local advertising and sales promotion, including special incentives. In short, all sales activities within the country were the direct responsibility of the subsidiary manager.

Costs. The subsidiary manager was responsible for all costs incurred within the country. This included all subsidiary administration and selling costs, as well as all warranty costs incurred by the dealers.

The Bases for Measuring Actual Performance. How well sales subsidiary managers met their responsibilities was measured in financial and nonfinancial terms.

Financial. Financial performance was evaluated by comparing actual performance with the profit budget prepared by the subsidiary manager and approved by headquarters management. In order to arrive at the figures for the profit budget, each year each subsidiary manager prepared: (1) a revenue budget based on budgeted prices, unit volumes, and accessory installations; (2) a cost budget based on the expected expenditures incurred directly by the subsidiary. These budgets, calculated in deutsche marks, were submitted to headquarters for review and approval. Budgets were approved after negotiating change, where such changes were deemed appropriate by the top operating management.

Subsequently, each subsidiary manager was provided with the following costs based on companywide budgets:

- Unit-variable cost by model.
- Unit-fixed manufacturing cost by model.
- Unit-special tool amortization, launching costs, and product development costs by model.
- Total allocated sales costs.
- Total allocated administrative costs.
- Total allocated assets.

On the basis of these figures, the managers prepared a profit budget for the subsidiary, stressing profits and returns on sales and assets.

Each quarter the actual costs and revenues were calculated, and the remainder of the year projected. Thus, each quarter there was an updated estimate of the profitability for the year. This estimate was compared to the original budget, and variances analyzed and explained. Each subsequent quarter was composed more of actual costs and revenues and less of projections. The final quarter compared the actual costs and revenues for the year with the original budget. Note that each quarter all items of costs and revenues were completely recalculated to reflect the latest figures for the year.

Nonfinancial Measures. The performance of subsidiary managers was also evaluated on the basis of three nonfinancial measures, as follows:

1. Market penetration.
2. Percentage recovery of price-level and exchange-rate changes. This was the relationship between sales-price increases and purchase price-level increases plus changes in the exchange rate of the local currency relative to the Deutsche marks.
3. Mix and option rates. This measured the improvement in the profits per car.

Events in 1980

In 1980, two events occurred that were not anticipated in the 1980 budget. First, the sale of vehicles fell significantly below budget as a result of the recession in Europe. Second, fixed manufacturing costs and launching costs seriously exceeded budget. As a result, beginning in the first quarter of 1980, major changes were made to all of the budgeted allocations. These shifts reduced the profitability of all marketing areas, with many areas even showing losses.

One of the subsidiaries that was most severely affected was VDW, Suisse. This situation led to a day-long discussion in April between Hans Weber, the financial director of VDW, Suisse, and Rolf Ernst, the finance director of VDW, A.G. The principal topic discussed in the meeting was the drop in profits and returns by VDW, Suisse, in spite of improvements in sales, volume and mix, and locally incurred costs. At the end of the discussion, Rolf Ernst asked Hans Weber to prepare a letter describing his objections to the accounting system and his reasons for these objections. This letter is reproduced as Appendix A.

On receipt of Weber's letter, Ernst assigned members of his staff to review two of the issues raised by Weber. Memoranda covering these issues are reproduced in Appendixes B and C.

Required

Assume that you were employed as a consultant to VDW. What changes would you recommend that VDW make to their system of measuring and controlling the sales subsidiaries?

APPENDIX A: VEREINIGTE DEUTSCHE WAGEN, A.G.

Mr. Rolf Ernst
Financial Director
Vereinigte Deutsche Wagen, A.G.
Munich, Germany

August 21, 1981

Dear Mr. Ernst:

Subject: Profit decline in VDW, Suisse

Our discussion of July 17 isolated three reasons for the decline in profitability of VDW, Suisse, from a budgeted 1980 profit of DM 13.9 million to a loss of DM 2.1 million. These were:

1. The variable costs increased because the sourcing of some models was changed from an assembly plant in Germany to an assembly plant in Italy. Not only are the variable costs considerably higher in Italy, but the plant utilization is much lower. This also increased fixed costs.

2. The worldwide sales of vehicles were 25% less than was anticipated in the budget. Because the vehicle sales of VDW, Suisse, was higher than budget, the subsidiary was assigned a much higher amount of allocated fixed costs.

3. Fixed costs were and are expected to be considerably higher than budget. In particular, development and launching costs of Model X, which had just been introduced, were considerably in excess of budget. This model is selling well in Switzerland and, consequently, VDW, Suisse, was assigned a relatively large proportion of these costs.

Problems

This situation distorts managerial performance and misrepresents the contribution made by this subsidiary, particularly in period-to-period comparisons.

Managerial Performance.   So far in 1980, VDW, Suisse has equalled or exceeded its budgeted goals on the items that it controls. Sales volume is somewhat above budgeted levels, the product mix and option rates are at budget, price recovery is only slightly below budget, and local selling and administrative costs are approximatley at budget. (The only costs above budget are warranty expenses. This resulted from unanticipated quality problems with Model X.) Yet the profit performance of VDW, Suisse, is DM 16.0 million worse than budget. The entire decline has been caused by factors completely beyond the control of management.

In our discussion, you assured me that management was measured on performance factors other than profit. This, however, creates a dilemma for management. Nonfinancial goals can often be met by taking action that may be contrary to the overall interests of the company. For example, we could increase the sale of Model X by offering special incentives, minimizing option installation, and increasing sales and promotional effort. In fact, we really should do this because it is our best defense against the threat of increasing Japanese imports. Yet if we were to do this, we would lower all the nonfinancial ratios except market penetration. Also, we would exceed our budgeted marketing costs. Not only would we change all of our ratios, but our profits would actually decrease! This occurs because the fixed cost per unit on Model X is so high that, if we lowered our price, we would sustain a loss on each unit sold. Yet, it would seem to me that any increase in volume would be desirable this year in view of the current amount of excess manufacturing capacity.

Subsidiary Performance.   As I indicated, this year VDW, Suisse, will show a loss, down from a DM 12.6 profit in 1979. This would seem to indicate that we are experiencing a profit slump. Yet, this is completely untrue. We are having our best year yet. The reason for the profit decrease is entirely due to causes outside of Switzerland, in particular the lower sales volumes in the rest of Europe. Does top management understand this? I find this situation very difficult to explain to our operating managers.

We agree that the problem is not an easy one and is largely compounded by lower overall business activity at source locations. It would seem to us, however, that because of these major fluctuations in accounted profit results, we need to review alternatives that more appropriately identify the true worth of profit center contributions. We realize, in the end analysis, that all fixed costs must be recovered, and satisfactory returns earned on all assets. For the present, however, it would appear that incremental profits are the appropriate decision profits. The presentation of data based on the present fully accounted conventions is totally accepted, and we recognize that it is not practical to calculate incremental profits for every market every month. Your present measurement, however, does not properly identify our true contribution and my operating management is very heavily criticized for actions that we believe were in the best interests of the company. We realize that the problem is not new but because of the magnitude of the aberration we suggest a coordinated corporate review be made as to how best to reflect data to management.

Best regards,

Hans Weber
Director of Finance

APPENDIX B: VEREINIGTE DEUTSCHE WAGEN, A.G.

Market Profitability Review—Fixed Market Concept

Market profitability is presently projected using the latest economic profits[1] less an allocation of fixed costs based on ratios calculated using the latest volume and cost estimates. Only fixed costs directly related to a market are allocated specifically. These represent about 20% of total fixed costs. The use of estimated actual volume to allocate fixed costs is termed the "variable market concept." Alternative methods would be the "fixed market concept," where allocations are based on budgeted ratios that remain fixed throughout the year and the "unit fixed cost concept," in which the budgeted amount of fixed costs is allocated regardless of volume or cost level changes.

The basic advantage of the fixed market concept is that performance in one market is not affected by sales performance in another market. The major

---

[1]Editor's note: Economic profit is revenue minus variable costs.

disadvantage is that movements from budget are amplified because volume changes are translated directly into economic profits. This can lead to substantial distortion in year-to-year comparisons within markets and intra-year distortions among markets as return in individual years differ from a fully accounted approach.

The variable market concept tends to have the opposite advantages and disadvantages of the fixed market concept. It results in the performance of one market affecting others but year-to-year comparisons at equal volume are not distorted.

The unit cost concept would avoid the problems of the above but could result in major differences between total corporate profits and operational profits if volume was substantially off budget. Such a large consolidation item would be unacceptable.

The use of a fixed or variable market allocation basis for fixed costs becomes a trade-off between the incentive advantages to managing directors under the fixed concept and the more representative trend profits that occur with the variable concept. A potential plan to reduce the financial disadvantages of the present methodology would be to change the primary measurement to a variable system, while maintaining the fixed system for performance measurement of general managers. Finance staff recommends implementation of the latter change for the 1981 budget, with all historical years restated. This could lead to situations where management presentations would show performance different from how the managing directors would be measured. If sales group prefers, performance measurement also can use the variable concept.

September 19, 1980.

APPENDIX C: VEREINIGTE DEUTSCHE WAGEN, A.G.

Market Profitability Review—Average Sourcing

At present, the product profit system details the cost of each vehicle in each market. The revenue and cost assumptions are provided by the relevant sales and manufacturing areas and reflect the actual vehicle sourcing pattern. As a result, the costs of identical vehicles assembled in different plants will vary because of differences in labor and material cost, freight patterns, plant capacity utilization, and other factors. This system provides an accurate estimate of the actual cost incurred in producing a specific vehicle in a specific plant, and offers the following advantages.

1. It provides an excellent base for financial analysis—all costs and revenues can be tracked from sales/manufacturing input.
2. It highlights problems—a comparison of variable cost data between sources can lead to the identification of cost-saving opportunities.

3. Proposals for product or capacity changes must be based on actual costs to evaluate the correct corporate profit effect.

An alternative to use of specific sourcing would be to provide cost data on an "average-source basis." The major advantage of such a policy would be to eliminate potential profit distortions that result from sourcing decisions that are not within the control of managing directors. Although this change has advantages for financial incentives, this value appears to be outweighed by the following weaknesses:

1. Elimination of sourcing variances from market profits would require average-source material, labor, overhead, and freight costs. This would require the development of theoretical costs. The development of these data would necessarily lead to cost increases.
2. The product system is fully computerized and does not have the capability to derive "average-source" costs without a major change to existing computer systems.
3. The use of "average-source" costs would mask specific pricing problems such as tax and duty in Scandinavian markets. In these markets, the tax and duty implications are a function of the transfer price charged by the national company owning the final assembly source. It is essential that specific tax and duty levels are reflected in pricing decisions to ensure full recovery of costs.
4. Even if average sourcing were used, intermarket comparisons would still include substantial factors outside the direct control of managing directors, such as exchange rates. Use of average sourcing could lessen attention to real issues such as source/sales exchange rate changes that require positive action.

Continued use of specific sourcing is recommended.

September 30, 1980

INDEX